The U.S. Accounting Profession in the 1890s and Early 1900s

Edited with an introduction by
STEPHEN A. ZEFF

GARLAND PUBLISHING, INC.

NEW YORK & LONDON 1988

For a list of Garland's publications in accounting,
see the final pages of this volume.

Introduction copyright © 1988
by Stephen A. Zeff

Library of Congress Cataloging-in-Publication Data

■■■■■■■■■■■■■■■■■■■■■■■■■■■■■■■■■

The U.S. accounting profession in the 1890s and early 1900s.

(Foundations of accounting)
Bibliography: p.
1. Accounting—United States—History. 2. Accountants—
United States—History.   I. Zeff, Stephen A.   II. Series.
HF5616.U5U18 1988   657'.0973   88-24443
ISBN 0-8240-6135-7 (alk. paper)

Design by Renata Gomes

The volumes in this series are printed on
acid-free, 250-year-life paper.

Printed in the United States of America

Contents

■ ■ ■ ■ ■ ■ ■ ■ ■ ■ ■

EDUCATION AND EXAMINATION

Introduction

■■■■■■■■■■■■■■■■

I became aware of the fragmented state of the literature on the early development of the U.S. public accounting profession in the course of conducting the research for my "14 leaders" article which appeared in the centennial issue of the *Journal of Accountancy*, in May 1987. To assist researchers who seek to understand this early development, I thought it would be useful to gather in one place most of the writings that portray the early decades of the profession. I have also included several papers on early U.S. accounting education. My purpose in this introduction is to place the authors of the articles and their contributions in a helpful perspective.

The papers included in this volume are of three kinds: contemporary accounts, recollections, and historical studies.

A.C. Littleton (1886–1974) fashioned his doctoral dissertation, completed in 1931 at the University of Illinois, into one of the most influential books on accounting history, *Accounting Evolution to 1900*. In a study entitled *Directory of Early American Public Accountants*, which was published in 1942 by the University of Illinois, Littleton combed the city directories of New York, Chicago, and Philadelphia for the period 1870–1899 in order to develop data that might be useful in analyzing trends among those who held themselves out as accountants. His research suggests interesting interpretations of the services which the practitioners purported to render, the factors that influenced trends in the number of accounting practitioners, and trends in the "professional mortality" of the practice entities.

James Thornley Anyon (1851–1929) emigrated to the United States in 1886 and joined the staff of what was to become the first major U.S. public accounting partnership, Barrow, Wade, Guthrie & Co.[1] He became a partner the following year, and he continued in this capacity for 42 years until his death at the age of 77. Within months of his arrival in the United States, he was instrumental in founding the American Association of Public Accountants. His *Recollections of the Early Days of American Accountancy, 1883–1893*, has been cited by many students of the early days of the U.S. profession. Anyon not only describes the early years of the Guthrie firm and his efforts to found an association of public accountants, but also sketches the character of those who practiced accountancy, the attitudes of lawyers toward the work of accountants, and the impact of the periodic visits by British accountants who were inquiring into the possible purchase of American breweries by British interests. His several anecdotes of personal experiences richly illustrate his characterization of the early days of the U.S. profession.[2]

George Wilkinson (1860–1932) was an indefatigable worker on behalf of the profession in the 1890s and early 1900s. He emigrated to the United States in 1890 and practiced successively in New York, Chicago, and Philadelphia. His name is linked with the founding of the Illinois Association of Public Accountants in 1897, the founding of the Federation of Societies of Public Accountants in 1902, the passage of the C.P.A. Law in Illinois in 1903, and the organization of the Congress of Accountants at the time of the St. Louis World's Fair in 1904. In the first of his three papers included in this collection, taken from the volume of proceedings from the Congress, Wilkinson discusses many of the issues that were facing the leaders of the young profession. One of the points on which he made some critical remarks, namely audit companies whose shareholders were other than accountants, provoked a response during the discussion session which followed his presentation.

In his other two papers in this collection, Wilkinson gives a historical rendering of the pioneering days of the public accounting profession in the United Kingdom, Canada, and the United States, with emphasis on the last, and a historical sketch of the early development of the accounting profession in Pennsylvania.

Ernest Reckitt (1866–1955), like Anyon and Wilkinson an émigré from England, is known for his 143-page typescript, *Reminiscences of Early Days of the Accounting Profession in Illinois*, which was published in 1953 on the occasion of the fiftieth anniversary of the Illinois Society of Certified Public Accountants. Reckitt's unique contribution is his description of the series of efforts to gain recognition and status for the accounting profession in Illinois, including the establishment of a School of Commerce in Chicago along the lines of those that had been installed in New York University and the University of Pennsylvania. Reckitt also explains how the Illinois Society's journal, *The Auditor*, which first appeared in 1904, resurfaced in November 1905 as *The Journal of Accountancy*.

James Don Edwards (1926–   ) completed a doctoral dissertation in 1953 at The University of Texas, which served as the basis for his book published in 1960 by Michigan State University, *History of Public Accounting in the United States*. The two articles by Edwards in this collection are early versions of Chapters V and VI in the book. Relying on a variety of primary and secondary sources (including several in this collection), Edwards examines the early evolution of practice units, professional bodies, the accounting literature, educational practices, and steps toward legal recognition of the profession, terminating his inquiry with 1913.

Mary E. Murphy (1905–1985), beginning in 1940 when she contributed three articles to *The Accounting Review* from her doctoral dissertation completed in 1938 at the University of London, wrote extensively on comparative trends in the accounting profession. Most of her writings dealt with the history of the profession in Britain and the United States. Among her articles were biographical studies of Sir Arthur Lowes Dickinson, Lord Plender, and Sir George Touche, three distinguished chartered accountants (the first two were Englishmen, the last a Scot). During all of her career, Murphy was an academic, teaching at Hunter College of the City University of New York and at California State University, Los Angeles (as it is now known). The selection included here from Murphy's many writings is a pair of chapters from her book, *Advanced Public Accounting Practice*, published in 1966 by Richard D. Irwin, Inc., in which she reviews developments in the U.S. profession in the 1890s and early 1900s against the backdrop of earlier and contemporary developments in Britain.

John L. Carey (1904–1987) was the chief administrative officer of the American Institute of Certified Public Accountants for almost four decades. His two-volume opus, *The Rise of the Accounting Profession*, published in 1969–70 by the AICPA, was much more than a memoir. It was a thoughtful and perceptive history of the organized profession of certified public accountants in the United States. Chapters 3,4, and 7 from the first volume of that work provide an interesting study, rich in contextual references, to the early development of accounting practice, the formative years of the organized profession, and the pioneering efforts to establish standards for entry into the profession.

C.A. Moyer (1908–), a longtime member of the University of Illinois accounting faculty, contributes an article in which he examines the state of U.S. auditing prior to the publication in 1904 of Robert H. Montgomery's adaptation of Dicksee's *Auditing.*

William Sutherland (1878–1973), a fellow Glaswegian of Arthur Young's, took employment with the firm of Stuart & Young, in Chicago, in 1903. He then joined the firm of Arthur Young & Company, formed in 1906, and in 1915 became a general partner. He retired from the firm in 1945. In Sutherland's brief recollections of his early days in the firm and the profession, he gives a vivid impression of what it means to be a pioneer—at a time when standards and a literature were nonexistent, and when "there was no clear understanding of the role of the public accountant."

Gary John Previts (1942–) and Barbara Dubis Merino (1939–) describe the development of accounting practice, the profession, the literature, and theory in the light of the political, financial, and regulatory crosscurrents of the times. In Chapters 4 and 5 from their *A History of Accounting in America,* published in 1979 by Ronald Press/Wiley, they are especially attentive to the milieu in which accounting emerged as a profession and as a field of serious inquiry.

Norman E. Webster (1869–1956) can perhaps be

called the unofficial chronicler of the U.S. profession. During the 1930s and 1940s, he contributed numerous articles and letters to the editor on historical aspects of the profession. In 1954, the American Institute of Accountants published his book, *The American Association of Public Accountants: Its First Twenty Years, 1886–1906*. Throughout his professional career, Webster practiced with a medium-sized firm in New York City. In the first of his three articles included in this collection, "The Meaning of 'Public Accountant'," Webster assembles quotations from writers in the 1880s, 1890s, and 1900s as evidence of informed views of the day on such questions as "what does the expert accountant do?" and "what is a public accountant?" Through the quotations, some of which are attributed to leaders of the accounting profession, a self-image of the profession in its formative years begins to emerge.

In Webster's second article in this collection, "Early Movements for Accountancy Education," he relates the unsuccessful effort of the American Association of Public Accountants to found the New York School of Accounts. The School actually enrolled seven students in 1893–94, its only year of existence. It failed to secure support from either the business community or the educational authorities. Webster characterizes the School as the "spiritual ancestor" of the School of Commerce, Accounts and Finance which was opened in New York University in 1900.

Jeremiah Lockwood (1891–1945) was a member of the accounting department of the Wharton School of Finance and Commerce, of the University of Pennsylvania, from 1914 until his death. In "Early University Education in Accountancy," Lockwood describes the contents of accounting courses offered in U.S. universities during the two decades preceding 1903, as well as the difficulties which the instructors encountered. Lack of suitable textbooks was a serious problem, and the low esteem in which accounting was held by academics elsewhere in the university was a source of disquiet. Lockwood reports that Henry Rand Hatfield, while at the University of Chicago, persuaded the Mathematics Department to offer a course in bookkeeping, in the belief that the department's unquestioned reputation "would remove some of the odium or reproach attached to a course on bookkeeping." The ability of accounting instructors to refine their courses and develop written material for use by their students was diluted by the expectation that they teach a variety of non-accounting courses as well.

Carl E. Allen (1895–1981), then at the University of Illinois and later a member of Lehigh University faculty, reviews the catalogues of 42 universities between 1900 and 1926 in order to document the increase, both in number and diversity, in the offerings of accounting courses.

Norman E. Webster, in "Some Early Accountancy Examiners," profiles the 29 accountant members of the nine Boards of Examiners for the C.P.A. certificate in existence in 1905. He traces their national origin and briefly describes their training and experience. The aim of his research was to understand the implications of the backgrounds of these examiners for the standards which they set for entry into the profession.

There is, to be sure, a degree of unavoidable overlap among the papers in this collection. Yet each of the authors presents his own interpretation, in the light of his particular perspective and experiences, of the early historical development of the U.S. accounting profession. Unfortunately, many facets of this early development are yet to be investigated. All of the pioneers of the profession died many years ago, and few, apparently, left personal papers that might be opened to scholarly study. Several of the major public accounting firms have published histories, but most have been written by partners of the firm and therefore do not represent objective and dispassionate inquiries. One that was written by a freelance writer seems to have been subject to approval by the firm prior to publication.

Several of the state societies of certified public accountants have sponsored histories. As might be expected, they vary considerably in quality. Most have been written by accountants whose work formed part of the record being presented. They were not objective historians. Nonetheless, their accounts represent interesting factual renderings of the early development of the profession in their respective states. Following is a list of the state society histories of which I am aware, in chronological order:

The Growth of Public Accountancy in the State of Virginia to December 1950, by W.P. Hilton (Virginia Society of Public Accountants Educational Fund, 1953).

The Story of Ohio Accountancy, by L.G. Battelle (Ohio Society of Certified Public Accountants, 1954).

Washington Society of Certified Public Accountants, 1904–1954, by Rodney D. White (Washington Society of Certified Public Accountants, 1957).

Iowa Society of Certified Public Accountants 1914–1960, by George A. Stephenson (Iowa Society of Certified Public Accountants, 1961).

History of Florida Institute of Certified Public Accountants, 1905–1963 (Florida Institute of Certified Public Accountants, 1963).

Fifty Years of Accounting in South Carolina, by N.E. Derrick (South Carolina Association of Certified Public Accountants, 1963)

History of the Professional Practice of Accounting in Kentucky, 1875–1965, by L.C.J. Yeager and Gordon Ford (publisher and publication date not disclosed).

History of the Oklahoma Society of Certified Public Accountants, 1918–1968 (The Oklahoma Society of Certified Public Accountants, 1967).

History of the West Virginia Society of Certified Public Accountants, 1919–1969, (West Virginia Society of Certified Public Accountants, 1969).

A History of Public Accounting in Maryland, by Stephen E. Loeb and Gordon S. May (Maryland Association of Certified Public Accountants, Inc., 1976)—Loeb and May are accounting academics.

Three Centuries of Accounting in Massachusetts, by William Holmes, Linda H. Kistler and Louis S. Corsini (Arno Press, 1978)—four chapters treat the history of the Massachusetts Society of Certified Public Account-

ants and predecessor bodies from 1910 to
1970.

*Texas Society of Certified Public Accountants: A
History, 1915–1981*, by James A. Tinsley
(Texas Society of Certified Public Accountants, 1982, revised edition)—Tinsley is a
professor of history.

*75th—A History of the Connecticut Society of
Certified Public Accountants, 1908–1983*,
(Connecticut Society of Certified Public
Accountants, 1983).

The First Seventy Five Years, by Tindall Cashion
(The California Society of Certified Public
Accountants, 1984).

Although the New York State Society of CPAs has not
published a history, it did issue a Fiftieth Anniversary
Commemorative Yearbook in 1947, which contains a
dozen articles on the history of the profession in New York
state.

In 1974, John M. Hunthausen completed a doctoral dissertation at the Universtiy of Missouri entitled "A
History of the CPA Profession in Colorado." Many of the
state societies have run historical articles in their journals,
or in the programs issued to commemorate important
anniversaries. Addresses of the state societies may be
obtained from the American Institute of Certified Public
Accountants, 1211 Avenue of the Americas, New York,
New York 10036.

As indicated above, several major accounting
firms have published histories. Most have been written by
elder or retired partners of their firms. The histories that I
have seen are as follows (listed in chronological order):

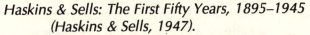

Haskins & Sells: The First Fifty Years, 1895–1945 (Haskins & Sells, 1947).

A Half Century of Accounting, 1899–1949—The Story of F.W. Lafrentz & Co. (F.W. Lafrentz & Co., 1949).

Price, Waterhouse & Co. in America, by C.W. DeMond (Price Waterhouse & Co., 1951).

Ernst & Ernst: A History of the Firm (Ernst & Ernst, 1960).

The First Sixty Years, 1913–1973—Arthur Andersen & Co. (Arthur Andersen & Co., 1974). This was a revision of a volume covering the first fifty years which was published in 1963.

Touche Ross: A Biography, by Theodor Swanson (Touche Ross & Co., 1972).

Haskins & Sells—Our First Seventy-five Years, by Arthur B. Foye (Haskins & Sells, 1979).

Peat, Marwick, Mitchell & Co.—85 Years, by T.A. Wise (Peat, Marwick, Mitchell & Co., 1982).

Pannell Kerr Forster—A Tradition of Excellence, A Commitment to Progress—A 75-Year Perspective, by Diana W. Wilding and C. Everett Johnson (Pannell Kerr Forster, 1986).

In addition, Lybrand, Ross Bros. & Montgomery published a special issue of its *L.R.B. & M. Journal* in 1948 dedicated to the first fifty years of the firm. Also, Arthur Young & Company published a 75th anniversary edition of *The Arthur Young Journal,* dated Spring–Summer 1969, which contains several recollections written by early partners of the firm.

Several volumes dealing with the careers of leading accounting practitioners constitute important parts of the literature on the early development of the U.S. profession. Apart from the aforementioned works by Anyon and Reckitt, the following should be cited:

Charles Waldo Haskins: An American Pioneer in Accountancy (Prentice-Hall, 1923).

Charles Ezra Sprague, by Helen Scott Mann (New York University, 1931).

Fifty Years of Accountancy, by Robert H. Montgomery (Privately printed, 1939).

Arthur Young and the Business He Founded (Personal Reminiscences) (Privately printed, 1948).

Reminiscences of a Certified Public Accountant, by Hermon F. Bell (Privately printed, 1959).

Memoirs and Accounting Thought of George O. May, edited by Paul Grady (The Ronald Press Company, 1962).

Thomas G. Higgins, CPA: An Autobiography (Privately printed, 1965). This work is, in large measure, a history of Arthur Young & Company.

I Remember, by Hassel Tippit (Privately printed, year of publication not given). Tippit, who died in 1978, was managing partner of Ernst & Ernst from 1948 to 1965, when he retired from the firm.

My Life and Times, by John B. Inglis (Privately printed, 1974).

Robert H. Montgomery: A Pioneer Leader of

American Accounting, by Alfred Robert
Roberts (Georgia State University, 1975).
John Raymond Wildman, 1878–1938, by Gary
John Previts and Richard F. Taylor (The
Academy of Accounting Historians, 1978).
*The Growth of Arthur Andersen & Co., 1928–1973:
An Oral History by Leonard Spacek* (Arthur
Andersen & Co., 1985).

Also of historical value, more for factual particulars
than for interpretations or recollections, is the most recent
compilation of biographical data for the members of the
Accounting Hall of Fame at The Ohio State University: *The
Accounting Hall of Fame: Profiles of Forty-one Members*,
by Thomas J. Burns and Edward N. Coffman (College of
Administrative Science, The Ohio State University, 1982).

Histories have also been prepared for two major
accounting departments in state universities:

*Sixty Years of Accounting Education on the Forty
Acres, 1912–1972*, by C. Aubrey Smith
(Austin, Tex: University Stores, Inc., 1974).
Deals with The University of Texas at Austin.
History of Accounting at Berkeley, by Maurice
Moonitz (Schools of Business Administra-
tion, University of California, Berkeley,
1986).

An encyclopedic, two-volume history of Beta Alpha
Psi, the professional accounting fraternity in U.S. universities and colleges, deals with early developments in accounting education: *Beta Alpha Psi, from Alpha to Omega*,
and *Beta Alpha Psi, from Omega to Zeta Omega*, by Terry

K. Sheldahl (Garland Publishing, Inc., 1982 and 1986).

Finally, a doctoral dissertation completed by a historian at Johns Hopkins University in 1985 will be of interest: "From Conflict to Consensus: The American Institute of Accountants and the Professionalization of Public Accountancy, 1886–1940," by Paul J. Miranti, Jr.

I wish to express my gratitude to the several authors and publishers for authorizing me to reproduce the works in this collection.

It is my hope that the papers collected in this volume, together with the references to book-length works mentioned in this Introduction, will be of assistance to students of the early history of the U.S. accounting profession.

Stephen A. Zeff
Rice University
February 1988

NOTES

1.   In 1950, Barrow, Wade, Guthrie & Co. merged with Peat, Marwick, Mitchell & Co., with only the latter's name surviving.

2.   Anyon's 68-page paper included in this collection is identical in all important respects to his three-part article, "Early Days of American Accountancy," published in the January–March 1925 issues of *The Journal of Accountancy.* The only salient omissions from the *The Journal of Accountancy* articles are several of the anecdotes.

The Profession

UNIVERSITY OF ILLINOIS
BULLETIN

VOL. 40   OCTOBER 13, 1942   No. 8

BUREAU OF ECONOMIC AND BUSINESS RESEARCH
BULLETIN SERIES No. 62

DIRECTORY OF EARLY AMERICAN PUBLIC ACCOUNTANTS

BY

A. C. LITTLETON

PUBLISHED BY THE UNIVERSITY OF ILLINOIS · URBANA

Published weekly. Entered as second-class matter at the post office at Urbana, Illinois, under the act of August 24, 1912. Office of Publication, 358 Administration Building, Urbana, Illinois. Acceptance for mailing at the special rate of postage provided for in Section 1103, Act of October 3, 1917, authorized July 31, 1918.

UNIVERSITY OF ILLINOIS
COLLEGE OF COMMERCE AND BUSINESS
ADMINISTRATION

CHARLES M. THOMPSON, Ph.D., LL.D., Litt.D., *Dean*

BUREAU OF ECONOMIC AND BUSINESS RESEARCH
H. K. ALLEN, Ph.D., *Director*

BULLETIN No. 62

3

DIRECTORY OF EARLY AMERICAN PUBLIC ACCOUNTANTS

BY

A. C. LITTLETON
Department of Business Organization
and Operation

PUBLISHED BY THE UNIVERSITY OF ILLINOIS, URBANA

1942

PREFACE

Two reasons prompted this study. It was hoped that the study of a sample of old city directories would provide quantitative data for judging the growth of public accounting in the United States. It was thought that biographical material could be found which, even though very brief, would show who among the rank and file were the men of most accomplishment and greatest leadership. Limited as the sample of directories is and incomplete as the biographies are, I think the data can be said to furnish a glimpse of an interesting section of an important era of American development.

The two decades 1880-1899 were preparatory and transitional years. They saw in the early years the expert bookkeeper, engaged in out-of-hours checking to detect possible fraud of whom the *New York Times* of January 16, 1877 could say "no cunning manipulation of accounts could deceive him. No fraudulent entry which failed sooner or later to reveal itself to his cold and searching vision." And they saw in the later years the professional accountant, registered under a Certified Public Accountant's law, engaged, among other things, in examining the accounts of half a dozen corporations preparatory to their being merged into a single organization.

This was the era in which many important accounting firms of today were founded. Some of these can be traced through the directories to the present. For example:

John Heins. 1879-89.
Heins & Whelen. 1890-92.
Heins, Whelen, Lybrand & Co. 1893-96.
Heins, Lybrand & Co. 1897-98.
Lybrand, Ross Bros. & Montgomery. 1898–
John Heins & Co. 1898–

It would be interesting indeed if more information were available about the evolution of specific firms and the changes that have taken place in accounting practices under the observation of their partners.

Biographical data were sought only for the years after 1884. The yearbooks of various organizations provided some facts; obituaries in periodicals provided others. *Who's Who in America* proved to be of little service, but volumes of the *Accountant's Directory* for 1920 and for 1925 were most useful.

I am indebted to the Research Committee of the Graduate School of the University of Illinois for the support they gave to the project

3

and to the Bureau of Economic and Business Research of the same institution for help with many details. I am particularly grateful to the men who obtained the original materials for me—H. T. Chamberlain of Chicago, P. H. Millichap of Philadelphia, and W. H. Childs of New York; and to some of the pioneers of the profession whose familiarity with the names of early accountants has been especially helpful—T. Edward Ross of Philadelphia, Ernest Reckitt of Chicago, and Norman E. Webster of New York.

A. C. LITTLETON

September, 1942

TABLE OF CONTENTS

7

I. GROWTH OF PUBLIC ACCOUNTING

The distinction between an accountant and a public accountant rests primarily upon the type of employment. The former's services are given to a single employer; the latter offers his services generally to the public and serves many clients. This does not mean that the private accountant's work is limited to simple clerical bookkeeping. He may do work that is graded all the way from clerical routine to comptrollership. In the higher grades, the individual may be as expert as any public accountant and often has responsibilities seldom borne by the latter. Nor is auditing itself outside the scope of the private accountant's work. Four hundred years ago the "Awdytour" was a trusted official in the English nobleman's household. But his auditing was confined to that one estate in the same way that a staff auditor today confines his activities to the affairs of his own corporation.

"Holding out to the public" came about gradually. In eighteenth century Britain, Italian bookkeeping (double entry) was gradually displacing the earlier "charge and discharge" records of feudal days and was still a good deal of a mystery to most people. Apparently it was baffling to some "bookkeepers" as well, for those most skilled in its intricacies were frequently called from their regular employment to untangle someone's records, to trace through the affairs of a bank-rupt, to audit some society's accounts, or to wind up a trust estate.

Some of the men in Scotland to whom such requests often came were: George Watson (d. 1723), cashier of a great mercantile house; Alexander Chalmers (d. 1759), accountant for the city of Edinburgh; James Bruce (d. 1825), also accountant for the city of Edinburgh; John Buchan (d. 1808), accountant to the post office of Scotland. Their long experience in important matters of accounts attested to their expertness and their places of trust testified to their integrity. These were the qualities that people would seek when they had emergency problems in accounting. And when the separate accounting problems of the public became numerous enough to occupy the entire time of experts, these men often left regular employment to offer their services generally and exclusively to the public. They listed their names in the directories accordingly and thus invited engagements. A few sample figures from the early city directories will indicate the year and the number of accountants listed.

Edinburgh: 1773 (6), 1774 (14), 1775 (15), 1778 (14), 1821 (58), 1834 (80).

Glasgow: 1783 (5), 1801 (6), 1807 (10), 1821 (16).

7

As the number of men thus holding out their services to the public increased, competition naturally produced a considerable variation in the quality of the "expertness" offered. And it is not at all surprising that the well-established practitioners should presently form organizations to indicate by membership the accountants who were particularly well qualified. After considering the matter for some years, the leading accountants of Edinburgh secured a royal charter in 1854 authorizing the society to call its members Chartered Accountants and to admit to membership by examination; Glasgow accountants followed in 1855, and those in Aberdeen in 1867. From 1892 the several Scottish societies made use of a joint examination. By 1904 the members of the Scottish societies numbered 906.

A few men were listing themselves as accountants in a similar way in the early directories of English cities. Some sample years are as follows:

London: 1776 (1), 1790 (1), 1799 (1).

Liverpool: 1783 (1), 1790 (5), 1796 (10).

Bristol: 1783 (2). Manchester: 1794 (2).

Sample years in the nineteenth century prior to 1840 show some increase in professional listing, but not a great deal. London: 1820 (44), Liverpool: 1832 (37), Bristol: 1830 (28), Manchester: 1831 (32). Figures for sample years between 1840 and 1870 indicate that a very real professional development took place during that generation.

London: 1840 (107), 1845 (210), 1860 (310), 1870 (464).

Liverpool: 1860 (91), 1870 (139).

Manchester: 1861 (84), 1871 (159).

Birmingham: 1861 (45).

This movement was greatly stimulated by corporation legislation in 1844, 1855, and 1862 which required company accounts to be audited. For this purpose the stockholders made ever-increasing use of professional accountants. And presently the accountants in the principal English cities organized professional societies as the Scottish practitioners had done.

Society	Date of society formation	Society membership in 1880
Liverpool	January, 1870	29
London	November, 1870	188
Manchester	February, 1871	103
Society of Accountants in England	January, 1873	286
Sheffield	March, 1877	32

These five societies merged to form The Institute of Chartered Accountants of England and Wales under a royal charter in 1880. At this time the total membership of the several societies was 638. Before February, 1881, Institute membership had risen to 1,025. Admission from 1882 was by examination.

American city directories yield similar quantitative data about the rise of public accounting in the United States. The sample here analyzed consists of three cities—New York, Chicago, and Philadelphia. These are the cities in which public accounting seemed to be concentrated in the early days. For each year from 1870 to 1899 the number of names listed as accountants is given in Table 1 and graphically presented in Chart 1.

11

TABLE I

TOTAL NAMES CLASSIFIED AS PUBLIC ACCOUNTANTS
(From city directories of New York, Chicago, and Philadelphia)

Year	Names	Year	Names	Year	Names
1870	28	1880	49	1890	125
1871	42	1881	50	1891	153
1872	42	1882	58	1892	192
1873	33	1883	52	1893	208
1874	46	1884	81	1894	225
1875	39	1885	91	1895	269
1876	40	1886	84	1896	287
1877	35	1887	100	1897	301
1878	38	1888	132	1898	316
1879	64	1889	119	1899	332

The pattern of growth here shown is not unlike that presented by the development of public accounting in Great Britain, although the time-periods are not very similar. The British growth was gradual up to about 1840; in the thirty years immediately following, the number of listed public accountants increased approximately fourfold. This expansion in the number of accountants roughly coincided with the period of rapid development of business corporations in Great Britain. In the United States the number of public accountants expanded very slowly until about 1884. Thereafter growth in numbers accelerated rapidly. In the next fifteen years the number of public accountants in the three sample cities increased fourfold. The change in this country also was coincident with a rapid development of business corporations.

Furthermore, there seems to be a time relationship between acceleration of growth in number of practitioners and the emergence of professional societies of accountants. In England the number of account-

12

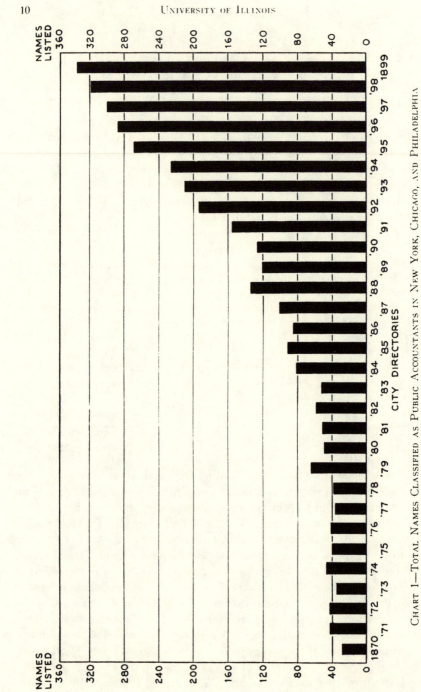

Chart 1—Total Names Classified as Public Accountants in New York, Chicago, and Philadelphia

ants increased markedly in the decade 1860-70 and numerous city societies of accountants were formed soon thereafter, to be merged into one in 1880. The American Association of Public Accountants, the antecedent of the present American Institute of Accountants, was formed in 1887, very soon after the real growth in number of practitioners began. Ten years later marked the beginning of state societies of C.P.A.'s, a movement that spread rapidly as state after state passed C.P.A. laws.

In both England and the United States the growth of public accounting has been marked by three stages: (1) The gradual appearance of experts in matters of accounting who offered a variety of skilled services, much of which was at first outside their regular employment. (2) The expansion of accounting services—especially auditing—and growth in the number of accountants under the impact of greatly increased business activities and the multiplication of corporations. (3) The formation of professional organizations whose principal function was to identify the most qualified practitioners through restricted membership, admission by examination, and distinctive titles.

13

II. AMERICAN DIRECTORIES ANALYZED

It has not been possible to examine early city directories for a large number of American cities. But it is believed that the data secured from the directories of New York, Philadelphia, and Chicago for 1850 to 1899 represent a very large proportion of the men in public practice in the half century during which American accountancy began its march toward a professional status.

Just to show that men did not begin to list themselves all at once as public accountants when this half century began, we may note a few names that appeared prior to 1850. David Franks, compiler of the first New York City directory (1786), listed himself in a display advertisement as "conveyancer and accountant at No. 66 Broadway." Benjamin Thomson advertised in the *New Jersey Journal* (Elizabethtown, April 21, 1795) that he kept "a conveyancing office . . . . where writings of every kind will be done on moderate terms; also farmers and tradesmen's books posted with accuracy and dispatch. . . . . " These men combined some phases of legal practice with some phases of accounting practice. Others combined teaching and practice. For example, James A. Bennett of New York was listed as an accountant in 1818-22, and as a teacher of bookkeeping in 1824-29; Benjamin F. Foster of Boston was listed as teacher in 1834 and as accountant in 1835-37.[1]

The file of available directories is almost complete for the two decades 1850-1869. For New York, volumes for nineteen of the twenty years have been found; for Philadelphia, the volumes for nineteen years were examined; for Chicago, all directories were available. Fifty-eight of a possible sixty annual directories give a fair picture of the number of accountants holding themselves out for clients. For New York in each of three years (1850, 1852, 1856) there were 14 names listed; in eight other years there were 7, 8, or 9 names; and in eight years there were 3, 4, or 5 names. The Philadelphia directories of this period showed 23 names in 1869, 12 in 1860, 10 in 1862, 4 in 1850, and for other scattered years three with 3 names, one with 5, and two with 7 names. Chicago lagged far behind with 8 names in 1854, 2 in 1865, and 1 in each of eight other years before 1870.

Appendix A presents the names in chronological order for each of the three cities, for the years 1850 to 1869.

To complete the survey of the growth in number of public accountants, Table II has been prepared. It shows that the fifteen-year period, 1870-1884, like the twenty-year period preceding it, experienced very

14

---

[1] Norman E. Webster, *Fiftieth Anniversary Celebration* (1937), pp. 104-5.

TABLE II

NUMBER OF PUBLIC ACCOUNTANTS LISTED IN CITY DIRECTORIES
1870-1884

Year	New York	Chicago	Phila-delphia	Year	New York	Chicago	Phila-delphia
1870	12	2	14	1885	47	8	36
1871	11	4	27	1886	45	6	33
1872	16	2	24	1887	55	13	32
1873	11	2	20	1888	68	16	48
1874	18	6	22	1889	61	19	39
1875	22	..	17	1890	66	24	35
1876	24	1	15	1891	83	31	39
1877	20	4	11	1892	96	41	55
1878	24	.	14	1893	107	51	50
1879	41	7	16	1894	112	58	57
1880	31	3	15	1895	138	64	67
1881	31	6	13	1896	147	77	63
1882	36	4	18	1897	163	81	57
1883	33	7	12	1898	173	81	63
1884	47	13	21	1899	183	71	74

15

small increases. The number in New York rose from 12 to 47, practically fourfold, but the total was still small. Progress in Philadelphia was much more irregular, and the listings in Chicago were almost negligible until 1884. The table also shows the changes for the next fifteen years, 1885-1899. In New York, the same rate of growth continued, the number increasing fourfold to reach 183 in 1899. The number in Philadelphia doubled, and Chicago made its real beginning, the names listed increasing ninefold, from 8 to 71.

The bulk of the information assembled consists of the alphabetical list of accountants and accounting firms in the three cities, 1850-1899, shown in Appendix B. But before completing the interpretive section certain observations drawn from a study of this list may be of interest.

Obviously many names will appear in the directory for several years. The total listed for New York in the directories examined was 2,276, but this total represented only 686 different individuals or firms. A few names appeared more than twenty times: James Simson (35), David P. Fackler (24), Thomas Bagot (23), John H. Allen (22), Henry M. Tate (21), Charles E. Townsend (21). Only 17 names appeared 15 times or more; 305 individuals (almost 45 per cent) appeared only once and 110 only twice. Frequently a name reappeared after an interval of one to ten years.

The total for Philadelphia was 1,098, representing 388 different individuals and firms. Some of the names most frequently repeated here were: John W. Francis (25), William W. Warr (25), Lucas E. Burke (23), R. F. Mustin (20). Only eight names appeared 15 times

or more, and 201 of the 388 individuals (a little more than one-half)
listed their names only once; 66 only twice.

For Chicago, only 10 names appeared 10 times or more; only one
appeared 17 times; one 14 times; and two 12 times. Of a listed total
of 726, there were 296 different individuals or firms, and of this last
number 156 (close to 53 per cent) appeared only once; 48 appeared
only twice.

If we strike a total for the three cities from 1850 to 1899, we find
some 1,370 different individuals or firms listed, of which number 662
appeared only once.

The high rate of "professional mortality" among those who tried
public accounting clearly indicates that the "bookkeeper out of work"
aspect was not wholly absent. But in the persistence with which a
number of individuals continued to practice there is evidence of success. Seventeen names in New York, 8 in Philadelphia, and 1 in Chicago are repeated 15 times or more. Evidently there were some whose
service continued to give satisfaction and whose experience continued
to broaden.

One other "test of longevity" will be given. Of 109 New York
names which appeared in the first twenty-five years, 12 (11 per cent)
were repeated six times or more. Of 188 New York names listed in
1899, there were 59 (30 percent) repeated six times or more. And
here it must be noted that the increase in rate of survival was probably
better than the comparative percentages suggest, because the study
terminated with the year 1899 and many names undoubtedly continued
to appear after that year.

The study shows some interesting facts about the number of practitioners that ultimately obtained a C.P.A. certificate. It is estimated
that 1,370 separate names appeared in the fifty-year period. Of this
total, 662 were found but once and 224 but twice. There was, therefore, a remainder of 484 names appearing three times or more. The
total number that obtained the C.P.A. was 211, a little less than half
as many as those who listed their names three times or more.

No study was made of the year in which the certificates were
granted; the New York law was not secured until 1896, that of
Pennsylvania in 1899, and that of Illinois in 1903. But the list was
checked to learn the earliest year in which each C.P.A. first listed his
name as a public accountant. Seven men who began practice in the
decade of the 1870's later secured the C.P.A. New York had three:
Edward Adams (1875), Thomas Bagot (1877), Robert M. Stratton,
Jr. (1872). The last named offers a curious case: his name appears
twice, once in 1872 and once in 1898, the year in which he obtained

the certificate. Philadelphia had four: John W. Francis (1871), John Heins (1879), Charles N. Vollum (1878), William A. Witherup (1872). Those who first listed their names in the decade of the 1880's and later became C.P.A.'s numbered 31 (New York, 25; Philadelphia, 4; Chicago, 2). A few of the names in this group that later became well known are: James Yalden ('84), Francis Gottsberger ('84), Charles E. Sprague ('85), James T. Anyon ('88), Charles W. Haskins ('88). There was a small group of 28 C.P.A.'s whose names appeared only as part of a firm name; they therefore could not be associated with any one year as individuals.

There remains the decade of the 1890's. Most of those who later obtained certificates listed their names for the first time in this period, 145 in all. Twelve of the names were in Philadelphia, 5 of these in 1893. Thirty were in Chicago, 16 of these in the two years 1896, 1897. The remaining 103 were listed in New York, 45 of them in three years, 1895 (18), 1896 (12), 1897 (15). The other 58 names for New York were scattered throughout the decade: '93 and '99 had 11 names each; '92 and '98 had 9 each; '91 had 8; '94 had 7; '90 had 3.

The concentration in 1895-96-97 is apparent. There is no clear reason why 65 (about 45 per cent) of the 145 later C.P.A.'s who first hung out their shingles in the 1890's should have done so in these three years. Perhaps the rumors of a public accountant's law in 1895 and the actual New York C.P.A. law of 1896 influenced men who had been practicing for some time without being listed to classify themselves in the directories. Perhaps recovery from the depression of 1893 was beginning to have some effect in increasing the demand for accountants. Yet the number of new names appearing in the directories was almost unchanging from 1892 to 1899: the increase ran close to 16 each year for the period, except for a large increase of 44 names in 1895. In the one year of 1895 there were 28 more names listed than the trend of 16 per year established before and after that year. Perhaps those three years marked the height of the surge in corporation reorganizations which were so characteristic of that decade and were so good a test of an accountant's skill. Whatever the full explanation may be, the fact is clear that a real impulse toward a professional status for accountants appeared in the decade of the 1890's and especially in the years 1895-96-97.

III. PROFESSIONAL ADVERTISING CARDS.

Public accountants announced their availability for engagements in various ways. The great majority merely listed their names in the classified section of the city directory, painted their names and occupation on their office doors, and depended upon the good reputation made by the quality of their work to bring them new engagements. A few made their names stand out in the printed list by the use of boldface type. Some printed a modest card in the directory or perhaps in some business magazine. Others—not many—published full-page display advertisements in varied type and bold headlines.

The samples given here were taken from the city directories of New York, Chicago, and Philadelphia, and from a few of the early business magazines. The items are of interest chiefly in the clue they may give to the kind of engagements that public accountants expected. The advertisements cannot be relied upon to picture the work that any one public accountant actually did. We may suspect that some had high hopes for real professional engagements but actually did considerable simple bookkeeping work. Others no doubt gave much of their time to real professional services which are barely mentioned in these advertisements.

A number of advertisers made strong statements such as "thirty years of experience," "established since 1861," "the oldest firm of public accountants in the United States." It is impossible, of course, to verify these statements now. But they could hardly have referred to so much experience in *public* accounting as they seem to do. The claims advertised were seldom supported by an early listing of the person's name in the directories. Several names first appeared only one year before the advertisement was published that claimed fifteen, twenty, or thirty years of experience. Several others were listed in the directory from five to eleven years before the card appeared. The advertisement in one case appeared fifteen years before the person's name was listed in a directory under the classification "Public Accountants." And in one case the claim of experience was clearly substantiated by the name's being listed as "public accountant" at the necessary earlier date.

Most announcements such as the ones shown on pages 17-19 probably represented a man who was an independent accountant at the time. But a few cards appeared in the 1880's which clearly indicated that the person named sought supplementary out-of-hours engagements. The editor of a business periodical, for example, announced

"Will undertake the audit, adjustment, and examination of accounts of corporations, public officers and merchants." A minor official of a bank ran a card as "Accountant," and an accountant in the office of a large railway company stated "partnership and other accounts carefully examined and accurately adjusted."

PROFESSIONAL CARDS:

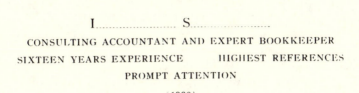

I................... S...................

CONSULTING ACCOUNTANT AND EXPERT BOOKKEEPER

SIXTEEN YEARS EXPERIENCE   HIGHEST REFERENCES

PROMPT ATTENTION

(1880)

19

W................... R...................

PROFESSIONAL ACCOUNTANT

NO. 150 ....STREET

ESTABLISHED 1866

(1880)

.... & ....

EXPERT ACCOUNTANTS

NO. 16 .... STREET

HIGHEST REFERENCES   PROMPT ATTENTION

(1881)

H................... B...................

CONFIDENTIAL, CONSULTING AND EXPERT ACCOUNTING

AND DETECTOR OF FORGED WRITINGS

PRACTICAL EXPERIENCE OF OVER THIRTY YEARS

(1888)

S .... F......................................

EXAMINING ACCOUNTANT
PARTNERS' INTERESTS ADJUSTED
JOINT STOCK BOOKS OPENED,
WRITTEN UP, AUDITED

(1889)

20

J .... M .... C ....

CONSULTING ACCOUNTANT, OFFICE ORGANIZATION
FACTORY COSTS OF PRODUCT.   CORPORATION INSTALLATION,
RAILROAD AND TRANSPORTATION
NO PRACTICE SOLICITED

(1891)

H .... C .... D ....

ATTORNEY AT LAW.   EXPERT ACCOUNTANT.
TWENTY YEARS EXTENSIVE PRACTICE IN MANUFACTURING,
WHOLESALE, BOARD OF TRADE, BANKING,
CORPORATION AND ESTATE ACCOUNTS

(1893)

C .... E .... F ....

PUBLIC ACCOUNTANT AND AUDITOR
.... BROADWAY
OFFICE HOURS—12:30 TO 1:30 P.M.
THOROUGH EXPERIENCE IN BANKING AND
RAILWAY EXAMINATIONS

(1893)

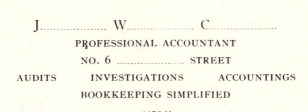

B.................. M.................. & COMPANY

EXPERT ACCOUNTANTS   PUBLIC AUDITORS

CONSULTING ACTUARIES

(1894)

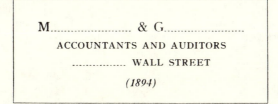

J.............. W.............. C..............

PROFESSIONAL ACCOUNTANT

NO. 6 .... STREET

AUDITS   INVESTIGATIONS   ACCOUNTINGS

BOOKKEEPING SIMPLIFIED

(1894)

21

M.................. & G..................

ACCOUNTANTS AND AUDITORS

.... WALL STREET

(1894)

Display Advertisements

1851

Practical bookkeeper and accountant. Opposite the Court House. Books opened, closed, posted. Bills and accounts made out. Bookkeeping in all its varied branches taught individually or in classes.

1875

Prepared to make statements for executors, examine corporation, partnership, industrial books and accounts of every description, open and close books, to attend to any and every kind of bookkeeping. Books posted monthly and trial balance taken at a trifling cost. Plans furnished for books for special purposes.

1880

Books opened and arranged for all classes of business in the most simple and concise manner. The rigid investigation of complicated and disputed matters, and the clear presentation of the results divested of technicality, a specialty. Particular attention given to the books of insurance companies, and the accounts of executors, estates in trust and bankrupt estates.

Display Advertisements (continued)
1880

Will render assistance to lawyers in the examination of accounts in litigation; aid agents and administrators of estates in adjusting accounts. Will give counsel upon improved methods of keeping accounts of incorporated companies, assist bookkeepers and business men in straightening out intricate and improperly kept books. Adjust complicated partnership accounts, examine books for stockholders and creditors.

1881

Consulting expert. Twenty years experience as bookkeeper, auditor and adjuster. Will audit and examine books of account for mercantile concerns and joint stock companies. Will undertake, the adjustment of complicated cases arising from partnership settlements and give advice upon adopting improved methods for special branches of business.

22

1882

Public accountant and expert. Complicated, disputed and confused accounts, also accounts of executors, trustees and estates investigated and stated. Books opened and closed. Suspected accounts confidentially examined. Partnership settlements made.

1886

Books opened and closed, commercial branches taught. Highly recommended by banks, business houses, export brokers. Proving arithmetic, detecting errors in trial balance, computing interest and discount, averaging accounts.

1887

H.............................. F......................................, public accountant and auditor, examines and reports on individuals, partnerships, corporation accounts, investigates and adjusts disputed accounts, acts as assignee or receiver, designs new books to meet special requirements. Books posted and balance sheets rendered, accounts audited, expert work for the courts, scientifically and faithfully performed.

1889

H—ave your books periodically audited.

B—usiness entirely confidential.

H—onest investigations scientifically conducted.
A—djustment of accounts for corporations or firms.
Y—our books opened, regularly superintended and closed.
E—xamination of erroneous accounts, a specialist.
S—tatements, trial balances, balance sheets and cost accounts.

1889

Embezzlement and forging are so much on the increase that they have become factors in business which none can with safety ignore; and yet, prevention (which really should be aimed at) is rarely hinted at. Practically there is only one method that can easily be put in operation. Have

Display Advertisements (continued)

your books of account drafted or reorganized by a man who understands how to make the books check themselves as far as possible, and then employ him to drop in at odd times without notice and thus keep up a constant supervision. If you desire further information, address, yours respectfully, J................................. W................................, consulting and expert accountant, No. 14...................... Street.

1889

Public auditor and accountant. Established 1864. Over twenty years practical experience. Best of references. Balance sheets proved and verified. Irregularities traced. Accounts kept for estates in trust. Banks and railway accounts a specialty.

1889

23

Fellow of American Association of Public Accountants with twenty years of experience, I am prepared to arrange books for any business. Accounts of estates examined and kept or prepared for court. Balance Sheets and Profit and Loss Accounts made. Partnership and disputed accounts adjusted. Confused accounts investigated and stated. Examination confidential. Competent assistants furnished to write up accounts.

1889

Expert accountant and auditor. Over twenty years expert practice in investigating suspected books and unraveling tangled books, in periodically auditing books and verifying balance sheets, in adjusting books, in terms of partnership agreement, corporation acts and by-laws, in planning and revising books, in preparing accounts for the surrogate and other courts.

1890

Qualified as an expert accountant by special training and examination; and by twenty years continuous experience in all branches of accounting and bookkeeping. No. .... Street, Telephone No. .... Assisted by a qualified staff of 18 expert bookkeepers. Experts supplied at low terms per day.

1890

Books of account and business affairs analyzed. Commercial and legal papers critically examined. Statements prepared for court. Special periodical audits and examination of books of banks, merchants and others, either for purposes of proposing improvement, or for the regular checking of the work of employees. Assistance rendered in the formation of joint-stock corporations. Receiverships and estates settled and reports of executors, administrators and guardians examined and audited. Large experience in trials involving complicated accounts and fictitious entries and forgeries.

1891

Are you satisfied with your books? Do they give a true condition of your business? If there is any doubt, give yourself the benefit of it and employ an accountant. Do you have a trial balance monthly? Or a balance sheet and analysis yearly? Do you know the percentage of gain on business

Display Advertisements (concluded)

done or on capital invested? If not, call on W........................ F.....................
J......................., accountant and auditor, No. 16............... Street. Thirty
years experience. An interview will cost nothing.

1891

Public accountant and auditor. Fifteen years practical experience, complications a specialty. Books and accounts opened, systemized, written up,
examined, adjusted, audited and balanced. Statements of Profit and Loss,
Balance Sheets, schedules and accounting for administrators, executors,
trustees, and assignees confidentially prepared. Highest testaments for
accuracy and simplicity of labor-saving systems. Assistant expert accountants and bookkeepers supplied at lowest terms per day. Consulting
accountant.

1892

24 This item was a display using half-page write-up taken from local paper
of two years prior in which the individual is named and described as "a
skillful professional accountant" engaged upon "the difficult task of unraveling and stating in a lucid manner" the accounts of a certain company
then in litigation. The enthusiastic newspaper reporter found that the
accountant performed his task in a way showing him "to be a master of
his profession" whose exhibits before the master in chancery were "models
of the bookkeeping and accounting art."

1894

F. W. R., No. .... Broadway (formerly with B...............................
W............................... & Co.). Railroad, industrial, banking, commercial,
corporation, syndicate, and general accountancy. Books designed, opened,
kept, examined, adjusted, audited and balanced.

1895

Accounting in all branches. Established 1883. Assisted by a qualified staff
of expert accountants, who have served for at least five years as chartered
accountants' assistants and who have passed the examinations of the
Institute of Chartered Accountants of England.

1896

Public accountants and auditors. Periodical expert examinations a specialty (special terms or contracts made for above). Investigation in matters of defalcation. Complicated accounts adjusted. Balance sheets and
statements of profit and loss prepared, certificates as to profits. Books
designed, opened, closed, balanced for any class of business. Schedules
and accounting for estates, executors, administrators, trustees, receivers,
assignees.

1899

Books correctly balanced regardless of size or number of months or years
since last trial balance was made. Experience on 500 ledgers. Average
speed posting 70 items per hour. $4.00 per day.

IV. ACCOUNTANTS AND ACCOUNTING FIRMS

The names obtained from the city directories of New York, Chicago, and Philadelphia for the half-century 1850-1899 are presented in one alphabet in Appendix B. The names for Chicago are preceded by one dash (—), and those for Philadelphia by two (— —) to make it easier to examine the list for one city alone if desired.

The figures immediately following a name, as 86-89, 95, 97, indicate the years in which that name was found in a directory. Where a period of years is shown (86-89), the name appeared in both terminal years and those between. Some names are shown in parenthesis, indicating that the name did not appear separately in the directory but there is reason to believe that the person was in practice in the city at the time. Usually this fact was indicated in a firm name elsewhere in the list.

25

A few items found in the directories under the classified heading of "Public Accountants" have been omitted. Some of these were obviously accountants' organizations: American Association of Public Accountants, Illinois Association of Public Accountants, Association of American Railway Accountants, National Association of Certified Public Accountants in the United States (N.Y., 1899). A few seemed to be organizations of bookkeepers, such as Corporated Accountants (N.Y., 1895-99), Original Society of Accountants (Chicago, 1898-99), Accountants and Stenographers Association (Philadelphia, 1897-99). Others were listed among accountants but little can be learned about their connection with accounting: Public Debt Adjustment Company (N.Y., 1890), Physicians Finance Association (N.Y., 1893-94), Commercial Bureau of Odd Fellows (Philadelphia, 1897), Philadelphia Financial Bureau (1894), Philadelphia Bureau of Accounting (1893-99).

A few other impersonal names remain in the list. In some cases it has been possible to indicate the names of the individuals who were the responsible heads of the firms. In other cases, nothing is known of the men who practiced under that firm style. (Expert Accountant Company, Chicago, 1892-93; International Audit Bureau, New York, 1898-99; New York Account and Adjustment Company, 1895-98; American Accounting and Bookkeeping, New York, 1896-97.)

Brief biographical data are given, when obtainable, for names appearing after 1884. Judging by these facts some twenty-five of the men listed might be considered outstanding for their active leadership in organization affairs, for building up important professional firms, or for their contributions to the literature of accounting and service as teachers. Obviously many men regarded as leaders may not have been

23

listed in the directories before the year 1900. For example, A. Lowes Dickinson was certainly an active leader in accounting affairs. But his name does not appear here because he did not come to this country from England until 1901. The profession is greatly indebted to many who were pioneers after 1900.

The asterisk (*) indicates a man with a C.P.A. certificate. The state is named; the year and the certificate number are given.

26

APPENDIX A

CHRONOLOGICAL LISTING, 1850-1869

NEW YORK

1850:
Burrows, William L.
Dubuar, Francis
Entz, John F.
Hargan, George
Hodgson, Edward W.
Isaacs, M.
Jenner, W. H.
Marsh, Christopher
Oakley, Robert S.
Quinn, Daniel
Richardson, Edward T.
Senior, Richard
Spellman, Samuel R.
Temple, Richard

1851-52:
Burrows, William L.
Griglietti, Charles A.
Isaacs, M.
Oakley, Robert S.
Spellman, Samuel R.

1852-53:
Brown, Constant H.
Churchill, William T.
Davis, Daniel B.
Douglas, Andrew
Ellard, Andrew
Griglietti, Charles A.
Isaacs, M.
Jones, Thomas
King, Samuel P.
Marsh, Christopher C.
Mills, William
Richardson, Edward T.
Scott, John F.
Watson, Richard

1853-54:
Douglas, Andrew
Dow, Martin
Griglietti, Charles A.
Hollermann, F. Van E., Jr.
Isaacs, M.
Maggi, Charles
Renville, Willis J.
Russell, W. W.

1854-55:
Freeman, John
Grighette, Charles (*sic*)
Groser, Louis B.
Hamel, Octavus
Isaacs, M.
Maggi, Charles
Renville, Willis J.
Russell, W. W.

1855-56:
(Missing)

1856-57:
Baker, Charles H.
Churchill, William T.
Darrow, William
Davis, Henry B.
Delaunay, Augustus
Dobbs, J. H.
Entz, John F.
Freeman, Alpheus
Hamilton, Francis
Hatt, John A.
Jones, Thomas
Merklee, John
Smith, Elias L.
Vogelsdorff, Maurice

1857-58:
Betts, James
Dobbs, J. H.
Jones, Thomas
Peckham, George
Queen, J.
Vogelsdorff, Maurice
Townsend, Walter

1858-59:
Foster, Benjamin F.
Marland, W. A.
Mitchell, G.
Parkin, Josiah
Townsend, Walter W.

1859-60:
Jones, Thomas
Lloyd, George W.
Parkin, Josiah
Simpson, James (*sic*)
Vogelsdorff, Maurice

1860-61:
Goodall, Augustus
Graham, Ralph
Graser, George
Jones, Thomas
Parkin, Josiah
Simpson, James (*sic*)
Wheeler, George

1861-62:
Jones, Thomas
Mason, William
Phillips, Alfred
Simpson, James (*sic*)
Townsend, Joseph

1862-63:
Bright, Richard E.
Henderson, James
Hohle, Moritz

Jones, Thomas
Simson, James

1863-64:
Bowes, William
Lloyd, George W.
Myer, George W. E.
Simson, James
Stoutenburgh, Alexander H.

1864-65:
Anderson, Frederick R.
Bryant, Stratton and Packard **27**
Miller, Isaac S.
Myer, George W.
Phillips, Alfred
Ryers, Lewis
Stimson, James (*sic*)
Stoutenburgh, A. H.

1865-66:
Miller, Isaac S.
Myer, George W.
Phillips, Alfred
Simson, James

1866-67:
Avery, William A.
Ryers, Lewis R.
Simson, James

1867-68:
Anderson, Frederick R.
Livingston, Charles M.
Marsh, Christopher C.
Oldershaw, Percival P.
Phillips, Alfred
Ryers, Lewis R.
Simson, James
Smithers, Henry K.

1868-69:
Bigood & Co.
Hansen, Lewis G.
Hobart, Henry C.
Livingston, Charles M.
Maude, Arthur A.
Phillips, Alfred
Simson, James
Smith, Frederick E.
Smithers, Henry K.

1869-70:
Hobart, Henry C.
Livingston, Charles M.
Maude, Arthur A.
Phillips, Alfred
Simson, James
Smithers, Henry K.
Warren, William E.

PHILADELPHIA

1850:
Hand & Pennington
Hervey, Robert
McCahan, John
Smethurst, Richard

1860:
Bowdle, Tristram
Burke, Lucas E.
Claghorn, William C.
Crittenden, S. H.
Depuy, J. Stewart
Hervey, Robert
Leeds, Barclay R.
Leidy, S. Snyder
Nathans, David
O'Donnell, Thomas
Penington, H. B.
Taylor, Thomas S.

1861:
Burke, Lucas E.
Claghorn, William C.
Crittenden, S. H.
Depuy, J. Stewart
Heppe, Philip H.
Leeds, Barclay R.
McDonald, William

1862:
Burke, Lucas E.
Chapouty, P.
Claghorn, William C.

Crittenden, S. H.
Depuy, J. Stewart
Duff & Co.
Groesbeck, John
Heppe, Philip H.
Leeds, Barclay R.
McDonald, William

1863:
Burke, Lucas E.
Chapouty, P.
Crittenden, S. H.
Glenn, B. F.
Groesbeck, John

1864:
Burke, Lucas E.
Chapouty, P.
Crittenden, S. H.
Geisz, Henry
Geisz, John
Glenn, B. F.
Groesbeck, John

1865:
Crittenden, S. H.
Glenn, B. F.
Graham, William H.

1866:
Burke, Lucas E.
Cole, Charles J.
Crittenden, S. H. & Co.

1867:
Crittenden, S. H. & Co.
Graham, William H.
Stahl, R. H.

1868:
(Missing)

1869:
Bowdle, Tristram
Burke, Lucas E.
Candelet, Allen
Crean, William
Dawson, Robert W.
Deitrich, S. V.
Gartley, Samuel W.
Graham, William H.
Hooke, Francis
Kerk, Augustus
Lembert, Gustavus
Lewis, John E.
Murray, Michael J.
Peirce, Thomas May
Ramsey, Alexander
Slack, Daniel W.
Spackman, John B.
Stahl, Rudolph H.
Steel, Edwin K.
Walsh, Michael L.
Warr, William W.
Waterman, T. A.
Winters, Adam J.

Note—No classified section for: 1851, 1852, 1853.
No accountants listed for: 1854, 1855, 1856, 1857, 1858, 1859.

28

CHICAGO

1851:
Woolley, James

1854:
Armstrong, G. B.
Barr, Robert
Dillingham, John
Keiller, Andrew
Keiller, John
Lloyd, James
Muir, W. T.
Tryon, W. A.

1856:
Pasdeloup, Francis

1857-58:
Ashwin, William M.

1858-59:
Tanner, Thomas A.

1864-65:
Ballingall, David

1865-66:
Ballingall, David
Lynch, James

1867-68:
Silke, J. Freeman

1868-69:
Silke, J. Freeman

1869-70:
Silke, J. Freeman

Note—No classified section for: 1850, 1851, 1852, 1853.
No accountants listed for: 1855, 1859-60, 1860-61, 1861-62, 1863-64, 1866-67.

APPENDIX B

ALPHABETICAL LIST OF ACCOUNTANTS AND ACCOUNTING FIRMS—1850-1899[a]

(Abbott, H. W.), legislative meeting, 1895.
Abels, Jacob, 94.
(Abraham) See Bagot & Abraham.
*Abrahams, John W. 92, 95, 96 (& Co. 95, 96); N.Y. C.P.A. 66 (1896); see Hooke and Abrahams, N.Y.
Abrahams, Smyth, Williams & Co., 94.
— Account, Audit & Assurance Company, 99.
Account, Audit & Assurance Co. Ltd., 99; (Anson O. Kittredge and others).
— Ackerman, (William K.) & Barrington, (Charles V.), 95.
— Adams, Alex. X., 92.
*Adams, Edward, 75-77, 79, 92-99; N.Y. C.P.A. 67 (1896).
Adams, George S., 94, 95.
— Adams, Geo. W., 84, 89, 90, 91.
*Aderer, Alexander (& Co.), 98, 99; d. 1924; N.Y. C.P.A. 424 (1909).
— *Adkins, William G., 96; b. Watertown, N.Y., 1855; Wis. C.P.A. 80 (1916).
Adriance, Thomas M., 72.
Ahearn, John F., 99.
— Aikin, William J., 94, 95.
Albert, Carl, 70.
— — Albertson, Eugene R., 89.
— Aldis, H. Charles, 92-99.
Allaire, Samuel Y., 84.
— *Allen, Edward, 97-99; Ill. C.P.A. 50 (1904).
Allen, John H., 78-99.
— — Allen, Robert B., 75-76.
Allen, Wm. H., 99.
Altman, Morris P., 99.
— American Accounting Company, 94-99.
American Accounting and Bookkeeping Company, 96, 97.
— — Amerman, John, 93.
Anderson, Archibald J. C., 88-99.
Anderson, Frederick R., 54, 67, 71-73.
— — Andrews, Adolph Y., 74.
Andrews, Lyman S., 82, 88-99.
Andrews, Norman S., 99.
*Angelo, William, 91-99; N.Y. C.P.A. 87 (1897).
— Annan, (John Dexter) & Company, 99.
Annan, (John Dexter) & Company, 99.
*Anyon, James Thornley, 88, 95-99; N.Y. C.P.A. 31 (1896); b. England, 1851; educ. Normal College, Manchester, England; U.S.A. from 1886; senior partner Barrow, Wade, Guthrie & Co. from 1887; helped organize Am. Assn. of Pub. Accts., 1887; its first sec., 1888; joint legisl. com., 1895; author, "Recollections of the Early Days of American Accountancy, 1883-1893" (1925).
— — Apple, Harry B., 94-99.
Appleton, E. J., 82.
— — Appleton, Samuel W., 93.
— Armstrong, G. B., 54.
*Arnold, Thomas E., 92-99; N.Y. C.P.A. 32 (1896); joint legisl. com. 1895.
*Ascher, Frederick, 91, 94-98; N.Y. C.P.A. 162 (1900).
— Ashwin, William M., 58.
— — Atkinson, James H., 97-99.

Audit Company of New York, 98, 99; see Edw. Ten Broeck Perine; also Alden W. Dunning.
— Audit Company of Chicago, 99; see Edward E. Gore and H. W. Roberts.
— Austin, William O., 99.
Avery, William A., 66.
— Axson, Charles W., 94.

— (Babcock) See Spencer & Babcock.
(Bacon) See Butler & Bacon.
— Badger, Horace H., 99.
Bagg & Weinberg, 97.
*Bagot, Thomas, 77-99; N.Y. C.P.A. 45 (1896); charter member N.Y. Soc. of C.P.A.'s.
Bagot (Thomas) & Abraham (J. W.), 97.
— Bailey, Fred N., 98.
— Baine, William C., 85-98.
Baker, Charles H., 56.
— Baker, John A., 84.
— Ballingall, David, 64, 65.
— — *Ballingall, Peter, 97-99; Pa. C.P.A. 36 (1900).
— — Banholzer, P. P., 91.
— Bard, Magoon & Co., 94.
— — Bargh, William, 95.
Barker, Abraham, 95.
Barker, J. Atwater, 97.
— Barker, John T., 92, 93.
Barker, William, 80.
Barnes, John E., 89-91.
Barnes, Willis G., 96-98.
— Barr, Robert, 54.
(Barrett) See Hopkins & Barrett.
— — (Barrington, Charles V.), see Ackerman and Barrington.
Barrow, Archibald C., 98, 99.
Barrow, Margaret, 97.
Barrow, John Wylie, 80-86; an actuary; first American partner in Barrow, Wade, Guthrie & Co.
Barrow, Wade, Guthrie & Co., 87-99.
— Barrow, Wade, Guthrie & Co., 91-99.
— — Bartalott, George, 88, 89.
Basley, Wm. D., 99.
— Bates, E. T., 91.
— — Baugh, William, 82.
*Beach, Oren M., 81-92; N.Y. C.P.A. 139 (1898).
— Bear, Sidney, 92, 93.
*Beaujon, Anton R., 95-98; N.Y. C.P.A. 33 (1896).
— Beck & Innes, 84.
— — Beidler, Page, & Biles, 90.
Benedict, Henry W., 75.
— — Bennett, Henry L., 95-99.
— — Bennett & Gross, 98.
— Benthen, Christopher, 87.
— — Benzon, John L., 70-72.
— — Bergan, William H., 95-99.
— — Bergmann, Charles C., 95, 96.
Bergtheil, Louis M., 85-91.
Bergtheil (L. M.), Horley (Thomas R.) & Co., 92.
Bergtheil (L. M.), Cook (Henry R. M.) & Co., 93-95.

29

[a]New York names set flush; Chicago names preceded by single dash; Philadelphia names preceded by two dashes.

*Carnrienke, John E., 97, 99; N.Y. C.P.A. 120 (1897).
— Carne, John Jr., 74.
*Carson, William, 86-91, 94-96; N.Y. C.P.A. 46 (1896).
Carter, Walter R., 79.
— Case, A. Porter, 97-99.
— — Castor, John B., 90.
— Cathrae, John H., 95, 97, 98.
— Challis, Arthur S., 96, 97, 99.
— — Chalmers, David B., 99.
*Chalmers, Rashleigh, 97, 98; N.Y. C.P.A. 144 (1898); see Skerten & Chalmers.
— — Chambers, Henry B., 96.
— Chapman, Charles C., 97.
*Chapman, Richard N., 92; N.Y. C.P.A. 2 (1896); member legisl. com., 1895; co-author of "American Accountant's Manual" (1897); see Broaker & Chapman.
— — Chapouty, P., 62-64.
*Charles, Edward C., 94-97; N.Y. C.P.A. 119 (1897).
— — Chase, Thomas, 89.
Cheney, Andrew G., 90-93, 97, 98.
*Child, Frederick Willis, 97-99; Conn. C.P.A. 4 (1908); b. Boston, 1844; member of the early Institute of Accounts; author, "Elements of Cost" (1887).
Church, Frank H., 93.
*Church, George H., 87-99; N.Y. C.P.A. 166 (1900).
Churchill, William T., 52, 56.
— — Claghorn, William C., 60-62, 70-79.
Clapp, William H., 95; legisl. meeting, 1895.
— — Clark, Frank T., 86, 88.
— Clark, George H., 90.
*Clarke, Andrew A., 91-94; N.Y. C.P.A. 15 (1896); legisl. meeting, 1895; see Smith, Reckitt, Clarke & Co.
Clawson, William H., 80.
— Clayton, J. F. & Co., 98.
— — Clement, Charles M., 88.
*(Clerihew, Alexander), N.Y. C.P.A. 90 (1897); see Whitehead, Clerihew & Driggs.
— — Coates, Edwin H., 72-74.
*Cockey, Edward T., 83-85, 87, 89-99; N.Y. C.P.A. 91 (1897); first president of the early Institute of Accounts, 1882.
Coffin, Edward H., 94-99.
— — Cole, Charles J., 66.
Cole, William H., 88.
Collins & Company, 72-76.
Collins, James R., 73-81.
Comer, John H., 76-79, 96-99.
(Comins) See Schultz & Comins.
*Conant, Leonard H., 96-99; N.Y. C.P.A. 3 (1896); b. Washington, D. C., 1856; eleven years a R.R. accountant; in pub. prac. from 1888; pres. Am. Assn. of Pub. Accts., 1899-1901; N.Y. C.P.A. examiners, 1900-03; com. on consolidation of Assn. and Federation, 1904.
(*Conant, Edward R.) N.J. C.P.A. 7 (1904); b. Lowell, Mass., 1854, d. 1926; grad. Lafayette Coll., 1876; R.R. accountant to 1893; thereafter in pub. prac. with his brother, Leonard H.
Conant & Crook, 93-95.
— — Condon, M. G., 95.
Congdon, Charles, 79-84, 86, 88.
Connelly, John J., 84, 89.
Conoley, Alex G., 98.
*Cook, Henry R. M., 92, 97-99; N.Y. C.P.A. 107 (1897); pres. Am. Assn. of Pub. Accts., 1892-93; assn. com. on organizing a school of accounts, 1892-93; joint legisl. com., 1895; prof. N.Y. Univ., 1900; N.Y. C.P.A. examiners, 1905-07; pres. N.Y. Soc. of C.P.A.'s, 1909-12; see Bergtheil, Cook, & Co.

— *Cooper, John Alexander, 91-96, 98, 99; Ill. C.P.A. 27 (1903); b. London, Eng., 1850; educ. Christ's Hospital, London; gen. accounting in London, 1865-71, and in U. S. A., 1873-90; in pub. prac. from 1890; charter member Ill. Assn. of Pub. Accts., 1897; vice-pres. Ill. Soc. of C.P.A.'s, 1907-10; pres., 1913; with Cooper, Winslow & Davis, Chicago.
Cooper, Walter G., 87.
— — Cooper, William F., 81, 84.
— — Corfield, Henry C., 86-88.
*(Corwin, Hamilton S.) N.Y. C.P.A. 56 (1896); d. 1922; charter member and first pres. N.Y. Soc. of C.P.A.'s, 1897; re-elected pres., 1914-17; with Patterson & Corwin, also Patterson, Teele & Dennis (N.Y.).
*(Cowan, James D.) N.Y. C.P.A. 587 (1912); see MacRae & Cowan.
Cowdrey & Franklin, 78-82.
Cowdrey, DeWitt C., 83, 84.
*Cowell, Louis P., 99; N.Y. C.P.A. 58 (1896).
Cox, James, 73-91.
— Coxon, Oliver, 95-99.
— — Crabbe, James H., 91, 92.
— Cragg, Harry, 87, 89, 91.
— — Craig, William B., 99.
Crandall, Levin, 84.
— — Crane, Edward T., 88-90.
Crapser, John M., 92-95.
— — Craven, John B., 91, 93-99.
— — Crean, William, 69
— — Crittenden, S. H., 60-67, 81-84.
— — Crittenden, Samuel W., 78, 83.
— Crittenton, Harlow, 85, 86.
Croad, Horatio J., 88-91.
— — Crocker, W. Eldridge, 92.
Crocker, Mark J., 95-99.
Cronyn, George H., 90, 93-95.
(Crook) See Conant & Crook.
— — Crook, Thomas B., 82, 84, 85, 93-95.
— Crowell, J. Herbert, 98.
Cullen, William G., 79-82, 86, 88-96, 98, 99.
Cummings, Frank G., 81.
— — Cushman, Charles W., 94-99.
*Cuthbert, Robert L., 95-97; N.Y. C.P.A. 16 (1896).
Cuthbert, Menzies & Company, 98, 99.
— Cuthbert, Boughey & Menzies, 99.

— Dafoe, William H., 95, 97, 98.
Dahlgreen, Charles G., 75.
— — Daly, Peter, 71, 72.
Dane, Silvan, 95-99.
— D'Arcy, Patrick, 97.
Darrow, William, 56.
*Davidson, Arnold, 97; N.Y. C.P.A. 17 (1896); b. Danzig, Germany, 1840; atty.
— Davidson, Edward G., 79.
— — Davidson, Jay C., 80-84.
*Davies, W. Saunders, 92-99; N.Y. C.P.A. 4 (1896); b. Liverpool, Eng., 1862; d. 1940; in U. S. A. from 1891; state legisl. com., 1895-96; pres. Am. Assn. of Pub. Accts., 1897; chairman com. on consolidation of Assn. and Federation, 1904; pres. Am. Inst. of Accts., 1916-17, and member of its council until 1940.
Davis, Daniel B., 52.
— Davis, George, 96.
Davis, Henry B., 56.
*Davis, Henry C., 93, 97-99; N.Y. C.P.A. 71 (1896).
Dawson, Miles M., 98, 99; b. Viroqua, Wis., 1863, d. Orlando, Fla., 1942; actuary; attorney; adviser to War Risk Insurance Bureau, 1917; author; prof. N.Y. Univ.
— — Dawson, Robert W., 69.
— — Dayton, O. M., 88, 89, 95.

33

34

Jones, Lewis D., 91-94; b. Manchester, Eng., 1859; d. 1899; chartered acct. (Eng.); a founder and first pres. of Ill. Assn. of Pub. Accts., 1897.
— — Jones, Samuel D., 99.
Jones, Thomas, 52, 56, 57, 59-62.
— *Joplin, J. Porter, 94-96; Ill. C.P.A. 2 (1903); b. Chippenham, Eng., 1859; d. Chicago, 1938; early experience in Bank of Nova Scotia; began pub. prac. in Chicago, 1888; twice vice-pres. (1904, 1912) of Ill. Soc. of C.P.A.'s, and twice its pres. (1905, 1911); vice-pres. Am. Assn. of Pub. Accts., 1905, and pres. of Am. Inst. of Accountants, 1914-16; pres. Walton School of Commerce; retired from practice in 1923; firm, Walton, Joplin & Langer.
— — Joseph, Gustav A., 95, 96.
— — Joslyn, Charles A., 97.
— — Joyce, John A., 72.
— *Judd, Frederick F., 87-91, 93-99; Ill. C.P.A. 59 (1904); charter member Ill. Assn. of Pub. Accts., 1897.
Judelsohn, Jacob, 90, 91.
— — Judelsohn, J., 85.
— Junes, Hugh, 77.

Kane & Peebles, 90.
**Kavanagh (John B.) & Sullivan (Thomas J.), 95-99; N.Y. C.P.A. 90 (1897); N.Y. C.P.A. 83 (1897).
— Keiller, Andrew, 54.
— Keiller, John, 54.
*Kelley, James N., 97-99; N.Y. C.P.A. 49 (1896); charter member N.Y. Soc. of C.P.A.'s and treas., 1898-1903.
— — Kelly, Henry, 84-96.
— Kelly, James N., 98, 99.
— Kelso, Samuel J., 98.
— *Kendall, William, 88, 92, 93, 98, 99; Ill. C.P.A. 84 (1904).
— — *Kennedy, Ridgley E., 93-99; Pa. C.P.A. 21 (1899); b. Newark, Ill., 1859; in pub. prac. after 1889.
— — Kennedy, William, 88-90, 93, 95.
(Kentworthy) See Gane, Jackson, Jeffreys, & Kentworthy.
*Kenworthy, Arthur W., 94-99; Ohio C.P.A. 75 (1909).
— — Kenworthy, Joseph W., 96; b. 1859; d. 1922; author "Bookkeeping" (1889).
— — Kerk, Augustus, 69, 72-79, 81, 85-91.
Kerr & Campbell, 89, 90.
*Kerr, James C., 93-95, 97-99; N.Y. C.P.A. 50 (1896).
Kerr, Thomas J., 91.
— — Keys Bros., 79.
— — Keyser, Nelson B., 92-95.
— Kidson, Buchanan & Co., 92-96.
— Kidson, Herbert & Co., 93-95.
Kimball, Wm. H., 98, 99.
King, Samuel P., 52.
— *Kingwill, Joseph H., 92-94; Calif. C.P.A. 12 (1907).
*Kinmonth, Alfred S., 93, 99; Conn. C.P.A. 6 (1908).
Kimmonth, Andrew J., 91, 92.
— — Kinsley, O. J., 90.
Kirstein, Henry, 93, 95.
*Kittredge, Anson O., 98, 99; N.Y. C.P.A. 121 (1897); b. Dayton, Ohio, 1848; d. Boston, 1903; charter member early Institute of Accounts; editor, 1886-1903; author; N.Y. C.P.A. examiners, 1899-1900; prof. of accg., N.Y. Univ., 1900; see Account. Audit & Assurance Co.
*Klaw, Aaron M., 95-99; N.Y. C.P.A. 130 (1898).
— Klinck, Henry G., 73.
— — Kline, J. Belmont, 84, 85.
Klopfer, Berthold, 87.

*Koehler, Theodore G., 96; N.Y. C.P.A. 76 (1897); b. Denmark, 1856; served in N. Y. State Senate, 1896-98, actively fostering the first C.P.A. legislation; organized "New York School of Accounts," 1896, for preparing C.P.A. candidates and directed the school for 25 years; author "Accounting Mentor of Theory and Practice" (1922), "The Accounting Quiz-Answerer" (1922).
— — — Kolb, Charles F., 85, 88-91.
Krugt, C. G., 98.
— — Kuckuck, Harry J., 98, 99.
— — — Kuen, John S., 86.
— *(Kuhns, Maurice S.), N.Y. C.P.A. 97 (1897); Ill. com. on legisl., 1903; see Safeguard Account Company.
— — Kummerer, Victor E., 90, 91.

*Lafrentz, Ferdinand W., 97-99; N.Y. C.P.A. 20 (1896); prof. of accy., N.Y. Univ., 1900; pres. Am. Assn. of Pub. Accts., 1901-03.
*Lamb, Fergus, 95-99; N.Y. C.P.A. 21 (1896).
— — Landell, William H., 82.
Lee, Samuel, 93-99.
Lee, Thomas B., 99.
— — — Leeds, Barclay R., 60-62.
— — Leidy, Byron, 71-76.
— — — Leidy, Channing, 72, 78, 80, 86-89.
— — — Leidy, S. Snyder, 60.
— (Leith) See Nelson & Leith.
*Lejeune, Capel Ellis, 89, 90, 92-99; N.Y. C.P.A. 39 (1896); legisl. meeting, 1895.
— — Lembert, Gustavus, 69-71, 73-75.
Lescher, Herman & Co., 93-96.
— Leslie, Henry T., 96, 97.
Levy, Julius E., 88, 89.
— — *Lewer, Charles, 93-99; Pa. C.P.A. 6 (1899).
Lewis, Alfred W., 91, 92.
Lewis, Frederick, 79-81, 83.
— — Lewis, John E., 69.
Lewis (Richard) & McGibbon (Brownell) 97-99.
*Lewis, Richard, 92-94; N.Y. C.P.A. 111 (1897).
Lindsay Reid (& Co.), 95; J. Lindsay Reid present at legisl. meeting, 1895.
— — Lindsay, Walter E., 95, 96.
*Lingley, Richard T., 96-99; N.Y. C.P.A. 127 (1897); b. London, Eng., 1873; later with Lingley, Baird & Dixon in N.Y.
— — Lippmann, Charles J., 94.
— — Lits, William H., 98.
— Litson, William T., 98.
Littlejohn, Frank B., 82-84, 95-99.
Livingston, Charles M., 67-84.
Lloyd, George W., 59, 63.
— — Lloyd, Herbert J., 73-76.
— Lloyd, James, 54.
Loder, Benjamin H., 86-91.
Lomax, Wm. V., 96, 97.
— Lombard, Willard C., 91.
*Loomis, John R., 91-98; N.Y. C.P.A. 51 (1896); b. Cambridge, N.Y., 1846; d. New York City, 1923; early in charge of accounting for International Paper Co. and comptroller for United Box Co.; charter member N.Y. Soc. of C.P.A.'s; 1904 with Loomis, Conant & Co.; later with Loomis, Suffern & Fernald; pres. early Institute of Accounts, 1898-1905; pres. Am. Assn. of Pub. Accts., 1903-06; vice-pres. Am. Inst. of Accts., 1922.
— Loss & Loss, 98, 99.
— Louderbach, William J., 92, 96, 97; b. Hamilton, N.Y., 1864; R.R. accountant, 1881-89; later with brokerage houses.
— — Lovejoy, A. F., 85.

35

Lucas, Newton C., 97-99.
— — Luckenbach, John L., 99.
Ludington, J. H., 89.
*Ludlam, Chas. S., 99; N.Y. C.P.A. 115 (1897); b. Chicago, 1866, d. 1934; R.R. accountant to 1895, then in pub. accounting with Haskins & Sells; com. on consolidation of Assn. and Federation, 1904; vice-pres. Am. Inst. of Accts., 1918.
— — Lukens, A. F., 97.
— — Lukens, Ezra, 74.
Luttman, Alfred & Co., 83.
— — Lybrand, Ross Bros. & Montgomery, 98, 99.
— — *(Lybrand, Wm. M.), Pa. C.P.A. 14 (1899); with John Heins, 1887; partner, 1891; later with Lybrand, Ross Bros. & Montgomery; treas. Pa. Inst. of C.P.A.'s, 1897-1901; pres. N.A.C.A., 1922.
Lynch, A. S., 93.

— MacBrair, Alexander, 92-98.
— — McCahan, John, 50.
— — MacCain, Robert, 98.
— McCall, W. A. Co., 93.
— McCarthy, Patrick A., 95.
— — McCausland, Craig, 87, 93-98.
— McClain, William C., 93.
McClintock, Wm. D., 91, 92.
— McClure, Thomas D., 95.
— — McConnell, J. S., 91, 92.
— McCulloch, C. H., 86, 89, 90.
McDonald, Benjamin A., 79.
— McDonald, J. H., 88, 89.
— — McDonald, William, 61, 62.
Macey, George R., 85-88.
— — McElwee, Isaac W., 94, 99.
— — McFaden, William W., 88.
— McGay, John H., 90-96.
*(McGibbon, Brownell), N.Y. C.P.A. 7 (1896); see Lewis & McGibbon.
McKain, Frank J., 97-99.
McKean & Hall, 87.
McKean, William B., 75-79, 83-86, 88-93, 97-99.
*McKenna, James A., 89-99; N.Y. C.P.A. 22 (1896); b. 1856, d. 1941.
*MacKenzie, John, 99; N.Y. C.P.A. 472 (1912).
— McKinney, Winfield S., 97-99; author, "Mercantile Accounting," 1907.
(McLaughlin, Rodney), incorporator Am. Assn. of Pub. Accts., 1887.
MacLean, Chas., 99.
— — McLeran, James B., 70, 71.
— McMullen, Charles H., 97.
— — McMullen, John S., 70, 71.
— — MacNeal, Bernard, 72.
MacRae (F. J.) & Cowan (James D.), 94.
*MacRae, Farquhar J., 92, 93, 97-99; N.Y. C.P.A. 23 (1896); incorporator and charter member N.Y. Soc. of C.P.A.'s, 1897, its vice-pres., 1899-1903, and pres., 1903-06; pres. Federation of Soc. of C.P.A.'s, 1903.
MacRae (F. J.), Gardner & Co., 95, 96.
MacRae, John, 89.
Maggi, Charles, 53, 54.
— Magill, Thomas J., 88-92, 95.
— (Magoon) See Bard, Magoon & Co.
— — Maher, John, 72-76.
— — Mann, Jacob, 88, 89.
*Manvel, Frederick Converse, 97-99; N.Y. C.P.A. 8 (1896); b. Greenwich, Conn., 1860; d. 1916; instrumental in C.P.A. legisl. in Connecticut; member state board of accountants, 1908.
— Marchand, G. S., 86-99, (& Co., 91-99); charter member Ill. Assn. of Pub. Accts., 1897.
Marden, George W., 76.
*Marin, (John C.), N.Y. C.P.A. 124 (1897); see Bragg & Marin.
— — Marks, Edward S., 91, 96.

Marland, W. A., 58.
— Marquand, Josiah Jr., 78.
Marsh, Christopher C., 50, 52, 67, 72, 76, 79-82.
— Marshall, Henry E., 94.
— Marston, J. G., 87-89.
*Martin, Andrew B., 85-94, 99; N.Y. C.P.A. 24 (1896).
Martin, Andrew B. & Clarence A., 95-99.
Martin Brothers, 82.
*Martin, Clarence, 85-94; N.Y. C.P.A. 25 (1896).
— — Martin, George R., 99.
Martin, Jacob, 99.
*Marwick, James, 96, 97; Ill. C.P.A. 103 (1907); b. Edinburgh, 1862; char. acct. Walker & Marwick of Glasgow, 1887; Vancouver, Can., 1893; U.S.A., 1894; later with Peat, Marwick, Mitchell & Co. (N.Y.)
Marwick (James) & Mitchell (S. Roger), 98, 99.
Masheder, Thomas, 98.
— Mason, George A., 91.
*Mason, John D., 93-96; N.Y. C.P.A. 122 (1897).
Mason, William, 61.
Mason, William E., 84.
Massa, Geo. F., 97-99.
— Matthern, C. Otto E., 83, 97-99; author, "Seven-account-system of Bookkeeping," 1876.
Maude, Arthur A., 68-71.
May, William A., 94, 95.
— — *Mead, Frederick Lockwood, 99; b. Camden, N. J., 1862; N.J. C.P.A. 43 (1904).
— Mechelk, E. C., 83, 84, 87-90.
(Menzies) See Cuthbert, Menzies & Co.
*Mercer, Charles J., 91, 93-99; N.Y. C.P.A. 9 (1896).
Merklee, John, 56.
— *Merrill, Clarence D., 97-99; Ill. C.P.A. 74 (1904).
— Metz, French W., 97-99.
Milbank, William J., 79, 89, 90.
— *Millard, Henry, 96; Ill. C.P.A. 46 (1904).
— — Millard, Henry, 97.
Miller, Isaac S., 64, 65.
— — *Miller, W. Harry, 85; Pa. C.P.A. 53 (1906).
Miller, William H., 75.
Milligan, Edward W., 93-97.
Mills, William, 52.
— Miner, John T., 95, 96.
Mirick, Mark C., 76, 79, 82-97; b. 1825, d. 1906; an incorporator Am. Assn. of Pub. Accts., 1887; legisl. meeting, 1895.
Mitchell, G., 58.
*(Mitchell, Simpson Roger), N.Y. C.P.A. 128 (1898); b. Glasgow, Scotland, 1860; char. acct. (Canada); see Hopkins, Mitchell & Co.; also Marwick & Mitchell.
Molloy, William, 79-91, 93, 95-98; b. Glasgow; char. acct. of Canada.
— — *Montelius, William E., 94-99; Pa. C.P.A. 9 (1899).
— Montgomery, J. Graham, 94.
— — *(Montgomery, Robert H.), Pa. C.P.A. 17 (1899); b. Mahonoy City, Pa., 1872; partner Heins, Whelen, Lybrand & Co., 1896; treas. Federation of Soc. of C.P.A.'s, 1902 and its sec., 1904; com. on consolidation of Assn. and Federation, 1904; pres. Am. Assn. of Pub. Accts., 1912-14; prof. of accountancy, Columbia Univ., 1912-24; pres. N.Y. Soc. of C.P.A.'s, 1922; Am. Inst. of Accts., vice-pres., 1927; pres., 1935-37; author, "Auditing Theory and Practice" (1912); "Income Tax Procedure" (1917); "Financial Handbook" (1933); see Lybrand, Ross Bros. & Montgomery.
Mooney, Stephen J., 97.
Moore, Louis B., 94.
— — Moore, S. Frank, 99.

— Morice, Frank H., 91-93.
— Morris, C. W., 88, 89.
— *(Morris, Charles E.), Ill. C.P.A. 55 (1904); b. Virginia, 1867; partner in Haskins & Sells.
Morton, Harry J., 98.
*Morton, Oscar E., 88-95, 97-99; N.Y. C.P.A. 78 (1897).
Mowton, William Edward, 74.
— — *Moxey, Edward P., Sr., 92-99; b. Phila., 1849, d. 1915; Pa. C.P.A. 30 (1899); a national bank examiner, 1891-1909; founded firm of E. P. Moxey & Co.; pres. Pa. Institute of C.P.A.'s, 1913-15.
— — — Moxey & Riley, 94.
— Mudge, Charles H., 96.
— — Mudge, Harry, 73.
— — Mueller, Louis, 87.
— Muir, W. T., 54.
Muller, Frederick J., 82.
Mullins, John P., 92.
— — Mundy, Charles I., 95.
Munro, Robert F., 86, 88; b. Scotland; later in cotton oil business.
— — *Murphy, Joseph C., 80, 84, 85, 90-92, 95, 97-99; N.H. C.P.A. 120 (1920).
— — Murray, Michael J., 69.
Musgrave, Wayne M., 99.
— — Musgrove, Thomas C., 72, 73.
— — Mustin, R. F. & Son, 73-75, 79, 84-99.
Mustin, Spenser C., 79.
Myer, George W. E., 63-65, 70, 80, 81, 83, 84.

Nathan & Bromberg, 97.
— — Nathans, David, 60.
— Neil, John F., 99.
— Nelson (Robert) & Leith, 99.
— *(Nelson, Robert), b. Glasgow, 1870; chartered accountant, 1893; Ill. C.P.A. 17 (1903).
Neumann, Paul C., 94.
Nevius, Peter I., 98, 99.
New York Accounting & Adjustment Co., 95-98.
— Nichols, William C., 96, 98, 99; see Butler & Nichols.
*Nicholson, Jerome Lee, 92-96 (& Co., 93, 94); N.Y. C.P.A. 190 (1901); b. Trenton, N.J., 1863; in pub. prac. from 1889; lecturer on cost accounting, Columbia Univ., 1912-17; chief, division of cost accounting, Bureau of Foreign and Domestic Commerce, 1917; consulting cost specialist, Federal Trade Commission; author "Factory Organization and Costs" (1909), "Cost Accounting" (1912), "Cost Theory and Practice" (1913), "Cost Accounting" (1918).
*Nield, Charles F., 96-99; N.Y. C.P.A. 79 (1897).
— *Nigg, Charles F., 90, 93-99; Ill. C.P.A. 66 (1904).
*Niles, Chas. E., 95-97; N.Y. C.P.A. 99 (1897); see Niles & Niles.
*Niles, Henry A., 96; N.Y. C.P.A. 59 (1896); b. Phila., 1865; admitted to bar, 1897; see Niles & Niles.
— — *Niles, Mary B., 93-99; Pa. C.P.A. 34 (1900).
Niles & Niles, 98, 99.
— Nisbet, P. L., 93.
— — Nixon, William, 74.
— Nolte, George H., 94-96.
— — Noonan, John S., 87.
— North, C. F., 95-97 (& Co., 95, 96).
North, Charles F., 91-94 (& Co., 91, 92).
— — (Nutt) See Falkenstein, Nutt & Co.
— Nyquist, Gustaf, 96.

Oakley, Robert S., 50, 51.
— — Oberer, George E., 75, 78-80, 82-86, 88, 89, 95, 96.

— — Oberteuffer, William C., 95-99.
— — O'Brien, Cornelius, 93.
O'Connor, John J., 96.
Odell, Thomas J., 86.
— O'Donnell, Charles W., 93, 94.
— — O'Donnell, Thomas, 60, 77, 84.
Ogden, Frederick & Co., 74.
— Oldershaw, Percival, 58.
Oldershaw, Percival P., 67.
— Oliver, William, 97-99.
— — Orrick, Newton L., 74.
Osborn, William J., 78.

(Packard, Silas H.), educator; member joint legisl. com., 1895.
— *Page, Frederick P., 95; Ohio C.P.A. 70 (1908).
*Page, Fred Palmer, 95-99; Ohio C.P.A. 70 (1908); b. Ipswich, Eng., 1859, d. 1940; A.C.A. (Eng.), 1884; F.C.A., 1904; in prac. New York from 1890; later with Sargent, Page & Taylor; New York partner in Deloitte, Plender, Griffiths & Co. from 1905 to retirement in 1920; see Sargent, Page & Taylor.
Page, George W., 79.
— — Page, Richard V., 98, 99.
— — (Page) See Beidler, Page, & Biles.
— Paine, Herman S., 96.
Palmer, William H., 87-91, 93, 94.
Parkin, Josiah, 58-60.
— — Parrish, William E., 90.
(Parsons) See Dean, Parsons & Buchanan.
— Pasdeloup, Francis, 56.
— (Paterson) See Broads, Paterson & Co.
(Paterson) See Glardon & Paterson; also Rea & Paterson.
*Patterson, Andrew S., 91, 92; N.Y. C.P.A. 41 (1896); charter member N.Y. Soc. of C.P.A.'s.
Patterson (E. C.) & Corwin (H. S.), 93-98.
Patterson (Andrew S.) Corwin (Hamilton) & Patterson (Stuart H.), 99.
*(Patterson, Stuart Hoyt), N.Y. C.P.A. 137 (1898); b. New York City, 1871; son of Andrew S.; with Patterson, Teele & Dennis, 1900-1905; later in bonds, banking, public utilities.
— Patterson, Frank & Co., 92.
Patterson, J. R., 96.
Paul, James M., 92.
— Paulsen, Andrew E., 96.
Paulsen, Wm. J., 98.
Peckham, George, 57.
(Peebles) See Kane & Peebles.
— — Peirce, Thomas May, 69, 71, 85; propr. Peirce's Union Bus. Coll., 1880; author "Manual of Bookkeeping," 1895.
Pendleton, Wm. T., 99.
— — Penington, H. B., 60.
— — (Pennington) See Hand & Pennington.
*Penney, John W., 95; N.Y. C.P.A. 100 (1897); see Wand, Edmonds, & Penney.
— — Pentlarge, Theodore, 94-97.
*Pentlarge, Theodore, 98, 99; N.Y. C.P.A. 129 (1898); b. Prague, 1846; in pub. prac. from 1876.
*Perrenoud, Gustavus F., 89-98; N.Y. C.P.A. 42 (1896).
*(Perine, Edw. Ten Broeck), N.Y. C.P.A. 636 (1914); b. Plainfield, N.J., 1870; officer in Audit Co. of N.Y., 1897-1908; deputy comptroller, State of New York, 1909-10.
— Perry, Edward C., 92.
— *Pfahler, Charles B., 96; Ore. C.P.A. 14 (1913).
*Phelps, Charles D., 91-99; N.Y. C.P.A. 43 (1896); b. 1855, d. 1927; bank accountant for 15 years; in public practice from 1889.

37

38

Schultz, Francis G., 72.
Schultz, R. E., 70, 79.
Scott, John F., 52.
(Scott) See Harney, Scott & Co.
(Scott) See Tremain & Scott.
*Searle, Harry F., 98, 99; N.Y. C.P.A. 131 (1898); b. Troy, N.Y., 1866, d. 1940; R.R. accountant; later, Searle, Oakey & Miller (N.Y.).
— — Secor, Ambrose T., 82-84.
Secor, Chas. A., 98, 99.
*Self, Edward, 93-99; N.Y. C.P.A. 52 (1896).
— — Selfridge, Robert K., 96.
— — — *Sellers, Alfred L., 95-99; Pa. C.P.A. 7 (1899).
*Sells, Elijah W., 96; N.Y. C.P.A. 10 (1896); b. Muscatine, Ia., 1858, d. 1924; honorary A.M. degree, Baker Univ.; honorary D.C.S. degree, N.Y. Univ.; R.R. accountant, 1879-92; with C. W. Haskins revised acct. system of U.S. Gov., 1893-95; established firm Haskins and Sells, 1895; charter member N.Y. Soc. of C.P.A.'s, 1897; pres. Am. Assn. of Pub. Accts., 1906-08; on com. to plan organization of Am. Inst. of Accts., 1915 and for many years a member of its council and executive com.; author, "The Accounting Profession."
Senior, Richard, 50.
— — Sexton, Townsend, 92-94.
Seymour, Norman, 86.
*(Shaible, Wm. G.), N.Y. C.P.A. 62 (1896); charter member N.Y. Soc. of C.P.A.'s.
Sharp, John A., 87-89.
— — Sharpless, Isaac, 87.
— — Shaw, George E., 97, 98; charter member Ill. Assn. of Pub. Accts.
— — Shaw, Samuel, 85.
— — Shawhan, J., 98.
Shearman, William P., 90-95.
— Sherman, Ward B., 96, 97.
*Sheridan, Frank J., 99; N.Y. C.P.A. 81 (1897).
— Sherwin, Judson G., 77.
— Sherwood, W. St. John, 71.
— — Shields, Jeffries F., 77, 78, 82, 84-99.
Sibley, Charles H. W., 79-90; an incorporator of Am. Assn. of Pub. Accts., 1887.
— — Siddall, Charles E., 93.
— Silke, J. Freeman, 67-71.
Silvester, Charles F., 90-96.
— Simon, H. & Co., 95, 96.
— — Simons, John P., 71.
— — Simpson, John L., 92.
— — Simpson, Thomas B., 88, 89, 91, 92.
Simson, James, 59-78, 80-82, 84-95.
Simson, Wm. T., 95, 96, 99.
— — Sinexon, Thomas, 75, 81, 90, 92-99.
Sizer, John M., 82.
Skerten & Chalmers, 95-99.
— — Slack, Daniel W., 69, 88.
Smallwood, George, 92-98.
— *Smart, Allen Rich, 97-99; Ill. C.P.A. 1 (1903); b. Peterborough, Eng., 1867; began pub. prac. in Eng., 1885; in U.S.A., 1891, with Barrow, Wade, Guthrie & Co. (partner in 1911); later formed Smart, Gore & Co.; first pres. Ill. Soc. of C.P.A.'s, 1904.
Smart, Allen R., 92, 93.
— — Smethurst, Richard, 50.
Smiley, Geo. P., 99.
— — Smith, Alex., 98.
*Smith, Charles B., 94-99; N.Y. C.P.A. 53 (1896); b. Bath, Eng., 1858, d. 1936; member Am. Assn. of Pub. Accts. from 1896.
— Smith, Cris F., 98.
Smith, Elias L., 56.
Smith, Francis A., 93, 94.
— — Smith, Franklin, 98, 99.

Smith, Frederick E., 68.
Smith, Henry C., 98, 99.
Smith, Howell, 82.
Smith & Inston, 88.
Smith, Jacob, Jr., 76.
*Smith, James Jaspar, 97-99; N.J. C.P.A. 10 (1904).
Smith & Moller, 90-93.
— Smith, Reckitt, Clarke & Co., 95-99.
Smith, Reckitt, Clarke & Co., 95-99.
— Smith, Reckitt & Co., 92-94.
Smith, Reckitt & Co., 92-94.
— Smith, Samuel C., 88.
Smithers, Henry K., 67-72.
— Smitz, Lee, 99.
Smyth, Cleveland H., 92.
Smyth, Wm., 98, 99.
(Smyth) See Abrahams, Smyth, Williams & Co.
— *Snyder, Carrie, 93, 94, 96-99; Ill. C.P.A. 61 (1904); co-author (with E. L. Thurston) "Universal System of Prac. Books" (1902).
— — Snyder, Joseph, 96.
Solomons, Herman, 76-80.
Somers, Frederick D., 72.
— Somerville, Charles, 90.
— Sorley, C. H., 95.
— — Spackman, John B., 69.
— Sparks, William, 98, 99.
*Sparrow, John Robert, 94-99; N.Y. C.P.A. 54 (1896); b. Brooklyn, 1859, d. 1921; legisl. meeting, 1895; pres. N.Y. Soc. of C.P.A.'s, 1917-19; with Sparrow, Harvey & Co., N.Y.
— Spear, Andrew Jr., 95-98.
Spellman, Samuel R., 50, 51.
— Spence, Robert, 99.
— Spencer & Babcock, 95.
— — Spooner, Walter, 88.
*Sprague, Charles E., 85; N.Y. C.P.A. 11 (1896); b. 1842, d. 1912; degrees, A.M., Ph.D.; teacher, 1864-70; prof. of accounting N.Y. Univ., 1900; with Union Dime Savings Bank for 30 years and its pres. in 1904; author "Philosophy of Accounts," 1907, based on his articles in The Bookkeeper, a periodical of which he was editor in the 1880's.
— — Stahl, R. H., 67, 69-71.
Stamford, Henry P., 91, 92.
— Stapleton, Edward J., 80.
— — Steel, Edwin K., 69.
— — Steel, Robert B., 78.
*Steenson, John F., 93-99; Pa. C.P.A. 41 (1900).
Stephens, George, 90-99.
— — Stephens, William A., 85-93.
Stephenson, Chas. F., 95.
— — *(Sterrett, Joseph E.), Pa. C.P.A. 12 (1899); b. Brockwayville, Pa., 1870; established firm Francis and Sterrett in Phila.; a prime mover in securing C.P.A. legisl. in Pa.; first sec. of Pa. Inst. of C.P.A.'s; chairman (with A. A. Ross and A. L. Sellers) of its com. on educ. which supervised evening classes in accountancy in Phila. from 1902 to 1904 when the work was taken up by Univ. of Pa.; the faculty of the school (1902) included R. H. Montgomery, W. M. Lybrand, J. W. Fernley and H. G. Stockwell; chairman of International Congress of Accountants, St. Louis, 1904; pres. Am. Assn. of Pub. Accts., 1908-10; member advisory tax board, Bur. Inter. Rev., 1917-19; treas. Am. Inst. of Accts., 1912-22.
— Stevens, J. B., 86, 87.
*Stevens, Richard F., 84, 88, 96-99; N.Y. C.P.A. 29 (1896); joint legisl. com., 1895; pres. Am. Assn. of Pub. Accts., 1893-96.

39

Walker, E. H., 87.
- - - - Walker, Edward J., 84-86.
- - Walker, James P., 96.
*Walker, Joshua, 94; Calif. C.P.A. 83 (1908).
Wallace, William S., 88, 89.
— — Walls, John J., 97.
— — Walsh, Michael L., 69.
- - Walter, Henry, 83, 84.
— Walterhouse, Oscar F., 99.
Waltermire & Co., 95.
- - - - Walton, Grace M., 92.
- *Walton, Seymour, 96; Ill. C.P.A. 3 (1903); b. New Orleans, 1846, d. Chicago, 1920; educ. at Williams College; cashier Fort Dearborn National Bank to 1893; in pub. prac. from 1893; with Griffin & Walton, 1895, Walton & Joplin from 1897; pres. Ill. Soc. of C.P.A.'s, 1907; prof. of accounting N.W. Univ., 1907-12; dean of Walton School of Commerce, 1917-20; editor "Student's Department" of Journal of Accountancy, 1914-20.
— — Wamalung, J. F., 99.
Wand & Edmonds, 92, 93.
Wand, Edmonds & Bouton, 95-99.
Wand, Edmonds & Penney, 94.
Wand, Sidney P., 97, 98.
- - Ward, Edward J. E., 95-98.
Ware, W. P., 71, 72, 74.
Waring, Viola D., 98, 99.
- - - - Warr, William W., 69-71, 73-94.
*Warren, Haynes L., 93-99; N.Y. C.P.A. 85 (1897).
Warren, William E., 69-71, 73-78.
- - — Warrington, James, 84-99.
Watrous, Halsted, 90-92.
— — Waterman, T. A., 69-71, 74, 82-84.
Watson, Charles, 79.
- - Watson, J. D., 87.
Watson, Richard, 52.
- - Watson, William I., 98, 99.
- - Webb, Henry, 74.
- *Webner, Frank E., 97; Ill. C.P.A. 51 (1904); b. Chicago, 1865; educ. in Armour Institute; gen. accg. C.&N.W. Ry. (1887); and Deering Harvester Co.; later head of own firm in Detroit and Washington; author "Factory Costs" (1911), "Factory Accounting" (1917), "Factory Overhead" (1924).
(Weinberg) See Bagg and Weinberg.
- Weinschenk, Maier, 79, 84, 88, 89.
Weiss (Wm. F.) & Johnson, 97, 98.
*Weiss, Wm. F., 99; N.Y. C.P.A. 141 (1898); b. Germany, 1861, d. New York City, 1939; came to U.S.A., 1880; in pub. prac., 1894; pres. N.Y. Soc. of C.P.A.'s, 1912; on council of Am. Inst. of Accts., 1916-19.
Weite, Joseph Jr., 96.
- - Welch, R. Kemp, 92.
Welsch, Wm., 99.
Wentworth, Frank P., 99.
West, Charles, 92, 95, 96.
West, George P., 90, 91.
- - Wheatcroft, S. Irvin, 94.
Wheaton, Fred S., 91-96, 99.
Wheeler, George, 60.
- - - - Whelen, Kingston G., 97-99; with John Heins, 1888-1896; see Heins & Whelen; also Heins, Whelen, Lybrand & Co.
White, Charles W., 72, 84.
- - - White, William, 96.
Whitehead (John W.), Clerihew & Driggs, 92-96, 98, 99.
*(Whitehead, John W.), N.Y. C.P.A. 103 (1897).
— Whitehead, James, 93, 94.
Whitman, George A., 80-85.

- - - Whitman, Henry F., 92.
Whitmore & Co., 97.
Whittemore, Geo. W., 99.
- - Wibert, William, 81.
- Wickens, Charles R., 98, 99.
*Wicks, Alfred H., 97, 98, 99; N.Y. C.P.A. 86 (1897).
- - Wiestling, John H., 89, 96.
- - - Wigand, E. O., 79.
Wiggins, F. A., 94-99.
- Wigham, Robert W., 94.
Wilde, George C., 99.
- - Wildman, James, 97.
Wile, David, 94.
- *Wilkinson, George, 96-99; d. 1932; Ill. C.P.A. 5 (1903); began pub. prac. with Veysey & Veysey, 1887; prime mover in organizing Ill. Assn. of Pub. Accts. in 1897, its sec., 1897, its pres., 1902; guiding spirit in calling convention of state societies in 1902 which resulted in formation of the Federation of State Societies of C.P.A.'s; first sec. of the Federation; sec. International Congress of Accountants, 1904, and chairman com. on consolidation with Am. Assn.
Wilkinson, George, 98, 99.
Williams, Edward D., 93.
- - Williams, George A., 98, 99.
- - - - Williams, Harry G., 95, 96.
- - Williams, Stephen T., 93, 94.
Williams, Stephen T., 99.
(Williams) See Abrahams, Smyth, Williams & Co.
- - - - Wilson, William L., 96-99.
- - Windsor, J. A., 89.
- - - Winters, Adam J., 69.
- - - - *Witherup, William A., 72, 94-99; Pa. C.P.A. 42 (1900).
—Wodrich, Henry J. D., 98, 99.
Wolfe-Brown, Francis, 97-99.
Wolff, Julius, 93.
Wolff, Moses, 96-99.
- Wood, Charles L., 99.
- - - Wood, Erskine H., 80.
- - - Wood, Francis M., 76, 80, 83-86, 88.
Wood, George, 96.
Wood, Philip, 97.
Wood, Raymond, 87.
- - — Wood, Thomas W., 97.
— Wood, William W., 99.
— Woodcock, Alfred K., 96.
— Woodruff, Edw. P., 81, 82.
— — Woodward, John W., 87.
Woodward, William A., 80, 81.
- - Woolley, James, 51.
— — Wright, Charles G., 98.
Wright, Prince Albert, 85, 87, 89-91, 95, 96; b. 1850, d. 1925; author "Bookkeeping Simplified" (1885).
- - - (Wunder) See Bullock & Wunder.

*Yalden, James, 84-88; N.Y. C.P.A. 138 (1898); d. 1905; an incorporator Am. Assn. of Pub. Accts., 1887, and its first pres. 1887-88; re-elected pres., 1891-92; joint legisl. com., 1895.
Yalden, Brooks & Donnelly, 89-93.
Yalden, Brooks & Walker, 94, 95.
Yalden, Walker & Co., 96-99.
- - - - Yarnall, William F., 94.
- - Yost, Herman, 98.
- - Young, Nathaniel L., 96.
- - *(Young, Arthur), Ill. C.P.A. 16 (1903); b. Scotland, 1863; member Ill. Assn. of Pub. Accts., 1897; see Stuart & Young.

Zimmerman, Seward, 94.

41

PUBLICATIONS OF THE BUREAU OF ECONOMIC AND BUSINESS RESEARCH

COLLEGE OF COMMERCE AND BUSINESS ADMINISTRATION
UNIVERSITY OF ILLINOIS

BULLETIN SERIES

1. Illinois Taxes in 1921. *(Out of print.)*
2. Illinois State Revenue, 1895-1920. *(Out of print.)*
3. The Tax Rates of Illinois Cities in 1921. *(Out of print.)*
4. Books About Shoes. *(Out of print.)*
5. Methods of Training Employees in Stores of Moderate Size. *(Out of print.)*
6. Books About Books.
7. The Statistical Characteristics of Bookstore Sales. *(Out of print.)*
8. The Method of Analyzing Business Data. *(Out of print.)*
9. The Current Ratio in Public Utility Companies. *(Out of print.)*
10. The Productivity Ratios of Public Utility Companies. *(Out of print.)*
11. The Natural Business Year. *(Out of print.)*
12. State Expenditures in Illinois, 1895-1924.
13. The Disposition of Income in Public Utility Companies.
14. Illinois Appropriations for Social and Educational Purposes.
15. The Earning Power Ratios of Public Utility Companies. *(Out of print.)*
16. The Nature of Cyclical Fluctuations in Electric Power Production Data.
17. Chicago as a Money Market.
18. Property Investments in Public Utility Companies.
19. The Automobile and the Village Merchant. *(Out of print.)*
20. The Sources of Public Utility Capital.
21. An Analysis of Bankers' Balances in Chicago. *(Out of print.)*
22. Books About Business Cycles. *(Out of print.)*
23. Stockholders' Equity in Chicago Banks.
24. Capital Stock, Surplus, and Undivided Profits of Chicago Banks.
25. The Determination of Secular Trends. *(Out of print.)*
26. Standard Financial Ratios for the Public Utility Industry. *(Out of print.)*
27. The Financial Plan of Gas Companies. *(Out of print.)*
28. An Analysis of Earning Assets of Chicago Banks. *(Out of print.)*
29. Balance Sheet Structure of Automobile Manufacturing Companies.
30. Seasonal and Cyclical Movements of Loans and Investments of Chicago Banks. *(Out of print.)*
31. A Test Analysis of Unsuccessful Industrial Companies. *(Out of print.)*
32. The Financial Plan of Department Stores.
33. The Banking Structure of the Seventh Federal Reserve District. *(Out of print.)*
34. A Community Labor Survey. *(Out of print.)*
35. The Financial Plan of Electric Light and Power Companies.
36. Grocery Wholesaling in Illinois from 1900 to 1929.
37. The Operating and Earning Power Ratios of Gas Companies.
38. A Market Research Bibliography. *(Out of print.)*
39. Investment Banking in Chicago. *(Out of print.)*
40. A Demonstration of Ratio Analysis. *(Out of print.)*
41. Business Mortality of Illinois Retail Stores from 1925 to 1930. By P. D. CONVERSE.

PUBLICATIONS OF THE BUREAU OF ECONOMIC AND BUSINESS RESEARCH

COLLEGE OF COMMERCE AND BUSINESS ADMINISTRATION
UNIVERSITY OF ILINOIS

BULLETIN SERIES (Concluded)

42. Operating and Earning Power Ratios of Electric Companies. By RAYMOND F. SMITH. *(Out of print.)*
43. The Expenditure of State Funds in Illinois. By M. H. HUNTER. *(Out of print.)*
44. A Survey of a Retail Trading Area. By FRED M. JONES. *(Out of print.)*
45. Costs of Township and County Government in Illinois. By M. H. HUNTER. *(Out of print.)*

44

46. Department Store Food Service. By INA M. HAMLIN and ARTHUR H. WINAKOR. *(Out of print.)*
47. Some American Proposals for War Debt Revision. By E. L. BOGART.
48. Legal Provisions Affecting Real Estate Tax Delinquency, Tax Sales, and Redemption. By M. H. HUNTER. *(Out of print.)*
49. Maintenance of Working Capital of Industrial Corporations by Conversion of Fixed Assets. By ARTHUR H. WINAKOR. *(Out of print.)*
50. Financial Aspects of Corporate Net Worth. By ARTHUR H. WINAKOR.
51. Changes in the Financial Structure of Unsuccessful Industrial Corporations. By RAYMOND F. SMITH and ARTHUR H. WINAKOR. *(Out of print.)*
52. Costs and Services of Local Government in Selected Illinois Counties. By H. K. ALLEN.
53. Capacity to Pay Current Debts. By ARTHUR H. WINAKOR.
54. A Balance Sheet of the Nation's Economy. By FRANK G. DICKINSON and FRANZY EAKIN. *(Out of print.)*
55. Banking Turnover and Facilities in Illinois. By ARTHUR H. WINAKOR.
56. The Financial Policies and Practices of Automobile Finance Companies. By HARVEY W. HUEGY and ARTHUR H. WINAKOR. *(Out of print.)*
57. The Tax System and Industrial Development. By GEORGE A. STEINER.
58. State-Chartered Savings, Building, and Loan Associations in Illinois, 1920 to 1936. By ARTHUR H. WINAKOR.
59. Trends in Rural Retailing in Illinois, 1926 to 1938. By ROBERT V. MITCHELL.
60. The Illinois Segment of the Nation's Economy for 1935: A Bookkeeping Picture. By FRANK G. DICKINSON and FRANZY EAKIN.
61. Control of Expenditures in the Local Governmental Units of Illinois. By H. K. ALLEN.
62. Directory of Early American Public Accountants. By A. C. LITTLETON.

BUSINESS STUDIES

1. Stock Control Methods. By H. W. HUEGY and R. V. MITCHELL.

SPECIAL BULLETINS

1. Price Lining of Men's Wear in a Retail Market. By FRED M. JONES.

OPINION AND COMMENT

This quarterly presents interpretative comments on current events.

RECOLLECTIONS

OF THE

EARLY DAYS OF AMERICAN ACCOUNTANCY

1883-1893

❦

BY

JAMES T. ANYON

MEMBER OF THE NEW YORK STATE SOCIETY

OF CERTIFIED PUBLIC ACCOUNTANTS

ASSOCIATE MEMBER OF THE INSTITUTE OF CHARTERED ACCOUNTANTS

IN ENGLAND AND WALES

MEMBER OF THE AMERICAN INSTITUTE OF ACCOUNTANTS

PRIVATELY PRINTED

1925

C

WRITER'S NOTE

✤

I HAVE *often been asked by accountants who not only take a deep interest in their profession as it is practiced to-day, but love to hear something of its distant past, to write an account of the early days of the profession in this country, its beginning over forty years ago, the quality and character of the men connected with it, the nature and extent of the work they did, and of course any odd or interesting personal experiences I met with during that early period. This request has been made of me I presume because I am supposed to be the oldest practicing accountant in the States, practicing I mean in a public capacity. On this point, however, I cannot make any positive statement. I have, therefore, written this account rather "by request" than for any other purpose, and I trust it may be of interest to some readers and probably in certain respects instructive.*

I wish to add that I do not claim any literary merit whatever for these writings. That is not my forte. They were composed mainly on the trains passing between New York and Atlantic City, and as railroad travelling is not as a rule calculated to produce an overabundance of inspiration, any faults in expression or defects in phraseology in this little work, must to a large extent be attributed to this circumstance. I hope therefore, these writings will be accepted just as they are and as the best I was capable of producing.

J. T. A.

46

PART FIRST

Beginning of the Profession—Establishment of the First
Public Accounting Firm, 1883—Personal Experiences in the
Early Days of the Profession, 1886-7—Formation of the
American Association of Public Accountants—My First
Long Business Trip.

PUBLIC Accounting in this country as a profession, I
have reason to believe, had its birth some time between
the years 1880 and 1883. I have been unable to find so
far the name of any firm or practitioner who posed as a Public
Accountant prior to that period. My present firm was established in the last of those years, namely, 1883, and in writing
these Recollections I hope I may be pardoned if before proceeding with the subject of the profession proper and its early
history, I first give a brief account of the circumstances
attending the firm's formation in that year and the initial
period of its existence. I wish to do this because the firm was,
more or less, an important element in the profession and its
development at that time.

Unlike a good many things when first conceived which
require thought and time and calculation before completion
is effected, the firm of Barrow, Wade, Guthrie & Co. was of
somewhat sudden and spontaneous creation. It was founded
in the year above named, by Mr. Edwin Guthrie and Mr.
Charles H. Wade, members of the firm of Thomas, Wade,
Guthrie & Co., chartered accountants of London and Manchester, England, and its formation came about in this way:

Mr. Edwin Guthrie, acting in the capacity of receiver in

[9]

the case of a certain bankrupt financial concern in England in the year named, found it necessary to proceed to this country to enquire into the value and status of certain property and assets which the bankrupt concern owned on this side. On arriving here his first thought was to find a good accounting firm whom he might employ to assist him in his investigations. He made enquiries in this direction and discovered that not only was the profession of accounting as it was understood and practiced on his side practically unknown in this country, but there was no such thing as a responsible accounting firm upon whom he could rely for any assistance he may require in his work. His attorneys in New York informed him that he did not need accountants, and that they would attend to all matters, both legal and accounting, in connection with his case.

The question might very properly be asked here "How did business firms and corporations get along in those days without the aid and service of auditors and accountants and, in their absence, who did this class of work so necessary and essential in these times?" The answer is: It was not done, because there was no one recognized as fitted by training and experience to do it. Fraud and embezzlement on the part of trusted employees, loss and confusion through defective accounting methods, and a rule-of-thumb way of arriving at important accounting results existed then, as to a lesser extent they exist now, but this was a condition that could not be helped and in consequence business men fumbled along without such aid, on the theory probably that "where ignorance is bliss" it would be folly to change that happy mental condition. And in the case of fraud in accounts, unless this came to light accidentally or through some other unusual circumstance the perpetrator was safe in the knowledge there was no special agency in existence to expose his wrong-doing, and gaily continued his practice without thought of interference. Inasmuch as the reverse of this condition, in the form of a set profession, had long been in existence in other countries, and fully recognized there as being of great value and importance to the business life of these countries, it seemed only a matter of time when a similar profession should take root and prosper in one so advanced and enlightened as this.

Mr. Guthrie fully recognized this condition and being a trained accountant and a thorough business man, saw an opportunity in this great and important business center, and he at once determined to establish an accounting practice in New York City, which, as far as he could then see, would be the first of its kind in this country.

49

In his efforts in this direction he met, through the good offices of his attorneys, a Mr. John Wylie Barrow of this city, an estimable American gentleman of culture and refinement, and held in the highest esteem by all. Mr. Barrow was an actuary rather than an accountant, and when Mr. Guthrie met him, his main business was in connection with certain British fire insurance companies, being employed by them to check the vouchers, and certify to the clerical accuracy of the monthly statements prepared by the Branches here before being sent to the home offices abroad. This work constituted his only practice.

After the necessary conferences and enquiries had taken place a partnership was formed in October, 1883, by and between John W. Barrow, Edwin Guthrie and C. H. Wade, known as Barrow, Wade, Guthrie & Co., Public Accountants, New York, the English partners supplying the necessary working capital.

The nucleus of this business was not large or important. It was merely the work (with some additional auditing modifications) hitherto done by Mr. Barrow for the insurance companies before referred to, together with the "hopes" of the members of the new firm that other matters of an accounting nature would develop in due season. Here then appeared to be the first step in the beginning of the great profession of public accounting in the United States of America.

After Mr. Guthrie had finished his work and left for his home in England, the firm opened offices in the old Equitable Building, and commenced practice, moving later on to 45 William Street, New York City. Mr. Barrow took in association with him as his chief assistant, one Oscar E. Morton who was, clerically speaking, a good man and had some knowledge of insurance work, but there is no evidence that his ability ran in any other direction. With this simple foundation the firm worked on in the even tenor of its way, keeping its own but gaining little, and the "hopes" of other matters developing, before referred to, materialized only to a very slender extent.

Business thus went on up to the Spring of 1886, when the English partners were notified by cable that Mr. Barrow had died and Mr. Morton was conducting the business of the firm in his place.

This news naturally came as a great shock to the others, and in the interest of the business, and to preserve and keep it intact, it was decided that Mr. Morton should be made a partner, and practically take the place and interest in the partnership of the one who had passed away. Matters thus proceeded apparently without any impairment till the early autumn of that year when certain reports reached Mr. Guthrie and Mr. Wade, which had the effect of reflecting somewhat on the integrity and loyalty of their new partner Morton, and as at the same time they received notification that it was the latter's intention to retire from the firm at the expiration of the requisite time notice, Mr. Guthrie determined to make another visit to this side and get the affairs of the firm properly adjusted.

He sailed in October, 1886, and brought me along with him

to act first as a senior assistant in the New York office and later as a partner. At the time of his sailing he did not know what subsequently proved to be the case, viz., that since the death of Mr. Barrow, Morton had been doing all that was possible to get the business in his own hands, and divert from the firm to himself individually the few clients whose patronage the firm enjoyed. As stated, Mr. Guthrie was not aware of these things at the time he left England and on arriving here, and presenting himself at the office of the firm on the morning of October 25, 1886, he was much surprised to be accorded a very frigid reception by his partner Morton. As for myself, the advent of my arrival at the office on the same day turned out to be somewhat of a dramatic event.

51

Monday, October 25, 1886, was probably the most momentous day in my life. It was the beginning of a new career, a new existence in a new and comparatively strange country. I had left behind me old and loved associations and new ones were to start from that time. Was the future to mean success or failure, that was the question uppermost in my mind, and not possessing a particularly sanguine temperament the answer was vague and indefinite.

I started from my hotel early in the morning of the date above given to find my way to the office of the firm, 45 William Street. The day was cold and gloomy and this circumstance naturally did not tend to lessen my general feeling of anxiety and loneliness. The new conditions and surroundings impressed me greatly. Everything was strange and novel compared to the quiet northern town in England from which I had come. The activity about the streets was greater; the people seemed more alert, active, and aggressive than those at home, and considering I knew no one from one end of the country to the other, I felt a veritable stranger, and almost an intruder. My anxious feelings can therefore be imagined when I entered the building of the firm in William Street.

I found there Mr. Guthrie conversing with Morton. Mr.
Guthrie attempted to introduce me to him, but he declined
to take any notice of this, and gruffly ordered me out of the
office. What followed is perhaps best expressed in the language of a complaint subsequently filed by Mr. Guthrie,
under the advice of his attorney, in the New York Supreme
Court praying that Morton be restrained from doing the
objectionable acts and things of which he was alleged in said
complaint to be guilty.

The complaint states:

52

"That the plaintiff Guthrie has employed in the service of
said co-partnership, James T. Anyon, and has ordered him to
work upon the business of the co-partnership at the place of
business in William Street, and that, upon said Anyon arriving
at the office to begin work, the defendant, Morton, ordered the
said Anyon to leave the office forthwith and called a policeman
to remove him but that, at the moment when the policeman
called, the said Anyon was not in the office, having temporarily
left the same;

"That, prior to the return of the said Anyon, the defendant
locked the doors of the outer office of the firm so that he could
not re-enter the office for the purpose of reporting to and talk-
ing with plaintiff Guthrie or receiving instructions from him;

"That the plaintiff Guthrie having duly applied to the defendant for the opportunity to examine the books of the firm,
the same were refused to him, the defendant referring him to
his lawyer, whom he did not name, as his only answer, except
that the said defendant did refuse to permit the plaintiff
Guthrie to examine the books.

"All the said acts occurred on the 25th day of October, 1886.

"And in addition thereto the defendant, Morton, did on the
said day instruct the chief clerk in the office of the firm, without reference to the right of entry of either the plaintiff
Guthrie or said Anyon, upon his leaving the premises, to lock
the door to the office, thereby excluding the plaintiff Guthrie
and the said Anyon, as well as such clients of the firm as might
wish to confer with them, from the use of the premises;

"That the relations between the plaintiff and the defendant are strongly unfriendly;

"That on the 26th day of October the defendant, Morton, locked the door of one of the firm's offices and has ever since prevented access thereto;

"That the plaintiffs are informed and believe that the defendant has endeavored to divert from the firm to himself individually the clients of said firm, so that on the termination of the firm the clients who now are, and have formerly, been the clients of the firm shall become his individual clients;

"That the defendant be enjoined to permit the said Anyon mentioned in this complaint to act under his employment as a clerk of the firm and to occupy during business hours, and such other hours as may be indicated by the said Guthrie, the premises occupied by the firm in William Street; and further, that any other clerks and assistants who may be employed in the business of the firm by the said Guthrie the defendant is enjoined to permit to occupy the said premises and not to interfere with them in any way whatsoever."

After the exciting events of this my first day at the office of the firm as above related, and for some days thereafter during which time I was confronted with the prospect of the reappearance of the policeman and his terrors, and when, moreover I expected Morton might decide to use physical force to settle his troubles and objections to my presence, I never lost courage nor was I afraid. Morton was a far bigger man than I and I could see that his heart was tempted often to get at me in a physical way, but fortunately he did not resort to this, and when I say fortunately, I mean fortunately for him as well as the good name of the firm, for I had plenty of pluck and in my inner heart had a secret feeling I would love to have had the encounter.

These difficulties and differences with Morton, involving also the settlement of the ownership of the goodwill of the business, resulted in Mr. Guthrie filing the complaint in the New York Supreme Court already referred to. In this com-

53

plaint he asked, among other things, for the appointment of a temporary receiver for the firm pending the adjustment of the several matters in dispute between the partners. A decision was later rendered by the court, granting the petitioner relief on all the points involved, and consenting to the appointment of a receiver. This receivership lasted several months, during which time all matters were settled, and Morton made his exit and disappeared as a figure in the affairs of Barrow, Wade, Guthrie & Co. for all time.

54

When the disturbing influences as above related had subsided somewhat, I turned my attention to practical business matters and particularly to an enquiry as to how the profession stood in New York.

I had left on the other side a profession full of vitality, one that was looked upon as an essential element of business life, and so recognized in every section of business activity. It need not therefore be a matter of surprise when I say that it was natural I should expect in this great and progressive country to find relatively the same conditions in the respect named as existed in the country I had left. A general survey of the situation, however, soon made the fact apparent that these conditions existed here only to a very limited extent, that public accounting was in its infancy and that it was little known or understood as a distinct profession.

As might be expected under such circumstances, my chief thought was to find out and become acquainted with the men then engaged in the profession, and to learn the kind and quality of work they performed. With this object in view I sought all available sources from which I might obtain the required information. A careful examination of the city directories, a scrutiny of the advertisements in the financial papers, enquiries from the few business men I had become acquainted with, and finally a talk with the firm's attorneys in the hope of obtaining some enlightenment on the subject, soon satis-

fied me that there were very few persons engaged in the profession, no more in fact than could be counted on the fingers
of one hand. There was a firm called Veysey & Veysey with
a staff of two or three assistants, another practicing under
the name of Jas. Yalden & Co., a man named Louis M. Bergtheil, one named H. M. Tate and another, I believe the best
of all, Geo. H. Church. In Philadelphia the late John Heins
seemed to be the only representative accountant in public
practice in that city, and in Boston a man named Rodney
McLaughlin played a corresponding part. These with a few
others who could not be determined or located at the time
appeared to be the sole exponents and representatives in this
great country of a profession that in a comparatively few
years was to become so important and essential to the needs of
the business world.

The next step was to put myself in communication with all
these men which I proceeded to do either personally or by
letter, pointing out to each one that I had just come to this
country from the other side to join them in the conduct of the
profession of accounting, that I was sure they would like to
see it better known, understood, and recognized by the public, and that with a view of considering what might be done
to attain this object I suggested that it might be desirable for
them to meet myself and Mr. Edwin Guthrie on a certain
appointed afternoon at the firm's office, 45 William Street, to
discuss the matter. One and all showed the greatest enthusiasm and interest in the proposal and agreed to attend the
meeting.

On the afternoon in question the gentlemen invited came
at the appointed time. There were about six or seven present
including Mr. John Heins who had purposely travelled from
Philadelphia to attend. They were not all practicing accountants, but all evinced a decided interest in the subject of
accounting. One of these was Colonel C. E. Sprague, presi-

55

dent of the Union Dime Savings Bank, 31st Street and
Broadway, New York. Colonel Sprague was a lover of anything connected with accounting and took a keen interest in
the fortunes of the profession. Several others professed to be
accountants but took no part in public practice. The situation seemed novel and at the same time interesting to those
present, and a general air of expectancy was apparent all
around.

After formal introductions to each other and to Mr.
Guthrie and the passing of the usual compliments, the meeting got down to business. Mr. Guthrie was asked to take the
chair and I to act as secretary of the meeting. Mr. Guthrie
gladly complied and proceeded to address those present, his
remarks being, in substance, as follows:

56

"That it was a great pleasure to him to be able to visit this
country again in connection with the affairs of his firm; that
it was a great privilege to him thus to have this opportunity
of meeting the accountants practicing in this and other cities;
that he was sorry, however, to find that the profession had
not materially progressed in public recognition, or in other
ways, since he was last here; that in England, on the contrary, the profession was on a very high plane; that it was
recognized as one of the leading professions—firms, corporations, banks, railroads and other financial and commercial
entities seeking the services of accountants in all phases of
activity; that the efforts of practicing accountants in this
country should be directed toward bringing about a similar
condition, and that he believed, some similar institution or
body to that now existing on the other side, viz., the Institute
of Chartered Accountants in England and Wales, could be
started here under the regulations of which competent accountants could practice and be recognized by the public as
fully qualified so to do."

It is needless to say Mr. Guthrie's remarks were listened to with great attention, and all freely admitted that his address had given rise to new life and zest and a keener desire for greater things. The meeting then settled down to business and discussion, and finally a resolution was proposed by Mr. Heins and put to the meeting to the effect that the accountants here present should form themselves into an association for the advancement and protection of the interests of the profession, and that the qualification for membership should be ability and fitness to practice in a public capacity.

This motion was seconded and it was further proposed (and I had the pleasure of making this proposal) that the name of this association be the American Association of Public Accountants. This resolution was passed unanimously, and thus came into existence in the month of December, 1886, the first organized body of professional accountants in the United States.

It is true there was a small body of men who, two or three years before this time, had formed themselves into an association devoted to the interests of accounting and bookkeeping called the "Institute of Accounts." This, however, was not strictly an accounting body whose members practiced in a public way. They were mainly bookkeepers and accountants connected with private firms and corporations, and others in similar lines of occupation banded together in this form for discussion and mutual benefit and improvement. I remember well there was quite a flutter of excitement among these members when they learned that Mr. Guthrie of London, England, and myself, as members of the Institute of Chartered Accountants in England and Wales, were here in the matter of promoting the interests of the profession on this side. They called a special meeting of the Institute for the purpose of inviting us to attend one to be called later in order to give us an official welcome. We attended and I need hardly say there was a full attendance and the welcome was com-

57

plete and sincere. They were an intelligent lot of men, intense and enthusiastic and took a deep interest in all that pertained to accountancy.

Early in the year 1887, I became a partner in the firm of Barrow, Wade, Guthrie & Co. along with a Mr. E. H. Sewell, an actuary, who was later retired, and as might be expected I was pleased and proud to be raised to this position.

The clients the firm had at this time were very few. The one we prized the most, and felt proud in keeping, was the New York, Ontario and Western Railway Co. This company was the first railroad in the United States to employ public accountants to act as auditors and to certify to the correctness of its annual statements to its stockholders. My firm has acted in this capacity ever since, and I believe there has never been any criticism of its accounting methods or any fault-finding with these statements on the part of its stockholders during all these years. Other clients we had were, The Royal Insurance Company of Liverpool; The British and Foreign Marine Insurance Co.; The London Assurance Corporation; the Sun Fire office; York Street Flax Spinning Co., and several others.

58

With this very moderate volume of business as a nucleus, I launched out as the head of the firm on my new career as a practicing accountant in this great United States of America, full of ambition, a love for my work, and a determination to make good. I had the advantage of being a fairly good accountant, but the disadvantage of being an Englishman, for the people generally, at that time, did not take very kindly to men of this nationality. They were looked upon as rather slow and stupid and while admittedly honest, were not considered over capable. Besides there was somewhat of a national feeling of prejudice against Englishmen, arising I think in the old Colonial days, which was still apparent. It was a fact, nevertheless, in spite of this feeling that if any real and important accounting work had to be done, it would in the majority of cases be given to the foreign trained accountant in preference to the native one. The usual explanation for this was that the giver of the work had greater confidence in the precision and accuracy of the work of the foreigner, and greater faith in the honesty of his conclusions. This may seem rather an odd statement to make, and while it was true then, it is gratifying to know this discrimination no longer exists even to a slight extent in these times, as both native and foreign-born accountants equally represent the highest point of efficiency and integrity in their professional work.

By reason of the limited amount of business my firm had to start with, as already stated, I could not afford to engage any assistant in the office beyond the employment of an office boy. I was, therefore, called upon to fill the several roles and discharge the duties of the following offices—Accountant, Acting Auditor, Correspondent, Cashier (this latter position did not take up much of my time for reasons quite obvious), Firm Bookkeeper, Writer of Reports, Traveller, Timekeeper, Computer of customers' bills for service, and in fact, everything but dusting the office desks, filling the ink stands, mailing the letters and doing other minor things which were the duties of the boy.

For the whole of this service, and the fact that I was a partner, my salary was fixed at $208.33 per month. My total annual income, therefore, was salary $2,500, and a proportion of the net profits of the firm, if there were any; and this I had very grave doubts about at the time. However, it was very gratifying to find that at the end of the first six months, viz., June 30, 1887, the operations of the firm including all the departments above referred to, resulted in a gross service credit of $4,842.08 and a net profit, after charging my salary of $1,250 for the half year, of $2,133.50. I state these particulars just to show how simple and moderate the business of an accounting firm was in those years compared to the many and wonderful firms of today.

Now how did I regard the future? A keen desire to make good and my firm a success, an ardent love for my profession and a resolve to seize every opportunity to have it better recognized, were the influences that dominated my business life and led me to believe the future was safe. In this spirit I was ready and willing to take up any professional work, at any time and go anywhere to do it, not just for the remuneration to be received but also because it appealed to me as meaning an advance in and better recognition of the profession I was devoted to. I remember well those early and younger days, full of ambition and enthusiasm, ready for anything. I felt I would cheerfully have gone to the North Pole in winter or amongst the savages of southern Patagonia in summer, if it was business to me and my small firm, and meant some advance in the profession itself, however small this might be.

As bearing upon what I have just said, the thought has occurred to me that I might be pardoned if at this point I digress a little from my main subject to tell the story of one of my early professional appointments involving a long trip away from New York, the first of its kind I had then made. I wish to do this not only because it will serve to illustrate what I have already stated, namely that I was willing to go anywhere at any time in the interests of business and the profession but also because the trip, full of novelty and unusual occurrences, was a most interesting experience and impressed me a good deal at the time, and its recital might also be of interest to others. I have purposely given the narrative in rather lengthy detail, and hope it may not prove too boring to the reader in this respect.

My appointment required me to proceed to a certain point

in the southern state of Alabama rejoicing in the unclassic name of "Mills Camp," my accounting duties being to verify certain figures and data pertaining to the operations of an extensive lumber business situated and conducted at that place.

I started from New York in the evening of a late autumn day, my objective point being the city of Chattanooga in the state of Tennessee, and there I arrived in the early evening of the next day. From that point I found I had to take a semi-local train going south to reach my final destination, the train, I learned, being scheduled to start at 9.00 P.M.

Long before that hour, having nothing else to do, I arrived at the designated railway station and proceeded to the waiting room. I found there were two, one having the word "White" inscribed over the door and the other the word "Colored." Being quite inexperienced in southern methods, I did not precisely know the difference between the two but selected the one marked "White" and walked in. The room was not by any means alluring in appearance. It might have been cleaned sometime during its past career but this certainly was not of recent occurrence. It was stained, grimy and forbidding, dimly lighted by two solitary gas jets, a wooden bench running round the place and an iron stove in the center. Here I sat to await the arrival of my train at 9.00 o'clock. That hour approached but there was no sign of anything, not even of any life about the station. I waited on, yawned, got nervous and still waited till nine-thirty, ten, ten-thirty, eleven, eleven-thirty and no train, and just before twelve o'clock, three hours late, came slowly lumbering and fussing into the station the belated object consisting of one snorting engine and three worn out looking coaches, and as for a sleeping car, not to be thought of.

I wish to say at this point that the ease-loving luxurious accountant of to-day must not imagine that travelling on the southern railways thirty-six years ago offered the same com-

61

forts as one finds now. Trains were slow and unaccommodating. Sleeping cars were known but not by any means the order of the day. Time and punctuality were elements hardly considered essential to good railroad management, the result being that trains were anything between two hours and, I was about to say, two days late in leaving or arriving at appointed places. I was very lucky, therefore, in being detained there only three hours after the schedule time.

I hurried to the platform and anxiously enquired of the man in charge of this transport if it stopped at Mills Camp. He replied it didn't, but if I wanted to get off at that point he would stop the train specially to accommodate me. I thanked him, asked him to do this, and also to be good enough to notify me when we arrived there. I also ventured to enquire if he knew whether or not there was a hotel at Mills Camp. He looked at me curiously with the shadow of a smile on his countenance and replied emphatically, "No there is not." Uncomfortable and uneasy I entered the car along with two other passengers and settled down on a hard rickety seat and waited. In the fulness of time the train started, hesitated, started again and finally got fairly under way, rumbling along at a slow monotonous gait which soon produced a feeling of drowsiness and I found myself alternately sleeping and waking. Thus we proceeded for some time when I became vaguely conscious of a gruff voice saying, "Say, mister, if you want get off this train at Mills Camp, I am stopping it only for you, you better get going." It was the gentle voice of the brakeman. I got up with a start, grabbed my bag, involuntarily took out my watch (it was half past two), and noticing the train was gradually slowing down hurried through the dimly lighted car to the door. It stopped and on a cheery "good night" from the brakeman who let me off, I alighted, not on the trim platform of the usual well regulated railroad station, but on the bare, wet, soggy ground.

62

I stood there till the train passed on and disappeared in the darkness, and I shall never forget the feeling that then came over me as I found myself standing utterly and completely alone in what appeared to me to be a lonely and abandoned place, not knowing just what move next to make. The night was intensely dark, a drizzling rain was falling, not a light was to be seen in any direction, no sign of life or anything indicative of man's existence anywhere. The silence of the place was oppressive, broken only by the distant sound of barking dogs and the occasional hollow mournful cry of some strange night bird in the adjacent forest. Through the darkness I thought I could distinguish the outlines of what seemed to me dense woods and nothing else. The whole surroundings had the atmosphere of desolation. I stood there practically motionless, not daring to venture one step in the black darkness for fear of the uncertainty of the situation. I did not call out for I felt the only response would be no more than an echo so I stood and remained silent. How long I was in that position I cannot now remember, possibly not long, but it seemed interminable till finally, to my great relief, I became conscious of some one approaching, evidently a man with a lantern, for I could see the thin streak of light passing through the air as he swung it to and fro in his walk. The light and the man drew near and then flashing the lamp suddenly on me, said, "I suppose you are the young man from New York which Mr. Howard, the manager, expected last night. He waited up for you till twelve o'clock, but as you didn't arrive went to bed and ordered me to watch out and take care of you till morning. My name is Williams. I'm one of the night watchmen in this camp so I'll try make you comfortable till morning. I think you better follow me." I obeyed and followed in the rain, the man and the light leading the way. Through side paths and by paths, through brushwood and fallen branches, over soft, wet, muddy ground, across open spaces, around

63

clumps of trees we went on for some considerable distance, no sound to be heard save the tread of our feet and the continued roar in the distance of the barking dogs, till on a sudden and abrupt divergence of our path I saw a bright fire burning on the ground in a space close to a thick forest some distance away. I said to my guide rather anxiously, "What is that?" "Well," he replied, "I suppose you know that this camp is worked by state convicts. We lock 'em up at night, but there is a few as behaves themselves so we let 'em make a fire outside and sleep around it. They're generally quiet and peaceful. That fire is where we're going to."

64

We arrived at the place designated and quite a sight presented itself. Around the fire, lying on the ground in all postures and scantily dressed, were a number of stalwart negroes sleeping. I felt an innate nervousness at this sight and said to the guide, "Mr. Williams, did I understand you to say these men lying around are state convicts?" He replied, "Yes." "What," I further asked, "is about the nature of their offenses?" "Well," he answered, "various. That big fellow over there that's snoring so loud got in a fight down in Texas and nearly killed his man with his knife. The fellow with the blue shirt on is in for horse stealing and I can tell you he was a dandy at that game. The chap next to him with the scar on his face is here for shooting up a saloon in Alabama City and killing the barkeeper. The others are about the same kind, but generally they behave pretty good here. "Now," he went on, "I've got my rounds to make and I'll leave you here. I'll be back in less than two hours and till then rest on this log and make yourself comfortable by the fire and on my return we'll walk up to the manager's house."

Before I had time to say a word he started off to make his rounds, the fallen dead branches on the ground crackling beneath his tread, and quickly disappeared in the gloom of the forest.

I have in my time been in situations of apparent danger and had pluck enough to get out unharmed, but I was never in one so uncertain and one that tested my courage quite so much as this. I will ask the reader to picture this rather unusual scene. I, a quiet every-day Englishman who up to this time had seen and experienced little beyond the simple and ordinary things in life, in an unknown and lonely region at half past three o'clock in the morning, sitting on a fallen log by a blazing fire in the open, huge bats circling around, in company with seven or eight cut-throats of the state, the rain falling copiously, wondering what the end of this adventure was going to be. I agree with the reader this was not exactly accounting work but it was part of the game and I was going to see it through.

I need hardly say I did not sleep. On the contrary, I kept wide awake, on the alert for any move that might be made by these men, but none was made, and as they lay there sleeping peacefully the familiar saying, "There is no rest for the wicked" came to my mind, but it did not seem to apply. Occasionally one would turn about to get an easier posture, open his big eyes for a minute, look around and again relapse into rest.

It was a great relief to me when the watchman came back about half past five and suggested we might then go to the manager's house.

The early morning light was faintly appearing in the east as we walked side by side over about the same character of ground as the night before. It was during this journey I learned the secret of the barking dogs. They were bloodhounds owned by the state, about six or seven of them, kept in chains at the manager's house during the day but allowed to go partially free at night to guard his home. The dogs were used by the officials of the camp to hunt convicts when any attempted to escape and while they were quiet and tractable

65

to those they loved and feared, were savage and cruel to strangers unless fully under control. As we drew near the house the din and excitement of these dogs became terrific. I felt genuinely afraid and involuntarily seized the arm of my companion who did not seem particularly affected. We finally reached the high barred gate of the house and to my great relief the manager appeared at the door with a huge dog whip in his hand and with a loud voice directed to the animals, ordered them to cease. At the sight of that whip and the commanding tones of their master, the hounds ceased, slunk slowly away and, while still excited, apparently became as gentle and passive as a parcel of subdued children.

The manager greeted me, made proper excuses for the inconvenience I had been put to and invited me into the house. There I took a short and needed rest and later, after breakfast was served, consisting of coffee, coarse bread and roast possum, I was ready to take up real accounting work. I stayed there three days and then left for home and I need hardly say I was truly glad to get back again to New York and civilization.

66

PART SECOND

American Association of Public Accountants—Quality and Personnel of the Practitioners—A Lady Client and the Writer—The Lawyer and his Client.

❖

I WILL now return to the fortunes and affairs of the American Association of Public Accountants. It soon became known around New York and adjacent cities that Public Accountants had taken steps to organize themselves as an association, and a number of letters and enquiries very soon came forward from persons interested in the movement asking what were the requirements for membership, the entrance fees, annual dues, etc. It must not be considered that all these enquiries came from persons connected with the profession of public accounting. Some filled positions as head bookkeepers in mercantile and manufacturing concerns; a few were men who apparently had no particular status in the respect named but who evidently loved accounting for itself and liked to be in association with those who understood and practiced it, while one or two were professors or teachers of bookkeeping who wished to be in touch with anything pertaining to the latter's progress and advancement. One letter was an enquiry as to what the association would charge for a certain piece of accounting work the writer required to have done. This was a good beginning and gave considerable encouragement.

All these things tended not only to give some little publicity to the movement, but also to steadily increase the mem-

[31]

bership of the association. At the date of the birth of the latter, December 23, 1886, its members numbered some eight or ten individuals, and from this time forward the increase was steady and continuous.

The interest therein of these members continued unabated. Each worked to do his own part, and all worked in one special direction, viz., to get public accounting better known and the association in a position whereby it would be recognized as having something of a legal status. This was eventually accomplished, and in August, 1887, the association became incorporated under the laws of the state of New York with the name and title of "American Association of Public Accountants."

The by-laws of the association were prepared, approved and adjusted, officers appointed and all other things done to facilitate the start of the association on its new career. Its first president was James Yalden, New York; vice-president, John Heins, Philadelphia; secretary, James T. Anyon, New York; and treasurer, W. H. Veysey, New York. Its offices were in the old Equitable Building, Rooms 50 and 51, for which the association paid no rent, said offices being the ones rented and occupied by my firm in the regular practice of its professional work.

The first council of the association, the members of which were selected to regulate and conduct its affairs, consisted of the following gentlemen:

AMERICAN ASSOCIATION PUBLIC ACCOUNTANTS

MEMBERS OF FIRST COUNCIL

James T. Anyon, New York City
Louis M. Bertheil, New York City

68

Geo. H. Church, New York City
John Heins, Philadelphia
Mark C. Merick, New York
Rodney McLaughlin, Boston, Mass.
C. H. W. Sibley, New York
William H. Veysey, New York
Walter H. P. Veysey, New York
James Yalden, New York

The by-laws of the association provided, amongst other things, that the members should be divided into two classes, styled, respectively, "Fellows" and "Associates," the Fellows to have the right to use after their names the letters "F.A.A." and the Associates the letters "A.A.A." to designate their degree of membership.

It was provided that "Fellows shall be (1) the original incorporators of the association and those who subscribe to the constitution and by-laws; and (2) all persons who have practiced as public accountants continuously for three years previous to their admission to membership in the association."

"Associates shall be all persons who obtain a certificate of their having passed the final examination hereinafter provided for."

The entrance fees payable by a "Fellow" were $100.00, one-half on admission and $50.00 on call of the council at any time after two months. By an "Associate" $75.00, viz., $25.00 payable on admission and the balance on call of the council any time after two months.

Other provisions in the by-laws concerned the powers of the council, meetings of the association, examinations, and so forth. One of the provisions appeared to be almost the equivalent of the council being called upon to make an annual inventory of its members who were actually in public practice. It read as follows:

"The council in every January or at any other time, and in such manner as they may deem reasonable, shall satisfy themselves that every member either continues to practice as a public accountant or continues in the employment of a public accountant, and on being so satisfied shall issue to such member a certificate of membership, for which there shall be paid to the council by each fellow $25.00 and by each associate $10.00. Such fee hereinafter styled "The Annual Certificate Fee" shall be due and payable in January of each year, or at the date of a member's election or admission, or beginning to practice, and until payment thereof no annual certificate of membership shall be issued. The Secretary shall keep a register of the members of the association, which shall contain their business addresses."

At the time of incorporation the association had thirty-one members of whom twenty-four were "Fellows" and seven "Associates." This number with a few others outside who for various reasons did not or could not join (the main one being that the payment of the entrance fee for the time being stood in the way) practically constituted the total exponents and representatives of the profession of accounting at that time in this country.

It must not be imagined, however, that all these were men in full professional practice connected with firms having regular located offices, the names inscribed on the door, and several assistant accountants as part of their staff as we find in these times. There were a few of this kind but not many. The majority had merely desk-room in other offices with no assistants, a few had their offices (mainly for reasons of economy) in the back parlors of their homes, while one or two others did not seem to have any visible address anywhere but when wanted were usually on hand.

It may be interesting at this point to study the character and standing of the men then engaged in the profession as a comparison with those who practice it at this time. They can be divided into two classes, the first consisting of a few who stood out somewhat conspicuously from the rest in reliability and proficiency, men who were imbued with the spirit of the profession, and by thought and experience had learned and acquired all there was to be known in connection with it as understood and practiced at that time. The first of these I think was John Heins of Philadelphia, a man who was by natural instinct an accountant, reliable, intense, and a gentleman. Geo. H. Church of New York was of the same type. James Yalden was a good accountant but lacked certain qualities to make him one of the best. Mr. Rodney McLaughlin of Boston, Mr. W. H. Veysey and Mr. C. W. Haskins of New York possessed many sterling professional qualifications but their knowledge was somewhat limited and I think placed them a little apart from the names first given. There were of course a few other undoubtedly good and proficient men whose names I need not specifically refer to.

The second class were by far the larger number, and in character and standing of a very mixed order. It will be interesting to study these.

With the limited amount of accounting work available on the part of the public and the relatively large number of accountants ready to take it, business was necessarily scarce, fees were few and far between, and the net result of the work performed was at the best meagre. This condition to a certain extent had its effect on the personal appearance of the class of practitioners I am referring to, the majority of whom certainly did not look exactly prosperous, and probably impressed prospective clients in that way. I remember the occasion of the first social meeting of the members of the American Association which I attended. The event was to take the form of a dinner to be held at the old Astor House in lower Broadway, New York. There were about fifteen or twenty members present, many of whom had evidently hired a dress-suit and white tie for the occasion; and taking them all round, their general appearance hardly suggested successful professional men. Nevertheless they all seemed happy, thoroughly enjoyed the occasion, made appropriate speeches, got full of dinner, enthusiasm and cocktails, and altogether had a splendid time.

Although full of zeal and ambition to excel, the average man of this class lacked personality and impressiveness. He failed to convey to the business man the conviction that he was an expert in his profession, or that he was especially expert in anything. He knew his business in a simple elemental way but possessed few ideas and little or no vision. My heart and sympathy often went out to these men. They had adopted as their calling in life a profession, the vastness and importance of which they had little or no conception. Nevertheless they loved their calling, for it appealed to them as interesting and in a way fascinating. Besides, they had a feeling it represented something really wanted in the business world and that sooner or later this something would take tangible form and be recognized. But these feelings were uncertain and indefinite and left them floundering as it were in an unknown region, vaguely conscious of its extent and importance. They were like the children the old philosopher refers to as "picking pebbles on the sea shore" while the great sea of accounting knowledge, unknown and unexplored lay before them. But they were ever ready and anxious to make any adventure on that sea to explore it and to learn, understand and master its secrets. This was nearly forty years ago and since that time they have mastered these secrets, and I may say the advanced American accountant of to-day in proficiency and a true knowledge of his profession stands second to none in the civilized world.

72

This primitive member of the new profession was satisfied nevertheless that he filled an important role in business life, and that in accountancy matters he was an authority. He felt, in any event, that he was in a class much higher than the usual commonplace bookkeeper, although the latter, on his part, had a feeling that the former was not a bit better than himself and, in a good many ways, not as good. He loved to discuss his business with brother accountants and in doing this usually dwelt on the simple little problems that cropped up in his every-day practice. But these were entirely bookkeeping problems and had no semblance at all to the higher questions, theoretical or practical, that constantly confront members of the profession in these days.

As illustrative of this simple condition I might relate an incident which happened at about the period to which I am referring. The occasion was an informal meeting of a number of accountants, and general accounting things were being discussed. The topic turned on the procedure necessary to be followed in the case of opening up the books of a new corporation, co-partnership or other business. One of the accountants present, who considered himself somewhat of an authority in these matters, and who had been freely expressing his views thereon, was asked by another how he would proceed to open up the books of a trust when a person had died and left an estate. He thought for a moment and then replied: "Well, I should say as there are funeral expenses, the cost of the burial lot, and opening up of the grave, that it would be as well first to open a 'Cemetery Account' and charge all these things to it, and in my opinion that's all there is in the matter."

There certainly were a number of oddities (I was about to say curiosities) among the "professionals" in those times. Here is another and rather amusing example.

The occasion was, as in the other case, an informal assembly of accountants met for general discussion. After a time

73

the conversation turned on the subject of the desirability of accountants being required to pass examinations as a test of their fitness to practice in a public way and as a basis for obtaining degrees in case laws should later be formulated to regulate the practice of the profession. There was general agreement and expression that this would be a good thing to do and one of the accountants present went so far as to state his views of the several subjects such examinations should cover. In his opinion, he remarked, the suggested examinations should embrace the following: English grammar and composition; arithmetic; elementary branches of mathematics; the theory and practice of bookkeeping and accounts and "I would further suggest," he continued, "that there be one or two other outside subjects, such as, one foreign language, say French or German, and the rudimentary branches of natural Philosophy and Physics." Just as the speaker uttered the word "Physics" an elderly accountant, sitting next to me, and who had been listening intently to what was being said, turned to me suddenly and eagerly remarked, "Mr. Anyon, I know I would pass easily on the subject of physics because I used to work in a drug store."

These professional gentlemen were usually referred to by the general public as "Experts" or "Expert Accountants" and sometimes as "Checkers." It was quite customary for them to advertise their calling in the daily papers and financial magazines, and these advertisements would run something like the following: "John Doe, Expert Accountant, Books written up and balanced, Tangled Accounts straightened out" and so forth. The word "tangled" did seem a favorite word to use, and appeared quite often in these advertisements. However, business men generally, notwithstanding, did not take very kindly to these new "experts" and the service they advertised. If some real accounting or bookkeeping problem had to be taken in hand, the average business man would often go to his lawyer, or better still, as costing less money, to his banker, and obtain the services of one of the bank clerks. Just as the general public was not particularly impressed with these experts, so bankers on their part had very little or no use for their services, while lawyers looked upon them more in the light of trespassers on their own business preserves than anything else, for lawyers in those times did or rather tried to do any special work in accounting matters that now falls to members of the accounting profession.

At the initial period I am writing of, and for a year or two thereafter, the profession did not advance in public favor to any pronounced extent. It did progress somewhat but not in a way and to a degree at all proportionate to the desires of those engaged in its practice. The reason for this I believe was partly the fault of the professionals and partly the fault of the public. The former seemed to be unable, mainly on account of their limited knowledge, to impress the latter that their services were anything different to that which pertained to bookkeeping, and the public on its part showed no disposition to be convinced that such a profession as public accounting was actually a needed one.

A little matter happened about this time which was quite encouraging. I had a request from the president of a large and well known trust company of this city (very prominent at this time) to see him on a business matter. I was very pleased to receive and comply with this request and presented myself at his office. He stated that for some time there had been a rather serious discrepancy in the trust company's books between the customers' deposit balances and the control account, which they had not been able to reconcile and requested me to take up the matter and endeavor to adjust same. I commenced the work and found after a short while a number of clerical errors and finally one of quite a large amount, $25,000, which sum had been posted in error to the credit of the account of one of the depositors, a man conducting a small business uptown, and which up to that date had not been discovered. I noticed also this error had been taken advantage of by the depositor who had gradually withdrawn considerable sums until the full credit had disappeared and the account became closed.

The error and the whole situation in regard to it at once became clear. I looked back and could see this man picking up his bank pass book one fine morning (after it had been returned to him by the bank, written up and balanced for the month) to be sure the small credit balance he expected to find was properly shown, becoming amazed and overwhelmed at the sight of a sum of $25,000 credited to his account representing a deposit he had never made, and a correspondingly large credit balance at his disposal. I could further see this man gazing at this balance, cogitating and wondering just what he should do and finally concluding he would keep quiet, lay low and await any possible notification from the bank that an error had been made. No such notification came forward, so he proceeded to gradually draw out the money, two, three, four thousand dollars at a time until the full amount was exhausted. On notifying the trust company officials of this situation, efforts were at once made to get into communication with this recent depositor, but it was too late, he had judiciously disappeared and like the discreet man he considered himself to be, left no address. Thus the trust company through the error referred to, lost the sum of $25,000. Now comes the sequel to this. About a week later the president of the company sent for me a second time and stated as follows:

"Mr. Anyon, I have been very much impressed with the great value of the accounting service you have recently rendered my company (as a matter of fact it was not accounting work at all. It was merely work that any intelligent 'checker' could have performed just as well as I) and I have decided to

find out from you if you would care to take a position in this
company as chief accountant or controller and have complete
charge of all our accounting matters."

The salary he mentioned was very liberal, much larger
than the income I then earned from my profession, but I had
to tell him that while I fully appreciated the offer of the position he had made me, particularly coming from such a source,
I was obligated under a partnership agreement to remain with
my present firm for a certain number of years, and as this
term had not then expired, I would, in consequence, be compelled to decline the offer.

I have already remarked that this incident, although small
in itself, created a feeling of encouragement, for I felt that
the work of the accountant when better known would tend in
each case to develop a larger recognition of the profession on
the part of business men we all desired. Here was the case of
a prominent man well known in business and financial circles
becoming satisfied by this individual experience that the work
of the professional man was actually of value, thus giving
rise to the conviction that as similar cases developed the profession would be benefitted and take one more step in the
right direction.

It is true there were some business men who had a fairly
good conception of the character of the profession, and saw
advantages in it which when better understood would undoubtedly be of benefit to business at large. On the contrary
there were a great many who had very mixed ideas as to just
what the business of the expert accountant was, and exactly
what he professed to do. Some considered that he was an experienced bookkeeper and no more, others looked upon him as a
man whose business it was to detect fraud, embezzlement and
stealing, and that his employment was of value only in this
direction, while quite a few had a vague idea that he was
merely a man of figures, a rapid and unerring calculator who

could add up two or three columns of figures at a time, could
tell you immediately the square or cube root of any given
number or say off-hand for example what one dollar put out
at six per cent compound interest per annum at the time
Columbus discovered America would amount to to-day. I will
give an example of this type. A lady called at my office one
day and announced that she wished to see me on an important
business matter. The lady in question proved to be the late
Mrs. Hetty Green, whom many will remember as being a
rather picturesque figure in this city some years ago. She entered
the office and after scrutinizing me fully and carefully said,
"I understand from Mr. Williams of the Chemical National
Bank that you are an expert calculator and figurer, and can
decipher accounts that are wrong." I hastened to assure her
that I was not a particularly quick or expert calculator, that I
was an accountant. "Well," she replied, "I suppose it's the
same thing and I'll tell you what I want," and thereupon set
out in a voluble and business-like way to state her case. She
was the residuary legatee under a certain will in a large estate
and was much dissatisfied with the acts and doings of the
executors and trustees of said estate and desired to know if I
was sufficient of an expert "figurer" or calculator to find out
and lay bare these wrongful acts. I informed her that as an
accountant I felt I could do this fully and satisfactorily, but
that it was not essential I should be an expert figurer and calculator to do the work properly. This did not seem to satisfy
the lady who evidently considered I had failed to prove my
case and that by my own showing I was not a fit and proper
person to take up her matter for I did not get the work. I
learned later she had engaged the services of one of the
Chemical Bank clerks, and probably he succeeded in unearth-
ing by his ability as a "rapid calculator" all the wrong acts
and doings of the executors and trustees of which she complained. There were many similar instances and each one

78

tended to indicate the somewhat distorted conception many people entertained of just what the accountant's work actually was.

It was therefore not only the character or rather lack of character as well as lack of knowledge on the part of the majority of accountants that tended to retard the advance of the profession in public favor, but another thing of equal importance, namely, the fact that practitioners seemed unable to create in the minds of business men the faith and confidence in their integrity and honesty which is the essence of the profession in these days, and there was some good reason for this.

I feel free to say that in those times there were many practitioners who did not seem fully to realize their responsibility to their profession, or to third parties who might be called upon to act on the results of their work. They did not consider themselves bound to precision and truth in the same degree or to anything like the same extent as their brother accountants of these days. It is most gratifying and satisfying in these times to see how careful and thorough accountants generally are in the presentation of the results of their work, and how strictly they adhere to truth and precision irrespective of the outcome or any outside considerations. Such was not entirely the case in those early days. It was not an uncommon thing to find accountants at times "stretching a point" in favor of their clients (mainly in matters relating to the preparation of statements for presentation to banks or the sale of a business) to show a financial condition more favorable than was actually the case, and in many instances clients expected them to do this. I remember on one occasion being called upon to check a statement which had been given to the National Park Bank by a borrower in order to obtain further credit (this statement had been prepared by the borrower's accountant) wherein an "asset" appeared for quite a considerable sum under the heading "Cash with Brokers." I found this item actually represented an aggregation of losses arising through speculative transactions of one of the partners in Wall Street, and the "Cash with Brokers" referred to was the total of the cash paid over by the firm from time to time to make good these losses. This was not an isolated case, there were many just like it and here is one probably a little more amusing.

A lawyer walked into my office one day with somewhat of an aggressive air, his manner indicating a certain degree of contempt for the situation generally. He abruptly started: "My name is so and so—I am the attorney for Mr. John Doe and I have here a statement you people got up for his company two weeks ago. I want to say to you, you haven't made up that statement in the way he told you to. You show more liabilities than his company owes; he has $12,000 notes receivable from his customers and you don't show a dollar for these (he had previously discounted these receivables at his bank), and worse still, he has over $30,000 of orders on his books, good orders, with a good profit in them, and you have put nothing in this statement for these at all. My client wants you people to make that statement right and when you've done that and included these things as they should be, Mr. Doe will pay you your bill but not before." Of course I waited until he had finished and then the reader can imagine how refreshing it was to be able to give him a full reply, informing him amongst other things that the only mistake that had been made in the matter was that he and his client had come to the wrong firm. It is of course to be understood that in all professions there are the good and the bad practitioners, the staunch, reliable and conscientious ones, and necessarily a number quite the reverse, and at the time I am referring to the profession of accounting had its due proportion of each of the classes mentioned. Time, training, and experience, however, I am glad to say, have worked decidedly for the good in this respect.

While on this subject, I would like to refer to what appears

to me to be a unique and exceptional feature as pertaining to
the profession of public accountancy, and which seems to set
it apart from other professions. I refer now to the work and
attitude of the professional accountant and the way these are
looked upon by the general public. In their minds his work, so
far as quality is concerned, must be faultless both clerically
and in principle. A mistake on his part must not be expected
or thought of. Men in other professions may at times be guilty
of error and their name and standing are not seriously im-
paired thereby, but the accountant is different; he must not
err, he is a man of precision and correctness—and error cannot be forgiven or overlooked. Besides, in his work and findings he must not be biased in any way in favor of his client,
but must keep in mind to the same degree the interest of any
second or third party who may be called upon to review the
results of his work; in other words, in his work, service and
findings he must act just as much for the other man as for his
client who alone engages and remunerates him, and in this
way only does he preserve his reputation and standing.

81

PART THIRD

Qualifications—Men of Figures—The Advent of English
and Scottish Accountants—Progress of the Profession—
James Stillman and the Writer—Legal Gentlemen and the
Profession—A Lawyer and the Writer—Sir Hardman Lever.

✣

IT IS interesting to note the qualifications of the average
practitioner in those old times judged in the light and requirements of modern accounting. His were simple and
restricted compared to the complex and advanced knowledge
of the accountant of to-day. Questions relating to such subjects
for example as the Principles of Costing, Sinking Funds, Reserves, Earned Surplus, Capital Surplus, Fixed and Liquid Assets, Capital and Income Charges, Invested Capital, Working
Capital, Depletion, Amortization, Obsolescence, etc., were very
indefinitely understood, and as a rule were hardly considered
matters coming within the scope of the accountant's practice.
Even the important subject of depreciation was in the same
class and failed to be dealt with in anything like a scientific
way. It was of course generally known what depreciation
meant but its application to practical accounting was no more
than partly understood. I have in mind the case of an "Expert" at that period who received his early training in the
office of one of the large railroad companies, being called
upon to testify in the matter of certain litigation connected
with one of these companies involving the determination of
the actual net earnings of the road in question for a specific
period. He was asked by counsel for the opposite side, evi-

dently to test his knowledge of the subject, to define the meaning of the words capital additions, betterments, extensions, replacements and renewals and how he would treat expenditures under these headings as between capital and income. He failed to give a satisfactory reply and was excused from further testifying on the ground that he was not a competent witness. Now while many accountants of moderate ability in these days could give a full and intelligent answer to these questions such were a little beyond the capacity and intelligence of the average practitioner of those days. I would be inclined to say that almost any modern young accountant just through his studies would have no difficulty in dealing with such questions and others of a like kind.

I will digress a little at this point to say a few words on the subject of "Figures" which happens to be one of my pet topics. In the old days, and as a matter of fact to a large extent in these, accountants were often looked upon and referred to as "men of figures." Now just what does this mean in the minds of those using the term? It means a man who deals in and loves figures for themselves, calculates, balances accounts, prepares elaborate statements, looks for errors, thinks figures, sometimes juggles them and always writes and talks them, and in proportion to his skill in this direction so does he consider himself a good and capable accountant. A man of such a type in his general practice is likely to base his findings and conclusions on the figures he finds on records rather than on the facts behind those figures. The latter are paramount, facts and truths automatically becoming secondary. If, for example, he sees on records he is examining a property asset standing at a certain value, he is prompted to accept such value as a truth because the figures say it is so.

The well trained and experienced accountant of to-day on the other hand is not a man of figures in the sense as above outlined. He is rather a man of facts and truths, and figures become subordinate and are used only as a means of expressing such facts and truths. In dealing with accounting matters he is not only skilled in what I may term the technique of accounting, that is figuring, balancing, adjusting and so forth, but understands and applies the fundamental principles governing accounts and their relations one to the other, knows the elements that properly enter into and constitute profits and losses, the underlying theories of capital and income and so on. In any account or statement put before him he does not take the figures at their face value. They are secondary and his thoughts at once center on the questions, what do they stand for, what are the actual facts and truths behind them, and proceeds to examine and adjust them accordingly. In other words, the accountant makes his figures fit in with the facts, the other man the facts to his figures.

Now there are a great many men of figures who imagine they are good accountants in practice to-day. There are also a great many good accountants. The former can usually be recognized by the nature of their reports, filled with figures, accompanied by wonderful and voluminous exhibits that bewilder the layman and leave him no wiser than he was before. The reports of the latter on the contrary are usually of a briefer character, giving such figures only as are needful to state required facts and essential things, and if necessary opinions and views on questions of use and interest to the client concerned. The difference between the two can probably be better expressed and understood if I state what a well known New York lawyer remarked to me some time ago. He said: "In the course of my professional practice I have seen and ready many accountants' reports, and what has always impressed me the most in reference to the majority of them is that they contain lots of figures but no brains." There's the whole of my argument in a nut shell, and before finishing I would like to say a few words to the young, rising and am-

84

bitious accountant of to-day who loves his profession. Don't allow yourself to be mesmerized by figures. I agree they are very alluring but be a little suspicious and don't trust them too much. Use figures as little as you can, remember your client doesn't like or want them, he wants brains. Think and act upon facts, truths and principles and regard figures only as things to express these, and so proceeding you are likely to become a great accountant and a credit to one of the truest and finest professions in the land. And one or two words also to those patrons of the profession who at times require important accounting work to be performed, select the man of brains and let the other man do the figuring. There are a few of the first kind and a great many of the latter and the result will be justified if the right one is chosen.

Toward the end of the year 1888 and the beginning of 1889, accountants in practice here experienced a feeling of much curiosity and surprise to find suddenly amongst them a number of English and Scotch accountants engaged in special and important accounting work in connection with a number of industrial undertakings located in this country. These accountants were the representatives of certain prominent London accounting firms who had been sent here to examine the financial condition and earning power of said undertakings on behalf of "English Syndicates" as they were then termed, formed over there to purchase American industrial properties of good standing which could show large earning power, the object being to incorporate and capitalize these under the English laws and float the securities on the English market. These operations were confined in the first place almost exclusively to American Breweries which in those days were undoubtedly large profit making undertakings. The first of these to undergo examination was the Kreuger Brewing Co. situated in Newark, N. J., which was later acquired by the "English Syndicate," and then followed a number of others, namely, the Rochester Breweries, San Francisco Breweries, Denver Breweries, St. Louis Breweries, Chicago Breweries and several others. I think the first industrial undertaking, not a brewery, examined by accountants and later taken over in the way referred to was the Otis Steel Company of Cleveland. This Company was subsequently repurchased by American interests and operates as an American company at the present time.

As will be seen, the accounting work necessary to be done in the process of acquiring these properties was great and important, and it was performed entirely by foreign accountants. This circumstance had a decided influence for good on the profession at large. In the first place, it had what may be termed an educational effect inasmuch as it gave American accountants more of an insight into the nature and responsibility of the work experienced accountants were called upon to perform, and how they went about doing it. In the second place, it opened the eyes of business men here for the first time to the fact that there existed an important and useful profession in regard to which they had known little or nothing previously, and in respect of which they saw advantages which in the future would undoubtedly enure to the benefit of business at large. At any rate the visit of these men having for its object the examination of the financial affairs of American commercial enterprises, intelligently and thoroughly going over their books and records within a limited time, and completing the work so as to be able to exhibit and report upon the financial conditions and earning power of such enterprises, was naturally a surprise to many and at the same time a novel and instructive experience.

The year 1890 and several years thereafter represented a period of undoubted development and advancement in accounting both in respect of a better knowledge of the profession and its requirements on the part of its practitioners, and also in the fact that bankers and financial men generally began to understand better the nature of its work and service. They were the first to perceive real merit and benefit in the employment of accountants in many business matters, and evinced a willingness to give the profession a larger recognition and to avail themselves of its services.

This feeling was further intensified by the fact that about the period I am referring to or possibly a little later a number of fairly large accounting firms sprang into existence and became established with offices mainly in the city of New York. Some of these firms were of English origin and others purely American. Amongst the former, and one of the first, was the firm of Jones, Caeser & Co. (afterwards Price, Waterhouse & Co. of London) established in 1890. I think it can safely be said that the profession received a pronounced impetus, and recognition became more general on the part of the public soon after the advent of this firm, mainly from the fact that it was later appointed as Auditors and Accountants to the U. S. Steel Corporation, an event that perhaps contributed more to creating a realization on the part of the business world here as to what accounting and auditing really meant than to any other circumstance up to that time. Of the American firms that a year or two later on became established and who quickly became prominent and important, and who are still enjoying these distinctions may be mentioned Haskins and Sells; Lybrand, Ross Bros. and Montgomery; Patterson, Teale and Dennis, and several others.

Another circumstance about this time also tended to the further development of the profession. A number of industrial concerns became incorporated under the laws of the various states, and their securities issued and offered to the investing public. In most of these cases bankers employed accounting firms practicing here to make examinations and reports on the financial condition and earnings of these under-

87

takings before offering the securities for public subscription. This work was usually reflected in the form of a short report or certificate given by the examining accounting firm of its findings, and published in the bankers' prospectus.

I believe the first industrial firm so incorporated whose securities were offered to the public with an accountant's certificate attached to the prospectus was the firm of John B. Stetson & Co. of Philadelphia early in the year 1891. Other industrial firms were incorporated in rapid succession and the services of professional accountants became general.

88

About this time also bankers turned their attention largely to the subject of the consolidation of industrial enterprises, that is, the merging of a number of separate companies engaged in identical lines of business into one parent corporation. Accountants were employed in connection with this work to verify the earnings of each company and together, and to ascertain other financial and operating data for the use of the bankers.

The first ones I think to undergo this process (other than U. S. Steel Corporation) were the Trenton Potteries, embracing several companies engaged in the manufacture of sanitary ware; the Herring-Hall-Marvin Company, representing three individual safe and lock companies, and the Union Typewriter Company consisting of five separate companies devoted exclusively to the manufacture of typewriting machines.

In the case of the latter company my firm was appointed to make the preliminary examinations and the work was taken in hand. The five separate companies involved were the Remington Typewriter Co., the Smith-Premier, the Dinsmore, the Yost and the Caligraph, these, I believe, representing the whole of the companies engaged in this line of business at that period.

The work embraced in these examinations was performed by myself with one assistant, and the report thereon finally completed and submitted. I will relate how I later became personally interested in this matter at the instance of a prominent and well-known banker of those days.

I wished to do this because it had been whispered in certain quarters that the head of the firm of Barrow, Wade, Guthrie & Co. was interested in the promotion of this Company and that, therefore, the report of that firm should be accepted in this light. Let us see how this coincided with the truth.

The principal for whom my firm was acting in this matter was Ex-Senator Fowler of Jersey City, who held options of purchase from these companies, and had the right thereunder to make full examinations. The report accordingly was directed and delivered to Mr. Fowler. About two weeks after its submission I received a request from Mr. James Stillman, then President of the National City Bank of New York to see him on a business matter.

I had heard in the meantime that Mr. Stillman was likely to become interested in this business and take a prominent part in its promotion and financing, and knowing that bankers generally did not have too much faith in the knowledge and reliability of men of my profession, I felt his object in wishing to see me was to satisfy his mind on this point and be assured the report was honest in its findings.

I called at his office at the bank in Wall Street as requested, and after some preliminary remarks he addressed me as follows: "I wish to talk with you about these Typewriting companies and the report you have recently made on them, copy of which I have here. I understand you personally visited each one of these plants and made the examinations yourself." I replied "I had." "I also understand that while this report is signed by your firm name, you individually wrote it." I said, "I did." He looked at me steadily and searchingly for a moment and then asked abruptly, "Do you believe in it, and are you willing to accept full responsibility for it?" I was a

89

little taken back by this question, wondering just what was in his mind, but answered, "I certainly do believe in it or I would not have written it and I am willing to take full responsibility." He seemed to be satisfied with this reply and said, "That is all I wish to know, and now I will tell you briefly what I intend to do. I am going to take up this business and incorporate it under the name of the Union Typewriter Company and arrange for its financing. There will be an issue of preferred stock and common stock, and I want you to subscribe for some of the preferred stock in your own name."

90

I naturally hesitated for a moment, fully conscious this was not just an invitation to subscribe, but practically a command that I do so. I still hesitated and finally said, "Mr. Stillman, I am sorry to say I am not a man of sufficient means to make an investment in this or in fact in anything at this time, otherwise I would be pleased to do what you ask." "That needn't trouble you at all," he promptly replied. "I will loan you the necessary money on your note with the stock as collateral." Again I hesitated for a time and then asked, "For how long?" "Just as long as you wish," he answered, "and I will charge you interest at the low rate of only five per cent." I have always been somewhat of a "sport" in a moderate way in matters such as this, and Mr. Stillman's attitude, sincerity and desire to meet all my objections impressed me so much that I finally said, "All right, I will subscribe for such reasonable amount as you think I should take, leaving this point entirely to you." "I am glad you have so decided," he replied, "and you will hear from me in the course of a few days."

I must confess I was somewhat puzzled at this conversation, and turning the thing over in my mind concluded that this evidently was the banker's way of testing my faith and sincerity in an enterprise formed on the basis of what I had personally written and vouched for.

About ten days after this interview a messenger from the

National City Bank presented himself at my office one morning, and handed me an envelope containing papers. These I found were a demand note for $20,000, a short letter requesting me to sign said note, collateral attached thereto consisting of 200 shares First Preferred Stock of the Union Typewriter Co. and 200 shares of common stock given as a bonus. This was something of a surprise to me, for here I was called upon to commit myself to an obligation much beyond my means, and for a sum far greater than I had ever thought of; but as already stated I was somewhat of a "sport," so I courageously signed the note and handed it back to the waiting messenger along with the collateral. Now I will go on to tell how splendidly Mr. Stillman carried out his part of the transaction.

91

Some time after this, while the note was still unpaid, a marked depression in business came over the country. Shares and securities of all kinds began to drop seriously in market value. A black cloud seemed to be hovering over the business and financial world, its effect being felt in all quarters. United States currency was for a time quoted at a premium. Banks refused in many cases to pay out currency for checks or would pay part in currency and part in a New York Clearing House check. In this condition of affairs I became much concerned about my own position and particularly the note obligation I was under with the bank. I expected each day to be notified my collateral had been sold with a request to make good at once the resulting deficiency. But none came and with much anxiety I decided to go and see Mr. Stillman and put myself in his hands. He received me pleasantly and on enquiring just what he wanted me to do, smiled slightly and said, "Nothing; I am not asking you for any money. I promised you you could pay back the loan whenever you wished and I intend to keep my promise. Pay the money whenever you are able to and till then, don't worry." Here was a man whose word was kept to the letter, and whose attitude and spirit in this transaction to one so small in the balance compared to himself, was something I could not readily forget.

Gentlemen of the legal profession were the last in line even moderately to recognize that accounting was a separate and distinct profession or that it played any very special role in the affairs of the business world. They persisted to the last in looking upon the accountant as no more than a well informed bookkeeper, and held a quiet contempt for his pretentions that he was anything else. As an example of this feeling I will relate a somewhat amusing incident which happened to me.

92

I was subpœnaed to appear and testify as an "expert" on behalf of the creditors in the case of a fraudulent bankruptcy where it was claimed that the debtor had illegally and improperly drawn large sums from his business to the detriment of his creditors at certain dates when he knew he was in a bankrupt condition. His attorney sought to prove that these drawings had not taken place; it was a fact, he admitted, that some moneys had been drawn by the debtor on or about the dates named, but that these were minor sums taken by the debtor for his own personal support and maintenance. After being put on the stand and certain direct evidence had been given, the debtor's attorney took me in hand. His preliminary abrupt question was, "You claim to be an expert bookkeeper?" I was a little surprised at this sudden and blunt question and slowly replied that "while I understood all about bookkeeping, both theoretical and practical, I was not exactly a bookkeeper." He came back at me again rather savagely: "It is your business to write up, balance and keep the books of others requiring service of this kind?" I replied again that this was not exactly my business—that I was a professional accountant, whereupon he quickly turned to the judge and said, "Your honor—I submit that this witness on his own showing is not a bookkeeper and therefore is incompetent to give evidence in this case and I move that the whole of his testimony be stricken out." The judge took a different view and smiling slightly requested him to go on with his examination. What followed was a little too funny not to relate. The attorney requested me to open to a certain page in the debtor's ledger (the cash book had previously mysteriously disappeared) wherein was found the debtor's personal account. He said, "I want you to look at that account and tell me if it is not a fact according to the account there shown that the debtor on such and such a date drew from his business $125.00." I replied that according to this account in the ledger before me on the date named the debtor had actually drawn the sum of $1,000.00; that the figure 125 was not the amount drawn but the page of the cash book from which the posting had been made. Here was the case of an otherwise bright attorney, who had evidently personally examined the ledger account of his client, taking the first column of figures he saw (which were the cash book posting folios) and had concluded these were the "large alleged drawings" his client had taken out of his business.

Lawyers in these days are not all like the one above, and while in many cases members of the legal profession do recognize the services of accountants as being of special value to them, this recognition is by no means general. This is unfortunate, for accountants are usually ready to consult members of the legal profession on special matters they may have in hand for clients to be sure their opinions and findings conform in every respect to the legality of the case at issue. On the contrary it is rarely the case that lawyers will seek the opinion of accountants in matters where law and accounting play an important part so as to be satisfied that their findings and provisions are in harmony with accounting principles and exactness. I have seen many cases where (mainly in the matter of the preparation of contracts and agreements in commercial affairs) attorneys have failed to prepare these so as to give full and proper effect to the accounting element contained therein. It is obvious that unless the legal part of these instruments fully harmonizes with the accounting part, and each fits in its place, dispute and trouble are likely to be the result and possibly expensive litigation. A very good example of what I am here referring to, viz., the value of accountants to lawyers can be given in the case of one of the former partners of my firm, Sir Hardman Lever, whose services were contributed by the firm to the British Government during the War in 1916. He was allotted to the Munitions Department of the Government and his services and knowledge as an accountant in the matter of interpreting, adjusting, and settling contracts made by the Government with contractors (these were no doubt correctly prepared from the usual legal standpoint) were such as to cause the saving to the Government of many millions of pounds sterling. This fact was openly stated during a debate in the British House of Commons and for such services he received high honors.

94

Sir Hardman Lever came to the firm from Liverpool, England, as an assistant accountant in the autumn of the year 1890. He was made a junior partner in 1898 and served the firm in that capacity up to 1922, when arrangements were made for his retirement which was finally effected in October of that year with the full approval of all the members of the firm.

The foregoing is given mainly to emphasize a point I have always had in mind, viz., that it would undoubtedly be to the advantage and interest of the two professions if accountants and lawyers acted reciprocally in cases of commercial and other matters where law and accounting together enter as elements.

PART FOURTH

[*Conclusion*]

The Profession and Its Probable Future

I DO NOT think it is necessary for me to trace the early days of the profession any further. This period began in 1883 and practically ended ten years later in 1893. From that time accounting became a real profession. The quality of the practitioner improved, the extent and diversity of his knowledge became greater, and altogether he gave to it a status and an atmosphere it had hitherto completely lacked, an atmosphere that carried with it knowledge, truth, precision, and reliability to an extent it had never before known. Then when these influences became apparent, and it was perceived that they formed the foundation and the real essence of the profession, the public, the banker, the lawyer and business men generally recognized that accountancy was a good and beneficial thing always wanted but which had not reached them till this time. And as the American business man is wise, intelligent, and alert at all times to adopt and take advantage of any beneficial and useful thing as it appears, so from this time on he became a patron of the profession and this patronage has grown and intensified to this day.

Probably to the average layman who, generally speaking, has still only a very indefinite idea what the profession represents, it would be interesting to him to learn just what this growth at the present time means. In the early stages of the profession in this country (1886 & 1887) the total gross earnings of all the accountants then in public practice (some 25 or 30 men) was roughly calculated at that time to be approximately $250,000 per annum. I believe I am safe in saying that a similar rough computation made at the present time would show the total gross earning of the profession to be in the neighborhood of something like thirty million dollars annually.

Therefore from the year 1893 I must leave to the pen of some other chronicler far more able than I to record the history of the profession and the interesting and far-reaching developments that later took place. He will commence probably by recording how the efforts of the members of the American Association of Public Accountants through the untiring efforts and patience of its members (the principal and most assidious one being Mr. Frank Broaker), to obtain some kind of legal recognition of the profession by the state, culminated in 1898 in the regents of the College of the State of New York having powers conferred upon them to grant certificates of qualification to accountants then in practice who could comply with the necessary requirements laid down by the Regents. He will proceed also to record when and under what conditions the New York State Society was formed and other societies in other states, and he will no doubt refer to what I think had a considerable influence for good on the profession and added greatly to the knowledge and proficiency of many connected with its practice, I refer now to the establishment of the School of Commerce, Finance and Accounts founded by the late C. W. Haskins then an active member of the well known firm of Haskins and Sells. This chronicler will also probably review the valuable accounting literature which began to appear soon after 1893 and to the establishment of the Journal of Accountancy a few years later. This then will be the beginning of the work of the chronicler as mine ends.

I do not wish, however, to finish this narrative without saying a few words on my own account in reference to the profession which I embraced nearly fifty years ago and which I have ardently loved all my life. I have loved it for its possibilities, its usefulness, its interesting problems, its exactness, for I look upon true accounting as an exact science. I have been in touch with it here from its inception, have seen its set-backs, its progress and development till it has become second to none as a profession in usefulness and importance in the land. I was always proud of it, particularly in its early initial period when I felt a real part of it, and it seemed to me to be like a child whose good name I was ever ready to defend. Any reflection cast upon its integrity I was ready to resent for I felt in a way it was personal.

That the profession will continue to progress, although it is already on an advanced and high plane, I have no doubt whatever. I believe the young professional accountant of today will be called upon for far greater things in the future than those that now constitute his daily practice. I believe it will eventually become apparent to men of the business world that the professional accountant (and when I say this I mean the real thing, the one who knows, who understands business principles and their relation to the theory and practice of accounting, the one who has matured in his knowledge born of long and varied experience) should have a place on the board of directors of all mercantile and manufacturing concerns in the country. I have seen so many cases in my time where losses through defective costing or accounting could have been prevented or materially lessened, where expensive litigation arising through contracts and agreements entered into without proper understanding and consideration for accounting principles, could have been avoided if the experienced accountant's knowledge had been availed of by his presence on the board. I believe the accountant will be called upon in

97

all cases where mercantile losses arise, not just to show the extent of these losses which he now does, but the real cause of them, how they might, through proper accounting methods and analysis, have been prevented or lessened and how they may be avoided in future operations. I believe further that accountants will be appointed receivers and trustees; that laws will eventually be enacted compelling all corporations and companies, all business and financial undertakings where the public and outsiders are interested, to have their operations audited, analyzed, and passed upon by legally authorized auditors qualified to do this work, and lastly that their services will be sought to audit and check periodically the accounts and records of municipalities and the departments of the federal and state governments. In other words true accounting, born of precision and exactness, will permeate in the future all mercantile and financial matters where truth, accuracy and honesty of purpose are the requisites.

When that time arrives the profession of accounting will at last have come fully into its own and although that day may not be far distant, I fear it is not for me to see.

98

The C. P. A. Movement and the Future of the Profession of the Public Accountant in the United States of America.

By GEORGE WILKINSON, C. P. A.

Secretary of the Federation of Societies of Public Accountants in the United States of America.

Acting under the instructions of the Committee on Arrangements, the official Scribe of the Federation of Societies of Public Accountants has prepared this paper. The Committee determined the title as follows: " The C. P. A. Movement and the Future of the Profession of the Public Accountant in the United States of America." The wording of the title indicates two distinct provinces, first the Historian, second the Architect. Three years ago a congress of Architects assembled here to draw up plans for the beautiful buildings and grounds of the World's Fair, in the very midst of which we are now assembled. Let us to-day constitute ourselves a Congress of Architects for planning the future of our profession. We are assembled here in due process of regular proceedings, all the public accountants in the United States of America have been invited to attend and those who have responded to the call and are here have equal rights. Surely no body of men ever met together with better right to make designs and to draw up plans for the future of their profession.

We have one great advantage: We have nothing to undo. What little tradition our profession in the United States has acquired in the very few years it has existed is good. We stand at the open door of the future which lies invitingly before us.

"THE C. P. A. MOVEMENT."

The history of the movement to secure State legislation establishing the degree of Certified Public Accountant, up to and including the year 1903, has been published in pamphlet form and, on the maxim of "silence gives consent," has been accepted by the profession in general, and by all those whose names are therein mentioned in particular, as a fair statement of the facts. Since that history was written we have to record the passage of a C. P. A. law in New Jersey and unsuccessful attempts in Ohio, Georgia and Louisiana.

Enough was said in that history of the trials and tribulations of various Legislative Committees, and of those enthusiasts who visited State Capitols and labored industriously to overcome the adverse prejudices of "hayseed" legislators. But for the sake of those who are unacquainted with that history, it might be well to recite the Roll of Honor and to remind you to-day that, but for the unselfish devotion to principle and the common good of others, displayed by the gentlemen named, "The C. P. A. Movement" had hardly yet taken root and certainly had never grown to be what we are proud to recognize in it to-day.

The thanks of the profession of the Public Accountants are due in no slight measure to these pioneers who bore the burden and the heat of the day, be it seven years ago or seven months. It affords us much pleasure to recite the names of:

> Frank Broaker, of New York;
> Charles N. Vollum, of Pennsylvania;
> Max Teichmann, of Maryland;
> Alfred G. Platt, of California;
> Cyril M. Williams, of Washington;
> J. Porter Joplin, of Illinois, and
> Frank G. DuBois, of New Jersey.

These are the names of the men who labored hard and long in the cause of C. P. A. There are others too. Many survivors are there who might claim the victory, but the few names mentioned should be gratefully remembered by us all, because they stand out prominently as the men who set aside their business and convenience for the good of others.

The States just named are those having C. P. A. laws in force. Eight other States have tried unsuccessfully to secure the passage of similar laws, and, nothing daunted, will try again and again until they succeed.

The first law passed was in April, 1896, in the State of New York, where the examinations are conducted and the certificates granted by Regents of the University of the State of New York. In Illinois, where the law was passed in 1903, the old established State University of Urbana conducts the examinations and issues the diplomas. In both cases the examination questions are prepared and the answers examined by three Certified Public Accountants who are members of the State Societies.

In other C. P. A. States the certificates are signed by the Governor, while the responsibility of conducting the examinations is vested in a State Board of Accountancy, composed of three Accountants, while in Pennsylvania and California two Attorneys-at-law are added to the board.

101

UNIFORM LEGISLATION.

Much has been said about "uniform C. P. A. legislation" and it is regarded as so essential to the future of our profession that its encouragement is embodied in the Constitution of the Federation as one of the "objects."

Model C. P. A. bills have been prepared with much care, and have been approved by the Executive Board of the Federation; one being known as "The University Bill," and the other as "The Board of Accountancy Bill." Possibly these models are not all they might be, but at the least they convey in a succinct form a very good idea of all that has gone before, in the way of State legislation recognizing our profession, with copious notes of the reason why.

BEST FORM OF C. P. A. LAW.

It is still a mooted point which of the two forms of C. P. A. law, so far enacted, is the better. There are a few Eastern States with Universities under the jurisdiction of the Legislature, but in several of the Western States the Legislature can prescribe the duties of the State Universities.

Where the University authorities are quite willing to assume the responsibility and the work involved, a law that constitutes the University of the State the examining body is considered to be the more desirable form of legislature, especially when the examiners are chosen from among reputable public accountants practicing in the State, as they invariably have been up to this date. Certificates issued by a State University carry more of the prestige that attaches to an educational degree, and the value of these will increase as successful examinations are held.

The bill providing for a Board of Accountancy, to be appointed by the Governor of the State, is frequently found expedient on account of the inability or reluctance of the State University authorities to assume the burden imposed by the act. The State Board form of law is also found to be easier of enactment, as it is better understood by the lawmakers and more in line with previous legislation erroneously supposed to be of the same class.

It has sometimes been said that the State Board law is open to the objection that it may be made subject to political influence. To entertain this view is to do an injustice to those who have labored hard in the cause. Thus far nothing like undue political influence has been noted. On every board so far, the Governors have appointed accountants in good standing to serve as examiners, and these boards have exercised their own best judgment free from political interference, so far as has become known. An excellent precedent to have inaugurated.

CLOSED DOOR IN NEW YORK.

In the State of New York the text of the law makes it a misdemeanor for any person to assume the title "Certified Public Accountant," or make any use of the letters "C. P. A.," within the State of New York, unless he holds a certificate *issued to him* by the Regents of the New York University.

The laws of Pennsylvania, Maryland, California and Washington have the same penalty clause. If a New York C. P. A. assumes to practice as such in Philadelphia, Baltimore, San Francisco or Seattle, he is committing a misdemeanor, and is liable to arrest upon the complaint of any citizen.

102

Thus stands the law, but only in the State of New York has there been any attempt to enforce the restriction. Learned counsel, who has made these laws his special study, rendered the opinion that the legal holders of C. P. A. certificates issued by other States could not be denied the use of their title so long as they designated the State whose certificate they held. All the alien C. P. A.'s are doing this in New York to-day.

So far each State has enacted a law for her own citizens alone. While taking pains to keep the aliens out the States previously named have forfeited control of all the C. P. A.'s imported from other States. This is quite a serious problem, especially in New York, because thither flock accountants from all States, many of whom claim rank with the best. Illinois, Pennsylvania and Maryland contribute a dozen C. P. A.'s actually practicing in New York City to my own knowledge. New York has no control over these. Their certificates can only be forfeited by the authorities that conferred them, and they are not permitted to belong to the New York Society. Any offense committed in New York would be without the jurisdiction of the home State of the offender.

OPEN DOOR IN ILLINOIS.

In Illinois the lawmakers have swung to the opposite extreme. In framing the bill for the law enacted in 1903, a provision, previously unheard of, was introduced. This opens the way for persons holding certificates issued by other States to practice as Certified Public Accountants in Illinois without going through any formalities. This wide open door is now recognized to be a mistake, as there is no way in which the State authorities or the Illinois Society of Certified Public Accountants can discipline an alien C. P. A. who may infringe the code.

It is only a question of time when the laws above referred to must be amended. The door should swing both ways, but should not open too far.

RECIPROCITY FIRST PROPOSED.

At the Annual Convention of the Federation of Societies of Public

Accountants held in Washington, D. C., on October 20th, 1903, a report was read by Max Teichmann, President of the Maryland Association of Certified Public Accountants, in which a proposition was brought out to have the law of the State of Maryland amended so as to provide that accountants certified by other States, upon coming to Maryland to engage in professional business, could, for a small fee, register their certificates with the Maryland State Board of Accountancy and thus secure all the privileges enjoyed by those who had passed the State examinations, always provided that the State whence such visiting C. P. A. might bring his certificate offered the same privileges to accountants certified in Maryland.

Mr. Teichmann met with the experience of most reformers. A long discussion ensued in which this newly born reciprocity doctrine was not encouraged. But Maryland sowed her seed in better places than appeared last October.

RECIPROCITY IN NEW JERSEY.

The next C. P. A. bill to be promulgated was in the State of New Jersey. The minute the bill appeared in the Judiciary Committee of the House of Representatives, an amendment was offered by a member of the house providing for the introduction of a reciprocal clause. The New Jersey law, as enacted last spring, provides for the issuance of a full C. P. A. certificate, without examination, to any person residing in the State who holds a valid C. P. A. certificate from another State where the like privilege is offered. The applicant must pay the full fee of $25, but the issuance of the certificate is at the absolute discretion of the State Board of Public Accountants.

RECIPROCAL REGISTRATION TO STAY.

The reciprocal registration feature has come to stay for the reason that it provides just the right measure of local control. Alien C. P. A.'s, who have registered their certificates with the local board, are accorded all the privileges and are subject to all the penalties imposed by the State laws. None others will be allowed to style themselves " Certified Public Accountants " within the borders of the State, or use the designation in any way.

It is not proposed to compel accountants to register in every State they may seek business in, but rather to provide a proper way in which a C. P. A. immigrating from one State to another can secure the privileges of and simultaneously become amenable to the local statute.

"C. P. A." AS A PROFESSIONAL TITLE.

The abbreviation C. P. A. has frequently been spoken of as a " degree," but there is no authority for this. Whether it shall become recognized as a diploma, a degree of learning or merely a license to practice, depends less upon the form of the law than upon the dignity with which the letters are upheld by the members of the profession and upon the merit of the technical examinations held.

It has been suggested that the letters C. P. A. constitute a specific professional title the equivalent for our profession of M.D. in medicine, D.D.S. in dentistry; LL.B. in law; also that the use of the courtesy designation of Mr. or Esquire might be eliminated as unnecessary, as in other professions referred to. The suggestion is most worthy of consideration as tending to elevate the title which has now become the recognized designation of our calling.

PROFESSIONAL STANDING.

During the early years of the C. P. A. movement grave doubts existed in the minds of some of the ablest accountants in the country as to the utility of a legal designation. "It will be an equalizer," they said. "The penny accountant on the side streets will be placed on a legal equality with the best in the land." They asked, "Why should I exert myself, or contribute funds, in behalf of legislation that will only benefit the little fellow?" These are the questions of the short-sighted men who call themselves "conservatives," because they are content with the existing order of things, so far as putting forth any personal effort goes, but who are generally found among those who are bemoaning their sad fate and complaining that their business is going to the "dimnition bow-wows."

The last three years have clarified the situation. Illinois, California, Washington and New Jersey have secured a place in the slowly increasing family of C. P. A. States. "The C. P. A. Movement" has set in simultaneously from both coasts and there is no stemming the tide. It is true that the little fellow has been benefited. In receiving his certificate he has felt the uplift of a legal designation; the best that is in him shall henceforth be devoted to the profession. But the accountant with the well-established practice has not suffered by the enactment of State laws, for what is good for the entire body works to the advantage of each of its members.

It it not contended that a mantle of wisdom is conferred with the diploma; but in receiving a certificate from the State an accountant becomes a member of a legally recognized profession, and is amenable to control of the properly constituted authorities. And with him come others—practically all the others. Their status is defined, in a year the exemption from examination ceases and an evolution is begun. The future will bring with it the survival of the fittest, while those who enter shall do so by the straight and narrow gate of examination. The more young men who enter the profession through the door of which the examiners hold the key, the stronger we shall become as a professional class.

FORMATION OF NEW SOCIETIES.

In pursuance of the policy of organization, avowed in the Constitution of the Federation, the Public Accountants have been called together in several States. With all the energy the Executive possessed, the work has been carried into the West and South, where the need of it appeared to be greatest; in every State where we could find a half dozen men, devoting their lives to the practice of accounting as a professional career, they have been called together. The doctrines of organized effort and the gospel of "C. P. A.-ism" have been preached; the work previously accomplished in the other States has been described, the advantages set forth, considerable enthusiasm has been aroused a' d local associations have been formed. The

104

number of members in some of these new societies is quite small, but a nucleus has been formed and in nearly every instance the seed sown by the Federation has taken root.

This work has been severely criticized by some of our professional brethren in the East, who have called the Apostle of organized effort a " walking delegate." Our New York critics can see no reason for carrying the gospel of " C. P. A.-ism " to the prairies, where the Public Accountant is not recognized as a professional man, but is regarded as merely a clever bookkeeper. It may be that the work done in some States is ahead of the times, that the enthusiasm displayed at the initial meetings, held under the direction of an enthusiastic missionary, has died down and little has yet resulted in the way of a permanent organization. But the seed sown *has* taken root; the future will yield the fruit. It will take time to finish this work, to cultivate the newly planted societies until harvest time, but one thing has certainly been accomplished: the new societies have been brought under the influence of the National organization and the men left in charge of the newly formed associations have been imbued with the ideals and ethics of the older societies.

If we are to advance our calling to the point where it shall be recognized by the Federal Government as a dignified and learned profession, we must advance by equal stride in every State—East and West, North and South. Our demand for recognition, to be heard in the legislative halls of our National Capitol, must come simultaneously from every section of the country.

FURTHER STATE LEGISLATION.

The question of seeking State legislation making audits compulsory has been much before Public Accountants' Societies in late years. Some accountants think that a proper equivalent of the English Companies Act should be sought in every State; but the fear is expressed that we are not ready to make any move in this direction yet.

Before we seek legislation that will make more work, we should firmly and fully establish the legal designation of C. P. A. After a majority of States and all the important ones have enacted C. P. A. laws, and the fact is recognized by the public that the best practitioners are certified, we can seek laws to compel corporations, in which the public are interested as investors, to have their balance sheets audited by legally recognized accountants.

The effect of making a premature effort to secure such legislation would be to attract to our calling a large number of persons whose lack of training renders them unfit to serve the public. There would be a great influx of worthless characters the minute it was known that any remunerative work had been created by the legislature.

THE ACCOUNTANT AS A BUSINESS ADVISER.

The most valuable service that the Accountant can render to his client lies along the lines of giving sound business advice. The accountant who is a good man of business acquires at every step of his career experience and business acumen that he can turn to the best account in serving his clients.

The accountant who is consulted on important business matters like agreements between companies, firms and individuals, or the adoption of new lines of business policy, is infinitely more valuable to the client than the mere man of figures. In our capacity as Auditors we are necessarily taken into the innermost confidence of our client, and what is more natural than that the accountant should be consulted in matters of management and the future policy of the business? The point is here: if the Accountant is individually competent to give good business counsel his advice will be sought. It therefore becomes most desirable that we should qualify ourselves by study and observation to become the adviser of our client more than the checker of our client's employees. Further, that we should favor the instructions of the rising generation of Accountants along lines of practical business utility as well as on technical subjects specified in State C. P. A. laws.

THE ACCOUNTANT AND THE PROMOTER.

The evolution of modern business methods has made the auditors' certificate so essentially a part of every prospectus for the flotation of a new stock issue that the relation between the accountant and his promoter-client has become one of much delicacy as well as great responsibility. In this connection it should be said that the Accountant's position should be absolutely independent of that of the promoter. This certificate should be an unbiased statement of facts, and of *all* facts, given under the exercise of the best judgment of which he is capable. Consideration, alike for his personal interests and the welfare of his profession, should teach him to abstain from any active participation in promotion. Above all, he should be most careful not to use veiled language as a cloak to hide the intrinsic facts. The Accountant who for love of gain, even if expressed in a reasonable fee for work performed, will withhold some essential facts from his client, and through his client from the investing public, is guilty of a crime, the effect of which is far beyond his ken.

The Accountant who engages in the promotion of companies ceases to be a public accountant and becomes a business man, a speculator. He forfeits his professional status the minute he loses his independent attitude, and if he continues to hold himself out to the public as a professional man of unbiased standing, he is guilty of misrepresentation which does himself and his profession an injury.

THE ACCOUNTANT'S RESPONSIBILITY.

In Great Britain the law holds the accountant both financially and criminally responsible for negligence and misrepresentation. There have been some notable suits for the recovery of damages and some criminal prosecutions in Great Britain, and these have tended to the employment of a greater degree of skill and care in auditing, and more caution in certifying. There is no law in the United States specifically holding auditors responsible, either in pocket or in person. A civil suit for damages or a criminal prosecution would have to rest upon evidence of direct fraud, wilful neglect or conspiracy, and would be difficult to secure, unless it could be proved to the jury that there had been *intent to do wrong.*

The responsibility of the accountant is professional and moral, not financial. If any penalties are to be provided for neglect or misrepresentation, they should be punitive and personal, involving the abridgment of privileges and individual freedom; the loss of reputation and professional standing; the forfeiture of certificates conferred by the State and by the society. The penalties should not be monetary so that they could be provided out of corporate capital.

FORFEITURE OF C. P. A. CERTIFICATES.

All the C. P. A. laws have sections providing for the forfeiture of the certificate by the same authority that conferred it, provided that sufficient cause be shown at a competent hearing of charges. So far as my information goes, no such proceedings have been held, and no forfeiture has been made. In history making we are young. Long may it be before there is occasion to invoke the power of the Governor of any of our States in this direction.

FORFEITURE OF SOCIETY MEMBERSHIP.

In like manner the by-laws of Accountants' Societies, or of most of them, provide for the forfeiture of membership for cause. So that the practical disbarment of men found guilty of wrong-doing is within our own hands. No thought of personal consequences should retard the prosecution of charges before the Directors of our Societies and before the C. P. A. Boards, when occasion for such action arises.

ACCOUNTANT NOT IN OTHER BUSINESS.

If we are to be considered as a professional class, it is highly desirable that accountants should not engage in any line of commercial or professional work inconsistent therewith. In this particular we can, with advantage, take a leaf out of the book of the older organizations in Great Britain, where it is specifically forbidden for members to engage in any other kind of business. For the present we must be content to encourage the observance of the principle in advance of the enactment of a law.

HIGH MORAL STANDING TO BE MAINTAINED.

One of the most vital considerations to the future of the C. P. A. degree, and hence to the entire profession, is that a high moral standard should be maintained in every State. If we are to make our calling honored and establish it as a learned profession we must maintain a high moral code, and we must find a legal way to keep out any black sheep that may stray in. A strongly expressed and rigidly enforced rule in respect to the moral character of candidates will always be a potent factor in securing public esteem. The New Jersey State Board of Public Accountants, in framing the rules under which examinations shall be held, have provided that all applicants for C. P. A. certificates shall make an affidavit that the statements therein contained are true, and one of the clauses states, in so many words, that the applicant has never been guilty of a crime. This is regarded as a wise provision, because the moral status is so difficult to determine in documentary form. This plan should be carried further. An applicant should be obliged to swear that he knows no reason why he is not a fit and proper person to receive a certificate from the State as a C. P. A. Should an applicant knowingly make a false statement in his application, it would not be difficult for the local authorities to have his certificate canceled, when it transpired that his standing was not good. To do this, it should be clearly defined what constitutes "good moral character." A man who has been found guilty of a crime by a court of competent jurisdiction cannot successfully claim to have a good moral character, unless subsequent judicial proceedings have cleared his name. A man will not knowingly misrepresent the facts in making application for a C. P. A. examination under oath. But in the stress of his desire for a certificate, he might stretch his conscience in filling out an application that he was not called on *to swear to*. If it should be found that an applicant had perjured himself, it would be an easy matter to cause the forfeiture of his certificate.

Examiners cannot be too careful in this regard. The man with unclean hands should not be suffered to take the examination. Admission to the examination room, where the technical examinations follow all other inquiries, should in itself constitute a certificate of good moral character.

EXAMINATIONS.

It has been suggested that this paper should contain a recommendation that the rules under which C. P. A. examinations are held should be uniform in their practical effect as far as possible.

The essential conditions that a model set of rules should provide are:

First, as to the Candidate. Citizenship in the United States, a good moral character and a clear record; graduation from high school or an equivalent education; age limit, 25 for the full certificate with right to practice as a C. P. A.; at least one year, and, later on, three years, of actual practice in the office of a Certified Public Accountant.

Second, as to the Examinations. These should be in writing and should be conducted with decorum in the presence of at least one of the examiners. A candidate, in order to pass, should receive at least seventy-five per cent. of the total counts allowed on each subject. Questions should be fairly stated without catches, and be so arranged as to demonstrate the practical and constructive ability as well as the technical knowledge of the candidate.

Third, as to the Subjects. If the subjects in which the applicants are to be examined are not specified in the statute, they should be defined in the rules of the Board, thus: " Auditihg," " Theory of Accounts," " Practical Accounting," " Commercial Law."

As the examiners who do the actual work are all practicing accountants, there is the greatest temptation to them to draw upon their own professional experience for difficult problems. This has been particularly the case in some recent examinations on the subject of " Practical Accounting." Examiners have repeatedly asked questions in recently held examinations that would defy the best accountants in practice to answer within the time limit. Therefore it is respectfully suggested to the Examiners, if you draw on your professional experience, gentlemen, *don't draw too deep.*

A suggestion was recently brought forward to have the questions before being used by the examiners scrutinized by some central bureau, to be conducted by a professor whose training and study should fit him for the difficult task and whose standing should place him beyond the reach of distrust, to the end that a uniform standard might obtain.

If such a bureau could be established under the auspices of the National Organization and could enjoy the co-operation of all the State C. P. A. examiners, or at least a majority of them, it would do much good in the direction of maintaining a high standard of examination. It cannot be denied that there would be room for abuse, for misunderstanding and for conflict of authority, also that State pride might interfere and raise obstacles. Some day this plan may be feasible.

AUDIT COMPANIES.

109

During the last few years a new form of conducting the accountancy business has been developed in the incorporated " Audit Company," of which there are several specimens in each of our largest cities. The remarks herein contained are applied to incorporated companies whose directors are not professional accountants. The plan is this: Half a dozen citizens who are engaged in business as bankers, merchants, lawyers, presidents of insurance or trust companies and the like, are induced to take some shares in an incorporated company and to become its directors. Flattering prospects are held out to them of profits to be made out of large accountancy business to be secured through the exploitation of their names and official titles, so they are " let in on the ground floor."

The names of the bankers and business men on the board are conspicuously advertised in city directories, trade papers, on the company's letter paper and elsewhere as a bait to draw business. It is obviously to the pecuniary benefit of the banker-director to send any business, over which he can exert an influence, to the audit company of which he is a shareholder, also to consent to a fee that he would call outrageous if charged by an independent accountant.

These questions follow: Can a corporation so organized fulfill the duties of the public accountant? Is it a proper custodian of the business confidence of the public? Is a corporation, whose directors are business men, without technical experience in the science and theory of accounts, really an accountant? Is it not a make-believe and a sham to call it an accountant?

In manufacture, trade or finance, the incorporated company has many advantages over the individual or the firm of individuals; among which may be mentioned, the limit of liability, the permanence of the corporation; the use of borrowed capital; the definiteness with which the company's position in the financial world may be ascertained; and the plan of government by which the brain power of several persons may be drawn upon. If these factors cannot be exercised for the good of the shareholders, where comes the benefit of incorporation?

In the business of the accountant some cash capital is necessary, but it plays the minor part, while brains, skill, personal integrity and technical experience are the controlling factors. The banker-director can certainly lend his good name to a corporation, but how can he acquire expert experience and technical skill as an accountant and dispense them to the corporation's customers?

The brain, the skill and the technical experience must therefore be hired, so an accountant is employed as manager; if he dies or leaves the company's employ, another is engaged to take his place, and the company goes on as before. Now how does the principle of responsibility apply to the incorporated audit company that gets into disgrace? Where shall the blame be laid? Shall the banker, the merchant, the insurance company's president, and the other professional directors on the board, be summoned before the local authorities, or shall the salaried accountant-manager be arrested?

If it comes to the worst the company is dissolved. The accountant-manager rents a new office, removes his staff and stationery, gets a new sign and starts all over again, under a new name, with nothing to identify him with his unsuccessful past.

The influence of incorporated audit companies is to commercialize the business and reduce it to the common level of trades and manufactures, while our influence exercised through the societies we belong to must ever be in the opposite direction, to lift it up, establish high ideals and secure its recognition as a learned profession.

THE FEDERATION OF SOCIETIES OF PUBLIC ACCOUNTANTS.

The National Organization of our profession is the " Federation of Societies of Public Accountants in the United States of America." It was organized at the National Capital on October 28th, 1902, and is, therefore, not quite two years old. The members of the Federation to-day are the State Societies of Public Accountants in Pennsylvania, Illinois, Maryland, Massachusetts, California, Ohio, Michigan, Georgia, Missouri, Minnesota and Washington. These Societies embrace a total membership of more than two hundred practicing public accountants. Each of these Societies is sovereign in its own realm and acknowledges allegiance to the Federation only in respect of matters National.

The Federation is governed by an Executive Board to which each Society contributes at least one member. Most of the executive work of this Board is delegated, under the by-laws, to an Executive Committee of five of its members, to which Committee are added the three Executive Officers.

The objects for which the Federation was formed may be stated briefly as follows: To bring the several societies of public accountants into friendly contact; to encourage the formation of further societies of public accountants; to encourage State Certified Public Accountant legislation on uniform lines; to secure Federal recognition of the profession of public accountant; to facilitate the training of young members of the profession and to further the interests of the profession in other ways. In pursuance of these objects the several Accountant Societies have been brought into close and cordial relationship, both at conventions and by correspondence; a dozen new societies have been formed; model C. P. A. bills have been compiled and promulgated; and this Congress has been brought together. So far the work has been formative; we are now ready to embark upon a useful career, " to further the interests of the profession of the public accountant generally."

THE AMERICAN ASSOCIATION OF PUBLIC ACCOUNTANTS.

Another National order, organized on entirely different lines, is the American Association of Public Accountants, incorporated under the laws of the State of New York in 1887. The Association has, according to the latest published list, 140 members, of whom about 100 are practicing public accountants. As an overwhelming majority of its members are in practice in New York, its meetings are held there and the members of its Board of Trustees reside or do business in Manhattan.

THE NEW YORK STATE SOCIETY OF CERTIFIED PUBLIC ACCOUNTANTS.

The largest State society is the New York State Society of Certified Public Accountants, with an even hundred members, all of whom have received C. P. A. certificates from the Regents of the University of the State of New York, and many of whom are simultaneously "Fellows" of the American Association. This New York State Society was a Charter Member of the Federation and remained such until June 13th last, when at a meeting of its members, held at the Waldorf-Astoria Hotel, a resolution was passed reading as follows: "*Resolved,* That this Society withdraw from this date from membership in the Federation of Societies of Public Accountants in the United States of America."

A certified copy of this resolution was transmitted to the Secretary of the Federation, but with it came no explanation of the summary action of the Society.

PROPOSED AMALGAMATION.

Since the unexplained withdrawal of the New York Society a movement has been set on foot to unite the Federation and the American Association. To that end a joint committee was appointed last June and has held three conferences.

A majority of this committee are in favor of a National Association of individual public accountants and of making certain amendments in the Constitution and By-laws of the American Association, designed to open the door to the members of all State Societies as such. The members of the joint committee representing the Federation hope to be able to bring about an amalgamation on very satisfactory lines.

FOR THE FUTURE.

And now, in closing, let me say a few words as to the future. There are several ways in which many, if not all, of us may embark our energies on behalf of the future of our profession. Let me call your attention to just three:

First: Attending the regular meetings of our respective State Societies, and there reading, or listening to the reading of, well considered papers on technical subjects, upon the preparation of which shall have been spent careful study and research.

Second: Attending gatherings of business men in other walks of life, bankers, lawyers, insurance men, and the reading of carefully prepared essays *of interest to them.*

Third: Assisting the Faculty of our State Universities by giving lectures to advanced students in accountancy and economics.

The attitude of indifference assumed by some accountants, who are habitually "too busy" to take up any kind of useful work, unless a fee is attached, is holding our profession back; while the zeal and enterprise of perhaps less gifted brothers, who are willing to work, is slowly but surely leading us on to higher planes. We are not all gifted in this direction, but the fact remains, however we may close our eyes to it, that each one of us has some inherent faculty for usefulness to others if he will but bring it forth.

ROBERT H. MONTGOMERY, C.P.A. (Philadelphia).—Mr. Chairman: I am quite sure that all of us have listened with a great deal of interest to Mr. Wilkinson's paper, and as it is desirable to have the discussion follow somewhat systematically, I would move you that the discussion be along three lines: (1.) "The C. P. A. Movement." (2.) "Audit Companies." (3.) "National Organization." These three headings have been suggested because it has been found that these three subjects are of special importance, and several of the members of the Congress expect to have something to say along these lines. I would further move that the discussion on each subject be limited to twenty minutes, and that no speaker be allowed to take more than five minutes unless by unanimous consent.

(Motion seconded; put to vote and unanimously carried.)

CHAIRMAN.—The discussion, then, is first upon "The C. P. A. Movement," and I would like to call upon Mr. Martin.

JAMES MARTIN (London).—Mr. Chairman, Ladies and Gentlemen: I will endeavor, in the course of the short time which has been allotted to me to say something on the first part of this subject, namely, "The C. P. A. Movement," and I take it that that includes the legislation which has so far taken place, and further attempts at legislation.

In the first place I hope Mr. Wilkinson will allow me to offer him my most cordial congratulations upon his paper. It does seem to me marvelous, that having regard to the fact that he goes to bed in the early hours of the morning, and is out of bed again before most of us are awake, that he has been able to prepare and to put before this Congress such an excellent paper.

I would like to take the opportunity of referring to that most interesting address we heard from Mr. Hyde at the opening of this morning's session. I think it very fortunate for us that Mr. Hyde's address was postponed from last night until this morning, as it seems to me that it has more bearing upon the subject that is now before us.

In the few remarks I shall offer you there shall be nothing of a controversial nature, as it would be discourteous both to you, as my host and to my fellow guests, were I to introduce anything in the nature of controversy to this assembly, but in dealing with the C. P. A. Movement in the United States of America I am compelled to refer to a movement for registration of public accountants in my own country. For reasons which I need not enter into here, that movement has not been successful in Great Britain and Ireland, but I am glad to say that it has had some measure of success in our colonies—in at least one of them. Finding that we could not come to any agreement in Great Britain and Ireland as to an act, which should register all public accountants, we turned our attention to Australia, and we were fortunate in the Colony of Victoria in getting all the different bodies of accountants to send a bill to be placed before their parliament. Unfortunately, Australia is dominated very largely by the working classes, and the working classes of Australia have nothing in common with professional men, and they brought our efforts to naught. Since then we have turned our attention to the latest acquisition of the British Dominions, namely, the Transvaal. Just before I left London to attend this Congress I had the satisfaction of receiving a cable to the effect that the Accountants' Ordinance had passed the Transvaal Legislature, and had received the consent of the High Commissioner on behalf of the Imperial Government.

I just want for a moment to compare your C. P. A. legislation with the act just passed through the Transvaal Legislature. Mr. Wilkinson stated in his paper that in the State of New York the text of the C. P. A. law makes it a misdemeanor for any person to assume the title of certified public accountant, or make any use of the letters C. P. A., unless he had a certificate from the New York University. That, I think, is the most stringent clause he was able to put before us. Now I don't think myself that that goes far enough. This is the text of the law as we have had it passed through the Transvaal Legislative Assembly:

After the passing of this Ordinance no person shall describe himself or hold himself out as an Accountant, or as a Public Accountant, or as an Auditor, or use any name, title, addition or description, or letters indicating that he is an Accountant by profession, or a Public Accountant, or an Auditor, whether by advertisement, by description in or at his place of business or residence, by any document, or otherwise, unless he is registered as a Public Accountant in pursuance of this Ordinance: Provided always that this Section shall not prevent any person employed exclusively at a salary on accounts and not carrying on business on his own account, from describing himself as an "Accountant" in respect of or in relation to his occupation.

The penalty for infringement is as follows:

Any person not registered as a Public Accountant in pursuance of this Ordinance and describing himself or holding himself out as an Accountant or as a Public Accountant or as an Auditor so as to contravene any of the provisions of Section 1 hereof shall be liable to a fine not exceeding one hundred pounds for each offence, and in default of payment to a period of imprisonment not exceeding three months.

It seems to me that that should be the object and aim of all legislation in regard to accountancy. It is all very well to say you protect the C. P. A. Movement, and that a man may not call himself a Certified Public Accountant, but directly you get your body of Certified Public Accountants in your State in good working order, you will find men spring up who will call themselves Accountants in some other description. What I think the American Accountants should aim at is that they should determine the path along which they intend to go. I don't mean that they should only go so far as they may think it is expedient to go, but they should look their policy full in the face and make up their minds to pursue it to the very end.

But I would make just this one suggestion to them, quoting from my own experience: that they should never allow the spirit of disunion to creep in anywhere. Unless the American Accountants unite themselves State by State, they will find that instead of pursuing a policy which will be for the advancement of each and all, they will be engaged in the very unprofitable process which has been described by an English Statesman as "ploughing the sand." (Applause.)

J. S. M. GOODLOE, C.P.A., of Columbus, O., (President of the Ohio State Society of Public Accountants).—Mr. Chairman and

Gentlemen: I am very glad to hear what Mr. Martin has to say. It is practically on the lines of what we tried to do in Ohio. Our proposed Ohio bill provided that any person who received the C.P.A. degree in any State in the Union, or who had received an equivalent degree in any country could have his certificate registered in Ohio and practice as a Public Accountant under the C. P. A. designation; but that no person should practice as a Public Accountant within the State who had not been so registered.

Now we have in Ohio at the present time a countryman of Mr. Martin's who is holding himself out as a Chartered Accountant. They advise me from over there that he is not a Chartered Accountant; he is not in the register. What protection have we under the present C. P. A. laws against this man? We welcome 115 genuine chartered accountants.

Chartered accountants stand at the top, as we all know. This man steals their reputation. He damns, if I may be allowed the expression, all of our good English friends. He has done more to hurt accountants in our part of the country than we can overcome in a long time. He is an embezzler; he is an impostor. Aren't we entitled to some protection against men of that class? Under our proposed bill it was to be given to us. We were severely criticised. Our honorable Secretary said it was a bad bill, so it didn't matter if we lost it. But I think we want to fight it on, even if we lose it again and keep on losing it. Rather lose a good bill than get one that simply says we can call ourselves C. P. A. We can go to some other State and take the C. P. A. degree. Some of us have done that. But the law of Ohio says that a man cannot practice medicine, cannot practice at the bar, without having passed an examination in the State of Ohio. If he passes his examination and submits proper credentials to the State Board of Examiners, he is admitted to practice without question. I think accountants should be in the same class. I believe our bill is in advance of any others.

HARVEY S. CHASE of Boston (Secretary of the Incorporated Public Accountants of Massachusetts).—Our Secretary, in his cheerful way, has referred to the old maids of Massachusetts, of whom I happen to be one, and while old maids are inclined often times to be a little slow still they have their good qualities.

In relation to the C. P. A. Movement as Massachusetts looks at it, and as I understand it, Massachusetts has preferred to wait until it could see what was happening in the other States before it took what it considered an extremely important and decisive step for C. P. A. legislation. Its opinion so far has been that it will be better to wait a little while longer before taking the step of the C. P. A. legislation, for the reason that the laws passed in the other States seem to us to be merely a single step. The Incorporated Public Accountants of Massachusetts have requirements of admission to their Society which are certainly much more stringent than that of any C. P. A. law which has been passed, or which could be passed at the present time. We require five years' experience in public accounting with the shingle out, and the passing of a careful examination as to morality and so on, before admission to the Association.

116

As Mr. Martin has put it, we need to look a long way ahead of what we are now looking at as C. P. A. legislation. C. P. A. as it now stands is a good thing, but we must remember that ninety-nine per cent. of the C. P. A. members in this country to-day are men who came in under the waiver clause; they have not passed any examination; they stand exactly as the I. P. A. do in Massachusetts. The title itself gives no strength so long as the men have not passed the examination and have come in—have been accepted, because they were well known and acceptable public accountants.

C. P. A. legislation requires a much more forcible handling of the whole matter than it has had so far. (Applause.)

HENRY MAGEE of Camden, N. J.—Referring to the remarks that have been made in relation to C.P.A. legislation, I have a special interest in the discussion, being from New Jersey, and special mention having been made of New Jersey by our distinguished Secretary.

I have made application recently for a C.P.A. certificate, and they not only wanted to know the date on which I was born, but they wanted to know everything I had done since that day. I do not wish to speak of that in a disparaging way at all. I only wish to state that there is some degree, and a considerable degree, of investigation in connection with the C. P. A. certificate. I have been practicing a number of years, and I had to state very thoroughly the various industries I had been connected with in my practice in that time, and the names of the prominent concerns— and they had to be prominent—for reference as to my application for a certificate. I learned further that they had written to my references, and thoroughly interrogated them in relation to the certificate. In other words, they seem to go thoroughly into the matter, and while I am not obliged to take an examination, I will be obliged to very exhaustively state the period of my experience, and also the variety of it.

Further in that connection, I have to state that four or five years ago, when the Pennsylvania law in regard to C. P. A. was passed, I then thought that it would be of no material use. I have been very busy since then, and although I have applied for examination under the Pennsylvania law I do not know whether there has been any examination since my application. Of the New Jersey law as passed I shall be glad to avail myself, and I feel sure it will be a great deal of benefit to me in my business if I secure the C. P. A. certificate. (Applause.)

FREDERICK A. CLEVELAND, Ph. D. (of New York City).—Mr. President. Gentlemen of the Convention: It has occurred to me that there is one flaw in the whole C.P.A. Movement that has not been properly eliminated, unless that elimination might come from the suggestion of Mr. Martin.

Mr. Chase has just said that in his State, while they have a very high standard for the title which the Society gives, one must practice at least five years with his shingle out before he can obtain that title; in other words, before they can have any control over him he must have practiced five years. Now there are the histories of a number of growing professions that we might refer to and in all of them the keynote of professional elevation has been one of control. The C. P. A. Movement has not been one primarily of control, but one of advancement and education, and it has been one of cultivating public professional ideas. Any regulation that we have is purely incidental and is not comprehensive. Now if associated with the I. P. A. Movement in Massachusetts, or the C. P. A. Movement in New York, or the other movements in other States, we have a local provision which has back of it the opinion of the profession, and which requires the registration of an Accountant before he is permitted to practice, the State then has control over him, and the profession can set standards for the State. And how can these standards be impressed on the State? Not only in matters of professional ideals, but in malpractice laws. There is no instrument in the hands of a profession to-day, whatever that profession may be, so effective as malpractice laws. Let not an accountant hold himself out as ready to accept business as a Public Accountant unless he registers, and then require of him that he become criminally and civilly liable for what he does; the penalty not only being civil and criminal responsibility, but the taking away from him of his right to practice in rescinding his registration. And I think that the whole profession can unite on such a movement, without respect to what our Societies for education and professional promotion may be. I think that is the first step towards a uniform movement in the education of the public and of the profession to a higher professional standing.

ALFRED G. PLATT, C.P.A., of San Francisco, Cal. (President of the California Society of Certified Public Accountants.)— Speaking for California, I desire to say that we attempted to get an act through there identically the same year that New York succeeded in 1896. We failed. We tried to get it in 1898 and again we failed. In 1900 we succeeded.

In drafting the act a great many thought it would be wise to incorporate in it some of the wording that occurs in the civil and penal codes of our State, where it alludes to expert accountants, such persons being authorized to be employed by boards of supervisors, grand juries, and appointed by Superior Judges. When we drafted the act we said that any citizen, at the age of twenty-one years, of good moral character, etc., passing the required examination, could style himself as " Certified Public Accountant or Expert Accountant."

The political code of our State provides for the appointment of Bank Commissioners, of whom there are four, and two of them must be expert accountants; the Building and Loan Commission consists of two members; both must be expert accountants. So we took that wording as being a pretty good foundation to work upon. Soon after that act was passed I had the pleasure of being appointed by the Governor one of the members of the State Board of Accountants.

Then we asked the opinion of our Attorney-General, and he went further than even we expected—he told us that under the Act we could make any restriction that we saw fit, or make any complaint that we might have to make against a person calling himself an expert accountant or a public accountant—we cannot deny a man the privilege of calling himself an accountant or auditor, but when he adds anything to that by way of qualification of a higher degree of competency, we have him. That comes under the misdemeanor clause. Several of these Audit Companies have come into the State to do business. Whenever I heard of them as Secretary of that Board I notified them and they retired. (Laughter.)

I want to say further that I think we ought to make up our minds to reject the word " expert." You don't call a lawyer an " expert lawyer." (Applause.) Call yourself a Certified Public Accountant, or a Public Accountant; as to expertness your client can best judge.

Under the interpretation of our act as given us by our Attorney-General, we have complete control of the issuance of the certificates, and we don't issue a C. P. A. certificate until a man has been in practice, holding himself out as a public accountant, exclusively practicing on his own account, as principal, for three years; he has to pass a good examination, seventy per cent.; and then bring in indorsements from five clients for whom he has done business for the past three years. We did that to prevent a graduate from a high school or a university, without the practical knowledge, from securing the certificate.

CHAIRMAN.—We will now proceed to discuss the second division: " Audit Companies."

THE SECRETARY.—A representative—the Vice-President or Treasurer, I think, of the American Audit Company, of Cincinnati, is with us this morning. We have asked him at a moment's notice to reply to this part of the paper. We had arranged with Mr. Stockwell, of Philadelphia, who is a member of our organization, to come here. He is a capital speaker, and we regret very much to learn that his wife is very seriously ill, and so he was unable to come. We must say in regard to Mr. Miller that he has had no time at all to prepare for this discussion. We have asked him to come up here and take the other side of the question.

JAMES ALBERT MILLER, of Cincinnati.—Mr. Chairman and Gentlemen: I feel it quite an honor to stand here in the place of one so well known as Mr. Stockwell is, and hardly feel that even at my best I could do anything which would at all justify my presence here.

I observe from the tremendous applause given the former speakers, that I am in a hopeless minority —I won't say hopeless; I will say minority.

While I thoroughly believe in anything and everything that will lift accountancy to the very highest standard, it did seem to me that this particular part of the paper presented by our Secretary, than whom no man I hold more highly in esteem, appeared to be more in the nature of a personal attack. I believe we cannot say to our fellow accountant how he must practice. I believe that we should have regulation as to the degree of ability and as to the character, and those things, and my many friends in the Ohio Society will vouch for me, I think, in that respect, but I do most heartily take exception to the remarks which have been thrust at audit companies. I cannot see very much difference between a company, we will say called the American Audit Company, and a corporation called John Smith & Company. We have many corporations of accountants practicing. I don't know many of them, but I· know there are some. The principle which I think should apply should be the efficiency and the ability of the men comprising such companies. Now the argument has been advanced that bankers and other men of affairs—merchants and manufacturers—could organize a Company, engage a manager who might be a C. P. A., who would surround himself with a number of inferior people to practice and make reports and audits and all that sort of thing. So can a firm. I could tell you of firms of accountants and individual accountants who have surrounded themselves with fairly incompetent men, and as principal this man would be allowed to take precedence over an Audit Company which might be surrounded with capable men in every particular. If I am not mistaken, our worthy Secretary was at one time employed by a corporation. I am not sure but that corporation still exists. I know of firms where the names used in the title belonged to men who have long since passed to their reward, and which firms are now controlled by any old fellow and he may sign that name and use it in his practice. I believe we should have a law which would make companies liable; I believe we should have a law which would make individual practitioners liable. I thoroughly believe in that, and I would be one of the first to encourage such legislation.

Now our worthy Secretary has referred i·o the flattering profits that have been held out as a bait to bankers and manufacturers. I have not had any such experience. He may have had—that I do not know. I do know this: that there are some individual practitioners and some companies, like John Brown & Company, practicing under names which are really not their own individually because it is a corporation. I contend this: that it is not absolutely necessary for a director in a bank who may be a shoe manufacturer, to know all about running a bank. He may not know a thing about the various exchanges that pass through that bank, but I do contend that he may be a good director of that bank, because he is a good business man in general. And I contend that a man may be a director in an Audit Company, and may be able in a general way—in a broad sense, to direct its affairs very capably and very satisfactorily.

I think, gentlemen, that it would have only been fair to have allowed the representatives of the Audit Companies to know in advance about such a discussion. The Secretary has said that the Executive Committee approved, if I quote him correctly, the criticism of the Audit Companies here to-day. We have no representatives of Audit Companies here to-day. We have had no caucus, nor agreed upon any particular plan of answer to these charges. But I should be very glad if the Secretary of the Federation and the Executive Committee would at some time arrange a conference and in advance notify the members of the Audit Companies, so that a general discussion might be had upon their merits. (Applause.)

JOHN EVERETT (Chicago).—I am really quite a stranger in this meeting, but all the talk about Audit Companies seems to have cast a reflection on me. I was the original Audit Company man. I organized the first Audit Company. They have been in business quite a number of years and will be in business quite a number of years to come. Don't worry about the manner in which we conduct our business. Let us work at this C. P. A. legislation and get that going along. Whether you want to conduct a partnership or an audit company or to do business as an individual has nothing to do with the C. P. A. Let that alone.

CHAIRMAN.—If there is no further discussion of Audit Companies we will now take up the Third division of the subject: " National Organization."

ARTHUR LOWES DICKINSON, F.C.A., C.P.A. (New York City).—Mr. Chairman and Gentlemen: I would like to say a few words to you as to the present status of the negotiations between the Federation of Societies of Public Accountants, The American Association of Public Acountants and the New York State Society of Certified Public Accountants, to which Mr. Wilkinson has referred in his paper.

The American Association Mr. Wilkinson has already described to you, and you will see that it is in fact the oldest organization of accountants in this country. It has existed for many years, with a constitution and by-laws which were at the time they were drawn up no doubt the highest ideal that could be conceived. But the profession went ahead faster than the Association, and Accountants from all over the country, feeling the need of a different organization, came together two years ago and formed the Federation. In the Federation scheme I believe we have the highest ideal at the present time of what a National organization should be. Since its initiation there has been considerable discussion as to the possibility of the two National Societies coming together. The result is that at the present time the American Association is quite alive to the fact that its present form of Constitution and By-Laws is not altogether that best suited to the needs of the profession and within the last few days a Constitution and By-Laws have been drafted upon which the representatives of the American Association and the Federation, will, I believe, be able to come to an agreement satisfactory to everybody, provided that both bodies will make certain concessions, as I believe they are prepared to do.

The importance of such an agreement is very great, because although the Federation is strong in the States outside of New York, the American Association is perhaps equally strong in New York State, and it is obvious that if the accountancy profession is to be united all over the country, you cannot have the State of New York, which is the biggest State and has the largest number of accountants, standing outside of that movement.

I would like to tell you how the plan stands at the present time. It is proposed to leave unchanged the name of the American Association of Public Accountants, which is now known all over the country as that of the oldest Society; in the opinion of some it is a more satisfactory name than the longer one which the Federation was partly forced into by the fact that the American Association at that time would not join its organization. Subject to a few minor details I think I may say that in the proposed plan the Name, Charter and Seal of the American Association are all that are left; and it will adopt a new Constitution and new By-laws.

In the objects as stated in the proposed Constitution the two main principles which the Federation has always had in view are incorporated, namely, the bringing together of the different State Societies, and the promotion of C. P. A. legislation, and added to that, is the essential principle that the National organization must not interfere with the local interests of the different Societies. It can advise and suggest, but local matters must be looked after by the State Societies, leaving the National body to attend to National affairs.

As regards membership, the suggestion is that the Societies shall join the American Association as Societies. Their individual members will become enrolled as individual members of the Association, but their voting privileges are restricted and can only be exercised through delegates who are to be elected once a year. The individual members of these Societies can attend the meetings and take part in the discussions, but they are bound by the votes of the delegates whom they have elected to represent them.

The American Association at present has some members who are not members of any State Society, and for one reason or another are not eligible for membership. Not being eligible does not mean that they are not good accountants and entitled to practice, but either that they are practicing in States which have no Societies or that they are not Certified Public Accountants and cannot become such without an examination, which to a man of any age or standing is a serious obstacle. Such men are eligible for membership in the American Association subject to their possessing certain qualifications, and they *must* be provided for in a National organization. The suggestion made and insisted upon by the Federation members of the Committee is that these Members-at-large, as they are called, as distinct from Society Members, must also vote through delegates and not as individuals, and a method be provided by which they can elect such delegates each year.

Second in importance comes the election of the governing body of the Society. At the present time, and for many years past, the American Association has been trying to be a National Association and to do as good work in that line as its Constitution and By-Laws would permit. But it has been mostly a New York Society. The whole of its Board of Trustees are drawn from New York and New Jersey, and all meetings are held in New York. That is not the condition that ought to exist in a National Society, and the draft amendments therefore provide that the Board of Trustees shall consist of the Officers, the Presidents of the State Societies as Vice-Presidents and nine other members, and that no more than three of such members shall be selected from members of the same State Society or from the members at large.

Moreover, in order to insure that the Officers shall be of the same representative character, it is provided that no more than one Officer, exclusive of Vice-Presidents, shall be members of the same State Society or be selected from the members at large unless elected thereto by a two-thirds vote.

Another feature is that there shall be low subscriptions for society members, viz., half that paid by the members at large. It is further suggested that in future no individual members shall be admitted to the National Association except as members of a State Society unless ineligible for that State Society, and members who wish to come in under that rule will have to bring forward evidence satisfactory to the Board of Trustees that they are not so eligible to membership in the Society of their State or District.

The organization of a National body on these lines will be the greatest thing ever done for the profession in this country, and if accomplished the credit will largely belong to our friend Mr. Wilkinson. He has not always agreed on the details of the subject, but he has always fought strongly for the essential principles. If it had not been for his efforts in the formation and growth of the Federation we should never have been to-day as near as we are to the attainment of our object, viz., the organization of a National Society embracing all practicing public accountants in the country. With a National organization the prospects of Federal recognition, whether by Federal Charter or under a Federal Corporation Act, or under Acts regulating Interstate Commerce, are better than they have ever been and with the aid of such a body, representing all the Accountants in the United States of America, it cannot be many years before we receive in some form or other National recognition.

CHAIRMAN.—We have a few minutes for further remarks. Failing that, the Secretary will have the floor to reply to the remarks that have been made in the discussion upon his paper.

GEORGE WILKINSON.—The Secretary is very reluctant to extend the time devoted to the discussion of this subject and he will endeavor to be brief.

A great deal of the discussion has been very convincing and really does not call for any reply. But there are one or two points that I would like to reply to. One of them is in connection with what our friend, Mr. Martin, of London, told us. I fear that he does not quite appreciate the difference between the Transvaal or any of His Majesty's Colonies, and the United States of America. In the Transvaal there is one government, one parliament, they have one High Commissioner, and ultimately they have one Monarch to look to. We have forty-five States and ninety houses of law makers, and these ninety houses of law makers don't look at it in Mr. Martin's way. They tell us, as they told me in 1897 when I went to Springfield, Illinois, to try and get a C.P.A. bill passed, they will not give us what they regard as a monopoly of the profession of the Public Accountant. Some of you will understand the phraseology of the member of the House who told me he " would like to know what youse fellows want; if youse want a lead-pipe cinch I am agin you." There is just the complication. If they think we want to put a fence around the profession of the Public Accountant they are " agin " us. If they think we only want something fair, they will give it to us. 125 There are seven States that have given us C.P.A. laws and the other States will do so in time. As soon as we have legislation in a majority of States, we shall have a profession and shall have an established degree of C.P.A. We shall never be able, in the United States of America, to get them to make laws that the accounts of all companies *must* be audited by Certified Public Accountants *only*. We shall never be able to pass laws that will permit none but Certified Public Accountants to *practice accountancy*. I am against the view expressed by Mr. Goodloe for that very reason. That was the reason they lost their bill. (Calls of " No, sir; no, sir.") One of the reasons you lost that bill. ("No. sir; no, sir.")

It is after all a question of expediency. What is the *best* thing we can do. Now, the best thing we can do, Mr. Martin told us, is to secure a monopoly of the business; but we *cannot* do it. Now let us do what we *can* do, and that is to establish the degree of C.P.A. Then we shall have a *profession* and can go to the law makers, and point to this profession, and say, " There is a profession that ought to be recognized. You ought to make these large companies in which the public are interested have their balance sheets certified by a C.P.A. who has a recognized standing in the community; then the public who buy their bonds and their shares will know something about them." That will appeal to the hostile legislator, but if you go to him and ask for " a lead-pipe cinch," he will repeat " I am agin you."

One word in regard to what Mr. Magee said about the New Jersey law. I am glad he did not speak in a spirit of resentment about it. I want to tell you that the New Jersey law is very different from all others. It is a simple law creating the "State Board of Public Accountants," and it gives them almost unlimited power. They can collect what fees they like and make whatever rules they like. No such law was ever passed for public accountants before. It would be a bad law unless they had a good Board; but they *have* a good Board and in their hands it is a good law. They have established rules, and by the carrying out of these rules they are going to have a splendid order of things in the State of New Jersey.

In regard to what Mr. Miller said, I am much obliged to him, on behalf of the Congress, for having jumped into the breach and filled the place on such short notice, which would have fallen to Mr. Stockwell of Philadelphia. I told Mr. Stockwell that I should attack Audit Companies on general principles, and he said he "would go for me." But, unfortunately, he could not come, and I think our thanks are due to Mr. Miller for the splendid way in which he took up the question of Audit Companies. I do not desire to make any personal attack upon anybody, and least of all on Mr. Everett, of Chicago, who established the Everett Audit Company, but I *am* against those audit companies whose directors are *not* accountants. I have not a word to say against those audit companies whose directors and whose shareholders are public accountants making a living out of the practice of accountancy in connection with that corporation. In some particular companies that I have in mind the Directors are all Certified Public Accountants.

In regard to what Mr. Dickinson says, I sincerely hope we can come together with the American Association. What we want, gentlemen, for our profession is one National organization. (Applause.) We want an organization that everybody can work for; that Pennsylvania, Illinois, Maryland, New Jersey, Ohio, Michigan, Missouri, Minnesota, Massachusetts, California, Washington, Colorado and Louisiana and all the rest of the States can stand by, that they will have confidence in, and to whose Council they all can say, "Go ahead; we don't want you to submit all the details to us: go ahead, armed with all the force we can give you." That is what we tried to build up in the Federation. When the New York State Society withdrew we had, as it were, our right arm and our right leg, if you choose, cut off, but we were still alive: we had a trunk and a head and we could hobble along on crutches. If we can regain the whole of our body and stand right at the head and take an active part to secure Federal recognition, I say *by all means let us do it.* I don't propose any longer to be the one juryman who speaks about " the obstinate eleven."

CHAIRMAN.—The Congress now stands adjourned until 2.30 p. m.

_____

A hasty luncheon was taken at the "Administration Restaurant" near the Assembly Hall.

127

The Genesis of the C. P. A. Movement

By GEORGE WILKINSON, C. P. A.,
Philadelphia, Pa.

Paper read at Pittsburgh Convention,
1927.

THE good Chairman of your General Executive Committee invited me to prepare a paper to be called "The Genesis of the C. P. A. Movement."

If this invitation is to be adequately complied with, it means that we must start at the very beginning. Let us first look at the title—just what is meant by the C. P. A. MOVEMENT? The term seems to me to denote the organized effort by practicing accountants to bring about the legal recognition of our chosen calling in the United States of America and to secure for our use a suitable professional designation. You all know that the Federal Government of the United States specifically disavows the responsibility of regulating the many varied trades and professions by which its citizens are making their living. Under our Constitution this duty rests with the several sovereign states which make up the Union.

Probably all of you know that every state of the Union and Alaska, District of Columbia, Hawaii, Philippines and Porto Rico have secured the enactment of C. P. A. laws at the hands of their duly elected law makers. As a movement it is now complete. It is a wonderful accomplishment; one that we may justly be proud of. And especially may we felicitate this great organization, at whose Sixth Annual Convention we are here assembled—The American Society of Certified Public Accountants.

It is my appointed task to tell you how this thing got started, who started it, and upon what basis it has been built.

It is a matter of common knowledge that the first C. P. A. law was enacted in New York State in 1896. I doubt if many of you Certified Public Accountants of today know how this came about and what lead up to it. In order to get a good start I would ask your permission to go a bit further back than the first legislative enactment referred to (1896), so as to see the cause from which this movement sprang. We must also learn how it came about that we are burdened with such a clumsy title involving the use of three words—Certified Public Accountant.

In pursuance of this quest we must first look to see what the other English-speaking countries had accomplished for our profession, prior to the date when our own more recent history begins, and we must see what bearing this had upon our own action here in America. We must first go to Scotland, then to England and lastly to the Dominion of Canada. These countries, each in turn, had established our calling on a legal basis before we acted. Indeed I think it fair to say that we inherited the idea of organization from our British ancestors.

For most of the data herein set forth, relating to the Scottish Accountants and their doings, I am indebted to the wonderfully interesting history edited and partly written by Richard Brown, C. A. of Edinburgh—(published in Edinburgh in 1905.)

In Edinburgh

The first definite move towards the formation of a society of professional accountants in Great Britain was a letter dated 17th January, 1853, by Alexander Weir Robertson, written to a dozen or more professional accountants in Edinburgh, inviting them to gather at his chambers to consider a move for "uniting the professional accountants of Edinburgh." As a result of the movement thus started there was formed the—"Institute of Accountants in Edinburgh."

This Institute, like the many state associations and societies of accountants, later organized in this country, was a voluntary association of individuals—a professional guild—pledged to the interest of public accountants.

At the first annual meeting of said Institute it was decided to apply to the British Government for incorporation by Royal Charter. It is interesting to note the language in which the petition to Her Majesty's Government was worded—it began:

"That the profession of Accountants, to which the Petitioners belong, is of long standing and great respectability, and has of late years grown into very considerable importance * * *"

The Royal Warrant for the incorporation of the Institute under the name of "The Society of Accountants in Edinburgh" was "given by Her Majesty's Court at St. James the 23rd October, 1854." It was signed by Lord Palmerston at the command of Her Majesty Queen Victoria.

In Glasgow

It was in the autumn of the same year that the accountants practicing in the West of Scotland made a similar move. Twenty-seven accountants who had been practicing in Glasgow a dozen years or more addressed a most respectful petition to fifteen of the older accountants, who had been practicing prior to 1841, requesting their older and more experienced brothers to take the initiative in a get-together move.

On 3rd of October, 1853, these two groups met and appointed a committee to take the necessary steps. A month later (14th November, 1853), they founded "The Institute of Accountants in Glasgow."

The following midsummer (6th July, 1854), half a hundred accountants practicing in Glasgow petitioned Her Majesty's Government to grant them a Royal Charter. And their petition began by assuring the government:

"That the profession of an Accountant has long existed in Scotland as a distinct profession of great respectability * * *" and much more.

On the 15th March, 1855, a Royal Warrant was issued constituting a body politic and corporate by the name of "The Institute of Accountants and Actuaries in Glasgow."

In Aberdeen

A dozen years later—(in 1867)—the Accountants in Aberdeen formed a society of their own and followed the lead of their older brothers in Edinburgh and Glasgow by securing a similar Royal Charter from the British Government.

Acting under the rights secured by the Royal Charters mentioned, the three Scottish Societies were the first to establish the use of the term "Chartered Accountant" and nailed down for their own use the two initial letters C. A. As we shall shortly see, the English and Canadian Chartered Accountants, who came into the field later, have been obliged to use other designating initials than these. Wherever you see these two letters after the name of an Accountant from Great Britain, you know he's from North of the Tweed.

In 1892, the three Scottish Societies entered into a joint agreement under which their rules for admission to membership in their respective societies were standardized. At that time the three bodies established a General Examining Board, which conducts the qualifying examinations for all three

129

130

societies. Since then they have worked harmoniously together and have raised the standard of qualification until it is, I have good reason to assure you, the highest in the world.

Admission to membership to these Scottish Societies is only obtained after service under formal articles of apprenticeship for five years, in the office of a chartered accountant, after diligent study of law and accounting and the passing of no less than three written examinations—Preliminary, Intermediate and Final.

Since the successful establishment of the professional designation of Chartered Accountant with the designating letters C. A., in Scotland, there have been several unsuccessful attempts by other associations of accountants to obtain a right to use these terms.

In each case the three original Scottish Chartered Societies have successfully resisted such assumption.

Due to the conditions described, members of the Scottish Societies throughout the English-speaking world are justly proud of their sole right to the use of those two letters—C. A.

In England

Accountancy as a separate professional calling seems to have first appeared in England at the beginning of the nineteenth century. There was a scattering of "accomptants," as they were called in London and here and there in different cities throughout England and Wales, as early as 1800.

The "Incorporated Society of Liverpool Accountants" was formed on the 25th January, 1870, closely followed on November 29, 1870, by the "Institute of Accountants" in London and by the "Manchester Institute of Accountants" in February of the following year.

On May 11, 1880, Her Majesty Queen Victoria, having been respectfully petitioned so to do, granted a Royal Charter to the then existing societies to unite in one body, called "The Institute of Chartered Accountants in England and Wales." Admission to this Institute, as Fellow Members, was allowed without examination to those accountants who had been in practice as principals for five years prior to January 1, 1879, also, as Associate Members, to those who had been employed for five years as a public accountant's clerk.

Admission to membership in the English Institute is at the discretion of the Committee of the Council and is obtainable only after a candidate has (1) passed a preliminary educational examination, (2) served an apprenticeship for five years in the office of a Member of the Institute, (3) passed an intermediate examination in bookkeeping, auditing, etc., and (4) passed a final

qualifying examination—after the apprenticeship has been completed.

From these particulars it will be seen that the tests of fitness imposed by the English Institute are very exacting. And they have continued so for forty-seven years.

Membership in The Institute of Chartered Accountants in England and Wales entitles a man to style himself a "Chartered Accountant" (in two words) and to use three designation letters F. C. A. if a fellow, and A. C. A. if an Associate. It does not entitle a member to use the two-letter designation of C. A. which, as before explained, is reserved for the Scottish Accountants.

In Canada

Having seen Chartered Accountants well established and royally chartered in Great Britain, I will ask you to take a mental hop to the Dominion of Canada.

John Hyde, F. C. A., then President of The Dominion Association of Chartered Accountants, speaking at the Congress of Accountants at Saint Louis in 1904, told us:

"We can trace back firms in the cities of Montreal and Toronto who had their origin as far back as sixty years; so that we may say that public accounting started in Canada as a profession about sixty years ago."

That means eighty-three years ago, looking back from today.

The Dominion Association of Chartered Accountants was incorporated under an act of Parliament of the Dominion of Canada, assented to by King Edward VII, on May 15, 1902. This Association comprises the entire membership of eight separate Associations and Institutes of Chartered Accountants in the various Provinces of the Dominion of Canada. This national association does not itself hold any examinations nor issue any title for its members.

In Montreal

As far back as November, 1879—well, before we began to agitate the question of getting together here in America—several of the older practicing accountants in Montreal held conferences to discuss the question of forming an Association. The result of these conferences was the formation on December 5, 1879, of the Association of Accountants in Montreal. This Association petitioned the Legislature of the Province of Quebec for an Act of Incorporation, which was granted on July 24, 1880.

This provincial charter gives the members of the Montreal Association the exclusive right to style themselves "Chartered Accountants" within the Province of Quebec. For an abbreviation of their title they may use the two

letters C. A. The Montreal Accountants have built up a sound value for their title by confining their membership to those who pass a severe examination set by a Committee of the Council of the Association. Later (1901), the By-laws required candidates before admission to membership to pass three successive written examinations—Primary, Intermediate and Final.

In Ontario

In December, 1879, several accountants practicing in Toronto formed an association entitled The Institute of Accountants and Adjusters of Ontario. After a couple of years, when the membership had increased to a hundred and fifty, it was decided to incorporate. A special act of the Legislature of the Province of Ontario was granted on February 1, 1883, giving the Toronto brothers the name of "The Institute of Chartered Accountants of Ontario." The membership of this Institute is now restricted to those in public practice, but is now composed solely of accountants who have passed a sound qualifying examination.

Under the present By-laws of the Ontario Institute three successive written examinations must be passed: (1) Primary (Educational) (2) Intermediate (Technical ability) and (3) Final (Qualifying.) Before passing the so-called final examination, five years' actual practice in accountancy work is required. Members may use the full professional title of "Chartered Accountant" and may use the abbreviation F. C. A. (if he is a Fellow) or A. C. A. (if he is an Associate.)

So much then for the Canadian Societies which antedated the earliest of our own efforts and whose accomplishments had a bearing upon "The Genesis of the C. P. A. Movement."

Other Canadian Provinces

There are six more recent Institutes of Chartered Accountants in Canada, namely:

The Institute of Chartered Accountants of Nova Scotia, incorporated on March 30, 1900.

The Institute of Chartered Accountants of British Columbia, incorporated in 1904.

The Chartered Accountants' Association of Manitoba, secured a charter on May 15, 1902; later became The Institute.

The Institute of Chartered Accountants of Saskatchewan, incorporated in 1920.

The Institute of Chartered Accountants of Alberta, incorporated in 1910.

The Institute of Chartered Accountants of New Brunswick, incorporated in 1916.

Examinations and Apprenticeships

Before starting the story of how our C. P. A. Movement came to be inaugurated, I would like to impress upon you, with much earnestness, the history of the Scottish, English and Canadian Societies in relation to Education and Apprenticeships.

When the accountants in Great Britain secured Royal Charters for their respective societies they naturally felt that they had taken a long step in the direction of erecting their calling to the dignity of a learned profession. But what has counted for more in the advance we have witnessed during the last fifty years has been the study and training of the younger generation under carefully supervised apprenticeships. Those entering into the profession during this period have brought with them a better educational equipment than their forefathers.

The Institute of Accounts

We have seen that the earliest move to organize Accountancy into a profession in any English-speaking country was in Edinburgh, the capital of Scotland—a little later in Glasgow, the metropolis of Western Scotland. We have also seen that Chartered Accountants have established themselves under local charters in all the Provinces of Canada. We may now come home to our own country.

The earliest recorded effort to establish our profession in these United States was the formation of a society in New York City in May, 1882, called the "Institute of Accountants and Bookkeepers."

This was in no sense a professional guild. It was a voluntary association of individual accountants engaged in various walks of life, a minority of them being professional accountants, who grouped themselves in a body for mutual advantage, mainly in an educational direction.

After some years the name of this society was changed to "The Institute of Accounts" and it became more than it was before—a scientific body. Its meetings were held on the 15th of each month during the season and usually included a lecture on some accounting or financial subject followed by a discussion. Major Henry Harney of New York was the President and was the moving spirit of the Institute for many years. Care must be taken to differentiate between this early educational body and the professional guild of much later date (1916), called the "American Institute of Accountants."

The membership of the old Institute of Accounts was not confined to New Yorkers, a scattering of its members being found in the Western and Southern States. The membership was small, even

for those early days, due to the fact that the Institute was conducted on somewhat exclusive lines. All applicants for membership had to pass an entrance examination as to general fitness and technical qualifications, while the senior grade of membership known as "Fellows," was only granted to those who succeeded in passing a pretty stiff practical and technical examination.

It must be clearly borne in mind that this was well before the passage of the first C. P. A. law. These early conditions are dealt with in this article, somewhat in detail, for the reason that this really was the foundation. In those early days, before the enactment of State Legislation establishing the C. P. A. designation—The Institute of Accounts issued to its Fellow Members, upon their passing the technical examination previously referred to, nicely engraved certificates,

giving them the right to style themselves "Certified Accountants."

These certificates were in a sense, home-made and had not the authority that our C. P. A. certificates now have, for the reason they were not supported by a legislative enactment of the State. Nevertheless they were the forerunners and were issued more than a dozen years ahead of the first batch of C. P. A. certificates. The Institute of Accounts, in New York, served a useful purpose in its day and was of much advantage to its individual members. It doubtless added no little to the general uplift we have all felt and presently profited by.

Early Action in Philadelphia

The first effort to secure the organization of a professional guild, solely composed of public accountants in these

---

TENTATIVE PROGRAM
SEVENTH ANNUAL CONVENTION
AMERICAN SOCIETY OF CERTIFIED PUBLIC ACCOUNTANTS
HOTEL ROOSEVELT, NEW ORLEANS, LA.

Monday, October 8

Registration

Tuesday, October 9

9:00 A. M. Meeting of Present Board of Directors

10:00 A. M. Meeting of State Representatives (Retiring and Incoming, but open to others)

12:30 P. M. Luncheon Meeting for New Board of Directors

2:00 P. M. Harbor Boat Ride (Including Dancing)

8:00 P. M. Masked Ball (A la Mardi Gras)

Wednesday, October 10

10:00 A. M. First Regular Session Address of Welcome Officers' Reports

11:00 A. M. Two Formal Papers

12:30 P. M. Recess

1:30 P. M. Golf, Bridge, Sightseeing

8:00 P. M. Musical Program

Thursday, October 11

10:00 A. M. Second Regular Session Reports of Committees

10:30 A. M. Three Formal Papers

12:30 P. M. Recess

2:30 P. M. Third Regular Session Business. Action on Officers and Committee Reports

3:00 P. M. Three Formal Papers

5:00 P. M. Recess

7:00 P. M. Visit to French Market

8:30 P. M. Annual Meeting of "The Order of Twelve" Annual Meeting of "Secret Order of Thirteen"

Friday, October 12

10:00 A. M. Final Regular Session Question Box. (Questions having been presented at prior sessions)

12:00 Noon New Business

12:30 P. M. Adjournment

2:00 P. M. Sightseeing Tours, Visits to Industrial Plants

7:00 P. M. Convention Banquet Introduction of Newly Elected Officers

The headquarters for the Convention will be at the Roosevelt Hotel, on the mezzanine floor of which an unusually attractive Business Show will be arranged. The detailed program will appear in the October issue.

132

United States, was made in Philadelphia in 1886. At that time some half dozen men had established themselves as public accountants in the City of Brotherly Love—John W. Francis (1869); Charles Nixon Vollum (1875); John Heins (1877); Laurence E. Brown (1882); and Hyland B. Hayes (1885). All of them have passed on to their reward. The first four named held several conferences at the office of Mr. Francis and decided to petition the Government of the Commonwealth for a charter as an educational institution to be called "The Chartered Accountants' Institute."

It was not then proposed to hold examinations nor confer titles, but rather to join hands in an effort to educate the public to the advantage of employing "persons thoroughly skilled and experienced as Public Accountants."

It happened that Edwin Guthrie of Manchester, a Fellow Member of the Institute of Chartered Accountants in England and Wales, was visiting America at the time, and was invited by Mr. Heins to come on to Philadelphia in December, 1886, and confer with his associates regarding the proposed State Society in Pennsylvania.

Having in view the prior rights established by the Chartered Accountants in Great Britain and in Canada, and the increasing recognition the imported designation was then securing on this side of the Atlantic, it was thought inexpedient to use the same term in America. After further discussion the effort to organize a state society in Pennsylvania gave way in favor of what promised to be of more far reaching usefulness, namely a national association of accountants which, of course, could only be brought out in New York City.

The American Association

On December 23, 1886—forty years ago last Christmas—upon the invitation of James Thornley Anyon, of Barrow, Wade, Guthrie & Co., Chartered Accountants, a meeting of accountants was held in the office of that firm in the old Equitable Life Building, New York City. There was then organized a voluntary association of individual practitioners which, on the motion of Mr. Anyon, was named "The American Association of Public Accountants."

On August 20, 1887, just forty years ago last month, that first professional guild of accountants in America secured a charter from the State of New York. For many years it continued more in name than in reality a national association, domiciled in New York as its charter required and governed by New York Accountants.

The Genesis of the C. P. A. Movement

We have seen what our older brothers in Great Britain had accomplished, first in Edinburgh, Glasgow and Dundee and later throughout England and Wales. We have seen that the British had secured for their own use the designation of Chartered Accountant with the two letters C. A. definitely reserved for the Scotch. And we have noticed that the British had invaded America and imported their titles with them. This distinction obtains to-day. Although there is no law against it, so strongly have we always observed the rights of our brothers over seas and across the border, that little or no attempt has ever been made in this country to use the term Chartered Accountant by anyone not a member of one of the British or Canadian Societies. Here then, we have the background—the underlying conditions of forty years ago.

In the United States, as we have seen, we had the Institute of Accounts (1882), issuing certificates of its own making; and we had the American Association of Public Accountants (1887), a New York State Corporation. These two were the only organized groups existing at that time.

Conception of the C. P. A. Movement

To the late Major Harney of New York City, President of the old Institute of Accounts is probably due the credit for initiating the effort to secure legislative action establishing the professional designation we use today. We know that some years before any definite action was sought at Albany, Major Harney had committed his ideas to paper, in the privacy of his own study at home. In the winter of 1894-1895, Major Harney prepared a draft of a bill, to be presented to the State Legislature, providing for a professional examination and for securing a distinctive title.

Under the authority of the By-laws of the Institute of Accounts, President Harney appointed Colonel Charles E. Sprague, A. M., Ph. D., President of the Dime Savings Bank of New York City, also an accountant and actuary of great ability, a committee of one to convey the draft bill to Albany and see what might be done toward having it made law by the State Legislature.

The Situation at Albany

Colonel Sprague took the now-historic draft straight to his old friend Hon. Melvil Dewey, State Librarian at Albany, who he knew could help the proposal along more than any one man. Major Harney's original draft for a bill contemplated the appointment of a State Board of Examiners by the Governor. Mr. Dewey, who was also Secretary of the Regents of the University of New York and whose counsel had been sought because of his long experience in Albany

and his political affiliations, strongly urged that it was inadvisable to add another board to the Governor's patronage. He recommended that the law be redrawn so as to place control of the examinations with the Regents of the State University, which institution had the equipment for holding such qualifying examinations as were contemplated. Mr. Dewey also pointed out that this course would give the proposal something of an educational character. This advice was regarded as sound and was accepted.

The Title

The next question—what shall the proposed legal designation be? The terms "Chartered Accountant" and "Certified Accountant," with the abbreviation of C. A. were most favored. At this stage of the discussion it was pointed out that the use of the term "Chartered Accountant," C. A., would conflict with the rights established forty years before by the Scottish Societies (1854), under Royal Charters which, as I have stated, were cheerfully recognized on this side of the Atlantic.

At the same time it was pointed out that the use of the term "Certified Accountant" would be an infringement of the established right of the Institute of Accounts (1882), many of whose certificates were then hanging in the offices of New York accountants. Moreover, with pardonable pride, the pioneers did not want to be copiers; rather would they be originators.

To meet these conditions the word "Public" was interpolated and the term—"Certified Public Accountant" was determined upon, with the designating letters, C. P. A., of which title we have during the ensuing years grown so proud.

Inscribe These Three Names

I wish to emphasize that the program I have described and which, mind you, was later embodied into law, was initiated by three men whom we should revere—permit me to repeat their names: Major Henry Harney, President of the Institute of Accounts of New York; Colonel Charles E. Sprague, President of the Dime Savings Bank of New York; Honorable Melvil Dewey, State Librarian, and Secretary of the Regents of the University of New York at Albany.

There are many other survivors of those most strenuous days who can rightfully claim some share of the victory, but my subject here today is "The Genesis of the C. P. A. Movement," and I'm here to tell you that the three men named conceived the idea and gave it birth.

The Regulatory Feature

But there were other forces at work in 1894. Acting independently of the Institute of Accounts, at a meeting of the American Association on February 12,

1895, Francis Gottsberger, presented a draft of a bill he proposed to send to Albany. It was entitled:

"A bill to authorize the Regents of the University of the State of New York to license Public Accountants, to provide for the registration of such licenses and to prevent unlicensed persons from practicing as public accountants."

The bill provided:

"that no person shall practice as a public accountant after the passage of this act unless he be licensed by the Regents of the University of the State of New York."

At a later meeting (February 28, 1895), Mr. Gottsberger reported that his bill for licensing public accountants had been introduced in the State Legislature and was being cared for by Senator David Bradley. In this latter proposal by Francis Gottsberger we have the genesis of another movement which seems quite recently to have taken root in some states—Maryland as the leading example—the effort to regulate the practice of accountancy by requiring all practitioners to qualify under a specific state law. Bear with me while I emphasize the essential point of difference between the two rival proposals brought forward in 1895. Shall we use the terms—Educational vs. Regulatory? On the one hand—the plan to procure a degree from the State University, initiated by the Institute of Accounts. On the other hand—the plan to license public accountants, initiated by the American Association.

The bill proposed by the American Association imposed a fine of a hundred dollars on any person found guilty of practicing in New York State as a Public Accountant unless he had received a license from the State University and had registered his license with the Secretary of State at Albany. No distinctive title was asked for in the Association's bill.

Two C. P. A. Laws Introduced

The American Association's bill happened to be the first to come before the Legislature, being introduced in the Senate at Albany on February 20, 1895, by Senator Daniel Bradley of Kings County, to whom it had been sent a week before by the American Association's Legislative Committee consisting at that time of Francis Gottsberger, William Sanders Davies and Richard M. Chapman. This licensing bill was referred to the "Committee on Literature."

Early in the following month (March, 1895), the bill sponsored by the Institute of Accounts was introduced in the Assembly by the Honorable Howard Payson Wilds, representing one of the Manhattan Island districts and an old-time personal friend of Colonel Sprague. This Institute bill provided that the Regents of the State University should make rules for holding examinations for persons applying for C. P. A. certificates. It was indeed practically the same as the New York law finally enacted.

Restrictive Clause Introduced

In the meantime, however, one important addition had been made to Major Harney's original draft. Section 4 of the Institute's bill as introduced provided that after July 1, 1896, only Certified Public Accountants (of New York State) should

"be appointed or employed to act as examiners of accounts, expert accountants or paid auditors by courts, administrators, receivers, state, county or municipal officers."

This Institute bill was referred in the Assembly to the "Committee on General Laws," where it encountered considerable objection mainly against the restrictive provision above quoted.

Two Rival C. P. A. Efforts

So we find two separate efforts being made by rival organizations of professional accountants, differing little in objective. The American Association's bill for a license, before the "Committee on Literature" of the Senate; the Institute of Accounts' bill for a title and with limited restrictions before the "Committee on General Laws" of the Assembly.

Meeting of Accountants

This was the setting when, on March 11, 1895, Francis Gottsberger and William Sanders Davies, members of the American Association's Committee mailed a notice to all practicing Public Accountants whose names were found in the business directory of the City of New York. This notice informed them that a bill "* * * the object of which is to have Public Accountants recognized and registered by the Regents of the University of the State of New York," had been introduced in the State Senate. The letter invited them all to attend a meeting at No. 111 Broadway on the afternoon of March 13, 1895.

Some forty-five accountants responded to the invitation and crowded into the dingy quarters of the Real Estate Exchange in the basement of an old-fashioned brick building adjoining Trinity Church yard, close to the head of Wall Street. (No. 111 Broadway.)

A majority of those present were not members of either the American Association or the Institute of Accounts; still it was thought desirable that Richard F. Stevens of Newark, N. J., President of the American Association, should take the chair. The late Thomas Cullen Roberts, for many years Secretary of the American Association, acted as Secretary of the meeting.

Committee of Fourteen

Both the Association's bill in the Senate and the Institute's bill in the Assembly were read and explained. Considerable interest was shown and much discussion ensued. A Committee of fourteen well-known public accountants was appointed to carry out the objects explained at the meeting. Eight members of this Committee were chosen from the membership of the American Association, three from the Institute of Accounts, three from those not affiliated with either body, with Mr. Gottsberger as Chairman. Upon calling for subscriptions to defray the expenses of securing the passage of legislation, thirty-eight New York accountants responded with subscriptions of $10 each.

The Committee of fourteen lost little time in determining that the Association's bill proposing a license, should be dropped and the Institute's bill proposing a title should be pushed. The committee also determined that an attorney should be retained to watch the progress of the bill through the Legislature.

The representatives of the American Association were: James T. Anyon, Frank Broaker, Wm. Sanders Davies, Henry R. M. Cook, T. Cullen Roberts, Richard F. Stevens, James Yalden, Thomas E. Arnold.

Those representing the Institute of Accounts were: Henry Harney, Charles Dutton, Charles Both.

The representatives of the non-member group were: S. H. Jenkins, Silas S. Packard and John E. Hourigan.

Sub-Committee

A sub-committee of five members consisting of Messrs. Francis Gottsberger, James Yalden, Henry Harney, S. H. Jenkins and Silas S. Packard, visited Albany while the Legislature was in session, together with Melvil Dewey, Secretary of the Regents, John E. Hourigan, a public accountant practicing in Albany, and E. G. Whittaker, the attorney who had been retained by the committee. The sub-committee appeared before the Assembly's "Committee on General Laws" to advocate the passage of the Institute's bill.

Here is where the C. P. A. Movement received its first serious set-back. Assemblyman Wilds, who had introduced the bill and had it referred to committee, would do nothing. He could not be persuaded to have it reported favorably to the House. In the meantime the session was getting well along. After a lot of difficulty Senator Bradley got the Senate's Committee to substitute the Institute's bill for his and report it favorably to the Senate. However, when the substituted bill came up for passage it secured only ten votes while eleven votes were recorded

133

134

against the measure, which, of course, never reached the Assembly. It was ascertained that what had killed the bill in the Senate was the provision of Section No. 4, "restricting employment in certain kinds of accountancy work to Certified Public Accountants under the act." Thus ended the first effort to secure legislation in favor of our profession in America.

The First C. P. A. Law

At its regular monthly meeting on November 12, 1895, the American Association of Public Accountants determined to introduce the bill I have described as the Institute's bill as soon as the legislature was in session. At the next meeting of the Association, on November 27, 1895, a committee consisting of Frank Broaker, James Yalden, first president of the Association (1887), and William Sanders Davies, was appointed to select a member of the State Legislature to have charge of the Accountants' bill which was then entitled, "An act to Regulate the Profession of Public Accountant." Frank Broaker, who was made chairman of the sub-committee, turned the bill over to Senator Albert A. Wray, of Brooklyn, who introduced it in the Senate on January 13, 1896, and had it referred to the "Committee on Judiciary."

This accountants' bill, as it was then called, had the support not only of the American Association but of the Institute of Accounts and of a considerable number of professional accountants unaffiliated with either body. Concurrently on January 15, 1896, a bill under the same title was introduced in the House by Assemblyman Marshall and was similarly referred to the "Committee on Judiciary."

An amendment was made in the bill while on its passage, having for its purpose the admission of semi-naturalized Britishers and other foreigners. The words interpolated follow the opening clause thus:

Any citizen of the United States "or person who has duly declared his intention to become such citizen * * *"

The bill was well taken care of in its passage through the assembly by Mr. Marshall and was carefully watched and guarded by the indefatigable Chairman of the American Association's Committee, Frank Broaker, who devoted all his time and energy to pushing the measure through to its final passage.

The bill passed the Assembly on April 3rd by an almost unanimous vote (120 to 1) and passed the Senate on April 7th. It was approved by Governor Levi P. Morton on April 17, 1896. A week later the American Association of Public Accountants passed a vote of thanks to Frank Broaker for the splendid work

he had done in securing the passage of the law.

Its Administration

Under the provisions of this law (1896) the Regents of the University of the State of New York made rules for the examination of persons applying for certificates as Certified Public Accountants, and appointed three accountants as examiners. After the first year the Examiners had to be Certified Public Accountants.

The law prohibits persons who are not certified by the New York University from styling themselves or their firms as "Certified Public Accountants," and provides that any violation of that provision shall be a misdemeanor. The law passed did not restrict the practice of Public Accounting in any way. It merely reserved the title for those who met the requirements.

The New York Waiver Clause

As in other states, soon to follow, the first Board of Examiners had not only to prepare the formal examination questions and to rate the answers, but had to pass upon the hundreds of applications for certificates under the waiver clause. Section 3 of the law as enacted provided definitely enough that—

"The Regents may, in their discretion, waive the examination of any accountant who shall have been practicing in the state on his own account for more than one year before the passage of this act."

In the face of this provision of the law, and probably in the exercise of their discretion, the Regents published a rule providing that exemption from examination should be granted only to candidates who could prove that they had "been in reputable practice as Public Accountants since January 1st, 1890." This rule set the preliminary standard of admission, up to a basis of six years' prior experience. The enforcement of the rule gave great dissatisfaction and caused much difficulty. Nevertheless this restriction was held to.

First Board of C. P. A. Examiners

The first board of examiners appointed by the Regents of the University was composed of Colonel Charles E. Sprague, whose early activities in framing the first C. P. A. bill have been related; Frank Broaker, who was elected Secretary of the board, and the late Charles Waldo Haskins, who was elected President. Upon these three men fell the unusually heavy duty of organizing the work of the examinations and at the same time of dealing with a great crowd of applicants.

There was of course a great rush of public accountants who had been genuinely practicing in New York City, and too, by a goodly number of outsiders

who strove in many artful ways to persuade the examiners that they really had the statutory requirements.

The first examination held under the law was conducted in New York City, on December 15th and 16th, 1896, and the first certificates to be issued to successful candidates at the written examination were granted to Edward C. Charles, Joseph Hardcastle, and William H. Jasper.

Within the first five years after the passage of the law, 169 certificates had been issued under the waiver clause; 93 certificates had been issued to those who had sat for the examination, while 115 candidates who sat for the examination failed to pass.

Some Accountants Were Sceptical

But it must not be supposed that all the public accountants who were genuinely eligible for the New York certificate availed themselves of the privilege of applying for same within the one year period prescribed by the law of 1896. Several New Yorkers, among them some of those in highest renown, did not take the movement seriously at the outset. I remember one of the leading professional accountants, still a prominent practitioner, saying to me:

"That C. P. A. business is nonsense, Wilkinson. All the penny accountants on the side streets will be applying for certificates under that absurd waiver clause."

And so they neglected their opportunity and later, when Frank Broaker, Secretary of the Board, pointed out to them that they were too late in filing their applications, they were wroth. Moreover, some of the British invaders had not at that time denoted their intention of becoming citizens of the United States.

Late Comers Shut Out

And so it came about that many good men and true, possessing all the qualifications required by law, found themselves without and looking for some way to get in. If some method could only be found to pry that big front door open again! But Haskins was obdurate and Broaker was obstinate (so they said) and there was "nothing doing." By this time the tide of C. P. A. legislation had set in from both coasts—Pennsylvania and Maryland and far off California had secured their C. P. A. laws—while New Jersey, Illinois, and Minnesota had made their initial but unsuccessful effort.

Waiver Door Reopened

And so we find on March 4, 1901, five years after the law had been passed, a bill was introduced in the House by Assemblyman Bennett, authorizing the Regents of the University to extend un-

(Continued on page 279.)

135

THE GENESIS OF THE C. P. A. MOVEMENT

(Continued from page 266.)

til 1st of September, 1901, the limit of time in which accountants, who possessed all the qualifications mentioned in the act, could file their applications for certificates under the terms of the original waiver clause. Many certificates were issued under this provision which was made law in April, 1901.

New York State Society

Almost immediately after the issuance of the earliest C. P. A. certificates, the New York accountants got together and organized a state association. On March 30, 1897, was organized the New York State Society of Certified Public

Accountants, which has grown to great proportions in membership and influence in the Empire State.

This addition made no less than three associations of professional accountants domiciled in New York City—The American Association, the Institute of Accounts, both claiming to be National in their scope, and the State Society just named.

Further Legislation Asked For

These three societies united in seeking further state legislation proposed to give them the right to select the members of the examining board, also to compel the Regents of the University to waive the examination of any applicant who had been in practice in New York State for one year or more prior to April 17, 1896. The latter point you will remember was a provision of the original law, but had been set aside by the Regents of the University. This bill was introduced in the House by Assemblyman Marshall on February 11, 1898, and was strongly backed in the Senate by Honorable T. G. Koehler, C. P. A. The bill passed the Senate by a vote of 30 to 7, but subsequently failed to pass in the Assembly.

The C. P. A. Movement in Pennsylvania

Within a month after the New York C. P. A. law was passed, namely, in May, 1896, Joseph E. Sterrett, of the firm of Francis and Sterrett, wrote to certain of the older accountants then practicing in Philadelphia, sending them a copy of the New York law and suggesting that the Commonwealth of Pennsylvania should make a move in the same direction. Among those to whom Mr. Sterrett wrote were the late Charles Nixon Vollum, John Heins, and Lawrence E. Brown. These three pioneers had established themselves as Public Accountants in Philadelphia in 1875, 1877, and 1882, respectively, and together with John W. Francis were substantially the recognized public accountants of that day in Philadelphia.

As Mr. Heins, who had the most extensive practice of those early years and the largest staff of assistants, was not in favor of taking any action along the line suggested, Mr. Sterrett's proposal came to naught for the time being. Not for long, however, did the movement falter.

The coming winter saw the earliest batch of C. P. A. Certificates gracing the walls of accountants' offices in Manhattan. The Philadelphians felt that they were being discriminated against because they had no handle to their names. Under date March 16, 1897, which you will pardon me for pointing out, was a week after the accountants in Chicago had feasted at the Wellington Hotel and started the ball rolling

in Illinois, John W. Francis and J. E. Sterrett acting jointly, addressed a second invitation to the pioneer accountants previously named and a few others, reading:

"Inasmuch as successful efforts are being made in several other states to secure, by legislative enactment, a wider range and scope for accountants, and also to provide a standard of qualification for persons entering the profession, we think it wise at this time to ask a few of the leading accountants of this city to discuss the subject and consider the advisability of taking some action along similar lines in our own state.

"We therefore cordially invite you to an informal meeting to be held at this office, on Tuesday evening, March 23, 1897, at 8 o'clock."

Mr. Sterrett was not taking any chance in having his second invitation turned down by Mr. Heins and so he got a young gentleman who was in close daily contact with that great man, to personally present his letter of invitation to Mr. Heins. As far as the record shows this little act of helpfulness was the first of many acts of unselfish devotion to the profession by one of our brother members in The American Society, Colonel Robert H. Montgomery.

Had John Heins persisted in his opposition to the C. P. A. movement in Pennsylvania it would likely have been quite a serious set-back. As it was he accepted the invitation. The meeting of accountants was held in the offices of Francis and Sterrett, Room 410 Penn Mutual Building, Philadelphia, the following week, but the minutes of the meeting do not record John Heins as being present. At this first meeting favorable consideration was given to the proposal to introduce a C. P. A. bill in the State Legislature, which was then in session, but no definite action was taken at that time.

A week later, on March 30, 1897, an adjourned meeting was held at the same place, when the same group of men organized the Pennsylvania Association of Public Accountants, and proceeded at once to elect John Heins, President, and J. E. Sterrett, Secretary.

At this inauguration meeting there were nine accountants present. A majority of them have passed on—Messrs. John W. Francis, John Heins, Charles N. Vollum, Hyland B. Hayes, and James W. Fernley. A minority are still living—Messrs. J. E. Sterrett, William M. Lybrand, Robert H. Montgomery have all migrated to Manhattan. Only J. D. Stinger remains in Pennsylvania.

After electing the officers just named the meeting proceeded to appoint an Executive Committee with instructions to make ready a draft of a C. P. A. bill. Said committee sought advice from ex-

Judge F. Carroll Brewster, learned in the ways of the Legislature.

The bill first proposed by the Pennsylvania Association authorized the Supreme Court of this Commonwealth to issue C. P. A. certificates and to appoint a board of three examiners. A committee consisting of Charles N. Vollum and John Heins was authorized to take the bill to Harrisburg and have it introduced as early as possible. It became Senate Bill No. 316 and was introduced on April 8, 1897, by Senator Brown. It turned out that the proposal to give the appointment of a State Board into the hands of the State Supreme Court was objectionable. The bill did not even pass the Senate. It was then too late to do anything in the House at that session.

November 30, 1898, found the Pennsylvania Association busy preparing for a second effort to secure their C. P. A. law. The revised bill provided for the appointment of a board of examiners by the Governor of the State. Considerable publicity was given to the matter of procuring a law and letters of endorsement were secured from many business and financial firms.

So great was the impetus given to the movement by Mr. Vollum, Chairman of the Executive Committee, that the Accountants' bill was the first to be introduced in the House of Representatives by the Honorable David L. B. Chew. It was referred to the Committee on "Judiciary General" and in a week's time was favorably reported to the House. The bill passed the House of Representatives on March 14th and the Senate on March 21st. It was signed by Governor William A. Stone on March 28, 1899. All this can be quickly related now, but it took an immense amount of work at the time. All this was cheerfully supplied by the late Charles Nixon Vollum.

The law provided for the appointment of a board of five examiners, of whom three must be Certified Public Accountants and two attorneys practicing in the State Courts. The subjects for the written qualifying examinations are Commercial Law and General Accounting. The examinations are held simultaneously in Philadelphia and Pittsburgh in November each year. The Governor of the Commonwealth signs the certificates.

The original waiver clause read in favor of accountants who had been practicing for three years prior to the act and who applied in writing within the first year. Under an amendment of the law approved June 4, 1915, a way was opened to bring under the jurisdiction of the law C. P. A's of other states practicing in Pennsylvania. The wording runs:

"* * * but certified public accountants of other states of the United States who have practised for five years prior to living in Pennsylvania may be certified at the discretion of the said board for certificates without any examination."

This is not a reciprocal feature. The full requirements of the Board of Examiners as to education and general fitness are insisted upon in respect of Certified Public Accountants from other states.

The C. P. A. Movement in Illinois

It is interesting to note how early the seed of organization began to take root in other states, after New York had blazed the way by securing the first law establishing the C. P. A. designation.

Acting under the urge to secure for themselves and brethren like recognition, the accountants in Illinois began their activities as early as February, 1897. One of the Chicago accountants had visited the office of Frank Broaker, Secretary of the newly-formed Board of Examiners, and had asked him for a form on which he might apply to the New York State University for a C. P. A. certificate. The candidate assured the Secretary of the Board that he had the practice requirements specified in the statute. He cited seven years' service, as Branch Manager, for no less than Barrow, Wade, Guthrie & Co., Chartered Accountants of New York. He grew profuse in his entreaties and arguments. Spoke Frank Broaker, C. P. A. No. 1:

"It's not for you, Wilkinson! If you fellows in Chicago want to become Certified Public Accountants, you had better get busy and have a law passed in your own state."

Forceful words! Prophetic words! Had the speaker the vision to see a long line of four dozen states each establishing the same designation of C. P. A.? As Frank Broaker had labored untiringly for many months to secure the passage of the first C. P. A. law it will be only fair at this late day to give him credit for his foresight, when he told the accountants of other states to get busy on their own. And that is just what happened.

Immediately upon my return to Chicago I went to see my friend and neighbor, Ernest Reckitt, and we together called upon R. S. Buchanan, one of the earliest accountants to establish an office in Chicago. We three sent out a joint invitation to all the public accountants, practicing in Chicago for five years or longer, to dine at the old Wellington Hotel on the evening of March 10, 1897. The only guide we had to determine who had the five-year qualification was the City Directory of 1892, plus our personal acquaintance which was very limited at that time.

Those who attended the dinner and became charter members of the Illinois Association of Public Accountants, were Lewis D. Jones, of the firm of Jones, Caesar & Co., George Shaw and R. S. Buchanan of the firm of Kitson, Buchanan & Co., Charles W. Hawley and Lawrence A. Jones of the firm of Hawley, Jones & Co., and Ernest Reckitt and George Wilkinson, later in partnership as Wilkinson, Reckitt, Williams & Co. Seven in all.

The first officers elected were Lewis D. Jones, A. C. A., President, and George Wilkinson, Secretary. The last named related his recent experience with the Secretary of the New York C. P. A. Board. Realizing the truth of Frank Broaker's pronouncement, the newly-formed association lost no time in appointing a committee to introduce and seek the passage of a C. P. A. bill at Springfield.

The bill provided that the Trustees of the University of Illinois should grant certificates to those who should pass the qualifying examinations. The waiver clause was to admit, without written examination, accountants who had five years' actual experience, of which at least two years must have been on their own account. The examining board, which was to function as a Committee of the University, was to report annually the receipts and disbursements under the act, and was to pay the excess of receipts to the State Treasurer. The bill was introduced into the Senate before the end of March, 1897, by Senator Dan Campbell, of Cook County, who secured its passage in that body. The Secretary of the Association, who had been constantly in attendance at the State Capitol, lost no time in rushing the Senate bill over to the House of Representatives, and there substituting it for the House bill, which he had previously gotten through committee.

A large number of favorable opinions had been secured from bankers, lawyers, manufacturers and business men generally, in Chicago, and other parts of the State. These letters were used as far as the limited time available would permit. It was confidently expected that Illinois was going to be the second state in the Union to enact a C. P. A. law. The biennial session of the State Legislature was by that time well along. In spite of every effort and much amateur lobbying, the bill could not be brought up, to be voted upon by the House, until the closing night of the session, when it was swamped in the final stampede. It was afterwards learned that the University authorities, at Urbana, had not favored the passage of the law, as they were unprepared, at that time, to handle what they deemed to be their share of the work.

In 1899 a very similar bill—still of the University type—was introduced in the Senate, where it was defeated early in the session. This second attempt was not vigorously supported by the Illinois Association. The bill could not be advanced to the House of Representatives and died through lack of interest.

Upon the assembling of the State Legislature in 1901 the Illinois Association held a meeting to discuss the advisability of again seeking C. P. A. legislation. About as much argument was advanced against taking any such action as in favor of so doing. It was reported that Pennsylvania and Maryland had secured their C. P. A. laws; that California was in the throes; that Minnesota, Wisconsin, Kansas and New Jersey had failed in their initial efforts and, more discouraging than any other news, Massachusetts had erected its own standard. Instead of following the lead of New York, Pennsylvania and Maryland, where C. P. A. laws had been enacted and were then in force, it was related that our brethren in Boston had decided, on February 14, 1901, to incorporate under the State laws as the "Incorporated Public Accountants of Massachusetts" and to build up a local reputation for the abbreviation — "I. P. A."

Such disturbing news, coming "from the effete East," swung the decision of the Illinois Association against renewing their twice-defeated efforts to secure legislation at Springfield. It was decided to let the session of 1901 go by without making any effort.

At the annual meeting of the Illinois Association of Public Accountants, held in Chicago in April, 1902, the following officers were unanimously elected: George Wilkinson, President; Ernest Reckitt, Vice President, and J. Porter Joplin, Secretary and Treasurer.

The new administration at once addressed itself to securing a C. P. A. law. The biennial session of the State Legislature was to assemble at Springfield in January, 1903, but the Directors of the Illinois Association were going to be in the field early this time. They were.

On July 8th, 1902, the president appointed a compact committee of three members, the late Henry J. D. Wodrich, of Chicago, being named as chairman. Mr. Wodrich's extensive personal acquaintance in both Houses of the Legislature made him an ideal chairman of the new committee. Unfortunately, before the beginning of the session, Mr. Wodrich was taken seriously ill and died in a few days. His death gave the Illinois Accountants a serious setback. The line of campaign had to be entirely changed. The committee was then enlarged and strengthened, until it was

(Continued on page 284)

138

bill creating a State Board of Public Accountants.

As soon as the General Assembly was in session at Springfield, a bill was introduced in both houses of the legislature providing that C. P. A. certificates should be issued by the Secretary of State, while the Governor should appoint the examining board. In the main the proposed bill was drawn on the lines of the Pennsylvania law, with two added provisions—(1st) The Secretary of State should maintain a register and charge a fee of $1 for each entry; (2nd) An annual renewal fee of $10 was to be paid by each C. P. A. without which his certificate would lapse.

Upon the executive officers of the association visiting Springfield, while this bill was in committee, it was found that a bill providing any additional patronage for Governor Yates, could not be passed, as he was "at outs" with the Assembly. By this time the session—very brief at the best—was well advanced. It was felt that energetic measures must be resorted to if the third attempt of the Illinois Association was to meet with success. Accordingly the membership of the Association, augmented by the addition of several new members, was pressed into service, while the executive officers of the association—especially J. Porter Joplin, the secretary, were constantly on the watch.

In view of the obstacle caused by Governor Yates' unpopularity with the Legislature, the Association's Committee deemed it best to swing back to the University form of C. P. A. bill.

A special sub-committee, consisting of J. Porter Joplin, Edward E. Gore, and George Wilkinson paid a hurried visit to Doctor A. S. Draper, President of the University of Illinois, at Urbana, to ask his approval of the proposed bill. To our relief we found that Dr. Draper had changed his view in regard to C. P. A. Legislation, moreover, that he was willing the State University authorities should assume the duties proposed for them.

And so it came that the Hon. James H. Wilkinson, an attorney-at-law in Chicago, and a member for Cook County of the Illinois General Assembly, introduced the bill in the House of Representatives, where it was soon passed by a large majority. It was at once confirmed by the State Senate and approved by Governor Yates.

The leading features of the law as enacted were: (1st) The University of the State of Illinois, situated at Urbana, undertakes to hold examinations and to issue certificates; (2nd) the President of the University shall appoint three examiners to serve one, two and three years, respectively, two of whom shall be Certified Public Account-

THE GENESIS OF THE C. P. A. MOVEMENT

(Continued from page 281)

fully representative of all the professional accountants who could be found in the State of Illinois.

After much earnest discussion, the enlarged committee decided to follow the lead of Pennsylvania and try for a

ants, and the third may be a Certified Public Accountant or an attorney at law; (3rd) the examination may be waived in favor of any Public Accountant who has had five years' experience, one of which shall have been on his own account in the State of Illinois, also in favor of any accountant who has had five years' experience, and who has passed an examination outside of the State of Illinois equivalent, in the opinion of the University, to the examinations to be held under the law; (4th) a fee of $25 is charged for the examination and certificate, and a remuneration of $10 a day allowed to each of the examiners in addition to his expenses. A further clause, not found in any other C. P. A. law, specifically provides that it shall be lawful for Certified Public Accountants of other states to practice as such and use their C. P. A. degree in the State of Illinois. The early work of carrying out the purpose of the C. P. A. law, prior to the organization of the board, was conducted, on behalf of the University of Illinois, by Dr. David Kinley, Dean of the College of Literature and Arts, who had been helpful to the Association's Committee in securing Dr. Draper's endorsement of the bill.

The law went into effect on July 1, 1903. The first examiners, appointed by Dr. A. S. Draper, President of the University of Illinois, were Ernest Reckitt, A. W. Dunning, and C. W. Knisely, all Fellows of the Illinois Association of Public Accountants. The first certificates were issued on October 5, 1903, to those who had qualified under the waiver clause, in respect of their previous experience of five years.

(To be continued)

139

The Genesis of the C. P. A. Movement

The C. P. A. Movement in Other States

It will not be possible, in the short time allotted to this paper to cover the whole situation and to relate to you the trials and tribulations of our professional brothers in securing the passage of C. P. A. laws in all the other states.

But I would like to ask you to bear with me as to a few of the earliest efforts, which, with your indulgence, may be brought within the scope of "The Genesis of the C. P. A. Movement."

Maryland

Our brothers in Maryland secured the enactment of their C. P. A. law on their first attempt. In this regard they are worthy of particular mention, as they stood alone for some years. By the time Maryland took hold of the matter, a great many accountants in Manhattan and one in Albany had their C. P. A. Certificates, while a couple of dozen had been issued to Philadelphians. On the other hand word had reached Baltimore that the accountants in Illinois, California, and New Jersey had failed in their efforts to secure a law.

The credit for initiating the C. P. A. movement in Maryland and of carrying it through belongs to the late Max Teichmann, who on June 1, 1899, wrote to all the public accountants practicing in Baltimore, inviting them to attend a meeting in his office for the purpose of forming a state organization with the object of securing the passage of a C. P. A. law. The Maryland Association started off at once with seven members, but recruited half a dozen more at the second meeting a month later.

Max Teichmann explained to the meeting what had been done in New York and Pennsylvania and asked the Association to back him up with their moral support in making a similar effort on their behalf. Mr. Teichmann had quite a wide and favorable acquaintance with members of the State Legislature and promised to secure the passage of a C. P. A. law single-handed and at once, if the Association would stand back of him. Friend Teichmann made good his promise, but he had a rough voyage in doing so.

The measure was introduced in the House by Representative Charles E. Siegmund, of Baltimore, in January, 1900. It was reported favorably by the Judiciary Committee, but was, at one time, actually defeated on the floor of

By GEORGE WILKINSON, C. P. A.,
Philadelphia, Pa.

Paper read at Pittsburgh Convention, 1927.

Continued from the September issue.

———————————————

the House. Representative Siegmund, a personal friend of Mr. Teichmann, was able to resuscitate the bill on some technical point and made it a special order of business for the following morning. As a result of some very special pleading and lobbying by the resourceful Max, the bill passed the House by a safe majority.

The House bill was then introduced in the Senate by Hon. John Hubner, the president of that body. The bill was mysteriously lost on two separate occasions, while on its passage through the Senate. Ultimately it emerged safely on the very last day of the session and was passed. The bill was approved by the Governor on April 10, 1900.

This original law provided for a Board of Examiners consisting of two public accountants to be appointed by the Governor from a list furnished by the Maryland Association of Public Accountants and of two practicing attorneys at law.

With the subsequent development of the C. P. A. movement in the State of Maryland time will not permit this little history to concern itself although it is of much importance to the profession. Suffice it to say that the original law was strengthened and re-enacted on April 11, 1916, still upholding the same title of Certified Public Accountants.

California

The accountants in California made a first effort to secure a C. P. A. law very soon after the enactment in New York State, but they met with no success at first. It was not until their third attempt that they succeeded. Right after Pennsylvania and Maryland had secured their laws, two old-timers in San Francisco, Alfred G. Platt and J. L. Fields drew up a bill for a State Board of Accountancy. It was first introduced in the Senate by Senator R. P. Ashe on February 15, 1901. It passed the Senate by a unanimous vote and was rushed over to the Assembly just in time to be made law before the end of the session. Governor Gage affixed his signature to the bill and made it law on March 23, 1901.

The bill as originally framed provided that the Governor should appoint five com-

petent and skilled accountants, who shall have been practicing in the state for five years prior to the passage of the act. This was amended by the Judiciary Committee of the Senate making three accountants on the Board.

The waiver clause provided for the issuance of certificates, without written examination, to accountants who had been practicing in California for three years prior to enactment. The 1901 law stood unchanged until 1913, when it was amended to include a new section establishing reciprocity with other states or foreign countries—

"provided, however, that such other state, territory or nation, extends similar privileges to certified public accountants of the State of California."

This reciprocity clause (adopted by California in 1913,) seems to be an elaboration of the idea embodied in the New Jersey law enacted in 1904.

Washington

The accountants practicing in Seattle and Tacoma joined in organizing on December 18, 1902, the Washington Association of Public Accountants. At the session of their State Legislature, immediately following, they were early on hand with their bill for a C. P. A. law. This bill was introduced by Representative Jones and was passed by the House on February 24, 1903. It was confirmed by the State Senate on March 5th, and was approved by the Governor a week later.

In this early success the Washington Association shares with the Maryland Association the honor and satisfaction of securing the passage of their law at the first attempt. This success was largely due to the diligence of George Shedden, E. G. Shorrock and C. M. Williams of Seattle, and L. G. Jackson, of Tacoma.

Under the very first provision of the law the Governor had to choose a Board of Accountancy from a list of fifteen accountants supplied to him by the Washington Association. The Washington law went into effect on June 11, 1903, and the first examination of candidates was held on September 14, 1903. The subjects set for the written qualifying examination were the same standard subjects set by other State Boards. The waiver clause read in favor of any citizen who had been a resident of the State for a year prior to the law, without requiring any previous accounting experience. This was regarded at the time as an undesirable feature, but the effect of it has long since passed off.

140

Minnesota

Another state to make an early though unsuccessful effort to secure a C. P. A. law was Minnesota. Late in the session of the State Legislature in 1899, a bill, copied from the New York C. P. A. law, was introduced in the Senate. It was too late to secure recognition.

In February, 1903, Herbert M. Temple of Saint Paul, prepared a second bill on the lines of the New York law except that five years prior experience were required under the waiver clause. This bill was introduced in the House on March 6, 1903, by Representative L. C. Simons. It was first referred to the "Committee on Public Accounts" by mistake. They wouldn't look at it. Later it was referred to the "Committee on Education," which indorsed the bill for passage. When it came up to be voted on, the bill failed to secure a quorum of votes and so was lost. On April 22, 1909, (ten years after their first attempt) the Governor of Minnesota approved an Act creating "The Minnesota State Board of Accountancy" containing the standard provisions of other C. P. A. laws of that period.

New Jersey

Possibly the accountants of New Jersey afford the most striking example of perseverance in keeping after the quest. Of the three unsuccessful efforts which preceeded the passage of the law little need be said. They had a state organization under the presidency of the late Richard F. Stevens of Newark, who in the early days had been president of the American Association. It was named the "Society of Public Accountants of the State of New Jersey." The three successive failures appear to have been due to lack of the requisite force behind the effort.

It was not until 1904, that the New Jersey accountants, at the hands of a legislative committee consisting of the late Frank G. Du Bois, William Sanders Davies and George Wilkinson, all three residing in New Jersey at that time, secured the passage of a law establishing the New Jersey State Board of Public Accountants which law was approved by Governor Franklin Murphy on April 5, 1904. Under this enactment the Governor appointed three New Jersey Certified Public Accountants to serve on the Board which makes its own rules both for the conduct of its routine business and for the holding of the examinations. The usual four subjects form the basis of the written examinations.

Massachusetts

Our professional brethren in Boston enjoyed a distinction all their own—that of holding back from the C. P. A. movement.

On February 14, 1901, the members of the "Massachusetts Society of Public Accountants" determined to incorporate under a State Charter as the "Incorporated Public Accountants of Massachusetts." They then took unto themselves the initials "I. P. A." They erected their own standard of qualification, requiring five years practical experience before admission to their society. In that and other ways they sought diligently to create a local reputation for those letters I. P. A.—while the rest of us were striving hard to build up C. P. A.

The first step taken by the Massachusetts brothers to get into line with the rest of the states was in 1909, when they secured what was called "the Massachusetts Registration Act." By that time no less than eighteen sovereign states throughout the Union had enacted laws definitely establishing the C. P. A. designation.

The Registration Act referred to provided that the Bank Commissioner should keep a register and should at his discretion admit to registry public accountants found by him to be fit, and should for a fee of $25, issue them a certificate stating that they were public accountants. The certificate was good for one year, and was renewable from year to year upon the annual payment of $5. This little act of five short sections was approved May 17, 1909. Still were the Bostonians outside of "The C. P. A. Movement."

At the next following session of the Legislature the Massachusetts Accountants secured the passage of "An Act Relative to Public Accountants," which provided, in nine lines, that public accountants, who had registered under the act of 1909, "shall be entitled to style themselves "Certified Public Accountants." This final act was approved by the Governor of the State on March 22, 1910.

Types of Laws in Force

There are now in force laws in every State of the Union also in the District of Columbia, Alaska, Hawaii, Philippine Islands and Porto Rico.

In every instance the title—call it "degree" if you will—is the same—CERTIFIED PUBLIC ACCOUNTANT—and everywhere throughout the United States and its dependencies, the designation C. P. A. means the same thing—namely a Professional Accountant who has met the legalized provisions of the state where he is conducting business and who has received, from the properly constituted authority, a certificate denoting that fact.

How are the states divided, as to the legalized authority to conduct the examinations?

Four laws are of the University Type: New York, Illinois, Montana, Kansas. In these four cases the State Universities appoint the examiners, chosen from the Certified Public Accountants under the law, who conduct the examinations and issue the certificates to those fully qualified.

In most cases the governors appoint the State Boards of Accountancy. Sometimes the certificates are granted by the governor and sometimes the certificates are issued by the boards thus appointed. Most boards consist of three members. Tennessee has seven, Pennsylvania six, California, Florida, Louisiana, Maryland, Michigan, Missouri, Oregon, Texas and Virginia have five each. North Carolina and Utah have four each. In most cases the boards are composed exclusively of certified public accountants, but the boards of Georgia, Illinois, Maine, Maryland, Michigan, Mississippi, Tennessee, Texas, Virginia and West Virginia each have one attorney member and Pennsylvania has two. Four boards have provisions for a special member: Maryland has an economist as one of its five members, Michigan has the governor as one of its five, Virginia has an educator as one of its five, and Pennsylvania makes its Superintendent of Public Instruction a sixth member.

Special Types

The provisions with regard to the appointment and control of the boards in the following states take them out of either the University or the Governor class:

In the District of Columbia the Board is appointed by and the duty of enforcement is placed in the hands of the Commissioners of the District.

In Idaho the Department of Law Enforcement serves as the Board of Accountancy.

In Indiana the State Board of Certified Public Accountants consists of the State Examiner and two deputy examiners of the Department of Inspection and Supervision of Public Offices.

In Nebraska two members of the Board are appointed by the governor and the third is the Auditor of Public Accounts.

In New Hampshire the registration of certified public accountants is in the hands of the Bank Commissioners.

In Oklahoma, the State Board of Accountancy consists of the State Examiner and Inspector, the Attorney General and one certified public accountant appointed by the governor.

In the Philippine Islands the Board of Accountancy is appointed by the Secretary of Commerce and Communications.

In South Dakota the Division of Audits and Accounts of the Department of Finance serves as the Board of Accountancy.

In Utah the Department of Registration has jurisdiction over the issuance of C. P. A. certificates and appoints three holders of C. P. A. certificates

141

The above map shows for each governmental unit the date when the C. P. A. law was enacted and the type of law as to administration.

142

who serve as a Board in direct charge of details with reference to the examinations.

In Vermont the State Board of Accountancy consists of the Auditor of Accounts, the State Treasurer and the Commissioner of Banking and Insurance.

In Washington the governor appoints an Accountancy Examining Committee upon the request of the Director of Licenses, who exercises all the powers and performs all the duties of the average board of accountancy except the conduct of the examination itself.

The Waiver Clause

Frequent mention has been made of the "Waiver Clause." In the initial stages of the C. P. A. Movement the exact terms under which existing practitioners should receive their certificates without examination were the subject of much discussion. This had been the case in Scotland in 1854, and in England in 1870, and more recently in the different provinces of Canada. Provision had to be made for the old timers, not only because they demanded it, but because the law-making authorities insisted on such a provision. In asking a legislative body to make a law providing for any control, even in the use of an entirely new professional designation, the proponents must persuade the law makers that there will be no infringement of existing rights. To

safeguard this it has always been found necessary to allow those in practice of a profession or those engaged in a trade, at the time the law is passed, to come in without restriction. The existing practitioners are given a limited time within which to file their formal applications.

It has usually been the aim of the existing practitioners to erect as high a standard of free admission at the outset as the law makers would stand for. On the other hand the law makers have nearly always wanted to cut the requirement down. In at least one case the previous experience requirement was entirely eliminated. As I have told you the New York C. P. A. law called for only one year's previous experience. In framing rules for the enforcement of the law the Regents of the University required five-years' previous experience. In other states the requirement of previous practice has been either one, three or five years.

We don't hear much about the "Waiver Clause" nowadays. It is practically a dead issue. While there is some danger that the waiver may be reopened by fresh legislative action, it is to be hoped that the national and state societies will succeed, as they have so far, in having such measures killed or vetoed.

What matters it today whether the earliest C. P. A. laws, passed twenty-five or thirty years ago, required one year of previous experience—or five?

The old-timers who came in through the open door and who are still among us today, in the active practice of the profession, have survived the intervening years by reason of their fitness.

What counts more in the upbuilding of our profession, is the manner in which the examinations are conducted.

First Conference of C. P. A. Examiners

At its regular monthly meeting on April 8, 1908 the New Jersey State Board of Public Accountants decided to invite the several State Boards of C. P. A. Examiners to meet, at the Marlborough-Blenheim Hotel, at Atlantic City, N. J., on October 19, 1908, "to confer in regard to matters of mutual interest." In view of the outcome the proceedings of this initial conference of examiners are of interest to the Certified Public Acountants of today, and are therefore made a part of this historical sketch.

In sending out the formal invitation, on behalf of the Board, I expressed the view that:

"The Conference of Examiners promises to be of benefit to all engaged in the most important duty of examining future members of our Profession, and its influence on the future cannot be over-estimated."

The following examining authorities were represented by one or more of their regularly appointed examiners—University of the State of New York, State Board of Pennsylvania, State University of Illinois and the State Boards of New Jersey, Ohio, Connecticut, G orgia, Rhode Island, Colorado. Fifteen examiners representing nine of the fourteen C. P. A. States, attended the conference and participated in its proceedings. After the usual preliminaries were over, and a chairman and a secretary had been elected, the meeting was thrown open for discussion. During the progress of the conference, Dr. Edward P. Moxey, C. P. A. of the Wharton School of Commerce and Finance, at the University of Pennsylvania, and a member of the Pennsylvania Institute, came into the meeting and was accorded the privilege of the floor.

At the suggestion of the promoter of the meeting, an expression of opinion, from each of the examiners present, was called for, as to whether a permanent association of examiners should be organized then and there, or whether an annual conference, such as had originally been proposed by George Wilkinson, would be the better plan.

On the subject of forming a permanent association the discussion ran something like this:

J. E. Sterrett of Pennsylvania—
"* * * I think we could accomplish great good by occasional conference. I don't see that a permanent organization would be of any real value. I doubt that it would have any authority which would make it worth while."

Charles N. Vollum of Pennsylvania—
"Mr. Sterrett has expressed my views. I don't think that a permanent organization would reach the desired end."

George Wilkinson of New Jersey—
"In favor of having an annual conference of the C. P. A. Examiners who are on the Boards at the time, and to hold this conference in the same place and at the same time as the Annual Meeting of the American Association of Public Accountants."

Joel Hunter of the Georgia State Board agreed with Messrs. Sterrett, Wilkinson and Vollum, that an annual conference of examiners would be the better plan.

W. A. Chase one of the examiners for the University of Illinois, agreed with the Pennsylvanians—in favor of an annual conference.

As other examiners present continued to express their views, it became evident that the Pennsylvanians were in a minority. The three examiners on the Ohio State Board being present were unanimously in favor of forming a permanent organization of examiners. Homer A. Dunn of New York joined in this view. Frank G. Du Bois and John E. Cooper of New Jersey felt strongly that way and so did the examiners pres-

ent from Connecticut, Rhode Island and Colorado. As a result of the discussion a committee was appointed to draw up plans for a "permanent organization of State Examiners."

At the adjourned meeting, held on the following day (October 20, 1908) designated as the "Second Conference," an organization was effected under the name of the "National Association of C. P. A. Examiners" and the election of officers was proceeded with. The first nomination for President was Mr. C. N. Vollum, C. P. A. of Philadelphia. who very promptly and very positively declined. This so-called "permanent organization" soon went to pieces.

Ultimately the view expressed by the Pennsylvanians has borne fruit. Today we find that a conference of examiners is held each year, at the time and place of the Annual Meeting of the American Institute of Accountants.

At the same pioneer conference of C. P. A. Examiners, held in Atlantic City on October 19, 1908, Harry T. Beers of Connecticut brought forward a suggestion:

"* * * to arrange as far as possible to have practically the same examinations held throughout the country, at the same time."

This suggestion similarly came to fruition. Of the whole family of C. P. A. States, thirty-four (34) are now using the standard questions prepared by the Board of Examiners of the American Institute. This development indicates wonderful progress, from a national viewpoint, as it makes for the maintenance of a uniform standard of qualification throughout the land.

143

The JOURNAL *of* ACCOUNTANCY

Official Organ of the AMERICAN INSTITUTE OF ACCOUNTANTS

| Vol. 44 | SEPTEMBER, 1927 | No. 3 |

Organization of the Profession in Pennsylvania*

BY GEORGE WILKINSON

In the January, 1925, number, an historical writer, to whom we shall refer more fully a little later, says, in a signed contribution to THE JOURNAL OF ACCOUNTANCY,

> "I have been unable to find, so far, the name of any firm or practitioner who posed as a public accountant prior to that period" (1880–1883).

It becomes, therefore, of more than passing interest to know who the real pioneers of our profession in the United States were, and where and when their efforts materialized. There seems to have been just a quartet of them in the city of Philadelphia. All of them have passed on to their reward.

In a booklet of eighty-seven typewritten pages, nicely bound and distributed to his chosen friends, Mr. T. Edward Ross and those associated with him in the effort, made a contribution of great value to the history of accountancy in Pennsylvania. The occasion for the compilation of this attractive little volume was the celebration of the twenty-fifth anniversary of the Pennsylvania Institute (in 1922).

The book referred to contains articles from the pens of half a dozen of our most valued members: (1) A brief history of the institute by Mr. Robert J. Bennett, secretary of the Pennsylvania Institute; (2) a report of the twenty-fifth anniversary proceedings, by the same writer; (3) half a dozen biographical sketches of certain deceased members, written by individual contributors, and (4) an extremely interesting essay entitled "Musings of a Quarter Century," by Mr. Joseph E. Sterrett.

From the biographical sketches referred to, we learn on very excellent authority who were the first men who offered

---

* An historical sketch prepared for the thirtieth anniversary of the formation of the Pennsylvania Institute of Certified Public Accountants, held in Philadelphia, June 14, 1927.

145

their services to the public in the commonwealth of Pennsylvania.

(First) The first person to establish himself as a public accountant in Pennsylvania was the late John W. Francis, who in 1869 ventured forth on untrodden ground, by opening an office as a public accountant in Philadelphia. Mr. Francis was a lovable old gentleman when most of us were boys—forty years ago.

(Second) The late Charles Nixon Vollum came second, when he opened an office as an accountant at 134 South Fourth street, in April, 1875, and sent out a modest bid for business, in the form of an attractive card, hand-written and multiplied photographically, explaining briefly just what he was prepared to do for the public. Mr. Vollum died on October 26, 1911. His name prevails today in the firm name of Vollum & Vollum, certified public accountants.

(Third) The late John Heins began to practise as an accountant in 1877, with an office on the second floor front of a stone-faced building at 235 Dock street, overlooking the original stock exchange which is still standing, now (1927) being used as a produce exchange. This was a very important section of Philadelphia forty years ago. Stephen Girard's old banking house, now standing tenantless, was close by, and the original Penn Mutual Insurance Company's building, where William Penn's life-size statue can still be seen, is on the adjacent corner. Mr. Heins' name still carries prestige for the members of the present firm of John Heins & Co.

(Fourth) The late Lawrence E. Brown opened an office at 430 Walnut street, in 1882. His original office at this address was in one of those old-fashioned but very substantial stone-faced residences with marble steps at the entrance door and an iron hand-rail. With his partners Mr. Brown established an honored name for the firm of Lawrence E. Brown & Co., certified public accountants.

THE FIRST EFFORT TO ORGANIZE IN PENNSYLVANIA

The earliest record that can be found of any effort to organize the profession of the accountant in Pennsylvania seems to be in 1886, when Mr. Francis had several conferences at his office with Messrs. Heins, Vollum and Brown looking to a plan of organization for their mutual protection and benefit. The plan was to organize a society and to seek a charter as an educational institution, under Pennsylvania law. The society was to be called "The Chartered Accountants' Institute."

The principal objects of the proposed society were:

> "to elevate the standing and advance the interests of public accountants; and to direct attention to the advantages offered by, and the safeguards attending, the auditing and adjusting of books and accounts by persons thoroughly skilled and experienced as public accountants, and of established personal reputation."

It was in December, 1886, that Mr. Edwin Guthrie, F. C. A., of Manchester, who was visiting the city of New York on the business of his firm, accepted Mr. Heins' invitation to visit Philadelphia, with the object of discussing the plan above referred to.

Mr. Heins introduced Mr. Guthrie to the late Mr. John W. Francis and together these three pioneers discussed the Philadelphia plan for a state society.

147

Mr. Guthrie strongly counselled Mr. Heins and Mr. Francis to use some other name than "chartered accountants," because, he pointed out, it would likely conflict with the use of that title in this country by English and Scottish accountants, visiting the United States on professional business. This loomed as a serious objection, at that time, for the reason that the most important and responsible business entrusted to public accountants in those days was given to visiting British accountants. Further than this Mr. Guthrie, having strongly in mind the success achieved in England by the organization (in 1882) under a royal charter, of the Institute of Chartered Accountants, strongly counseled a nation-wide association, in preference to a state society.

It is not of record that Mr. Guthrie, on the occasion of his visit to Philadelphia, met Mr. Charles N. Vollum, Mr. Lawrence E. Brown, nor Mr. Hyland B. Hayes, who had an office at 110 South third street. Upon returning to New York Mr. Guthrie related to his partner (Mr. James Thornley Anyon) his experience at Philadelphia. It is remembered that he stated he had been able to find but two accountants in the City of Brotherly Love.

GENESIS OF AMERICAN ASSOCIATION

In the January, 1925, number of THE JOURNAL OF ACCOUNTANCY there began an interesting, ingenuous and intimately descriptive article by Mr. James Thornley Anyon, chartered accountant and C. P. A., of New York.

In a prefatory note, Mr. Anyon admits that he is "supposed to be the oldest practising accountant in the United States."

Knowing whereof he speaks, permit the present writer to say that unquestionably Mr. Anyon is the dean of our profession.

Mr. Anyon enjoys the further remarkable distinction of having stood at the head of his firm for no less than forty hard-working years. In 1887 Mr. Anyon became the head of the firm of Barrow, Wade, Guthrie & Co., first established in New York in 1883.

In his own intimate and conversational style, Mr. Anyon tells The Journal readers of his arrival in the city of New York and of his presenting himself at the office of Barrow, Wade, Guthrie & Co., 45 William street, New York, on October 25, 1886.

Also of his strong desire to meet his professional brethren in America—if he could find any. He intimates that his diligent inquiries in that regard disclosed to him "that there were very few persons engaged in the profession—no more than could be counted on the fingers of one hand."

Mr. Anyon goes right on to say, "There was a firm called Veysey & Veysey with a staff of two or three assistants. . . ." This old firm of Veysey & Veysey, long since out of existence and only a memory in connection with the earliest days of accountancy, was composed of William H. Veysey, an old English gentleman who never foreswore allegiance to Queen Victoria, and his oldest son, Walter H. P. Veysey. The senior partner established himself as a public accountant in New York in 1866, and was, I have always believed, the first practitioner to do so.

Permit the present writer to introduce the three assistants referred to: first, James Nicholas Kelly, who served for many years as treasurer of the New York State Society of Certified Public Accountants; second, George Wilkinson, whose employment with the firm began January 20, 1887, and third, George Johnston, a colored porter and office boy. Some of the earliest meetings of the trustees of the American Association occurred in the office of Veysey & Veysey. The writer well remembers Mr. Anyon (the first secretary) and Mr. James Yalden (the first president) coming to the office of Veysey & Veysey to hold one of those trustee meetings.

Mr. Anyon goes on to write:

> "In Philadelphia the late John Heins seemed to be the only representative accountant in public practice."

This may have been the report which the late Edwin Guthrie had brought back from Philadelphia, just before Christmas forty years ago, but it certainly left out of the picture those three stalwarts, John W. Francis, Charles N. Vollum and Lawrence E. Brown, who, as we have seen, had established themselves in Philadelphia as public accountants in 1869, 1875 and 1882 respectively.

Continuing his narrative Mr. Anyon tells how he invited all the accountants he found trace of to a conference in his office in New York, including one man from Boston (a Mr. Rodney McLaughlin).

> "On the afternoon in question the gentlemen invited came at the appointed time. There were six or seven present, including Mr. Heins who had purposely traveled from Philadelphia to attend."

Mr. Edwin Guthrie, F. C. A., of Manchester, England, was invited to take the chair and Mr. James T. Anyon, who also hailed from Lancashire, was elected secretary of the meeting. After a full discussion, it was unanimously resolved, on the motion of Mr. John Heins, that those present form themselves into an association "for the advancement and protection of the interests of their profession." It was further resolved, and this time on the motion of Mr. J. T. Anyon, that the name of the new society should be "American Association of Public Accountants."

Thus, on December 23, 1886, was formed the first professional guild of accountants in the United States, with an aggregate membership of less than a dozen.

On the 20th of August, 1887, those charter members of the association who happened to be citizens of the United States joined in signing a certificate of incorporation, expressing therein their desire "to associate themselves for social and benefit purposes." Mr. Anyon and Mr. Veysey, being unrepentant British subjects, could not join in the petition.

The late Mr. James Yalden of New York was the first president of the association, followed in 1889 by the late John Heins of Philadelphia, who continued in the chair for three years.

Of the eight original signatories to the certificate of incorporation, only two above named remained members of the association after a dozen years. Of the original group of members only three—Mr. J. T. Anyon, Mr. George H. Church and Mr. W. R. Blackman—are alive today.

The principal objects for which the association was created are stated in its articles of incorporation to be:

> "to associate into a society or guild for their mutual benefit and advantage the best and most capable public accountants practising in the United

States; and through such association to elevate the profession of public accountants as a whole. . . ."

The charter of the association was finally issued on September 22, 1887. It required that the association's place of business should be in the city of New York. In order to make the membership nice and select, the original by-laws provided that the entrance fee should be an even hundred dollars. In the first year there were thirty-one members. In a dozen years, when the initiation fee had come down to the present popular price of twenty-five dollars, there were sixty fellow members. This latter number included Mr. John Heins and Mr. John W. Francis of Philadelphia, while the present writer was the only member at that time who lived in Chicago.

150

With the years that follow this history has naught to do, as Philadelphians bore no part of the responsibility. The American Association was virtually, as well as legally, a New York corporation—domiciled in New York and governed by New York accountants.

ORGANIZATION IN PENNSYLVANIA

The first law establishing the professional designation of certified public accountant—C. P. A.—was passed in New York on April 7, 1896, and was approved by the governor of the Empire State a month later. Immediately after this important happening, we find the movement getting under way in the Keystone State. In May, 1896, Mr. J. E. Sterrett sent to certain other Philadelphia accountants, among whom were the late John Heins, Lawrence E. Brown and Charles N. Vollum, copies of the bill just then enacted in New York state and suggested that Pennsylvania should make a move in the same direction. Mr. Francis and Mr. Brown supported the proposition, but Mr. Heins was not in favor of doing any such thing. Nothing was done at that time.

A year later, the New York C. P. A. certificates having come out, an actual start was made in Philadelphia. In a letter dated March 16, 1897, and signed jointly by the late John W. Francis and by J. E. Sterrett, these pioneers wrote their professional brothers:

"We think it wise at this time to ask a few of the leading accountants of this city to discuss the subject and consider the advisability of taking some action along similar lines in our own state. We therefore cordially invite you to an informal meeting, to be held at this office, on Tuesday evening, March 23, 1897, at eight o'clock."

We have it on good authority that Mr. Sterrett fully measured the difficulty of promulgating such a radical departure in our most conservative city. Obviously it would be an advantage to secure the coöperation of the big, little man at 508 Walnut street, so Mr. Sterrett took the precaution to present personally his letter of invitation to Mr. John Heins, then ex-president of the American Association of Public Accountants. The letter was handed by Mr. Sterrett to Mr. Heins' personal attendant—no less a personage than Robert H. Montgomery—who at once secured a private interview for the missionary. Thus was Mr. Heins won over against his personal prejudice to accept an invitation to the meeting.

At the initial meeting, held as scheduled, there was a sentiment in favor of setting the legislative machinery in motion at Harrisburg, even if failure might result on the first trial. After a general discussion, the meeting was adjourned for a week. At the adjourned meeting, held on March 30, 1897, Mr. John Heins showed up. It was then determined to organize an association of individuals, to be known as the Pennsylvania Association of Public Accountants. Mr. John Heins was elected president and Mr. J. E. Sterrett was elected secretary.

After appointing a committee of two to draft a constitution and set of by-laws for the new association, the meeting got busy with a first effort to secure a law recognizing our profession. After another week's adjournment, the committee brought in its recommendation for a C. P. A. bill.

It should here be noted that while our brothers in Illinois were struggling, early in March at Springfield (the state capital), to secure the passage of a law similar to that enacted in New York, under which it was proposed that the state university at Urbana should hold the examinations, our own association, here in Pennsylvania, acting under legal advice from the late Judge F. Carroll Brewster, was seeking a bill authorizing the supreme court of the state to issue certificates and appoint a board of examiners. The chief justice had expressed his willingness to fall in with this provision of the proposed law.

A committee consisting of Mr. John Heins and Mr. Charles N. Vollum lost no time in getting things started. Bill No. 316 was introduced in the senate on April 8, 1897, by State Senator Brown. The following evening the legislative committee reported to the newly formed association, expressing a confident hope that

151

the bill would pass the senate within ten days. Alas! The provision in the bill in regard to the state supreme court turned out to be a stumbling block. So much so that the bill failed to pass the senate and had to be abandoned for the 1897 session.

Two years went by.

A meeting of the Pennsylvania Association was held November 30, 1898, at which a new proposal for a C. P. A. bill was discussed. The revised bill, relieved of its supreme court handicap, called for a state board to be appointed by the governor.

C. P. A. LEGISLATION IN PENNSYLVANIA

152

With the convening of the state legislature in January, 1899, the Pennsylvania Association again got busy with its legislative programme. While Illinois and New Jersey accountants had visited Springfield and Trenton respectively, with like aims in view, and with equal lack of success, Pennsylvania kept in the lead, being second only to New York in actual accomplishment.

The very first bill to be introduced in the house of representatives at Harrisburg, by the Honorable David S. Chew, in the session of 1899, was the association's bill for the establishment of a state board. It was referred at once to the committee on judiciary general and a week later was reported favorably to the house.

The active work of looking after the bill at Harrisburg was placed in the hands of the late Charles N. Vollum, chairman of the executive committee of the Pennsylvania Association, who worked most untiringly to secure the passage of the bill.

In the meantime literature explaining the purpose of the proposed law was extensively circulated by the association. The endorsement of leading business men, of judges and of lawyers was freely given and broadcast. The bill passed the house on March 14th and the senate a week later. It was signed by Governor William A. Stone and became law on March 29, 1899.

This, then, was the second C. P. A. law to be enacted and the first one creating a state board of examiners. It has been largely copied by other states.

And what of the harvest?

The American Institute's year-book for 1926 gives a complete list of the examining boards of all the forty-eight states of the union, of the District of Columbia and of Alaska, Hawaii and the Philippine Islands—fifty-two legislative enactments and every one of them establishing the same professional designation— certified public accountant. And in every state but six, the conduct of the examinations rests in the hands of certified public accountants.

CHANGE IN NAME

Following the passage of a C. P. A. law in the commonwealth of Pennsylvania, the attention of our members was at once turned to the desirability of embodying the word "certified" in the name of the association. This object was fully accomplished on October 15, 1900, when the name of the association was changed to Pennsylvania Institute of Certified Public Accountants. Amendments in the constitution and by-laws were made to accord with this change.

153

PENNSYLVANIA CHARTER SECURED

On the 25th day of April, 1904, the Pennsylvania Institute having grown to be a healthy youth of seven years, our older brothers, of whom a majority have since departed this life, joined in signing a certificate of incorporation.

A month later (May 24, 1904), a charter was issued, under the act of April 15, 1874, signed by a judge of the court of common pleas for the county of Philadelphia and duly recorded by the recorder of deeds. This charter has ever since served the institute as its constitution.

EARLY ACCOUNTANCY EDUCATION

The first formal examination, prescribed by the Pennsylvania C. P. A. law of 1899, was held on November 13, 1899. Three candidates, all of them from Pittsburgh, sat for the written examination: two passed, one failed. Very soon it was realized that there was pressing need, here in the Keystone State, for some sound, dependable course of education in accountancy subjects. The Pennsylvania Institute soon realized that the upbuilding of our calling into a profession must come through education, far more than through legislation. The younger generation must come forward with a better preliminary training than the pioneers had brought to bear. To meet this need, in the summer of 1902, the council of the institute authorized the formation of classes for the study of the four subjects specified in the C. P. A. law.

169

PENNSYLVANIA NOT FAR BEHIND NEW YORK

Let it not be thought that Pennsylvania was far behind New York in the matter of establishing classes for the training of its young citizens in accountantship. These two principal states moved almost simultaneously in this important development. The accountancy classes conducted at the university building in Manhattan by Dean Joseph French Johnson and his faculty of educators were inaugurated in 1901, under the auspices of the New York State Society of Certified Public Accountants, by its then president, the late Charles Waldo Haskins. Students' evening classes were established here in Philadelphia in September, 1902, under the supervision of the institute's committee on education, with Mr. J. E. Sterrett, as chairman, together with Mr. Adam A. Ross and the late Alfred L. Sellers, as secretary. These classes were organized primarily for the purpose of affording technical instruction to assistants engaged in the offices of members of the institute. The restriction was not strictly enforced, because each member of the institute had the privilege of nominating, from outside of his office, a student who wanted to become a practising accountant—may be.

The fee for the full course was set at ten dollars, payable in two equal instalments. To supplement the fund thus collected from the students, the institute appropriated a hundred dollars from its treasury. Volunteer instructors were enrolled from among the leading members of the institute, the classes being held during the evenings in the offices of their respective firms. The subjects taken up and the instructors lecturing thereupon were:

Theory of accounts,	R. H. Montgomery
Practical accounting,	W. M. Lybrand
Auditing,	J. W. Fernley
Commercial law,	H. G. Stockwell

PIONEER EDUCATIONAL WORK IN PENNSYLVANIA

The actual work of these evening classes began October 20, 1902, and continued through that winter and the next. Hours, eight to ten. Two subjects each evening. This educational work, like all pioneer efforts, was not without its difficulties. The instructors had not at that early date acquired much facility as lecturers, but what they lacked in experience they made up in enthusiasm and perseverance. On the other hand, the students presented some unforeseen difficulties, due to their varying ages

154

and their more varying experience. But as these students, though comparatively few in number, were prompted by a keen desire to better their educational equipment and were devoting their leisure to these studies of their own volition, good progress was made from the beginning.

At the end of the first winter's work, the chairman of the committee made a favorable report to the council of the institute, in which it was intimated that the work would be continued the next winter, with the same four instructors. The second season's work was even more successful and the movement gathered impetus.

When the institute's committee on education came to make its second annual report on this work, it wrote, referring to the instructors:

155

> "These gentlemen have given generously of their time and energy, in carrying forward this important department of the institute's work. Their names constitute a roll of honor as the teaching staff of the first school of higher accounting to be established in this state."

EDUCATIONAL CLASSES TURNED OVER TO UNIVERSITY OF PENNSYLVANIA

By the spring of 1904 negotiations had been successfully carried out, with the faculty of the Wharton School of Accounts and Finance and with the trustees of the University of Pennsylvania, under which the educational classes, so successfully inaugurated by the Pennsylvania Institute, were turned over to the university as a going concern. Subsequent to that date this important educational work has been carried on, as part of the regular curriculum of the university, to the upbuilding of our profession in this state.

Dr. Edward Sherwood Mead was appointed director of the Wharton School of Accounts and Finance and bestowed a great deal of zeal thereupon. The real active operation of the university evening classes began on the evening of the 30th of September, 1904, when Herbert G. Stockwell, attorney at law and C. P. A. of Pennsylvania, was placed in charge of the classes in advanced accounting for the first year of the new school.

But it was our good friend Dr. Edward Preston Moxey who assumed, and who has maintained, the major burden of the work, being in charge of the accounting classes. Ever since then and up to this day, Dr. Moxey, still a young man, has carried on this work—twenty-three years.

When the institute's evening accountancy classes were ceded to the Wharton school, certain members of the institute undertook to guarantee the expenses of conducting the classes—advertising, light, heat, janitor services and the like—for the first winter season, but the guarantors were never called on for any money.

PLAN FOR THE FEDERATION FIRST PRESENTED TO PENNSYLVANIA

In the autumn of 1902, when Pennsylvania was in the throes of inaugurating students' evening classes, a missionary from the west arrived in Philadelphia and was invited to establish his quarters in the offices of a firm of accountants in the Stephen Girard building, on Twelfth street. This person explained that he had lately been elected president of the Illinois Association of Public Accountants; that a special committee of that association had been authorized to consult the several existing state societies as to forming a national body of professional accountants. The name proposed by the Illinois Association was "The Federation of Accountants."

Provided the brethren in the City of Brotherly Love endorsed the plan, the missionary from the west would carry on; would visit Baltimore and Boston. Indeed, he hoped to muster courage enough to invade Manhattan.

An informal evening meeting of the institute was held and the president of the Illinois Association was given an opportunity to explain his plans, which were summarized thus:

"to link the several existing state societies together, under one control, for mutual protection and advantage; to promote additional state societies of public accountants; to encourage uniform state C. P. A. legislation; and ultimately to secure recognition from the federal government."

It was pointed out that accountants practising in the west did not feel that the old-established American Association of Public Accountants, domiciled as it was in New York and governed by a New York board, was fulfilling its avowed calling as a national institute.

THE FEDERATION IDEA ACCEPTED BY PENNSYLVANIA

Being always ready to support a movement for the betterment of the profession, the Philadelphians endorsed the plan of federating the existing societies and promised to send delegates to the forthcoming convention at Washington. In due course official action of the institute was taken and two delegates were appointed —Mr. Robert H. Montgomery and the late Mr. A. R. Barrett.

The first convention was held at the New Willard Hotel in Washington on October 28, 1902, and was an immediate success. Many practitioners had prophesied that nothing formative could be accomplished at the first convention. The scoffers were surprised to find that what they expected would take two or three meetings was accomplished in one day. Permanent officers were elected, constitution and by-laws were adopted and the whole works was completed. The business which took the most time was naming the infant. All the delegates present wanted to participate in the christening, and not merely as spectators. Each group added something to the name, until in the end the poor baby was overburdened with the following: The Federation of Societies of Public Accountants in the United States of America.

157

At a meeting of the Pennsylvania Institute, held on November 25, 1902, resolutions were passed that the Pennsylvania Institute become a member of the federation.

At each of the following annual conventions of the federation and of the meetings of its directors, Pennsylvania was always represented and took an active part in the work.

At the succeeding annual conventions of the federation, in 1903 and 1904, it was established that

> "The several state societies of accountants, without forfeiting any of their sovereign powers, in their own states, could work, hand in hand, under one executive, in all matters related to the Washington government, both legislative and executive branches. Hand in hand for the common good of all."

As it turned out, the life of the federation was disproportionate to the length of its name. It can not be doubted, however, that while its name was dropped after its second year, the good work it accomplished has not been lost to the profession. Through the work of the federation, from 1902 to 1905, the principle was firmly established that the interests of the profession demanded and that the members of the profession would support a national organization of accountants.

THE CONGRESS OF ACCOUNTANTS AND THE PENNSYLVANIA INSTITUTE

At the annual banquet of the Pennsylvania Institute, held at the Hotel Bellevue on May 27, 1904, one of the guests was the secretary of the Federation of Societies of Public Accountants, who had been invited by the toastmaster of the occasion—Mr. William M. Lybrand—to speak in regard to the proposed congress of accountants, to be held under the auspices of the Louisiana Purchase Exposition, at St. Louis, in the following September. After narrating something of his recent visit to St. Louis, and after describing some of the architectural beauties of the exposition buildings and the scope of the exposition, the secretary of the federation said:

> "The official bulletin of the exposition company announces there will be held on the fair grounds—"International congresses of learned men from everywhere." This is where we come in! The executive committee of the federation has authorized the announcement of a programme for a congress of professional accountants, to be held in the Hall of Congress, in the fair grounds, during the last week of September."

158 After enumerating the several states where associations of accountants had been organized, each one of which was expected to contribute some members of the congress, and after telling of the arrangements already made by the committee on arrangements, the secretary went on:

> "Other professions, the most dignified and learned, have held national congresses, but this will be the first national meeting of professional accountants ever held in the United States of America.
> "The Pennsylvania Institute has stood out most prominently in encouraging the federation, from the very inception, and has been conspicuous in good works, on its own account. . . ."

The secretary concluded a long address by extending, on behalf of the federation, a most cordial invitation to the members of the Pennsylvania Institute to attend the congress of accountants at St. Louis, in September, 1904. That the invitation was enthusiastically accepted was shown by the outcome. Four members of the Pennsylvania Institute took a prominent part on the committee on arrangements for the congress and themselves contributed greatly to the success of the conference. These were Messrs. William M. Lybrand, Robert H. Montgomery, Joseph E. Sterrett and Charles N. Vollum.

The contribution of the Pennsylvania Institute to the success of the congress was notable. Mr. J. E. Sterrett was elected permanent chairman of the congress of accountants.

Chairman Sterrett's opening address to the members of the congress of accountants gave a vivid insight, as well as an accurate history, of what had been accomplished, up to that date, on behalf of the profession of the public accountant in America. This address, appearing in full in the official record of the congress, makes most interesting reading today.

A valuable contribution to the literature of our profession was the paper read by Robert H. Montgomery, one of the delegates from Pennsylvania, recommending uniform practice in the accounts of public-service corporations.

Another special feature of the congress was a cash prize given for the best essay on the mode of conducting an audit, to be written and read at the congress by a clerk regularly employed on a salary by a public accountant firm. The prize was won by Mr. Walter A. Staub, then of Philadelphia, whose treatise is considered a valuable and permanent contribution.

BRITISH AND CANADIAN SOCIETIES AT THE CONGRESS

Mr. Francis William Pixley, F. C. A. of London, barrister-at-law, fellow and past president, represented the Institute of Chartered Accountants in England and Wales.

159

Mr. James Martin, F. S. A. A., of London, for many years its secretary, represented the Society of Accountants and Auditors, Incorporated.

The several Canadian accountancy organizations were each represented by delegates chosen from among their own members.

It is within the scope of this historical sketch to follow the development of the national organization, for the reason that the Pennsylvania Institute has always played a prominent and well considered part in such development.

At a regular meeting of the American Association of Public Accountants, held on January 10, 1905, in the city of New York, the constitution and by-laws of the association were amended so as to

(1) Take into membership, as society fellows, the entire membership of the several societies and associations in the federation.

(2) Adopt substantially the form of government of the federation.

In this way the two rival organizations were merged. The name of the association was retained, the essential structure of the federation was maintained.

By proper action of its council, and of its members, taken on April 17, 1905, the entire membership of the Pennsylvania Institute became society members in the American Association of Public Accountants, from October 1, 1905. The Federation of Societies of Public Accountants came to an end. It is a pleasant memory to many of us. It served a useful purpose.

At the annual meeting of the reformed national association, held at the Hotel Astor in New York on October 17, 1905, separate societies came bodily into the American Association from the following states: New York, New Jersey, Pennsylvania, Ohio, Illinois, Maryland, Tennessee, Minnesota, California, Massachusetts, Missouri, Washington, Colorado, Georgia and Michigan. At the meeting in question every one of these states was represented by delegates, bearing credentials from their respective societies.

This reformed national body continued from 1905 to 1916 inclusive. During that period the great majority of the members continued to carry their membership in the national body through their respective state societies. These society members attended the annual meetings of the American Association, at the hands of their respective delegates annually elected to that duty.

PITTSBURGH BRANCH OF THE PENNSYLVANIA INSTITUTE

On November 25, 1913, our professional brothers in Pittsburgh, taking advantage of a permissive regulation in the by-laws at that time, held a meeting to organize a Pittsburgh branch of the Pennsylvania Institute. Membership of the branch was to be restricted to members of the institute residing, or doing business, in Pittsburgh. The council of the institute duly received a formal application from the new Pittsburgh branch, for approval by the institute, under the then existing by-laws, and on January 22, 1914, the application was approved.

This Pittsburgh branch, which seems to have lasted about a year, had little more than a nominal existence, largely because of the small membership. Its passing left the western part of the state, as before, without any local organization.

THE PENNSYLVANIA DOOR THROWN OPEN

On June 4, 1915, Governor Brumbaugh affixed his signature to an amendment of the Pennsylvania C. P. A. law, under which discretion was given to the board of examiners to recommend for certificates, without written examination, certified public accountants of other states, who had been in practice five years, and who established bona-fide offices in Pennsylvania.

This provision of law opened the door to a large number of certified public accountants of other states to active membership in our Pennsylvania Institute. Particularly was this felt in the western part of the state, where many accountants had established themselves and sought to use C. P. A. titles secured from other states.

In the spring of 1915, several Pittsburgh accountants got together in an effort to form an independent local organization to represent the profession in the western part of the state. This movement crystallized in a meeting to organize a new body to be called the "Accountants' Society of Western Pennsylvania," whose membership should be open alike to certified public accountants of any state and to non-certified men. This proposal was regarded by the council of the institute as inimical to the welfare of our profession. The president of the institute, Mr. Herbert G. Stockwell, counseled more thought and discussion. Further committee work ensued. Finally the proposed western society came to naught.

161

In the summer of 1915—a dozen years ago—the institute's committee on by-laws struggled earnestly with proposed amendments to the by-laws to bring about a division of the membership east and west—a chapter in Philadelphia and a chapter in Pittsburgh. Under this 1915 proposal the membership was to be widened to take in as chapter members men who were not eligible as members of the Pennsylvania Institute. After a great deal of work and discussion this proposition was submitted to a meeting of the institute on January 17, 1916, and was disapproved.

After another year's time, namely on January 15, 1917, the by-laws of the institute were amended and our present article IX on local chapters was adopted. This ten-year-old by-law provides a method for the formation of local chapters within the membership of the Pennsylvania Institute, wherever a nucleus of seven members is grouped.

Five years after this provision for local chapters had been worked out and adopted, the first such chapter was organized—in Pittsburgh—on April 13, 1922. And a flourishing organization it has become, suitable to the progressive city and district it serves. The chapter elects its own executive officers: chairman, treasurer and secretary, and its own governing body called the executive committee. The chapter makes its own by-laws, subject to approval by the council, and is in undisputed charge of its own field, its own policy, its own finances and its own meetings. Such matters as relate to the enforcement of the C. P. A. law, to state or federal legislation and to intercourse with other state societies remain the province of the Pennsylvania Institute—the state society—whose council carries on as heretofore.

PHILADELPHIA CHAPTER

Up to last spring the members of the institute residing in the eastern part of the state and those outside of the state had contented themselves with the old order, under which the institute held quarterly stated business meetings and monthly meetings of its members during the winter season for the reading of papers on subjects of professional interest followed by discussion thereupon. These meetings have been attended by a fair number of Philadelphians.

It was inevitable that a feeling should grow up among those who had affiliated with the Pittsburgh chapter, that they had been relegated into a subordinate body while the Philadelphians had held together the institute itself.

At the annual meeting of the Pennsylvania Institute, held in Philadelphia, April 20, 1925, Mr. Frank Wilbur Main of Pittsburgh, a member of the state board of examiners, brought fraternal greetings to the institute from the Pittsburgh chapter, and told of the success of its work in the western part of the state and of its weekly luncheon meetings with discussions. In the course of his remarks Mr. Main brought forward the suggestion that there should be a rearrangement of the by-laws of the institute to provide for chapters in various sections of the state, including Philadelphia and Pittsburgh. Mr. Main expressed his belief that the day was not far distant when additional chapters would be organized in Harrisburg, Wilkes-Barre and Scranton.

It remained for Gardner W. Kimball, while vice-president of the institute and chairman of its meetings committee, to carry out the plan. After a further revision of the by-laws, on April 7, 1927, five years after Pittsburgh had stepped out on its own, the Philadelphians organized a chapter of their own, leaving the institute—the parent organization—in charge of state-wide matters in the commonwealth of Pennsylvania, with but one meeting of members each year.

At the present writing seventy-one members of the institute are definitely affiliated with the Pittsburgh chapter while one hundred and eighty-nine belong to the Philadelphia chapter. This leaves a small minority of members of the institute who have not denoted their wish to belong to either chapter and are therefore members at large. These can fraternize annually if they attend the annual meeting of the institute.

Under the latest amendment to the by-laws the officers and council governing the affairs of the Pennsylvania Institute are distributed as between the two chapters approximately on the basis of membership—east and west. This year the president of the institute is a Philadelphian while the vice-president resides in Pittsburgh. It has been arranged that the next annual meeting shall be held at Bedford Springs, near Pittsburgh. The Pittsburgh chapter will then have the right to put forward a member of its own for president, while the Philadelphians will have to content themselves with the vice-presidency.

163

ENFORCEMENT OF THE C. P. A. LAW

As previously intimated, it remains the province of the Pennsylvania Institute to police the state, in an effort to enforce the C. P. A. law.

Since the enactment of June 4, 1915, previously referred to, under which an accountant registered as certified public accountant in another state, after establishing residence or office in Pennsylvania, may, at the discretion of the board of examiners, be granted a C. P. A. certificate by the governor of the commonwealth, no others are permitted to use the C. P. A. designation in Pennsylvania.

This has proved a very wise provision as it definitely limits the use of the C. P. A. designation within the commonwealth to those who hold certificates signed by the governor. Formerly an alien C. P. A. was permitted to use his imported title by simply designating, by initials, the state from which he had received a certificate. There have, of course, been several infringements, but these have been so adroitly handled by the institute's most competent secretary that there has so far been no necessity to bring any one to trial before the courts.

The Pennsylvania Institute of Certified Public Accountants, as the state society, will carry on with its policy of maintaining a high standard of professional conduct and through the medium of its council and its committees to advance the interests of the profession throughout the commonwealth of Pennsylvania.

REMINISCENCES OF EARLY DAYS

OF THE ACCOUNTING PROFESSION

IN ILLINOIS

by

ERNEST RECKITT, M.S., C.P.A.

Published in 1953 by the

Illinois Society of Certified Public Accountants

Chicago, Illinois

during its Fiftieth Anniversary Year

"I hold every man a debtor to his profession; from the which as men of course do seek to receive countenance and profit, so ought they of duty to endeavor themselves by way of amends to be a help and an ornament thereunto."

Francis Bacon

166

THE AUTHOR

Ernest Reckitt was born in Hull, England, October 8, 1866. He studied at the Victoria University of Manchester, England, and received his degrees of Bachelor of Science and Master of Science from that university, continuing his studies at Göttingen University in Germany. He came to the United States in 1890 and located in Chicago.

Mr. Reckitt has practiced public accounting since 1891. In 1897 he and George Wilkinson organized the first society of public accountants in Illinois under the title of the Illinois Association of Public Accountants with fourteen char- ter members. The chief object of the Association was to secure the passage of a C.P.A. law in Illinois. The efforts of the Association were finally successful in 1903 by which time its membership had increased to 54. Mr. Reckitt served as president and vice president of the Association during its six years of life.

Mr. Reckitt holds Illinois C.P.A. certificate No. 4. The University of Illinois appointed him as a member of the first board of C.P.A. examiners in which capacity he served for four years. He was one of the charter members of the Illinois Society of Certified Public Accountants and was elected to honorary membership in 1927. He was president of the Society for the year 1910-11 and vice-president of the American Institute of Accountants for the year 1923-24. He has served on numerous committees of both the Society and the Institute. It was while he was historian of the Society from 1940 to 1949 that he was asked to write these "Reminiscences", which were completed in 1948. Their publication is a part of the observance of the fiftieth anniversary of the first accountancy law in Illinois and of the founding of the Illinois Society of Certified Public Accountants in 1903.

169

PREFACE

by Jackson W. Smart, CPA

It is difficult for those of us who are in public accounting today to appreciate the lack of understanding and public acceptance of our profession fifty years ago. All of us owe a tremendous debt to the pioneers who laid the foundation for what we now have.

There are many men who have given unsparingly of their time and their efforts to make public accounting an important factor in our present economic and social life. Mr. Reckitt not only has done his full share in this respect but was able to make a contribution which many of the others could not. He had a college education, and a social and cultural background which gave him an opportunity to further the interests of public accounting outside of his business associations. The wide acquaintanceship which he enjoyed among business leaders and other professional men was important in the development of the stature of public accounting today, and also most helpful in attracting into our profession the best type of young men.

He has always had a great love of public accounting and a pride in it. His pleasure in accounting has primarily been an unselfish one. It has had more to do with being a part of a new profession that he was proud of than merely a vehicle for the making of money. It is the intellectual honesty and fundamental integrity of our early members which have given us our heritage. Our profession in Illinois is particularly fortunate to have had Mr. Reckitt, and other men of his calibre, identified with it in the early days. Too often we take too much for granted and do not think about what has gone before.

The book which Mr. Reckitt has written is of great interest to all of us in that it makes us stop and think and appreciate some of the efforts and trials with which the older members of our profession have been confronted.

171

INTRODUCTION

"O wad some power the giftie gie us
To see oursel's as ithers see us"

The world is indebted to the great Scottish poet, Robert Burns, for many wholesome truths, one of which, quoted above, should ever be borne in mind. The succeeding lines of the verse from which this quotation is taken makes it very clear that the poet had in mind our failings and not our virtues, if perchance we were thus favored. May it now, however, be true, though I imagine only on rare occasions, that the reverse application of this saying can arise and some "power" might have "the giftie" to tell us of some virtues of which we had not been even aware and thus spur us on to still greater accomplishments.

Be that as it may, looking back more than fifty years and having had the privilege of being a co-worker and associate of those pioneers in our profession in the State of Illinois who gave so freely of their time, energies and abilities, I know that not one of them realized at that time the high quality of their efforts nor the sound foundations upon which they were building. History, however, will give these Founding Fathers high credit for their vision as to the future great possibilities of our profession.

It will therefore be my endeavor as a historian to record in these pages the activities of those men who organized in 1897 the first society of practicing public accountants under the name of "The Illinois Association of Public Accountants"; who after six years of strenuous work succeeded in securing the Certified Public Accountancy Act in 1903; who then organized in 1903 our present Society, "The Illinois Society of Certified Public Accountants," and initiated many other important contributions to our profession, so that their successors who are now practicing may better appreciate their heritage.

172

1

How "ithers" looked upon the work carried out in the early days
by the pioneers of our profession, it is indeed fortunate that I find among my
papers a copy of the article written by Homer S. Pace, a distinguished and
highly respected Certified Public Accountant of New York, which appeared in
the May 1927 issue of "The American Accountant."

To read, learn and inwardly digest the following excerpts of this
article, cannot fail to be of the greatest interest and may, I trust, spur us all
to be worthy successors of the pioneers of our profession.

"An inspiring record of accomplishment and constructive
work is disclosed by a study of the history of the Illinois Society
of Certified Public Accountants and of its predecessor, the Illinois
Association of Public Accountants.

173

"Claim is made, and apparently the claim is well founded,
that the Illinois accountants were first to form a state association
as a professional guild. Promoters of that state organization,
which came into existence March 10, 1897, may well be called
pioneers.

"From the time of its formation the Illinois organization
began to make an enviable record of constructive action in the
betterment of the profession, through constant attention to the
training of the coming generation of accountants, as well as to
the establishment and maintenance in Illinois of the highest
standards of accounting practice.

"From the beginning, practitioners in Illinois have devoted
much time and effort to public service. The historian is struck
by this fact immediately. Members of the organization were apparently among the earliest in this country to realize that public
accountants, by reason of their training and their places of responsibility in the life of their community, are in a position to
perform valuable public service that enhances their standing
and increases the stature of their profession and of their professional bodies. Illinois accountants were quick to recognize
their responsibilities and opportunities as quasi-official public
servants, and the record shows that they have met their responsibilities fully.

"Today there is found in Illinois one of the strongest organizations of professional accountants in the country, numbering 380 members (Note - in 1927) a great force for good in financial, industrial, and commercial circles - a force that has
been directed intelligently and applied wisely, thanks to careful
leadership and to a sense of loyalty on the part of the entire
membership. Because of the prominent part that the organizea
C.P.A.'s of the state have taken in important financial, legisla-

2

tive, and business matters, and because of the complete co-operation of the Illinois Society with the bankers and business and trade organizations of the state, the profession in Illinois enjoys the full confidence of the business and banking world and is on a high plane in public estimation.

"All this has not been accomplished without a carefully planned and well executed program. A policy that is at once aggressive and conservative seems to have marked the career of the organization. It has produced results that have been noted with interest by other state societies, and many features of the Illinois program have been emulated in other states.

"Closely interwoven with the history of the Illinois organization are the names of many men who have won for themselves places of distinction in the accounting world. Several of these practitioners have, in fact, become national figures.

"The inspiration that brought about the organization of the first association in Illinois probably came from New York, which had enacted a certified public accountant law in 1896 and was issuing certificates early in 1897 to those entitled to receive them. One writer describing the beginning of the Illinois movement says:

'The movement to organize a professional society in Chicago was initiated by George Wilkinson as the direct result of a visit to New York City in February, 1897, where he found other old timers exhibiting their newly acquired certificates from the University of New York. Indeed he went hotfoot from the private office of Frank Broaker (to whom the first certified public accountant certificate was issued), who had said to him, 'Wilkinson, if you fellows in Chicago want to be certified public accountants, you had better get busy and have a law passed in your own state.' And so it came about.

'Mr. Wilkinson went at once to see his friend and neighbor Ernest Reckitt, and they together called upon R. S. Buchanan. These three brother accountants, whose offices were in the same building, invited all the public accountants who had been practicing in Chicago for five years to gather at a dinner at the Wellington Hotel on March 10, 1897, when those present organized the first state society of public accountants.

'Lewis D. Jones, a chartered accountant, senior member of the firm of Jones, Caesar & Co., and representing in this country the firm of Price, Waterhouse & Co., of London, was elected president. He continued in that office until his untimely death in February, 1899.'"

My story begins with my first entering our profession in Chicago in the year 1891 as a senior accountant in the employ of Messrs. Barrow,

Wade, Guthrie & Co., but also touches on some of those events which had a direct influence on our profession in Illinois prior to that date, and carries forward the history to about the year 1912, a period of twenty-one years. Others must continue the story from the year 1912 up to date and it should be written by those who were more active in the subsequent affairs of our Society than I. While my interest in the affairs of our profession has never abated (my activities in our profession after 1912 to 1926 being more concerned with the American Institute of Accountants and its predecessors) I insisted on resigning as a director of the Society in 1912, having been an officer or director of the Illinois Association and Illinois Society since 1897, a period covering fifteen years. In 1912, or thereabouts, many of the directors felt that a policy of rotating the members of the Board should be inaugurated, a very healthy policy in my opinion, thus bringing into the management of the Society new blood and new ideas. These younger members of the Board have carried our Society to new heights of success, and it should be from the pen of one of these that the history since 1912 be recorded.

175

In concluding this introduction I desire to express my high appreciation of the assistance I have received from the special committee appointed by the directors of our Society in 1947 to edit and recommend changes in my original manuscript. Their recommendations have been most helpful. The members of this committee, consisting of Robert O. Berger, Chairman, Robert C. Brown and John A. Stolp, have given most generously of their time and experience. I also desire to express my appreciation to the firm of Lybrand, Ross Bros. & Montgomery for undertaking the typewriting of my original manuscript. I am, of course, particularly pleased that the Illinois Society authorized the publication of my manuscript during the observance of the Society's fiftieth anniversary.

CHAPTER 1

CHICAGO IN 1891 AND PRIOR

"Weep not that the world changes - did it keep
A stable changeless state, it were cause
indeed to weep"

Bryant in "Mutation"

I believe it may be accepted as axiomatic that the success of a new undertaking in any community depends very largely upon the character of its citizens. The rapid growth of our profession in Chicago, even in its primitive stages, was largely due to the fact that the businessmen of those days were alert to any new ideas possessing merit.

While not having any direct bearing upon the history of accountancy in the State of Illinois, I believe it may be of interest to briefly describe the type of men and the character of the city in the year 1891 and years following, to about the year 1900, for unquestionably we are the heirs of those pioneering days. Furthermore, the younger generation who do not know this picture of Chicago may not realize the many improvements of the past fifty years. There is certainly some analogy between the crudities existing in 1891 in the city's life and conditions and the crudities of our own professional work of the same period, and equally it may be said that as our city has grown both in its size and the beauty of its buildings, parks and boulevards during the past fifty years, our profession has had a similar growth in the recognition of our profession and the quality of the services rendered.

In 1891 the population of the metropolitan area of Chicago was approximately 1,300,000; today it is about 4,000,000, or over three times that of 1891. Of that population in 1891 a very large percentage had been born in other communities and consisted for the most part of people of a pioneering character, people who had possessed the courage of starting life in new sur-

5

roundings, willing to meet hardships and to hew for themselves and their families an independence and a livelihood. Little wonder that, with these fine attributes of character, combined with the natural advantage of location, the City of Chicago grew rapidly into a prosperous center for the entire Middle West. And because such people had of their own experience known the difficulties and hardships of a life in new surroundings, they were, in my opinion, interested in assisting other newcomers to make a successful start in their business or profession. This attitude was probably due to the fact that the fast growing city required a steady immigration of workers to fill the demands of its rapidly growing industries, for as I remember Chicago in those days we had few problems arising from unemployment.

Because of these conditions it was comparatively easy to secure access to and an interview with the heads of business concerns, who in those days, did not find it necessary to hide themselves in any "Sanctum sanctorum," for such asylums of refuge from the public hardly existed. The proprietor of a business or a president of a company usually had his desk in the open office with no defenses in the shape of "information desks" in order to keep him from the intrusion of strangers, and while undoubtedly this condition may have had some drawbacks, it made business pleasant for all concerned. This is mentioned, not with any thought of criticizing the conditions of today which are necessarily so different from those in the past, but rather to explain why the members of a new profession such as ours met with such a comparatively quick response from and easy Entre' to the businessmen of those times. We had a story to tell and we were given the opportunity of telling it and proving that we could be of a very distinct service to the community.

It must not be inferred from the foregóing paragraph that the businessmen of 1891 were any more virtuous than those of today, for, if anything, the reverse might be nearer the truth. Human strengths and weaknesses do

6

not change a great deal in the course of fifty years. The financially successful men of 1891 were shrewd, and in some cases were hard task masters and
possessed a code of ethics which left much to be desired. Those were the
days of secret rebates in respect to railroad freights and other dishonest
practices were not infrequent. These conditions were largely corrected by
government legislation which became pronounced with the turn of the century.

Enough has probably been now said concerning the character of
the people in Chicago in 1891. In the main, I suppose they averaged about the
same then as now, some saints, many sinners and a very large percentage of
good, kindly, and honest men and women who lived quiet and decent lives,
bringing up their children in the love of God, their country and their neighbors.
President Lincoln said that God must love the common people for he made so
many of them, and I am thankful to say that it was my good fortune to have
known many of them, and the memory of their lives is the best antidote to
pessimism.

It may be interesting to consider briefly the changes during the
past fifty years in respect to the hours of work and the character of our pas-
times, for here we do find great differences. Business hours were long,
leàving less time to recreation. Today we have a minimum wage and a maximum hour law. In 1891 a sixty hour week was not unusual and no overtime
was paid. It, of course, was not an entirely healthy situation, but probably
since then the pendulum has swung too much to the other direction. A man
working sixty hours a week had little time for sports or games, and in 1891
there were few who could indulge in such recreations.

The two great games that were most popular in 1891 were foot-
ball and baseball, but the "grown-ups" did not play games, they only watched
them. Tennis was indulged in by only a very few, while basketball was unknown.

7

Looking back it seems to me that most of us got our exercise in gardening, hunting and fishing. This also was the "Horse and Buggy Age" not only in a metaphorical manner of speech but as an actual form of quiet recreation. In my own experience one of the greatest treats was when I hired a buggy or surrey on a Sunday afternoon and drove around the parks accompanied by my wife and children.

One of the first golf courses laid out in the Chicago area was at Glenview in 1896 and shortly after that the Onwentsia course at Lake Forest, but it was then only a game for the rich. Strange as it may seem, horseback riding and swimming in or sailing on Lake Michigan were only moderately indulged in. We all worked six days in the week, and it was only after several years after golf had become so popular that Saturday afternoons became a holiday. What a difference to the present conditions when many businessmen do not attend their office any part of a Saturday. The race tracks were very popular then, as they are today, in addition to which trotting horses were much in vogue. The race track afforded the public accountant some special investigations into frauds, by reason of the defalcations of "trusted employees" who tried the "get rich quick" method of gambling.

As an offset to this lack of sports, I think people were more neighborly than they are now, as people lived almost exclusively in houses, apartments being practically unknown. Attendance at Church, Masonic, and other lodges also afforded much of our social activity, for moving pictures and the radio did not then exist.

It is probable that the greatest changes in our lives during the past fifty years have been due to the extraordinary advances of science. Up to 1891 science had given us the steamboat and steam engine, both stationary and locomotive, the telegraph and cable, but we depended upon gas and oil for lighting our streets and homes.

The telephone and the typewriter were in their infancy. Accountants' reports prior to 1892 were usually written in longhand, so that good handwriting was a necessary accomplishment. I have a very vivid memory of having to prepare, in my own handwriting, three copies of a long report dealing with an audit of a large packing house in Kansas City, but after that experience I purchased a typewriter, hired a stenographer and typist and then taught her how the exhibits and schedules should be set up and the whole report bound up. Mr. George Wilkinson, who later became my partner and who was such an important factor in the advancement of our profession, told me that about the year 1890 when he was in the employ of Barrow, Wade, Guthrie & Co., in their New York office, Mr. Anyon, the senior partner, purchased a typewriter. Mr. Wilkinson, being of a mechanical turn of mind, began to play with it and having mastered some of its intricacies wrote a whole report on it. Mr. Anyon was delighted and requested him to write another report on the typewriter, but Mr. Wilkinson, very wisely, seeing that his mechanical aptitude might result in his becoming an expert typist instead of a public accountant, refused to have anything more to do with this great adjunct to an accountant's service to his client.

Humorous stories are told of the introduction of the typewriter into business houses. Like all new inventions, there was a considerable amount of criticism and inertia before it was accepted as an economic factor in office operation. Some business men used to say, "Why should I pay $125.00 for a machine when I can buy a pen for two cents." Some people were insulted when they received typewritten letters, even as today some people seem to think it is improper for their friends to write them typewritten letters of a social character. One man received an answer to a typewritten letter somewhat as follows: "I do not think it was necessary for you to have your letters to me taken to the printers and set up like a handbill. I have attended school and I

9

know writing, reading and arithmetic, and you sure insult my intelligence by supposing I cannot read handwriting."

In 1891 we had no electricity either for lighting our homes or for other domestic purposes, no motor cars, trucks or tractors, and of course no aeroplanes. Moving pictures, radios and marconigrams were yet to be discovered. What a difference from today when we have pictures in our newspapers of the scenes of the day before from all over the world! It was only about twenty-five years ago I attended a notable dinner at the Union League Club for the purpose of listening for the first time over the radio to the music and singing at the grand opera at the Auditorium Theatre about a quarter of a mile away, but the only sounds that could be heard were some terrifying squeaks and the whole affair was a "flop."

However, notwithstanding the lack, during the "nineties" and the first decade of this century, of the many means of entertainment now enjoyed, as also the use of the many labor-saving devices now part of the enjoyment of most business offices, I am old fashioned enough to believe we had just as good a time as we all believe we have now, and perhaps we had a better time, for our pleasures cost but little, most of them being such as we created for ourselves.

In conclusion a brief-word concerning the office buildings in what is termed "the loop" may be of interest inasmuch as it deals with the subject of obsolescence from an accounting point of view.

I have seen from the year 1888 to date, a period of sixty years, the erection of every structure facing on La Salle Street from Randolph Street to Jackson Boulevard and including the Board of Trade Building. I have seen two buildings not only erected but also torn down as being obsolete; namely, the Woman's Temple Building on the southwest corner of La Salle and Monroe Streets and the Masonic Temple on the northeast corner of State and Randolph

Streets. The life of these buildings was supposedly over fifty years, but actually their financial life was much less for the reason that they were losing money for their owners for at least ten years prior to their demolition.

To Certified Public Accountants there is an interesting lesson to be learned from these facts; namely, that in the case of business buildings, obsolescence and not "wear and tear" is the chief and all important factor in the calculation of rates for depreciation.

This lesson turned out to be a valuable one in my practice. Prior to about 1924, the Treasury Department had never admitted obsolescence as a factor in calculating depreciation on buildings, though they admitted it in the case of machinery. Clients of mine owned the North American Building at the northwest corner of State and Monroe Streets, but not the land on which the building was erected. However, they had a ground lease for a ninety-nine year period. In the preparation of their income tax returns they had taken a depreciation rate of 2-1/2 per cent. Four or five years after the building had been completed, examiners from the Income Tax Department claimed that as there was a ninety-nine year lease, and as unquestionably from a purely physical standpoint the building could stand up for ninety-nine years, only a one per cent rate for depreciation would be permitted. Mr. Louis Eckstein, one of the owners, sent for me and on my recommendation he decided to fight not only this claim but several others of minor importance. Mr. Alden was then the head of the Income Tax Department in Chicago, and at a hearing shortly after the circumstances narrated above, all the claims of his staff were overruled, except the claim in respect to depreciation which was so fundamental and important it had to be referred to Washington. I was fortunate in being able to secure on the legal side the services of Mr. Albert L. Hopkins. In due course Washington sent two representatives to hear this case.

In the meantime, I had prepared a "brief" covering this whole

182

11

subject, much of it taken from my own experience in the City of Chicago. I cited case after case of buildings once profitable being no longer so, due to newer buildings with better facilities having been erected, thus taking away the tenants of the older buildings; also how in certain cases the older buildings had to be wrecked. The case of the City of Los Angeles was also cited as an illustration that over night the whole shopping center of the city moved to an entirely new location. Eventually we won our case, as it was based upon facts which could not be controverted.

This case is known among lawyers as the North American Building Case, and it was the first time that the Income Tax Department at Washington acknowledged obsolescence of buildings as a factor in arriving at depreciation.

CHAPTER 2

Book-keeping and Accounting Methods in 1891

"Thus times do shift, each thing his turn does hold;
New things succeed, as former things grow old."

Herrick in "Ceremonies for Candlemas"

In the year 1494 Lucas Pacioli printed the first text on Double
Entry Book-keeping. A translation from the Italian into English was made
in 1914 by John Bart Geisjbeek, a Certified Public Accountant of Denver,
Colorado. Briefly it may be stated that Pacioli's records consisted of (i)
what used to be termed the "Day Book," in which all transactions were entered as they occurred, whether they were for cash received or disbursed,
or for goods sold or bought, or for returned merchandise; and (ii) a ledger
similar in principal to what we use today, to which each and every Entry in
the "Day Book" was posted, Debit and corresponding Credit. Pacioli introduced the use of such impersonal accounts as Cash, Merchandise, Expense,
etc.

The use of the Day Book continued for many years and in fact
I remember distinctly seeing such a record in England when I was about 18
years of age, but instead of posting direct from the "Day Book" to the
Ledger, the entries in the Day Book were transcribed into the Cash Book,
Sales Book, Purchase Journal and General Journal as might be necessary,
so as to arrive at Cash Balances, Total Sales, Total Purchases, etc.; the
General Journal being used to provide a place for recording all other Entries.
I do not remember having seen a "Day Book" in use in the United States, but
in 1891, the only book-keeping records in general use were those listed above,
and these were always bound books, usually very heavy and cumbersome to
handle and of course always written up in ink. All letters, invoices, etc.,

184

13

were written with what was termed Copying Ink and copies were secured by the slow process of placing the originals with a damp cloth, in a Copy book of thin paper, and using a press in order to bring sufficient pressure so that an impression of the original would be transferred on to the paper of the Copy-book. From this copy book, the entries in the Sales Book were made, showing date, name of customer and the total of the invoice and sometimes columns in order to distribute various classifications of sales.

The bound ledgers usually contained anywhere from 500 to 1000 pages, probably half of which would be used for the larger accounts, one page to each account; one quarter of the pages would be divided into two parts, so that each page would record the transactions of two accounts and the last quarter of the pages divided into four parts. As it was quite impossible when starting a new ledger to determine with any accuracy the number of pages that an account might finally require before another ledger was opened, it was quite customary to find that an account was forwarded to some other page. Naturally all pages in such ledgers were numbered and an account started on page 10 might, when that page was full of entries, be forwarded to page 99, then to page 150, then to 209 and so forth. This procedure necessitated the use of an index to show the page numbers of each account; but such indexes were not always used, in which case the book-keeper was supposed to enter at the bottom of the page, the new page number to which the account was car-ried. Often, however, no notation was made as the book-keeper knew the new page number of the current account. From the above it will be seen that the public accountant making an audit would have many difficulties locating the accounts, much time being lost thereby.

The introduction of loose-leaf ledgers by Ira W. Rubel and the Baker Vawter Company was probably one of the most valuable aids to modern books of account, both concerns acquiring patents on these devices.

14

The first time that the name of Baker Vawter & Co. appeared in the Chicago classified directory was in 1897 in which this company described itself as "Devisers of Business Systems", but it was not until 1901 that it advertised its Loose-Leaf Records. Shortly thereafter a Mr. Gifford Jones secured other patents which were also well-known as Jones' Perpetual Ledgers. These concerns were for many years the largest manufacturers of Loose-Leaf Records.

The use of loose-leaf forms for books of original entry came a few years later, for at first it was considered too dangerous to use them for fear of substitutions of the original pages by new pages, for the purpose of covering up fraud by entries differing from those contained on the original page, and that in consequence such books of account would not be accepted as evidence in a Court of Law.

The introduction of "loose leaves" in a binder was not entirely original with Baker Vawter & Company, though I believe they may have been the first concern to use "loose leaves" as a Ledger. I am indebted to Maurice S. Kuhns, one of the oldest members of the Illinois Society for the following account of the original concept of loose leaf records.

"Edward C. Page and James B. McCleery, two entry clerks employed by Selz, Schwab & Co. a well known wholesale shoe house conceived the first practical loose-leaf system which completely eliminated the use of the old-fashioned order book and in March 1883 secured a patent on this invention (No. 273,301) which was acquired by Rubel Bros., Chicago printers. Mr. Maurice S. Kuhns of Horne & Kuhns, public accountants of Boston had patented or originated the Safeguard Ledger, a form of ledger which was very well known and used by many business concerns, and used largely at first by banks and known as "The Boston Ledger". In the year 1885 Rubel Bros. and Horne & Kuhns joined forces and in 1890 organized the Safeguard Account Co., in which company the original patentors Page and McCleery were employed as book-keepers. Later the Safeguard Account Company organized (for the purpose of printing their forms) The Workman Mfg. Co. in Chicago, which is a prosperous concern still doing an extensive business, and the Safeguard Account Company was taken over by Mr. Kuhns under the name of M. S. Kuhns & Co. Certified Public Accountants."

15

With a few exceptions, notably in the case of Insurance Companies and Agencies, no control accounts were kept, and in order to secure a trial balance the balance of each and every account in the ledger had to be arrived at, such trial balance consisting of all impersonal accounts, customers and creditors accounts.

As all entries were in ink it was necessary that the book-keepers and clerks wrote legibly and as there were no adding or calculating machines in those days, the book-keeper had to be rapid and accurate with figures.

Special columns in books of original entry were in vogue in 1891 and prior thereto, but their use was quite limited. The balance of the cash account appearing in the cash book usually consisted of cash in the bank or banks, plus the currency and coin in the cash drawer. The value of an Imprest system was little known. This lack of systematic control was a great aid to dishonest cashiers in covering up shortages and the fact that usually the cashiers also frequently kept the General Ledgers, assisting them in any manipulation of the records.

What is commonly known as a Voucher System in conjunction with Voucher Journals became very popular about the year 1897. The adoption of Check Vouchers and The Voucher Journal were distinct improvements in book-keeping methods, but like many good things the use of Voucher Journals with its innumerable columns was overdone. These records were bound books, each page being about 18" by 14" containing at least 200 folios. When opened such a record would be three feet or more wide, and would contain as many as thirty columns, many of such columns only having three or four entries in a month. The time taken in carrying forward the total of each column with consequent chances of error, was, of course, much more than if each item in those columns which were little used, had been posted direct, while the clumsiness and weight of the record was a serious hindrance to rapid work. On one occasion when I was requested to make a special investigation, the book-keeper, with much pride, informed me that all entries of whatsoever kind, were entered in one book, there being a column for every impersonal account they carried. In the center of each page there was a space of about three inches for describing the entry and on each side were columns "ad infinitum" both debit and credit. I was informed that the great advantage of this monstrosity was that it took the place of a general ledger, and that by taking off the total of each column, you secured a balance sheet and profit and loss account. It almost required a hoist or a powerfully built man to get this book from the vault to the book-keepers desk.

The use of cards for carrying ledger accounts came into vogue, if I remember rightly, about the year 1900 or a bit later.

In the majority of businesses there were no systematic means of arriving at the cost of goods manufactured and even when a cost system had been installed there existed many shortcomings due to the limited development of this most important subject. In 1891 John Mann, a chartered accountant of Glasgow, Scotland, wrote a very interesting book on this subject (it was a "natural" that a Scot would deal with it) which I had the privilege of studying about the year 1893. This may have been the cause of my taking a great deal of interest in this matter, for I appear to have written an article on the subject which was published in the Journal of Accountancy in the year 1909. An examination of the number of articles and books listed in the 1920 number of The Accountants Index under the caption of Cost and Factory Accounting showed a total of about 325, of which however only seventeen had been published prior to the year 1900.

Also in 1891 a book was published entitled "Cost Records of Pratt & Whitney", but the lack of literature on this subject would indicate that prior to 1900 there must have been little interest in this most important

17

phase of our professional work which has now become such a factor in the success of manufacturing concerns in the United States.

Andrew Carnegie (also a Scot) was one of the first pioneers in the introduction of Cost Accounting, maintaining a considerable staff in his Cost Department and he attributed his great financial success to his knowledge of his costs in the steel industry.

The Westinghouse Air Brake Company and the National Cash Register Company had, to my own knowledge, installed cost accounting as important factors in their plants as early as 1896 for it was my privilege to bring their cost methods up to date several years later.

In the early years of the twentieth century John Lee Nicholson, Clinton H. Scovell and Frank E. Webner contributed much towards improvements in Cost Accounting by their books and articles.

The disastrous results of a lack of any appreciation of the fundamental necessity for a Cost System may be offered at this time.

About the year 1915 I was engaged to investigate the financial condition of a corporation engaged in the manufacture of stationary engines and boilers and to report to its bankers the causes why this concern, though at one time financially strong, had in later years shown heavy losses and was having difficulty in meeting its obligations. These losses appeared to have commenced at the time that the company started to manufacture boilers, theretofore it having confined its activities solely to building engines.

I discovered that the company's cost department had distributed the total factory expenses on the basis of the direct labor of each department. In the case of engines, due to the use of "Automatics," direct labor was small and factory expenses were high, while in the case of boilers the reverse situation existed. The result was that the cost department had reported the cost of engines much lower than the true cost and the cost of boilers higher than the actual.

As selling prices were largely based upon these erroneous costs, the engines which were sold resulted in an actual loss. On the other hand the selling prices of boilers, being based on erroneously high costs, resulted in a shrinkage of these sales, due to competition of other concerns quoting lower prices.

In the foregoing paragraphs an attempt has been made to describe the book-keeping and cost accounting methods in 1891 up to 1900 and even later. Comparing these conditions with methods now in use, the advances have been spectacular. The introduction of mechanical devices has, in large measure, been responsible for this situation, among which may be mentioned type-writers with adding machine attachments, loose leaf-books of account, calculating machines of many varieties, Hollereth and similar machines using punched cards and International Business Machines for the purpose of securing statistical information and manifolding devices for many purposes.

These, and others which might be mentioned, together with the development of cost accounting technique, have indeed revolutionized the book-keeping procedures in the past fifty years. Another very noticeable change is in the personnel of the office employes. Fifty years ago it was a rarity to see any woman employed in an office; today a very large proportion of office employes are women who became most proficient in handling the office machines referred to above.

190

CHAPTER 3

Public Accounting in Illinois in 1891 and Prior

"The old order changeth, yielding place to new"

Tennyson in "The Passing of Arthur"

In a previous chapter I have attempted to describe briefly the
types of people living in Chicago in 1891 and its buildings, etcetera. These descriptions have had little connection, if any, with the practice of our profession, but on the other hand they may have prepared the way for a comparison
of the conditions of today with those of fifty years ago or more. If the City
of Chicago was just emerging in 1891 from a past which was in some respects
crude, certainly we should not be greatly surprised to find that the profession
of accounting and auditing was on about the same footing at that time.

Inasmuch as I did not start practice as an accountant until 1891,
it has been necessary for me to delve into whatsoever records I could find
in order to give any facts of interest concerning those who advertised themselves as accountants in 1891 and prior thereto. As there was no literature
of any kind to assist me in this search, I determined to examine the Chicago
City classified directories, beginning with the first ever published and gradually working up to the year 1891. I was informed there were only two complete sets of such directories in the City of Chicago, one in the Chicago Public
Library and the other at the Historical Society Building in Lincoln Park near
North Avenue, both of which represented gifts to those institutions by the
Reuben H. Donnelley Corporation.

I was expecting to find that this research would be most uninter-
esting, for the compilation of statistics is notably dry as dead men's bones and
in this particular case the analogy was somewhat apt. Fortunately I was very
pleasantly surprised for I found much of interest and amusement in glancing

over the pages of these supposedly dry tomes.

The first Chicago directory ever published was in 1839 (109 years ago), and was called "Fergus' Directory of the City of Chicago." It contained 71 pages, of which 32 pages gave the names of all householders in the city, about 1,600 in all. It would seem that just prior to the printing of this directory there had been an election for mayor (Chicago became incorporated as a city in 1837), the opposing candidates being Wm. B. Ogden and John H. Kinzie. The 1839 directory gave a complete list of those who had voted at that election and for whom each had cast a vote. It is evident there was no Australian form of ballot in those days.

But it was the reading of the advertising matter contained in these early directories that afforded entertainment and threw some light on the character of the people 100 years ago. Evidently people at that time were as gullible as those of today. A certain Dr. Tew in a half page advertisement admits he is a wonderful phrenological and magnetic examiner, that he may be consulted at his residence in all cases of nervous or mental difficulty and that his remedies will enable him to relieve and cure any case of monomania, insanity or recent madness; that he can give correct and true delineations of mental dispositions of different persons which will be in every way profitable to all who wish to understand the mysteries of their own natures and how they may use their attributes to the best advantage. Dr. Tew's style of writing may be out of date, but we have our Dr. Tews today, only they call themselves by other names.

The 1850 directory possesses some special interest, for it gives the population of Chicago as:

Whites - males	11,978
Whites - females	10,698
Colored	378
	23,054

21

During the next year, 1851, the population of Chicago increased to 28,000, and in 1854 it was 66,000, a very rapid growth in three years. It was in the 1854-1855 directory that we find for the first time a classification of "Accountants" with eight names listed underneath. The names of these men, however, never appear in later directories. Mr. A. C. Littleton of the School of Commerce of the University of Illinois (who made an exhaustive examination of another classified directory, published by a different concern than that at the Historical Society) informs me that an 1851 Directory gives the name of a certain James Woolley under the classification of Accountants, and the 1856 directory a Francis Pasdeloup. In the 1857-1858 directory there appear the names of two men under the classification of "Accountants." Then there was a long gap of six or seven years with no names of accountants in the directories. In the year 1865, however, a certain David Ballingall appears as the sole representative of our profession and from that time onward, there have always been accountants who could afford to pay the fee of having their names listed in the classified directory. Never more than seven names, however, appeared until the year 1884, when there were thirteen; in 1885, eight; in 1886, six; in 1887, thirteen; in 1888, sixteen; in 1889, nineteen; in 1890, twenty-four and in 1891, thirty-one.

An examination of those classified directories from the year 1865 to 1891, inclusive, (a period of twenty-seven years) shows there was a total of ninety-seven different persons listed as "accountants." Of these ninety-seven persons, fifty practiced for one year or less, eleven for two years, three for three years, one for four years, two for five years, one for six years, two for seven years and one for eight years, leaving a balance of twenty-six who were still in practice after the year 1891. Of these twenty-six accountants, one, Mr. Charles J. Bishop, had practiced continuously since 1871, a period of twenty years, and he continued in practice until the close of

1895. This gentleman must have been quite the most outstanding accountant in Chicago in his time, having practiced for twenty-five years up to the time of his death or retirement. Summarizing the length of years that these twenty-six accountants had been in practice up to the close of the year 1891, we find

In practice for 20 years	1
In practice for	7 years	1
In practice for	6 years	1
In practice for	5 years	2
In practice for	4 years	1
In practice for	3 years	4
In practice for	2 years	9
In practice for	1 year or less	7
		26

Among these twenty-six names were the following individuals or firms who either in their own name or through their partners were charter members of the Illinois Association of Public Accountants which was founded in 1897:

Name	Started Practice
J. L. Marchand	1886
Frederick F. Judd	1887
William Fries	1889
Henry Butler	1890
Price Waterhouse & Co.	1890
(Lewis D. Jones)	
Barrow, Wade, Guthrie & Co.	1891
(George Wilkinson)	
John Alexander Cooper	1891
Smith, Reckitt & Co.	
(Ernest Reckitt)	1891

The statistics given in the foregoing paragraphs tell a sad story of the heavy professional mortality of men listed as public accountants prior to 1891. This condition was due chiefly to the fact that most of them were not qualified to practice as public accountants. Undoubtedly, for the most part, they were bookkeepers who temporarily were out of jobs, who thought they could keep the "wolf from the door" by holding themselves out as "expert

accountants." In other cases they may have been regularly employed as bookkeepers during the day, adding something to their income by extra work during evenings and Sundays.

An example of the type of work carried out is well illustrated in
the following advertisement appearing in the 1881 classified directory by a
Mr. Franks in which he also states that his office hours are from one to two
PM and that he handles:

> "Complicated disputed and confused accounts; also accounts with
> executors, trustees and estates in assignments investigated and
> stated. Books opened and closed. Suspected accounts confiden-
> tially examined. Partnership settlements made."

The 1888 classified directory contains the following advertisement of Francis W. Holbrook, whom I met many years ago. He was probably
in his day one of the better known public accountants in Chicago of his type.
He states:

195

> "Confidential, Consulting and Expert Accountant
> and
> Detector of forged writings.
> Practical experience of over 30 years.
> Former general manager and holding full
> power of attorney from late firm of
> A. T. Stewart & Co."

Another somewhat enlightening fact brought out by an examination of the names of men advertising themselves as accountants is that in the
majority of instances it is the home address of the advertiser that was given,
indicating the very transitory nature of the accountant's work. I recall very
vividly being frequently asked by my acquaintances of those earlier years
whether or not I was still in practice as an accountant, for it seemed to be
the unanimous opinion that no one adopted our profession as his life's work
but merely used it as a stepping stone to some other and more lucrative
employment.

24

It may now be asked what was the character of these accountants of 1891 and prior and what was the nature of their accounting engagements. The answer to this question is so admirably described in the book published by Mr. James T. Anyon in 1925 entitled "Recollections of the early days of American Accountancy 1883-1893," that in the succeeding paragraphs I propose to quote excerpts from this fascinating history. Mr. Anyon's narrative specifically dealt with the conditions he found in New York City in 1886, and could be applied with equal truth to the conditions I found had existed in Chicago prior to 1891 and as a matter of fact for several years thereafter.

As will be later described in chapter 5 with the origin of The American Association of Public Accountants, Mr. Anyon came to the United States from Manchester, England, in 1886 and became a partner in the firm of Barrow, Wade, Guthrie & Co. in the following year. Probably no other man did more for our profession in New York and Illinois in its early years than Mr. Anyon and it therefore seems especially befitting that the following quotation from Mr. Anyon's book should conclude this chapter:

"It must not be imagined that all the members were men in full professional practice connected with firms having regular located offices, the names inscribed on the door, and several assistant accountants as part of their staff as we find today. There were a few of this kind but not many. The majority had merely desk-room in other peoples' offices, a few had their offices, mainly for reasons of economy, in the back parlors of their homes, while one or two did not seem to have any visible address anywhere, but when wanted were usually on hand.

"At this time (1886 to 1890) the profession did not advance in public favor to any pronounced extent. It did progress somewhat but not to a degree at all proportionate to the desires of those engaged in its practice. The reason for this was partly the fault of the accountants and partly the fault of the public. The former seemed to be unable, mainly on account of their limited knowledge, to impress the latter that their services were anything different to that pertaining to bookkeeping, and the public on its part showed no disposition to be convinced that such a profession as public accounting was actually a needed one. The public accountants were usually referred to by the general public as 'Experts' or 'Expert Accountants' and sometimes as 'Checkers.' It was quite customary for them to advertise their calling in the daily papers and fi-

25

nancial magazines, and these advertisements would run something like the following, 'John Doe, Expert Accountant, Books written up and balanced, Tangled Accounts straightened out and so forth.' The word 'tangled' seemed a favorite word to use and appeared quite often in these advertisements. However, business men generally, notwithstanding, did not take very kindly to these new 'experts' and the service they advertised. If some real accounting or bookkeeping problem had to be taken in hand, the average business man would often go to his lawyer, or better still, as costing less money, to his banker and obtain the services of one of the bank clerks. Just as the general public was not particularly impressed with these experts, so bankers on their part had very little or no use for their services, while lawyers looked upon them more in the light of trespassers on their own business preserves than anything else, for lawyers in those times did or rather tried to do any special work in accounting matters that now falls to members of the accounting profession.

"The average public accountant in the very early days of our profession, although full of zeal and ambition to excel, lacked personality and impressiveness. He failed to convey to the business men the conviction that he was an expert in his profession or that he was especially expert in any thing. He knew his business in a simple elemental way but possessed few ideas and little or no vision. They had adopted as their calling in life a profession, the vastness and importance of which they had little or no conception. Nevertheless, they loved their calling, for it appealed to them as interesting and, in a way, fascinating. Besides, they had a feeling it represented something really wanted in the business world and that sooner or later this something would take tangible form and be recognized. But these feelings were uncertain and indefinite and left them floundering as it were in an unknown region, vaguely conscious of its extent and importance. They were like children the old philosopher referred to as 'picking pebbles on the seashore' while the great sea of accounting knowledge, unknown and unexplored, lay before them, but they were ever ready and anxious to make any adventure on that sea to explore it and to learn, understand and master its secrets.

"This primitive member of the new profession was satisfied nevertheless that he filled an important role in business life, and that in accountancy matters he was an authority. He felt, in any event, that he was in a class much higher than the usual commonplace bookkeeper, although the latter, on his part, had a feeling that the former was not a bit better than himself and, in a good many ways, not as good. He loved to discuss his business with brother accountants and in doing this usually dwelt on the simple little problems that cropped up in his everyday practice. But these were entirely bookkeeping problems and had no semblance at all to the higher questions, theoretical or practical, that constantly confront members of the profession in these days.

"It is true there were some business men who had a fairly good conception of the character of the profession and saw advantages in it which when better understood would undoubtedly be of benefit to business at large. On the contrary there were a great many who had very mixed ideas as to just what the business of the expert accountant was and exactly what he professed to do. Some considered that he was an experienced bookkeeper and no more; others looked upon him as a man whose business it was to detect fraud, embezzlement and stealing, and that his employment was of value only in this direction, while quite a few had a vague idea that he was merely a man of figures, a rapid and unerring calculator who could add up two or three columns of figures at a time, could tell you immediately the square or cube root of any number or say off-hand, for example, what one dollar put out at six per cent compound interest per annum at the time Columbus discovered America would amount to today.

"In the old days, and as a matter of fact to a large extent in these (1925), accountants were often looked upon and referred to as 'men of figures.' Now just what does this mean in the minds of those using the term? It means a man who deals in and loves figures for themselves, calculates, balances accounts, prepares elaborate statements, looks for errors, thinks figures, sometimes juggles them and always writes and talks them, and in proportion to his skill in this direction, so does he consider himself a good and capable accountant. A man of such a type in his general practice is likely to base his findings and conclusions on the figures he finds on records rather than on the facts behind those figures. The latter are paramount. If, for example, he sees on records he is examining a property asset standing at a certain value, he is prompted to accept such value as a truth because the figures say it is so. The well-trained and experienced accountant of today on the other hand is not a man of figures in the sense as above outlined. He is rather a man of facts and truths, and figures become subordinate and are used only as a means of expressing such facts and truths.

"It was, therefore, not only the character or rather lack of character as well as lack of knowledge on the part of the majority of accountants that tended to retard the advance of the profession in public favor, but another thing of equal importance, namely, the fact that practitioners seemed unable to create in the minds of business men the faith and confidence in their integrity and honesty which is the essence of the profession these days and there was some good reason for this. Some practitioners did not seem fully to realize their responsibility to their profession, or to third parties who might be called upon to act on the results of their work. They did not consider themselves bound to precision and truth in the same degree or to anything like the same extent as their brother accountants of these days. It was not an uncommon thing to find accountants at times 'stretching a point' in favor of their clients (mainly in matters relating to the preparation of statements for presentation to banks or the sale of a business) to show a financial condition more favorable than was actually the case, and in many instances clients expected them to do this. It is most gratifying and satisfying in these times to see how careful and thorough accountants generally are in the presentation of the results of their work and how strictly they adhere to truth and precision irrespective of the outcome or any outside considerations."

199

CHAPTER 4

History of the Profession of Public Accountants from 1891 to 1897, together with some personal reminiscences

"When time who steals our years away
Shall steal our pleasures too,
The memory of the past will stay
And half our joys renew"

Moore "Song"

It is the purpose of this chapter to cover the rapid growth of our profession during the period 1891 up to 1897 when the Illinois Association of Public Accountants was organized and the causes of that growth.

For the sake of brevity in this and subsequent chapters I shall refer to "The Illinois Association of Public Accountants" as "The Illinois Association", and to its successor in 1904 named "The Illinois Society of Certified Public Accountants" as "The Illinois Society".

A perusal of the preceding chapter reveals that in the U.S.A. before the years 1890 and 1891 there were, with a very few exceptions, no public accountants as that term is now understood and most certainly our profession had received no recognition by the leaders of business enterprises. Yet by the year 1897, in the brief period of six or seven years a great change had taken place and our activities were largely recognized as inherently pertaining to a profession.

The reason for this actually began prior to 1891, probably about the year 1888 when British capital, seeking to secure higher rates of profits than were possible in Great Britain, was invested in large enterprises in the United States.

As is well known, prior to 1890 our profession had been legally recognized, first in Scotland and soon thereafter in England and Wales; a body of well trained accountants existed and the independent auditor was

29

elected by the stock-holders of corporations.

It naturally followed that when British capital secured the control of certain businesses in the United States, British professional accountants were sent to this country to audit such concerns, for the purpose of reporting their findings on their return to Great Britain. This being a somewhat costly matter due to traveling and hotel expenses, the following British firms of accountants opened branch offices in the United States, believing that, not only would they, thereby, give better and more economical services to their British clients, but also that through new contacts with purely American capital they would expand their practice.

201

> Price, Waterhouse & Co.
> Deloitte, Dever, Griffiths & Co.
> Broads, Patterson & Co.

The firm of Barrow, Wade, Guthrie & Co., an off-shoot of the British firm of Thomas, Wade, Guthrie & Co. had opened an office in New York City in 1883, but in doing so it was for other reasons than those given in the foregoing paragraph. Mr. Guthrie may, however, have had the vision to foresee the future possibilities of his profession in this country through the investment of British capital which later became an accomplished fact and in which his firm also participated.

Prior to 1888 British capital in the United States was largely invested in Fire Insurance Companies, Railroads, and Farm Mortgages. Due to the fact that all British fire insurance companies paid promptly all losses incurred in the Chicago fire in 1871, while many of the American fire insurance companies failed to meet their similar obligations, the British companies captured a large amount of this business and correspondingly expanded.

It was the custom of these British fire insurance companies to send their auditors to the United States, but in the early nineties they en-

gaged as their auditors British firms having offices in this country to conduct
monthly audits. Thus, in my own firm (my partner A. W. Smith being a Chartered Accountant) was included among our clients the London Assurance
Corp'n, the Northern Assurance Company, the Queen Insurance Company
and the London and Lancashire Fire Insurance Company.

In 1888 to 1890 British capital was especially attracted by investments in Breweries as will be noted by the list of breweries submitted
below, showing date of registration on the London Stock Exchange.

Each of the following companies was composed of from two to
fifteen individual breweries. Both the original investigations and subsequent
audits for a considerable length of time were made by British Chartered
Accountants.

Bartholomay Brewing Co., Rochester, N.Y.	April 11, 1889
St. Louis Breweries, Limited	Dec. 6, 1889
City of Chicago Brewing & Malting Co.	June 2, 1890
San Francisco Breweries, Limited	Unknown
City of Baltimore United Breweries, Ltd.	Nov. 8, 1889
Milwaukee & Chicago Breweries, Limited	Dec. 31, 1890
United States Brewing Co.	May 20, 1889
New York Breweries, Limited	Aug. 11, 1889
New England Breweries, Limited	Mar. 27, 1890
Denver United Breweries, Limited	June 10, 1889
Cincinnati Breweries, Limited	Oct. 29, 1889
Springfield Breweries, Limited	Mar. 27, 1890
Washington Breweries, Limited	Apr. 12, 1888
Indianapolis Breweries, Limited	Nov. 8, 1889
Chicago Breweries, Limited	Apr. 9, 1888

In addition to the Breweries listed above, other audits undertaken by British Accountants in the early 90's included:

Boston United Gas Co.
Procter & Gamble
American Sugar Refining Co.
Pratt & Whitney
Chicago Junction Railway & Union Stock Yards Co.
New York Belting & Packing Co.

(All of the above information, both as to Breweries, and other
companies is based on information contained in the "London Stock Exchange

31

Intelligence" for the year 1896.)

It will, therefore, be realized that our profession from 1891 (and before) to 1897 had received a great impetus due to the investment of British capital and also by the excellent character of the audits made by British Chartered Accountants. This development necessarily attracted many other concerns controlled by American capital to a realization that they should adopt the British custom of engaging public accountants to audit their books and to prepare and certify the financial statements in the annual reports. These new conditions necessarily increased the clientele of firms of accountants having no affiliations with Chartered Accountants in Great Britain.

While public accountants in New York City were the first to enjoy a steadily increasing growth and a recognition of the value of engaging qualified firms, it was not long before we, in Illinois, also derived substantial benefits, so that in the period covered in this chapter, great gains accrued to those accountants who maintained offices in Chicago. It is for this reason that the investment of British capital in the United States must form an important place in any history of accounting in Illinois.

In addition, our profession in Illinois was materially strengthened by the opening of offices in Chicago by Price, Waterhouse & Co. in 1890 and in 1891 by Barrow, Wade, Guthrie & Co. In 1892 Mr. Arthur Young, coming from Scotland, arrived in Chicago in order to oversee the interests of certain Scottish investors. In 1904 Mr. Young and Mr. Stuart opened an office as independent accountants in Chicago under the firm name of Stuart, Young & Co. which two or three years later became Arthur Young & Co., Mr. Stuart retiring. It was also about the year 1894 that Mr. Frank M. Boughey, a Chartered Accountant, arrived in Chicago as a representative of Broads, Patterson & Co. of London, England.

The organization of the Illinois Association in 1897 (see Chapter

32

6) was therefore a natural corollary in the advancement of the interests of public accountants in Illinois.

The author hopes he may be forgiven if he now takes the opportunity of referring to one or two of his personal reminiscences during the years 1891 to 1898. He believes that these episodes may serve to illustrate some of the conditions and difficulties in those early days of our profession. The last episode is given for the purpose of showing the progress and recognition of our profession.

In 1891, and for some time thereafter, the members of our profession were, by quite a number of people, looked upon as a type of detective in the discovering of defalcations, or as "lightning calculators" especially qualified in the finding of errors in books of account.

During this period it was frequently a sad and pathetic experience to find defalcations and other irregularities. It may sound like an exaggeration, but it was my experience that approximately in every three new audits we would discover defalcations in every two. This condition was undoubtedly due to the fact that no audits had ever been made prior to that time, no fidelity bonds placed on trusted employes, no internal check was made of cash receipts and disbursements and in numerous cases the cashier also kept the general ledger and journal. In smaller concerns he also kept the customers' ledgers.

Cashiers and book-keepers felt it was a reflection on their characters if an accountant was called in to make an audit, their belief being that public accountants were never engaged unless a defalcation had been discovered or suspected. In the year 1893 or thereabouts, I was requested to make an audit of a large retail coal concern. The office staff was courteous but cold to my staff. After the audit was completed the office manager, who was also the cashier, told me that at first he and the other employes had felt outraged

204

33

when informed that outside accountants had been engaged to conduct an audit, but that now he was delighted an audit had been made, for prior to that time his employer did not know whether he was honest or not, but now his employer knew he was honest. It was this same concern that later engaged the services of Mr. David J. Levi, when the cashier referred to above had resigned. Mr. Levi, then by no means a young man, but ambitious to increase his knowledge of accountancy, informed me he was most desirous of becoming a Certified Public Accountant. I encouraged him in this worthy object, with the result that after a course of study he passed the C.P.A. examinations in 1906 receiving Certificate No. 93. He later became a member of the staff of Walton, Joplin & Co. and an instructor in the Walton School of Commerce.

205

Another episode illustrating the ignorance of "the man on the street", was somewhat quaint, for I failed to secure the audit of a concern manufacturing "mouse traps" for the reason I had never audited a similar concern before that time and therefore did not have the necessary experience.

The final episode, illustrating the reverse of those described and showing the progress of our profession, occurred when I was invited to make a "spot audit" of the books of account of the City of Chicago. I believe that this engagement was the first time that any city government in the United States had ever had its books audited by independent public accountants.

On April 6, 1897 Carter H. Harrison II was elected mayor of the City of Chicago. Desiring to secure a competent and honest man as Controller he offered this responsible post to his good friend, Mr. R. A. Waller. Mr. Waller, while not seeking this position, felt it was not only a civic duty to accept, but an obligation to his friend, Mr. Harrison.

In November or December of 1898 Mr. Waller, who was one of my clients, telephoned, asking me to come over to the City Hall, as he wanted to discuss with me some matter of importance. On arriving there he told me he

34

desired to have a "spot audit" of the City's accounts, but he also said that he realized such an examination would necessarily have to be limited in its scope, as he had only $2,500.00 in his "Contingent Fund" subject to his discretionary use, and therefore my remuneration would be limited to that amount. He went on to say that he knew it would cost me considerably over $2,500.00 but assured me that he would see to it that I would secure so much publicity from this engagement that I would, eventually, make up many times any monetary loss I might incur.

I agreed to start the audit immediately and about twelve men were busy on this assignment for a period of two to three months. Unfortunately, about a month after I started this audit, Mr. Waller died from an attack of pneumonia, so I lost a good friend, who would have secured for me the publicity I might have been entitled to. As I remember it I paid out in cash about $7,500.00 (equivalent today to $15,000.00 or more) in salaries alone, making a loss of $5,000.00.

I do not propose to outline in any detail the scope of this examination, but among other irregularities a deficiency of half a million dollars was discovered in the special assessment fund. Another irregularity brought to light by this audit was the chaotic condition in respect to the payment of bonds and coupons. In this latter case, on requesting to examine the actual bonds and interest coupons over a period of one year, we were shown a vault where all bonds and coupons paid during a number of years were lying in a disordered mass. To have attempted to put them in numerical order, so as to commence any audit, would have been a greater task than Hercules undertook in cleaning out the "Augean Stables". On reporting the situation to Mr. Waller or his successor, Mr. Kerfoot, it was decided to let "Bygones be Bygones" and to inaugurate better methods which would prevent in the future those irregularities which, it was feared, had existed in the past.

My report on the deficiency of $500,000.00 in the Special Assessment Fund created considerable notice in certain circles and eventually was given such wide publicity that a leading civic organization in Chicago insisted that a detailed investigation ought to be made by some reputable firm of public accountants to cover all matters related to special assessments. Our investigation had necessarily only touched the high spots and was only detailed in respect to the listing of the balances of all assessments, both debit and credit, from 1871 (the date of the Chicago fire, all records prior to 1871 having been destroyed in that fire) to the date of our audit.

Certain firms of public accountants were therefore requested to make tenders on a contract basis for a detailed investigation of all assessment records both in the Controller's office and also in the City Clerk's office, where the original assessment rolls were kept. My firm, of course, also received an invitation to make a bid, but having such a thorough knowledge of the intricate mess of these assessment accounts, I turned down this request. I, however, well remember stating that a bid of $200,000.00 would not be too high to conduct such an investigation.

The firm of Haskins & Sells made the lowest bid and was therefore engaged to conduct this investigation. Mr. Sells informed me many years later that this audit resulted in a considerable financial loss to his firm which, however, was largely offset by detailed investigations of other city departments on a "per diem" basis, which included the inauguration of improved systems of accounting so that future audits could be more intelligently conducted.

Haskins & Sells thoroughly earned this further recognition and it was to the credit of the "City Fathers" that they gave Haskins & Sells the opportunity of recovering some of the loss on the original contract.

CHAPTER 5

Dealing with the organization of the American
Association of Public Accountants and the passage of the first C.P.A. law in the United States.

"Great oaks from little acorns grow."

Old Proverb

No history of our profession in Illinois would be complete unless
it included an account of the organization of the American Association of Public Accountants in the City of New York in the year 1887, for it was largely
responsible in 1896 for securing the passage of the first Certified Public Accountancy Act in any state of the Union.

208

One of the immediate effects of the passage of this law was the
organization of the Illinois Association of Public Accountants in the year 1897
by accountants in Chicago who desired, through that society, to secure a similar C.P.A. in the State of Illinois.

As pointed out in Chapter 4 the accountancy profession in Illinois
had been much indebted to the accountants in New York in the years 1890 to
1897 and we who are practicing as C.P.A.'s today (1948) should be interested
in learning something concerning the birth of the American Association of
Public Accountants and of the men who took part in this creative work.

Prior to 1886 a few public accountants in Philadelphia had been
in practice, namely John Heins, Lawrence E. Brown, who had a staff of approximately a dozen men, John W. Francis who had started practice in 1869
and Charles N. Vollum who had practiced since 1875. Mr. T. Edward Ross of
the firm of Lybrand, Ross Bros. & Montgomery in a letter published in the
Journal of Accountancy appearing in its March 1925 issue wrote that he became a member of the staff of John Heins in 1887 in which letter he stated
that he was well acquainted with all of the accountants named above and also

37

cognizant of their plans to organize the first professional society of accountants in the United States. It was their idea that this society should be devoted to education in accounting under the name of "The Chartered Accountants Institute." Meetings were held in the office of John W. Francis and it was decided to apply for a charter. Mr. Ross in his letter states that the minutes of this meeting, almost, if not entirely complete, are now in the possession of the American Institute of Accountants.

Mr. George Wilkinson in an article appearing in the Journal of Accountancy in September 1927, on the occasion of the thirtieth anniversary of the Pennsylvania Institute of Certified Public Accountants corroborated the statements of Mr. Ross.

209

At this crucial time in the history of our profession, by a fortunate coincidence, Mr. Edwin Guthrie, of Manchester, England, was visiting this country for the second time in the interest of his firm in New York City of Barrow, Wade, Guthrie & Co., being accompanied by Mr. James T. Anyon who came to this country to take over the management of the New York City office. Both Mr. Guthrie and Mr. Anyon felt that there was a great need for the organization of a national organization of public accountants similar to the Chartered Accountants' Society in England and for the consummation of this plan, they had communicated by letter to various public accountants in New York City, Philadelphia and Boston, Mr. John Heins being one of them. It would appear that Mr. Heins then invited Mr. Guthrie to meet him and other public accountants in Philadelphia to discuss the project outlined by Mr. Guthrie and the latter arrived there just prior to the time that the Philadelphia accountants were about to apply for the state charter of the Chartered Accountants' Institute. The result of this meeting was that Mr. Guthrie persuaded the Philadelphia public accountants that a local state society devoted purely to education was not the answer to the advancement of our profession on a national basis, so the application for a state chapter was abandoned and Mr. Heins and his associates threw themselves whole-heartedly in support of a national organization under the name of the "American Association of Public Accountants."

Credit for the organization of this Association must therefore be given not only to Mr. Guthrie and Mr. Anyon but equally to John Heins and his associates in Philadelphia.

For a detailed account of the events that took place after Mr. Guthrie had met Mr. Heins and other Philadelphia public accountants we must turn to a book published by Mr. James T. Anyon in 1925 in which he gives his "recollections" of the organization of the American Association of Public Accountants and of other matters connected with our profession about the year 1886, as well as a brief sketch of those events that brought Mr. Guthrie to the United States in 1883 and 1886. Inasmuch as Mr. Anyon's "Recollections" were written nearly forty years after the events described and at odd times while he was traveling by train, he must be forgiven for omitting any reference to Mr. Guthrie having met Mr. Heins in Philadelphia and the prior activities of the public accountants in that city to organize a society as already described in this chapter, but in general (with a few modifications) his "Recollections" may be accepted as showing the limited appreciation of our profession by business and professional men at that time.

Mr. Anyon was a man, as the older members of our profession will remember, of great initiative, energy and ability. His history was written in a style that made his book a pleasure to read, indicating a sense of humor and a keen insight into the failings of our profession in its earlier years.

Inasmuch as both Mr. Guthrie and Mr. Anyon played such an important part in the organization of the American Association of Public Accountants it is deemed most expedient to give in this chapter excerpts from his book telling something of Mr. Guthrie's visits to America, the founding of the firm of Barrow, Wade, Guthrie & Co. in 1883, and of those events which followed Mr. Guthrie's first meeting Mr. Heins in 1886 in the creation of the Association.

Mr. Anyon was a member of the staff of Thomas, Wade, Guthrie & Co., Chartered Accountants practicing in Manchester, England, when in 1883 Mr. Guthrie, acting in the capacity of Receiver of a bankrupt concern in that country, visited the United States to investigate the character of certain assets located in the U.S.A.

Mr. Guthrie, on arriving in New York City, immediately made enquiries to secure the names of reputable public accountants, but discovered that not only was the profession as it was understood and practiced in Great Britain practically unknown in this country, but that there was no such thing as a responsible accounting firm upon whom he could rely for any assistants he might require. His attorneys in New York informed him that he did not need accountants, but that they would attend to all matters, both legal and accounting, in connection with his case.

The question, very properly asked, was, "How did business firms and corporations get along in those days without the aid and service of auditors and accountants and, in their absence, who did this class of work so necessary and essential in those times?" The answer was: It was not done; because there was no one recognized as fitted by training and experience to do it.

It was apparent to Mr. Guthrie that it was only a matter of time when the profession of accountancy as practiced in older countries would "take root and prosper" in a country as enlightened as the U.S.A. and he determined to establish an accounting practice in New York City, which, as far as he could see, would be the first of its kind in this country.

In his efforts in this direction he met, through his attorneys, Mr. John Wylie Barrow, an estimable American gentleman of culture and refinement, who was held in the highest esteem by all. Mr. Barrow, however, was an actuary rather than an accountant, whose main business was in connection with certain British fire insurance companies, being employed by them to check the vouchers and certify to the clerical accuracy of the monthly statements prepared by the Branches before being sent to the Home offices. This activity constituted his only practice.

In October, 1883, after necessary conferences and enquiries, a partnership was arranged between John W. Barrow, C. H. Wade and Edwin Guthrie under the name of Barrow, Wade, Guthrie & Co. The nucleus of this business was not large or important, for it consisted merely of the work hitherto done by Mr. Barrow with "hopes" that other matters of an accounting nature would develop in due season. Here then appeared to be an early step in the beginning of the great profession of public accounting in the United States of America.

After completing the American partnership arrangements Mr. Guthrie returned to England, offices were opened in the old Equitable Building in New York City and an assistant was engaged. With this simple foundation the firm worked on in the even tenor of its way, holding its own but gaining little, and the "hopes" of other matters developing materialized only to a very slender extent. Business thus went on up to the spring of 1886, when English partners were notified that Mr. Barrow had died and that the assistant was carrying on the business of the firm. It was anticipated that Mr. Morton, the assistant, might be made a partner in the United States business

41

in place of Mr. Barrow, but on learning that Mr. Morton intended to leave their employ in order to go into independent practice, Mr. Guthrie determined to again visit New York so as to get the affairs of the firm properly adjusted, and he arrived in New York in October, 1886, bringing with him Mr. James T Anyon to act first as a senior assistant in the New York office and later as partner.

Shortly after Mr. Anyon's arrival in New York he started an enquiry as to how our profession stood in New York. He had left in England a profession full of vitality, one that was looked upon as an essential element of business life, and so recognized in every section of business activity, but he found that these conditions existed in the United States only to a very limited extent; that public accountancy was in its infancy and that it was little known or understood as a distinct profession. A careful examination of the city directories, a scrutiny of the advertisements in the financial papers and enquiries from a few business men satisfied Mr. Anyon that there were very few persons engaged in our profession, no more than could be counted on the fingers of one hand. (This was undoubtedly an understatement by Mr. Anyon.) In New York City there was a firm called Veysey & Veysey with a staff of two or three assistants, another firm practicing under the name of Jas. Yalden & Co., while George H. Church, Louis M. Bergtheil and H. M. Tate practiced as individuals. In Philadelphia, John Heins appeared to be the only representative accountant in public practice, and in Boston a man named Rodney McLaughlin played a corresponding part.

After having thus secured the names of accountants practicing in New York, Philadelphia and Boston, Mr. Anyon put himself in communication with them either personally or by letter, pointing out to each one that he had just come to this country to join them in the conduct of the profession of accounting and that he was sure they would like to see it better known, understood and recognized by the public; that with the view of considering what might be done to attain this object he suggested it might be desirable for them to meet Mr. Edwin Guthrie and himself on a certain appointed afternoon at their firm's office at 45 William Street. One and all showed the greatest enthusiasm and interest in the proposal and agreed to attend the meeting.

On the afternoon of December 23, 1886, the gentlemen invited came at the appointed time. There were six or seven present including Mr. John Heins of Philadelphia. They were not all practicing accountants, but all evinced a decided interest in the subject of accounting. One of these was Colonel C. E. Sprague, president of the Union Dime Savings Bank. He was a lover of anything connected with accounting and took a keen interest in the fortunes of the profession. Several others professed to be accountants but took no part in public practice.

214

After formal introductions, the meeting got down to business. Mr. Guthrie was asked to take the chair, and Mr. Anyon acted as Secretary of the meeting. Mr. Guthrie then addressed the meeting, stating among other things that in Great Britain the profession was on a very high plane and that it was recognized as one of the leading professions; that the efforts of practicing accountants in the United States should be directed towards bringing about a similar condition and that he believed an institution or body similar to that now existing in England, (The Institute of Chartered Accountants in England and Wales) could be started in the United States, under the regulations of which competent accountants could practice and be recognized by the public as fully qualified so to do.

Mr. Guthrie's remarks were listened to with great attention and all freely admitted that his address had given rise to new life and zest and a keener desire for greater things. Finally on motion of Mr. Heins, which was seconded by Mr. Anyon and carried unanimously, a resolution was adopted

that the accountants then present should form themselves into an association

for the advancement and protection of the interests of the profession under

the name of the American Association of Public Accountants and that the

qualifications for membership should be ability and fitness to practice in a

public capacity.

At the date of its birth, December 23, 1886, the American Asso-

ciation of Public Accountants was without any legal status and numbered some

eight or ten individuals. It soon became known around New York and adjacent

cities that public accountants had taken steps to organize themselves as an

association with the result that many enquiries were received from persons

interested in the movement asking what were the requirements for member-

ship, the entrance fees, annual dues, etcetera. The interest of the members

continued unabated, all working in the direction of making the profession better

known and raising it to a position whereby it would be recognized as having

something of a legal status. This was eventually accomplished, and in Aug-

ust, 1887, the Association became incorporated under the laws of the State of

New York with the name and title of "American Association of Public Account-

ants." Its first officers were: President, James Yalden of New York City;

Vice President, John Heins of Philadelphia; Secretary, James T. Anyon; and

Treasurer, W. H. Veysey, of New York City.

At the time of incorporation, the Association had thirty-one mem-

bers of whom twenty-four were "Fellows" and seven "Associates." This

number, with a few others who for various reasons did not or could not join

(the main reason being the payment of the entrance fee for the time being)

practically constituted the total exponents and representatives of the profession

of accounting at that time in this country.

Mr. Anyon, in his book, records the fact that he became a partner in the firm of Barrow, Wade, Guthrie & Co. in the year 1887. Their clients were at that time very few, but the client they prized most was the New York, Ontario and Western Railway Co., the first railroad in the United States to employ public accountants to act as auditors and to certify to the correctness of its annual statements to its stockholders, which engagement lasted for many years. In addition, the firm audited the accounts of several British fire and marine insurance companies.

Mr. Anyon also states that in launching out as the head of the firm he was full of ambition, a love for his work and a determination to make good, qualifications for success that are equally necessary today for a young certified public accountant.

216

He, in a somewhat amusing way, went on to say that though he could modestly admit he was a "fairly good accountant," he had the disadvantage of being an Englishman, for at that time people generally did not take very kindly to men of that nationality. Englishmen, he states, were looked upon as rather slow and stupid, and while admittedly honest, were not considered overly capable. Besides, there was somewhat of a national feeling of prejudice against Englishmen, arising from the old colonial days, which was still apparent. It was a fact, nevertheless, in spite of this feeling, that if any real and important accounting work had to be done, it would in the majority of cases be given to the foreign trained accountant in preference to the native one. The usual explanation for this was that the client had greater confidence in the precision and accuracy of the work of the Britisher and greater faith in the honesty of his conclusions. Mr. Anyon, however, then states (and it must be remembered that he is writing nearly forty years later), "This may seem rather an odd statement to make, and while it was true then, it is gratifying to know this discrimination no longer exists even to a slight extent in these times, as both native and foreign-born accountants

45

equally represent the highest point of efficiency and integrity in their professional work."

In concluding this narrative of Mr. Anyon and his important part in the organization of the American Association of Public Accountants, I want to quote two paragraphs from his book as an illustration of the old adage that "great oak trees from little acorns grow."

> "By reason of the limited amount of business my firm had to start with, as already stated, I could not afford to engage any assistant in the office beyond the employment of an office boy. I was, therefore, called upon to fill the several roles and discharge the duties of the following offices - accountant, acting auditor, correspondent, cashier (this latter position did not take up much of my time for reasons quite obvious), firm bookkeeper, writer of reports, traveller, time-keeper, computer of customers' bills for service, and in fact everything but dusting the office desks, filling the inkstands, mailing the letters and doing other minor thing which were the duties of the boy.

217

> "For the whole of this service, and the fact that I was a partner, my salary was fixed at $208.33 per month. My total annual income, therefore, was $2,500.00 and a proportion of the net profits of the firm, if there were any. I state these particulars just to show how simple and moderate the business of an accounting firm was in those years compared to the many and wonderful firms today."

For the purpose of recording the history of accountancy in the state of Illinois the activities of the American Association of Public Accountants from 1886 to 1894 has little to offer of any interest, other than the account given in the foregoing paragraphs. In the year 1894, however, I find that the first efforts to pass a C.P.A. law were undertaken.

I believe it is commonly believed that the American Association of Public Accountants was the activating and only body of accountants responsible for the passage of the first C.P.A. law in the United States. This is not entirely correct, for a share of the honor of securing this legislation must also be given to the "Institute of Accounts."

The Institute of Accounts was established about the year 1882, very soon after the formation of the Institute of Chartered Accountants of

England and Wales. It was a scientific body and in no sense a trade-union, and one of its objects was the introduction of a law which would establish public accounting as a legally recognized and regulated profession in the State of New York instead of a self-constituted body of men practicing accountancy.

On the other hand, the American Association of Public Accountants was a professional guild composed solely of public accountants practicing in several states, including a scattering of members on the Pacific Coast, though a large majority practiced in New York.

It was during the winter of 1894-1895 that a rough draft of a Bill providing for a professional examination was prepared by Major Henry Harney, the President of the Institute of Accounts, who had many years before committed to paper some of his ideas along these lines. Major Harney, acting in conformity with the by-laws of the Institute, appointed Colonel Charles H. Sprague, as a "committee of one", to convey the draft of such a Bill to Albany in order to find out what could be done towards having it enacted by the State Legislature. Colonel Sprague visited Albany and immediately got in touch with his friend, Mr. Melvil Dewey, the eminent Librarian and Secretary to the Regents of the University of New York.

The original draft of the Bill called for the appointment of a board of examiners by the Governor, but as it was deemed inadvisable to add another political board and as Mr. Dewey believed that the enforcement of the law should be placed under the jurisdiction of the Regents of the University, which body had the machinery for conducting examinations, this change was adopted. Furthermore, he pointed out that this course would give the proposed measure something of an educational character.

In the meantime, and acting independently in every respect, several members of the American Association of Public Accountants prepared a draft for a Bill which provided "that no person shall practice as a public accountant after the passage of this Act unless he be licensed by the Regents of the University of New York." This Bill was introduced in the Senate on February 20, 1895 and it was referred to the Committee on Legislation. Two weeks later the Institute's Bill was introduced into the Assembly and it provided that the University of the State of New York should make rules for the examination of persons applying for C.P.A. certificates and this Bill was in every respect practically the same as the law subsequently passed.

After these two Bills had been introduced in the Legislature, a notice, purposely unsigned, was sent out by Mr. Gottsberger, assisted by Mr. William Sanders Davies, to all practicing public accountants whose names appeared in the current classified directory of the City of New York informing them that Bills had been introduced in the Legislature and asking them to attend a meeting at 111 Broadway on March 13th, 1895. About sixty accountants attended this meeting, at which Mr. Richard F. Stevens of Newark, New Jersey, acted as Chairman. It was stated that two Bills had been introduced, one in the Senate and one in the Assembly. Each of these Bills was read and after considerable discussion a committee of fourteen was appointed to carry out the objects of the meeting, eight of whom were members of the American Association of Public Accountants, three from the Institute of Accounts and three not members of either body.

The committee decided that the Association's Bill be withdrawn and that the Institute's should prevail and an attorney should be engaged to watch the progress of the Bill through the two houses of the Legislature. The Bill was reported upon favorably by the Senate committee, but when it came up for passage by the Senate it only received ten votes and was therefore never passed.

At its November 1895 meeting the American Association appointed a committee, consisting of Frank Broaker, Chairman, James Yalden and William Sanders Davies, to renew the effort to secure the passage of a C.P.A. Bill. Mr. Broaker sent the proposed Bill to Senator Albert A. Wray of Brooklyn, who introduced it in the Senate January 13, 1896 and it was referred to the Committee on Judiciary. It was, of course, also introduced in the Assembly, passed by both houses and received the approval of the Governor of the State on April 17, 1896.

The success of this Bill was largely due to the indefatigable efforts of Mr. Frank Broaker who devoted all his time and energy to pushing this measure to its final passage and thus earned the thanks of our entire profession, and it was possibly in appreciation for this that he was given Certificate No. 1 as a Certified Public Accountant of the State of New York.

It may be of interest to note that the first board of examiners consisted of Colonel Charles E. Sprague, Frank Broaker and Charles Waldo Haskins.

This chapter, while not exactly constituting a History of Accountancy in the State of Illinois is descriptive of those events which had so much influence on the welfare of our profession in Illinois, and for that reason I have included it in these pages.

After the passage of the New York C.P.A. law and the encouragement it gave to public accountants in the United States, other states soon took steps to secure similar legislation, as shown below:

Pennsylvania
The first attempt was defeated in 1897, but a C.P.A.
law was enacted March 29, 1899, largely through the
efforts of Mr. J. E. Sterrett and Mr. Charles N. Vollum.

Maryland
Law enacted April 10, 1900 on first attempt, largely
through efforts of Mr. Max Teichman.

California
  Two first attempts failed, but third attempt

successful March 23, 1901.

Washington
  Law enacted March 12, 1903

Illinois
  Attempts to secure law in 1897 and 1899 both

failed, but successful on May 15, 1903.

221

CHAPTER 6

The Illinois Association of Public Accountants
1897 to 1904

"Making all futures, fruits of all the past"

Edwin Arnold in "The Light of Asia"

I was chatting a few days ago with a very well known Certified
Public Accountant, a man probably in his early fifties, the subject of our conversation being this history of accounting in the State of Illinois which I am
now writing. In this conversation it developed that he had absolutely no knowledge that there had ever been any association of public accountants prior to

222   he passage of the Certified Public Accountancy Act of 1903 and prior to the
organization of the present Illinois Society of Certified Public Accountants.
If a man of the character I have described was ignorant in this matter, I think
it quite possible that a large majority of the members of the Illinois Society
are similarly in ignorance. This being the situation, one naturally feels inclined to ask the question of those who have no knowledge of how they, today,
enjoy the privilege of placing the letters C.P.A. after their names, "How did
it happen that they possess this privilege and why is it they have enjoyed the
blessings of a sound education in the science of accounts?" Did a sudden
miracle happen in the year 1903 and the C.P.A. law come down from heaven
as a special gift to mankind?

      The answer to this question is that a few farseeing and enterpriz-
ing public accountants, only fourteen in number, organized the Illinois Association of Public Accountants on March 18, 1897; almost succeeded in passing a C.P.A. law in that year, and after six years of strenuous labor, with
the assistance of new members, succeeded in the final accomplishment of
their most pressing endeavor, the passage of a C.P.A. law in Illinois. So that
the reader, who may thus far have had the hardihood to read this history, will

appreciate the birth-pangs of the Illinois Association in 1897, let me submit
some of the difficulties encountered by those who were in practice in those
early days. In the first place, how was it that only fourteen men were charter
members of the Association in this city having a population of over one and a
half million people?

In a preceding chapter I have already outlined the almost complete absence of any proficient members of our profession prior to the year
1890 and also the lack of understanding on the part of business men, bankers
and lawyers as to the character of public accounting as a profession. I have
also in the same chapter shown the steady advances made during the years
from 1891 to 1897 resulting in many new firms of accountants opening offices
in Chicago which undoubtedly strengthened our profession. Nevertheless it
was left to only fourteen men who had the vision and courage to organize the
first Illinois Association of Public Accountants. The names of those men
and their affiliations in case they were partners of firms are given below:

223

> Frank M. Boughey
> R. S. Buchanan of Kidson, Buchanan & Co.
> Henry F. Butler (Resigned April 8, 1902)
> John A. Cooper
> S. B. Foster of Price, Waterhouse & Co. (moved away and
>   resigned July 1, 1899)
> William Fries (resigned in 1899)
> Charles W. Hawley of Hawley, Jones & Co.
> Lawrence A. Jones of Hawley, Jones & Co.
> Lewis D. Jones of Price, Waterhouse & Co. (Died February 1899)
> Frederick F. Judd (Resigned April 8, 1902)
> G. L. Marchand (Resigned in 1898 due to illness)
> Ernest Reckitt of Smith, Reckitt & Co.
> George E. Shaw of Kidson, Buchanan & Co. (moved away and
>   resigned April 29, 1898)
> George Wilkinson

A few practicing accountants of excellent reputation appeared to be lukewarm
towards this new association on its first attempt to secure the passage of a
C.P.A. law and did not join the Association until it had demonstrated its quality and dogged determination to carry on, but in 1898 and 1899 they came into

the fold and supported the Association's endeavors in many valuable ways.

That only fourteen men were found willing to become the charter members of the Association will be better understood by a study of the following statistics gleaned by the author from a detailed study of the Classified Chicago Directory.

As of January 1, 1892, there were only twenty-six individuals and firms who had been in practice prior to that date. In the years 1892 to 1897, inclusive, 132 more men had begun practice as public accountants, making a total of 158 including those in practice on January 1, 1892; yet at the close of 1897 only 92 were still in practice and in 1904 of these 158 there were only 29 still in practice, as shown in the following table summarized by years:

Year	In Practice Jan. 1, 1892, and subsequent additions	Still in practice Dec. 31, 1897	Still in practice in 1904
Jan. 1, 1892	26	20	12
1892	20	8	2
1893	11	2	-
1894	18	5	2
1895	30	13	6
1896	26	17	5
1897	27	27	2
	158	92	29

The figures submitted in the above table clearly demonstrate a professional mortality rate of large proportions due to the fact that many men who thought that they were capable of practicing as public accountants were, through inexperience or other causes, quite unable to make good and dropped by the wayside, so that of the 158 only 29 were able to build up a practice. When, therefore, early in 1897 Mr. George Wilkinson and the author of this history conceived the idea of organizing an association, we knew fairly well the standing of those accountants whom it would have been useless to approach, and our efforts were therefore directed to those who had been in practice for several years.

During the six years after the formation of the Association seven of the charter members, as will be seen by reference to Appendix A, had died or moved away from Chicago, leaving only seven of the original fourteen still in practice at the close of the year 1903. It was, therefore, a god-send to the Association and to the welfare of our profession that 53 new members, some of them of a very high calibre, were elected during the years 1898 to 1903. In Appendix A is given a complete list of all members, including the charter members who had been elected up to the year 1903, totaling 67 men, of whom 13 had died or resigned, leaving 54 in practice when the Association gave up its charter in 1904 and the Illinois Society of Certified Public Accountants took its place.

225

It will be of considerable interest to glance over the names of these 54 members, for it includes many who have been, and some who are still, shining lights in our profession not only in Illinois but throughout the United States, such as Seymour Walton, J. Porter Joplin, Allen R. Smart, C. J. Marr, George Wilkinson, J. B. Niven, A. Lowes Dickinson, Charles Waldo Haskins, Elijah W. Sells, Arthur Young, George O. May, R. O. Berger, Edward E. Gore and W. Ernest Seatree. It is also to be noted that out of these 54 members, 21 were partners or members of the staff of Price, Waterhouse & Co., a splendid contribution to our profession by that firm.

The first meeting to organize an association was held March 10, 1897, at the Wellington Hotel which stood on the northeast corner of Jackson Boulevard and Wabash Avenue, a very noted hostelry, famous for its good meals, but long since disappeared from the scene. The following persons were present, all of whom had been in practice as public accountants continuously for the prior five years: R. S. Buchanan, Henry F. Butler, Charles A.

Hawley, Lawrence A. Jones, Ernest Reckitt and George Wilkinson. The first board of directors consisted of all of the above except Lawrence A. Jones.

An application for a certificate of organization under the name of The Illinois Association of Public Accountants was filled out. A committee of three was appointed to draw up the by-laws and another committee appointed to take the necessary steps to secure through the Illinois State Legislature, an Act to regulate the profession of public accountants.

On March 18, 1897, the Department of State of the State of Illinois granted the charter which created the Illinois Association of Public Accountants.

On April 20, 1897, George Wilkinson was instructed to go to Springfield, Illinois, and he was empowered to use the funds of the Association to the best of his judgment in furthering the passage of the "Bill for an Act to regulate the profession of Public Accountants" then pending before the State Legislature. The history of the various activities in 1897, 1899 and 1903 for legislation to create a Certified Public Accountancy Act are given in the next chapter, as they are of such importance as to deserve special consideration.

On June 8, 1897 at a meeting of the board of directors the following officers were elected:

> Lewis D. Jones   President
> Ernest Reckitt   Vice-President
> George Wilkinson   Secretary and Treasurer

Membership in the Association required the following qualifications:

(a) Any person above the age of twenty-five who had been engaged in reputable practice as a Public Accountant in the State of Illinois for a continuous period of three years immediately preceding the date of his application;

(b) Any member of the Institute of Chartered Accountants of England and Wales in good standing, in practice in Illinois for one year immediately preceding application;

(c) Similarly any Fellow of the American Association of Public Accountants of New York;

(d) Similarly any person holding membership in any other Association solely composed of Public Accountants outside the State of Illinois.

Entrance fees were stated to be $25.00 and annual dues $20.00.

The following rules also appear to have been adopted:

"A member may be excluded or suspended up to two years after due hearings if:

1. He violates any of the By-Laws of the Association applicable to him;

2. He is convicted of a felony or misdemeanor, or is finally declared by any Court of competent jurisprudence to have committed any fraud;

3. He is declared by any Court or authorized Commission to be insane;

4. He is held by the Board of Directors on the complaint of any person aggrieved, whether a member or not, to have been guilty of any act or default discreditable to a public accountant;

5. He shall cease to practice as a public accountant for a consecutive period longer than two years;

6. He fails to pay any dues, assessments or other sum payable by him to the Association under the By-Laws for three months after the same has become due.

Of the above rules, only number four can be described as in any way pertaining to "Rules of Professional Conduct," but as its terms were more general than specific it was difficult to enforce.

While discussing rules governing professional ethics prior to 1904, it may be of interest to study the progress made after that year by the Illinois Society of Certified Public Accountants.

No changes in the rules appear to have been adopted until October 13, 1908, though Mr. John A. Cooper had recommended a more detailed definition of rules of professional ethics as early as June 15, 1907. The new rules appear to have closely followed those which had been adopted by the American Association of Public Accountants, a copy of which we submit below:

1. No member shall allow any person, not being either a member of the Association, or in partnership with him as a public accountant, or in his employ on a salary, to practice in his name as a public accountant.

2. No member shall directly or indirectly allow or agree to allow a commission, brokerage or other participation by the laity in the fees or profits of his (the member's) professional work.

3. No member shall directly or indirectly accept or agree to accept any part of the fees or profits of the professional work of a lawyer or any commercial brokerage, bonus or commission whatsoever as an incident to work in which such member is professionally engaged.

4. No member shall engage in any business or occupation conjointly with that of a public accountant, which in the opinion of the Board of Directors is incompatible or inconsistent therewith.

5. No member shall certify to statements, exhibits, schedules or other form of accountancy work, the preparation of which was not carried on entirely under the supervision of himself, a member of his firm, one of his staff, a member of this Association or of a similar Association of good standing in foreign countries.

6. No member shall perform accountancy work, payment for which is by arrangement upon the contingency of the result of litigation or other form of adjustment.

In addition, Article VIII was added covering provisions for a Trial Board, the mailing of notices at least thirty days prior to the trial of all parties involved, and that a three-fourths vote of the directors present would have to be necessary for any decision in the case.

It is interesting to compare the rules of professional ethics as shown in the foregoing paragraph with our present code. It will be noted that the earlier code contains no reference to advertising, competitive bidding and many other matters as now contained in our present code. Still it was a good beginning and laid a foundation for future development as our profession grew.

In examining the minutes of meetings up to November 1899, it would appear that apart from efforts to secure C.P.A. legislation little was

228

done to keep up the interest of the members, of which there were then only
twenty-three, though directors' meetings were held fairly regularly. At a
meeting of the Association held November 23, 1899, this situation was discussed and it was decided that frequent meetings of all members should be
inaugurated, not only for the purpose of securing a continuing interest, but
also to serve an educational purpose.

The committee appointed to suggest a program reported at the
November meeting as follows:

1. That regular monthly meetings of all members be held and announced thereof, including the nature of the paper to be read,
   be sent to all members and that after such papers had been
   presented, discussion regarding same should be encouraged

2. That a salaried reporter be present who would prepare a
   typewritten statement of such discussions to be turned over
   to the Library Committee;

3. That a Library Committee be appointed, the duty of which
   would be to secure speakers at such meetings and to prepare for publication such papers with discussions thereon
   with power to curtail or exclude portions of such papers,
   but not to alter the effect thereof;

4. That the Secretary of the Association should forward such
   papers and discussions thereon, after having been edited by
   the Library Committee, to each of the publications in our
   profession, namely: "The Accountant" of London; "The
   Public Accountant" of Philadelphia; "The Financial Times"
   and "Business," both of New York City; "The Book-keeper"
   of Detroit; "The Chicago Banker," etc.

5. That each member of the Association should receive copies
   of such publications;

6. That members of the Chicago Bar Association and the
   Chicago Bankers Association should be invited to read papers
   before meetings of members, which papers should be printed
   and copies of same mailed to every recognized member of
   our profession who might be interested;

7. That members of the Association should read papers before
   the two Societies named above, and also before a meeting of
   the American Association of Public Accountants in New York.

While this action did not accomplish all that it had set out to do, it
did accomplish much of its intent, as will be seen by the following resume of

229

papers read and published.

Date	Title	Author
Dec. 12, 1899	"National Legislation for the Public Accountant"	John A. Cooper
Feb. 13, 1900	"The Public Accountants' Assistants"	Ernest Reckitt
Mar. 13, 1900	"Cui Bono"	Seymour Walton
Apr. 10, 1900	"Commercial Investigations"	Allen R. Smart
May 8, 1900	"Charter Accountants and their Examinations"	Henry Wilkinson
Nov. 13, 1900	"Corporate Dividends"	Charles C. Reckitt
Apr. 9, 1901	"Workings of the C.P.A. Law in New York State"	Charles Waldo Haskins
July 9, 1901	"Depreciation of Plant"	George Wilkinson
Feb. 28, 1902	"The Duties and Responsibilities of a Public Accountant"	A. Lowes Dickinson
July 8, 1902	"Proposed Organization of a Federation of Societies of Public Accountants"	George Wilkinson

Commenting on the above, "Mr. Henry Wilkinson" was the father of George Wilkinson and the paper was read by the latter, as his father resided in England. The "Charles C. Reckitt" who wrote on "Corporate Dividends" is a brother of the author. Charles C. Reckitt was trained as a lawyer in England and was partner of the author for several years until he retired to enter into another activity in February, 1903.

The practice of holding more meetings of the members proved to be a strong force in holding together the membership and it was continued for many years, as will be realized by a study of the minutes of meetings of the Illinois Society of Certified Public Accountants.

The printed syllabus for the season 1909-1910 announced in advance the date of each meeting to be held, the name of the speaker and the subject of his address. It may be worthwhile to give excerpts of this syllabus, for it indicates the steady growth of our profession and the high character of the speakers.

1. "The Development of Accountancy as a Profession," by J. E. Sterrett, C.P.A., President of the American Association of Public Accountants.

2. "A Central Bank of Issue," by George E. Roberts, President of the Commercial Bank of Chicago.

3. "Corporation Audits from the Controller's Viewpoint," by William M. Reay, C.P.A., Controller of the International Harvester Company.

4. "Governmental Supervision and its Effect on the Profession of the Public Accountant," by Robert H. Montgomery, member of the firm of Lybrand, Ross Bros. & Montgomery.

5. "The C.P.A. Degree, Now and Hereafter," by Edward E. Gore, C.P.A.

6. "The Accountant as an Expert Witness," by Charles F. Lowy, attorney at law.

One of the greatest difficulties which members of our profession experienced in its early stages was that of finding assistants, both seniors and juniors, who were competent and reliable. Personally I found it best to engage young men who had some knowledge of bookkeeping, of good character and possessing potentialities of intellectual attainments, and to train them myself by active supervision. While, naturally, the men thus engaged did not always measure up to the requirements outlined above, and who therefore after a brief engagement had to be discarded, yet by and large it proved to be the only method of building up a permanent and competent staff.

Notwithstanding our attempts to train men so that we could slowly build up a permanent staff, those early years were especially difficult when, through special investigations suddenly arising or during the busy season, it became necessary to add temporary employees to the staff. There were a few men available more or less experienced in accounting but somewhat unreliable due to their personal habits, who were well-named "Floaters," working intermittently for several firms as special occasions arose. There-fore, in the year 1901, to help this situation, the Illinois Association organized an "Employment Bureau" at which such "Floaters" would register when not otherwise employed. When a member of the Association found it necessary to engage temporary employees he would call up this central bureau and thus secure the services of one or more of these "Floaters" if they were free. The Secretary of the Association was to all intents and purposes the manager of this Bureau, keeping all the necessary records. I do not recall how long this Bureau functioned, but possibly a few years until the difficulty of secur-ing temporary employees had lessened.

232

Another most important activity affecting the accountancy pro-fession throughout the whole country and for which the Illinois Association was largely responsible, was the creation of an organization known as the "Federation of Societies of Public Accountants," which may be said to be the father of our present American Institute of Accountants. The American As-sociation of Accountants was founded in 1887 and its activities are fully covered in chapter five. While our profession was indebted to its earlier ac-complishments, it was to all intents and purposes a local New York State So-ciety. Apparently it had little interest in accountancy as a profession outside of the State of New York, even though it numbered in its membership a few practicing public accountants outside of that state. This attitude of isolation created a strong prejudice against the American Association by some of the leading public accountants in New York City, but especially among public ac-countants outside of the State of New York. It was felt that a real active na-tional organization was vital to the needs of all practicing accountants within the United States to promote the interests of our profession, and also in the organization of State Societies, where none existed, and in the passage of Certified Public Accountancy laws in such states.

At the meeting of the members of the Illinois Association held July 8, 1902, George Wilkinson read a paper entitled, "Proposed Organization of a Federation of Societies of Public Accountants." I believe the original idea of organizing such a Federation was entirely due to his foresight, but he was very ably supported by public accountants in Philadelphia, (notably by the members of the firm of Lybrand, Ross Bros. & Montgomery and Mr. Sterrett); in New York City (by members of the firm of Price, Waterhouse & Co.); and in Boston (by Mr. Harvey Chase).

A more detailed account of the events that led to the organization of this "Federation" will be found in chapter ten which also covers an account of the first Congress of Accountants held in St. Louis on the occasion of the Louisiana Purchase Exhibition in the year 1904, which was the direct result of the formation of the Federation.

233

In concluding this chapter it may be interesting to note that in the initial stages of the Illinois Association it was not always an easy task to maintain one's faith in the final outcome and success of our undertaking.

Immediately prior to October 24, 1898, the total membership, through deaths, changes of residence and resignations, had reached its lowest ebb, there being only ten members. Many good public accountants practicing in Chicago had held aloof from joining this young organization (See Appendix A); the first attempt to pass a C.P.A. law had failed and a second attempt was being contemplated when on October 24, 1898, one of the directors, resigned both as a director and as a member, stating in his letter of resignation:

> "I have experienced a change of opinion as to the benefit to be derived by public accountants by such a measure," (the C.P.A. law then contemplated) " as I am satisfied that many irresponsible men will through political influence (and in some cases through a money consideration) be given a certificate that they should not be entitled to and that the name of a C.P.A. will not carry any great weight when brought before the public, but will in some cases be considered a reproach."

Attempts to secure a reconsideration on the part of this member were un-availing at that time, but it is only fair to record that on January 10, 1901, he sought reinstatement which was granted.

Looking back nearly fifty years and comparing the present pros-perity and high standards of our profession with the lugubrious prophecies contained in the letter just quoted, I think we may appreciate better the faith and fortitude of those few men who carried on notwithstanding the many dif-ficulties which had to be overcome. It was these same men who were largely responsible for the passage of the C.P.A. law in 1903 and for the early devel-opment of the small but growing organization which has, over the years, done so much towards the educational and ethical standards of our profession. The title of C.P.A. is, and always has been, an honorable one and it may be of in-terest to know that out of the more than 2800 C.P.A. degrees granted by the University of Illinois up to June 1945 only two men have forfeited their cer-tificates on account of misconduct.

This, I maintain, is a wonderful record. It speaks most highly for the care and watchfulness of those whose duty it has been to investigate the character of the applicants for the C.P.A. examinations. It also demon-strates that the men who aspire to become Certified Public Accountants are, in the main, those of an earnest and serious type of character, and who, by reason of their training in the offices of Certified Public Accountants, have been inculcated in the value of high ideals.

After the effective date of the C.P.A. law, on July 1, 1903, the Association's activities were directed mainly to matters pertaining to the "Federation of Societies of Public Accountants," which are dealt with in a subsequent chapter; to the organization of the new "Illinois Society of Cer-tified Public Accountants" and to winding up of its own organization. At a meeting held October 13, 1903, a committee, composed of Edward E. Gore,

Allen R. Smart and Seymour Walton, was appointed to devise a plan for the creation of the "Illinois Society of Certified Public Accountants."

The last meeting of the "Illinois Association of Public Accountants" was held on June 14, 1904, for the purpose of effectuating its dissolution.

This may be the appropriate place for listing the names of the officers of the Illinois Association for each of the years during its existence.

Term of Office	President	Vice-President	Secy-Treas.
1897-1898	Lewis D. Jones	Ernest Reckitt	George Wilkinson
1898-1899	Lewis D. Jones*	Ernest Reckitt	George Wilkinson
1899-1900	John A. Cooper	Ernest Reckitt	Lawrence A. Jones
1900-1901	John A. Cooper	Ernest Reckitt	Lawrence A. Jones
1901-1902	John A. Cooper	George Wilkinson	Lawrence D. Jones
1902-1903	George Wilkinson	Ernest Reckitt	J. Porter Joplin
1903-1904	Ernest Reckitt	Henry W. Wilmot	J. Porter Joplin

* Mr. Jones died in February 1899 and Mr. Reckitt served as Acting President for the balance of the Association's year.

CHAPTER 7

The Passage of the Certified Public Accountancy
Act of 1903 with Description of Prior Attempts '

"No Bill, however inoffensive, will go through a
legislative body on its own weight. The way is
uphill from start to finish and has many
sharp turns, some of them mighty dangerous."

The above quotation is taken from a pamphlet written by George
Wilkinson published in 1903, and he certainly had every reason to know its
truth. He spoke not only from his own experience, but he also spoke for all
the public accountants who were engaged in the struggle to secure the C.P.A.
law for the State of Illinois from 1897 to 1903.

As already stated in a previous chapter, the immediate object of
organizing an Association of Public Accountants in Illinois in 1897 was to secure the passage of a Certified Public Accountancy Act similar to that already
secured by public accountants in the State of New York. It was, however, six
years after the first attempt in 1897 before we were finally successful.

In this chapter it is proposed to give an outline of the activities
of the Illinois Association to secure this legislation.

The 1897 Attempt for a C.P.A. Law

The Illinois Association of Public Accountants received its charter
as of March 18, 1897 and at a directors' meeting held on April 20, 1897 George
Wilkinson was instructed to go to Springfield and was empowered to use the
funds of the Association to the best of his judgment in furthering the passage
of the C.P.A. law which had already been introduced in both Houses of the
Legislature. Reference to the annual report covering the first fiscal year of
the Association indicates that not more than $164.01 was thus expended.

Fortunately Mr. Wilkinson had friends and clients in Springfield, among whom were Mr. Charles Ridgely, the President of The Ridgely National Bank, and Mr. A. A. Billingsley, both of these men being very influential in Illinois politics. Four days after the date of the charter (March 22) Mr. Wilkinson wrote Senator Frederick Lundin requesting the favorable consideration by his committee in the Senate of a Bill entitled, "An Act to regulate the profession of Public Accountants," and stating that a similar Bill was now in force in the State of New York and under consideration in several other states. It was, of course, pointed out that Illinois public accountants would be discriminated against in a disadvantageous manner in competing with Certified Public Accountants of other states if they did not possess the same standing.

237

On March 22nd Mr. Wilkinson wrote to his friends, Mr. Ridgely and Mr. Billingsley, requesting their cooperation and assistance and on March 24th he arrived in Springfield, armed with letters from many reputable Chicago business men supporting this campaign, one of which was a letter from Mr. R. E. Brownell, of the Chicago Chamber of Commerce, addressed to Mr. Netterstrom, the Chairman of the Senate License Committee. From this date Mr. Wilkinson spent a large part of his time in Springfield so as to secure this much desired legislation.

The chief difficulty was encountered through the fact that a large majority of the members of the House were from rural districts and small towns who had no comprehension of the importance of the legislation which was being sought. The Bill for this legislation was unfortunately introduced in the House by a Mr. Hunter, a "green" country member from a dairy district, whose sole ambition was the passage of a Bill to prohibit any coloring of "Butterine," as it was then called, now better known as "Margerine."

The Bill, however, was passed by the Senate through the activities of Senator Campbell, and looking over the copies of letters written by

66

Mr. Wilkinson there is one dated May 13th, addressed to Mr. Lawrence Kilcourse of the House of Representatives, in which it appears that the latter had decided to promote the Senate Bill No. 209 which had been passed, and to drop the House Bill No. 556. It was thus hoped that this action, by securing the leadership of Mr. Kilcourse, would overcome the lethargy of Representative Hunter, already referred to.

The delay in securing prompter action in the House was, however, fatal, for it was impossible to have the third reading of the Bill until the last night of the session and though Speaker Curtis had promised the Bill would come up at that time and would undoubtedly be passed, it failed for the reason that due to the merriment and jollification, which in those days, (and possibly ever since on similar occasions) prior to the immediate return home on the following day by all the representatives, there was no quorum in the House, only sixty-five being present, while a quorum necessitated seventy-seven members present.

Thus, our first attempt, after the most strenuous efforts, came to naught.

It may be of interest at this time to state that outside of the City of Chicago there were only ten men practicing in the State of Illinois; namely, one in Decatur, two in East St. Louis, two in Elgin, one in Moline, one in Quincy, one in Rock Island, one in Springfield and one in Bloomington. These men all gave us their hearty cooperation in our attempt to secure a C.P.A. law in 1897.

Appendix B gives a copy of the Bill it was hoped might be passed, and which was similar in form to that passed in the State of New York.

The 1899 Attempt for a C.P.A. Law

In the summer of 1898 the Board of Directors determined to

238

make another effort to secure the passage of a C.P.A. law at the forty-first session of the Illinois Legislature beginning early in 1899, though the Society at that time had only twelve members, two less than at its organization. The officers of the Society were Lewis D. Jones of Price, Waterhouse & Co., President, Ernest Reckitt, Vice-President, and George Wilkinson, Secretary and Treasurer. It was believed that the failure to secure the passage of a C.P.A. law in 1897 was entirely due to our not having had sufficient time for the preparation of the proper publicity and education of the members of the legislature as to its importance.

For this reason it was decided to make our plans well in advance in order to secure favorable action.

At the fall election in 1898 all our members did everything they could to assist in the re-election of Senator Dan Campbell, who had been so helpful to us in the attempt for a C.P.A. Act in 1897. Senator Campbell was duly re-elected and he wrote expressing his appreciation of our assistance.

In the meantime the members of the Association secured a large number of valuable endorsements, as to the importance of a C.P.A. law, from leading bankers throughout the State of Illinois and from many of the influential lawyers in Chicago. Printed copies of the proposed law, (identical to the proposed 1897 law (See Appendix B)) with the names of the endorsers and their favorable comments thereon, were sent to every member of the legislature and also to all the bankers throughout the state asking them to use their influence with their local representatives in the legislature.

I have before me, at this writing, a copy of this printed circular, on the front page of which was a copy of the proposed law and on the back page was a list of twenty bankers living in many Illinois cities who had endorsed the proposed law as necessary, together with their comments.

In addition to these printed endorsements the following endorsements, written in later, are of interest.

Harry Rubens, a leading member of the Chicago Bar Association, wrote:

> "I have examined the Bill for an Act to regulate the profession of Public Accountants, and am heartily in favor of its passage. I have had frequent occasions to employ accountants and have always been compelled either to employ London accountants who had a branch office in New York, or Certified Public Accountants of New York. If the Act were passed, the reliable accountants of Chicago, and other places in the State, could become Certified Public Accountants, and then the necessity of going beyond the State for accountants would cease."

Luther Laflin Mills, another eminent member of the Chicago Bar Association, wrote:

240

> "I heartily favor the enactment of legislation to regulate the profession of Public Accountants and have no doubt that the adoption of the Bill for that purpose, now pending in the legislature of Illinois, would be of great public benefit."

Among the printed list of endorsements by bankers, probably the most emphatic was that written by James B. Forgan, then the First Vice-President of The First National Bank of Chicago, and later its President for many years. His prophetic endorsement is given below:

> "I heartily approve of the foregoing bill as being a step in the right direction. The certificate of a 'C.P.A.' as to the correctness of accounts, public or private, will carry weight with it, which that of a self-designated expert cannot have; in much the same degree that an M.D.'s diagnosis carries more weight than that of a self-educated unprofessional healer.

> "As time advances and the public becomes educated to the meaning of Certified Public Accountants, and the necessity for them, a professional reputation will undoubtedly have been established by those holding University certificates that will attract to them the great bulk of the business requiring their service, just as lawyers attract the legal and M.D.'s the medical. Their work will carry with it the professional standing and weight, which, without such a law, it lacks in the estimation of business men.

> "I think there is a business necessity existing for the establishment of recognized public accountants, whose reports can be received as carrying with them the weight of competence on the part of the expert, and the Bill will be a step toward that end."

These circulars and endorsements produced excellent results and everything appeared favorable to a final victory for the Bill.

Promptly on the assembling of the legislature in January 1899 active operations were begun by the Illinois Association and as soon as the various legislative committees were organized, our Bill was introduced in the Senate by Senator Dan Campbell, a personal friend of Mr. Lawrence A. Jones, one of our members, and a little later it was introduced in the House by Representative Linn K. Young, a personal friend of Mr. Frederick F. Judd, also one of our members.

Inasmuch as in 1897 our attempt to secure a C.P.A. law had met with little opposition in the Senate, while it failed for passage in the House, our chief efforts were now concentrated on educating the House members to the importance of this proposed legislation, but unfortunately the Senate members were not given the attention they deserved. In this we undoubtedly erred, believing that with the backing that Senator Dan Campbell gave the proposed law and the ease with which the 1897 law had been passed by the Senate, we could await the prompt passage of the law in the House before concentrating our campaign on members of the Senate.

241

Senator Dan Campbell again took an active interest in the Bill and advanced it rapidly in the Senate; in fact, as it turned out, too fast, so he was asked to hold back further action until the House Bill had been acted upon; but on February 28, 1899, in spite of that request and evidently through some misunderstanding or misadvertance, the Senate Bill was brought up for final action by Senator Campbell and it was defeated by a vote of thirteen "Ayes" against twenty-three "Nays."

During this whole time Mr. Wilkinson, who had done such a marvelous job in 1897, was absent on business in Philadelphia and we certainly missed his guiding presence.

On March 8, 1899 the Bill was introduced in the House by Mr.

Linn K. Young and it was favorably reported upon by the Judiciary Committee, but thereafter Mr. Young ceased to have any interest in this legislation. As it was a rule of the House that once a Bill had been introduced it could not be advanced by any other member than the introducer, the Association was left with no other alternative than to urge Mr. Young by correspondence, and by visits to Springfield, to take active measures for its advancement. This he lamentably failed to do and the legislative session closed without any further action on the part of Mr. Young.

It should be noted that while the Bill had been lost in the Senate, the Bill could have been re-introduced by substituting the House Bill for the Senate Bill, but Mr. Young's lack of interest in the House Bill made this course of action impossible.

And thus the second attempt to secure a C.P.A. law failed, even though it had been supported by so many bankers, lawyers, etc., and after so much preliminary planning and endeavors of the members of the Association.

The Certified Public Accountancy Act of 1903 (See Appendix C)

Four years elapsed between the second attempt to secure a C.P.A. law in 1899 and our final success. This was not because the members of the Association had become downhearted by reason of two failures, but rather it was believed that the Association should grow in strength before any further attempt should be made.

At the time of the first attempt in 1897 our membership was only fourteen; in the second attempt, as of January 1, 1899, it was only twelve, so it was actually an accomplishment to have secured so much support from bankers, lawyers and business men. Furthermore, these efforts, though unsuccessful, had done much to make our profession better known throughout

242

the state and may also have had an influence in securing new members to join the Association.

By January 1, 1901 our membership had increased from twelve, as of January 1, 1899, to twenty-seven and it did not even then include many reputable practicing accountants; hence the directors did not believe it advisable at that time to make a third attempt. This is evidenced in reading the minutes of a meeting of the directors held on January 15, 1901 when a letter from Mr. Edward E. Gore, then of the Audit Company of Chicago, (but who was not a member of the Association at that time) was read, in which he asked if the directors had any objection to his attempting to secure C.P.A. legislation at the session about to commence. The record shows it was the opinion of the Board that no such action should be taken at that time.

However, on July 8, 1902 at a quarterly meeting of the Association, (at which George Wilkinson had read a most interesting paper dealing with a proposed Federation of Societies of Public Accountants, the object of which, among other things, was to secure national legislation) there was a discussion on the subject of the Association once more trying to secure a C.P.A. law for the State of Illinois. The following resolution was then passed:

> "Whereas the States of New York, Pennsylvania, Maryland and California have passed C.P.A. laws and other states are known to be contemplating similar action:
> It is the sense of this meeting that the best efforts of all the members of this Association be put forth to secure the passage of a C.P.A. law at the next session of the Legislature of the State of Illinois, and that the President (George Wilkinson) be requested to name a committee to prepare and draft a Bill for a C.P.A. Law and submit the same to an adjourned meeting of the members of the Association to be called by the President."

This resolution was ratified at a meeting of the members held on August 18, 1902, on the motion of Allen R. Smart and seconded by A. Lowes Dickinson, two members voting against it. The President thereupon appointed Henry

J. D. Wodrich as chairman of the committee, as proposed in the foregoing paragraph, inasmuch as he had a large personal acquaintance with members of both houses of the State Legislature. While the minutes of this meeting failed to state the names of the other two members of this committee, if my memory be correct they were Allen R. Smart and J. Porter Joplin.

Mr. Wodrich's sudden and untimely death in December, 1902, gave a serious setback to these plans and the line of campaign had to be entirely changed. The Legislative Committee was then enlarged so that it would be fully representative of all the accountants practicing in the state and not merely of those accountants who were members of the Association. To carry out this object, Edward E. Gore of the Audit Company of Chicago and Maurice S. Kuhns of the Safeguard Account Co., neither of whom at that date being members of the Association, (though they became members on March 16, 1903) were added to the membership of the Legislative Commitee, George Wilkinson being, of course, also as an "ex-officio" member.

The members of this committee were most active, giving much of their time to promote the passage of the C.P.A. law, not only in Chicago, but by their presence in Springfield when the legislature was in session. I think, also, that without in any way detracting from the credit due to the other members, special mention and praise should be accorded to Mr. J. Porter Joplin who was in almost constant attendance at the legislative session in Springfield.

At a meeting held on December 19, 1902 the Legislative Committee was authorized to make arrangements with Senator Dan Campbell by which the latter would nominate some well qualified person who would make it his duty to watch the interests of the Association in the passage of a C.P.A. law.

During this time the Association had secured the active and most valuable cooperation of Messrs. Gore, Kuhns, Dunning and Knisely, all of

244

whom were the active heads of audit companies, and therefore ineligible to become members of the Association. It is, in my opinion, quite doubtful whether the C.P.A. law of 1903 would have passed without their cooperation, especially the experience and time contributed by Edward E. Gore.

Therefore, at a meeting held February 2, 1903 the by-laws of the Association were amended so that members, officers or employes of incorporated companies doing business as public accountants were eligible as members of the Association. As a direct result of this amendment to the by-laws, the following accountants, all connected with audit companies, were elected members of the Association on March 16, 1903:

A. W. Dunning of the Audit Company of New York
Edward E. Gore of the Audit Company of Chicago
Maurice S. Kuhns of the Safeguard Account Company

and on May 2, 1903 Mr. C. W. Knisely, of the Illinois Audit Company, was also elected. Each of these men contributed largely to the success of the campaign for a C.P.A. law.

As soon as the legislature was organized the Bill was introduced simultaneously in both Houses. This Bill, as prepared by the Legislative Committee, differed considerably from the Bills of 1897 and 1899, for it provided that certificates should be issued by the Secretary of State instead of the University of Illinois; that the Governor of the State of Illinois should appoint the Board of Examiners whose members were to be public accountants who had been practicing three years or more, and whose successors must be Certified Public Accountants. The waiver clause provided that accountants with five years of previous experience might be certified without examination.

While the approval of this Bill was still pending in the Senate and House Committees, George Wilkinson, J. Porter Joplin and another member of the committee visited Springfield to watch over the advancement of the Bill.

To their consternation they discovered that the Bill as introduced, providing for the appointment of the Board of Examiners by the Governor of the State, could not, in all probability, be approved by the Legislative Committees. Evidently there was a strong feeling on the part of members of the legislature that the measure as first introduced would merely give Governor Yates another Board, affording him another opportunity for political patronage.

The members of our committee immediately rewrote the whole Bill, spending a large part of that night in its preparation and the next morning submitted it to President Draper of the University of Illinois, inasmuch as the Bill as rewritten gave the University the power to appoint the Board of Examiners instead of the Governor of the State, and he gave it his approval. This Bill was passed on May 15, 1903 and became effective on July 1, 1903, a copy of this Bill appearing in Appendix C.

246

One of the most important factors in securing the passage of this Act was the splendid cooperation of Dr. David Kinley, who, I believe, was at that time Secretary of the courses in Commerce recently inaugurated at the University of Illinois. Being a Scot, he knew the value of recognizing the accounting profession by suitable legislation, having been brought up among Scottish Chartered Accountants. He was therefore enthusiastic in promoting the legislation we were attempting to secure. Dr. Kinley later became the President of the University of Illinois and served as such for many years with great distinction.

As a member of the first Board of Examiners under the C.P.A. law, it was my privilege to come into close contact with Dr. Kinley, and to discuss with him some of the problems incidental to putting into effect certain provisions of the law. Dr. Kinley's interest in our profession never ceased and his name should ever stand high in the annals of our profession.

On May 19, 1903, four days after the passage of the Act, the an-

nual meeting of the Association was held and action was taken to have letters
of appreciation mailed to Senators Dan Campbell and Wilkerson for their as-
sistance and cooperation. In addition, it was resolved that the Secretary of the
Association should write to Dr. Kinley informing him of the passage of the
Act, and assuring him of the desire of the Association to cooperate with the
University of Illinois in every way.

The following resolution, prepared by Edward E. Gore, was also
unanimously adopted:

"Whereas an Act of the General Assembly of the State of Illinois,
soon to become in full force and effect, provides that the University of Illinois shall appoint a Board to undertake the examination
of, and the granting of certificates, to such persons desirous of becoming Certified Public Accountants, as may make application for
such examination, and
Whereas such Act provides that such Board of Examiners shall
consist of three members, at least two of whom shall be practicing public accountants, and
Whereas such Act leaves to the University of Illinois the limita-
tion of the term of office of the members of such Board of Examiners, and
Whereas The Illinois Association of Public Accountants caused
such Act to be considered by the legislative body, and was instrumental in securing its enactment into law and feels a deep
interest in the execution of the provisions thereof, now therefore
be it
Resolved That The Illinois Association of Public Accountants, in
Annual Meeting assembled, does tender to the University of Illinois its assistance and cooperation in the work of making such
Act effective and productive of the greatest possible usefulness,
and be it further
Resolved That in the opinion of this Association, the rules to be
adopted by the University of Illinois for the carrying into effect
of the provisions of this Act, should provide that the terms for
which examiners shall be appointed shall not exceed two years
and shall be so arranged as to give opportunity for change in the
membership of such annually, and be it further
Resolved That this Association respectfully submits to the favorable consideration of the University of Illinois, the following
names as being those of public accountants, the selection of any
of whom as members of the Board of Examiners would, in the
opinion of this Association, result in the Law being carried into
effect with credit to the University and with benefit to the profession of Public Accountancy

Frank M. Boughey	R. S. Buchanan
John A. Cooper	A. W. Dunning
Edward E. Gore	C. W. Knisely

247

76

Maurice S. Kuhns   John Leith
George O. May   F. K. Parke
Ernest Reckitt   Seymour Walton
and Henry W. Wilmot

and be it further
Resolved That a copy of this resolution properly attested be communicated to Dr. David Kinley, Dean of the School of Commerce and Accounts of the University of Illinois."

Undoubtedly in accordance with the above resolution the University of Illinois appointed the following accountants as its Board of Examiners:

Ernest Reckitt for one year, but reappointed for another term of three years

Clarence W. Knisely for two years, but reappointed for another three years

Alden W. Dunning for three years.

The University, however, decided to make the term of an Examiner three years instead of the two years recommended in the foregoing resolution, but in order to make a change in the composition of the members of the Board of Examiners each year, the terms of one year and two years in the case of Ernest Reckitt and Clarence W. Knisely, respectively, were in both cases extended to another three years.

As in the case of all C.P.A. laws, there was a provision for the granting of C.P.A. certificates under what has been called a "Waiver Clause" to public accountants who had been continuously in practice for five years immediately prior to the passage of the Act, with some other necessary qualifications. A complete knowledge of the terms upon which certificates under the Waiver Clause could be secured may be gained by turning to Appendix C, paragraph 3. The intent of this Waiver Clause was in two respects somewhat obscure and in order to clarify it, the University of Illinois ruled:

"(i) That a senior accountant, being an employe of a firm of public accountants and fulfilling the other requirements contained in paragraph 3, was in fact practicing on 'his own account' and

248

"(ii) That practicing public accountants and members of
their staffs, also fulfilling the other requirements contained
in paragraph 3, but not residing within the State of Illinois,
were eligible to receive the C.P.A. Certificate, provided that
the individual or partner maintained offices within the State
of Illinois."

A similar ruling had been made by the University of the State of

New York (and possibly by other states) for I had received my C.P.A. certif-

icate from that state in 1896 or 1897, though not residing there.

Naturally some controversy arose as to the issuance of C.P.A.

certificates without any written examinations and it was believed by some

that a Waiver Clause might result in a few public accountants of little ex-

perience being able to style themselves as Certified Public Accountants.

It was, of course, obvious that, as the first Board of Examiners

would not necessarily be Certified Public Accountants, a Waiver Clause was

essential and logical in order to operate. It was also realized that if any

accountant received a C.P.A. certificate under the Waiver Clause who was

not worthy of it through inexperience, he would soon fall by the wayside and

cease to practice. As a matter of fact, as it later developed, this was what

actually occurred, but there were very few of such cases.

During the four years, 1903 to 1906, inclusive, ninety-four C.P.A.

certificates under the Waiver Clause were issued and since the year 1906

another nine, making a total of 103. These figures are those reported to me

by the Committee on Accountancy of the University of Illinois in a letter they

sent at my request, dated January 6, 1947. Of these 103 certificates forty-

seven were issued to members of the Illinois Association of Public Account-

ants and sixty-six to practicing public accountants who had not been such

members. Most of the latter had been practicing in Chicago either individu-

ally or as members of staffs of public accountants. There were also a few

Certified Public Accountants or Chartered Accountants not necessarily residing in Illinois, among whom may be mentioned Louis G. Peloubet, Elijah W. Sells, George O. May, James Marwick, Simpson Roger Mitchell, Joseph E. Sterrett and John B. Niven.

As of September, 1949 of these 103 Certified Public Accountants who received their certificates under the Waiver Clause, seventy-five are definitely known to have died, thirteen cannot be traced, (some of them may have died or retired, their names no longer appearing in the 1945-1946 Year Book of the Institute) and fifteen are definitely known as living, among whom are:

Maurice S. Kuhns* of Chicago

Edward Frazer of Kansas City, Missouri

George O. May of New York City

R. O. Berger of Chicago

Harold Benington, now residing in Washington, D. C., but formerly of Chicago

James Hall, New York partner of Peat, Marwick, Mitchell & Co.

John Franklin Forbes of San Francisco

John B. Niven of New York City

Ernest Reckitt of Chicago

* Died October 10, 1949

The Committee on Accountancy of the University of Illinois publishes annually a register of all persons who have received Illinois C.P.A. certificates. In the latest register, covering the period up to date, it would appear that about 2,950 certificates had been issued. The Year Book of the Illinois Society for the year 1946-1947 shows a membership in excess of 1,200. Assuming that 200 Certified Public Accountants have died since receiving their certificates and that of the present membership of the Illinois

Society 60 were not Illinois Certified Public Accountants, it would appear likely that there are 2,750 Illinois C.P.A.'s still living and of that number only 1,150 were members of the Illinois Society. The register referred to indicates that many Illinois C.P.A.'s are no longer residents of Illinois, while others are not practicing, having taken positions in other lines of work. Nevertheless, the above statistics would indicate that there must be a large number of Illinois Certified Public Accountants who are eligible for membership in the Illinois Society.

This may be an appropriate place to refer to the fact that some women have also won favorable recognition as Certified Public Accountants. Miss Carrie Snyder started practice as a public accountant in 1893 and became a Certified Public Accountant under the waiver clause in 1904, receiving certificate No. 61. She carried on her practice for many years, I believe, until a short time before her death.

Miss Florence L. Sivertson was the next woman to succeed Miss Carrie Snyder as a Certified Public Accountant, winning her C.P.A. degree by written examination in 1918, certificate No. 190. Miss Sivertson is still active in her work as an accountant and she was the first woman to be elected a member of the Illinois Society. There were in 1947 at least sixteen other women who are also members of the Society.

Historical Sketches of Some of the More Prominent
Members of the Illinois Association of Public
Accountants During the Period from 1891 to 1903

"Where is the heart that doth not keep
Within its inmost core,
Some fond remembrance hidden deep
Of days that are no more."

Ellen C. Howarth in "'Tis but a little flower"

252

I propose in this chapter to give brief sketches of a few of those members of our profession in Illinois who stand out in my memory as being the foremost leaders in the growth of our profession in the period from 1891 to 1903 and especially in connection with their work which resulted finally in the passage of the C.P.A. law in 1903.

In a short history of those days it is quite impossible to describe the work of each and every one of those who so ably gave their time and money. If their names are not now referred to in this chapter, it is not because their services should be ignored, so I therefore submit a complete list in Appendix A of the membership of the Illinois Association of Public Accountants from the date of its organization in 1897 up to the time that the Illinois Society of Certified Public Accountants was organized in 1904, showing the date of their election as a member.

Inevitably in an organization of this character there were those who were more prominent in leadership than others, who from various causes had more time or opportunity to give of their time and money. By reason of my own activities I was able to make closer contacts with some members than with others equally worthy of notice, whom I did not know so well.

It can, however, be truthfully stated that all members were imbued with a unity of purpose and determination which created success. Looking back these many years I cannot remember any serious dissensions. Differences of opinion as to certain policies arose from time to time, but those differences were discussed in a friendly spirit and a united action determined.

GEORGE WILKINSON

Mr. Wilkinson was born in or near Manchester, England in 1856. As a young man he was sent to Shanghai, China, in the employ of British banking interests and he resided there for some years before coming to the United States about 1888. His first engagement as a public accountant was with the firm of Veysey & Veysey, followed by his employment as a Senior Accountant with the firm of Barrow, Wade, Guthrie & Co. Mr. Wilkinson must have progressed successfully in that capacity for in November, 1891 he was sent to that firm's Chicago office as its manager.

In 1895 he resigned and started to practice as an independent accountant under his own name until about 1902, when he entered into partnership with me and a Mr. John J. Williams under the name of Wilkinson, Reckitt & Williams, Mr. Wilkinson taking charge of the New York and Philadelphia offices of the firm. This partnership was dissolved about the year 1912, in a most amicable spirit and Mr. Wilkinson again started to practice as an independent accountant chiefly in the City of Philadelphia until his death in 1931 at the age of 75 years.

It was in 1892 that I first met Mr. Wilkinson when he was the Chicago manager of Barrow, Wade, Guthrie & Co. but it was not until 1895 that we really became well acquainted and a friendship began which lasted until his death.

As a qualified public accountant George Wilkinson ranked high, for his past experience in the science of accounting and his further training with Barrow, Wade, Guthrie & Co. had been excellent.

It is not, however, as a qualified accountant that his name appears first in these brief historical sketches but much more on account of his activities as the chief promoter in the organization of the Illinois Association of Public Accountants in 1897 and the success of this Association in securing the C.P.A. Law in 1903 with the assistance of other practicing public accountants. In addition to these valuable activities he probably did more than any other man in promoting the growth of our profession throughout the United States and in the organization of the Federation of Societies of Public Accountants in 1902, culminating in the first Congress of Accountants held in St. Louis, Mo. in 1904, full details of which are given in Chapter 10.

My opinion as expressed above, might be considered by some as a prejudiced one, for George Wilkinson was my life-long friend and my partner for ten years, but this opinion is not only mine but was that of most public accountants active in our profession, some of whom, I am glad to say are still living. I refer to Mr. William M. Lybrand, T. Edward Ross and Col. Robert M. Montgomery.

He was capable now and then, of short bursts of temper, for "he could not suffer fools gladly," but his energy and zeal knew no bounds and he never permitted himself any relaxation when the interests of our profession were at stake, even if his own financial interests suffered in consequence.

In his later years he withdrew from the activities to which he had given so much, leaving to younger men the "White Man's Burden" and also in order to attend more to the building up of his clientele, for his sacrifices for the benefit of our profession had necessarily affected his personal finances.

No attempt will be made in this chapter to outline in detail all the many activities of Mr. Wilkinson, for a perusal of the succeeding chapters deal

254

fully with his accomplishments and the debt that our profession owes him.

J. PORTER JOPLIN

Mr. Joplin was born in England on March 23, 1859, the son of a
Baptist minister who was a close friend of the Reverend Spurgeon, a very
noted Evangelist of those days. When Mr. Joplin was six years old his family
moved to Nova Scotia where his father had been sent to take charge of a Baptist Church, Mr. Joplin, however, being sent back to England for his education. At the age of twenty-one he went to Boston and was employed by and
kept under the wing of Colonel Lee Higginson who was a leading financier and
the founder of the Boston Symphony Orchestra.

Mr. Joplin, while in the employ of Lee Higginson & Co., was sent
to Colorado and other western states, as well as to Florida, in the interests
of that firm, making financial investigations until about the year 1893. He then
came to Chicago and started his practice as a public accountant, being associated with Seymour Walton in 1896 under the firm name of Walton, Joplin &
Co. He lived to the age of seventy-nine, passing away on December 24, 1938.

Mr. Seymour Walton and Mr. J. Porter Joplin made a grand team
in all the activities of the Illinois Association, and its successor The Illinois
Society, in the early years of our profession.

An account of Mr. Walton's contributions to our profession is
given hereafter, but it is only fair to add that such activities on his part
would have been seriously impeded, if Mr. Joplin had not been equally interested.

Undoubtedly in the years 1902 and 1903, when Mr. Joplin was
giving so much time to secure the passage of the 1903 C.P.A. law and also
acting as Secretary of the Illinois Association, it was necessary for Mr. Walton to give more time to their clients, while the reverse situation arose when

Mr. Walton gave so much of his time to the editorship and the publishing of "The Auditor" and to the organization of the Northwestern University School of Commerce. In any case they made a great team, each supplementing the work of the other.

Not only was Mr. Joplin a guarantor against any loss that the Northwestern University might incur in the first three years of the operation of the School of Commerce, but was one of the largest donors of cash towards the erection of the present building on Chicago Avenue housing that School.

Mr. Joplin was not only a man of the highest integrity, but the possessor of sound judgment in his professional life. He was rather the type of man usually described as "self-effacing" and modest. He was one of the most dependable persons I ever had the privilege of knowing. As an illustration of his innate modesty, when he, as Secretary of the Illinois Association, rendered a report at the annual meeting held on May 26, 1903 of the activities of the Association resulting in the passage of the C.P.A. law he never referred to his own share in that success, but gave the most credit to Mr. George Wilkinson and Mr. Edward E. Gore. The omission of the time he had himself given was immediately noted by others and a resolution was offered and unanimously carried, giving unstinted praise to Mr. Joplin for his services.

In 1902 and later Mr. Joplin also gave much of his time to the organization and conduct of the "Federation of Societies of Public Accountants" which later was merged with the American Association of Public Accountants under the name of the latter Society, as more fully set forth in Chapter 10.

SEYMOUR WALTON

While Mr. Walton was not so active as his partner, J. Porter Joplin, in those activities which culminated in the passage of the 1903 C.P.A. law (for after all one partner must carry on the professional work of a firm

if the other partner is so deeply engaged in the promotion of our profession)
we owe a great debt of gratitude and appreciation for his devotion to the cause
of the education of accountants after the year 1903.

It would probably be difficult to find two men of such entirely different temperaments and characters as George Wilkinson and Seymour Walton, the former being a great organizer and of the aggressive type, while Mr. Walton was a great educator and of a quiet dignified character. The success of any organization requires men of different personalities to make a strong efficient team, and the Illinois Association was thus blessed.

Mr. Walton was born in New Orleans in 1846 and he inherited the ideals and culture which we connect with a refined Southern gentleman and in his personal appearance he certainly looked the part. Physically, as I remember him, he looked frail, but nevertheless he possessed an indomitable spirit which carried him to success in whatever he sought to accomplish. He died in 1920 at an age of about 74, beloved by all who had the privilege of knowing him.

Mr. Walton's training had been that of a banker and in that capacity he came to Chicago to become an officer of the Fort Dearborn National Bank. This bank was, in 1922, absorbed by one of the larger banks, the Continental and Commercial Bank.

Apparently Mr. Walton resigned his official position with the bank about the year 1893, for his name appears for the first time as a public accountant in that year as a partner in the firm of Griffin & Walton. In 1896 he entered into partnership with J. Porter Joplin under the firm name of Walton, Joplin & Company, a happy association which lasted for many years and an honorable name still in practice.

I remember vividly my first meeting both Mr. Walton and Mr. Joplin, being accompanied on that occasion by George Wilkinson, and the courteous reception accorded to us when we expressed the hope that they would join the Illinois Association of Public Accountants. Our visit appears to have borne fruit, for Mr. Joplin joined the Association on October 17, 1898 and Mr. Walton on August 30, 1899.

Two activities of Mr. Walton stand out especially, both of which have been of great benefit to our profession and both of which should be recorded in any history of our profession in Illinois.

Probably no one put in so much time and energy as Mr. Walton in the organization and editorship of the monthly magazine sponsored by the Illinois Society, entitled "The Auditor," to which he contributed many articles on accountancy subjects. A special chapter (No. 11) in this history is devoted to "The Auditor" in which it is pointed out that the first number appeared in September, 1904.

The other great achievement of Mr. Walton was his participation in the foundation of the Northwestern University School of Commerce, which, with assistance of other practicing public accountants and some leading business men, was founded in the year 1908, Mr. Walton being appointed the first professor in "the theory and practice of Accounting." This association of Mr. Walton with the University lasted for two or three years when he founded "The Walton School of Commerce" which has continued ever since as a prosperous concern now under the ownership of Mr. Langer, C.P.A.

A separate chapter (No. 12) in this history is devoted to the organization of the Northwestern University School of Commerce setting forth the efforts of the Illinois Society to have such a school created, beginning with the year 1905, to its final success in 1908.

EDWARD E. GORE

Born near Carlinville, Illinois, in 1866, Edward Everett Gore had an early heritage of prosperity and success. His father, David Gore, was a farmer, a founder of the Illinois Agricultural Association, and later a state senator and State Auditor. Possibly this is why Edward E. Gore read law and, during the administration of Governor Altgeld, became one of the youngest Justices of the Peace in Illinois. His own honeymoon was scarcely over before he was presiding at the marriages of his contemporaries. In 1893 he became chief of the Building and Loan Department of the State Auditor's Office, and in 1895 he took over the additional duties of chief of the State Banking Department. Thus he acquired that knowledge of law and accounts which was the foundation of his future profession, and that understanding of the ways of politicians which he later turned to the advantage of that profession.

259

Lured to Chicago by the promise of a job, he brought his growing family to the south side and established them there, only to find that promises can be broken. In the face of this catastrophe he first set himself up as a public accountant in 1897, taking desk space in an office with three young lawyers. Later he joined the Audit Company of Chicago and became its President, but returned to practice under his own name, realizing that public accounting could not properly be carried on by a corporation. He became a member of the Illinois Association of Public Accountants March 16, 1903. From 1908 to 1910 he deserted public accounting to be the Vice-President of the Assets Realization Company, but at the end of that term he returned to his chosen field, joining Allen R. Smart, who was the resident partner in Chicago in the firm of Barrow, Wade, Guthrie & Co. Mr. Smart and Mr. Gore served as partners in this firm until 1922 when they organized their own firm under the name of Smart, Gore & Co. This firm operated until 1927 when, with the friendliest feelings on both sides, the partners separated. Mr. Smart then organized the firm of Allen R. Smart & Co., and Mr. Gore, the firm of Edward Gore & Co. It was during this period that Mr. Gore became one of

88

the founders of a unique nationwide affiliation of accounting firms known as Pace, Gore & McLaren. He continued, however, to practice under his own name until his death in 1935.

If George Wilkinson was a great organizer and Seymour Walton a great educator in our profession, Edward E. Gore was a past master in dealing with our politicians in Springfield. His experience along these lines, his large acquaintance, and his capacity for making friends among those active in Illinois politics were most valuable aids in securing the passage of the C.P.A. law in 1903, and in keeping it on the books thereafter. And this was done, as he once said, "without expenditure of any funds for the benefit of members of the legislature." Without Mr. Gore's assistance, it is questionable, in my opinion, whether this law would have been passed in 1903, notwithstanding the valuable work of George Wilkinson, J. Porter Joplin and others.

Mr. Gore's services to our profession did not cease with the passage of the 1903 C.P.A. law. For several years he served as a director of the Illinois Society. In 1904 he was its Secretary and Treasurer, and the minutes of the Society in those years bear testimony to his fine penmanship. He became President of the Society in 1906. During those early years he was one of the guarantors of the Northwestern University School of Commerce, and one of its volunteer lecturers. Throughout his life he was devoted to the cause of professional accountancy, and in 1923 he became President of the American Institute of Accountants.

Mr. Gore's services were not confined to his profession. He was equally well known for the public and patriotic services he so freely gave. He received citations for his work on liberty loan drives during the first World War. He served a term as President of the School Board in La Grange, Illinois, where he lived. He was active in the Chamber of Commerce of the United

States. He was one of the founders, and for many years the President, of the Chicago Crime Commission. For fifteen years he was an active member of the Chicago Association of Commerce, and in 1922 he became the first professional accountant to be elected President of that organization. During this time he was instrumental in arbitrating a disastrous street car strike in Chicago, and in this activity he displayed such courage that it was felt necessary to place a police guard around his home. In writing of his services to the Chicago Association of Commerce, Mr. C. W. Judd, its acting business manager, said, "His contribution to the public good in the way of time and energy cannot be measured." The fact that his presidency of the Association, and the outstanding success of his administration, reflected great credit on the accounting profession in Chicago, led his fellow members of the Illinois Society to hold a testimonial dinner in his honor at the Blackstone Hotel, following his term of office.

261

But most of all Mr. Gore loved people. Wherever he went, even abroad, he would look up accountants and call on them, and because of this he was probably one of the most widely known accountants of his time. Because of his genial personality and kindly wit, he was constantly in demand as presiding officer, toastmaster and speaker. I have never heard Mr. Gore criticize any man in an unkind spirit. I have never heard him complain of his own afflictions, although he had them, but he was always ready to go out of his way to perform good and charitable deeds for others.

JOHN ALEXANDER COOPER

Mr. Cooper was born in England and as a boy was sent to the "Blue Coats School" in London.

This school was a very old institution and the students had to wear the type of clothes which prevailed centuries ago of a medieval character, consisting of long blue cloaks and knickerbockers, yellow stockings and buckled shoes. Mr. Cooper was quite proud of having been a student of this school and he had a right to be, for it had turned out many boys who later became famous.

As a young man he came to the United States and entering the employ of the Pullman Company, he advanced to a position of considerable responsibility in its accounting department.

Leaving the Pullman Company he started to practice as a public accountant in Chicago under his own name as early as 1890 or 1891. Mr. Cooper was a charter member of the Illinois Association and received his certificate to practice as a Certified Public Accountant in 1904. He remained in active practice until a year or so before he died in 1926 at the age of about eighty years.

No account of our profession in its early years would be complete without some words of appreciation of the quite unique character of Mr. Cooper. Being of British birth myself, I think I can say, without any disparagement of Mr. Cooper, that he was a typical "Johnnie Bull." Nevertheless, we all loved him in spite of some of his idiosyncracies and admired him for never letting go of anything he got his teeth into.

Due to his practicing wholly by himself, without a partner, it was difficult for him to take any leading part in any campaign for the passage of C.P.A. legislation, but he was always ready to carry out any task specifically assigned to him.

We are, however, especially indebted to Mr. Cooper for his interest in and devotion to the subject of "Professional Ethics." He carried on this activity with great success, not only in the Illinois Society, but also in the American Association of Public Accountants. In the early years there was only a limited appreciation of professional ethics in the United States and much was lacking in its practice. Mr. Cooper was unquestionably an outstanding influence in the improvement of professional ethics.

M. S. KUHNS

Mr. Kuhns, the senior partner of M. S. Kuhns & Co. deserves recognition in this history for his assistance in the passage of the C.P.A. law in 1903; also for being a pioneer in the introduction of improved forms of bookkeeping records. (See Chapter 2). He began his career as a public accountant in the city of Boston in 1886. In the year 1890 he moved to Chicago, retaining his Boston office and an office in New York City which had been opened in 1888. He is, therefore, probably the oldest practicing public accountant in the Illinois Society at this time.

263

After the New York C.P.A. law was passed in 1896 he became a Certified Public Accountant of that state. On coming to Chicago, he was active in, and possibly the founder of, "The Chicago Association of Accountants and Book-keepers," organized for the interchange of ideas on accounting problems. Mr. Kuhns became a member of the Illinois Association on March 16, 1903, and immediately became active in promoting the passage of the Illinois C.P.A. law. He was one of the members of a committee, including George Wilkinson, Edward E. Gore, J. Porter Joplin, and Allen R. Smart, which went to Springfield to persuade the Illinois legislators of the necessity and advisability of the passage of this law.

When the Bill was presented, it had been referred to the Judiciary Committee, of which Mr. McKinley (later United States Senator from Illinois) was chairman. It appears that the Judiciary Committee invited the Accountants' committee to appear before it in order to determine on the necessity or otherwise of the passage of a C.P.A. law. As Mr. Kuhns was the only Certified Public Accountant (New York State) of the Accountants' Committee, he was requested to be the spokesman for this group. Mr. Kuhns appears to have done a very good job in the presentation of our claims for recognition. However, after addressing the Judiciary Committee at some length to the dismay of the committee, the chairman, Mr. McKinley, pounded the table saying he had heard enough. For a moment Mr. Kuhns and the other members felt that their efforts had been in vain and that another session of the legislature had passed without any progress having been made, but they were greatly relieved when chairman McKinley went on to state, "I am for this Bill and will do everything in my power to have it passed at this session of the legislature."

In addition to his activities as a public accountant, Mr. Kuhns was the founder of the Workman Mfg. Co., which took over the business of the Safeguard Account Co., manufacturing books of account on a large scale. He also was the founder and President of the National Chess Federation of the U.S.A., he himself being an excellent player of this ancient game.

ALLEN R. SMART

Mr. Smart was born in Peterborough, England, on October 21, 1867 and started his accountancy career in 1885 in the office of his brother in that city. By the year 1891 he had arrived in New York City and had been engaged as a senior accountant with the firm of Barrow, Wade, Guthrie & Co. In 1895 Mr. Anyon, the senior partner of the firm sent Mr. Smart to Chicago as manager to succeed George Wilkinson who had just resigned in order to practice on his own account. Mr. Smart remained as head of the Chicago office of that firm until 1922, a period of 27 years.

From 1922 to 1926 he was a partner in the firm of Smart, Gore & Co., after which he practiced under the name of Allen R. Smart & Co., his two sons being associated with him, until his death on February 8, 1940 at the age of seventy-three.

Mr. Smart became a member of the Illinois Association of Public Accountants on October 18, 1898 and was an important factor in its success. He was a member of the Legislation Committee appointed for the purpose of securing prompt action by the Illinois Legislature in the passage of the C.P. A. law in 1903, also serving on other committees.

These services were recognized by his election as President on the founding of our present organization, the Illinois Society of Certified Public Accountants, and he was also presented by the first Board of Examiners with Certificate No. 1.

I believe that Mr. Smart was one of the first to insist that all of 265 his senior accountants should not only study for the C.P.A. examinations but also to take such examinations. He also added to accounting literature a number of articles of much interest, the chief of which I remember being his address to the members of the Association on April 10, 1900 on "Commercial Investigations" and his article in the Journal of Accountancy in 1906 entitled "Accountants as advisers to the manufacturer."

Apart from his high standing as a Certified Public Accountant, his judicial temperament was recognized by all who knew him. He possessed that rather rare quality, after listening quietly to all the "pros" and "cons" of any discussion, of summing up the factors and reaching a sound judgment based upon logical conclusions. Finally he was a genial and a good friend, always willing to give good counsel to those who sought his advice.

<u>LEWIS D. JONES</u>

and a brief mention of others associated with
<u>Price, Waterhouse & Co.</u>

During the life of the Illinois Association from 1897 to 1904 there had been a total of sixty-seven members (see Appendix A), of which twenty-three were partners or members of the staff of Price, Waterhouse & Co. It would therefore seem appropriate that, in giving a brief sketch of Lewis D. Jones, mention should be made of a few others associated with that firm during the seven years, in order to record the continuance of the firm's interest and participation in the Illinois Association and the C.P.A. movement after Mr. Jones' untimely death in February 1899 while serving his second term as President of the Association.

In 1890 Mr. Lewis D. Jones and Mr. William J. Caesar, both then in the London office of Price, Waterhouse & Co., were sent to the United States to open agencies of the London firm in New York and Chicago for the purpose of looking after the existing work of the firm for British clients interested in American enterprises or branches of British concerns and to undertake to develop also a clientele originating in America. The New York and Chicago agency offices were opened practically simultaneously in 1890 and for several years Mr. Jones was resident in New York and Mr. Caesar was resident in Chicago. During that time Mr. Jones frequently spent long periods in Chicago, where much of the American business for British clients was undertaken, and in the spring of 1894 he definitely transferred his residence to Chicago and Mr. Caesar moved to New York. As of January 1, 1895 the American firm of Jones, Caesar & Co. was established which acted as agents for the London firm of Price, Waterhouse & Co. and gradually developed an American clientele. This arrangement continued until the American firm of Price, Waterhouse & Co., Certified Public Accountants, was established a few years later in a form which, I understand, is substantially preserved today.

Thus Mr. Jones had been identified with the accounting practice in Chicago and Illinois since 1890. He was a charter member of the Illinois Association of Public Accountants and was elected its first President. Mr.

Caesar, the New York partner of the firm, became a member of the Illinois Association in October, 1900 but resigned in 1903, after he had retired from the American firm and left the United States to reside in Paris, France.

Some of the charter members of the Illinois Association had had only limited public accounting experience at that time; hence it was a great asset to this young Association to have in Mr. Jones, as its first President, an eminent Chartered Accountant of England and Wales, well grounded in British accounting experience, standards and ethics. Other Chartered Accountants who were charter members were Frank M. Boughey, in practice on his own account, and George E. Shaw, a partner of Kidson, Buchanon & Co. The membership, in the Illinois Association at its inception, of these chartered accountants was a most valuable influence in giving the Association a high standing at the outset. It was a great misfortune to the Association that Mr. Jones was suddenly taken ill and died early in February, 1899. He was a brilliant accountant and a man of fine character, esteemed by all who knew him; and though gentle in nature he was firm in upholding high professional standards.

267

Following Mr. Jones' death, Mr. Charles J. Marr, who had been in the Chicago office of the firm since August, 1895, became Chicago manager and was admitted as a partner of the firm not long afterwards. He was elected as a Director of the Illinois Society on its formation in 1904. Mr. Henry W. Wilmot, who became a partner in the New York office in July, 1899, was transferred to Chicago temporarily in March, 1900 and immediately joined the Illinois Association of which he served as Vice-President for the year 1903-1904. He returned to the New York office shortly afterwards. Mr. A. Lowes Dickinson, who succeeded Mr. Caesar as senior partner of the American firm in July 1901, promptly joined the Illinois Association and was frequently in Chicago. He was one of the ablest public accountants in the United States during his residence in this country and he contributed much to the literature of our profession.

Mr. George O. May, who was transferred from the London office to the New York office in July, 1897, joined the Illinois Association in 1902 and is still a member of the Illinois Society and very active in our profession. He always had a deep interest in the profession in Illinois and addressed many of the meetings of that Society throughout the years on subjects of timely interest. He succeeded Mr. Dickinson as senior partner of the firm in 1911.

Mention should be made of two early members of the supervising staff of the firm who were admitted as such to membership in the Illinois Association in January, 1899, and later became prominent in the profession on their own account - namely, Mr. John B. Niven who established the firm of Touche, Niven & Co. and Mr. Louis J. Peloubet, one of the founders of Pogson, Peloubet & Co. His son, Maurice E. Peloubet, has been a partner in that firm for many years and takes a very active part in the affairs of the American Institute of Accountants.

Other members of the firm of Price, Waterhouse & Co., who were managers or supervising accountants during their membership in the Illinois Association but who later became partners were George R. Webster, who joined the Illinois Association in February, 1903, Robert O. Berger in March, 1903 and W. Ernest Seatree in April, 1903. Mr. Seatree was elected President of the Illinois Society in 1908 and Mr. Berger was elected to that office in 1914.

268

CHAPTER 9

The Illinois Society of Certified Public Accountants
1903 to 1912

"Arts and Sciences are not cast in one mould,
but are found and perfected by degrees, by
often handling and polishing."

Montaigne

Prior to the dissolution of the Illinois Association of Public Accountants, a committee consisting of Edward E. Gore, Allen R. Smart and Seymour Walton had been appointed in order to organize a new Society to be composed entirely of Certified Public Accountants (see Chapter 6).

A charter was applied for under the laws of the State of Illinois and was issued under date of November 6, 1903. The first meeting was held May 17, 1904 at which the charter was signed, a set of by-laws adopted and a tentative Board of Directors and officers were elected, namely:

Directors - John A. Cooper, Edward E. Gore, J. Porter Joplin, Charles S. Ludlam (the Chicago partner of Haskins and Sells), C. J. Marr (the Chicago partner of Price, Waterhouse & Co.), Ernest Reckitt and Allen R. Smart

Officers - Allen R. Smart, President
J. Porter Joplin, Vice-President
Edward E. Gore, Secretary and Treasurer

At the first regular meeting of the Society held on July 5, 1904 the election of the directors and officers named above was confirmed, as also the by-laws.

As stated in Chapter 6, when the Illinois Association disbanded and gave up its charter it had 54 members. Six of these members did not elect to apply for certificates as Illinois Certified Public Accountants under the waiver clause and action on one was temporarily deferred, thus leaving only forty-seven men receiving such certificates, all of whom became members of the Illinois Society.

Between the date of the organization in 1904 and October, 1906, a period of slightly over two years, seven new members had been elected, but this gain was offset by a loss of seven members who, through death, moving away from Chicago or lack of interest, had resigned, thus leaving only forty-seven members in 1906.

In this and subsequent chapters I propose to give a history of the main activities of the Society from 1904 to 1912. The later chapters, because of their importance, are dealt with separately as follows:

270

1. The continued cooperation with the "Federation of Societies of Public Accountants" which had been organized in the year 1902, due in large measure to members of the Illinois Association of Public Accountants, as outlined in Chapter 6. Chapter 10 gives a more detailed history of this Federation.

2. The publication of the magazine known as "The Auditor" promoted by the Illinois Society at its meeting held on August 24, 1904, which was the fore-runner of the "Journal of Accountancy" and Chapter 11 gives an account of this subject.

3. The creation of the Northwestern University's School of Commerce, details of which appear in chapter 12.

4. Cooperation with the Chicago Association of Commerce through its Subscription Investigation Committee for the audit of all philanthropic institutions desirous of securing the approval of the Chicago Association of Commerce, details of which appear in chapter 13.

Other activities of the Society from 1904 to 1912 of some interest are now submitted:

Illegal Use of the Title of Certified Public Accountant

After the passage of the Illinois C.P.A. law, as will be easily understood, certain cases arose when public accountants, not certified, nevertheless advertised themselves as such. In such cases the Illinois Society took prompt action to stop this illegal use of the C.P.A. degree. With one exception the offenders voluntarily corrected their previous malpractices.

In the case of the exception referred to above, legal action had to be taken and the offender was found guilty and fined $25. After this little or no difficulty arose in respect to the illegal use of the designation of Certified Public Accountant, but another more technical point was settled, as described in the following paragraph.

Certain firms advertised themselves as Certified Public Accountants in the Chicago Classified Directory, yet only some of the partners were certified, others were not. The Society took the position that a firm should not use the title of "Certified Public Accountants" unless all partners were "certified" and there has been no difficulty on this point since that time as far as I am aware.

A Proposed Organization of a National Association of Certified Public Accountants

The American Association of Public Accountants had always numbered among its members, after the passage of the New York State C.P.A. law in 1896, certain men who were not Certified Public Accountants in any state. When the American Association was merged with the Federation of Societies of Certified Public Accountants late in 1904 or early in 1905, under the title of the American Association of Public Accountants but adopting the form of organization of the Federation, one of the problems to be worked out was what should be the status of those who were not Certified Public Accountants because they practiced in states having no C.P.A. laws. The answer was that they should retain their membership under the title of "Members at Large."

In December 1907 an article written by Mr. C. N. Vollum, a member of the Pennsylvania Institute, appeared in which he strongly recommended the organization of a National Association of Certified Accountants, for the reason that so many of the accountants who were members of the American Association were not Certified Public Accountants (see Volume V of the

"Journal of Accountancy," pages 100 to 106).

In 1908 the Pennsylvania Institute of Certified Public Accountants also felt that the inclusion of these "Members at Large" was an anomaly and proposed that a National Association of Certified Public Accountants should be organized composed solely of Certified Public Accountants. The Illinois Society, with its wisdom and caution, opposed this plan and at its meeting on June 9, 1908 passed a resolution which I quote as follows:

1. "Formation of such a new society would result either in the abandonment by Certified Public Accountants of memberships in the American Association, leaving that body one of ordinary accountants but retaining all the prestige of its 21 years of existence with its close affiliation in the past with certified members or else there would result the concurrent membership by certified public accountants in both organizations.

2. "It is the reasonable hope of all accountants that all the more important States of the U.S.A. will shortly pass C.P.A. laws, with the result that virtually all of the members of the American Association will be able to obtain the title of Certified Public Accountant from their own State and thus secure the consummation of what the Pennsylvania Institute desired to secure.

3. "Therefore the Illinois Society is not in favor of taking any radical action at this time but proposes that a by-law be adopted by the American Association absolutely prohibiting the admission as a "Member at Large" of any person whomsoever from any State having a C.P.A. Law and also of any person to its membership through the medium of a Society in a State not having a C.P.A. Law, if that person is a Certified Public Accountant and has not connected himself with the Society in the State from which he obtained his certificate.

4. "The Illinois Society is of the opinion that this course will eventually make the C.P.A. membership in the American Association the largely predominant element and will reduce the Non-C.P.A. membership to a negligible quantity.

5. "The Illinois Society has already adopted a resolution declining to ratify the election as a "Member at Large" of any person from the State of Illinois and intends to propose, and will attempt to have adopted, an amendment to the By-Laws of the American Association as indicated in this resolution."

The terms of the above resolution were duly acted upon by the

101

American Association and became a part of its rules and thus a duplication of Societies was avoided. In due course of time those who had been "Members at Large" became Certified Public Accountants.

However, in the year 1921 the "American Society of Certified Public Accountants" was organized and it published a monthly magazine called "The Certified Public Accountant." This Society secured a large membership of Certified Public Accountants, many of whom also were members of the American Institute of Accountants. This duplication of effort finally resulted in the American Institute of Accountants' assimilating the membership of the American Society of Certified Public Accountants and the latter organization was disbanded, this uniting of effort proving of much benefit to the profession as a whole.

273

Privileged Communications

This subject was introduced by John A. Cooper at a meeting of the Society on November 26, 1904 and, as far as I am aware, this was the first occasion this important matter was discussed. Therefore, I believe that the Illinois Society should receive the credit for the first recommendation that accountants might have the same privileges as those extended to lawyers, doctors and ministers and that all confidential information secured through their audits and investigations for their clients should be equally privileged in respect to giving evidence in a Court of Law. At a meeting of the Illinois Society held on May 12, 1908 a discussion of this important subject again took place and a resolution was passed that the Society should attempt to have a law enacted giving Certified Public Accountants the same privileges as doctors, etc., in respect to such confidential information.

While there is nothing in the minutes of the Society's records to show that the action recommended above was ever followed up at that time, the publicity given to it undoubtedly resulted in other state Societies working towards similar endeavors. In the August 1911 issue of the "Journal of Accountancy" appears an article by John B. Geijsbeck, a Certified Public Accountant of Denver, urging the necessity of securing laws in all states, giving immunity to accountants from contempt of court if they refused to divulge the financial affairs of their client, inasmuch as such information was of a purely confidential character.

It appears, however, from the investigation I have made that no state passed any law granting this immunity until the year 1924. On page 456 of Volume XXXXII of the Journal of Accountancy covering the year 1924 we find that the State of Maryland passed such a law which read:

274

> "Except by express permission of the person employing him, or of the heirs, personal representatives or successors of such person, a certified public accountant, or public accountant or person employed by a certified public accountant or public accountant shall not be required to, and shall not voluntarily disclose or divulge the contents of any communication made to him by any person employing him, audit or report on any books, records or accounts in rendering professional service; provided that nothing in this section shall be taken or construed as modifying, changing or affecting the criminal laws of this State or the bankruptcy laws."

It would also appear from another article appearing in the same issue of the "Journal of Accountancy," that a few other states had also secured similar legislation as that of the State of Maryland.

It was not, however, until 1931 that the Illinois Legislature passed a law granting the same relief as given by the Maryland Legislature.

Notwithstanding the state laws affecting Privileged Communications, Judge Murray Hulbert, of the United States District Court for the Southern District of the State of New York, ruled in April, 1937 that accountants are not privileged and that they can be compelled as witnesses to disclose any matters pertaining to their clients' affairs and that if they refuse to do so, they could be held in "contempt of court."

Committee on Terminology

The Illinois Society very early in its history, namely, on January 5, 1909 (realizing that many popular accounting terms required more accurate definitions, and that there were duplications of terms, thus creating confusion in the minds of the public as to what the real meaning was) adopted a resolution which recommended the desirability of the appointment of a committee to report on the definitions of professional nomenclature. Definite action was taken at the Denver convention of the American Association of Public Accountants held in September, 1909 at which time a resolution was adopted requesting the President, Mr. J. E. Sterrett, to appoint a special committee to study the whole subject of nomenclature and make a report thereon. Mr. Sterrett then appointed as members of such a committee: Seymour Walton, Chairman; James T. Anyon and Edward L. Suffern, all Certified Public Accountants, and the following economists: Allen Ripley Foote of Columbus, Ohio; Professor Stephen Gilman of the University of Wisconsin and Dean French Johnson of the New York University School of Commerce.

275

This topic of nomenclature has been the subject of further investigation ever since and various committees have reported their findings from time to time.

Audit Companies

While the original Illinois Association of Public Accountants welcomed the valuable assistance given by the managers of four large audit companies in securing the passage of the C.P.A. law and amended its by-laws so as to make members of the staff of audit companies eligible as members of the Association, (see chapter 7) yet it was believed that an audit company was not a proper medium for professional activity, and there was much discussion during the first few years of the Illinois Society on this subject.

When the Illinois C.P.A. law was passed, fourteen audit companies were in existence, four to six of which had an extensive clientele. With possibly one exception they have all gone out of business many years ago.

However, in the year 1904, and prior thereto, this question of audit companies was a real problem to those of us who practiced as firms. This is illustrated by a discussion on this subject at the Congress of Accountants held at St. Louis, Missouri, in September, 1904:

George Wilkinson addressing the Congress stated in part:

"During the last few years a new form of conducting the accountancy profession has been developed in the 'incorporated audit company,' of which there are several specimens in each of our largest cities. The remarks herein contained are applied to incorporated companies whose directors are not professional accountants. The plan is this: Half a dozen citizens who are engaged in business as bankers, merchants, lawyers, presidents of insurance or trust companies and the like, are induced to take some shares in an incorporated audit company and to become directors. Flattering prospects are held out to them of profits to be made out of large accounting fees to be secured through the exploitation of their names and official titles, as they are 'let in on the ground floor.' The names of the bankers and business men on the Board are conspicuously advertised in the City Directories, trade papers, etc., and on the company's letter paper and elsewhere as a bait to obtain business. It is obviously to the pecuniary benefit of the banker, director, etc., to send any business, over which he can exert an influence, to the audit company of which he is a shareholder, also to consent to a fee that he would call outrageous if charged by an independent accountant.

"These questions follow: Can a corporation so engaged fulfill the duties of the public accountant? Is it a proper custodian of the business confidence of the public? Can a corporation, whose directors are business men, without technical experience in the science and theory of accountants really act as an accountant? Is it not a make-believe and a sham to call it an accountant?

"The influence of incorporated audit companies is to commercialize the profession and reduce it to the common level of trades and manufacturers, while our influence, exercised through the Societies we belong to, must ever be in the opposite direction, to lift it up, establish high ideals and secure recognition as a learned profession."

In concluding a discussion of the subject of audit companies, I may state that there existed a real fear, whether rightly or not, that the reports prepared by the manager of the audit company might find their way into the hands of the directors of such companies and thus cease to be confi-

276

dential. However that might be, the denunciation of audit companies by George Wilkinson, as quoted above, and the arguments he advanced against them were of such a strong character that the audit company method of accounting practice of the character outlined above has been discontinued.

Advertising

In the early years of our profession from 1891 onwards it was an almost universal custom for practicing accountants to advertise in the classified city directory. In justice to most of these accountants the advertisements were confined to conservative wording, merely giving the name of the firm, name of partners, the post office address and telephone number, occupying about one quarter of a page or less. There were, however, others who overdid it, taking half or a full page and publicly admitting their great experience at considerable length.

At a meeting of the Illinois Society held November 26, 1904 Mr. C. J. Marr, Chicago partner of Price, Waterhouse & Co., led a discussion on "Should accountants advertise?" At that time there existed no authoritative code of professional ethics and it was much later that the American Institute of Accountants made specific rulings in respect to advertising. Many men on starting practice as public accountants felt that the only way that they could secure clients was by advertising and it was also believed by the Board of Directors of the Society that while individual cards in the directory might not attract new clients except to a very limited extent, the advertising of a number of accountants in the classified directory would publicize our profession as a whole. I do not remember the exact year, but the Board of Directors, in order to discourage the advertising matter of individual practicing accountants, took a whole page in the name of the Illinois Society and listed the names of all of its members. The uselessness of attempting to build up a practice by advertising is, I believe, now fully realized by men starting to practice.

CHAPTER 10

An Account of the Organization and Activities of
the Federation of Societies of Public Accountants
which also Sponsored the First International
Congress of Accountants Held in September, 1904 at the
Louisiana Purchase Exposition in St. Louis, Missouri

"In union there is strength"

Old Proverb

The above title, it will be noted, covers two topics, yet they are so closely related that it seems best to include both in one chapter. For the sake of clarity, however, each topic will be treated separately as far as it may be possible.

I Organization and Activities of the
Federation of Societies of Public Accountants

In chapter 6 of this history reference has already been made to the fact that the American Association of Public Accountants, founded in 1887, had, after it had secured the passage of the C.P.A. law in the State of New York, failed to realize its opportunity of not only representing all of the reputable public accountants scattered throughout the United States as a central and national body, but it had also failed to undertake the promotion of C.P.A. legislation in other states of the Union. These conditions were the cause of a very critical attitude on the part of public accountants outside of New York towards the isolationary policies of the American Association of Public Accountants, as then constituted.

The birth of this Federation demonstrates, as will be proved by a perusal of this chapter, that it was inspired by the Illinois Association of Public Accountants and should therefore appear as a most important part of this history.

At the quarterly meeting of the Illinois Association of Public Accountants held on July 8, 1902 George Wilkinson, who was then its President, delivered a most memorable address entitled, "A Proposed Federation of Societies of Public Accountants" which would be a national organization, one of its purposes being to secure national legislation to regulate our profession and confer a national title of Certified Public Accountant.

I believe that this idea and inspiration was entirely due to George Wilkinson, and in several addresses by leading public accountants outside of Illinois at the Congress of Accountants held at St. Louis in 1904, this was acknowledged.

It is also a matter of local pride that the Illinois Association so ably supported George Wilkinson in this endeavor to arouse the interest of public accountants outside of the State of Illinois, as shown in the following resolution unanimously adopted at the meeting held July 8, 1902:

> "Whereas it appears to be desirable to form a National Federa-
> tion of Accountants to be composed of representatives of the
> several existing Societies and associations of public account-
> ants throughout the country.
> Therefore be it resolved that the President be and he is here-
> by requested to name a committee of five members of this As-
> sociation to draft a plan for such National Federation and that
> such committee shall have the power to incur any necessary
> expense thereon subject to the approval of the directors."

In pursuance of the above resolution Charles W. Haskins, A. Lowes Dickinson, Allen R. Smart, John A. Cooper and Ernest Reckitt were appointed members of this committee, George Wilkinson, as President of the Association, being a member "Ex-officio." This committee immediately took the necessary steps to secure a charter under the laws of the District of Columbia and notified all State Societies of the objects sought by the proposed Federation, requesting that each State Society send delegates to a convention to be held in Washington, D. C. on October 17, 1902. The charter was duly granted early in October and the meeting on October 17th was held for the purpose of organization. The Illinois Association sent John A. Cooper and Allen R. Smart as delegates, and J. Porter Joplin and Ernest Reckitt as alternates. At this meeting George Wilkinson was elected the Secretary of the Federation.

The plan of organization of the Federation called for memberships of State Societies and not of individuals, and its government was vested in the delegates elected by the State Societies. This form of organization was continued for many years after the amalgamation of the Federation with the American Association of Public Accountants, and until, I believe, in 1916, when the change of name to the American Institute of Accountants, and the change to a membership of individuals instead of by Societies were adopted.

The activities of the Federation were devoted to the organization of new State Societies of Public Accountants, assisting such societies in the passage of uniform C.P.A. laws and making the necessary preparations for a Congress of Accountants to be held in St. Louis, Missouri in September, 1904 on the occasion of the Louisiana Purchase Exposition.

When this Congress met in St. Louis, the Federation, though only two years after its organization, had made great progress in the objects for which it had been created. Twenty State Societies had been organized, eleven of which had become members of the Federation. Of the remaining nine societies, the New York Society, though originally a member had temporarily withdrawn from the Federation, the New Jersey Society had never become a member and seven Societies, while not members at the date of the Congress, were anticipating becoming members and actually became members shortly thereafter.

In the following tabulation details are given of the standing of all Societies at the date of the Congress and also showing the names of all States having public accountants who attended the Congress. This statement has been prepared from the printed official record of the addresses made by Joseph E.

Sterrett and George Wilkinson before the Congress.

States having C.P.A. Laws	States having Societies of Accountants		Members of Federation in Sept. 1904	States having Representatives at Congress in Sept. 1904
	C. P. A.	Other		
New York	New York			New York
Penna.	Penna.		Penna.	Penna.
Maryland	Maryland		Maryland	
Calif.	Calif.		Calif.	Calif.
Washington	Washington		Washington	Washington
Illinois	Illinois		Illinois	Illinois
New Jersey	New Jersey			New Jersey
		Mass.	Mass.	Mass.
		Ohio	Ohio	Ohio
		Mich.	Mich.	Mich.
		Georgia	Georgia	Georgia
		Missouri	Missouri	Missouri
		Minn.	Minn.	Minn.
		Tenn.		Tenn.
		Oregon		Oregon
		Kentucky		Kentucky
		Iowa		Iowa
		Louisiana		
		Wisconsin		
		Indiana		
	7	13		
7	20		11	16

In the last half of the year 1904, negotiations for the merger of the Federation with the American Association of Public Accountants were entered into. On January 10, 1905 the American Association amended its Constitution and By-Laws by adopting those of the Federation except as to a few minor details, and thus making it actually, and not only in name, a national organizatior

At a meeting of the Illinois Society held April 25, 1905 the following resolution was adopted:

"Whereas the American Association of Public Accountants did on January 10, 1905 amend its Constitution and By-Laws so as to become a national body, representing all Societies, Resolved That the Secretary be and is hereby authorized to make the necessary application to the American Association of Public Accountants, in accordance with Article II, Section 9 of its Constitution to become a Society Member thereof from October 1, 1905."

282

All other State Societies, including the New York Society of Certified Public Accountants which had theretofore taken no part in the Federation, then took similar action to that of the Illinois Society of Certified Public Accountants.

Actually what had happened was that to all intents and purposes the Federation of Societies of Public Accountants continued to live under the new name of the American Association of Public Accountants.

At the Congress of Accountants certain addresses by prominent public accountants were given which throw a further light on the birth and activities of the Federation and it is believed that excerpts from such speeches should find a place in this chapter.

Mr. J. E. Sterrett, a C.P.A. of Pennsylvania, (at that time practicing under his own name in Philadelphia and later as a partner in the firm of Price, Waterhouse & Co.) as Chairman of the Congress of Accountants gave the opening address and said in part:

"In common experience with other growing movements when central organization is lacking during preliminary stages, it was soon found that larger development created a series of problems insoluble by local organizations working independently and the feeling began to arise that some sort of relationship should be brought about between these local Societies. It remained for Mr. George Wilkinson, the

111

president of the Illinois Association to write on this subject a paper
and to read it before a meeting of the Illinois Association of Public
Accountants on July 8, 1902. Mr. Wilkinson reviewed concisely and
clearly the situation as it then existed, showing the isolation of the
several Societies and their impotence in affairs of a national character. Like a true prophet he did not rest content with a lamenta-
tion over present ills but proceeded to unfold a plan for the co-or-
dination of all existing organizations by the formation of a Federation of Societies of Public Accountants. Here, for the first time,
the thought of such a form of association was given concrete expression."

Mr. Sterrett then quoted the resolution adopted by the Illinois As-

sociation of Public Accountants at its meeting held on July 8, 1902, already re-

ferred to in this chapter. Continuing he said:

"The subject awakened wide-spread interest and the plan prepared
was presented to a convention held in the City of Washington on
Tuesday, October 28, 1902. Only elected delegates (and alternates)
of all the established Societies were present, and an organization
was formed under the title of the Federation of Societies of Public
Accountants in the United States of America. So the delegates of
that first general convention of public accountants practicing in
the United States met, many of them strangers, but all of them very
much in earnest, and there officially stamped with their approval
what is now generally known as 'The Federated idea.'

283

"While the plan outlined by the Washington Convention of 1902 is
now generally recognized as embodying in its essential features
the proper basis for national organization, it is a matter of regret
that one Society, the American Association, did not agree to it and
has since held aloof. It is also regrettable that the New York State
Society during the past year, for reasons mostly of a local character, which it is hoped will prove only temporarily affected, has
felt constrained to withdraw from its rightful place as the head of
all federated societies. It, however, is most satisfactory to be
able to state that negotiations are now being conducted with a
very fine prospect of accomplishing a practical, honorable union
of all these bodies. The march of progress cannot at this day be
stayed by the defection or isolation of any one State, but by hearty
cooperation of all, its pace can be accelerated, and to this end it
is earnestly desired that all differences of opinion may be quickly
adjusted, and that the entire program, with a solid front and even
step may address itself to those more weighty matters that are
now calling for its best thought."

On the following day George Wilkinson delivered an address en-

titled "The Certified Public Accountancy Movement," and in introducing the

speaker, Mr. Sterrett made the following remarks:

"We now come to one of the most interesting parts of our program.

One of the prime objects of this Congress was that of bringing us together in order that we might discuss matters of common interest relating to our profession. To bring some of these concretely before you, a paper has been prepared with a great deal of care. It has been discussed by members of the Executive Committee of the Federation and it will be presented to you this morning. It certainly is not necessary to say very much about the gentleman who has written this paper. You will know him. He has been active in every field of effort; first in the local society in Illinois; one of the prime movers there in all the good work that Society has accomplished; and to him more than to any other man is due the organization of the Federation which we feel has done such a noble work during the past two years. And you know, too, the relation he has borne to this Congress. How he has worked day and night, literally giving up his professional duties, subordinating everything to the task that was upon him in arranging for this Congress; I know you all appreciate what he is and what he has done and are waiting with much interest to hear his paper."

284

And, with the above quotation of Mr. Sterrett's introductory address of George Wilkinson's paper, I will close the first part of this chapter, except to state that the Illinois Association of Public Accountants, especially through its honored member, supported by its members, had proved itself to be a pioneer in all matters relating to the advancement of our profession.

II Congress of Accountants

This Congress, the first in the history of the accounting profession, of an international character, was held in St. Louis, Missouri, on September 26, 27 and 28, 1904. It was, as already stated, sponsored by the Federation of Societies of Public Accountants which for several months had been perfecting plans to make it an outstanding success. I have already described in some detail the part played by George Wilkinson in this project, but no man, however able and enthusiastic, could or should be given credit for the results obtained, and the names of others should be recorded as outstanding. I have particularly in remembrance A. Lowes Dickinson and George O. May of Price, Waterhouse & Co., J. E. Sterrett, William M. Lybrand, Adam A. Ross, Robert H. Montgomery, all of Philadelphia, Harvey S. Chase of Boston and Elijah W. Sells of Haskins & Sells.

The international character of this Congress may be appreciated by submitting a list of the names of the guests who came from outside the United States:

Francis William Pixley, past President of The Institute of Chartered Accountants of England and Wales, the author of the well-known book on auditing.

James Martin, (later Sir James Martin) the Secretary of the Society of Accountants and Auditors in Great Britain and Ireland.

John Ballantyne Niven, representing the Scottish Societies of Chartered Accountants. His father, Alexander T. Niven, was one of the organizers of the Society of Accountants in Edinburgh in 1854. John B. Niven came to the U.S.A. in December, 1897 as a member of the staff of Price, Waterhouse & Co. in its Chicago office. In August, 1900 he established the American firm of Touche, Niven & Co. He was elected the President of the American Institute of Public Accountants in 1924.

285

John Hyde, President of the Dominion Association of Chartered Accountants.

F. H. Macpherson, Vice President of the Institute of Accountants of Ontario.

John W. Ross representing the Montreal Accountants Society.

E. Van Dien of Amsterdam, Holland.

In addition to those guests, four Chartered Accountants of Canada attended the Congress.

To demonstrate how widespread the interest of Public Accountants was in the Federation, I submit below a list of the number of accountants from each state and the District of Columbia attending the Congress.

Missouri	18
Illinois	17
Ohio	11
New York	10
Pennsylvania	6
Tennessee	3
Kentucky	3
Michigan	2
New Jersey	2
California	2
Washington, D.C.	2
Minnesota	1
Oregon	1

114

```
Iowa . . . . . . .  1
Georgia . . . . .  1
Massachusetts.    1
                 81
```

The large number registered from Missouri was naturally due to the Congress being held in St. Louis.

St. Louis, being unfortunately noted for its very hot summers, it had been decided to hold this Congress late in September when the climate would be more endurable, but by one of those freaks of nature, a bad heat wave struck that city at the very same time as the Congress was held, the temperature each day being 100 degrees or more. To add to these discomforts, the headquarters of the Congress were in a recently-constructed hotel, the screens on the windows fitting very badly, with the result that what with the heat and fighting mosquitos, our nights were by no means pleasant.

Notwithstanding the fatiguing nights and the hot busy days, everybody, I believe, thoroughly enjoyed their visit to St. Louis and was entranced with the buildings and the exhibits of the Louisiana Purchase Exposition. Happy friendships were developed, many of which lasted for many years.

The high-spots of the Congress chiefly centered in the character of the addresses given and the discussions that followed. It may be of interest to give a list of the papers read during this Congress, complete copies of which may be found in a book in the library of the American Institute of Accountants giving a very complete account of this Congress. These addresses are listed in the order that they were delivered.

1. Municipal Accounting by Elijah W. Sells

2. A Brief History of the Movement Toward Uniform Municipal Reports and Accounts in the United States by Harvey S. Chase

3. The Municipal Balance Sheet by H. W. Wilmot of the firm of Price, Waterhouse & Co.

286

4. Revenues and Expenses as Distinguished From Receipts and Disbursements in Municipal Accounting by F. A. Cleveland

5. Appropriations in Respect to Municipal Accountancy by Ernest Reckitt

6. Practice of Accountancy in Canada by John Hyde of Montreal

7. The C.P.A. Movement by George Wilkinson

8. The Duties of Professional Accountants in Connection with Invested Capital both prior to and subsequent to the Investment by Francis W. Pixley of London, England

9. The Importance of Uniform Practice in Determining the Profits of Public Service Corporations where Municipalities have the Power to Regulate Rates by Robert H. Montgomery

10. The Profession of Public Accounting by William M. Lybrand

11. The Profits of a Corporation by A. Lowes Dickinson

12. The Mode of Conducting an Audit by Walter A. Staub

287

In connection with the last named paper prepared by Walter A. Staub, it should be explained that several months prior the Executive Committee of the Federation had offered a prize of $50 for the best article on the subject of "The Mode of Conducting an Audit" by any senior accountant in an office of practicing public accountants and it appointed a committee of three to determine the best paper dealing with this subject. Four papers were presented to the committee and that submitted by Mr. Staub was, in every respect, far superior to the others, so he received the prize of $50 and his paper was read at the last session of the Congress. That the judgment of the committee was sound is supported by the fact that Mr. Staub became a highly valued partner in the firm of Lybrand, Ross Bros. & Montgomery and his death a year or so ago was lamented by all who knew him, not only as a learned accountant but as a man of the highest character.

The Congress, after concluding its business sessions on September 28th, celebrated at a banquet, at which Harvey S. Chase acted as toastmaster, and a better toastmaster could not have been found. In this same capacity he served on many other occasions with a sparkling wit that endeared him to all who had the pleasure of attending these conventions.

Towards the close of this banquet, Alfred G. Platt of San Francisco on being asked by the toastmaster to make a speech, explained that the matter on which he would claim the attention of the Congress and their friends was the presentation of a silver loving cup to George Wilkinson, the Secretary of the Federation and the promoter of this Congress. Mr. Platt paid a glowing tribute to Mr. Wilkinson, and to the unceasing endeavor and hard work which he had devoted to making the Congress a success and also to the earnest endeavors that he had put forth in organizing the Federation. Mr. Platt said that all practicing accountants should be proud of such a man in their ranks and on behalf of all accountants expressed the admiration, love and goodwill which they all felt for him and wished him every success and prosperity, with good health to his wife and himself.

Mr. Wilkinson was so surprised and overcome at the unexpected honor conferred upon him that it was some time before he could find words to reply, but finally recovering himself he expressed his thanks and appreciation for the handsome gift in his usual genial manner and thanked the accountants, and especially his colleagues, Robert H. Montgomery, A. Lowes Dickinson and George O. May, for their active labors and their never-tiring devotion to help him. He also wished to publicly express his thanks to his business partners, Ernest Reckitt and John J. Williams, and especially to his life partner, Mrs. Wilkinson, for their forbearance with him and their great help when things at times looked dark and when the success of the enterprise was by no means assured.

288

CHAPTER 11

"The Auditor" and "The Journal of Accountancy"

"Knowledge is of two kinds, we know a subject
ourselves or we know where we can find information upon it."

Boswell's "Life of Johnson"

It may not be fully known by the Certified Public Accountants of
today (1948) that the "Journal of Accountancy," of which our profession is so
justly proud, was the offspring of a magazine named "The Auditor," which
was first published under the management of the Illinois Society of Certified
Public Accountants in September 1904.

It is undoubtedly true that, as our profession grew in strength and
numbers, some magazine would, in all probability, have been forthcoming and
in fact it would have been absolutely necessary to have a mouthpiece of our
professional activities and education. However, the fact remains that it was
the Illinois Society that first published a magazine of such a high character
and secured such a large readers' interest that it created a demand on the
part of the members of our profession to take over the goodwill of "The Auditor" under the name of "The Journal of Accountancy."

Long before the first publication of "The Auditor" at least ten
other magazines which featured accountancy, although not exclusively, had
been published and from October 1898 to June, 1900 William Hobson Vollum
of Philadelphia, published "The Public Accountant" devoted purely to the interest of our profession. These magazines, however, appear to have been,
for the most part, short-lived and were in no way responsible for the creation of "The Journal of Accountancy" in 1905.

In the following paragraphs I propose to give a brief account of
the business activities of "The Auditor" as recorded in the minutes of meet-

ings of the Illinois Society.

At the meeting of the Board of Directors of the Illinois Society held August 22, 1904, consideration of a project for the publication of a magazine, which would represent the interests of our profession, was fully discussed and a resolution was adopted authorizing the appointment of two committees to assume (i) the editorial control and (ii) to supervise its business management.

The first magazine appeared in September, 1904, and at a meeting held September 13, 1904, it was decided to have 900 extra copies in order to mail a copy to every public accountant in the United States and another 200 copies to be taken to the Congress of Accountants to be held in St. Louis later that month.

On November 8, 1904, the Secretary was instructed to mail 1,000 extra copies of the October issue for circulation among public accountants in the U.S.A. and to arrange that the November issue should be 7,000 to include mailing to bankers, etc.

At the December 10th meeting it was decided that after the December issue the format of the magazine should consist of 32 pages and that all accountants in the U.S.A. should be asked to subscribe and to do whatever they could to increase its paid circulation so that the magazine could secure admission to the mails as "second class matter." The Secretary was instructed to mail copies of the magazine to all banks having a capital of $100,000.00 and over in the central, western and southern states at the expense of the Society.

At the meeting of the Board held May '9, 1905, Edward E. Gore presented a letter from Robert H. Montgomery, Secretary of the Federation, under date of April 29, 1905, which outlined a plan of an organization of an incorporated company to undertake the publication, in the near future, of a monthly magazine to be known as "The Public Accountant" or "The Accountant." This letter intimated that terms would be considered under which "The Auditor" might be merged with this new enterprise. It was resolved that Edward E. Gore and Allen R. Smart should confer together as to the reply to be sent to Mr. Montgomery.

At the meeting of the Illinois Society held on August 8, 1905, the affairs of "The Auditor" were discussed. The members were then advised that negotiations were in progress under which the publication of the magazine would be assumed by the Accountancy Publishing Company of New York not later than November 1, 1905.

On September 12, 1905, the following resolution was adopted:

291

"Resolved that the President and Secretary be and they are hereby authorized and directed on behalf of the Illinois Society of Certified Public Accountants to assign to the Accountancy Publishing Company, a New York corporation, all the name, goodwill, subscription lists, property, rights and demands of and appertaining to a certain publication called 'The Auditor' (save and except such Accounts Receivable as may be due and unpaid upon the books of 'The Auditor,' on the first day of November, 1905, which are specifically reserved unto the Illinois Society of Certified Public Accountants) and all the right, title and interest of the Illinois Society of Certified Public Accountants in and to said publication called 'The Auditor,' together with a covenant on the part of the Illinois Society of Certified Public Accountants to refrain from conducting or editing any similar publication under the same or any similar name so long as the publication of a similar journal or organ is continued by the Accountancy Publishing Company; the said assignment and covenant to be in consideration of the issue to the said Illinois Society of Certified Public Accountants by the said Accountancy Publishing Company of five thousand dollars par of the common stock of the said Accountancy Publishing Company and for the further consideration that the said Accountancy Publishing Company shall assume any liability for unexpired subscriptions existing at the time of taking over the said 'The Auditor';
Resolved further that the President and Secretary be and they are hereby authorized and directed in behalf of the Illinois Society of Certified Public Accountants in consideration of one dollar, to assign to the American Association of Public Accountants, a New York corporation, four thousand dollars par of the common stock of the Accountancy Publishing Company."

It will therefore be noted that the Illinois Society first received

120

five thousand dollars par of the stock of the Accountancy Publishing Company and then made a gift of four thousand dollars par of that stock to the American Association of Public Accountants, (which had assimilated the membership of the Federation), thus retaining one thousand par of the Accountancy Publishing Company's common stock.

At the meeting held on May 8, 1906, it was reported that the Accountancy Publishing Company had a claim of $840 against the Illinois Society for having paid sundry liabilities of the Illinois Society incurred in the publishing of "The Auditor," and that this claim was settled by the Illinois Society transferring an equal amount at par of the stock of the Accountancy Publishing Company.

In the last number of "The Auditor" the following announcement appeared:

> "With this number of 'The Auditor' we take pleasure in advising our friends and subscribers that we have arranged to issue our paper in the future under the name of 'The Journal of Accountancy,' with offices at 32 Waverly Place, New York, and with such material enlargement, both of form and space, as will enable us to cover the broadening field of the public accountant's work more fully than we have found it possible to do under present conditions. The Journal will be a monthly magazine of some eighty pages of reading matter and twenty pages of select advertisements. The first number will be issued about October 31, 1905, and subscribers to 'The Auditor' will be supplied with the paper in its new form for such a period as their unexpired subscription may entitle them."

Referring briefly to the character and high quality of the articles published in "The Auditor," it is only necessary to state that men like A. Lowes Dickinson, Francis W. Pixley (Chartered Accountant), William H. Roberts, Frederick A. Cleveland, Charles N. Vollum, Seymour Walton and other well-known accountants, prepared and had articles published in the magazine which are still worthy of study.

CHAPTER 12

The Northwestern University School of Commerce

"I went into the temple there to hear
The teachers of our law, and to propose
What might improve my knowledge or their own"

Milton's "Paradise Regained"

In December, 1905 the Illinois Society of Certified Public Accountants took its initial step to found a "School of Commerce," with its headquarters in the central part of Chicago, but it was not until June, 1908 that its
efforts in this direction met with success.

Other Schools of Commerce had been opened prior to that date, 293
notably "The Wharton School of Finance and Commerce of the University of
Pennsylvania," in Philadelphia, which, I believe, was the oldest school of this
character in the United States, and the organization of "The New York University School of Commerce, Accounts and Finance" on October 2, 1900, with its
headquarters in the University Building in Washington Square, New York City.

Before giving any account of our experiences in Chicago, I believe
a brief digression may be permitted with a specific purpose in view, which
will appear later, concerning the New York University School referred to
above.

It was largely due to the inspiration and efforts of Charles Waldo
Haskins, who became its first Dean, that this School of Commerce was started.
As may be well known, Mr. Haskins had entered into a partnership with Elijah
W. Sells on March 4, 1895 under the firm name of Haskins & Sells, and both
of these men had become members of the Illinois Association of Public Ac-
countants in November, 1901.

The life story of Mr. Haskins, who did so much for our profession
and who accomplished so many other things in his short life of only 51 years,

may be found in a book published by Haskins & Sells in 1923.

Apparently, prior to the formation of the New York University School, referred to in a foregoing paragraph, other attempts in this direction had been made, for on page 64 we read:

> ". . . . it must not be understood that this was the first effort made to secure the co-operation of an American University and, because the idea was a good one and represented a real need, that it had but to be brought before the attention of the proper authorities to be at once welcomed with open arms. The idea of a course in accounting had earnestly and eloquently been presented to other leading educational institutions, but they disdainfully drew closer around them the robes of their sacred scholasticism, that they might not be tainted by the desecrating touch of commercialism, and, like the Pharisee of old, passed by on the other side. It requires vision to realize a great truth in the dawn of its youth and to accept it; it requires vision to fight for such a truth and to battle on courageously till victory is achieved."

294

As in most new ventures, difficulties had been encountered the first one or two years after the school was founded, for we find that Leon Brummer, a prominent Certified Public Accountant of New York and a devoted ally in the movement to get the school organized, who was also a teacher from the beginning, writes:

> "I know that, judging from my own class, the accounting knowledge of the students was so ungraded; the knowledge of the teacher and his ability to teach was so uncertain; and the confidence of the scholars, who were continuously asking for instruction in higher accountancy, was so wanting, that nothing but the persistent efforts and the personal encouragement and glorious example of Charles Waldo Haskins kept the School from following in the footpaths of those which had gone before."

Despite all the hardships, struggles, discouragements and obstacles, (writes Mr. Sells) the new venture conquered and flourished and within a few years this, the youngest school in the University, had the largest enrollment of students. It not only performed fine, loyal, direct service to the profession in the number of young men it trained to take their places with splendid equipment and high ideals in the ranks of Certified Public Accountants, but the school itself became an exemplar and an inspiration to other schools, more or less similar, started in other parts of the country.

That the foundation and the activities of the New York University School of Commerce, Accounts and Finance was an inspiration to the members of the Illinois Society of Certified Public Accountants, there can be no question, and its success made it much easier for those of us in Illinois who were desirous to found a similar school in Chicago. Gone were the prejudices and fears of commercialism, as related earlier in this chapter, which had been obstacles that the New York accountants had to overcome. Furthermore, we had influential and sympathetic friends to assist us, such as Dr. David Kinley of the University of Illinois, Mr. Arnett, the Controller of the University of Chicago, Dr. Earl D. Howard who had come from the Wharton School of Finance and Commerce to be associated with the Northwestern University and Professor Hotchkiss, also of the Northwestern University.

Nevertheless, we had difficulties of another sort to overcome, as will be seen in the following pages, the chief of which (strange as it may appear from later developments) was the fear of the Trustees of the Universities approached that a School of Commerce would be financially unprofitable and a cause of losses in their revenues and expenses.

The first reference I can find in regard to the establishment of a School of Commerce in Chicago appears in the first issue of the "Journal of Accountancy" in November, 1905, (pages 71 and 72) which I will quote verbatim:

> "The University of Illinois has recently addressed a series of questions to the public accountants registered in that State, soliciting an expression of opinion as to the practicability of maintaining a 'School of Accounts' in Chicago. We have not been advised of the result of these inquiries, but believe that there are 75 to 100 young men, just entering upon business life, who would be glad to avail themselves of the opportunity to study accountancy under such auspices. The graduates of such a school would be largely sought after for engagements

124

as assistants and when their book knowledge had been supplemented by more or less experience, their services should be of great value to established practitioners.

Since the passage of the C.P.A. Bill there has been an increasing interest among office men, which has lead many of them to desire the degree, not always for the purpose of practicing as public accountants, but principally with the desire of acquiring a better knowledge of higher accounting for its own sake as well as the greater prestige that the degree will give them. In consequence of the demand thus created for instruction in the subjects covered by the C.P.A. examinations, several schools of accountancy have been started which are fairly well attended and the State University has taken up the question of establishing a department of accountancy in Chicago. As the University is situated in a small city in the center of the State, it was found impossible to reach a large number who would like to take the course, and who could not afford the time necessary to go to Urbana to attend the regular sessions. It has been proposed that the department be transferred to Chicago, and that the sessions be held in the evenings, so that persons regularly employed during the day may be able to take the evening courses. The demand for this instruction would undoubtedly be large enough to make the course a success, if the University can find a way to waive the requirements for a 'high school' diploma which is now a requisite to matriculation. The members of the Illinois Society of Certified Public Accountants are all willing to help the movement and it is hoped that the University will be able to make a beginning this winter."

On December 1, 1905, soon after the article quoted above, there was a meeting of the Board of the Illinois Society at which there was a discussion of the subject of the establishment of a School of Commerce by the University of Illinois. The minutes of this meeting included a copy of a long letter addressed to the Trustees of the University pointing out the success of a similar School of Commerce in New York City operated by the New York University, and of the Wharton School of Finance and Commerce of the University of Pennsylvania. This letter stated that as the Wharton School had 307 students, Chicago, having a much greater population than Philadelphia, could easily attract to the proposed school a much greater body of students. The Illinois Society offered to guarantee $500 a year for two years to the support of such a school in its initial stages, when a small deficit might occur, and to give a prize, each of those years, of $100 to the student in the senior

296

grade with the highest average marking in the accounting course; also to assist in the educational work by a series of lectures by members of the Society.

It was stated that at least one hundred students paying $60 per annum for the course could be secured, thus giving a revenue of $6,000, sufficient for the engagement of two permanent teachers, one in accountancy and one in law, the lectures to be given in the evenings at the building owned by the University at Michigan Avenue and Twelfth Street in Chicago.

A response to this letter was read at a meeting of the Board held April 10, 1906 which stated that the University could not immediately take any action in respect to the proposed School of Commerce, but would have to await action by the State Legislature in 1907.

297

Nothing further being possible, the Illinois Society had to patiently mark time until the Illinois Legislature would convene early in 1907, but in anticipation of that event, it held a meeting on December 27, 1906, at which Dr. David Kinley was a guest. At this meeting the following resolution was unanimously adopted:

"Whereas the University of Illinois has established (at Urbana) a school intended to provide for the higher education of men in the Science of Finance, Commerce and Accounts, and

Whereas the said University is desirous of extending its course of instruction in this School to the end that the same may be more complete and productive of more beneficial results to its students, and

Whereas the Illinois Society of Certified Public Accountants is fully advised of the aims, purposes and accomplishments of the said University in the School referred to, therefore

Be it resolved That the Illinois Society of Certified Public Accountants in meeting assembled, heartily endorses the methods of the University of Illinois in the conduct of its School of Commerce, Finance and Accounts and that said Society will use its best efforts to secure from the General Assembly of the State of Illinois at its next session, an appropriation of $5,000 per annum for the use of said University in Urbana in extending its courses of instruction on business subjects, and

Be it further resolved that the Illinois Society of Certified Public

126

Accountants favors an additional appropriation by the General Assembly for the use of said University of $10,000 per annum for the establishment and maintenance of a night school of Commerce, Finance and Accounts in the City of Chicago, the same to be wholly under the jurisdiction and control of said University of Illinois, and

Be it further resolved that the members of the Illinois Society of Certified Public Accountants pledge themselves to do all in their power to secure action in favor of the appropriations above stated by the various social and commercial organizations of the City of Chicago."

For many, many years, and even to this day, what is termed "Down State" (meaning all counties of the State of Illinois outside of Cook County in which the City of Chicago is located) has for some absurd reasons been antagonistic to any legislation which would benefit Chicago. Whether or not that was the cause why the appropriation of $10,000, referred to above, failed to receive any approval by the Illinois Legislature, I cannot definitely say; but the fact remains that the University of Illinois found it impossible to undertake the opening of a School of Commerce in Chicago.

It was not, therefore, until November, 1907 that it was possible to renew our efforts to secure a School of Commerce operating in Chicago, this time through the Trustees of Northwestern University.

At the meeting on November 5, 1907, Seymour Walton, who was then the President of the Illinois Society, reported he had addressed a letter to Dr. Earl D. Howard of the Northwestern University regarding the establishment in Chicago of a School of Commerce. He also reported he was keeping in touch with Dr. Howard, who was willing and anxious that the Illinois Society should cooperate with the Northwestern University and the Chicago Commercial Club in the inauguration of such a school.

As an immediate result of the meeting on November 5th, another meeting was called to be held November 26th, and attending the meeting were Dr. Howard of Northwestern University and Professor Arnett of the University of Chicago.

Mr. John A. Cooper, as Chairman of the Committee on Education, then submitted his report as to progress, in which he outlined subjects to be studied by students in each of a three year course. The President, Mr. Walton, then called upon Dr. Howard to address the meeting. Dr. Howard reported that, as already stated by Mr. Cooper, a plan for the inauguration of a night school under the auspices of the Northwestern University, the Chicago Commercial Club and the Illinois Society of Certified Public Accountants had been outlined by him and submitted to the Executive Committee of the Chicago Commercial Club, which had promised to take up the matter at an early date. Continuing, Dr. Howard stated that in his opinion the expense of conducting such a school would be about $6,000 the first year and the plan involved obtaining guarantors to this amount by September next, at which time it is proposed to open the school, such guarantors to form an executive body for the management and control of the school; that the Northwestern University was willing to give free of charge the use of its downtown building for this purpose, at least for the first year. Dr. Howard spoke at some length on the advantages to be derived by the members of the Illinois Society from the institution of such a school and spoke most interestingly of his past experience with the Wharton School in Philadelphia.

The meeting was also addressed by Professor Arnett of the University of Chicago, who supported the plan as outlined and stated that both he and the members of the faculty of the University of Chicago would be pleased to cooperate.

A letter was then read in which Dr. David Kinley of the University of Illinois wished every success to this movement.

At the next meeting of the Society on December 24, 1907, Mr. John

A. Cooper submitted a draft of a circular which it was proposed to issue to prospective guarantors of the "School of Commerce" which was being organized. The following resolution was then adopted:

"Resolved that the Society become a guarantor to the extent of $500.00 per annum covering a period of three consecutive years from September next, conditional upon the Society being represented upon the Executive Committee and subject to ratification at the next general meeting of this Society."

At the meeting of the Society on March 10, 1908 Mr. John A. Cooper had to report that the response from businessmen who had been asked to become guarantors had been most disappointing and he suggested that in order to make up the requisite guarantee of $5,000 all members be requested to obtain guarantees from one or more of their clients, "preferably those who are employers of the class of men who would be likely to become students."

While the minutes of the meetings of the Illinois Society do not make any reference to it, between the meeting held on March 10, 1908 and the date of the next meeting on June 9, 1908 nineteen Certified Public Accountants and a few businessmen, notably Joseph Schaffner of the well-known firm of Hart, Schaffner & Marx, each guaranteed $300 to provide for any losses incurred by the Northwestern University in the operation of the school. Thus the Certified Public Accountants guaranteed a total of $5,700, or $700 in excess of the minimum amount requested by the University, while businessmen guaranteed a sum of probably another $3,000. At the end of the first year each guarantor had to make good to the extent of about $150 on his pledge; at the end of the second year about $75. The third year the University made a gain, so that the guarantors were no longer called upon.

In passing it may be interesting to note that for many years the School of Commerce has been, I believe, one of the most financially profitable of the several schools conducted by the University.

I have before me a letter from the Dean of the School of Com-

300

merce giving an official list of the Certified Public Accountants who became

guarantors, which I submit below:

Harold Benington	Stephan T. Mather
R. S. Buchanan	S. Roger Mitchell
John Alexander Cooper	Luman S. Pickett
A. Lowes Dickinson	Ernest Reckitt
Edward E. Gore	Elijah W. Sells
J. Porter Joplin	Allen R. Smart
William Kendall	Joseph E. Sterrett
Charles S. Ludlam	Seymour Walton
James Marwick	Henry W. Wilmot
Arthur Young	

The representatives of the Illinois Society on the Executive Com-

mittee of the School of Commerce were John Alexander Cooper, J. Porter

Joplin and Allen R. Smart.

In a report that I made at the 1911 annual convention of the

American Association of Public Accountants on the work of the Northwest-

ern University School of Commerce, I stated in part:

"The Growth of the Northwestern University School of Commerce
continues to be a source of great satisfaction on the part of the
members of the Illinois Society who were so largely responsible
for its creation. Below is submitted a statement showing the
growth of this school since it was first started:

Year 1908 to 1909	235 students
Year 1909 to 1910	362 students
Year 1910 to 1911	539 students

The faculty of the School of Commerce includes the following
members of the Illinois Society:

Seymour Walton, Professor of Theory of Accounting

Arthur E. Andersen, Lecturer on Intermediate Accounting

Charles H. Langer, Lecturer on First Principles of Accounting."

The School of Commerce, as also the Illinois Society, was indeed

fortunate in the type of men of such high calibre as lecturers from its very

commencement.

Arthur Andersen gave many years to the interests of the school as a lecturer, and it is interesting to note that a few years before his untimely death, he had served the University on its Board of Trustees.

The statement given in a foregoing paragraph of the number of students in the first three years of the school is most instructive as showing a healthy and steady growth right from the start, but appears insignificant when compared with 7,582 students who were enrolled in the fall semester of 1946, as reported to me by the Registrar of the School, consisting of 7,034 evening students and 548 full-time students.

In concluding this chapter it should be also recorded that many Certified Public Accountants contributed most generously towards the cost of construction of the present beautiful building on the downtown campus on Chicago Avenue, now housing the School of Commerce.

302

CHAPTER 13

The Subscriptions Investigating Committee of the
Chicago Association of Commerce

"Nothing has such power to broaden the mind
as the ability to investigate systematically and
truly all that comes under thy observation in life."

Meditations of Marcus Aurelius

The above maxim, taken from the writings of the great philosopher, may not have any special application to the subject of this final chapter, but, I believe, it is an appropriate quotation as embodying all that has gone before in this narrative. No profession has a greater power to broaden the mind than that of the public accountant who conscientiously gives his talents to investigate and report upon the many and varied activities which come within his sphere. This, in turn, gives the public accountant an especial responsibility to give the public, in all welfare and philanthropic work, the benefit of his broad experience.

It may be most justly said of our profession that it has met this responsibility in many ways, and one of these, which I now propose to describe, has been its support of the Chicago Association of Commerce and more particularly of its Subscriptions Investigating Committee.

It is noteworthy that two of our members have been honored by their election as Presidents of the Chicago Association of Commerce, having also served on some of its committees in an outstanding manner. I refer to Edward E. Gore and George W. Rossetter. Mr. C. R. Whitworth was also a director of the Association and served on various committees.

The Subscriptions Investigating Committee was organized in 1910, a committee of ten of the members of the Chicago Association of Commerce including Mr. Granger Farwell as Chairman, being appointed. The purpose of this committee was to devise and inaugurate a systematic method of securing all necessary information in respect to those charitable organizations that were appealing for funds for their support.

In Chicago, as in all large cities, there were alleged charitable institutions which were of a fraudulent character; others were conducted by well-meaning people with little or no business or welfare experience, while in a few cases there were duplications of effort. In this last category it was hoped that a merger would effect economies in administration. It was the object of the Subscriptions Investigating Committee to give, when called upon by members of the Association, such information as would enable their members to form an intelligent opinion of the worth or otherwise of any charitable institution appealing for their support.

In order to devise the best methods of procedures the Committee created an Advisory Council of men and women who had made a life study of the social problems of the day and it also sought the cooperation of the Illinois Society of Certified Public Accountants to assist it in all matters pertaining to the audit of all institutions desiring to secure its approval.

It so happened that in 1910 I was President of the Society and I presume that was the reason I was asked to become a member of the Committee as a representative of our profession and for the purpose of securing the cooperation of our profession in the furtherance of its efforts. I accepted the invitation to become a member of the Committee and it was my privilege to continue as a member for many years.

Realizing my responsibility and the necessity of securing the cooperation of all reputable members of our profession, an informal meeting was promptly called at which there was present a large number of the principals of firms of Certified Public Accountants and it was unanimously and enthusiastically agreed that the support of the Committee afforded our profession an opportunity for public and civic service.

At this meeting a committee of five was appointed to meet the members of the Subscriptions Investigating Committee to formulate plans, first, by which those charitable institutions desiring to secure the approval of the Chicago Association, could secure an audit of their affairs by reputable accountants at the lowest reasonable cost and second, by which no firm should be burdened by too many of such assignments, but rather that such assignments be spread in such a manner that all accountants would participate in this work. The Committee had found out that numerous institutions objected to an audit on the grounds that they could not afford the cost. The agreement between the Committee and the Accountants provided that such audits should 305 be carried out at a fixed nominal per diem rate so that it would be difficult for any institution to object to an audit on grounds of expense.

After several meetings a definite plan of procedure was adopted, which I reported to the annual convention of the American Association of Public Accountants held in San Francisco in September, 1911. This report appeared in the Journal of Accountancy, so it is not therefore necessary to refer to these plans any further, except to state that the "Gentlemen's Agreement" between the participating members of our profession for the audit of charitable institutions was eminently satisfactory for all concerned. It was especially appreciated by Chicago Association of Commerce, and the plan as outlined above continued for several years and until the necessity for its operations ceased to exist.

It will be of interest to know that the Subscriptions Investigating Committee, later supported by the Community Fund, is still actively functioning along the same plans as those laid down in 1910; in fact the forms used which must be filled out by the Auditors are almost identical with those first prepared, with the further requirement that a copy of the Auditor's annual report be also submitted.

Finally, it may be stated that the activities of the Subscriptions Investigating Committee not only eliminated in a short time many fraudulent so-called charitable institutions, or others that were badly managed, thus saving many thousands of dollars to the citizens of Chicago and its suburbs, but that it strengthened the worthy charities by the publicity it gave them through the Year Book published by the Committee in which all charitable institutions that had secured approval were listed.

It is well said that "Charity begins at home." The Illinois Society by following this precept as outlined in this chapter, has performed a worthwhile service.

306

APPENDIX A

List of members of the Illinois Association of Public Accountants showing dates of election, resignation or death if prior to 1904 and names of firms with whom associated, if not practicing under their individual names

Date	Name	Resignation or death	Partner or member of staff of
3/18/97	Frank M. Boughey		-
	R. S. Buchanan		Kidson, Buchanan & Co.
	Henry F. Butler	Resigned 4/8/02	-
	John A. Cooper		-
	S. B. Foster	Resigned 7/1/97	Price, Waterhouse & Co.
	William Fries	Resigned 1899 Discontinuance of Practice	
	Charles W. Hawley	Resigned 10/24/98 Reinstated 1/10/01	Hawley, Jones & Co.
	Lawrence A. Jones		Hawley, Jones & Co.
	Lewis D. Jones	Died Feb. 1899	Price, Waterhouse & Co.
	Frederick F. Judd	Resigned 4/8/02	-
	G. L. Marchand	Resigned 1898 Illness	-
	Ernest Reckitt		Smith, Reckitt & Co.
	George E. Shaw	Resigned 4/29/98	Kidson, Buchanan & Co.
	George Wilkinson		-
10/17/98	J. Porter Joplin		Walton, Joplin & Co.
	Allen R. Smart		Barrow, Wade, Guthrie & Co.
1/10/99	Charles C. Reckitt	Resigned 2/10/03	Smith, Reckitt & Co.
	Henry J.D.Wodrich	Died Dec. 1902	Audit Co. of Illinois
	C. J. Marr		Price, Waterhouse & Co.
	L. H. Peloubet	Resigned 4/8/02	Price, Waterhouse & Co.

307

Date	Name	Resignation or death	Partner or member of staff of
	J. B. Niven		Price, Waterhouse & Co.
	R. J. Evans		Price, Waterhouse & Co.
	Edward Stanley		Price, Waterhouse & Co.
	Henry Millard		Price, Waterhouse & Co.
	R. O. MacDonald		George Wilkinson
	Roddam Cant		Smith, Reckitt & Co.
	Edward Morgan Mills		Price, Waterhouse & Co.
8/30/99	Arthur Young		Stuart, Young & Co.
	Seymour Walton		Walton, Joplin & Co.
12/12/99	John J. Williams		Smith, Reckitt & Co.
10/9/00	Wm. J. Caesar	Resigned 1/30/03	Price, Waterhouse & Co.
	Henry W. Wilmot		Price, Waterhouse & Co.
11/13/00	Charles S. Ludlam		Haskins & Sells
11/12/01	A. Lowes Dickinson		Price, Waterhouse & Co.
	Charles Waldo Haskins	Died Jan. 1903	Haskins, Sells & Co.
	Elijah W. Sells		Haskins, Sells & Co.
	Charles L. Brown		Walton, Joplin & Co.
1/20/02	Charles U. Stuart		Stuart, Young & Co.
6/19/02	Herman J. Dirks		Smith, Reckitt & Co.
	F. W. Sprung		Smith, Reckitt & Co.
	A. W. Rugg		Smith, Reckitt & Co.
8/11/02	C. A. McKeand		Barrow, Wade, Guthrie & Co.
	L. S. Pickett		Barrow, Wade, Guthrie & Co.
	Richard F. Ring		Barrow, Wade, Guthrie & Co.

308

APPENDIX A

Date	Name	Resignation or death	Partner or member of staff of
	A. J. Stallings		Price, Waterhouse & Co.
	R.F.S. Ring	Died 1902	Not known
12/29/02	Arthur Bentley		Price, Waterhouse & Co.
	George O. May		Price, Waterhouse & Co.
1/20/03	William M. Reay		Price, Waterhouse & Co.
2/10/03	George S. Webster		Price, Waterhouse & Co.
3/16/03	R. O. Berger		Price, Waterhouse & Co.
	A. W. Dunning		Audit Co. of New York
	Edward E. Gore		Audit Co. of Chicago
	M. S. Kuhns		Safeguard Account Co.
4/20/03	Edward Allen		Not known
	John Leith		Nelson, Leith & Co.
	Robert Nelson		Nelson, Leith & Co.
5/2/03	C. W. Knisely		Audit Co. of Illinois
	F. K. Parke		-
5/19/03	Charles P. Carruthers		Price, Waterhouse & Co.
	E. Sydney Coleman		Price, Waterhouse & Co.
	Edward Fraser		Price, Waterhouse & Co.
	W. Ernest Seatree		Price, Waterhouse & Co.
	George A. Turville		Price, Waterhouse & Co.
7/15/03	A. F. Rattray Greig		-
	William Sparks		Not known
10/13/03	John Lowrie		

A BILL
FOR AN ACT TO REGULATE THE PROFESSION OF PUBLIC ACCOUNTANTS

(Introduced in 1897 and again in 1899)

SECTION 1. Be it enacted by the People of the State of Illinois repre-sented in the General Assembly, That any citizen of the United States, or person who has duly declared his intention of becoming such citizen, residing or having a place for the regular transaction of business in the state, being over the age of twenty-five years, and of good moral character, and who shall have received from the Trustees of the University of Illinois, at Champaign, a certificate of his qualifications to practice as a public expert accountant as hereinafter provided, shall be styled and known as a Certified Public Account-ant; and no other person shall assume such title or use the abbreviation C.P.A.; or any other words, letters or figures to indicate that the person using the same is such Certified Public Accountant.

SECTION 2. The Trustees of the University of Illinois, at Champaign, shall make rules for the examination of persons applying for certificates un-der this act, and shall appoint a board of three examiners for the purpose, which board shall, after the year 1899, be composed of Certified Public Ac-countants. The Trustees shall charge for the examination and certificate such fee as may be necessary to meet the actual expenses of such examina-tions, and they shall report annually the receipts and expenses under the pro-visions of this act to the State Auditor, and pay the balance of receipts over expenditures to the State Treasurer. The Trustees may revoke any such cer-tificate for sufficient cause after written notice to the holder thereof, and a hearing thereon.

310

APPENDIX B

SECTION 3. The Trustees may in their discretion waive the examination of any persons possessing the qualifications mentioned in Section 1, who shall have been continuously for more than five years, before the passage of this act, practicing as Public Accountants, two years of which shall have been on their own account, in this state, and who shall apply in writing for such certificate within one year after the passage of this act.

SECTION 4. Any violation of this act shall be a misdemeanor.

311

ILLINOIS CERTIFIED PUBLIC ACCOUNTANT
LAW - 1903

312

SECTION 1. That any citizen of the United States, or person who has duly declared his intention of becoming such citizen, residing in or having a place for the regular transaction of business as a professional accountant in the State of Illinois, being over the age of twenty-one years, of good moral character, being a graduate of a high school with a four-years' course, or having an equivalent education, and who shall have received from the University of Illinois a certificate of his qualifications to practice as a public expert accountant as hereinafter provided, shall be styled and known as a "Certified Public Accountant" and no other person shall assume such title or use the abbreviation "C.P.A." or any words or letters to indicate that the person using the same is a certified public accountant.

SECTION 2. The University of Illinois shall determine the qualifications of persons applying for certificates under this act, and shall make rules for the examination of the same, and for this latter purpose shall appoint three examiners, at least two of whom shall be skilled in the practice of accounting and actively engaged therein in the State of Illinois, and the third shall be either an accountant of the grade herein described or an attorney skilled in commercial law.

The time and place of holding the examinations shall be duly advertised, for not less than three consecutive days, in one daily newspaper published in each of the places where the examinations are to be held, not less than thirty days prior to the date of each examination.

APPENDIX C

The examinations shall be in "Theory of Accounts," "Practical Accounting," "Auditing," and "Commercial Law" as affecting accountancy.

The examinations shall take place as often as may be necessary in the opinion of the university, but not less frequently than once a year.

SECTION 3. The University of Illinois may, in their discretion, under regulations provided by their rules, waive all or any part of the examination of any applicant possessing the qualifications mentioned in section 1 who shall have had five successive years' previous experience as a public accountant previous to the date of application, who shall apply in writing within one year after the passage of this act, and who shall have been practicing in this State as a public accountant, on his own account, for a period of not less than one year next prior to the passage of this act; also to any person who shall have been actively in practice as a public accountant for not less than five years next prior to the passage of this act, outside of the State of Illinois, who shall have passed an examination equivalent, in the opinion of the University of Illinois, to the examination to be held under the provisions of this act.

313

SECTION 4. (a) The university shall charge for the examination and certificate a fee of twenty-five dollars ($25.00) to meet the expenses of such examinations. This fee shall be payable by the applicant at the time of filing his application.

(b) The examiners appointed by the University of Illinois shall be paid for the purposes of this act for the time actually expended in pursuance of the duties imposed upon them by this act, an amount not exceeding ten dollars ($10.00) per day, and they shall be further entitled to their necessary traveling expenses. All expenses provided for by this act must be paid from the receipts under this act, and no expense incurred under this act shall be charged against the funds of the university.

(c) From the fees collected under Section 4, the University of Illinois shall pay all the expenses incident to the examination held under this act, the expenses of issuing certificates, the traveling expenses of the examiners, and their compensation while performing their duties under this act.

SECTION 5. The university may revoke any certificate issued under the provisions of this act, for unprofessional conduct or other sufficient cause, provided that written notice shall have been previously mailed to the holder of such certificate twenty days before any hearing thereon, stating the cause for such contemplated action, and appointing a date for a full hearing thereof by the university; and, provided further, that no certificate shall be revoked until a hearing shall have been had.

SECTION 6. If any person shall represent himself to the public as having received a certificate as provided in this act, or shall assume to practice as a certified public accountant, or use the abbreviation C.P.A., or any similar words or letters to indicate that the person using the same is a certified public accountant, without having received such certificate; or if any person having received a certificate as provided in this act, and having thereafter lost such certificate by revocation as herein provided, shall continue to practice as a certified public accountant he shall be deemed guilty of a misdemeanor and upon conviction thereof shall be fined a sum not exceeding two hundred dollars ($200) for each offense: Provided that nothing herein contained shall operate to prevent a certified public accountant who is the lawful holder of a certificate issued in compliance with the laws of another state, from practicing as such within this State, and styling himself a certified public accountant.

314

143

THE EMERGENCE OF PUBLIC ACCOUNTING IN THE UNITED STATES, 1748-1895

JAMES DON EDWARDS

Assistant Professor, Michigan State College

M OST OF THE HISTORIES of accounting have begun with Assyria and Babylonia, leaped over the many countries to Italy in the days of Pacioli, then hurried across Europe to devote their remaining space to the origin and growth of public accountancy in Great Britain. By the time these authors had covered the period from the South Sea Bubble to the organization of the British societies during the third quarter of the nineteenth century, they had exhausted their space and gave but little thought to the United States.

The story of the accountants who blazed the trails for the accounting profession in our country can only be inferred from brief, infrequent references and this paper may be considered as covering the "ancient" history of the American profession. The date 1895 was chosen to end this period since prior to this time success had not been achieved in getting legal recognition for the profession. Even so, several accounting firms had been formed, but there is no record of any attempt to have the practice of public accountancy recognized on a national level as a profession by the men engaged in public practice.

EARLY AMERICAN ACCOUNTANTS AND THE FUNCTIONS THEY PERFORMED

British Accountants Sent to the United States

Richard Brown of Edinburgh, in his *History of Accounting and Accountants*, published in 1905, leads one to believe that British accountants had visited the United States before the American Revolution.

A great commercial crisis visited Glasgow in 1777 as the result of the revolt in the previous year of the North American Colonies, with which part of the world the trade of the city was closely identified.

Mr. Walter Ewing Macloe of Cathkin who was designated in the earliest issue of the Glasgow directory as "Merchant and Accountant" was, we are told, from the esteem and confidence in which he was held, employed to wind up some of the largest and most important of the bankruptcies which occurred in that unfortunate year.[1]

It is known that James Ewing, son of Walter Ewing Macloe, acquired possessions in the West Indies, and one wonders if some of the Britishers who may have come for specific accountancy engagements did not remain here and establish themselves to serve American merchant business of Philadelphia, Boston, New York, and Charleston. If so, it may be inferred that a few Americans availed themselves of the abilities and experience of these visitors. No dates have developed as facts of the earliest visits by Scottish accountants to the colonies on behalf of British traders and of the later permanent migration of British accountants to this country.

If there were public accounting engagements in the American colonies during the eighteenth century, they were doubtless performed in one or more of the commercial towns on the Atlantic seaboard during one of the commercial crises, and they were probably connected with some of the principal businessmen of that time.

Functions of Early American Public Accountants

Some early references to men performing the functions of public accountants in the

315

---

[1] Richard Brown, *A History of Accounting and Accountants* (London: T. C. and E. C. Jack, 1905), p. 199.

316

United States have been found, the earliest of these references being dated 1748. In that year, Benjamin Franklin sold his interest in the firm of Franklin and Hall, a printing company, to David Hall for £18,000. The money was to be paid to Franklin in eighteen annual installments amounting to £1,000 each, subject to a final accounting for the contributions and withdrawals of the partners. This period expired in 1766 when ·Franklin was in London as colonial representative. James Parker had been Franklin's partner in New York for several years, so Franklin asked him to act as his representative in the final settlement with Hall. He made an inventory and valuation of the equipment and materials and presented a report which he entitled "State of your Accounts with Mr. Hall."

There is no proof that James Parker was in practice as a public accountant. Nevertheless, this may have been the first public accounting engagement in the American Colonies. Parker's report has been deposited in the Library of Columbia University.[2]

On January 11, 1786, *The New York Directory*, the first such volume issued for the City of New York, was published. The publisher, Shepard Kollock, advertised the directory as showing national, state and municipal officers, ministers, bank officers, Columbia College professors, physicians, lawyers, tradesmen, etc. One of the announcements in the directory read as follows:

David Franks Conveyance and Accountant No. 66 Broadway begs leave to return his sincere thanks to his friends and the public and hopes the cheapness of the following will continue him their favors.[3]

Then follows the advertiser's charges for

drawing a release, a bond, and a power of attorney, but fees for services as an accountant were not stated.

A similar reference of a public accountant is found in an advertisement which appeared in the *New Jersey Journal* of Wednesday, July, 8, 1795, printed and published by the same Shepard Kollock at Elizabethtown, New Jersey. The advertisement reads:

Notice

A conveyance office and office of intelligence will be opened by the subscriber on Monday next, in the brick house of William Shute, Esq., formerly occupied by Cortland Van Ansdaler; where writings of every kind will be done on moderate terms; also, farmers and tradesmen's books posted with accuracy and dispatch, and those who do not understand the method of keeping their books will be shown the form.

Benjamin Thowson
Elizabethtown, April 21, 1795.[4]

The public practice of accountancy seems to have been combined most commonly with teaching and writing on the subject of bookkeeping. The advertisements also indicate that some individuals were performing the duties of accountants and lawyers at the same time.

The following display advertisement indicated the functions performed by the public accountants in the United States during the last half of the nineteenth century.

1851

Practical bookkeeping and accountant. Opposite the Court House. Books opened, closed, posted. Bills and accounts made out. Bookkeeping in all its varied branches taught individually or in classes.[5]

According to this advertisement the accountant did some systems work but was primarily a bookkeeper and probably re-

[2] Norman E. Webster, "Public Accountancy in the United States," in *Fiftieth Anniversary Celebration* (New York: The American Institute of Accountants, 1937), p. 104.
[3] *Ibid.*, p. 105.
[4] "Early Days of Accountancy," *The Journal of Accountancy*, October, 1913, p. 311.
[5] A. C. Littleton, *Directory of Early American Public Accountants* (Urbana, Illinois: The University of Illinois, 1952), p. 19.

sorted to teaching to supplement his income.

The New York City directories give the name of James A. Bennet for the following years:

1818–1820, Accountant, 48 Fulton Street
1821–1822, Accountant, 12th Avenue
1824–1829, Teacher in Bookkeeping, 97 John Street
1830–1831, Teacher in Bookkeeping, 39 Arcade
1833–1835, Teacher in Bookkeeping, 73 John Street[6]

Among those who were included in the directories was Benjamin F. Foster, of Boston, who was listed as a teacher in 1834 and as an accountant in 1835–1837.

Probably the first person to call himself a public accountant in Pennsylvania was John W. Francis, who opened an office in Philadelphia in 1869. Some years later Mr. Charles Nixon Vallum opened his office as an accountant in 1875 also in Philadelphia. He sent out as a bid for business an attractive card, handwritten and multiplied photographically, explaining briefly just what he was prepared to do for the public.[7]

1875

Prepared to make statements for executors, examine corporations, partnerships, individual books and accounts of every description, open and close books, to attend to any and every kind of bookkeeping. Books posted monthly and trial balance taken at a trifling cost. Plans furnished for books for special purposes.[8]

John Heins, who was later to play a primary role in the organization of the American Association of Public Accountants, began to practice as a public accountant in downtown Philadelphia in 1877.

Another one of these advertisements

which indicates the widening scope of the accountant's functions appeared thirty-six years after the 1851 display:

1887

H..... F....., public accountant and auditor, examines and reports on individuals, partnership, corporation accounts, investigates and adjusts disputed accounts, acts as assignee or receiver, designs new books to meet special requirements. Books posted and balance sheets rendered, accounts audited, expert work for the courts, scientifically and faithfully performed.[9]

The advertiser seemed to perform a very wide variety of functions compared to that of thirty years before. The emphasis in 1887 was on auditing business records and issuing reports, whereas in 1851 the accountant or bookkeeper was concerned with the more routine matters of posting and closing accounts. In the advertisement the individual was available to render clerical help in that he was willing to make statements for his clients. The accountant in the latter case was available for work of a professional nature.

During the early 1890's the railroad companies in the United States were having financial difficulties. When one of these, the Norfolk and Western Railway, had a receiver appointed by a federal court, Price, Waterhouse and Company through its agent and predecessor, Jones & Caesar, were engaged to make a detailed examination of the company's accounts. This was the first of several railroad engagements undertaken by this firm.

Several other audits prior to amalgamation were brought to the firm of Jones & Caesar during the last decade of the nineteenth century.[10] These mergers continued even though the Sherman Anti-Trust Act had been passed in 1890.

During this period engagements such as those by Jones & Caesar, later Price,

---

[6] H. C. Bentley, *A Brief Treatise on the History and Development of Accounting* (Boston: Bentley School of Accounting and Finance, 1929), p. 27.
[7] George Wilkinson, "Organization of the Profession in Pennsylvania," *The Journal of Accountancy*, September, 1927, p. 162.
[8] A. C. Littleton, *Directory of Early American Public Accountants*, p. 19.

[9] *Ibid.*, p. 20.
[10] C. W. DeMond, *Price, Waterhouse and Company in America* (New York: The Comet Press, Inc., 1951), p. 5.

317

Waterhouse Company, helped establish the profession. It was not yet a frequent occurrence for accountants to be called in regularly for auditing engagements. In the engagements incident to mergers, the accountants would audit the books of all the enterprises to be consolidated. Along with the audit the accountants would assist in determining the basis for recording the assets and equities of the companies.

Formation of Accounting Firms

A natural development from practicing as individuals was for two or more accountants to associate themselves in a partnership. Accountants probably formed partnerships in imitation of other professions such as medicine and law, or following the precedent set by British accountants.

A firm called Veysey and Veysey was established in New York in 1866. The senior partner, William H. Veysey, an Englishman who never forswore allegiance to Queen Victoria, established himself in New York in that year. His oldest son, Walter H. P. Veysey, was associated with him.[11]

This firm had several assistants, employed by them prior to 1880, who were to become leaders in the development of the profession. Two of these men were James N. Kell, who later served as treasurer of the New York State Society of Certified Public Accountants, and George Wilkinson, who later became very active in the organization of the national organizations.

In Cincinnati, a firm was listed under the caption of "Accountants Bureau" in the 1876 directory. The firm was composed of Nelson, Shepard and Cooke, who were described as expert accountants.[12]

One of the oldest if not the oldest national firm, Barrow, Wade, Guthrie and Company, was established in October, 1883, in New York. From the earliest days of this firm engagements were taken in different sections of the United States. As far as can be determined the accounting firms prior to this date were local to their operations. Mr. Guthrie had come to this country on business while acting in the capacity of receiver of a bankrupt financial concern in England. Guthrie was also a representative of the firm of Thomas, Wade, Guthrie and Company, Chartered Accountants, of London and Manchester. While visiting in the United States, it was evident to this trained accountant that there was an opportunity to establish a firm in this country. He joined with Mr. John Wylie Barrow, of New York, an actuary, who checked the branch statements of insurance companies in this country before forwarding them to England, as the American partner.

Prior to Mr. Barrow's death in 1886, the firm took in another partner, Mr. Oscar E. Morton. But when Mr. Guthrie returned to this country with Mr. James T. Anyon, whom he had employed to work in the New York office, he was faced with a lawsuit brought by the resident partner. After the suit was settled, Mr. Anyon assumed the duties of the firm in this country and became an outstanding individual in the development of public accountancy.[13]

All the names of the partners in the James Yalden and Company are not known, but James Yalden was listed in the 1883 telephone directory, and in 1891 he was listed under Yalden, Brooks and Donnelly; and in 1895 under Yalden, Brooks, and Walker. Security offerings in the New York *Times* showed that ac-

[11] George Wilkinson, "Organization of the Profession in Pennsylvania," *The Journal of Accountancy*, September, 1927, p. 162.
[12] Norman E. Webster, "Public Accountancy in the United States," in *Fiftieth Anniversary Celebration*, p. 107.
[13] James T. Anyon, "Early Days of American Accountancy," *The Journal of Accountancy*, January, 1925, 2.

318

counts were certified in 1890 by Deloitte, Dever, Griffiths and Company and by Price, Waterhouse and Company.

Samuel Lowell Price, of Price Waterhouse and Company, was a moving spirit in the formation of the Institute of Accountants in London in 1870. He was active in this organization until it was absorbed by the Institute of Chartered Accountants in England and Wales, incorporated by Royal Charter in 1880. All three partners, Price · Waterhouse and Holyland were fellows of the Institute of Accountants.

Work in the United States was undertaken by the firm as early as 1873, and thereafter visits to this country were made with increasing frequency.[14] During the next decade there was considerable activity in the conversion of privately owned businesses into public companies and a report on earnings, signed by some well known accountant, became an indispensable part of the prospectus advertising the offer to the public. During this period London financiers were seeking opportunities for investment of funds abroad, and as a result the undertakings by the firm, particularly in America, were increasing. With the amalgamation of a group of American breweries into the Bartholomay Brewing Company of Rochester, New York, audits were made of the accounts of the constituent companies. Sheath and Fowler, and members of the staff of Price, Waterhouse and Company were sent to the United States to carry out the work involved in the merger proceedings.

The period during which these representatives of English public accounting firms came to audit the accounts of American breweries was the beginning of a new era in American enterprise, an era which witnessed a wide expansion of business. But the great value of the work referred to English accountants resulted in the opportunity for training Americans taken on their staff, many of whom had practically no experience before this time in public accounting. This work gave them experience in a fairly wide field of accounting activity.[15]

The importation of the above mentioned professional skills and subsequent training of American apprentices resulted in the emergence of American counterparts to the existing English present firms. One of the first of these firms was Price, Waterhouse and Company which originally operated under the name Jones, Caesar and Company. The first American office of Price Waterhouse and Company was opened under the latter name in New York in September, 1890. The Chicago office was opened in February, 1892.

In 1893 the first of the midwestern firms was opened by Arthur Young in Chicago. The firm was known as Stuart and Young.

Then came the founding of Haskins and Sells on March 4, 1895, in New York. The two founding partners, Charles Waldo Haskins and Elijah Watt Sells, had met while serving on a committee investigating the operations of the Executive Department at Washington after the panic of 1893.[16]

A note in *The Accountant*, in 1899, states that two of the best known firms of English chartered accountants opened branch offices in Chicago in the year 1891 and transferred to them their Western business.[17] Unfortunately the names of these firms were not given in the announcement, but Mr. Jones and Mr. Caesar were operating in the United States as agents of

319

---

[14] C. W. DeMond, *Price, Waterhouse and Company in America*, p. 5.

[15] *Ibid.*, p. 10.
[16] Charles W. Haskins and E. W. Sells, *The First Fifty Years, 1895–1945* (New York: Privately Printed, 1947), p. 5.
[17] "The Public Accountant in Chicago," *The Accountant*, April, 1899, 395.

Price Waterhouse and Company of England and had several accounts in the Chicago area, including the stockyards. Mr. Jones first came to this country in 1891 and established an office in Chicago; therefore this might have been one of the offices mentioned as branch office of English Chartered Accountants.

PROFESSIONAL ORGANIZATIONS

Institute of Accountants and Bookkeepers

Just as it was natural to form partnerships it was also a natural move for an occupational group to form an organization, even though the groups were formed for social as well as professional benefits.

The first accounting organization in the United States was the Institute of Acountants and Bookkeepers of the City of New York, incorporated July 28, 1882. The name or the organization was shortened to the Institute of Accountants on June 23, 1886. Its objects and purposes, as stated in its certificate of incorporation, were:

the evaluation of the profession and the intellectual advancement and improvement of its members:

1st, By the discussion in its councils of technical knowledge and commercial practice;

2nd, By aiding its members in the performance of their professional and social responsibilities.[18]

Although the Institute of Accountants and Bookkkeepers was active during twenty-five years or more, very few records of its activities remain except its charter, its by-laws, a few notices, and some news items in the accounting journals of that period. These records show that its membership included a considerable number of accountants in public practice and that for its highest class of membership, applicants were required to pass examinations which were described as severe. Its aims, at least

during the first decade of its life, appear to have been almost wholly devoted to education for accountancy and the provision of accounting literature. So far as is known, this was the earliest effort to provide educational opportunities for the profession in America.[19]

American Association of Public Accountants

After the organization of accounting firms and the establishment of collegiate schools of business, it became clear to a few men of vision that the profession then known as "expert accounting" was a profession essential to the proper conduct of business. Those men who claimed to be experts in "matters of accounts" were few in number, had no means of increasing their number or maintaining high standards of practice for their own benefit and the benefit of the public, and had no legal status or means of controlling the profession. It was not until 1886 that the first steps were taken to organize accountancy on a professional basis.

As has been noted, Mr. James T. Anyon arrived in New York City from London in October, 1886, to enter the firm of Barrow, Wade, Guthrie and Company. After the death of Mr. Barrow, Mr. Anyon turned his attention to an inquiry into the standing of the profession of accounting in New York. Mr. Anyon made the following statement:

I had left on the other side a profession full of vitality, one that was looked upon as an essential element of business life, and so recognized in every section of business activity. It need therefore not be a matter for surprise when I say that it was natural I should expect in this great and progressive country to find relatively the same conditions in the respect named as existed in the country I had left. A general survey of the situation, however, soon made the fact apparent that these conditions existed here only to a very limited extent, that public accounting was in its infancy and that

320

[18] Norman E. Webster, "Early Movements for Accountancy Education," *The Journal of Accountancy*, May, 1941, 443.

[19] *Ibid.*, p. 443.

it was little known or understood as a distinct profession.[20]

It was in early December, 1886, that Mr. Edwin Guthrie, F.C.A. of Manchester, who was visiting the city of New York on the business of his firm, accepted Mr. John Heins's invitation to visit Philadelphia. Heins was one of the most prominent accountants in Philadelphia. The object of the meeting was to discuss a plan to organize public accountants into a society with the following objectives:

to elevate the standing and advance the interest of public accountants; and to direct attention to the advantages offered by, and the safeguard attending, the auditing and adjusting of books and accounts by persons thoroughly skilled and experienced as public accountants, and to establish personal reputation.[21]

The society was to be called the "Chartered Accountants' Institute," but Mr. Guthrie strongly counseled Mr. Heins and Mr. Francis to use some other name than "Chartered Accountants." He pointed out that it would conflict with the use of that title in this country by English and Scottish accountants visiting the United States on professional business. This seemed to be a serious objection, because the most important and responsible business entrusted to public accountants in these days was given to visiting British accountants because of the large amounts of foreign, primarily English, investments in this country. Also, Mr. Guthrie felt that a national organization, such as the Institute of Chartered Accountants (1882); would serve these purposes better than a state society.

Mr. Anyon immediately invited all of those present at the first meeting as well as all interested accountants to meet with him and Mr. Edwin Guthrie at the firm's office, 45 William Street, to discuss "the matter of making the profession better known, understood, and recognized by the public, and what might be done to attain this object."[22]

On December 22, 1886, six or seven persons attended such a meeting. Mr. Guthrie was asked to take the chair, and Mr. Anyon was asked to act as secretary of the meeting. Both gentlemen complied, and Mr. Guthrie addressed those present. Among other things he said,

that it was a great privilege to him thus to have this opportunity of meeting the accountants practicing in this and other cities; that he was sorry, however, to find the profession had not materially progressed in public recognition, or in other ways, since he was last here; that in England, on the contrary, the profession was on a very high plane; that it was recognized as one of the leading professions—firms, corporations, banks, railroads, and other financial and commercial entities seeking the service of accountants in all phases of activity; that the efforts of practicing accountants in this country should be directed toward bringing about a similar institution or body to that now existing on the other side, viz., the Institute of Chartered Accountants in England and Wales, under the regulations of which competent accountants could practice and be recognized by the public as fully qualified so to do.[23]

A resolution was proposed by Mr. John Heins, who had come from Philadelphia to attend this meeting, to the effect that the accountants present should form themselves into an association for the advancement and protection of the interests of the profession, and that the qualifications for membership should be ability and fitness to practice in a public capacity. It was further proposed (Mr. Anyon states that he had the pleasure of making this motion) that the name of this organization be the American Association of Public Accountants. The motion was carried unanimously

321

---

[20] James T. Anyon, *Recollections of the Early Days of Accounting, 1883–1893* (New York: Published by the Author, 1925), p. 16.
[21] George Wilkinson, "Organization of the Profession in Pennsylvania," *The Journal of Accountancy*, September, 1927, 163.

[22] James T. Anyon, "Early Days of American Accountancy," *The Journal of Accountancy*, January, 1925, 7.
[23] *Ibid.*, p. 7.

and thus came into existence on December 23, 1886, the first organized body of professional accountants in the United States.[24] This organization consisted of some eight or ten individuals whose interest continued unabated. All worked to get public accounting better known and the association in a position to become recognized as having a legal status. Their efforts were finally successful when, on August 20, 1887, the Association became incorporated under the laws of the state of New York with the name and title of "American Association of Public Accountants."[25] A copy of the Association's certificate of incorporation was published in the American Institute of Accountants *Fiftieth Anniversary Celebration.*

All of the American citizens present signed the certificate of incorporation. Mr. Anyon and Mr. Veysey, being British subjects, could not join the petition. Of the eight original signers of the certificate of incorporation, only two remained members about a dozen years later—Mr. John Heins and Mr. James Yalden.[26]

The bylaws of the association were prepared and adopted on February 8, 1888, at a general meeting of the members of the Association. A council meeting immediately followed, at which time the following officers were elected:

President
James Yalden, New York
Vice-President
John Heins, Philadelphia
Treasurer
William H. Veysey, New York[27]

The first Council of the association, the members of which were selected to regulate the conduct of its affairs, consisted of the following men:

James T. Anyon	New York
Louis M. Bertheil	New York
George H. Church	New York
John Heins	Philadelphia
Mark C. Mirick	New York
Rodney McLaughlin	Boston, Mass.
C. H. W. Sibley	New York
William H. Veysey	New York
Walter H. P. Veysey	New York
James Yalden	New York[28]

The bylaws of the association provided that the members should be divided into two classes, "Fellows" and "Associates," the Fellows to have the right to use after their name the initials "F.A.A." and the Associates the letters "A.A.A." to designate their membership status. It was provided that

Fellows shall be (1) the original incorporators of the association and those who subscribe to the constitution and by-laws; and (2) all persons who have practiced as public accountants continuously for three years previous to their admission to membership in the Association.

Associates shall be all persons who obtain a certificate of their having passed the final examination hereinafter provided for.[29]

At the time of incorporation the association had thirty-one members, of whom twenty-four were fellows and seven associates.[30]

ACCOUNTING LITERATURE AND
EDUCATION FOR ACCOUNTANCY

Early Bookkeeping and Accounting Books

James Bennett, one of the earliest American writers on bookkeeping, published his first book, *The American System of Practical Bookkeeping*, in 1814. This

322

[24] *Ibid.*, p. 8.
[25] T. Edward Ross, "Random Recollections of an Eventful Half Century," *The Journal of Accountancy*, October, 1937, 268.
[26] Sanders W. Davies, "Genesis, Growth and Aims of the Institute," *The Journal of Accountancy*, August, 1926, 105.
[27] Robert H. Montgomery, *Fifty Years of Accountancy* (New York: Ronald Press Company, 1939), p. 63.

[28] James T. Anyon, "Early Days of American Accountancy," *The Journal of Accountancy*, February, 1925, 84.
[29] James T. Anyon, *Recollections of the Early Days of American Accountancy*, 1883–1893, p. 33.
[30] James T. Anyon, "Early Days of American Accountancy," *The Journal of Accountancy*, February, 1925, 85.

book met with popular response and was highly recommended by merchants, bank presidents, and others.

In 1818, Bennett published a revised edition for use in schools. The title page of this edition shows him as:

James Bennett, A. & M., Professor to the Accountants' Society of New York, late a professor to the Accountants' Society of Pennsylvania, Late President of the Accountants' Society of New York, and member of Medico-Chirurgical Society of the State of New York.[11]

He probably states this to promote his book. No other references to the organizations in which he claimed membership could be found.

The following quotations are from his book:

Natural and mathematical instruments are supplied and students will have access to a choice library. An excellent, mounted telescope for observing Satellites of Jupiter and for other astronomical purposes.[22]

The annual commencement of Bennetts' Public Lectures on Bookkeeping is on the first Monday in October, and a new class commences on the first Monday of each of the succeeding months, including April; as the lectures close annually on the 1st of May.[33]

Terms for an unlimited attendance, with the practice, $15 to be paid in advance. For private instruction, which is given at all times, $25 including books for practice. The private instruction is given in the daytime throughout the year.[34]

Mr. Bennett makes the following statement as to his ability and accomplishments:

The author has instructed in the Science and Art of Bookkeeping a far greater number of grown persons than any other person in any other country or age of the world; he has instructed persons from thirteen different nations of the earth.[35]

Another teacher-author-accountant was Benjamin F. Foster, of Boston, who was

listed in 1834 as an instructor. From 1835 to 1837, he was listed as an accountant. He was also a writer.

In 1837 Christopher C. Marsh, of New York City, published a *Lecture on the Study of Bookkeeping with the Balance Sheet*, the title page of which contained the following statement:

To Merchants and Others
Complicated Accounts Adjusted:
Opinions given on disputed points relating to accounts;
Books opened and commenced.[36]

George N. Comer, of Boston, published *A Work on Bookkeeping* in 1842. His card as Accountant stated:

Offers his services for the adjustment of disputed and complicated accounts, Insolvent and Other Estates ... and all business pertaining to that of an accountant, executed with fidelity and dispatch.[37]

It is clear, therefore, that these early American authors and teachers sought engagements as public accountants. It is probable that persons from other activities, especially from banking and insurance, were from time to time called in for public accounting service. After 1840, one begins to find mention of men whose principal occupation was that of public practice of accountancy.

In 1852, Christopher C. Marsh published *Bookkeeping in Spanish* in California. A. G. Beck was secured as a professional translator because of his friendship for Marsh and his familiarity with the subject matter of Marsh's book. According to a letter dated May 20, 1888, from Beck's son, Francis E. Beck, who was one of the earliest members of the American Association of Public Accountants, A. G. Beck was in public practice as an accountant in Los Angeles from 1852 to 1878.[38]

323

---

[11] H. C. Bentley, *A Brief Treatise on the History and Development of Accounting*, p. 27.
[22] *Ibid.*, p. 27.
[33] *Ibid.*, p. 27.
[34] *Ibid.*, p. 28.
[35] *Ibid.*, p. 28.

[36] Norman E. Webster, "Public Accounting in the United States," in *Fiftieth Anniversary Celebration*, p. 106.
[37] *Ibid.*, p. 106.
[38] *Ibid.*, p. 107.

Nineteenth Century Bookkeeping and Accounting Education

Mr. Bennett, mentioned previously as one of the early authors, also had a school which offered instruction in bookkeeping and related subjects. The following statement was made concerning his school:

The school established by Bennett for the teaching of bookkeeping and mathematical science, in New York City in 1818, is doubtless the first accounting school in the United States.[39]

Attempts were made as early as 1851 to found a school of commerce at the university level. This attempt was made at the University of Louisiana but was apparently abandoned in 1857. In 1868, the University of Illinois established a school, the name of which became the School of Commerce two years later. The purpose of this school was to prepare men for the tasks of business. Bookkeeping was one of the subjects taught. In 1880 the Board of Trustees discontinued the school since

the attempt to construct a University School of Commerce along the lines of a business college have proven unsuccessful. The school had done little more than to prepare clerks and bookkeepers. It had not been realized that the function of a university school of commerce was to prepare for future leadership in economic enterprise, not for clerkship.[40]

The first business college of record offering instruction in accounts and related subjects was the Bryant and Stratton School, established in 1853.[41] Schools of a similar nature began to be established in the major cities on the East coast.[42]

The United States was the first country to recognize accounting as a proper subject or discipline to be given a place in the university curriculum. The earliest known definite plan for the establishment of a collegiate school of business in the United States is described in a report made by President Robert E. Lee in 1869 to the trustees of the institution that later became Washington and Lee University. President Lee died the next year and his proposal was not carried out.[43]

The honor of establishing the first American collegiate school of business belongs to the University of Pennsylvania. Mr. Joseph Wharton gave $100,000 in 1881 to establish the Wharton School of Finance and Economy in Philadelphia.[44] The name was later changed to the Wharton School of Commerce and Finance.

American Association's Educational Effort

On February 10, 1892, while James Yalden was president of the Association and Henry R. M. Cook was vice-president, a special meeting was called to consider a charter for an educational institution; the meeting was held at the office of the president. The vice-president, who it appears was also chairman of a committee on Albany "to find out the particulars," was authorized to go to Albany "to find out the particulars." At Albany the committee was advised by Melvil Dewey, Secretary of the Board of Regents, to present to the regents a petition for a charter for the proposed institution, embodying an outline of its form of organization, a statement of the provisions to be made for its financial stability, the curriculum which it would offer to its students, and probably the names of the persons who would constitute its faculty.

---

[39] H. C. Bentley, *A Brief Treatise on the History and Development of Accounting*, p. 28.
[40] Jeremiah Lockwood, "Early University Education in Accounting," THE ACCOUNTING REVIEW, June, 1938, 132.
[41] Norman E. Webster, "Early Movements for Accountancy Education," *The Journal of Accountancy*, May, 1941, 441.
[42] James B. Lovette, *History of Accounting in the United States* (unpublished typescript, American Institute of Accountants Library, New York), p. 14.

[43] H. C. Bentley, *A Brief Treatise on the History and Development of Accounting*, p. 28.
[44] Emanuel Saxe, "The Role of the Society in Accounting Education," in *The New York State Society of Certified Public Accountants, Fiftieth Anniversary* (New York: New York State Society of Certified Public Accountants, 1947), p. 21.

On February 20, 1892, Harry A. Briggs, Richard F. Stevens, and the Committee on Charter were constituted as a Committee on Curriculum which reported on March 5, 1892, that it had agreed upon the course of study. On that date a fund of $5,000 was provided; on April 6, 1892, John L. N. Hunt was asked to take the chair of commercial law.[45]

A copy of this petition or of the curriculum is not known to exist. However, subsequent records indicate that the petition asked for a charter for a college of accounts, with the power to confer degrees, to have a guaranty of $5,000 against deficits, to offer the courses provided for in the curriculum, and to be under the direction of the American Association of Public Accountants. The petition was endorsed by several hundred bankers, corporations, firms, and individuals of note and sent to the regents prior to May 21, 1892, because on that date the Committee informed the members that action would be taken on the petition in Albany on June 8, 1892.[46]

The minutes of the regents' meeting contain this statement:

... and after discussion, on motion of Regent Doane, it was voted that the Secretary be instructed to inform the petitioners in the matter of the American Association of Public Accountants of New York that the regents are not prepared to endorse the whole proposal in their petition, but are ready to open examinations for such persons as desire to become public accountants.[47]

The members of the Association's Charter Committee went to work immediately on a revision of the petition. The task was completed and the revised petition was presented to the members of the Associa-

tion on December 8, 1892, when Mr. Cook submitted copies of the petition and the proposed curriculum. The proposed curriculum can be found in an article by Mr. Norman E. Webster in the May, 1941, *Journal of Accountancy.*

Even with the energetic sponsorship of the Association, the school was not a success. Though the school itself was a failure, the movement promoted by it was a success. Soon after the temporary charter expired on December 14, 1894, the regents' willingness to open examinations as early as 1892 paved the way for two bills which finally blossomed into the first state laws which set up the professional designation of Certified Public Accountant.

FIRST LEGAL RECOGNITION PROPOSED FOR THE PROFESSION

In 1895 the accountants in California and New York were seeking legislation to obtain legal recognition and the licensing of public accountants. Early in 1895 in New York, both of the then existing accounting societies, the American Association of Public Accountants and the Institute of Accountants and Bookkeepers, had bills introduced in the legislature. The Association appointed a committee to promote the passage of suitable legislation, which was prepared by Francis Gottsberger, and introduced on February 20. The Institute's bill was prepared by Henry Harvey early in March.[48]

The Institute's bill provided for the examination of candidates for certificates as Certified Public Accountants.

Section I of the bill stated:

Any citizen of the United States and a resident or doing business in the State of New York, over the age of twenty-one years, and of good moral character who shall have received from the Uni-

---

[45] Norman E. Webster, "Early Movements for Accountancy Education," *The Journal of Accountancy,* May, 1941, 443.

[46] "A College of Accountants—Petition for It Sent to the University Regents," *The Accountant,* June, 1892, 520.

[47] Norman E. Webster, "Early Movements for Accountancy Education," *The Journal of Accountancy,* May, 1941, 444.

[48] Norman E. Webster, "Background of the New York State C.P.A. Law of April 17, 1896, and Its Subsequent Amendments," in *The New York State Society of Certified Public Accountants, Fiftieth Anniversary,* p. 32.

versity a certificate of his qualifications, to practice as a public expert accountant, shall be styled and it shall be a misdemeanor for any person not holding such certificate to assume the title of certified public accountant, or to use in connection with his name the letters C.P.A.[49]

Both the bills of the Association and the Institute contained restrictive provisions which, however, differed materially in their application. The Association's bill provided

that no person shall practice as a public accountant after the passage of this act unless he be licensed by the Regents of the University of the State of New York.

The Institute's bill provided

that after July 1, 1896, only certified public accountants should be appointed or employed to act as examiners of accounts, expert accountants or paid auditors by courts, administrators, receivers, state, county or municipal officers.

Before the end of the legislative session, the Association's bill with its restrictions of practice to those licensed by the Regents was withdrawn. The Institute's bill was defeated in the Senate because of the provision limiting practice to Certified Public Accountants.[50]

SUMMARY

It seems evident that more than seventy-five years ago some men in large cities called themselves public accountants. They audited or "checked up" books with

the object mainly of discovering or preventing irregularities rather than for constructive work, although systems work was undertaken. Somewhat later the foreign shareholders and bondholders of a number of large enterprises, mainly but not exclusively railroads, desired that the accounts should be audited and sent out auditors from England to perform such services.[51] This practice led to the opening of offices in the United States by English and Scotch auditors; some of the early firms were established in this way. American accountants gave increasing competition.

The earliest accounting organization, The American Association, was formed with the purpose of raising the professional standards and "for social and benefit purposes." Early attempts to elevate the profession by means of collegiate instruction in accounting for those wishing to enter the profession were unsuccessful. Wharton's School of Finance and Economy, however, was formed in Philadelphia, and accounting was included in its curriculum.

The desire on the part of the members of the profession to receive recognition was carried to the New York State Board of Regents. With the Board's willingness to administer examinations an attempt was made to secure legal recognition from the state. The first attempt in 1895 to get legislation for the legal recognition of Certified Public Accountants failed, but during the period to follow the public accountants continued their efforts with considerable success.

---

[49] "History of the American Institute," in *Fiftieth Anniversary Celebration*, p. 7.

[50] Norman E. Webster, "Background of the New York State C.P.A. Law of April 17, 1896, and Its Subsequent Amendments," in *The New York State Society of Certified Public Accountants, Fiftieth Anniversary*, p. 32.

[51] Edward L. Suffern, "Twenty-five Years of Accountancy," *The Journal of Accountancy*, September, 1922, 174.

PUBLIC ACCOUNTING IN THE UNITED STATES, 1896–1913

JAMES DON EDWARDS
Assistant Professor, Michigan State College

THE first legal recognition of the certified public accounting profession took place during the period 1896–1913, along with many other features which aided the evolutionary development of the profession. This paper deals with some of the early firms, still in existence, which have since acquired national reputations. The expansion of accounting education will be discussed as well as the organizations which were formed.

FIRST C.P.A. LAW AND OTHER LEGISLATION

New York Legal Recognition

After the failure to get the legislature of the State of New York to pass public accounting legislation in 1895, the American Association and the Institute of Bookkeepers and Accountants united behind the Institute's bill from which the restrictive provision, which would have permitted only certified public accountants to practice public accounting, had been deleted.

The next year, the Association appointed a committee of three to press for the Institute's bill. Its members were Frank Broaker, William Sanders Davies, and James Yalden. Mr. Davies stated that he worked for the bill only in New York City, that James Yalden was inactive, but that Frank Broaker spent nearly all his time in Albany and that without his efforts and that of his partner, Mr. Richard M. Chapman, of the firm Broaker and Chapman, the bill would not have passed on April 17, 1896.[1]

The following is the text of the first C.P.A. law enacted:

Chapter 312. Laws of 1896
Passed Assembly 3 April, 1896; Passed Senate 7 April, 1896.
Signed by Governor 17 April, 1896
State of New York

An Act to Regulate the Profession of Public Accountants.

The people of the State of New York, represented in the Senate and Assembly, do enact as follows:

Section 1. Any citizen of the United States, or person who has duly declared his intention of becoming such citizen, residing or having a place for the regular transaction of business in the State of New York, being over the age of twenty-one years and of good moral character and who shall have received from the Regents of the University a certificate of his qualifications to practice as a public expert accountant as hereinafter provided, shall be styled and known as a Certified Public Accountant; and no other person shall assume such title, or use the abbreviation C.P.A. or any other word, letters or figures, to indicate that the person using the same is such Certified Public Accountant.

Section 2. The Regents of the University shall make rules for the examination of persons applying for certificates under this act, and may appoint a board of three examiners for the purpose, which board shall, after the year eighteen hundred and ninety-seven, be composed of Certified Public Accountants. The Regents shall charge for examination and certificate such fee as may be necessary to meet the actual expenses of such examinations, and they shall report annually their receipts and expenses under the provision of this Act to the State Comptroller, and pay the balance of receipts over expenditures to the State Treasurer. The Regents may revoke any such certificate for sufficient cause after written notice to the holder thereof and a hearing thereon.

Section 3. The Regents may, in their discretion, waive the examination of any person possessing the qualifications mentioned in Section 1 who shall have been for more than one year before the passage of this Act, practicing in this State on his own account, as a public accountant, and who shall apply in writing for such certificate within one year after the passage of this Act.

Section 4. Any violation of this Act shall be a misdemeanor.

Section 5. This act shall take effect immediately.[2]

[1] Norman E. Webster, "Background of the New York State C.P.A. Law of April 17, 1896, and Its Subsequent Amendments," in *The New York State Society of Certified Public Accountants Fiftieth Anniversary,* New York: The New York State Society of Certified Public Accountants, 1947, p. 33.
[2] N. Y. Laws, 1896, Ch. 312.

This was the first legislation in the United States to create the professional designation "Certified Public Accountant."[3]

Acting under the authority of this act the Regents of the University of the State of New York appointed Frank Broaker, C. E. Sprague, and Charles Waldo Haskins to be the first board of examiners under the new Public Accountants Act.[4] The following conditions had to be met by each candidate before a certificate could be issued under the rules of conduct. He must be at least twenty-five years of age with three years' satisfactory experience in the practice of accounting, one of which shall have been in the office of an expert public accountant. The examinations were to cover the theory of accounts, practical accounting, auditing, and commercial law.[5]

The examinations were given under the auspices of the New York State Board of Regents by an appointed board of examiners from the public accountancy profession. These examinations were under the control of the administrative board of all the educational facilities of the State of New York.

Efforts at Federal Regulation

Many of the prominent practicing public accountants in these years felt that the profession of accountancy needed federal recognition and regulation. They based their argument largely on the fact that accountancy was to a very large extent interstate. All of the large firms of public accountants, the arguments went, practiced in more than one state—in some cases in foreign countries. If the accountant re-

ceived recognition from the national government, he would be able to practice in interstate commerce uninterrupted. The profession desired a license which all states would recognize.

It was pointed out by Mr. Sells that no such confusion existed in the practice of the professions of law and medicine neither of which, generally speaking, was of the same interstate character as that of the profession of accountancy.[6]

The difficulty of getting the Congress of the United States to take action on legislation pertaining to one profession was one reason for not pushing for federal legislation. Then, too, several states—for example, California, Pennsylvania, Florida, and Maryland—had C.P.A. legislation in force, and Congress would be very reluctant to pass a law which might invade states' rights. Therefore, the idea of securing Congressional action on professional accountancy was given up or failed to gain acceptance.

Legislation in Other States

After the passage of the New York Act, public accountants in other states sought their own state laws. The accountants in New York were eager to forward information on their Act and give assistance to other state organizations. The Pennsylvania law was enacted in 1899; the Maryland law in 1900; the California law in 1901; the Illinois and the Washington laws in 1903; the New Jersey law in 1904; and the Florida and Michigan laws in 1905.

Additional state legislation recognizing the accountancy profession was passed in Colorado in 1907; in Georgia, Connecticut, Ohio, Louisiana, and Rhode Island in 1908; in Montana, Nebraska, Minnesota, Massachusetts, and Missouri in 1909; in Virginia in 1910. Then in 1911 West Vir-

---

[3] C. W. Haskins and E. W. Sells, *The First Fifty Years, 1895–1945* (New York: Privately Printed, 1947), p. 8.

[4] "Accountancy in the States," *The Accountant*, June, 1896, p. 504.

[5] Charles W. Haskins, *Accountancy; Its Past and Present*, an address delivered before the American Institute of Accountants, January 25, 1900 (unpublished), p. 21.

[6] C. W. Sells, "The Accountant of 1917," *The Journal of Accountancy*, February, 1907, p. 298.

ginia and in 1912 Vermont passed their laws. The next year Nevada, North Carolina, North Dakota, Oregon, Tennessee, and Wisconsin succeeded in obtaining C.P.A. legislation.

In each of these states the accountants banded together in a society, and the society in each state was affiliated with the American Association. By the end of the first decade of the twentieth century, there were about one thousand members of the Association.

First Violation of C.P.L. Law

In 1898 the first violator of the New York C.P.A. law was brought into court. The suit resulted from the publication of the following advertisement in a New York newspaper. This incident happened even before any other state had enacted a C.P.A. law.

Accountant—a certified public accountant, highly recommended, will write up books, prepare trading accounts, make investigations etc., terms, $6 per diem, or accept permanent situation with firm or corporation—Certified Accountant, Herald.[7]

Authorities checked to find out that this advertisement had been inserted by a Mr. John Fenton. He pleaded ignorance of the 1896 Act as passed by the New York Legislature and offered a full apology. Further, he stated to the authorities that he was a member of the Society of Accountants and Auditors of England, but after a check had been made, his name was not found among the list of members.

When Fenton appeared in court he pleaded guilty to the charge of using the professional designation "Certified Public Accountant" without having been licensed to practice by the New York State Board. He was fined $35.00 or ten days in jail for the violation. The conviction of the viola-

tor of this law was made only nine days after the violation.[8]

C.P.A. EXAMINATIONS, CERTIFICATION, AND PROFESSIONAL EXPANSION

Analysis of First C.P.A. Examination

The first examination was given by the New York Board of Examiners on December 15 and 16, 1896.

The first section of the examination on the theory of accounts was given on December 15, 1896—9:15 A.M. to 12:15 P.M. The candidates had to answer five specific questions and any five of the other questions. The first question pertained to the essential principles of double-entry bookkeeping as contrasted with single-entry. This section of the examination contained questions asking the candidate to distinguish between accounts—Revenue account, Trading account—and to define such terms as fixed assets, cash assets, stock, capital, and loan capital.

Practical accounting was given in the afternoon from 1:15 to 4:15 P.M. The candidate had to answer two specific questions and had a choice of any two of four other questions.

The first question required a statement of affairs, and the second question was a partnership problem. These two questions had to be answered.

The third problem concerned the opening of the books of a company after the company had been purchased at a receiver's sale. A balance sheet was to be made from the ledger accounts. Problem number four was a partnership liquidation problem. The fifth problem was a foreign exchange problem, and the sixth was a joint venture problem.

The auditing examination was the following day from 9:15 A.M. to 12:15 P.M. Ten questions had to be answered by the

329

---

[7] "Accountancy in the States," *The Accountant*, April, 1898, p. 349.

[8] *Ibid.*, p. 349.

candidate, five required, and a choice of five from seven remaining questions. These questions pertained to the duties of an auditor, and the principal points to which an auditor should direct his attention while auditing a corporation. The examination then went into specific questions in regard to auditing cash payments and receipts as well as other specific audit procedures.

The examinee had to make a grade of 75 out of 100 on each section of the examination to receive a passing grade. The examination seemed to cover the functions which the public accountant performed during the 1890's.

The present-day C.P.A. examination covers the same areas mentioned in the sections of this first examination. The current examinations cover a longer period of time (two and a half days) with longer sessions than did the first examination. The technical portion of the test has been set at the level of a senior accountant. Thus, the emphasis now is on accounting matters with much less time devoted to bookkeeping.

As a result of the first examination held under the auspices of the Regents of the State of New York under the authority granted in the first C.P.A. law, fifty-six certificates were issued. The records of the American Institute of Accountants show that all of these certificates were issued by waiver. In fact, it was two years later before a certificate was issued upon examination, evidently because the examination papers were unsatisfactory. Some accountants at this time began to refer to the C.P.A. as a degree. Webster says that "degree" was used because the certificates issued were from the State Board of Education of New York, and secondly, the initials were written after the name as are the letters of academic degrees.[9] As generally

understood, it was not a degree but a certificate of professional proficiency. Mr. Frank Broaker (Broaker & Chapman) was issued Certificate No. 1; Mr. Chapman, partner in the same firm, Certificate No. 2; Mr. Sanders Davies, Certificate No. 4; and certificates were also granted to Messrs. James T. Anyon and S. Lever, both with Barrow, Wade, Guthrie and Company of New York.[10]

Examinations—Thirty Boards

Twentieth century accountants were not satisfied with the method of examining candidates for the certificate. There was little uniformity in the requirements of the various state boards, of which there were thirty in 1913, and it was felt by some members of the profession that the C.P.A. examinations did not deserve to rank along with examinations in law and medicine.[11]

The following extract from an editorial in the July issue of *The Journal of Accountancy* reflects the opinion of the profession:

It has long been a reproach to the Accountancy profession in the United States that the examinations proposed for admission into the profession are exceedingly elementary and in no way comparable with the examinations for admission into the other learned professions. The examinations everywhere consist of questions in four subjects: theory of accounts, practical accounting, auditing, and commercial law. The questions in commercial law can readily be answered after a few days "cramming" from some elementary textbooks, such as White or Gano. The auditing questions require a mastery of Dicksee's auditing and little more. The theory of accounts examination usually asks of the candidate a number of elementary definitions, for example, "What is a consignment account," "Define and differentiate real and nominal accounts or controlling and specific accounts"; or such a question as this is

---

[9] Letter from Norman Webster, Chairman of the History Committee of the American Institute of Accountants, to James D. Edwards, dated October 16, 1951.

[10] "Accountancy in the States," *The Accountant*, January, 1897, p. 99.

[11] Edward S. Meade, "Established Preliminary Examinations in Law and Economics," *The Journal of Accountancy*, January, 1907, p. 193.

asked "State briefly the proper manner of conducting the following kinds of accounts: Bills receivable, Bills payable, Shipment accounts."

These are questions in bookkeeping, and their answer demands no very high order of intellectual attainment. The questions in practical accounting are of a different nature. They are almost without exception, problems of simple arithmetic which the student is required to express in "technical form." The problems themselves ordinarily present not the slightest difficulty, provided the meaning of the examiners can be clearly determined. Their expression is generally a matter of taste. A variety of methods are available if the examinee selects one which may or may not suit the examiner.

As a result of this condition, a singular situation is presented. With few exceptions, candidates for the C.P.A. degree passed the examinations in commercial law, auditing, and theory of accounts generally with high marks. Very few, however, pass the examination in practical accounting. The reason for this condition is not far to seek. It is because the first three subjects are generally too elementary to be set as a condition of examination into a profession, and because the examination in practical accounting demands of the candidate the working out of puzzles rather than the solution of problems. Even interpreted in the most kindly spirit, the practical accounting examination is an examination for accountants' assistants and not for accountants. We do not wish to be misunderstood as universally condemning all the examination questions set by the state boards of accounting examiners. As a general proposition, however, we believe that our characterization is correct.[12]

Examination Results

During the years covered in the period from 1896 to 1913, we find that a majority of the certificates issued to those in the public practice of accountancy were waiver certificates. Actually the first C.P.A. certificates issued by examination according to the American Institute's records were in 1898. The following table reflects the number of certificates issued by states by years, whether on examination, by waiver or reciprocity

---

[12] *Ibid.*, p. 194.

ORIGINAL C.P.A. CERTIFICATES ISSUED*

Year	Examination	Waiver	Reciprocity	Total	Cumulative Total
1896		56		56	56
1897		70		70	126
1898	6	1		7	133
1899	9	35		44	177
1900	16	25		41	218
1901	15	70		85	303
1902	37	24		61	364
1903	58	41		99	463
1904	67	31		98	561
1905	36	20		56	617
1906	58	20		78	695
1907	62	28	11	101	796
1908	56	229	4	289	1,085
1909	115	108	8	231	1,316
1910	201	117	8	326	1,642
1911	122	47	11	180	1,822
1912	108	9	2	119	2,021
1913	89	139	16	244	2,265

* Source: American Institute of Accountants.

331

Firms—Newly Established and Branch Offices

With accounting practice moving more and more to the area of business operations, Price Waterhouse & Co. opened the following offices during this period: St. Louis, in November, 1901; Pittsburgh, in May, 1902; and San Francisco, in November, 1904.[13]

Some significant auditing engagements which this firm handled are presented here. In December, 1897, the firm Jones, Caesar and Company (later Price Waterhouse & Co.) accepted an engagement from J. P. Morgan & Company to make examinations of the accounts of all constituent units which were to form the American Steel and Wire Company of New Jersey. This audit was one of the first examples of the employment of public accountants during the preliminary stage leading to the negotiation of merger agreements. The consolidation was finally completed by John W. Gates in 1899 after the recovery from the recession of 1897.[14]

---

[13] Letter from C. W. DeMond, Partner in Price Waterhouse and Company, dated May 6, 1952.
[14] C. W. DeMond, *Price Waterhouse and Co. in America* (New York: The Comet Press, Inc., 1951), p. 34.

On February 17, 1902, the stockholders of United States Steel Corporation elected Price Waterhouse & Co. as auditors of the company. The United States Steel Company was the first important industrial company to fix a policy of having the auditors elected by stockholders rather than selected by the officers or directors. The first audit certificate issued by the corporation for the year 1902 was accompanied by a certificate of chartered accountants signed by the firm.[15]

In 1906, Stuart and Young was dissolved because of disagreements between the partners, and the firm was reestablished under the name Arthur Young and Company, opening its office in 1911. It became a firm practicing on a national level two decades later.[16] The firm attributes its growth into a national organization to the many special jobs which were directed to it when the United States entered World War I. Many of these special jobs related to investigation of companies owned by alien enemies of the United States.[17]

Haskins and Sells opened offices in Chicago on December 1, 1900, in Cleveland and St. Louis in 1902, in Pittsburgh in 1903, in Baltimore in 1910, and in San Francisco in 1912.[18]

Lybrand, Ross Brothers and Montgomery was founded on January 1, 1898, in Philadelphia. In 1902, Mr. Montgomery was given permission by the partners to open a New York office. A Pittsburgh office was set up in 1908, and a Chicago office in 1909.[19]

In the last year of the period covered by this paper, Arthur Anderson, head of the accounting department at Northwestern University in Chicago, became a partner in Anderson, DeLong and Company.[20]

With over twenty-two hundred certified public accountants in the United States by 1913, it would seem safe to assume that there were several hundred public accounting firms. Most of these firms were probably operating in a single city. Some of the more active firms were operating throughout regions of the United States. It would be reasonable to say also that there were competent public accountants practicing in states which did not have public accounting laws.

EDUCATIONAL ACTIVITIES OF THE PROFESSION

Education and Accountancy

It was early recognized that the upbuilding of the accountancy profession must come through education, far more than through the enactment of C.P.A. laws alone. With this idea in mind, in the summer of 1902, the Council of the Pennsylvania Institute authorized the formation of classes for the study of the four subject areas in the field of Public Accounting.[21]

These classes were organized primarily for the purpose of affording technical instruction to assistants engaged in the offices of members of the Pennsylvania Institute. The restriction was not strictly enforced, because each member of the Institute had the privilege of nominating a student, not an employee, who wanted to become an accountant. The subjects taken up and the instructors lecturing thereon were:

Theory of Accounts, Robert H. Montgomery,

---

[15] *Ibid.*, p. 60.

[16] Arthur Young and Company, *Arthur Young and the Business He Founded* (New York: Privately Printed, 1948), p. 15.

[17] *Ibid.*, p. 30.

[18] Charles W. Haskins and E. W. Sells, *The First Fifty Years, 1895–1945*, p. 5.

[19] William M. Lybrand, Adam A. Ross, T. Edward Ross, and Robert H. Montgomery, *Fiftieth Anniversary* (Privately Printed, 1948), p. 3.

[20] Charles W. Jones, "A Chronological Outline of the Development of the Firm," *The Arthur Anderson Chronicle*, December, 1943, p. 8.

[21] George Wilkinson, "Organization of the Profession in Pennsylvania," *The Journal of Accountancy*, September, 1927, p. 162.

Practical Accounts, W. M. Lybrand,
Auditing, J. W. Fernly,
Commercial Law, H. G. Stockwell,

These classes actually did not begin until the evening school was started on October 20, 1902.[22] By the spring of 1904 negotiations had been successfully carried out with the faculty of the Wharton School of Accounts and Finance and with the trustees of the University of Pennsylvania, to turn the educational classes established by the Institute over to the University. Some members of the Institute guaranteed the expenses of conducting the classes for the first winter season, but the guarantors were never called on for any money.[23]

In 1900, the Council of New York University established in that institution a "School of Commerce, Accounts and Finance."[24] Members of the profession felt that steps should be taken to secure the cooperation of some educational institution which would establish a course in accountancy to train students to fill future needs for trained assistants.[25] The institutions were skeptical as to the feasibility or advisability of such a step, but at length, heeding the urgings of the committee, New York University instituted the course major in 1901. The Board of Regents appointed C. W. Haskins as the dean of the new school.[26]

The tentative course of study, as worked out by the New York State Society's committee, included (A) Accounting (Theory of Accounts, Practice in Accounting, and Auditing); (B) Finance (Money and Banking, Exchange, and Stocks and Bonds); (C) Commercial Economics (Statistics, Taxation, Public Debt, and Economic History); and (D) Commercial Law. These had been recommended at the meeting of the society in New York on December 10, 1900.

Dean Haskins's aim was "to bring together in the school such a corps of trained educators and practicing accountants as would meet the requirements of the State Board of Examiners under the Law of 1896."[27]

The need for technical literature in those early years was pressing. Very little had been written in this country, and schools were dependent upon the English works, which—while valuable—were not wholly adaptable to use in this country.[28]

In the year 1900, thirteen universities and colleges gave courses in accounting for which college credit was given. They were Dartmouth College, Drake University, Harvard University, Louisiana State University, University of Pennsylvania, Temple College, Agricultural College of Utah, University of Vermont, West Virginia University, and University of Wisconsin.[29]

Of the thirteen schools offering courses in accounting, only four (Agricultural College of Utah, Dartmouth, New York University, and Temple College) had a course listed under the title of auditing.

The first course in C.P.A. problems and questions, as such, appeared in New York University's catalog during the period 1905–1910. It may be said that the introduction of a course called C.P.A. problems closely followed the passage of the State

333

---

[22] *Ibid.*, p. 170.
[23] *Ibid.*, p. 171.
[24] Arthur H. Woolf, *A Short History of Accountants and Accountancy* (London: Gee and Company, 1912), p. 188.
[25] Edward L. Suffern, "Twenty-five Years of Accountancy," *The Journal of Accountancy*, September, 1922, p. 177.
[26] "Accountancy in New York State," *The Accountant*, September, 1901, p. 983.

[27] Emanuel Saxe, "The Role of the Society in Accounting Education," in *The New York Society of Certified Public Accountants Fiftieth Anniversary*, p. 23.
[28] Edward L. Suffern, "Twenty-five Years of Accountancy," *The Journal of Accountancy*, September, 1922, p. 178.
[29] C. E. Allen, "The Growth of Accounting Instruction since 1900," THE ACCOUNTING REVIEW, June, 1927, p. 150.

C.P.A. laws in almost every case.[30]

After 1905, it was decided to publish a journal which would make the accounting papers given at the conventions available to the public and the profession for educational purposes. The Accountancy Publishing Company was formed for this purpose.[31] The common stock went to the old Federation and to the Illinois Society. The preferred stock was sold to prominent public accountants in New York and Philadelphia by Robert H. Montgomery, Secretary of the Federation of Societies of Public Accountants.[32]

334

In November, 1905, the first issue of the *Journal of Accountancy* was published as the official organ of the profession. The co-editors were Professors Joseph French Johnson, of New York University, and Edward S. Meade, of the University of Pennsylvania. For a time these gentlemen accepted preferred stock in payment of their salaries.

The first *Journal* reviewed the status of the profession:

Within the last decade accounting has made rapid strides. Several states have formally recognized it as a profession by providing for examinations leading to the degree of Certified Public Accountant. Five of the largest American Universities have organized instruction in Accountancy. A large number of the most important railroads and industrial corporations subject their books to periodical audits by Public Accountants. Banks, trust companies and insurance companies have more recently adopted the same plan as a guarantee of security to depositors and policy holders, and the best method of protection against fraud. Manufacturers are calling upon public accountants to install cost systems, banks are requiring borrowers to secure accountants' certificates to the statement submitted as a basis for credit, and states, municipalities and public institutions in constantly increasing numbers are engaging the services of the profession to introduce systems and order into their affairs. These indications of the growing appreciation of Accountancy are the source of gratification and encouragement to its members; and there is no doubt that they will receive even more substantial recognition in the future.[33]

Once the amalgamation of the Federation and the Association became official, many if not all of the accountant-stockholders donated their preferred stock to the American Association of Public Accountants. At the annual meetings of this organization in 1908 and 1909, additional capital was obtained because the editor reported that the *Journal* would not be on a self-supporting basis for three years. Then in January, 1912, A. P. Richardson became editor and in the same year the Association assumed direct control of the *Journal* with the cooperation of the Ronald Press Publishing Company.[34]

PROFESSIONAL ORGANIZATIONS

American Association of Public Accountants

On April, 18, 1896, some ten years after the Association was formed and at the time the first public accounting law was enacted and approved by Governor Levi P. Morton, the Association, according to the American Institute of Accountants, had only forty-five active members, distributed geographically as follows: New York, 37; Massachusetts, 3; California, 2; and Georgia, Illinois, and New Jersey, 1 each.[35]

National Society of Certified Public Accountants

The legal recognition of the accounting profession in New York led to the incor-

---

[30] *Ibid.*, p. 155.

[31] Sanders W. Davies, "Genesis, Growth and Aims of the Institute," *The Journal of Accountancy*, August, 1926, p. 107.

[32] Robert H. Montgomery, *Fifty Years of Accountancy*, New York: Ronald Press Company, 1939, p. 69.

[33] Editorial, "Present Status of the Profession," *The Journal of Accountancy*, November, 1905, p. 1.

[34] W. Sanders Davies, "Genesis, Growth and Aims of the Institute," *The Journal of Accountancy*, August, 1926, p. 107.

[35] *Fiftieth Anniversary Celebration* (New York: The American Institute of Accountants, 1937), p. 7.

poration of a National Society of Certified Public Accountants in the United States in 1897. Anyone holding a certificate from the University of the State of New York was eligible for membership. The objects of this society were to unify in one body all Certified Public Accountants practicing in the United States, to exchange professional knowledge by means of lectures and to establish a professional library, and to secure legal mutual recognition of the letters C.P.A., by and between all of the United States of America. Mr. C. W. Smith was the first president of the National Society of Certified Public Accountants. Sixty-seven accountants were admitted to membership.[36]

The organization was short-lived because in 1899 the National Society and the American Association merged into one organization. The merger was a great advantage to the membership of both groups as well as the profession as a whole.[37]

Founding of the Federation

In July, 1902, at a meeting of the Illinois Association of Public Accountants, Mr. George Wilkinson read a paper in which he set forth the great need of establishing a definite relationship among the local state societies, which at that time showed little unity of purpose in affairs of a national character. He suggested a plan for the coordination of all existing organizations by the formation of societies of public accountants.[38] In much the same line of thinking—searching for a means of maintaining the standards set by the new laws—the practitioners in several states formed societies; even in some states where laws had not yet been passed, practicing accountants also formed societies. It was also pointed out by Mr. Wilkinson that accountants practicing in the West did not feel that the old, established American Association of Public Accountants, domiciled as it was in New York and governed by a New York board, was fulfilling its avowed purpose as a national institute.

The first convention of "The Federation of Societies of Public Accountants in the United States" was held at the New Willard Hotel in Washington, D. C., on October 28, 1902. At this meeting a constitution and bylaws were accepted, and permanent officers were elected. The officers were Charles Waldo Haskins, president; George Wilkinson, Secretary; and Robert H. Montgomery, Treasurer.[39]

The objects of the Federation were defined in its Constitution. They were as follows:

(a) To bring into communication with one another the several Associations and Societies of Public Accountants, organized or to be organized under the laws of the several States of the United States of America; (b) to encourage the formation of State Associations of Public Accountants in States where they do not exist; (c) to encourage State Certified Public Accountant legislation on uniform lines; (d) to secure Federal recognition of the profession of the Public Accountant; (e) to facilitate and assist the training of young members of the profession, and to establish a uniform standard of efficiency in federal societies; (f) to disseminate throughout the United States a general knowledge of the objects of the Federation and of the utility of the Public Accountants in the industrial and financial development of the country; and (g) to further the interests of the profession of the Public Accountant generally.[40]

Though the Federation existed only from 1902 to 1905, it was clear that the in-

335

[36] "Accountancy in the States," *The Accountant*, September, 1897, p. 858.
[37] "Accountancy in the States," *The Accountant*, August, 1899, p. 889.
[38] James B. Lovette, *History of Accounting in the United States* (unpublished typescript, American Institute of Accountants Library), p. 14.

[39] Edward L. Suffern, "Twenty-five Years of Accountancy," *The Journal of Accountancy*, September, 1922, p. 179.
[40] Richard Brown, *A History of Accounting and Accountants* (Edinburgh and London: T. C. & E. C. Jack, 1905), p. 277.

terests of the profession demanded and the members of the profession would support, a national organization of accountants.[41]

First International Congress

The Federation arranged the first International Congress of Professional Accountants in connection with the Louisiana Purchase Exposition, or World's Fair, held at St. Louis, Missouri, in September, 1904.[42]

The President of the Illinois Society of Public Accountants and one of the organizers of the Federation, George Wilkinson, was elected Secretary of the Congress. He was the organizer and director of all the affairs of the Congress.

Joseph E. Sterrett, a prominent public accountant of Philadelphia, was permanent chairman of this First Congress. In his introductory address, Chairman Sterrett referred to the negotiations which were then under way to effect a Union of the two existing "national" accounting organizations, including the state societies as well.

Ninety-one members attended this first International Congress in 1904.[43]

Communication on Merger

In the course of time it became apparent that if the profession desired to achieve its proper place in the business community, it could not rely on accomplishing this means by state legislation alone because there were only seven C.P.A. laws by 1904, almost nine years after the New York law. Accountancy was not a local profession, even then, but was practiced nationwide, and as time went on the need for professional standards became more and more apparent. Both the American

Association of Public Accountants and the New York State Society of Certified Public Accountants addressed letters to the Federation at the St. Louis Congress.[44]

At a meeting of the executive board of the Federation held during the Congress, the Secretary presented a communication from the Secretary of the American Association of Public Accountants and one from the Secretary of the New York State Society expressing the opinion that there should be one national organization in which all public accountants should be represented by delegates. Both secretaries recommended the formation of a joint committee to consider ways and means of bringing this about.

A joint committee of nine was consequently appointed, composed of the following: W. Sanders Davies, Chairman; Duncan MacInnes, Franklin Allen, representing the American Association of Public Accountants; A. Lowes Dickinson, George Wilkinson, and Robert H. Montgomery, representing the Federation of Public Accountants. This joint committee agreed upon a plan of consolidation under which the American Association of Public Accountants would be the continuing organization after certain necessary amendments were made of its constitution and bylaws.

One National Organization after the Merger

In 1905, as a result of efforts of the joint committee of the two organizations, the goal of one national organization was reached. The constitution of the American Association of Public Accountants after the merger of the two organizations provided for membership by virtue of membership in a State Society of Public Accountants and also for individual membership; the latter membership provided for

---

[41] George Wilkinson, "Organization of the Profession in Pennsylvania," *The Journal of Accountancy*, September, 1927, p. 173.

[42] James B. Lovette, *History of Accounting in the United States*, p. 14.

[43] Norman E. Webster, "Congress of Accountants," *The Journal of Accountancy*, February, 1921, p. 104.

[44] Carl H. Nau, "The American Institute of Accountants," *The Journal of Accountancy*, February, 1921, p. 104.

336

those public accountants practicing in states which did not have State societies. The new Society, even with the old association's name, was not organized to supplant the various state societies of Certified Public Accountants, nor was it formed to supplant the C.P.A. laws of the various states. It had its genesis, rather, in the effort to supplement both state legislation and state societies, and was a partial remedy at least for the recognized defects which had developed in former programs attempting to establish professional standards and professional solidarity by enacting statutes and the issuance of certificates.[45] The amalgamation of the societies was an attempt to nationalize the profession, with a centralized control from within itself, in place of the former scattering control which lacked uniformity both in aims and ideals and was influenced by outside conditions as well as by professional considerations.[46]

The constitution of the new society, the first national organization, was adopted; the purposes of the society, as stated therein, follow:

1. The bringing together in friendly contact of the different state societies and members of the profession.
2. The encouragement and unification of C.P.A. legislation. In this organization the principle was adopted that the national organization should not interfere with the local interests of the different states, but at the same time should cooperate with the constituent societies in all practicable ways.[47]

The purpose of the merger was further set forth in the words of President John R. Loomis of the American Association of Public Accountants:

---

[45] Carl H. Nau, "The American Institute of Accountants," *The Journal of Accountancy*, February, 1921, p. 105.
[46] *Ibid.*, p. 105.
[47] J. Edward Masters, "The Accounting Profession in the United States," *The Journal of Accountancy*, November, 1915, p. 351.

This occasion celebrates the culmination of what is perhaps the most important movement ever inaugurated in the interest of the profession of public accountancy in this country—the fusion of the several societies constituting the Federation of Societies of Public Accountants with the American Association of Public Accountants. The American Association of Public Accountants stands at this time as the grand national body, representing practically all public accountants throughout the United States. Its objects are the elevation of the profession and the spreading of a knowledge and recognition of the utility and necessity for the public accountant in the industrial and financial development of our country. It is an organization that every society can stand by and that every member can work for. The hopes and plans of the past are now measurably realized, and upon a basis of absolute cause for rejoicing—the promise of the future is most encouraging.[48]

During the following years the program of the Association reflected a great interest in education for accounting. The educational committee made an effort to impress upon the members of the Association the importance of cooperation with the universities and colleges. It also suggested that the members of the Association contribute their services, whenever the opportunity arose, as instructors and lecturers.

In these years the American Association of Public Accountants continued to foster rapid development of the profession by acting as spokesmen for the profession when the need arose, and it continued its efforts to obtain legal recognition in all the states which had not yet enacted C.P.A. laws.

SUMMARY

The late 1880's represented a period of undoubted development and advancement in accountancy both in better knowledge of the profession and its requirements, and

337

---

[48] "History of the American Institute," in *Fiftieth Anniversary Celebration* (New York: The American Institute of Accountants 1937), p. 9.

in the fact that financial men generally began to understand the nature of its work and service.

Another trend that tended to further the development of the profession was the incorporation of industrial concerns under the laws of the various states. The securities of these corporations were issued and offered to the investing public. In many of these corporations, public accounting firms were employed to make examinations and reports on the financial condition and earnings of these corporations before their securities were offered for public subscription. The first industrial

firm so incorporated whose securities were offered to the public with an accountant's certificate attached to the prospectus was the firm of John B. Stetson and Company of Philadelphia.[49]

By 1909, the accountancy profession had gained such favor among businessmen that corporations of the better class were of their own volition adopting the practice which had become obligatory in England under the Companies Act of 1900, of retaining public accountants to make periodic audits.

[49] "Accountants as Directors," *The Journal of Accountancy*, March, 1940, p. 165.

Chapter One

Heritage of the American

Accounting Profession

FROM THE AREA of London known as the City, and from Edinburgh and Glasgow, came the chartered accountants who established professional accounting in the United States in the 1890's. They were sent by British owners of American companies, ranging from manufacturing enterprises on the East Coast to orange groves in California.

British Accounting Societies

It appears that George Watson, who was born in Edinburgh in 1645, was the first professional accountant in the United Kingdom.[1] The initial step in the formation of a professional body of accountants was taken in Edinburgh, in January, 1853, when a circular was sent to a number of local practitioners asking them to consider this project. From this meeting emerged the Society of Accountants in Edinburgh, established in 1854, when it applied for a royal charter. This document was signed by Lord Palmerston at Queen Victoria's command on October 23, 1854, thus creating the first accounting society in the United Kingdom and, indeed, in the world.[2] Later, accounting societies were formed in Glasgow and Aberdeen.

Public accounting did not develop in England at the same time or in the same manner as in Scotland. The Scottish legal structure affecting the

---

[1]David Murray, *Chapters in the History of Bookkeeping and Accountancy* (Edinburgh: Jackson, Wylie & Co., 1950), p. 52. In 1695 Watson was appointed the first accountant of the newly founded Bank of Scotland.

[2]The Charter recited, in the Latin of the court, that the duties of an accountant in Scotland "required great experience in business, very considerable knowledge of the law and other qualifications which can only be obtained by a liberal education."

1

estates of bankrupts and other unincorporated persons, and the practice of the courts of justice were on an entirely different basis from those in England. The real impetus to the English accounting profession was provided by the Companies Act of 1862 and the Bankruptcy Act of 1869. By offering liberal provisions for the formation of joint stock trading companies, the first-named measure created a demand for English public accountants to serve as auditors and liquidators. The Bankruptcy Act, by abolishing the Official Receiver, paved the way for the appointment of receivers by creditors, who generally chose professional accountants for such posts.

In January, 1870, the Incorporated Society of Liverpool Accountants was organized—the first professional body in England. This society was followed by the formation of five associations in other parts of England.[3] By 1880, these bodies had a total membership of 638. On March 4, 1880, a draft charter was approved by Her Majesty, and the formal grant under which all five societies became merged in The Institute of Chartered Accountants in England and Wales occurred May 11, 1880.[4] Other English societies were formed in succeeding years, the largest being the Society of Incorporated Accountants and Auditors, set up in 1885. The Institute of Chartered Accountants in Ireland followed three years later.

All of the accounting societies in the United Kingdom examined candidates after they had completed an apprenticeship under articles in a chartered accountant's office. What articled clerks learned was acquired from experience and by personal direction by individual practitioners to whom the clerks were apprenticed. The periodical, *The Accountant,* was published from October, 1874, and now has a worldwide circulation. In 1892, an English chartered accountant, Lawrence R. Dicksee (1864-1932) wrote his classic volume, *Auditing: A Practice Manual for Auditors,* and summarized in it the auditing principles and procedures then followed in the United Kingdom.[5] This book is herein referred to as it was brought out in an American edition in the early 1900's; it was used as the basis of American practice for many years.

---

[3]The Institute of Accountants in London, established November 29, 1870; the Manchester Institute of Accountants, February 6, 1871; the Society of Accountants in England, January 11, 1873; and the Sheffield Institute of Accountants, March 14, 1877.

[4]The preamble to the royal charter stated that "the profession of public accountants in England and Wales is a numerous one and their functions are of great and increasing importance in respect of their employment in the capacities of Liquidators acting in the winding-up of companies and of Receivers under decrees and of Trustees in bankruptcies or arrangements with creditors and in various positions of trust under Courts of Justice and also in the auditing of accounts of public companies and of partnerships or otherwise."

[5]Dicksee served as lecturer and later professor of accountancy at the London School of Economics from 1904 to 1926. He wrote books on auctioneers' accounts; depreciation, reserves and reserve funds; garage accounts; gas accounts; hotel accounts; mine accounts; and solicitors' accounts.

The English Auditor's Duties

The question of the professional accountant's duties first came before the English courts in *Leeds Estate Building and Investment Co.* v. *Shepherd* (36 Ch. 787), in which Mr. Justice Sterling enlarged an auditor's responsibilities beyond the mathematical accuracy of the balance sheet. In essence, the justice stated that the auditor should not confine himself merely to ascertaining that this statement was mathematically accurate but that he should, in addition, discover whether it was substantially accurate. The decision in the *Leeds* Case was far-reaching, and portions of it were preserved in later Companies Acts.[6]

341

Pioneer British Accounting Firms

William Welch Deloitte (1819-98) was one of the early public accountants to establish his practice in the City of London; his office operated from 1845, and his contribution to English railway accounting was notable.[7] His firm, which became Deloitte, Plender, Griffiths & Co., grew into an international organization.

Accounting historians have traced the development of many British accounting firms, formed in various parts of Scotland, England, Ireland and Wales. Only one firm, it is believed—Cooper Brothers & Co.—maintained its name unaltered from 1857.[8] It is now connected with Lybrand, Ross Bros. & Montgomery, CPAs, in an international accounting partnership.

Although most of the engagements of the early British accounting firms were concerned with bankruptcy, some of their partners traveled to Russia, to the European continent and to South Africa and South America on company and governmental appointments. As one example, John G. Griffiths was retained by the Khedive Ismail of Egypt during the inquiry of Stephen Cave into the financial condition of that country.[9] The governmental appointments of British chartered accountants, even today, fill the pages of *The Accountant*, and it is a tradition for them to receive knighthoods and other recognition from the Crown for their services.

---

[6] Other cases of this same period affecting auditors included *Le· Lievre and Dennes* v. *Gould*, 1893 (1 Q.B. 491); *In re London and General Bank* (No. 2), 1895 (2 Ch. 673); and *In re Kingson Cotton Mill Co.* (No. 2), 1896 (2 Ch. 239).

[7] James Kilpatrick, *Deloitte, Plender, Griffiths & Co.: Some Notes on the Early Days of the Firm* (London: Wyman & Sons, 1942).

[8] *A History of Cooper Brothers & Co.: 1845-1945* (London, privately printed, 1954).

[9] *Deloitte & Co.: 1845-1956* (Oxford, privately printed, 1958), pp. 58–59. Also see speech of Edwin Waterhouse, president of The Institute of Chartered Accountants in England and Wales, reprinted in *The Accountant*, May 13, 1893, pp. 440–45.

In the 1890's, one British chartered accountant, George A. Touche, visited the United States on numerous occasions in connection with actual or prospective British investors in American industrial securities. He also established one of the oldest accounting firms in the United States and Canada (now Touche, Ross, Bailey & Smart), and affiliated with another London accounting firm in a South American partnership.

Accounting historians would do well to read Galsworthy's *Forsyte Saga* because it describes the years of opulence in Britain and the power in the City of London. In this period—the 1880's and 1890's—the limited liability company dominated the business scene, and public accountancy achieved the status of a profession. The services of chartered accountants, then as now, were used in the formation of limited companies, and in their administration, reorganization, and liquidation. In this period, too, the professional accountant won the confidence of the government, shareholder, banker and man in the street. The early years of British public accounting afforded practitioners a matchless opportunity to advance principles and procedures from rudimentary levels and to conceive an ethical code which became the standard of public accountants everywhere. Although they participated in many capital issues, accountants made it a practice to inquire into the type of directors with whom they were to be connected. They withheld their reports on some occasions, or qualified them, because of the financial data supplied to them. Thus, they established a reputation for high ethical standards which stimulated their growth in numbers and prestige in the United Kingdom, and in recognition overseas.

The British and American Financial Patterns

Financial resources of British industrialists were sufficient to meet the demands for capital to finance new enterprises. However, in the United States the function of securing funds for industrial expansion accrued to investment bankers. The practice followed by British banking institutions was to avoid the establishment of a purely American firm. Instead, they sent to the States representatives steeped in the tradition of British banking, who were required to report at regular intervals on their work. The organization of J. & W. Seligman & Co. in New York in 1862, and of Dabney, Moore & Co., predecessor of J. P. Morgan & Co., two years later, marked the inception of American banking houses which maintained strong European connections.[10]

Although J. P. Morgan continued to deal extensively in foreign exchange and the sale of American securities in foreign markets, from 1875 forward his attention was directed increasingly to domestic invest-

---

[10]The Seligman firm emerged from a mercantile business, originally scattered throughout the U.S. and in 1857 combined in one New York house engaged in the importation of clothing. In 1862, this firm was converted to a private bank. A branch was opened in Frankfurt in that year, and another two years later in London.

ment finance. During and after this period he applied his own special technique of banking control to industry, a development accelerated by industry's growing demand for capital and the separation of ownership from management. This concentration of industrial control was closely paralleled by a centralization of financial control—an interrelation which first appeared in the railroad field.

The Londoner, H. Osborne O'Hagan, was one of the first individuals to embark on an active career of company promotion and consolidation.[11] He introduced the present practice of underwriting new issues. Although he never visited the United States, O'Hagan's underwriting activities from 1882 to 1924, as head of The City of London Contract Corporation Ltd., were equally numerous in Britain and America. A large amount of accounting work was involved in company promotion. O'Hagan enlisted the services of a number of English accounting firms, both to prepare preliminary figures which he used in his negotiations with prospective vendors, and to audit the accounts of companies in the process of amalgamation.[12]

American Brewery Mergers

O'Hagan was especially active in promoting the merger of breweries in this country. In all of these companies he introduced English brewers as directors. Companies were capitalized to yield 12–15 percent on their ordinary shares over and above debenture interest and preference dividends.[13]

As an important aspect of the merger of these American breweries, an audit was made by public accountants; in many cases these were agents of London firms of chartered accountants. The work required the determination of the financial position and earnings of each enterprise for a number of years, the calculation of net floating assets under certain purchase contracts and of amounts due to vendors, and the preparation of accounting records of all the merged companies. In the case of one Chicago brewery merger the fees for this range of accounting activities, carried out early in the 1890's, totaled $4,000.

Public accountants, upon completion of this work, frequently sug-

---

[11]H. Osborne O'Hagan, *Leaves from My Life* (London: John Lane The Bodley Head Ltd., 1929), 2 vols. Also see obituary notice, *The Economist*, (May 8, 1929), p. 1115.

[12]In the case of the Britannia Works, which was contemplating a merger with the Eastman Kodak Co., O'Hagan instructed Turquand Youngs & Co., chartered accountants, to examine the books for a period of five years and to prepare material to be included in the prospectus. This merger was never realized, since the British shareholders refused to sustain their chairman's decision to join forces with the American company.

[13]Robert I. Swaine, *The Cravath Firm and Its Predecessors, 1819–1947* (New York: Privately printed at Ad Press, Ltd., 1946), Vol. I, pp. 424–72, gives a description of the first project, which was the purchase of three breweries in Rochester, New York, and other projects.

gested to the managements of the companies that monthly cost sheets should be prepared to provide accurate statistics concerning the operations of each plant. These cost sheets were the first effort on the part of public accountants to combine work sheet detail with cost data. They were prepared from trial balances, statements showing movements in inventories, and reports furnished by each plant to the head office. They provided financial statement data and also cost details for beer and bottling. Important accounting matters, such as depreciation of fixed assets, valuation of inventories, and differentiation of capital and revenue charges, were stated on the monthly cost sheets, subject to adjustment at the time of the annual examination. Copies of the sheets were sent to local brewery managements and to the London brewers who were serving as American company directors.[14]

344

Some accounting historians have written about the arrival of representatives of British accounting firms to audit the accounts of British-owned American enterprises.[15] One of the able writers of the period was James T. Anyon, CPA. His recollections indicate that practitioners believed the brewery audits would stimulate the expansion of the American profession and lead to greater investment of British capital in other areas of the American economy. This prophecy actually was realized in the years before the First World War.

American public accountants, who were earning relatively small incomes and enjoying little recognition as professional men at the time of the brewery audits, received encouragement from the knowledge that British investors insisted upon a thorough examination of companies in which their money was to be placed.[16] Moreover, American public accountants gained a new insight into the duties and responsibilities of auditors as well as the principles and techniques of British business operation. Chartered accountants who came to the States before 1900 drew on a background of professional training and affiliations not enjoyed in the United States. They supported a high ethical code in the conduct of their duties, drew on experience of auditing a variety of companies, and actually advanced the American profession in business and governmental circles.

---

[14]The report rendered to one brewery in 1894 indicated that the theory of depreciation was not thoroughly understood by company bookkeepers. It read in part: "We would suggest that whenever a horse dies or is transferred the stableman should at once report the same to the bookkeeper, as in some instances we have found that the stock of horses cannot be agreed at the end of the year."

[15]Firms employed by English promoters included Broads, Patterson & Co.; Deloitte, Plender, Griffiths & Co.; Hart Bros., Tibbets & Co.; Monkhouse, Goddhard & Co.; and Price Waterhouse & Co.

[16]The following auditor's report, prepared in London in 1895, was contained in the annual directors' presentation: "We have examined the above Accounts with the Books and Vouchers of the Company, and find the same to be correct. We approve and certify that the above Balance Sheet correctly sets forth the position of the Company."

The annual balance sheets of the American breweries were frequently prepared and signed in London. They followed the British form, still in evidence today, stating the liability and capital accounts on the debit side and the assets on the credit side. These statements were presented in both pounds and dollars. Unfortunately, the British investments in some American breweries did not prove successful because of the enactment of "dry laws" in some states and the 1893 panic.[17] In 1894, one London brewing syndicate experienced difficulty in meeting dividends on its shares and proposed to reduce depreciation charges to the extent necessary to provide a profit sufficiently large to cover dividends. The London accounting firm which had originally conceived the depreciation policy for the American companies resisted any modification of the annual depreciation charge and some American financial papers supported its stand.

345

The intimate connection between banks and breweries, always evident in the United Kingdom, was never found in America. In Britain, for instance, it was customary for brewers in London and the provinces to receive their customer's money on deposit at interest, and this banking facility was extended to the friends and connections of their customers. This formed the nucleus upon which many of the provincial banks started and, in London, Barclays and other banks were in close touch with the brewing interests.

Other Early American Auditing Engagements

By far the greatest number of auditing engagements in the 1890's was for one-year examinations. Much of the work was of a routine nature for which billings were at the rate of $6 to $10 a day. The total fees for most American accounting partnerships were disappointing. British fees for professional services concurrently were much larger than those customarily received by American public accountants, a situation resulting from the fact that professional accounting in the United States did not then have the prestige attached to the British profession.

The periodic examination of bank records by public accountants in this country was of infrequent occurrence, in contrast to the invariable annual audits of British banking institutions. When an auditor was engaged for this type of work here, his presence had to be shrouded in the deepest secrecy until his report was published so depositors would not become suspicious and start a disastrous run on the bank.

Numerous engagements were received by public accountants from American land, mortgage and investment companies which were owned

---

[17]However, English syndicates continued to hold their original investments in the brewing mergers consummated in the U.S. in 1889–91. In February, 1919, in fact, English investments in American breweries amounted to $54 million, represented by debentures and preferred and common stock.

or financed by British interests. As a result of the 1893 panic, however, defaults on mortgages were general, and American public accountants were appointed agents of English receivers—discharging the duties of collecting rents, paying taxes, and selling properties. Monthly insurance work was carried out by auditors on instructions from London home offices. Although many of these audits were of a routine nature, they proved of value in training staff members in cash examinations. To provide an invariable approach to each annual audit of the American branches of London insurance companies, detailed audit programs were prepared which embraced the steps to be covered and required the signature of each assistant assigned to the engagement.

346 The financial returns accruing to British public accountants from their American branch offices or agents were somewhat disappointing at this period. This was a deciding factor in the closing of some British offices in the States around 1900. The chartered accountants who remained continued to serve British clients in the main, and their transition to American organizations was achieved only gradually by the conversion of agency arrangements to American partnerships, sometimes perpetuating the names of the British agents in America and sometimes continuing the British style. These developments occurred simultaneously with the establishment of firms composed of individuals whose professional experience had been obtained in the United States. These two types of partnerships—one inspired by British tradition, the other stimulated by business expansion in America—formed the pattern of American professional accounting.

Gradual Recognition of the American Public Accountant

In his recollections of accountancy in America from 1883-93, James T. Anyon, CPA (1851-1929) writes that American practitioners "seemed unable to create in the minds of businessmen the faith and confidence in their integrity and honesty which is the essence of the profession." Anyon was trained in Britain and he felt that "certain accountants [in the States] stretched a point in favor of their clients [mainly in matters relating to the preparation of statements for presentation to banks or for the sale of a business] to show a financial condition more favorable than was actually the case; and in many instances clients expected them to do this."[18]

Anyon emphasized that questions relating to the principles of sinking funds, reserves, earned surplus, capital surplus, fixed and current assets,

---

[18]James T. Anyon, *Recollections of the Early Days of American Accountancy; 1883-1893* (New York: Privately printed, 1925).

capital and income charges, invested capital, working capital, depletion and amortization were not always understood by American practitioners and, in fact, were not considered part of an accountant's practice. He writes, however, that gradually "the quality of the practitioner improved, the extent and diversity of his knowledge became greater, and he gave to his profession a status and atmosphere that carried with it knowledge, truth, precision, and trustworthiness to an extent it had never before known."

The business cards of American public accountants in the 1880's and 1890's indicated that these men were willing to undertake a wide range of duties for which they would charge a modest fee. A typical card of this period read:

Having had a wide and varied experience in accounts I would respectfully inform you that I am prepared to make out all statements correctly and administrators' or executors' accounts, examine corporation, copartnership or individual books, and generally attend to any and every kind of bookkeeping. Books posted monthly and a trial balance taken at a trifling cost. Plans furnished for books for special purposes. Prompt attention and very modest charges.

Acceptance of the theory that an annual audit of accounts was a necessary adjunct of scientific company management was achieved largely by the efforts of pioneer accountants who traveled throughout the United States, examining the accounts of American companies formed or supported by British capital, and acquainting all sections of this country with the value of their services. By the end of the last century, a deeper appreciation of the functions of the public accountant was apparent in the United States. The change was coupled with an increase in the incorporation of American companies and in the offering of their securities for sale to the public. Bankers began to employ auditors to examine and report on the accounts of these new companies, and it became customary for the latter to prepare, at the end of their examination, a short report which was published in the banker's prospectus.[19]

Always insistent upon absolute accuracy in accounting documents, British public accountants feared that the absence of detailed checking as an essential part of American auditing practice would necessitate a decided modification of their firms' statements and procedures to meet American business conditions. They realized that the synthetic audit generally employed in the United Kingdom, beginning with original data and working forward to summarized results, emphasized minute checking of accounts, with infinite effort devoted by the British auditors

---

[19]John B. Stetson & Co. of Philadelphia was the first company to utilize the services of accountants in this manner in 1891, receiving a report prepared in manuscript form with tissue press copies made from it.

to ascertaining that each statement which he examined complied exactly with the law.[20]

This detailed checking never had been adopted in the United States as part of the customary auditing procedure. By insisting upon professional engagements being carried out by members of their own staffs, rather than by auditors employed in the United States, British accounting partnerships were convinced that British auditing standards would be followed in a country—the United States—where public accounting was in an initial phase of development. As an additional assurance of strict adherence to the tenets of their firms, some chartered accountants instructed their American representatives to send all working papers and draft reports covering American companies to London for approval and signature. In cases of special complexity, British chartered accountants visited their American branch offices.

Scientific accounting in companies, as it is defined in modern times, was not generally known in the period 1880-1900. Practitioners devoted many hours to locating errors and balancing accounts. At least one writer, early in the 1890's, urged the adoption of the British system of a compulsory, periodical audit of company accounts by outside auditors who were not of the stereotype attributed to bank examiners.[21] It was emphasized, on more than one occasion, that bank examiners were notoriously incompetent, appointed through political influence rather than for their merits, and sometimes, for a large fee, persuaded to write unduly favorable reports.

Beginning in the 1880's, occasional references were made to public accountants who had audited the records of companies issuing securities; usually prospectuses contained the reports of these companies. The custom of including the accountant's report in the prospectus gradually became general practice in the United States, but readers found that the practitioners mentioned most frequently were either British firms or partnerships of British origin which had established branches or affiliated partnerships in New York, Chicago, or other cities. Later, several American accounting firms were established on a sound basis, and they shared in this new phase of work, so closely correlated in its expansion with the growth of industry.

Railroads and Their Auditors

The steady rise in the number of public accountants was accompanied by increased recognition of the auditors' duties. These changes were mo-

[20]Stanley W. Rowland, *A Reconsideration of Auditing Methods* (London: Gee & Co. (Publishers) Ltd., 1934), pp. 5-6: "It is not an unfair criticism to say that the general conception [the synthetic process] has resulted in emphasis being laid on arithmetical phenomena. The conception has colored legislation which governs us and it has determined the public estimate of our functions."

[21]J. Lindsay Reid, "A Needed Profession," *North American Review* (October, 1894), pp. 510-12.

tivated by and closely correlated with shifts in the nation's business and commerce. They were especially stimulated by the railroad reorganizations subsequent to 1893, which placed heavy responsibilities on the shoulders of professional auditors.

During the period in which receivers were outlining solutions to problems of actual management of the bankrupt roads, numerous committees were working to discover bases on which to establish their plans of reorganization.[22] Many of the important accounting duties accruing to these committees were transferred by them to professional accountants. The professional men—bankers, attorneys and accountants—had few historical precedents to guide them in their vital tasks. The development of the theory and practice of railroad reorganization is considered by many economists to be an outstanding example of American ingenuity.[23]   349

The techniques evolved by the financiers and other individuals most closely concerned with the return to solvency of American railroads were noteworthy both for the originality of concept and for the amount of securities involved. In their own design of auditing procedures to cover inadequate or poorly maintained records, accountants provided the basic data upon which reconstruction plans were executed. They ascertained whether or not the published reports of the roads in the years preceding the failures were a fair presentation, concerning themselves not only with the technical accuracy of the books but also ascertaining whether or not the depreciation accounts were adequate. In addition, auditors decided whether the rolling stock claimed by the companies to be in usable condition actually was in use or in good order. They also checked all the rentals of leased lines, and insurance policies, to see if the old managers had protected the railroads' contractual rights.

In railroad reorganizations, additional facts were supplied by special traffic accountants who worked independently or in collaboration with public accountants. The special task of the former involved the determination of the relative and separate earning capacity of various parts of the railroad system. This was a highly important task, because only by the classification of subsidiary lines and leased lines according to their past earning capacities could the reorganization committees determine what sections of the system should be retained and what parts relinquished.

In all railroad bankruptcy cases, reorganization committees arrived at their decisions with the assistance of elaborate reports furnished them by accountants, engineers, and traffic experts. Through a perusal of the important data contained in these documents, the committees were able to calculate the amount of money which had to be expended in the immediate future to increase the earning capacity of the insolvent lines. With

[22]Edward S. Meade, "The Reorganization in Railroads," *Annals of the American Academy of Political and Social Science* (March, 1901), pp. 25–63.
[23]Arthur S. Dewing, "The Theory of Railroad Reorganization," *American Economic Review* (December, 1918), pp. 774–95.

the expert advice of their legal counsel, committee members finally conceived a reorganization scheme which was predicated upon a statement of the financial aspects of reconstruction. After this plan received wide distribution, a formal reorganization agreement was signed which incorporated the essential changes in funded debt and in capitalization of the new structure. In it the new name of the venture was stressed, with the title "railroad" usually being changed to "railway" and "company" to "corporation."

Poor's Manual for 1884 stated that almost $4 billion—practically all the capital stock of American railways—represented water.[24] Within the fifteen-year period from 1888, 423 American roads with a total mileage of 43,770, representing more than $2.5 billion of capital, went into bankruptcy. In later years, historians had little difficulty in finding the causes for the widespread railroad failures. The panic of 1893 revealed the uncertain financial condition of many of the largest systems; and the impartial examination of their affairs, following concerted efforts for reconstruction, indicated that the insolvent lines were greatly overcapitalized. In addition, this examination disclosed that the bonds of these lines were inadequately secured; that some of their traffic agreements and leases were more of a burden than a help; and that in some instances, they had been badly, even fraudulently, operated.

One line, the Norfolk & Western, failed primarily because of overexpansion. A friendly federal court was petitioned to appoint receivers and a bondholders' committee was set up in London and Amsterdam; the latter was responsible for the employment of Price Waterhouse & Co. to make a detailed examination of the road's accounts.[25] Within fifteen months of the receivership, the final plan for reorganization had been published, a comprehensive document which provided an effective method for restoring the line to solvency.[26] The Norfolk road followed the English procedure under which company auditors were elected by company shareholders. Annual reports indicated that in successive years from 1897 until 1921, Price Waterhouse & Co. was elected professional accountant of the company.[27]

The railroad audits included not only the general books of a system

---

[24]Carl Hovey, *The Life Story of J. Pierpont Morgan* (London: William Heineman, 1912), p. 126.

[25]Six months after the receivership, the secretary of the bondholders' protective committee announced that "at the instance of the committee a thorough investigation and exhaustive report of the accounts of the company for the last three years has been made by the accountants, Messrs. Price Waterhouse & Co., the result of which save for some modifications of minor importance, is considered by the committee as confirming the accuracy of the company's own reports and accounts." See *Railway Age and Northwestern Railroader* (August 16, 1895), p. 406.

[26]*Railway World* (April 4, 1896), p. 328.

[27]A complete file of Norfolk & Western Railroad annual reports is available in the Hopkins Library at Stanford University.

but also the accounts of various companies and the cash accounts of several treasurers. They frequently raised questions of importance concerning the maintenance of proper accounts and the adoption of sound principles. One dilemma was the amortization of bond discount in cases where bonds were issued for reorganization purposes. A practice was followed by which this discount was charged to capital, while discount on bonds subsequently issued, to provide funds for additions and betterments, was to be amortized over the life of the issue.

Another question concerned the entries covering new equipment purchased; some railroad managements and public accountants, for instance, deciding to charge all such equipment to fixed asset accounts and to credit such accounts with items withdrawn from service. In the absence of a body of literature in the field of railway accounting, transport boards and their legal advisers turned to public accountants for answers to questions involving book entries and financial statements.[28]

351

Before 1887, the only important regulation of American business enterprise was that exercised by state commissioners over railroad companies. This control, however, was inconsistent because individual states did not have jurisdiction over all of the companies, their regulations applying only to lines in an intrastate position. In April, 1887, the Interstate Commerce Act became effective, with its implementing body possessing authority to require annual reports from the carriers subject to its regulations and to exercise some measure of accounting control. While reports were received, compiled, and analyzed by the ICC from that year forward, only a slight degree of accounting uniformity was secured initially through the medium of required reports.[29]

One serious omission in the early ICC regulations concerned depreciation. Although the commission, in its report for 1888, had included a form of profit and loss statement which referred to repairs or renewals of ties, rails, roadway, locomotives, and cars as part of operation, no specific mention was made of depreciation as an annual charge against operations or of the unsatisfactory practice observed by many railroad companies of basing the amount of depreciation on the amount of profit earned in any year.[30]

---

[28]The relations between company managements and public accountants were intimate, meetings were frequent, and discussions were spirited. To this close liaison both parties made a contribution and from it each derived a benefit—managements learning much about the intricacies of accounting and auditing, and accountants acquiring a knowledge of corporate finance and business administration.

[29]I. L. Sharfman, *The Interstate Commerce Commission* (New York: The Commonwealth Fund, 1935), Vol. iiia, p. 69.

[30]By way of contrast, it should be mentioned that the first circular recommending a system of accounts for telephone companies, sent out by the Bell Co. in 1884 to its various local licensee companies, recommended the establishment of depreciation reserves. Depreciation expense was regarded as an operating expense, in this manner, a 10 percent composite rate being suggested. See Charles A. Heiss, *Accounting in*

(Continued on next page)

Realizing that the regulation of railroad companies could be secured only by the control of the financial statistics of these companies, public accountants helped to lay the foundation of accurate company accounts and annual reports. The more important aspects of this foundation later were incorporated in measures taken, early in the 20th century, to reinforce the powers of the ICC, and to extend these powers to other public utilities and into other jurisdictions. In expressing their belief that the success of administrative regulations rested upon honest, understandable, uniform, and consistent accounts, practitioners did much to advance the cause of consistency and authenticity in American railroad accounts. Moreover, they furnished incontrovertible proof that these accounts, involving broad and comprehensive questions of public policy, were of great importance to the nation's prosperity.

352

Mergers and Consolidations

The accounting firm of Patterson & Corwin covered the books of General Electric Co. by a report dated April 18, 1898. This company had been organized in 1892 of competing companies and capitalized at $50 million. It was a Morgan combination.

With the revival of business in the mid-nineties, Morgan was encouraged to extend his abilities to the steel industry. Early in 1898, he instructed the public accounting firm of Jones, Caesar & Co. (affiliated with Price Waterhouse & Co.) to examine the accounts of all units of the American Steel and Wire Co. of Illinois. During this engagement, various technical problems arose, including the reconcilement of the large excess of appraisal values over book values of fixed assets in connection with adjusted accounts prepared for merger purposes. The auditors' problems of placing the accounts of all constituent companies on a comparable basis were finally resolved because the Morgan firm decided not to proceed with the consolidation. In 1899, however, John W. Gates approached J. & W. Seligman & Co. with the request that negotiations be reopened. Jones, Caesar & Co. audited the accounts of the original fourteen companies and of eleven additional wire plants.

In the late 1890's, various firms of public accountants aided financiers in mergers leading to the American Bicycle Co., American Hide & Leather Co., American Malting Co. (later the American Malt Corporation), Chicago Pneumatic Tool Co., and National Tube Co.

Although the professional relations between public accountants and banking and legal firms in the 1890's had an important influence on the development of the American accounting profession, these relations were

---

the Administration of Large Business Enterprise (Cambridge: Harvard University Press, 1943), pp. 12–14. Bell system accounts were covered by an 8-page manual in 1890. When Heiss gave his paper in 1943, a 130-page manual was used.

often subjected to strain because of the ethical stand taken by the accountants. In some cases, this stand led auditors to decline to provide the usual certification of accounts; in others, it necessitated their withholding a certificate until the valuation of inventories was placed on a satisfactory basis. In this manner their American practice and goodwill were established and placed on a level commanding the respect of legal and banking circles.

Maintenance of a rigid code of technical and ethical conduct, usually over a period of several months of audit before a proposed consolidation was consummated or abandoned, was difficult, as accountants were not able to sustain their positions on controversial issues by reference to authoritative sources. Thinking processes had to be directed to the outline of accounting principles to meet complex corporate situations, while tactical procedures were evolved to assure the adoption of these principles by financial and managerial interests. More than they realized, accountants played an important role in the evolution of accounting and auditing principles, and in providing the basis for professional organization and solidarity.

353

Bibliography

A History of Cooper Brothers & Co.: 1854–1954. London: Privately printed, 1954.

ANYON, JAMES T. *Recollections of the Early Days of American Accountancy: 1883–1893.* New York: Privately printed, 1925.

BROWN, RICHARD. *A History of Accounting and Accountants.* Edinburgh: T. C. and E. C. Jack, 1905.

CARR-SAUNDERS, A. M., AND WILSON, P. A. *The Professions.* Oxford: Clarendon Press, 1933.

CLAPHAM, J. H. *An Economic History of Modern Britain.* 3 vols. Cambridge, England: University Press, 1926, 1932, and 1938.

COLE, G. D. H. *British Trade and Industry.* London: Macmillan & Co., Ltd., 1932.

COOPER, ERNEST. "Fifty-Seven Years in an Accountant's Office," *The Accountant* (October 22, 1921), pp. 553–63.

COUSINS, DONALD. "The Advance of Professional Education," *The Accountant* (October 1, 1949), pp. 356–60.

Deloitte & Co.: 1845–1956. Oxford: Privately printed, 1958.

"Early Development of Accountancy in New York State," *New York Certified Public Accountant,* (March 1949), pp. 157–62.

"Fifty Years," *Accounting Research* (November 1948), pp. 22–23.

GREGORY, T. E. *The Westminster Bank through a Century.* 2 vols. London: Oxford University Press, 1936.

HASKINS, CHARLES W. *Business Education and Accountancy.* New York: Harper & Bros., 1904.

JORDAN, WILLIAM G. *Charles Waldo Haskins: An American Pioneer in Accountancy.* New York: Prentice-Hall, Inc., 1923.

KILPATRICK, JAMES. *Deloitte, Plender, Griffiths & Co.: Some Notes on the Early Days of the Firm*. London: Wyman & Sons, 1942.

LITTLETON, A. C. *Directory of Early American Public Accountants*. Urbana: University of Illinois Bureau of Economic and Business Research, 1942.

MEADE, EDWARD S. "The Reorganization in Railroads," *Annals of the American Academy of Political and Social Science* (March, 1901), pp. 25-63.

MONTGOMERY, ROBERT H. *Fifty Years of Accountancy*. New York: Privately printed by The Ronald Press Co., 1939.

MURPHY, MARY E. "Arthur Lowes Dickinson: Pioneer in American Professional Accountancy," *Bulletin* of the Business Historical Society (April, 1947), pp. 27-38.

_____ "British and American Institutes' Effect on Present Accounting Practice in the Two Countries," *Journal of Accountancy* (August, 1952), pp. 202-44; and (September, 1952), pp. 328-35.

MURRAY, DAVID. *Chapters in the History of Bookkeeping and Accountancy*. Edinburgh: Jackson, Wylie & Co., 1930.

NEW JERSEY SOCIETY OF CERTIFIED PUBLIC ACCOUNTANTS. *Fifty Years of Service: 1898-1948*. Newark: the Society, 1948.

REID, J. LINDSAY. "A Needed Profession," *North American Review* (October, 1894), pp. 510-12.

"Recollections of an Old Accountant," *The Accountant* (September 5, 1914), pp. 268-72.

ROSS, T. EDWARD. "Random Recollections of an Eventful Half Century," *LRB & M Journal*, Vol. 18 (1937).

ROWLAND, STANLEY W. *A Reconsideration of Auditing Methods*. London: Gee & Co. (Publishers) Ltd., 1934.

SHARFMAN, I. L. *The Interstate Commerce Commission*. 3 vols. New York: The Commonwealth Fund, 1935.

STACEY, NICHOLAS A. H. *English Accountancy: 1800-1954*. London: Gee & Co. (Publishers) Ltd., 1954.

SWAINE, ROBERT T. *The Cravath Firm and Its Predecessors, 1819-1947*. 2 vols. New York: Privately printed at Ad Press, 1946.

The New York State Society of Certified Public Accountants: 1897-1947. New York: the Society, 1947.

"These Forty Years," *LRB & M Journal*, Vol. 19, 1938.

WATERHOUSE, EDWIN. "Some Aspects of Liquidation under Recent Legislation," *The Accountant* (October 27, 1894), pp. 946-50.

WEBSTER, NORMAN E. (compiler.) *The American Association of Public Accountants: Its First Twenty Years*. New York: AICPA, 1954.

_____ "What Is a Public Accountant?" *New York Certified Public Accountant* (November, 1944), pp. 667-76, (December, 1944), pp. 703-15.

WILKINSON, GEORGE. "Organization of the Profession in Pennsylvania," *Journal of Accountancy* (September, 1927), pp. 161-79.

Chapter Two

Founding Fathers of the American Accounting Profession

EARLY STEPS TAKEN by public accountants in the United States to achieve professional solidarity were faltering and, in some cases, doomed to failure. After a preliminary meeting of accountants at the Astor House, the Institute of Accountants and Bookkeepers in the City of New York was incorporated in July, 1882, with the following objectives:

To elevate the standing and advance the interest of public accountants; and to direct attention to advantages offered by, and the safeguards attending, the auditing and adjusting of books and accounts by persons thoroughly skilled and experienced as public accountants, and of established personal reputation.[1]

The society later shortened its name to the Institute of Accountants. Its membership included accountants who were not in public practice, but a considerable number of its charter and later members were in this field. Membership was open to all individuals who could pass rigid examinations, and institute certificates, although not supported by legislative enactment, permitted members to title themselves certified public accountants. In 1897, the institute endeavored to establish itself on a national basis but its efforts ended in failure. The general public had little conception of what public accounting implied, and refused to accord it recognition as a profession. The importance of this initial effort at professional organization accrues from the fact that the institute introduced fitness tests for those seeking membership, emphasized the role of the

---

[1] Norman E. Webster, "Public Accountancy in the U.S.," in *American Institute of Accountants Fiftieth Anniversary Celebration, 1937* (New York: AICPA, 1938), pp. 101–9. The minutes and other records of the association covering the years 1886 and 1887 are in the archives of the American Institute of Certified Public Accountants.

public accountant in business affairs, and worked to secure the enactment of state laws recognizing the accounting profession.

Achievement of an Organized Profession

A significant contribution to the promotion of professional unity was made by a Lancashire man, James T. Anyon, CPA, referred to in Chapter 1. Anyon was the American representative of Barrow, Wade, Guthrie & Co., public accountants, and he invited all practicing accountants to his New York office late in December, 1886, to discuss the possibility of organizing an American professional society comparable to The Institute of Chartered Accountants in England and Wales. Deserting their somewhat slender practices, six men appeared at the appointed place and Edwin Gutherie, who was visiting in this country, was accorded the chair because of his long experience as a member of the council of the English institute.

In his talk, Guthrie explained that when he had visited America three years earlier he had discovered almost no accountants in practice, and that the profession since that time had not progressed materially in public recognition. He described the steps taken by English practitioners to attain organization and recognition. After prolonged discussion, John Heins, CPA, who had come from Philadelphia for the meeting, introduced a motion calling for the establishment of an association dedicated to the advancement and protection of the interests of the profession. James Anyon moved that the name of the new society should be the American Association of Public Accountants. Upon the adoption of these motions, the first society of public accountants was formed in the United States.

The certificate of incorporation of the association, signed August 20, 1887, contained the following statement of aims:

> The particular business and object of such society is to associate into a society or guild for their mutual benefit and advancement the best and most capable public accountants practicing in the United States, and through such association to elevate the profession of public accountants as a whole, and to promote the efficiency and usefulness of members of such society, by compelling the observance of strict rules of conduct as a condition of membership, and by establishing a high standard of professional attainment through general education or otherwise; and to transact such business as may be necessary and incident to the establishment and conduct of an association for the foregoing transactions.

James Walden, CPA, was chosen as president, Heins as vice-president, Anyon as secretary, and William H. Veysey, CPA, as treasurer of the new association. As the founding fathers of the American profession were familiar with the designatory initials of The Institute of Chartered Accountants in England and Wales, they divided the membership of the

American body into "Fellows" and "Associates," choosing the letters F.A.A. for the original incorporators of the organization and for those who subscribed to its constitution and by-laws, and also for all persons who had obtained a certificate stating that they had successfully passed the examinations set by the association.

Contrary to expectations, the new group did not enjoy activity on a national basis for a number of years. The state societies of accountants which were organized from time to time tended to concentrate their efforts upon securing state CPA legislation, rather than furthering a national society.

Three years after its formation, the association had only sixty members, and its activities were largely controlled and motivated by New York accountants. Some of its members had no offices of their own but rented space in some obscure building or used back parlors of their homes for professional quarters. Fees were uniformly low. Accountants of this period were noted for their ability and integrity, and they were anxious to establish their profession on a firm, nationwide, ethical basis. Few of them, however, elicited public respect; all were handicapped by insufficient professional training and experience. When meetings were called to discuss professional matters, conversations tended to center on bookkeeping questions, such as the proper method of opening books for a partnership or a corporation, and the correct entry for discounting a customer's note.

Professional Growing Pains

At its 1894 meeting, however, the association directed attention to the development of accounting standards by resolving: "That the method of stating assets and liabilities on a balance sheet should be in the order of quickest realization . . . making the total of the same and balance with the Surplus or Capital properly apportioned to the partners or stockholders as may be."

At this same meeting detailed consideration was given to ethical questions, with the following resolution adopted: "That all members of the Association be prohibited from advertising in any shape or manner their vocation and calling and setting forth the nature or special features of their business, but that the insertion of a card in any regular authorized journals or papers indicating their profession and giving address, etc., is permissible."

Professional accounting organizations continued to engage in wishful thinking rather than action relative to the enactment of suitable legislating which would both recognize and promote the profession, bestow merit upon worthy practitioners, and permit them to use a descriptive title which would serve to separate them from nonqualified persons.

357

Perceiving that more progressive action would have to be taken, the president of the Institute of Accountants during the winter of 1894-95 had drafted a bill providing for the professional education of accountants and the securing of the title for them of certified public accountant. Under this bill, which was to remain unaltered in future years, except in a few administrative details, the regents of New York State would be placed in charge of the CPA certificate examinations.

The American Association of Public Accountants also had introduced a bill in 1895, but neither this measure nor the institute bill became law. In November, 1895, however, the association again introduced a bill which was signed by Governor Levi P. Morton on April 18, 1896, and became law on August 17, 1896, as an Act to Regulate the Profession of

358 Accountancy in the State of New York.[2] The first board of examiners consisted of Chairman Charles Waldo Haskins, CPA, of the public accounting firm of Haskins & Sells, a leader in the profession and in education for the profession; Frank Broaker, CPA, of the CPA firm of Broaker & Chapman, the person who deserved the most credit for enactment of the measure; and Col. Charles E. Sprague, Ph.D., president of the Dime Savings Bank and author of the classic volume *The Philosophy of Accounts*.[3]

Under the New York law, the right to use the title "certified public accountant" was held out as a distinction to public accountants who voluntarily proved their right to it by satisfying the state requirement, and there was no provision for recognition or regulation of practitioners who did not seek the CPA certificate or who were unable to satisfy requirements therefor. This was a permissive type of legislation, not following British accounting societies in regard to the manner of conferring titles. In the United States, also, the authority became vested in the state government, in contrast to the United Kingdom, where this function was discharged by the chartered accounting societies. Both American and British legislative measures were voluntary, neither seeking to restrict nor to regulate the practice of public accounting except in the use of titles.

This permissive type of legislation was followed by other states and territories until 1924, when modern regulatory measures were introduced in Maryland and later in seventeen other states, setting minimal standards of competence for all individuals seeking entrance to the accounting profession. Waiver clauses have cast their doubtful shadows over professional development from time to time, but standards have been raised

---

[2] Henry A. Horne, "The History and Administration of Our Society," in *New York State Society of Certified Public Accountants, Fiftieth Anniversary Number 1897-1947*, pp. 5-14. See also Norman E. Webster, "Background of the New York State CPA Law of April 18, 1896, and Its Subsequent Amendments," *ibid.*, pp. 30-33.

[3] Walter N. Dean, "The Role of the State Board of Examiners in the Development of Accountancy in New York," *ibid.*, pp. 49-66.

in some instances, such as in New York in 1938, when a college degree was made prerequisite for admission to that state's CPA examination.

The growing pains of the American accounting profession, experienced in the 1890's and in the beginning years of this century, were essential to professional maturity and public recognition. A debt is owed by the present generation to those farsighted practitioners in Eastern cities and, more recently, in the Middle and Far Western sections of the country, who worked for state legislation and state societies. Without their efforts, American professional accounting would lack the cohesive organization long enjoyed in the United Kingdom, and the unification of principles and standards which were important aspects of development of public accounting in the twentieth century.

359

Reciprocity of CPA Certificates

The question of reciprocity of CPA certificates remained a debatable issue within the profession in the period from 1900 to 1910. The issue was argued pro and con by American CPAs, with the view expressed by the minority that nationality should not become a governing factor in the admission of accountants to the profession. The controversy continued and in 1904 a particularly lively session of the New York State Society of Certified Public Accountants (formed March 30, 1897) considered the proposition of extending membership privileges to out-of state CPAs. A vignette of this meeting shows fifty practitioners at dinner at Mouquin's, one of the city's gathering places for epicures. At this session, John R. Loomis, CPA, proposed an addition to Section 3 of the New York State Society's by-laws, as follows: "Any person holding a CPA Certificate under the laws of any State other than New York, and who is in active practice of his profession as a public accountant, and who resides or has a place of business in the State of New York, may become a member of this Society." This motion, however, was voted down by the assembled practitioners. In 1908, during his term as president of the New York Society, Loomis transmitted a letter to the regents of the University of the State of New York which contained the society's resolution extending the privileges of the New York law to CPAs in other states who could provide satisfactory evidence that their educational background was equal to that demanded by the Empire State.

Professional Standards

In the first decade of this century, the reputation of British chartered accountants practicing in the United States was unassailed, and their membership in recognized British professional bodies entitled them to respectful attention on the part of fellow-practitioners and businessmen.

Some American companies favored the employment of British-trained accountants.[4] This trend was noted by some struggling "native sons" who bitterly resented what they termed intrusion into their sacred professional precincts. No one was more aware of prevailing conditions in this country than the English periodical *The Accountant*. It counseled forbearance in the face of the "general prejudice on the part of the American public in favor of British professional accountants, which American practitioners may well hope to remove eventually by patient well-doing."[5]

For almost the first five years of this century, little attention was devoted by the American accounting profession to the formulation of standards of ethical practice. However, after the American Association of Public Accountants began to publish the *Journal of Accountancy*, in November, 1905, a definite trend was evident toward the clarification of basic tenets of conduct in both editorial comment and signed articles.

Throughout his professional life, Joseph E. Sterrett, CPA, aligned himself with all movements devoted to the elevation of accounting standards. He played a prominent part in the formation of the Pennsylvania Institute of Certified Public Accountants and the enactment of the Pennsylvania CPA law, and he was honored by appointment to the state board of examiners, and served as chairman of the Pennsylvania Institute's Committee on Education which arranged for evening courses in higher accounting at the University of Pennsylvania.[6] Sterrett delivered many papers on the necessity of outlining a professional code for CPAs. His efforts led to the American Association's by-laws including rules of conduct for the first time in 1907.

A National Federation

In 1902, George Wilkinson, CPA, then president of the Illinois Association of Public Accountants, reviewed the situation as it then existed, pointing out the isolation of the state societies and their inability to cope with national affairs. He unfolded a plan for the coordination of all existing organizations by the formation of a federation of societies of public accountants. A committee consisting of A. Lowes Dickinson, CPA, John A. Cooper, CPA, Allen R. Smart, CPA, Charles W. Haskins, CPA, and Ernest Reckitt, CPA, was set up to draft a plan for such a federation. All of these men, with the exception of Haskins, had been born in England. The plan offered by the committee was presented to a convention

---

[4]*Journal of Accountancy* (April, 1907).

[5]*The Accountant*, September 4, 1909, reprinted in *Journal of Accountancy* (October, 1909), pp. 452–53.

[6]Sterrett served as secretary of the Pennsylvania Institute from 1897 to 1900 and as president from 1904 to 1906. For a more complete record of his activities, see T. Edward Ross, "Random Recollections of an Eventful Half-Century," *Journal of Accountancy* (October, 1927), pp. 256–78.

held in Washington, D.C., in October, 1902, attended by duly elected delegates of all the established societies, and an organization titled the Federation of Societies of Public Accountants in the United States of America was established. Officers were elected and a constitution and by-laws adopted. Subsequently the scheme was submitted to the constituent societies for ratification. As honest differences of opinion existed, the constitution and by-laws adopted differed from the project first prepared by the Illinois Association committee.

A statement of the federation's purposes follows:

> To bring into communication with one another the several associations and societies of public accountants, organized or to be organized under the laws of the several States of the United States of America; to encourage the formation of State associations of public accountants in States in which they do not exist; to encourage State certified public accountant legislation on uniform lines; to secure Federal recognition of the profession of the public accountant; to facilitate and assist the training of young members of the profession, and to establish a uniform standard of efficiency in Federated Societies; to disseminate throughout the United States a general knowledge of the objectives of the Federation and of the utility of the public accountant in the industrial and financial development of the country; to further the interests of the profession of the public accountant generally.

361

Officers of the federation were Charles W. Haskins, CPA, president; George Wilkinson, CPA, secretary; and Robert H. Montgomery, CPA, treasurer. As Haskins died shortly after assuming office, Farquhar J. MacRae, CPA, president of the New York Society, was chosen to fill the unexpired term. The contribution of the federation to the advancement of the American profession cannot be overemphasized.

First International Congress of Accountants

Under the auspices of the federation, the first International Congress of Accountants was convened in September, 1904, on the grounds of the Louisiana Purchase Exposition in St. Louis.[7] A. Lowes Dickinson, CPA, was chairman of the Committee on Arrangements; he nominated Joseph E. Sterrett, CPA, as chairman, and George Wilkinson, CPA, as secretary,

---

[7]*Official Record of Proceedings* of the International Congress of Accountants, September 26–28, 1904, p. 231. Among the honored guests were Francis W. Pixley, immediate past president of The Institute of Chartered Accountants in England and Wales; James Martin, secretary, Society of Incorporated Accountants and Auditors; John B. Niven, of New York, representing the Society of Accountants in Edinburgh; John Hyde, president of the Dominion Association of Chartered Accountants; John W. Ross, president of the Association of Accountants of Montreal; W. T. Kernahan and F. H. Macpherson, president and vice-president, respectively, of the Institute of Chartered Accountants of the Province of Ontario; E. van Dien, representing the profession in Holland; and Captain Percy Atkin, British Commissioner of Education and Social Economy.

of the Congress, while George O. May, CPA, served as chairman of the Local Planning Committee.

The 1904 International Congress was one of the most important accounting conferences ever held in the United States.[8] It was convened at a time when the American Association had a membership of only 140, living in 15 states, of whom 81 held certificates; the New York Society, a membership of 100; and the state societies which were members of the federation, 200.

Amalgamation of Societies

Participants in the 1904 International Congress reached the decision that the American Association of Public Accountants and the Federation of Societies of Public Accountants in the United States of America should be amalgamated, with the purpose of attaining greater professional solidarity.[9] A committee worked out a plan under which the association was the continuing organization after amendment of its constitution and by-laws.[10] Just one year and one month after the International Congress, in October, 1905, the merger was effected under a constitution which provided for individual and state society memberships, with the objectives of elevating the profession and spreading the knowledge of the CPA's usefulness in the business world.

The twenty-first annual meeting of the association in October, 1908 proved to be the largest gathering yet held by the group.[11] More than 230 delegates, members, and guests registered, including 40 representatives of British and Canadian accounting societies. At that time, the association had a membership of 734 (U.S. population 70 million) consisting of the members of the various state societies affiliated with the national

362

---

[8]Only a few copies remain of the limp, leather-bound de luxe edition of the Proceedings of the 1904 Congress, containing invaluable photographs and signatures of the participants. Edited by A. Lowes Dickinson, it is a document of unusual historical importance.

[9]At that time practitioners without CPA certificates were more numerous than those possessing them. The federation had grown slowly chiefly because it admitted only one society from each state, and only if it were composed wholly of public accountants, with at least seven regular members. As each state enacted its own CPA law governing practice within its limits, and as there was marked divergency between these laws and almost no reciprocity between states, serious doubt had been expressed as to the ultimate success of the federation.

[10]The committee consisted of W. Sanders Davies, chairman, Franklin Allen and Duncan Macinnes, representing the association; A. Lowes Dickinson, Robert H. Montgomery, and George Wilkinson, representing the federation; and L. H. Conant, Charles W. Ludlam, and T. P. Ryan, representing the New York State Society.

[11]See, for instance, "Railroad Accounting in Relation to the Recent Rulings of the Interstate Commerce Commission," read by Prof. Henry C. Adams, in charge of Statistics and Accounts, ICC: "Accounting Practice and Procedure," by A. Lowes Dickinson (later expanded into a book of the same title); and "The Accounting of Industrial Enterprises," by William M. Lybrand. Reprinted in *Journal of Accountancy* at intervals in 1908 and 1909.

group, and of certain other individuals, not members of any affiliated society, who were known as members at large. Sixteen of the states—California, Colorado, Connecticut, Florida, Georgia, Illinois, Louisiana, Maryland, Michigan, New Jersey, New York, Ohio, Pennsylvania, Rhode Island, Utah, and Washington—had enacted CPA bills; while four other states—Massachusetts, Minnesota, Missouri, and Tennessee—although they had attained no such legislation, maintained associations of practitioners affiliated with the American association. Of the former number, however, CPAs of Connecticut, Florida, and Utah were not yet connected with the national body. As the internal laws of each state varied radically relative to matters with which accountants were concerned, it was only questions of general professional interest which came under the purview of the association, such as bringing the different states into communication one with another, and encouraging the passage of CPA laws and the formation of state CPA societies.[12]

363

The American Association of Public Accountants was the only society of practitioners until 1917 when its name was altered to the American Institute of Accountants (membership at that date, 1,150). The American Society of Certified Public Accountants was formed in 1921 as a federation of state societies of CPAs. In 1936 it was merged with the institute, with the institute agreeing to support the CPA certificate by restricting membership to CPAs and to maintain close cooperation with state societies of CPAs.

In 1957, the institute's name was altered to the American Institute of Certified Public Accountants. Membership on April 1, 1965 reached 51,876. This compares with a total in 1944 of 5,722 and in 1964 of 50,211. It is the only national organization of CPAs in the United States today.

It is interesting to note that as of August 31, 1964 there were 87,890 CPAs in the United States. At that date, there were 58,511 members of state societies of CPAs.

With a large budget and staff, the institute endeavors to maintain nationwide interest in public accounting in all segments of the community. It also coordinates the 128 local chapters of state societies of CPAs in a national program to enlarge public concern with accounting, financial reporting and terminology; taxation and tax practice; uniform CPA examinations and educational and experience requirements; application of ethical codes to CPAs; testing and internship training of accounting students; recruitment and training of CPA staff personnel; maintenance of library facilities, research and technical information ac-

---

[12]Even at this date New York would not grant reciprocity to out-of-state CPAs. Not until 1912 was an amendment to the New York law passed, under which Joseph Sterrett, William Lybrand, and Robert Montgomery, with one or two other practitioners, were granted their New York CPA certificates, after which the barriers were raised again. In the course of time, reciprocity between states became the rule rather than the exception.

tivities; publication of professional materials; organization of national and regional meetings; promotion of good relations with the public through dissemination of information; and cultivation of close working relations with other professions, stock exchanges, and government agencies.

No federal legislation exists today in this country which restricts public accounting practice. However, a number of states have some type of regulatory legislation covering CPAs.

An ideal of the AICPA has always been to eliminate, or at least to reduce, the wide diversity of requirements for CPA certificates. Practically all states require that an accountant have some professional experience before being permitted to sit for the Uniform CPA Examination. In several states, however, this experience is permitted to follow the examination. The type, quality, and duration of the professional experience are seldom specified by state law.

The institute administers and grades the Uniform CPA Examination for all states. In May, 1965, 15,211 candidates sat for the examination.

There is little uniformity relative to interstate practice. An institute committee has tried to encourage the elimination of barriers to interstate practice by CPAs, and to promote wider acceptance of the principles of interstate practice approved by the institute's council. In September, 1956, the council adopted the following long-range legislative program:

1. The public welfare, which is affected by the activities of CPAs and of persons calling themselves public accountants or using similar designations, justifies the enactment of licensing laws which establish measures of control and standards of competence for professional accountants.

2. Ultimately all professional accounting work should be performed by certified public accountants, who have satisfied educational and experience requirements and have demonstrated competence by passage of examinations. Ultimately all other persons should be prohibited from using the term public accountant or any other term which may be taken to mean that the person so designating himself is competent to practice accountancy at a professional level.

3. The attainment of the ultimate objective of limiting the professional practice of accountancy to CPAs in terms of timing and of the manner of accomplishment must be decided by each state in the light of existing circumstances and without pressure from outside the state for immediate action.

4. Constitutional provisions require that persons in practice as public accountants as principals when a licensing law is enacted must not be deprived of their means of livelihood. Such persons must therefore be permitted to register, and in so doing should become subject to control and to provisions for revocation of their licenses for unprofessional conduct.

5. After the initial licensing of public accountants no further registration should be permitted except for those who acquire the CPA certificate by examination, since the public would be confused by the perpetual licensing of two classes of professional accountants under similar titles but with different standards.

6. In the states which have adopted a licensing law, reopening the registration of public accountants would be contrary to the public welfare, since it would attribute professional competence to persons who had not demonstrated such competence.

7. Only certified public accountants or public accountants subject to control under licensing provisions should be permitted to sign financial statements with any wording indicating that they have expert knowledge of accounting or auditing.

8. No one should be prevented from doing accounting work for more than one employer, provided he does not hold himself out as a certified public accuntant or public accountant, or does not sign financial statements in a manner which adds to their credibility.

9. Free passage of CPAs and other licensed public accountants across state lines in response to the needs of their clients should not be impeded by legislation. 365

Firm Organization and Personnel Policy

One of the questions facing the profession in the early years of this century was that of assuring junior and senior accountants permanent employment and adequate salaries. Although compensation varied among CPA firms and between localities, generally speaking, juniors received salaries ranging from $70 to $125 a month, while seniors earned $150 to $200. In addition, overtime was paid, men in the former category receiving 50–70 cents an hour, while seniors were paid $1 or more. A daily expense allowance, usually $4, was granted to men assigned to out-of-town engagements. Managers—those in complete charge of an important audit and with authority to sign checks, quote fees, and engage assistants—received as much as $300 monthly with an overtime rate of at least $1.50, and a bonus in many firms based upon annual profits. The annual bonus of one staff member was $15!

Several New York CPA partnerships approached Harvard University seniors, offering to employ them at an initial salary of $60 per month for the first year, $80 for the second, and $100 for the third, provided that the individuals selected proved proficient in the art of acounting. The salary scale for holders of postgraduate degrees was $80, $100, and $125, respectively. Men employed were expected to remain with the CPA firms for at least three years, a period sufficient to qualify them for the New York State CPA examination.

British-trained public accountants expressed some doubt that the graduates of American universities, without the benefit of service under articles, would prove adaptable to professional requirements. Staff members chosen were impressed with the fact that they were expected "to do whatever they were told to do and to devote any spare time that they had to reading up subjects in connection with the profession which they proposed to adopt," in the words of a partner of one CPA firm. Continuing, in his words: "Men straight from college know nothing as a rule about business and there is no office work in which they ought not to a certain extent share, including copying letters and straightening files."

To recognize the contribution of experienced men as well as to indicate opportunities of advancement to able recruits, some CPA firms divided their staff members into four classes, based upon range of experience and years of service. Most firms, also, defined the methods by which the annual profits were to be calculated, each stating that after deducting from the net fees all business expenses, interest on capital at a fixed percentage, and salaries of partners, junior and senior managers, a portion of the balance of profits should be set aside and credited to bonuses. From these bonuses were paid certain sums to all members of the staff who had been employed for a period of at least one year, with the remainder usually distributed to staff members who had rendered special firm services.

Under the legal documents motivating the separate organizations, partners were construed in some firms as general partners, without reference to the earnings of the office to which they were assigned. In other agreements, members of the CPA firm had a strong incentive to increase the number of appointments in their particular offices, as their earnings were directly correlated with the expansion within their areas. It should be noted that the latter system was and is followed by many British chartered accounting firms, which sometimes even today organize a separate partnership to cover the practice in a certain part of England or Scotland, or in some overseas country or countries.

Each CPA firm placed a certain value upon its goodwill, selling a portion of it to any person admitted to its ranks, and in some cases the new partner was given a nongoodwill interest of a certain percentage of future profits. In calculating the goodwill, a figure representing the average profits for a certain number of years, usually three, was agreed upon, the new partner acquiring a designated portion of this goodwill and being guaranteed annual minimal profit, sometimes fixed at $5,000. Provision was made for the revision of the interests of old and new partners at periodic intervals and, in the case of firms established by British chartered accountants, for the modification of the profit-sharing ratios accruing to the British firms from their American professional affiliates. In the early years of this century, the British share of profits derived from the American practice of these partnerships was much larger than that allocated to their partners in the United States, but as the years elapsed this ratio was reversed, the individuals immediately responsible for American engagements receiving the major portion of the profits. Eventually, in some instances, the British share was eliminated entirely, the American partnerships purchasing the goodwill in their respective firms held by the firms which had been responsible for their original formation.

The task of selecting firm managers and partners was a delicate one,

366

which was not based on modern theories of personnel administration. Rather, promotion to the upper levels was gained through long service, sometimes in an administrative capacity but more often in the field, a partner's intimate knowledge of the respective qualifications of his staff acquired through engagements jointly executed. The requisites which were considered essential included high personal and professional standards, unswerving honesty and devotion to duty, the certificate of an American or a British accounting society, experience in public accounting, training in the firm's techniques and standards, a pleasing personality and a mature, professional viewpoint, the ability to get along with firm personnel and with clients, and the capacity of representing the firm in the community.

367

Professional Education and Training

It was early recognized by American public accountants that a formal educational program should be adopted preparatory to practice. The November, 1899 meeting of the New York State Society of CPAs empowered the president to confer with the trustees of New York University with the aim of establishing courses for persons desiring to enter the profession and to become certified public accountants. On October 1, 1900, fifty men heard Charles W. Haskins, CPA, deliver his first lecture as dean and professor of the history of accountancy at New York University's new School of Commerce, Accounts, and Finance.

Haskins' course used British literature. The average age of students enrolled in it was about thirty years. Practitioners who took a prominent part in the early years at NYU included W. Sanders Davies, CPA, F. W. Lafrentz, CPA, Farquhar J. MacRae, CPA, John R. Loomis, CPA, John B. Niven, CPA, Samuel D. Patterson, CPA, Elijah Watt Sells, CPA, and Edward L. Suffern, CPA.

During the fall of 1902, the Pennsylvania Institute's Committee on Education, Joseph E. Sterrett, CPA, Chairman, arranged evening classes at which Philadelphia CPAs lectured to a group of fifteen students. The teacher-practitioners were Robert H. Montgomery, CPA, Theory of Accounts; William M. Lybrand, CPA, Practical Accounting; J. W. Fernley, CPA, Auditing; and H. G. Stockwell, CPA, Commercial Law. This Evening School of Accounts and Finance, which met in the office of Lybrand, Ross Bros. & Montgomery, CPAs, was the first educational institution of highest rank to prepare candidates for the CPA examination. In September, 1904, it was incorporated in the Wharton School of Commerce of the University of Pennsylvania. In 1918, Robert H. Montgomery, CPA, accepted a professorship of accounting in the Columbia University School of Business.

Edwin Gay became the first dean of the Harvard Business School in 1908, and accounting thereafter received emphasis in the curriculum.

Professor Henry Rand Hatfield of the University of California aided the educational process by preparing the text *Modern Accounting,* published in 1908, and rewritten as *Accounting: Its Principles and Problems* in 1927.

The Professional Pattern

At the turn of this century, the greatest part of American business enterprise was of limited size and scope. Most audits were of a routine nature. There were numerous unqualified accountants in practice. The few auditing companies which had been formed were frowned upon by the profession as a type of organization which sought to eliminate the personal responsibility inherent in any professional endeavor. State societies of CPAs were striving to formulate and maintain qualifications for members and for standards of practice.

Audits were not carried out on a regular basis. Even at this period, senior and junior accountants entered a client's door separately to avoid suspicion being cast on the financial soundness of the company. They were sometimes referred to as "those business ferrets." Generally, audits concentrated upon complete verification of all entries in journals, the footings of journals, and the checking of posting to ledger accounts. The CPA also checked subsidiary records and ascertained that all transactions had been recorded in the books. He did not attempt, however, to examine inventories or to read directors' minutes. It was not until much later that it became customary for him to accept books which had been balanced by his client's staff, to make test examinations of entries, and to devote a portion of his time to an evaluation of the client's system of internal control.

Practitioners believed that the profession should be permitted by law to evolve its procedures, with reliance being placed at all times upon the individual and his ethical standards. Recognition of the profession in this country was hastened by the decision in *Knoxville* v. *Knoxville Water Co.* (212 U.S. 1) in which the U.S. Supreme Court accepted allowances for depreciation as legitimate expenses in the operation of public utility companies—a step forward in the recognition of accounting principles as well as of certified public accountants.

There was no uniform adherence to standards of auditing or of account maintenance throughout the United States, a direct contrast to practice under the Companies Act in Britain. Reports prepared by American CPAs commonly contained the minimum number of words, frequently reading as follows: Audited and Found Correct. The initials E. and O.E. were added—standing for errors and omissions excepted. In this way, public acountants protected themselves from mathematical errors and errors of omission in clients' books.

The provision of adequate data for stockholders and bondholders of a going concern or for a sales basis, the certification of statements to

368

bankers for credit purposes, the statement of information for bankruptcy or litigation, the examination of public utility and municipal bonds—all of great importance today—were only beginning to enter the auditor's experience before World War I. Completeness, frequency, promptness, and comparability of financial statements, as these qualities are now defined and discussed in subsequent chapters of this book, were then unknown as the main objectives of the auditing examination. A number of cases, however, involving alleged professional negligence had been tried and they held the accountant was not liable to third parties, a position previously taken by the English courts. As a whole, however, little attention was devoted to the acounting profession by the American judiciary.

It became customary for CPAs to ascertain that the accounting data underlying financial statements were accurate and that the statements themselves satisfied legal requirements and personal standards as to form and content. This condition was counterbalanced, however, by a definite trend on the part of some business managements to reveal the minimum of financial information, even to their stockholders, for fear of informing competitors. The need for protecting investors, through the establishment of basic accounting and reporting standards, had not been instilled in the consciousness of either the governing body or the public.

At this period, the balance sheet and the income statement received equal attention from investors. In Britain, however, concentration was placed largely on the balance sheet, as it was the only statutory document required by law. The interest of the American investor in the income statement, as a means of ascertaining the earning capacity of his company and therefore of estimating the value of its stock, did not prevail to the same degree in the United States as it does today. Little comparison could be made of financial statements because of confusion in terminology, inclusion of items under ambiguous headings, and differences in the underlying structure of the accounts supporting the statements.

The initiation of the movement to secure more complete disclosure of important company data in financial statements did not occur to any marked degree before the first World War. Auditors' reports, now of uniform content, had not been subjected to searching inquiry and remained on a voluntary basis. The New York Stock Exchange had not begun to promulgate accounting requirements pertaining to companies with listed issues. The cooperation between the exchange and the AICPA, which was to occur some years in the future, was not at that time considered to be of importance. Yet CPAs did stress acceptable accounting principles, as can be seen from the following statement of a board member of one corporation: "His [the CPA's] sound and experienced judgment was of great value to our corporation. He inducted into the minds of our board of directors many fundamental principles which should properly be observed in the presentation of the affairs of a corporation through its accounts and likewise in the composition of accounts. We were profited materially from his counsel and advice."

Although CPAs utilized English terminology in their reports, some of them did not appear to understand the more technical aspects of accounting. They were handicapped too, by business managements who would not always admit that depreciation of their companies' fixed assets actually had occurred. Some companies maintained the ineffective merchandise account into which were posted purchases, sales, discounts, expenses, and old and new inventories. It was customary to include in the profit and loss account any additions to fixed assets if profits were sufficient to stand such a charge. A few companies carried all their fixed assets in one account at the value of $1, and posted all items of a doubtful nature to an account titled "Items in Suspense." Others combined tangible and intangible assets in their balance sheets and merged these items under the title of "Plant."

370

Various engagements tended to attract attention to the profession. In 1893, the Dockery Commission was created to investigate the operating methods of the executive department of the government and to recommend improvements and economies in these methods. Charles W. Haskins, CPA, and Elijah Watt Sells, CPA, were selected by the commission as full-time investigators. After new systems of accounting and auditing were installed in various departments, the two public accountants formed a firm bearing their names in March, 1895.

The insurance investigation made by a joint committee of the New York State Assembly in 1905 led to the appointment of Price Waterhouse & Co. and Haskins & Sells to make a thorough study of the records of the Equitable Life Assurance Society and the New York Life Insurance Company. Later an investigation of the U.S. Post Office was made by Deloitte, Plender, Griffiths & Co. and Jones, Caesar, Dickinson & Wilmot. Close connections were maintained by the accounting profession with the Interstate Commerce Commission from 1906 and with the national taxing authority from 1909.

An important legal decision was rendered in 1905, *Smith* v. *London Assurance Corporation* (96 N.Y.S. 820), in which the New York Supreme Court stated:

> Public accountants now constitute a skilled professional class, and are subject generally to the same rules for liability for negligence in the practice of their profession as are members of other skilled professions, and such is doubtless the law.

So much uncertainty existed in the business community concerning the duties and responsibilities of auditors that Dean David Kinley of the University of Illinois, in the same year, solicited answers to the query: "What is a public accountant?" A representative number of replies follows:

A person skilled generally in commercial affairs, and particularly in the accounts relating thereto, who places his services at the disposal of the public.

—A. Lowes Dickinson

A public accountant is one engaged professionally in the practice of accountancy; the term accountancy being understood to cover all forms of investigations of accounts for the determination of financial conditions, detection of frauds or prevention thereof, or for whatever purpose data obtained from the accounts may be required.

—William M. Lybrand

A person skilled in accounts and commercial ways offering his service to the public in auditing, making examinations, designing, installing, and advising concerning accounts.

—Joseph E. Sterrett

A professional accountant, whose services are available to the public for a fee or per diem remuneration, as may be arranged. To be successful he must be honest, diplomatic, fearless, versatile, indefatigable, experienced, perspicuous and skilled in his craft.

—George Wilkinson

As there were no American texts in the field of auditing, practitioners in this country attempted to adapt material contained in British volumes written by Lisle and Pixley to American conditions. Inevitably, conflicts arose which were not resolved until 1905, when Robert H. Montgomery, CPA, brought out an American edition of Lawrence R. Dicksee's *Auditing: A Practice Manual for Auditors,* a standard English volume. Montgomery has paid tribute to A. Lowes Dickinson's securing Dicksee's permission for an American edition. Dickinson himself wrote the volume *Accounting Practice and Procedure,* originally published in 1913, which summarized current trends in the United States.

During the formative period of public accounting in America, practitioners saw the profession established in various sections of the nation. In addition, they witnessed the attainment of a certain growth of power and the promise of further development in acceptance of accounting as a profession.

Early efforts to weld American public accounting into one organization, at once endowing it with the high ethical standards and the scholarly literature it merited, have not been forgotten by those CPAs who have written about the pioneers of the profession. Those who came after the founding fathers discovered the professional groundwork to be well laid. Their task then and now was to secure enactment and improvement of CPA legislation, to advance technical education and writings, and to attain the further refinement of accounting and auditing theory and practice.

Bibliography

Arthur Young and the Business He Founded: Personal Reminiscences. New York: Privately printed by Arthur Young & Co., 1948.

BRUMMER, LEON. "The Inception and Foundation of the School of Commerce, Accounts, and Finance," *Journal of Accountancy* (February, 1911), pp. 250–55.

Colliers Weekly, November 7, 1908.

DEAN, WALTER N. "The Role of the State Board of Examiners in the Development of Accountancy in New York," in *New York State Society of Certified Public Accountants, Fiftieth Anniversary Number, 1897–1947,* pp. 59-66.

Editorial, *The Accountant,* September 4, 1909, reprinted in *Journal of Accountancy* (October, 1909), pp. 452–53.

Editorial, *Journal of Accountancy* (November, 1906), pp. 39–41.

Fiftieth Anniversary, Lybrand, Ross Bros. & Montgomery, 1898-1948. New York: Privately printed by the firm, 1948.

Financial Record, June 10, 1896.

HEIMBUCHER, CLIFFORD V. "Fifty-Three Jurisdictions," *Journal of Accountancy* (November, 1961), pp. 42–50.

HORNE, HENRY A. "The History and Administration of Our Society," in *New York State Society of Certified Public Accountants, Fiftieth Anniversary Number, 1897-1947,* pp. 5-14.

MURPHY, MARY E. "Notes on Accounting History," *Accounting Research* (January, 1950), pp. 275–80.

Official Record of Proceedings of the International Congress of Accountants, September 26-28, 1904.

ROSS, T. EDWARD. "Random Recollections of an Eventful Half Century," *Journal of Accountancy* (October, 1927), pp. 256–78.

STAUB, WALTER A. "Mode of Conducting an Audit," *Financial Record* (November 2, 1904), pp. 42–45.

Thirtieth Anniversary Book, New York State Society of Certified Public Accountants. New York: the Society, 1927.

WEBSTER, NORMAN E. "Public Accountancy in the United States," in *American Institute of Accountants Fiftieth Anniversary Celebration, 1937.* New York: American Institute of Accountants, 1938, pp. 101–9.

———— "What Is a Public Accountant?" *New York Certified Public Accountant* (November, 1940), pp. 703–15.

WILKINSON, GEORGE. "The CPA Movement and the Future of the Profession of the Public Accountant in the United States of America," *Financial Record* (November 2, 1904), pp. 25–28.

372

CHAPTER 3

Accounting Practice at the Turn of the Century

Profound economic and social changes were taking place in the United States. The country had emerged from the Civil War with a predominantly agricultural economy. The transcontinental railroads had been completed only a few years after the war. Vast western territories remained to be explored. Invasion of these areas by cattlemen, sheep herders, miners and farmers involved decades of Indian fighting. In fact, it was only a year before the Association's formation that the Apache chief, Geronimo, surrendered to the government.

The United States was a young country, and the accounting profession was a mere infant. But things were on the move. Iron mines, steel mills, and oil wells were added to meat-packing, textile manufacturing and breweries as major industries—along with railroading and shipping. By 1900 the country was one of the world's greater manufacturing centers, as well as a major center of extractive industry. Yet the value of farm products even then exceeded the value of industry's.

The industrial development, however, was marred by financial abuses. Over-capitalization and speculation in the securities markets caused panics in 1873 and 1893. Watered stocks of railroads became a national scandal. Monopolistic tendencies provoked concern. And exploitation of the working class brought on the labor unions and the first big, violent strikes.

Cries for reform were heard in the land, and they were not long in being answered.

At the time the American Association of Public Accountants was organized Congress passed the first Interstate Commerce Act—and, three years later, enacted the Sherman Antitrust Act. While it was years before these laws were adequately enforced—partly due to the reluctance of the Supreme Court to embrace the new theories—the beginnings of federal regulation of business were visible.

374

With the assassination of McKinley in the fall of 1901, Theodore Roosevelt became, at the age of 43, the youngest man ever to reach the highest office in the land. He was a liberal-conservative—a "progressive." He accepted the new industrial order, but recognized its excesses. He felt that government regulation was necessary. He knew it was impossible to turn back the economic clock, and though heralded as a "trust-buster," he recognized the inevitability of combinations in business. The only answer, in his view, was a corresponding increase in governmental power over big business.

The Sherman Antitrust Law was being evaded. The "trusts" were buying up companies to the point of monopoly of entire industries. Common stocks of the trusts were unloaded on the public by the bankers, competition was crushed, and prices then soared.

Roosevelt persuaded Congress to set up a new Department of Commerce and Labor to gather facts needed for enforcement of the antitrust laws. Railway regulation was broadened. The Interstate Commerce Commission's powers were extended from railways to steamship, express and sleeping-car companies. The Commission was also empowered to prescribe maximum rates and to set up a uniform system of accounting—the first use of accounting by the federal governent as an instrument of regulation.

In 1905 there was an investigation of the great insurance companies which also led to reform and regulation.

Big business was here to stay, but it was also here to be regulated.

Nature of Accounting Practice

What was the practice of accounting like in those early days, and what kind of people were they who practiced it? The records are incomplete, but they provide some clues. 375

Advertisements by accountants of the late nineteenth century reflect one type of accounting service in that time. A circular refers to "planning and remodeling books for business firms, preparation and adjustment of partnership accounts, and more especially the periodical auditing and verification of books and statements as a safeguard not only against fraud but against error."*

Another article stated, "The duty and service of the public accountant are by no means limited to the matter of searching out and reporting upon the possible shortages in the cash and securities of trusted employees. The proper departmenting of accounts, the planning of books and formulas, assisting and advising in the general organization and duties of office, so that proper safeguards and methods may be adopted to insure correctness with dispatch . . . are also parts of the duty and service of the specialist in this line."

Another firm of accountants offered to advise clients on "how

---

*NOTE: For much of the information which follows relating to the period 1886-1905, credit is due to Norman E. Webster's *The American Association of Public Accountants—Its First Twenty Years,* American Institute of Accountants, 1954.

single articles are to be priced in order to yield a required percentage of profit."

Still another accountant's circular pointed out "the advantage to any business of proper books of account correctly opened and thoroughly kept . . . and the advantage of regular and systematic auditing of accounts . . . the only existing safeguard against errors, and fraud."

The emphasis of smaller accounting firms was on accounting aids to management—bookkeeping systems, statement preparation, and audits to detect irregularities. In smaller businesses audited financial statements for third-party use were rarely necessary.

However, there was another, and more important, phase of practice not reflected in advertisements—the auditing of the large corporations, many of which by mergers became rapidly larger.

An Early Accounting Firm

For example, the clients of Barrow, Wade, Guthrie & Co., the first English firm established in New York, included the New York, Ontario and Western Railway Company, which James T. Anyon[1] said was the first railroad in the United States to employ public accountants to act as auditors and to certify to the correctness of its annual statements to its stockholders. Other important clients were British insurance companies with operations in the United States, and a textile concern in New York. The going wasn't easy at first. Mr. Anyon's book states candidly that at the end of the first six months of his tenure in 1886 the operations resulted in a "gross service credit" of $4,842.08, and a net profit, after charging his salary of $1,250.00 for the half year, of $2,133.50.

---

[1] James T. Anyon, *Recollections of the Early Days of American Accountancy 1883-1893.* James T. Anyon, New York, 1925.

The amount of business was so limited that Mr. Anyon could not afford to engage any assistant, except an office boy. He, therefore, did everything himself, except dusting, filling the ink stand, mailing letters and running errands, which were the duties of the boy.

The British Invasion

In the late 1880's more English and Scottish chartered accountants appeared in New York, representing prominent 377 British accounting firms. They were sent to examine the financial condition and earning power of American industries which English syndicates had purchased, and whose securities were floated on the English market.

The presence of these British colleagues provided the American accountants, according to Mr. Anyon, with a greater insight into the nature and responsibility of professional accounting work. Bankers and financial men also began to understand better the nature and value of accounting and auditing.

Some of these British firms established permanent offices in the United States. After Barrow, Wade the first to do so was Price Waterhouse & Co., already firmly established in London, which in 1890 and 1891 sent two agents, Jones and Caesar, to reside in this country. For a while they practiced as individuals, then as Jones, Caesar & Co., but to all intents and purposes they were Price Waterhouse in America, and eventually the entire American practice was absorbed under the latter name.

American industrial concerns were beginning to incorporate under the laws of the various states, and their securities were offered to the American investing public. Bankers usually employed accounting firms to make examinations and reports on the financial condition and earnings. Consolidation of industrial enterprises, to the extent permitted by the antitrust laws, also became popular, and accountants were employed to examine the earnings of the companies which were to be combined, but most of the important auditing work at first went to the British firms.

A typical certificate of the early days is the following, covering the accounts of St. Louis Breweries Ltd., signed in London by Price Waterhouse & Co.:

> We have examined the above accounts with the books and vouchers of the company, and find the same to be correct. We approve and certify that the above balance sheet correctly sets forth the position of the company.

In 1899, Jones died, and in 1900 Caesar retired. London offered the senior partnership of the American firm, which soon reverted to the name of Price Waterhouse & Co., to Arthur Lowes Dickinson. Dickinson was a superior man. He held a master's degree from Cambridge University, and was both a chartered accountant and a Fellow of the Institute of Actuaries. In addition, he had an attractive personality and extraordinary leadership capacity. He had a strong interest in elevating the status of the accounting profession, and played a prominent part in strengthening the professional organizations in the United States.

In 1902 Price Waterhouse & Co. was elected, by shareholders of the United States Steel Company at their first annual meeting, as auditors of the company, which the firm continues to be to this day. The auditor's certificate issued in 1903 read as follows:

> We have examined the books of the U.S. Steel Corporation and its Subsidiary Companies for the year ending December 31, 1902, and certify that the Balance Sheet at that date and the Relative Income Account are correctly prepared therefrom.
>
> We have satisfied ourselves that during the year only actual additions and extensions have been charged to Property Account; that ample provision has been made for Depreciation and Extinguishment, and that the item of "Deferred Charges" represents expenditures

reasonably and properly carried forward to operations of subsequent years.

We are satisfied that the valuations of the inventories of stocks on hand as certified by the responsible officials have been carefully and accurately made at approximate cost; also that the cost of material and labor on contracts in progress has been carefully ascertained, and that the profit taken on these contracts is fair and reasonable.

Full provision has been made for bad and doubtful accounts receivable and for all ascertainable liabilities.

We have verified the cash and securities by actual inspection or by certificates from the Depositories, and are of opinion that the Stocks and Bonds are fully worth the value at which they are stated in the Balance Sheet.

And we certify that in our opinion the Balance Sheet is properly drawn up so as to show the true financial position of the Corporation and its Subsidiary Companies, and that the Relative Income Account is a fair and correct statement of the net earnings for the fiscal year ending at that date.

379

When U.S. Steel was organized in 1901 through consolidation with a number of other enterprises, the lawyers and bankers wished to present to the stockholders the accounts of the parent company alone. Dickinson insisted that consolidated accounts were necessary, and supporting statements and schedules were provided. To a large extent, United States Steel established a standard for financial reporting during the early years of the century. The disclosure of significant facts and figures, in which Dickinson played an influential role, contributed to a realization on the part of the business world of the importance of accounting and auditing.

In 1905 the life insurance business was put under the spotlight of a public examination, as a result of widespread publicity about the internal difficulties of some of the larger companies. A Joint Legislative Committee of the State of New York was appointed for the investigation. Legal counsel was Charles Evans Hughes. The newly elected chairman of the Equitable Life Assurance Society engaged Price Waterhouse & Co. and Haskins & Sells to make a thorough examination of the past transactions of this large insurance company in order to ascertain its condition at the time he assumed office. The New York Life Insurance Company also engaged the two firms for similar purpose. The reports were signed by Price Waterhouse & Co. as chartered accountants, and Haskins & Sells as certified public accountants.

Early American Firms

380   Haskins & Sells, one of the oldest native American accounting firms, was founded in 1895 by Charles Waldo Haskins and Elijah Watt Sells.

Haskins, after some years in private accounting work, had begun the public practice of accounting in New York City in 1886. Sells' previous experience had been in accounting work for railroads in the Midwest. His last post in 1893 was as secretary and auditor of the Colorado Midland Railway.

The two founding partners met in 1893, having been designated as experts to assist a Congressional commission investigating the operating methods of the Executive Department in Washington and to recommend improvements and economies.

Mr. Haskins was the first president of the New York Board of Examiners of Public Accountants, and also the first president of the New York State Society of Certified Public Accountants. He took a leading part in the founding of the School of Commerce Accounts and Finance of New York University, becoming its first dean.

Mr. Sells was also active in professional affairs. He was one of the organizers of the first International Congress of Accountants, and for two years he served as president of the American Association of Public Accountants.

Robert H. Montgomery's book, *Fifty Years of Accountancy*[2]

---

[2] Ronald Press Company, New York, 1939.

throws much light on the nature of accounting practice in the formative days of the profession. Montgomery was a native-born American, and the firm of which he became a member, Lybrand, Ross Bros. & Montgomery, founded in 1898, had no British origin. But Montgomery readily conceded that he benefited much from his association with Dickinson and the other Englishmen and Scots who were among the pioneers.

Montgomery, who became an outstanding leader of the profession, was employed at the age of 16 as an office boy by John Heins, a public accountant of Philadelphia, then president of the American Association of Public Accountants, which had been organized only two years before.

381

Montgomery said, "As office boy, I would have gained an insight into all the secrets of the national organization if there had been any secrets. The activities were few. Often I sent a telegram that there would be no quorum, hence no meeting."

Montgomery became a junior accountant with the Heins firm, spending much of his time checking postings from one book to another.

In the early days, prior to the turn of the century, many financial statements of both large and small businesses had the symbols "E.O.E." in the lower left-hand corner. It meant "Errors and Omissions Excepted." So many of these statements were erroneous, wrote Montgomery, that it gave rise to one of the favorite jokes of his contemporaries, "The real meaning is Errors and Omissions Expected."

Montgomery also said that his firm in the early days frequently verified all of the transactions in the books, wrote "audited and found correct," and did not make a single constructive suggestion. He felt it wrong to accept fees for routine checking of footings and postings, without finding errors sufficient to pay for the accountant's time.

When an audit was started the accountants were handed what were known as all the books of account: ledgers, journals, cash, purchase and sales books, with canceled checks and paid bills. When the accountants verified the entries and vouched all the payments, they were pretty much through with the job.

Later the Heins firm began to analyze the trial balance, and look at shipment books, cash-sales records and other evidences of transactions which might not have found their way into the books with which the auditors were furnished. Often they were refused access to subsidiary records, but they kept insisting, because they found many defalcations they were not supposed to find, which would not have been discovered by checking the formal books of account.

The accountants were not supposed to know much about inventories, but they tried to learn what they could. Montgomery said that the first time he asked to see the insurance policy covering the stock in process and on hand, "I might as well have thrown a bomb." But his rule was that if there was any reluctance to show him what he wanted to see, he would keep on asking—"or else." In some cases auditors were not permitted to read the minutes of boards of directors. The mere fact that permission was denied was a cause for suspicion.

One of the reasons for detailed checking was that the instructions often included bringing the books into exact balance. Frequently the books of businesses had been out of balance for months or even years, and the discovery of the errors was a terrific task. One junior accountant would call off an amount from a ledger to another junior who compared it with an item in a book of original entry. One hollered the amount, and the other ticked it off. The function was known as "holler and tick."

It gradually became apparent that when the books were in balance the integrity of the records could be determined by comprehensive tests as well as by verifying all items.

Out-of-Town Work

Accountants traveled a good deal in those days, since their firms had not established branch offices in many different parts of the country. Some of the conditions in which they worked were primitive. James T. Anyon told of a visit to a place called Mills Camp in Alabama in the 1890's. His train was hours late, and he arrived at midnight in a desolate part of the country where there was no railway station, but where he was allowed to dismount from the train. A night watchman met him and allowed him to sleep, in the rain, around a roaring fire among a group of convicts who were working at the camp. When morning came he was allowed to go to the house of the manager, where he was given coffee, and found other civilized amenities.

Robert Montgomery described a job in Vicksburg, Mississippi, where there was no hotel. He and his companion camped out in the mill. They drank and bathed in the muddy waters of the Mississippi. On another engagement, Adam Ross and Montgomery spent six weeks in a town in the mountains of North Carolina. They occupied a double bed and used one washbowl. In the morning the water was frozen. To finish the job on time, they worked nights and Sundays and all night on the final day. The cooking was so bad that they lived on boiled eggs—six or eight a day!

Montgomery's tireless service in the professional organizations will be mentioned frequently in this book. He wrote, "My personal opinion is that it is far easier to rise in one's trade or profession by attendance at meetings and by friendly intercourse with those in the same line as ourselves than in any other way."

Professional Pioneers

Many other firms which later became prominent were founded in the late nineteenth and early twentieth centuries.

It was, of course, an advantage to these early accounting firms to be on the scene when the American economy was in the first stages of its great industrial growth. They formed important connections with influential bankers, lawyers and industrialists which in many cases led to rapid expansion of the practices of these firms.

But it must be remembered that many other firms which came on the scene about the same time did not prosper, and have long since been forgotten. Those that survived were able to deliver the goods. Their partners were not wealthy men at first. They worked hard, held to high standards, gave their clients valuable service, and through sound internal policies developed strong organizations of their own.

In spite of the head start enjoyed by these firms, many other firms which were founded much later have also achieved great success through application of the same formula.

In those pioneering days from 1886 to 1906, some of the American accountants were jealous of their British colleagues, who seemed to be favored by the bankers, and thus obtained many of the most lucrative engagements. In retrospect, however, the accounting profession clearly gained much from the presence of the English and Scottish chartered accountants.

They brought with them a background of discipline, professional training, standards, and professional pride, derived from the simple fact that in their home countries the profession had already been organized for 20 years or more, and had attained status and recognition. This in turn was due to the industrial development in Great Britain, and the acquisition of investment capital in that country which preceded similar developments in America by roughly half a century.

The chartered accountants were self-confident, since they knew their jobs; they were articulate, and were generally well educated. They were hard workers and astute businessmen. For the most part they were dedicated to high standards, and earnestly desired to enhance the status of their profession in their adopted country.

The same things can be said of the native American accountants who followed their example and had the vision to see the opportunities in the young profession. It is not surprising that some of these pioneer firms developed into the large national organizations of today.

The partners of the larger firms became comparatively well-to-do. They had time also to give to the affairs of the infant professional organizations.

The contributions of these men are too numerous to be described individually. In the aggregate they were invaluable. If they had chosen to devote their attention exclusively to the development of their own practices, without concern for the accounting profession as a whole, that profession would not enjoy the status which it has today.

385

CHAPTER 4

386

The First "National" Association

W HILE the organization of a national professional accounting society was inevitable, it might have been delayed for many years if it had not been for a visit to New York by an Englishman in 1883.

In that year Edwin Guthrie, of the firm of Thomas, Wade, Guthrie & Co., Chartered Accountants of London and Manchester, England, was receiver in bankruptcy of a financial concern in England. He found it necessary to come to the United States to ascertain the value and status of certain property and assets which the bankrupt concern owned in this country. He intended to employ an accounting firm here to assist him, but could not find one.

Being a perspicacious gentleman, Mr. Guthrie saw an opportunity to establish an accounting practice in New York, which as far as he then knew would be the first of its kind in the country. He met an actuary named John Wylie Barrow, and with him organized in 1883 the firm of Barrow, Wade, Guthrie & Co., Public Accountants, New York, the English partners supplying the necessary working capital.

In 1886 Barrow died. Mr. Guthrie then brought to this country James T. Anyon, a senior assistant and a chartered accountant of England, who became the partner in charge of the firm in New York.

Mr. Anyon, a stranger in a strange land, looked about for American colleagues in his chosen profession. He found a firm called Veysey & Veysey, with a staff of two or three assistants, a James Yalden & Co., and several individual practitioners. In Philadelphia John Heins appeared to be the leading accountant in public practice, and in Boston Rodney McLaughlin was similarly situated.

387

Since Mr. Guthrie had remained in New York to provide for the conduct of the firm's practice there, Mr. Anyon arranged for him to meet the accountants with whom Anyon had become acquainted.

Six or seven individuals attended the meeting, including Mr. Heins of Philadelphia.

Mr. Guthrie expressed his pleasure at meeting the American accountants, but indicated regret that the profession here had not attained much public recognition. He said that in England, on the contrary, the profession was on a high plane, being recognized as one of the leading professions. He suggested that a body similar to the Institute of Chartered Accountants in England and Wales should be started in the United States.

Since the English Institute had been in existence for only six years, Mr. Guthrie's allusions to the high standing of his profession may have involved some poetic license, excusable on the grounds of national pride.

Nonetheless, his suggestion was received with enthusiasm. It was moved and seconded that the accountants present at the meeting should form themselves into an association for the advancement and protection of the interests of the accounting profession, and that the qualification for membership should be ability and fitness to practice accounting in a public capacity.

At first, it was proposed to select as a name, "The Chartered

Accountants' Institute." However, Mr. Guthrie strongly advised the use of some other name than "chartered accountants." He pointed out that this would be likely to conflict with the use of the same title in the United States by English and Scottish accountants who might visit the United States on professional business for clients in Great Britain. This loomed as a serious objection at that time, since the most important and responsible engagements entrusted to accountants in those days were given to visiting British accountants.

Accordingly, it was resolved to organize a society entitled the American Association of Public Accountants. A committee was appointed, a second general meeting was held, the Association was incorporated, a constitution was adopted, and a Council and officers were elected. The certificate of incorporation was filed on September 20, 1887.

The first president was James Yalden, the vice president was John Heins, the secretary was James T. Anyon, and the treasurer was W. H. Veysey. At this time there were 31 members— 24 fellows and seven associates. Fellows were persons who had practiced as public accountants continuously for three years prior to their admission to membership.

Most of the members and associates merely had desk space, with no assistants, and some had offices in their homes. A few had firms with regular offices, names on the door, and several staff assistants.

The formation of the Association did not immediately change things very much.

The new society had to struggle for survival. It was the first American organization intended to represent the public practitioners of accounting. But whereas the English Institute had started with more than 1,000 members, there were few public accountants in the United States from which to draw membership. The Association was also the first organization to aspire to national coverage, but the bulk of its members were in New York, and transportation being what it was, the Association had little to offer those in other parts of this vast nation.

Legal Base Lacking

There was nothing in the United States similar to the required statutory audit of corporations in England, which had greatly stimulated the development of the accounting profession there. Nor did the United States provide a Royal Charter, which automatically had given status to the chartered accountants of Scotland and England. The Institute in England had actually introduced a system of examinations as early as July 1882. It was not until 1897 that any professional accounting examinations were required in the United States— and those only in the State of New York.

389

There was no recognized title for qualified public accountants here. There was no native accounting literature to speak of, nor any system of education and training for young accountants.

The first two years of the tiny American Association were occupied with internal affairs. Where matters stood in 1889 is reflected in the address of President James Yalden:

> The profession of accountancy having hitherto been but little known in the United States, and the recognized want of a well-organized body of professional and public accountants, whose ability, character, and strict business conduct could be relied upon, being called for by the leading commercial and financial representatives of the country, led to the formation of our Association— the lines being taken mainly from the older countries, notably England, in the formation and the ruling and conduct of our Order.
>
> It is much to be regretted that our Association is not stronger in number. At the present time we have but 25 fellows, and seven associates, which I am sure you will agree is not enough to give the Association that standing and recognition we all desire, and it is of paramount importance to the profession that some means should be adopted to increase our membership.

But things moved slowly. By 1892 the membership had increased only to 35. The Association had no employees. Everything was done by volunteers. The officers were required to spend a good deal of time and energy on mere administrative details—the arrangement of meetings of trustees and members, the writing of minutes, the sending out of notices and invitations to membership, discussion of amendments to bylaws, debates over proposed activities, and efforts to obtain publicity and recognition.

Nor did the Association have the field entirely to itself. There were various organizations of bookkeepers and accountants in New York, among the most vigorous of which was the Institute of Accounts. Its members were mostly accountants in private employment, but included a number of public accountants, among whom were even some of the leading members of the Association.

Societies of public accountants had also been organized in a number of the states. From time to time the Association was faced with the competition of other national organizations, though they were short-lived. The most influential of these was the Federation of Societies of Public Accountants in the United States of America (the state societies).

At times the leaders of the Association must have been tempted to throw in the sponge. By January 1894, its membership had grown to 48 fellows and 17 associates. But in January 1896, the membership had dropped again to 27 fellows and five associates.

Adventure in Education

Over a period of several years in the early 1890's, the Association invested an enormous amount of its scarce resources, and the time and energy of its members, in efforts to establish a school or college of accounting where young men could be trained for the profession.

The certificate of incorporation of the American Association included as one of its objectives "establishing a high standard of professional attainments through general education and knowledge and otherwise."

In 1892 the Association began an effort to establish a college of accounts with degree-conferring powers, under the jurisdiction of the Regents of the University of the State of New York and the immediate guidance of the Association. The project was supported by a number of business and financial leaders. *The New York Times* commented editorially on the proposal. A delegation from the Association attended a hearing before the Regents on June 8, 1892. But the petition for a charter for a college of accounts was not approved by the Regents. This august body resolved that it was not prepared to endorse the entire proposal of the petition, but was ready to open examinations for such persons as desired to become public accountants.

The Association returned to the attack with better preparation. In December 1892 it presented another petition to the Regents for a charter to establish a professional school to be known as the New York School of Accounts. The petition stated that $5,000 had been subscribed as a guarantee of support for the school; that suitable accommodations had been leased; and that all necessary furniture, books and supplies would be provided within a reasonable time. The petition was supported by a resolution of guarantee, an outline of a proposed curriculum in detail, and a paper elaborating the reasons for the establishment of such a school, the proposed method of financing it, the qualifications of the proposed board of trustees and other details.

This time the effort was successful. The Regents granted a temporary charter for two years. A dean and faculty were appointed, members of the Association were designated to lecture, and letters and prospectuses were sent to several thousand prospective students.

Alas, this herculean effort was doomed to failure.

At a meeting of the faculty of the school in June 1894, the following resolution was passed:

> Resolved, That in the opinion of the faculty it is unadvisable to continue the School of Accounts, and they recommend that the Trustees take such action as they may decide upon to surrender the charter to the Board of Regents or otherwise. Carried.

In September 1894, at a meeting of the trustees of the school, Richard F. Stevens, president of the Association, reported:

> Our members gave freely of their time and experience, and everything that the Association could do with the limited means at its command was done. A year has passed since its inception, and what has been accomplished? A class of seven pupils have gone through the year's course, that is all, not a businessman has come forward to aid us in any way, the whole burden has fallen upon the shoulders of a few members, now disheartened and disillusioned, the Board of Regents of the University has stood silent and aloof, not a word has been said about commissioning or licensing our members, and communications addressed to them on the subject of legalizing the profession by legislative enactment have remained unanswered. The members, under this state of affairs, naturally have ceased to take an interest in the school, the professors have resigned or been slack in their attendance, the scholars supine, and further continuance of the school, in its present status, seems idle.

392

The school was abandoned. However, several proprietary schools of accounting were started a few years later, quite likely as a result of the Association's pioneering effort. The growing interest in accounting education also led the universities to establish courses in the subject.

The Wharton School of Commerce and Finance had been established at the University of Pennsylvania in 1881, and the introduction of accounting instruction there encouraged the growth of public accounting in Philadelphia. The School of Commerce, Accounts and Finance of New York University was established in 1900, on the initiative of the New York State Society of Certified Public Accountants. In 1902 the Association established an annual scholarship of $100 at the New York

University School, which was gratefully acknowledged by the University authorities.

In 1906, the Pace Institute of Accountancy was founded, which survives today as Pace College, now a degree-granting institution.

The unsuccessful efforts of the American Association in the field of education at least started some ripples by pointing up the need, and the need was finally filled in better ways than those originally attempted. The question of "licensing our members" had also arisen in connection with this adventure in education—and that was to be the subject of successful action.

The First CPA Law

The idea of legislative recognition of the public accounting profession had fascinated members of the Association from the beginning. Tentative approaches to the Board of Regents had not received encouraging responses. But in 1894 a serious attempt was made to have a bill enacted by the New York State Legislature.

Several draft bills were prepared by different individuals— and argued over. A Mr. Gottsberger wrote his own bill and put it in the hands of a senator, apparently without submitting it for approval of the Association. The Institute of Accounts, most of whose members were privately employed, but some of whom were also public accountants, also drafted a bill and had it introduced in the Assembly.

Failure because of conflicting bills was feared. A "Committee of Fourteen" was formed, and a meeting of all interested public accountants was held in New York to discuss the situation. The committee included representatives of the American Association, the Institute of Accounts, and public accountants belonging to neither organization. The bills already introduced were read at this meeting.

The Gottsberger bill was restrictive. It prohibited practice as a public accountant in New York without a license, and provided the means by which such licenses could be obtained.

The other bill (by the Institute of Accounts) was permissive. It provided for the issuance of a certificate to practice as a "certified public accountant," but did not restrict the practice of public accounting to persons who obtained this title.

There ensued a long debate in which various opinions were expressed as to the merits of the two bills. Apparently, the Regents had expressed a preference for the permissive bill. The minutes of the meeting state, "Richard M. Chapman thought that of the two bills . . . the one endorsed by the Regents was the most desirable to act upon. . . ."

Meetings were held in Albany with the secretary of the Board of Regents, and with a committee of the Assembly. Finally the Association endorsed and approved, with some amendments, the permissive bill providing solely for the issuance of the CPA certificate.

The bill was defeated in the Senate.

Nothing daunted, the accountants renewed the effort in 1896. The Committee of Fourteen rallied all interested accountants in support of identical permissive bills in the Senate and Assembly. Representatives of the Association appeared at the legislative hearings. The bill became law on April 17, 1896. It provided for issuance of a certificate conferring the title "certified public accountant" upon qualified persons, and prohibited use of that title by others. It provided for examination of applicants but included no education or experience requirement. "Waiver certificates" could be issued without examination to public accountants already in practice.

The passage of this law marked the beginning of an *accredited* profession of accounting in the United States.

The question has often arisen as to why the title "certified public accountant" was selected.

It was no doubt a temptation to adopt the term already established in Great Britain—"chartered accountant." But it was pointed out in the discussions of this subject, as Mr. Guthrie had done ten years before, that this would conflict with the rights established by the Scottish societies, and later by the English, under Royal Charters. Moreover, the pioneers in the United States, with native pride, probably did not want to be accused of copying the British. In addition, the term "public accountant" was already fairly well established in the United States, and the simple addition of the prefix "certified" seemed to meet with general approval. It is also possible that the American Association of Public Accountants favored preservation of the last two words in its own title.

By the end of 1905, New York had issued 332 CPA certificates, of which 155 were issued by examination, the remainder by waiver.

395

The passage of the CPA law in New York was swiftly followed by similar legislation in other states, notably Pennsylvania (1899), Maryland (1900), California (1901), Illinois (1903), Washington (1903), New Jersey (1904), Florida (1905), and Michigan (1905).

The Struggle for Identification

The members of the American Association of Public Accountants had a compulsive desire for recognition. This was natural and understandable. They knew that they had skills which were useful to the community. They knew that their colleagues in Great Britain had already achieved professional status and a considerable degree of prestige. The Association members were impatient for wider opportunities for service in the United States, and for the public respect which they felt was due them as experts in a field which deserved, even if it had not yet attained, the title of "profession."

Yet in the view of most of the public they were indistinguishable from bookkeepers. In 1902, a publication known as *Business World* published a letter in which the writer said plaintively, "The term accountant to the public signifies bookkeeper." This feeling persisted for a long time. Robert H. Montgomery was fond of saying, humorously, "The public thinks a public accountant is a bookkeeper out of a job—who drinks."

It is not surprising, then, that much of the energy and financial resources of the new Association was directed to publicizing the profession. A committee on advertising was formed in 1888. Thousands of dollars were spent on advertising in the following years.

Booklets were printed and widely distributed containing the bylaws, objectives and membership of the Association. Paid advertising in contemporary business and financial newspapers and magazines described the services of accountants, the profession's objectives and the nature of its organization. Membership-promotion materials were distributed by the thousands.

Individual accountants, including members of the Association, also advertised their services through circulars distributed by mail and advertisements in periodicals. In England, the Institute of Chartered Accountants had begun as early as 1881 to stamp out advertising and "touting" for business, though it was over 20 years before the practice entirely died out. On occasion *The Accountant* (London) made critical remarks about "touting" by American accountants.

In 1893, at a meeting of the American Association, W. Sanders Davies offered a resolution "that the indiscriminate soliciting of business by the issue of touting circulars is unprofessional and unworthy of the profession of public accountants, and it is further resolved that a copy of the foregoing resolution be transmitted by the secretary to each member of the Association."

This action was characteristic of Mr. Davies. He had come to New York from England in 1891, and established a local firm—still flourishing as Davies and Davies—in which his son and grandson became partners. Sanders Davies was a man of uncompromising integrity, devoted to the highest standards of conduct. He was genial, humorous and fearless. Over a span of more than 40 years he was a tireless worker in the national organizations, a member of the governing bodies, twice serving as president.

However, his resolution of 1893 was laid on the table.

But in 1894 the Association adopted the following resolution:

> That all members of the Association be prohibited from advertising in any shape or manner their vocations and calling; and setting forth the nature or special features of their business, but that the insertion of a card in any regular authorized journals or papers indicating their profession and giving address, etc., is permissible.

There is no indication that this admonition was ever enforced, or that it succeeded in eliminating undesirable advertising, although it doubtless had a restraining effect on many of the members.

Although one of the objectives of the American Association of Public Accountants was to compel "the observance of strict rules of conduct as a condition of membership," no such rules were formulated in the first twenty years.

For one thing, the membership was so small that formal complaints against members by other members might have generated personal hostilities which would have torn the organization apart.

Nevertheless, the records indicate that the trustees of the Association were conscious of the importance of professional conduct, and actually did take disciplinary action in at least a few instances. Some applications for admission were refused on ethical grounds. One complaint or question which had official attention apparently caused the voluntary separation of a member.

Lack of Technical Standards

Very little was done in the first 20 years to develop standards of accounting and auditing. The first technical meeting held by the Association occurred in 1892. The subject was uniformity in practice. The main speaker proposed that at each meeting one or more members present a paper designed as a model for universal adoption on some phase of practice, which, after being discussed, would be laid over until the next meeting when it would be rejected or adopted: "As soon as sufficient matter be thus accumulated, it should be published in book form, with proper table of contents, index, etc., and placed on the shelves of every fellow member as the code of the Association."

This was an ambitious plan which showed awareness of the need for codification of standards of practice. It was too ambitious, however, to come to fruition.

The next record of a technical discussion was in March 1893. The preparation of balance sheets was the subject. In June 1893 papers were read on trading and profit-and-loss accounts.

Then there was a gap. No doubt the members were giving all their attention to the school fostered by the Association, and thereafter to the effort to secure enactment of the New York CPA law.

In June of 1893 a resolution was adopted to the effect that members be requested to present papers connected with the profession of accountancy at the regular meetings of the Association. In the following three years, 13 technical papers were presented, which were published in one or another of three contemporary financial magazines: *The Financial Record, Business,* and *The Banking Law Journal.*

Apparently, however, these technical meetings also died a natural death.

In 1901 the president of the Association called attention to the need for instructive literature related to the accounting profession in the United States.

There were British books on accounting, but most of those published in the United States were on bookkeeping. Little had been written primarily for the use of public accountants.

In 1902 there was a discussion by the trustees of the Association on the desirability of establishing a library. Thirteen books were acquired, mainly by gifts.

With regard to periodical literature, *The Accountant* (London) was apparently widely read in the United States. Technical articles on some aspects of accounting were also occasionally published in various business and financial magazines in the United States.

The 1904 Congress

399

The outstanding event of the first 20 years was the first International Congress of Accountants held in St. Louis, simultaneously with the Louisiana Purchase Exposition, in 1904.

The initiative for the Congress came from George Wilkinson of Chicago, who as president of the Illinois Society of Public Accountants had organized in 1902 the Federation of Societies of Public Accountants in the United States of America. He became the secretary of the Federation, and was a moving spirit in organizing the 1904 Congress.

Accountants in many of the states had organized local societies, though most of them were small. The American Association in 1904 had only a little over 250 members, with a heavy concentration in New York. Nearly one-third of its members had come from abroad, mostly from England and Scotland, and many of these were chartered accountants.

England was generally unpopular in America at the turn of the century. James T. Anyon, in writing of his early experiences, said that he had the disadvantage "of being an Englishman, for the people generally, at that time, did not take very kindly to men of this nationality. . . . There was somewhat of a national feeling of prejudice against Englishmen, arising I think in the old colonial days, which was still apparent. It was a fact nevertheless in spite of this feeling that if any real and important accounting work had to be done, it would in the majority of cases be given to the foreign-trained accountant in preference to the native one."

No doubt because of this preference, the native American accountants, particularly outside of New York, had some latent feelings of hostility toward the "foreigners," which may have carried over in some measure to the Association.

In any event, the Association was not doing much for the members outside New York, and this probably stimulated the organization of the Federation.

Meanwhile, the New York State Society of Certified Public Accountants had been organized in 1897, following enactment of the CPA law a year earlier. Many members of the Association naturally obtained CPA certificates, and some of them joined the New York State Society. But the Association had other members who were public accountants in states where CPA laws had not yet been enacted. Yet the bulk of its membership was in New York, and there is evidence that some of its leaders feared that the New York State Society would be competitive. They suggested, unsuccessfully, that the Association remain as the representative society of all public accountants.

A comparison of memberships showed that some CPAs belonged both to the American Association and to the New York State Society, some CPAs belonged only to the Association and not to the State Society, some CPAs belonged to the State Society but not to the Association, and the Association contained some accountants who were not CPAs!

Further to complicate the scene, the New York State Society chose not to join the Federation.

In these chaotic circumstances the International Congress in St. Louis provided a rallying point. The energetic George Wilkinson brought together all three organizations in a common cause. It was the first truly national meeting of professional accountants in the United States. The international flavor added glamour. Representatives from England, Canada and Holland attended.

It was a large meeting for those times. There may have been somewhat more than 150 persons present.

Arthur Lowes Dickinson was chairman of the committee on arrangements, George O. May was chairman of the local committee, and Joseph E. Sterrett was permanent chairman of the Congress. Other participants who later occupied prominent positions in the professional organizations were: William M. Lybrand; Robert H. Montgomery; John B. Niven; Ernest Reckitt; Elijah Watt Sells; and Walter R. Staub. Some of them had been active in the Federation, others in the Association.

Joseph E. Sterrett first came to national prominence as chairman of this Congress. He had joined the staff of a pioneer accounting practitioner in Philadelphia, John W. Francis, in 1891, and became Francis' partner in 1893.

Sterrett was instrumental in the organization of the Pennsylvania Association of Public Accountants in 1897, which following passage of the CPA law in that state changed its name to the Pennsylvania Institute of Certified Public Accountants. Sterrett became president of the state association, a member of the State Board of Examiners, and chairman of the committee on education. In this capacity he initiated the Evening School of Accounts and Finance, which later was merged with the Wharton School of Commerce of the University of Pennsylvania.

Francis died, and Sterrett continued the practice in his own name. In 1902 he had become interested in the Federation of Societies of Public Accountants, of which Arthur Lowes Dickinson, the head of Price Waterhouse & Co., was president in 1904. The friendship of these two men resulted in amalgamation of Sterrett's practice with Price Waterhouse & Co., Sterrett becoming a partner of the firm in 1907. He later moved to New York.

Sterrett's capacity as a negotiator, together with his competence and his personal sincerity, idealism and persuasiveness, made him one of the great leaders of the profession in his time.

The program of the 1904 Congress was largely devoted to technical papers, followed by discussion. Both papers and discussion were subsequently published in the official record, which must have been one of the most important professional accounting publications thus far produced in the United States.

In all respects, the Congress was a grand affair, and it undoubtedly contributed in many ways to acceleration of the progress of the profession in the following years.

Notably, the Congress laid a foundation for merger of the Federation with the Association a year later. All members of state societies associated with the Federation were admitted to the Association. Other national groups disappeared from the scene. A truly national organization of professional accountants was emerging.

In 1905 also, arrangements were made to take over a magazine launched by the Illinois Society, under the title *The Auditor*. The name was changed to *The Journal of Accountancy*, the first issue of which appeared in November 1905. It has been published ever since, under the editorial control of the American Association and its successor organizations.

In spite of disappointments and discouragements the Association had stuck to its guns. The little band of leaders who did most of the work kept on trying, and in the second decade their efforts began to be rewarded. They knew what it took to create a profession and they developed momentum in the right direction.

By 1906, the end of the first 20 years, the survivors could look back with satisfaction on their efforts. Their Association had become a going concern. It had 341 members and associates, from 25 states and two foreign countries. To be sure, the majority—200 of the members—resided in New York. But the foundations of a nationwide profession were being laid.

CHAPTER 7

Education and CPA Standards

T HE lack of adequate technical and ethical standards was not the only serious weakness in the structure of the aspiring accounting profession prior to 1917.

The standards for admission to the profession—for accreditation as a competent public accountant—were all over the lot. While accounting practice followed business activities across state lines, and while bankers and government agencies were beginning to urge uniformity in auditing and accounting, the requirements for recognition as a professional accountant were in the hands of the states which had enacted CPA laws. From state to state these requirements, including the level of examinations, ranged from very good to very poor.

Membership in the American Association, following the 1905 merger with the Federation, was attained mainly through membership in an affiliated state society. Where there were no CPA laws as yet, the state societies consisted of public accountants who had passed no examination at all, and whose education and experience had not been effectively evaluated by any common measurement device.

This untidiness was especially galling to the Association's leaders in the light of the shining examples across the Atlantic —the Scottish and English chartered accountants—whose societies and institutes had by 1905 established elaborate systems of training and examinations for those who sought the chartered accountant title.

These rigorous requirements were largely responsible for the prestige of the British accountants, which overshadowed that of the Americans—even in the United States.

404   If the Association had been able to secure authority comparable to that conveyed by the English Institute's Royal Charter, it is quite likely that the apprenticeship system established by the English chartered accountants would have been imitated in the United States. In that event the teaching of accounting in colleges and universities might have been delayed for many years—until the apprenticeship system proved unworkable, as it certainly would have in this country, and indeed may ultimately prove to be in England.

But the old Association was in no position to set itself up as a "qualifying body." Not only had it no legal authority to do so, but it had a hard enough time to attract members when the only requirement for admission was a few years of undefined experience in public accounting. In the circumstances the best way to create a supply of qualified recruits was through some formal educational process.

Efforts to Improve Accounting Education

It will be recalled that one of the first major efforts of the Association was an abortive attempt to establish a school of accounting. This failed, but it demonstrated the need, and several proprietary schools, as well as a few recognized universities, set about filling the vacuum.

The Association's interest in accounting education continued through the years.

At the 1907 annual meeting, Joseph French Johnson, Dean of the New York University School of Commerce, Accounts and Finance (and, incidentally, editor of *The Journal of Accountancy*) read a paper on accountancy education.

He said that ten years before only one university had recognized accountancy in its catalogue—the Wharton School of Finance at the University of Pennsylvania. However, in the past ten years a dozen or more institutions had followed the Wharton School's example: New York University in 1900, and then the Universities of Wisconsin, Illinois, California, Chicago, Michigan, Vermont, and Kansas, the Cincinnati School of Commerce and Accounts, and Harvard University. In addition, Dartmouth College had founded its graduate business school, The Amos Tuck School.

405

Dean Johnson predicted that in the next ten to 15 years CPAs would be receiving training not only in the use of figures, but in subjects that covered the whole field of the science of business. "I do not believe," he said, "the profession will receive the recognition from the public which is its due until we recognize the fact that a very broad and liberal education, a thorough education, is necessary to its professional practice." Five university professors commented on Dean Johnson's paper. All of them supported the idea of broader and better training of accountants at the universities.

From 1908 to 1916 the Association's committee on education—for most of the time under the chairmanship of Waldron H. Rand, head of his own firm in Boston—submitted a series of impressive reports. It kept close track of additions to the list of institutions which taught accounting, just what courses were being taught, what the Association's members thought should be taught, and related matters.

For example, in 1908 the committee reported the creation

of the Harvard Graduate School of Business Administration, and stated that several well-known members of the Association were among the lecturers. It also reported that several institutions had been added to the list of those providing instruction in accounting: Northwestern University, and the Universities of Minnesota and Colorado. In Boston an evening School of Commerce, Accounts and Finance had been established in connection with the YMCA. In St. Louis a new College of Law and Finance included accountancy in the curriculum.

In 1911 the committee reported results of a survey of all state universities and other institutions which had over 100 instructors or 1,000 students. The objective was to find out the exact status of higher education in commercial subjects, and particularly accounting. An elaborate questionnaire had been developed and sent to 100 institutions. Forty-three replies were received, from which it was learned that The Amos Tuck School, the Harvard Business School and 16 other institutions were giving courses in accounting and commerce.

In 1913 the committee reported results of a survey of Association members' opinions as to the subjects which should be included in the education of a certified public accountant. Commercial law, auditing, theory of accounts and economics attracted the largest number of votes. Finance, banking, organization management, penmanship and commercial arithmetic came next. (In contrast with attitudes of later days, English was not mentioned among all the other subjects suggested!)

The committee also presented an analysis of the requirements for the CPA certificate in those states which had passed CPA laws up to July 1913. The analysis showed wide variation in education and experience requirements, as well as variation in the subject matter of the examinations.

In 1916 the committee for the first time submitted a report on the experience requirement. A questionnaire had been sent to the state boards of accountancy, most of which indicated that they did not equate bookkeeping with practical accounting experience, that education in accounting was not deemed to be the equivalent of actual public practice, and that experience gained as a junior staff assistant with a reputable firm of public accountants was acceptable.

The 1916 report also described "laboratory" methods adopted in some of the colleges and universities which gave accounting courses.

A notable example was the accountancy laboratory installed at Columbia University, under the direction of the ubiquitous Robert H. Montgomery. The laboratory consisted of accounting records and some complete sets of books of business enterprises which had been discontinued by dissolution or bankruptcy. In addition there were a few "model" sets of books and collateral records, such as minute books, stock certificate books, and transfer books. 407

The laboratory also included a file of annual reports and statistical data from leading companies, together with organization charts, descriptions of systems in use, and similar material. Also the laboratory was expected to maintain an exhibit of office appliances, bookkeeping machines, and so on. All this was designed to give the student contact with the real world of accounting, as well as with the theory of the subject.

At New York University, John R. Wildman, both a teacher and a partner of Haskins & Sells, proposed a plan under which the student would be called upon to do accounting work under the supervision of a CPA, mainly in the audit of various charitable organizations, which it was said as a rule could not afford to pay for such service. In this proposal was the seed of the "internship programs" later attempted in conjunction with the formal educational process.

The Association's hardworking committee on education performed a useful service. By repeated questionnaires and correspondence, it continually reminded the university community of the profession's keen interest in accounting education. This undoubtedly encouraged the introduction of the subject in more and more institutions.

Furthermore, the committee's surveys identified significant interrelationships—between CPA requirements and education, for example, and between education and experience. These re-

lationships involved thorny problems which remained un-
solved for many years to come, but they were made sufficiently
visible to permit a start toward solutions.

Professional Literature

In those days there was not much technical literature with
which teachers and students could work.

One of the most valuable contributions by the Association
was its sponsorship of *The Journal of Accountancy*. It was the
principal medium—virtually the only medium for many years
—for the interchange of information, ideas and opinions among
both schools and practitioners throughout the nation.

From the time of the Association takeover in 1905 the *Journal* had the benefit of intelligent and imaginative editorial
guidance. The first editors were Dean Johnson, of NYU, and
Dr. Edward Sherwood Meade, Director of the Evening School
of Accounts and Finance, University of Pennsylvania. In 1912
A. P. Richardson, the new secretary of the Association, assumed also the post of editor. However, Dean Johnson continued as consulting editor until 1915.

The leaders of the Association were also the mainstays of
the *Journal*. Volume 1, No. 1, published in November 1905,
contained excellent articles by Messrs. Sterrett, Dickinson and
Montgomery.

Although the editors complained periodically, as editors are
wont to do, about the lack of enough manuscripts of high
quality, the content of the *Journal* in its first decade was sur-
prisingly good, considering its limited circulation and its financial difficulties.

It was first published by the Accountancy Publishing Company which was controlled by the Association. Stock in this
company was sold to members of the Association.

By 1909 the circulation of the *Journal* was almost 2,000, but in 1910 it had sunk to 1,625, including only 219 members of the Association—much to the disappointment of the leaders. The magazine was having trouble in making ends meet. However, by 1914 circulation had risen to nearly 5,000, and almost half of the Association members had become subscribers.

An arrangement was then made with The Ronald Press Company, which contracted to publish the *Journal,* with editorial control remaining in the Association.

In 1916 the magazine had become a going concern. This was its most prosperous year to date. For the past three years it had been on a paying basis. Circulation was maintained at about 5,000, and advertising volume had grown. Profits were divided between The Ronald Press Company and the Association, which received some $2,900 as its share, of which $1,160 was devoted to payment of debts of the Accountancy Publishing Company. This practically wiped out the obligation to the creditors of that organization.

Aside from the *Journal,* however, there was an embarrassing paucity of American accountancy literature.

The most important book available was the American edition of *Auditing: A Practical Manual for Auditors,* by Lawrence R. Dicksee, professor of accounting at the University of Birmingham, England. The American version was edited by the amazing Robert H. Montgomery.

Dicksee's *Auditing,* first published in 1892, was a standard work on the subject in England. But so large a part of it was occupied with analysis of English court decisions and discussion of English practice that it was not applicable to the United States. Mr. Montgomery's adaptation contained only those portions adapted to American needs. Later American editions evolved into "Montgomery's *Auditing.*"

The *Journal* for February and April 1908 carried articles on accounting literature by Leo Greendlinger, instructor in accounting at New York University. He said, "We not only do not possess a body of accountancy literature that could be called American, but if we inquire in some of our libraries or book stores for accounting books we generally receive the answer, 'You mean bookkeeping books.' "

The articles listed the available accounting literature for study or reference. In all they described some 130 books, including many dealing with special industry accounts, a number of books on cost accounting, and a number on auditing, prominent among which was Montgomery's American edition of Dicksee's *Auditing*. However, even some of the books included in this list were of English origin.

The extension of accounting courses in colleges and universities and the emergence of a number of distinguished accounting professors were soon to result in a number of textbooks and other publications, some of which became classics. In 1908 and 1909, for example, several outstanding books on accounting were published which served as a basis for instruction at the universities, and to a considerable extent as authority for practitioners for many years to come. They were Charles Ezra Sprague's *The Philosophy of Accounts*, William Morse Cole's *Accounts—Their Construction and Interpretation*, and Henry Rand Hatfield's *Modern Accounting*.

In the first 30 years of its existence, however, the American accounting profession had little native technical literature with which to work.

The CPA Movement

As a sponsor of the first CPA law, the Association was naturally dedicated to the enactment of similar legislation throughout the nation. Through merger with the Federation in 1905 the Association became in effect a federation of state societies. Inevitably it was the Association's official policy to encourage and assist state societies in bringing about enactment of sound CPA legislation. To this end, its committee on state legislation drafted a model CPA law.

The numbers of states enacting CPA laws increased rapidly. Almost every year one or more states were added to the list. By 1914 there were 33 "CPA states," and it was predicted that by 1916 there would be 40.

But gradually there were signs of disenchantment on the part of the Association's leadership with the diversity of requirements in the various laws, with questionable administration in some cases, with wide fluctuations in the level of the examinations among the states, and with the difficulty of establishing reciprocity among the states. Thoughts turned again to the desirability of obtaining recognition of the profession by the federal government.

The Association tried to prevent enactment of undesirable CPA laws, but occasionally failed. Sometimes it was not informed early enough. Sometimes, no doubt, its advice was ignored. Sometimes state societies were simply not strong enough politically to prevent enactment of objectionable provisions.

A case was cited in which CPA certificates originally issued without examination—"waiver certificates"—were made available to anyone who had any bookkeeping experience. In another instance an amendment to an existing law, subsequent to issuance of waiver certificates at the time of enactment, permitted issuance of CPA certificates without examination on affidavit that candidates had been in public practice for five years. Efforts to lower standards were not uncommon, and political influence on legislatures and on state board appointments was a cause of constant concern.

Even sound laws were not always well administered. Some state boards were too lax, others too tough. There were cases in which circumstances strongly suggested that state board members who were practicing accounting deliberately limited the number of CPA certificates issued—in order to minimize competition with themselves!

In 1908 a banker, James G. Cannon, addressed the American Association's annual meeting on "The Relation of the Banker to the Public Accountant." Described as a sincere friend of the profession and a bank president of influence, Mr. Cannon criticized the results of the requirements for the CPA certificate. He stated that of 617 candidates who tried the CPA examination in New York over a ten-year period, 409 were rejected. Possible reasons, he suggested, were a monopolistic intention on the part of the examiners or those who influenced them, "catch questions" in the practical accounting part of the examination, and inadequacy in the education or training of the candidates.

In 1913, the New York State Education Department reported: "There were 134 candidates who took the CPA examination, six of whom have passed in all topics." Two reasons were suggested for the failures: lack of education and training on the part of the applicants, and the character of the examinations themselves.

412

On the first count the New York State Regents stiffened the requirements for admission to the CPA examination, by providing that a candidate must have had five years' experience in the practice of accountancy, at least two of which must have been in the employ of a certified public accountant in active practice, in no less grade than that of a junior accountant.

The *Journal* applauded this change as one that would eliminate a large proportion of the unqualified applicants who were likely to fail the examination. However, the editorial did suggest that candidates who had done advanced work at schools of the highest type, "such as the Graduate School of Business Administration at Harvard—to take an illustration at a safe distance," might get credit for two years against the experience requirement.

On other occasions spokesmen for the profession deplored the elementary nature of the examinations for the CPA certificate in some states. It was said that the examinations were often too simple to serve as a standard for admission to a profession. A pleasing contrast was noted in the questions set by the Pennsylvania Board of Examiners of Public Accountants. Passing this examination, it was said, would require more than "cramming in three subjects and guessing in a fourth."

Reciprocity among the states was another goal toward which

the Association struggled with varying success. It was not until 1913, 17 years after enactment of the New York CPA law, that an amendment was enacted permitting issuance of New York CPA certificates to CPAs of other states. Yet, as the *Journal* said, "A large percentage of the practicing accountants [in New York] had been CPAs of other states, and while there was no reciprocity clause in the New York law it was impossible for those accountants to obtain the New York degree unless they elected to take the examination—an alternative not seriously to be considered by men who had already fulfilled the requirements of other boards."

The Association's committee on state legislation in 1916 recommended that the Association endorse the principle of reciprocity among states, without regard to place of residence. "The practice of accounting is so largely of an interstate nature," said the committee, "that we believe this matter should receive the careful consideration of an action on the part of the Association."

However, the variations in preliminary requirements and in the level of examinations enormously increased the difficulty of achieving reciprocity on a broad scale. States with higher standards were naturally reluctant to issue certificates to CPAs of other states whose standards were notoriously lower.

A hopeful sign appeared in 1916. The state boards of examiners in Missouri and Kansas collaborated in the preparation of a single CPA examination to be used in both states. Said the *Journal*, "The harmonious way in which this cooperative method has been brought about should encourage other states, particularly those which are near neighbors, to put into practice a principle which tends toward that uniformity of standard which is the aim of every friend of CPA legislation."

This incident may have started the thinking which soon led to the beginnings of a uniform written examination, ultimately adopted by all state boards of accountancy.

In addition to screening candidates, state boards had to concern themselves with unauthorized use of the initials "CPA."

In New York in 1913 a magistrate decided a case against

413

certain public accountants who were using the letters "CPA" after their names without having complied with the provisions of the CPA law. It was held that the use of the letters "CPA" was permissible only to persons who had complied with the law; that a person could not use the letters "CPA" in New York simply because he was a CPA of another state; and that although a firm name was used by public accountants, and one of its members was a certified public accountant, the letters "CPA" could be used only with his individual name.

At the time this evidently was an important precedent. "For many years," the *Journal* noted, "it has been a moot point whether or not the title authorized by the act could be restricted to those persons holding the degree under authority of the state in which they practice."

414

Even before such basic questions as this had been settled, even before some states had enacted CPA laws, even before the public had begun to learn the difference between a CPA and a public accountant, there was talk of restricting the practice of accounting to certified public accountants.

The regulation of the practice of law and medicine was cited as precedent. Naturally the idea had strong appeal. It was utterly impracticable at this stage of the profession's development, but it was bound to be tried out before long—and to become a source of internal conflict.

As the historic year of 1916 approached, the CPA movement, from a national viewpoint, looked extremely untidy. The prospect of uniformity of standards seemed hopeless. Time, energy and money were being expended by state societies, and to a lesser extent by the Association, on legislative and administrative problems which seemed almost insoluble. It appeared that little progress was being made in meeting the urgent needs for better education and training, higher standards of competence, and strengthened public confidence in CPAs.

More and more frequently mention was made of the possibility of federal CPA legislation.

And so decisions were made and steps were taken which in a few years resulted in splitting the profession in half. It took

15 years to put it together again. The experience was painful, but instructive.

In any event it settled some things, and in the end provided a foundation for the growth and development of the profession on a scale beyond the wildest dreams of those who were about to try a new approach to its problems.

415

The Accounting Review

VOL. XXVI JANUARY, 1951 NO. 1

EARLY DEVELOPMENTS IN AMERICAN AUDITING

C. A. MOYER

Professor, University of Illinois

IT IS NATURAL that recent developments in auditing receive considerable attention from accountants. However, early developments and an examination of the influences which brought about these early changes, in addition to being interesting in themselves, may lead to a better understanding of what is happening in the present and may offer clues to what future trends may be. The literature and other information available which relates to auditing in America up to about the beginning of the twentieth century seem to indicate that auditing was then completing its first major phase of development.

The first audits in America were of course patterned after the British general audit. In fact, much of the auditing work was done by visiting British auditors retained by British investors in American corporations. It is generally recognized that auditing in Great Britain had been instituted to a great extent by specific statutory requirements. The principal function of an audit was considered to be an examination of the report of stewardship of corporation directors, and the most important duty of the auditor was to detect fraud. The search for defalcations resulted in a minute, painstaking check of the bookkeeping work done by the employees of the client. Almost all of the time of the auditor's staff was devoted to checking footings and postings in detail, in looking for bookkeeping errors, and in comparing the balances in the ledger with the trial balance and with the statements.

This detailed type of audit was no doubt well-suited to British needs at the time. No attempt will be made in this discussion to trace the influences which led to the extensive general audit required by statute in Great Britain. It is probably sufficient to point out that the early industrial history and the practices of early corporations in Great Britain were primarily responsible for the establishment of required audits in connection with reports to stockholders.

Inasmuch as statutory audits were not present in America, and British auditors were available to do much of the work, the accounting profession grew slowly in this country in the nineteenth century until near the turn of the century. A study of occupational directories[1] shows that in New York City, 31 local practitioners were listed as public accountants in 1880, 66 in 1890, and 183 in 1899. In the city of Chicago only 3 were listed in 1880, 24 in 1890, and 71 in 1899. Display advertisements published in the same directories

---

[1] "Directory of Early American Public Accountants," Bulletin No. 62, Bureau of Economic and Business Research, University of Illinois, 1942.

give some idea of the type of service offered to the public.

> "Complicated, disputed and confused accounts, also accounts of executors, trustees and estates in assignment investigated and stated. Books opened and closed. Suspected accounts confidently examined. Partnership settlements made" (1881).
>
> "Books opened and closed, commercial branches taught. Highly recommended by banks, business houses. Proving arithmetic, detecting errors in trial balance, computing interest and discount, averaging accounts" (1886).
>
> "Railroad, industrial, banking, commercial, corporation, syndicate, and general accounting. Books designed, opened, kept, examined, adjusted, audited and balanced" (1894).

Announcements of this nature indicate to some extent the nature of American auditing during this early period and also reflect the influence of British auditing upon early American practice. In the first edition of his text,[2] Robert H. Montgomery, a contemporary observer, called the early audits "bookkeeper audits." The program of examination usually consisted of vouching all cash disbursements, checking all footings and postings, checking the ledger to the trial balance and the trial balance to the financial statements (pp. 80–81). He estimated that three-fourths of the audit time was spent on footings and postings, whereas experience had shown that three-fourths of the defalcations were hidden by failures to account for income or cash receipts (p. 258).

In a backward look over his career[3] the same author later repeated the opinion: "Much of our time in those days was consumed in the endless checking of postings from one book to another" (p. 14). "Frequently books had been out of balance for months or years, and the finding of the errors was a terrific task. . . . In some audits, and not only small ones, we verified

every footing and every posting" (p. 19). The auditor fifty years ago . . . "was little recognized because the matters which were referred to him were relatively unimportant and this unimportance tended to reduce him to the level of a clerk" (p. 316).

Little auditing literature appeared in America during the nineteenth century, but the small amount available does throw some light upon the changes taking place.

H. J. Mettenheim's *Auditor's Guide* appeared in 1869. Its sixteen pages hardly furnish a guide to auditing. Suggestions are given for preventing fraud: require all entries to be clear, full, explicit; rule in money columns to prevent slovenly work; make it the duty of the cashier to have a voucher for every payment; require a record of the detailed composition of every bank deposit. Directions are given so the proprietor can audit his own cash book "as an easy and pleasant summer recreation": test the cash book additions; look for forced balances, for offsetting errors, for payments on spurious notes payable, and for charges to merchandise of expenses that should go to the bookkeeper's personal account.

G. P. Greer's *Science of Accounts*, published in 1882, contained some significant sections, some of which are summarized below:

> General remarks: Proof should be sought outside the books in the statements of debtors and creditors themselves for comparison with the books; for example, call in the pass books of the depositors in a bank under audit. Watch for omitted postings from the books of original entry; where totals are not passed through the journal, omissions easily occur. When the receipts and disbursements pass through the hands of a treasurer and cashier, and different collecting or disbursing clerks, the accounts should be arranged to check and prove each other. All obligations of the corporation should be authorized by vote of the directors. All payments of large amount should be made by check or draft on a bank of deposit.
>
> Capital stock: Critically compare the original issue and subsequent issues with the

---

[2] *Auditing Theory and Practice*, Ronald Press, New York, 1912.
[3] *Fifty Years of Accountancy*, privately printed, 1939.

journal entries and stock ledger. Compare transferred stock with the stock ledger, transfer book, cancelled certificate, and stub outstanding. Compare the stub total with the capital stock account, "great care being taken to detect, if possible, the overissue of stock, if any there be, or any errors in the transfer and cancellation of legitimate shares." Analyze and compare the reserve fund and surplus profits with the dividend account, the amount of net profit, and the requirements of statutory law.

Cash: Trace receipts to sources, and payments to purposes for which disbursed; count and scrutinize the cash on hand, verify cash on deposit by bank pass book or official statement.

Accounts receivable: Trace to origin and check the valuation estimated; as to accounts past due or long unsettled, inquire regarding the cause, and investigate the parties' standing.

The author also describes procedures to be followed for examination of real property, losses other than regular expenses, accounts and bills payable, and bills receivable. He describes the inter-comparison of ledger, trial balance, closing entries, balance sheet, and profit and loss statement, but does not mention footings and postings. Apparently he does not attempt to describe a "complete audit" as it was known at that time, but it is significant that the procedures suggested involve the securing of evidence outside the books for certain of the assets and liabilities. This outline indicates that something different than a "bookkeeper audit" was being developed.

New York State adopted its first CPA law in August, 1896. A book of unofficial answers to examination questions appeared soon after several examinations had been given. This was *The American Accountant's Manual* by Broaker and Chapman. One of the questions on auditing was this: "In an audit where an exhaustive detailed examination of the books is not stipulated or not practicable, what examination is essential to assure their general correctness?" The authors' answer was:

"An audit under limitations may imply any degree of thoroughness from an exhaustive examination of every detail to a mere cursory review of generalities, the object of each particular audit and the opportunities afforded in each case governing the extent to which it may be carried.

"However, to insure the general correctness of the accounts, the footings of all the books of original entry should be verified, journal entries of an exceptional character scrutinized, and the postings to all nominal, representative and special accounts, both as to aggregate amounts and separate items, should be checked. An audit, to be at all effective, should also include the examination of vouchers for all cash payments and the verification of the final cash balance.

"While such an audit is distinguished by the commission to check the postings to the individual customers' and creditors' accounts throughout, it is practicable where advanced systems of bookkeeping are employed to agree them in the aggregate, and it is advisable in any event to call over a few of the postings to the individual accounts covering a day here and there, and in like manner to examine invoices for purchases, and check extensions for a partial test of their accuracy."

It should be noted that "in an audit where an exhaustive detailed examination of the books is not stipulated or not practicable" it was still considered necessary to foot all books of original entry, to check all postings to the general ledger, and to vouch all cash payments. However, it was considered acceptable procedure to reduce the time required, by omitting or merely testing the postings to the personal accounts, and similarly examining only part of the invoices for purchases, and checking only part of the extensions.

F. S. Tipson, a New York CPA, published his *Auditing* in 1904, in which he used the auditing questions given in New York from 1896 to 1902. Several of the questions involved conditions where it was not feasible to conduct a complete examination. His answers showed some shortening of the program by sampling, but indicated that all books of original

419

entry should be footed, and that the cash book transactions should be vouched completely. Also, "the balance sheet should be taken in hand, to see that it is a fair expression of the Assets and Liabilities of the business as of the date it bears on its face."

By the end of the nineteenth century the literature and practice reflected quite clearly the direction being taken in American auditing as British audit procedures became adapted to American needs. A memorandum of interim work done in advance of a year-end audit, which was copied by permission from the files of one of the oldest firms in this country, probably shows the changes taking place more clearly than does the literature. The work performed covered nine months of the client's business ending September 30, 1900.

420

> Counted cash on hand.
> Checked bank reconcilements.
> Checked vouchers with cash book, also deposits to bank, and pay roll into cash book to October 23, 1900.
> Checked postings of monthly total from cash book to general ledger from January 1 to September 30—also postings of general ledger column in cash book to general ledger for July, August, and September.
> Checked postings from Journal to General Ledger for July, August, and September, and monthly totals from Journal to General Ledger for nine months ending September 30.
> Checked monthly totals of Invoice Book to General Ledger for nine months ending September 30.
> Checked monthly totals from Returns Book to General Ledger for period.
> Checked Sales Ledger monthly totals to General Ledger for period. .
> Checked Settlement Book monthly totals to General Ledger for period.
> Checked entries from Settlement Book to Cash Book for January, February, and March.
> Checked monthly totals of Stock Journal to General Ledger for period.
> Checked footings of monthly summaries in Invoice Book.
> Analysed following accounts:
>> Merchandise account.
>> Manufacturing account.

> General Expense account.
> Machinery account.
> Boston Improvement account.
> New York Improvement account.
> Verified footings of Pay Roll for July, 1900.
> Checked following trial balances:
>> General Ledger.
>> Sales Ledgers Notes Receivable.
>> Stock Ledger (returned products).
>> Stock Ledger (Consignments).
>> Agencies (product).
>> Accounts Payable and Agents Ledger.

It should be noted that postings were checked completely only for monthly totals to the general ledger; other postings were checked for three months. The only footings checked were the monthly summaries in the invoice book, and the payrolls for one month. A number of important accounts were anlayzed. This technique was not emphasized in contemporary writings, but its use was expanded rapidly in practice.

A book of selected articles under the title of *The Science and Practice of Auditing* was compiled in 1903 by E. H. Beach and W. W. Thorne. This book reproduced some of the few contributions which had been written in this country on auditing but did not present a unified, comprehensive treatment of the subject. Most of the material was very compact and stressed the mechanical details of auditing. For example, the opening paragraph of the "general program or auditing plan" contained in an article by the two authors reads as follows:

> "Check all postings, at least all those in the cash book and nominal and private ledgers. Vouch the cash book and petty cash book; check the additions thereof; verify the balances at bank and on hand. Check the ledger balances and additions of all ledgers; where all postings are not checked, compare the balances of each ledger with the corresponding adjustment account."

The conclusion is inescapable that no important American auditing literature had appeared up to this time. It is obvious however, that the "bookkeeper audits," modeled after British general audits of directors' stewardship and directed toward discovery of defalcations, did not continue to be typical American audits. Frank G. Short, a professional accountant who has had extended experience in auditing practice in the United States, describes this transition as being a change from detailed audits to test audits. Auditors incorporated the idea that "it was not necessary to make a detailed examination of every entry, footing, and posting during the period in order to get the substance of the value which resulted from an audit . . . the second phase of the development of auditing retained the viewpoint of the detailed auditor, but resulted in a less total quantity (and cost) of detailed audit work."[4]

Although the adoption of sampling procedures probably represented the most important development in auditing during this period, other changes were beginning to appear, as indicated in the preceding references. Account analysis was playing a more important part in the audit program. This development also seems to represent no departure from the point of view of the detailed auditors, for it seems to represent originally a substitute for the enormous quantity of detailed audit work formerly done in audits.

A third development during this period does seem to portray the beginning of a difference in point of view by the auditor. Methods adopted for verification of transactions by securing of evidence outside the records of the client implies that auditors were finding it desirable and necessary to consider more than mere clerical accuracy and detection of fraud. Closer examination of the valuations of assets and liabilities also reflects the beginning of the assumption by the profession of broader audit objectives.

[4] "Internal Control from the Viewpoint of the Auditor," *The Journal of Accountancy*, Sept., 1940, p. 226.

These developments did not just happen. Although the first audits in the United States were patterned after British audits, changes occurred gradually which represented adaptations of earlier procedures to American business conditions and American needs. Some of the many factors which had an influence on early American auditing are discussed briefly below.

Great Britain had found it desirable to require statutory audits. The United States was a new, expanding country with little industrial history behind it, and with no such requirements. In this country it was necessary that the benefits derived from an audit be apparent to a client in order that he would be willing to incur the cost of such an engagement. The detailed procedures followed in Great Britain soon were found to be too costly to clients who could decide for themselves whether or not an auditor was engaged. Consequently testing or sampling methods for checking footings and postings were introduced and more and more widely adopted as time passed. The necessity of reducing the audit time spent on checking bookkeeping details became more apparent as American businesses increased in size.

The many corporation mergers effected during the last decade of the nineteenth century increased the complexity of business operations in the United States and gave a considerable impetus to the accounting profession. For example, 199 consolidations or mergers were completed between 1885 and 1900; of these 78 were completed in 1899. The separate interests of the several established companies to be combined needed reliable data in order that the combination would be accomplished in an equitable manner. Dependable data on such things as earnings, property values, debts, and financial trends were needed, and professional accountants were called upon to supply this information. A new and broader opportunity for service thus opened up for American public accountants. Not only were they called upon to conduct audits of different scope and purpose than formerly, but also they often installed accounting systems for merged companies, assisted in reorganizations, and prepared statements for concerns in receivership or in bankruptcy.

Another important factor in this early period was the increasingly wide use of single-name paper for short term loans in place of other methods of short-term borrowing such as bills of exchange and trade acceptances. No attempt will be made to examine here the conditions after the Civil War which led to the widespread business practice of granting cash discounts and the resulting use of direct personal loans from banks. It is significant, however, that this method of short-term financing led to the

need for credit investigations. The services performed by professional accountants in this connection began to affect the procedures followed.

From this brief survey it will be evident that by the beginning of the twentieth century American auditing was still in an immature stage. Yet growth and change were taking place. Local conditions had brought about some new developments in procedure, most of which reflected the desire and the necessity of reducing the audit time spent on an engagement. Beneath the surface, however, the possibilities of audit services relating to the growing separation of management and owners, to credit granting, to system installations, and to various financial matters, were beginning to transform the detailed examinations of the bookkeeper's work into auditing as we have come to know it.

North Carolina, by retired partners Thomas G. Higgins and A. V. McPhee. The results of that meeting and an earlier interview, under the title "A Conversation with William Sutherland at the Age of Ninety," appeared in the Winter 1968 issue of this JOURNAL, from which the following excerpt is drawn.

WHEN WE GO BACK to the year 1903 we are going back, a long way in the accounting profession. I can dramatize this by pointing out that I arrived in Chicago a couple of months before the first Illinois CPA law was enacted and about eight months before the Illinois Society of Certified Public Accountants was organized.

So the first thing you must understand is that there was literally no accounting profession in existence in 1903—no established body of accounting theory that one could turn to, no precedents, and of course no "authorities." Whatever textbooks were then in existence dealt for the most part with double-entry bookkeeping, with very little being said about the theory and logic of accounting.

In the early days of the century there was no clear understanding of the role of the public accountant, and of course he had no status. Most people, I think, viewed him as a skilled bookkeeper who was an expert in figures and who might be called in in the event of irregularities or if the books were out of balance.

Companies in those days were very secretive, and most corporate officials had a strong conviction that accountants should be refused unlimited access to the books and records. It was a battle sometimes to see a contract or examine board minutes, although this battle was nothing compared with the inevitable battle that ensued when the accountant insisted on making disclosures in financial statements. I had some frightful experiences. Three or four times I was threatened with dismissal from jobs, and on two occasions I had to appeal to the board of directors. I was even threatened with physical violence on more than one occasion.

In those early days there was not much uniformity in accounting standards and procedures. Different companies handled similar transactions in different ways. Property exhaustion is a good example of this. Some companies provided for depreciation, others did not. Where there *was* a depreciation provision it was seldom calculated in any kind of systematic manner. Usually the amount provided was arbitrary and varied considerably from year to year, depending more or less on the whims of management. Likewise with capital expenditures—there was little uniformity between companies as to items capitalized and items charged to expense.

By today's standards the information contained in financial statements around the turn of the century was meager indeed. Of course there was not the present-day need for financial information. There were few outside investors, and many companies were still controlled by the original owner-manager group. Yet despite these inadequacies it is interesting to recall

423

Early Days of the Firm and the Profession

by William Sutherland

In 1967, just prior to William Sutherland's ninetieth birthday, he was interviewed at his home in Pinehurst,

32

how the quality of financial reporting improved from year to year, and of course this improvement is still going on.

Did our firm do much auditing work in its early days?

No, initially the firm's principal business was acting as agents for some British investment companies and placing money in real estate loans for some of the Scottish life insurance companies. Some of these investments were highly speculative. In those days there was not the emphasis on safety that there is today.

It was Stuart who had the aspiration to practice public accounting. He seemed to sense the growing need for accounting services in a country which was rapidly becoming industrialized. But while Stuart had the idea, not much auditing work developed until Arthur Young himself took charge. When I got to Chicago in 1903 the firm was pretty well on its way to developing an accounting practice, and as I recall it there was a staff of perhaps twenty people. I might say that I was more than surprised when I got to the Monadnock Building to find the firm listed in the notice board on the ground floor as "General Agents."

Could you tell us something about the competence of the audit staff in those early days?

It was not too good. You must remember that it wasn't until after World War I that the colleges and universities in America began to teach accounting and auditing seriously. Until the early 1920s our principal source of trained acountants was Great Britain. We obtained some competent men from that source, but the supply was limited and we had to fill in with men who had little experience other than some bookkeeping. I might also say that a lot of our early practice involved investigations and work in connection with mergers and consolidations. This kind of work was entirely outside the experience of the Britishers prior to their coming to the United States. In my own case, I came up against hundreds of problems for which there were no precedents whatever. We were pioneers, and I had the feeling on a number of occasions of being thrown into a lake and having to learn to swim or else.

424

William Sutherland (center), just before his ninetieth birthday in January 1968, with Thomas G. Higgins (left) and A. V. McPhee.

4 PRELUDE TO THE MODERN AGE

426

As more details are learned about the 1880's and the 1890's it becomes ever clearer that a great many occurrences in the last double decade of the nineteenth century played an important part in making it possible for accounting in the twentieth century to be what it is. [A. C. Littleton, 1946]

Political and Social Environment in the Gilded Age

Many consider the post World War II period as a time of unprecedented growth and change in American life. A study of the changing economic, social, political, and technological environment of the post–Civil War era indicates that these years were also ones of high opportunity, intense activity, and national achievement. It was the era of manifest destiny in the West beyond Missouri and unity among farmers of the Great Plains with the birth of the grange movement. In the East it was a time of capital intensive industrialization and urbanization as steam power and machinery brought about important changes in the demand for labor. The South, staggered by the consequences of the Civil War, submitted to a period of "reconstruction."

World power was on the horizon as the American nation moved away from a century-long tradition of isolation in global affairs. Inventions such as the incandescent light, patented by Thomas Edison in the 1880s, and the telephone, first used in Boston in 1876, foretold important changes. It was also an era of Scott Joplin's ragtime, Victorian morality, and the birth of the American golf, with the first club forming in New York City in 1888.

Youth found inspiration in "Horatio Alger" success stories about young people who turned pennies into fortunes through hard work and unceasing application of their talents in the marketplace. It was all at once the age of P. T. Barnum's showmanship, the industrial "robber barons," and unbridled competition among vast enterprises that were to form the first business trusts.

Cities swelled with the waves of Ellis Island immigrants who had viewed the Statue of Liberty as they entered New York harbor. The statue had been dedicated in 1886 as a gift of the people of France. In the thirty years spanning 1860 to 1890 America's population doubled from 31 million to 62 million (Schlesinger 1939: 132). By 1880 some business historians suggest, American had become a metropolitan economy although the population had not shifted to a predominantly urban pattern and would not for another thirty years.   427

Social Philosophy

During these decades before the turn of the century, businessmen were relatively unencumbered by government involvement in the carrying out of their pursuits. Americans held to the traditional belief of laissez-faire, the right of citizens to be left alone in their economic activities. This posture, combined with the rapid industrialization and growth of businesses, seemed justified in the hope of the benefits anticipated from economies of scale. Before the century ended, the misdeeds of laissez faire, cut throat competition, and the creation of trusts and monopolies would popularize the movement for a countering system of government regulatory controls over utilities and other major businesses that affected the interstate domain. Yet, these early government powers, once attained, would not be widely applied to check the abuses of corporate power until the early years of the twentieth century.

The model for the modern integrated industrial concern developed from the post–Civil War railroad merger movement, one of the most notable amalgamations being the creation of the New York Central System in 1867. Such combinations, it was demonstrated, made it possible for the public to receive better service at apparently lower prices. With the opening of the West, keynoted by the completion of the transcontinental railroad in 1869, it became possible for Americans to benefit from the superior efficiency of large scale rail operations. Travel from New York to Chicago had been cut to twenty-four hours from fifty hours as a result of Cornelius Vanderbilt's consolidation of the New York Central. Americans could travel coast to coast in a week versus months by ship. But an indirect price for this speed and efficiency included abuses such as corruption of public officials, watering of corporate stock, and manipulation of securities in unregulated stock markets, effectively transferring business control from the owners to the managers of corporations. Americans, however, still eschewed direct government involvement in the conduct of business. The potential for growth and the prospects of unlimited business opportunity supported the popular sentiment for unrestricted individual freedom in business (Cochran 1942: 122–123).

428

In January 1882, the Standard Oil Trust was formed and a new vehicle for consolidating corporate operations was initiated. The trust device was the brainchild of Samuel C. T. Dodd. After considering and discarding several forms wherein the Standard Oil Corporation could devise a legal structure to incorporate all its operations, Dodd recommended to Standard officials that they create a corporation in each state in which Standard had a major investment. Superimposed on these state corporations would be a "corporation of corporations,"—a trust, which would be, in terms of control, the only important vehicle. The trust would hold the voting stock of the subsidiary companies; trust certificates would be issued to the companies on a percentage basis according to the amount of stock contributed, and the management of the entire organization would reside in the trustees of the trust. The trust afforded Standard the opportunity to develop complete vertical integration of operations, including barrel making, pipelines, selling agencies, storage facilities and byproducts merchandising.[1] (Gressley 1971: 5).

Railroads, followed by more oil and then steel companies, were organized along the lines of the trust. Trusts also were formed in tobacco, sugar and coal. The money trust, banks, was the financial soul of the gilded age just as the railroads were the economic heart. Even as late as 1898, approximately 60 percent of the listings on the New York Stock Exchange were railroad securities. Federal legislation ultimately banned the trust vehicle, but large integrated corporations were then consolidated in other ways via modified legal frameworks, such that by 1901 the first billion dollar "super consolidation," the United States Steel Corporation, came into existence.

The Constitution and Case Law

In 1888 the Supreme Court affirmed that the protection under the due process clause of the Constitution was not, like that of the privileges and immunities clause, confined to citizens, but extended to all persons, including corporations. This decision reflected an earlier court ruling which recognized the corporate entity as an "artificial person," thereby extending the civil rights of the corporation to a point of practical advantage. Even smaller business operations began to adopt the corporate form. Prior to this, the corporate form had been of benefit mostly to financial institutions, insurance companies, railroads, and a few major industrials, with a major segment of American enterprise conducted in the partnership or proprietary form.

The Fourteenth Amendment, enacted in 1868 primarily to establish the Civil Rights of the recently freed slaves, also afforded the means for expanded federal involvement in the area of regulation of corporations. Corporations were "legal persons" and the Fourteenth 429 Amendment restricted states from discriminatory regulation against such corporate persons. In substance, states were preempted from regulating interstate corporations. The passage of the Fourteenth Amendment and the subsequent enactment of the Sherman Antitrust Law brought into effect the federal movement to regulate interstate corporations.

Urban workers and labor organizations grew in number and strength during this period. The long span of the post–Civil War period (1865–1890) saw hourly wages rise by nearly two-thirds. In the face of the continuing drop in the price level (deflation), "real" wages therefore increased even more. Labor groups combined to form the American Federation of Labor (AFL). At first numbering approximately 150,000, the AFL would increase to over 500,000 by the turn of the century and represent 90 percent of the skilled labor population. This increased strength of organized labor via unions sparked popular concern about shifts in power just as did the rise of the corporate trust structure. The 1890s were marked by violent strikes, including the Homestead Steel Strike in Pennsylvania and the bloody Pullman strikes in Chicago where workers seeking redress on wage reductions confronted government troops in the streets.

The Politics of the Gilded Age

A panic originating in the European money markets spread to the United States in 1873 causing corporate credit to crumble. This, when combined with the rumors of corruption in the federal government, brought about major economic disturbances (Fels 1951).

More than 5,000 concerns failed, and losses mounted to $220 million, a significant amount in those days. Three million workers were unemployed and farmers found that their grain could not be sold on the wheat markets. Conditions were aggravated by the revelation that several members of President Grant's administration held stock, for which they had never paid, in the Credit Mobilier, a holding company which had constructed the Union Pacific Railroad. The shares had been distributed by a congressman and an officer of the company, with the intention of receiving protection from government inquiry into company affairs.

430

The cloud of popular mistrust created by this scandal within the federal bureaucracy was to linger until the election of 1896. The 1896 election was one of the most intensely fought in American history. The East saw William Jennings Bryan as a threat to society as they knew it. His platform championed the free coinage of silver and opposed the gold standard. The election of 1896 resulted in a significant political realignment. Two years earlier, in 1894, the Republicans had secured control of the House with the largest gain in a congressional election in the nation's modern history. In that year the Democrats failed to return a single member to Congress in twenty-four states. The presidential race of 1896 revealed equally strong shifts in sentiment which favored the Republicans. An analysis of this change, although complex, revealed that it was caused largely by workers and immigrants who had blamed the Democrats for the severe depression sparked by the panic of 1893. Workers were suspicious of the economic interests of the farmers and organized western political elements (Hoffman 1956).

The panic of 1893, an intense contraction, was one of the most severe depressions in the history of the United States. Unemployment in manufacturing and transportation mounted to over 9 percent of the work force.

Although there may be dispute as to whether the 1880s or the 1890s was the period during which the economic momentum switched from agrarian to industrial, it is important to recognize that these decades together provide the formative influence for our culture in industrialized America.[2] For example, this era witnessed the birth of the modern city. Census data reveal that the number of cities with 8,000 or more inhabitants increased from just 280 in 1880 to over 500 by 1896. Many cities doubled in size and some, such as Chicago, showed spectacular rates of growth.

In the West, under the sponsorship of the Homestead Act, the population was drawn to farming and ranching. The "Go West Young Man" fever created the western version of a corporate buccaneer, namely, the cattle baron. Ambitious ranchers underwrote a series of Indian wars, and fought to free the land from native influence. Investors were attracted to the cattle industry in large numbers by the late 1870s. Subscribers to the stock in cattle companies were of varied ages and backgrounds: Boston dry goods merchants, land speculators, and southern land owners (Gressley 1971: 71). Mining speculation also attracted eastern investors, including stock brokers and other merchants from the midwest (Brewer 1976).

The Birth of the Modern Capital Market

After the 1870s, the failure of the gold supply to keep pace with money growth demands generated by industrial expansion enhanced the position of the investment banker who was skilled in managing and providing both cash and capital. Bankers controlled important power to determine and direct major economic decisions affecting capital structure, scope, and existence of developing businesses. Investment banking during the period between 1873 and 1884 in particular was characterized by the actions of J. P. Morgan. Initially in partnership as Drexel and Morgan, the operation was renamed J. P. Morgan and Co. in 1895. Morgan's first successful major venture was in 1879 when he became involved in marketing overseas stock for the Vanderbilt family to provide capital for the expansion of the New York Central, yet preserving control for the family. In exchange for his services he came to be appointed a member of the New York Central Board of Directors. Morgan's influence over this period through the year 1900 provides a guiding thread to the elements that affected the capital markets.

Railroads and their financing were the center of attention in the capital markets. The funds for railway construction came from bank credit and foreign exchange supplied by European investors. Every new burst of railway construction was met by a corresponding burst of investment from abroad, including England, Holland, and Germany. A boom that lasted from 1866 to 1873 was fueled by such investment; and when the depression of 1873 struck it took a heavy toll of foreign investors. By 1887 another depression had hit. English investors sold off to American investors at greatly reduced prices, the result being that Americans had gained ownership in the railroads at a small portion of the original investment. It was established that foreign investors had lost heavily, perhaps over $250 million on railroad bonds alone.

The House of Morgan survived the economic panics of the 1880s and 1890s. This survival itself enhanced its reputation and prestige. During the failures and panic of 1893, Morgan's money, expertise and organizational abilities aided many shaky railroad capital structures. Morgan put into effect reorganizational plans that permitted many of the railroads to survive. The essence of his reorganizational plan was to scale down fixed liabilities and exchange them for stock. If bondholders were unwilling to exchange their bonds for stock, they were persuaded to take bonds of lesser yield (Chamberlain 1974: 173).

It is impossible to consider this period of American industrialization without being drawn into a controversy that has engaged historians for the past half century. The names Morgan, Vanderbilt, Durant, Stanford and Fisk evoke a certain popular resentment because some industry leaders of the late nineteenth century were characterized as "robber barons." Were they robber barons or captains of industry? Josephson, who coined the robber barons term in a book of that name, electrified and outraged readers with what appeared to be indisputable data about the shameless buccaneers of capitalism. Yet historians note that the alleged predatory acts were accomplished only through collusion with and assistance from government officials.

432

The most important case in point is revealed in the story of the Credit Mobilier, the financial holding company that built the Union Pacific Railroad. The Mobilier scandal was brought to light by members of the House of Representatives and was a type of nineteenth century "Watergate." One of the House investigators summarized the situation by saying, "With absolute fairness we have striven to obtain the truth and in the sentence I declare in all the history, I never saw a scheme of villainy so profoundly arranged, so cunningly carried forward, so disastrously executed as this one disclosed in the report now submitted to the House." The corruption reached into all branches of President Grant's administration and into the offices of various members of Congress (Green 1959).

Not only through the Mobilier but in other ways during this era, railroad companies had received substantial subsidies from federal and state agencies. The Erie Railroad combine including Gould, Fisk and Drew made their fortunes through secret stock manipulations only because the New York legislature was dominated by public representatives whom the Erie group was known to control. Central Pacific Railroad's control over the legislature in Sacramento, California, ultimately led to that state's government granting monopolies over certain prize routes.

Yet not all of the railroads or their entrepreneur promoters were embroiled in this type of government sponsored chicanery. Unprotected and competitive railroads, such as those owned and controlled by Vanderbilt and Hill, grew without government-aided monopolies and were also known to be as profitable to their stockholders and probably less costly to their shippers. Although the eastern roads did not depend on illicit subsidies financed by taxpayers, they were characterized by sharp and often vicious competition for routes, in turn affording these roads the benefits of a legal monopoly without having to obtain the sanction of the government.

To assess the developments in this period, marked by the birth of many rail and industrial empires, it is important to consider that it may have been impossible to raise the large quantities of scarce capital required by such operations had it not been for the intense promotion of early entrepreneurs. The economy's appetite was almost boundlessly growth oriented. The success of investment bankers in early corporate promotion is suggested by statistics that by 1893 there were 1,250,000 shareholders out of a population of 62 million people in the United States. (This can be contrasted with the ownership for the post–World War II information in Figure 8-2.) The strong will and tactics of this early group of "captains of industry" in large part accounted for the establishment of an efficient corporate form of enterprise in a period when any other form of organization, given the nature of the market, might not have similarly provided for growth. 433

In 1889 the daily *Wall Street Journal* began publication, assuring a comprehensive source of investment news to supplement other weekly published sources. By 1890 tickers and telephones were commonplace and it was possible to instantaneously transmit stock trading data to points far beyond Wall Street. By the turn of the century New York's Wall Street was about to emerge as the leading location of international finance surpassing London's Lombard Street. This rise in the influence of American capital markets came quickly and at the hands of but a few men, with little or no governmental regulation. These men virtually controlled America's business life: Morgan in banking and finance, Rockefeller in oil, Vanderbilt in railroads, Carnegie in steel. These were the titans amidst the tycoons, men whose annual incomes were in the millions, who paid no income taxes, and whose control over organizations and battles with one another for the whole industrial empire are legend (Sobel 1965: 158).

A colorful insight into this group is found in a early biography of the Vanderbilt family. Commodore Vanderbilt had a personality about which no single statement could be more revealing than the following found in the text of a letter the old commodore sent to a competitor. "'You have undertaken to cheat me,' he wrote, 'I won't sue you for the law is too slow. I'll ruin you.' And he did" (Campbell 1941). The commodore's fortune, as did Carnegie's and Rockefeller's, ultimately provided the funding for a major private university.

Although one cannot condone their swashbuckling techniques, it is difficult to readily condemn them either. The force of the work ethic and the pace of change and opportunity nearly a century ago are not clearly perceived today. These forces were likely more complex and competitive than one can appreciate today and were an influence that shaped outcomes of countless entities beyond the enterprises of the "robber barons" themselves.

434

The economic environment of this era was also influenced by the fact that throughout the post–Civil War period there was a gradual but steady increase in purchasing power of the dollar brought about by general price deflation. Furthermore, the economy was beginning to change character. By 1880 the United States had entered into a metropolitan style economy characterized by the growth and significance of industrial urban areas as key points of demand, distribution, and political influence.

In addition to the East's industrial cities and capital markets, it is also important to recognize that in this era of manifest destiny, crops, land, mining, and cattle also played an important role in the functioning of the American capitalistic system. Both eastern and European investors were attracted to western mines, ranches, and cattle as investments. Furthermore, the abundant American wheat harvest of 1879 offset the disastrous European crop failures which had resulted from poor weather. This led to the export of millions of bushels of wheat per day and served as the source of an agricultural boom that finally led the American economy out of the serious depression which had lingered since 1873. Without these western investments and the strength of American agriculture, it is difficult to expect that our economy would have had a balanced attractiveness to investors at home or overseas.

The history of eastern investments in western mortgage companies, land, and cattle is interesting and involved. The conservative lending policies of major eastern capital sources led them to protect their customers from sustaining substantial losses in western investments. But, because they did not venture into high risk-return situations, the involvement of the conservative New York money sources did not in itself account for the entire capital of western ventures.

As the westward movement gained momentum after the Civil War, the demand for mortgage credit grew rapidly; at the same time, credit funds also grew rapidly in the East and in Europe. Important amounts of these funds were attracted by the temperament and potential of the West. Perhaps it was in part that the eastern investors were enchanted by the potential of the cattle industry, although researchers suggest that investments in cattle arose because the eastern investors had originally made investments in other areas of the West, usually mining, railroads or real estate. As such, investment in cattle was a part of an "associative spirit." Investors in the cattle industry included merchants, bankers, financiers, and industrialists, although there was also a small group of professional men. Names commonly found include those such as Marshall Field, the Chicago merchant; Teddy Roosevelt; August Busch; and David Goodrich.

435

By the end of the 1800s both the western manager and the eastern investor had learned a modicum about the economics of the cattle business. Expenses were closely scrutinized and curtailed, dividends were postponed as necessary, and improved procedures of operation were being adopted. Only when these business procedures were followed did cattle companies show an accounting ledger based profit. Intensive investment in the cattle industry from 1882 to 1885 represented the high point of activity. The low point came from 1886 to 1888 followed by a short period of recovery and a much larger resurgence from 1898 to 1900.[3] Thereafter, the cattle industry in the plains underwent a radical change wherein ranching became increasingly locally controlled.[4]

In 1884 following a panic in the economy, a Democrat was returned to the White House for the first time since the end of the Civil War. Whether this reflected public disenchantment with an administration tied to the Credit Mobilier or whether it indicated a new populism is not clear. Nearly simultaneous with the changing mood which brought the Democrats into power, there was a decline in the use of the trust as a device to direct the growth and expansion of corporations. Although trusts continued in existence through the turn of the century it was in the mid-1880s, perhaps in response to the panic of 1884, that the consolidated holding corporation began to emerge as an alternative to the trust as an operating and control mechanism.

With the creation of the Interstate Commerce Commission (1887) and the passage shortly thereafter of the Sherman Act (1890), the days of laissez-faire were coming to a close. These actions communicated a message that the federal government would respond to popular political pressures to curb the abuses of unrestrained competition and corporate monopoly. It would not be, however, until the early years of the twentieth century that the provisions of these laws would be enforced to the extent that there would be a curb on widespread trust abuses and monopolistic practices.

Accounting Reports, Financial Disclosure and Regulation

436

Financial reports before the turn of the century reflected the influence of the railroad corporation, the trust form of business, and the large manufacturing corporation. This section considers the format, content and influence of financial reports of the period including regulatory and legal aspects, the role that accounting systems played in internal administration of large organizations, and attempts by the private and public sectors to establish uniform accounts.

To consider this era without focusing on railroads would be inappropriate and ineffective, for railroad securities were the dominant factor in the capital markets. Increasing public interest in understanding railroad reports gave birth to financial analysis before the turn of the century. Among the early pioneers of financial analysis were Thomas F. Woodlock, John Moody, and a proponent of need for publicity of corporate accounts, Henry Clews. It was Clews, a noted author in financial circles, who suggested that expert accountants in the private sector could provide the requisite service needed for appropriate publicity of the corporate accounts. He stated that publicity could be accomplished by the employment of skilled accountants because certified results of their examinations would be accepted as conclusive. Thomas Woodlock's book, *The Anatomy of a Railroad Report*, was published in 1895 and acknowledged by others, including Moody, as a popular and authoritative presentation on the subject matter of railroad operations and financial reports.

Analysis of financial statements by banks, credit establishments and other institutions was an activity that affected the entire economy as evidenced by the fact that by 1900 there were more than a million individual stock owning investors.

Moody, a pioneer financial analyst, noted concern over matters of secrecy. In *How to Analyze Railroad Reports*, Moody observed that until the early 1890s balance sheet secrecy was a distressing characteristic of financial statement disclosure by railroads. For example, during the 1870s and 1880s the New York Central Railroad rendered no annual reports to its stockholders. Also, in responding to an inquiry from the New York Stock Exchange for financial information, the Delaware, Lackawana and Western Railroad, whose stock was also traded on the Exchange responded ". . . the Delaware, Lackawana and Western Railroad makes no report, publishes no statements, and . . . (has) not done anything of the kind for the last five years." (Sobel 1965: 85)

The secrecy surrounding financial affairs was cited in a 1900 government report on the subject. The report noted that "while the chief evil of large corporations is a lack of responsibility of the directors to the stockholders . . . the directors . . . practically never make reports to the individual shareholders for periods." The public's concern over disclosure was evidenced in a passage which appeared in the *Railroad Gazette* (January 6, 1893): "The annual report of a railroad is often a very blind document and the average shareholder taking one of these reports generally gives up before he begins."

437

Another common feature of accounting systems of this age was the use of the "private ledger" which was an account book equipped with a lock and key wherein were kept the capital expense accounts, the record of officers' salaries, controlling accounts of sales and purchases, and any other cumulative accounting information the firm desired to keep confidential. A partner or trusted employee posted the essential figures from the usual accounting records and only this person saw the trial balance and knew the condition of the important accounts (Roberts 1975).

British trained accountants in America had a convenient and authoritative set of examples, which could be modified and applied to the American scene from such sources as the British Companies Acts. A replacement method became widely adopted, under which the asset cost remained as book value, without regard for depreciation. An expense account was used to even out the differential in charges resulting from costs of renewal and maintenance. The Remington Arms Company, for example, showed no depreciation on their financial statements until after the turn of the century (Williamson 1952: 120, 402). Another factor affecting the development of an appropriate method for valuation of fixed assets in quasi-public corporations was the occurrence of a general price level decline in America. During the period of 1875 to 1900 there was an increase in purchasing power such that the historical cost values assigned to fixed assets, if not adjusted in book value for "wear and tear" or other loss in value, were in effect being *written* up by deflation. In addition to matters of technical accounting, political considerations significant to

AUG. 17, 1880.]

Let us add all these equations together into one, grouping those of the same letter.

$$(17.) \quad \begin{aligned} &(I + i_3 + i_5) \\ &+ (K + k) \\ &+ L \\ &+ U \\ &+ (V + v) \\ &+ W \\ &+ P \\ \\ &+ x_3 \end{aligned} \quad = \quad \begin{aligned} &(i + i_4 + i_6) \\ &+ k \\ &+ L \\ &+ U \\ \\ \\ &+ P \\ &+ Q \\ &+ x \\ &+ R \\ &+ Y \\ &+ Z \end{aligned}$$

80. Chronicles Transformed to History.—Examination will show that this grouping process has given us the materials for a history of each department of the business.

All the increase and decrease of cash, for example, is denoted by the terms $i_2 + i_3$ on one side, and $i + i_4 + i_5$ on the other.

31. Posting.—The grouping process is called in book-keeping "posting." The matter of the journal is re-written in a form known as the "**Ledger.**"

32. The Ledger.—This form of the equation differs from the journal in this: it allots a page or space, called an account, to each department of the business, just as in the above equation we alloted a line to each letter. The account must have two sides (just as the equation has,) one for the "debits" and one for the "credits." The journal is gone through line by line and dissected; each amount in the Dr. column is transferred to the Dr. side of the account named on the same line of the journal; each amount in the Cr. column is transferred to the Cr. side.

(*Continued.*)

THE READING RAILROAD COMPANY'S BOOKS.
(*Concluded.*)

The following is a copy of the last report made by the President and Managers for the information of stockholders, which was submitted January 12th, last past:

Dr. GENERAL BALANCE-SHEET OF THE PHILADELPHIA AND READING RAILROAD COMPANY, NOVEMBER 30, 1879. Cr.

CAPITAL ACCOUNTS:		CAPITAL ACCOUNTS:		
Railroad	$6,318,877.58	Total mortgage loans *		$7,903,877.94
Depots	4,194,711.39	6 pr. c. § debent'e loan, 1886-93, coupon	1,195,500.00	
Locomotive engines and cars	9,855,442.94	7 " § deb. conv " 1870-90	88,000.00	
Real estate	7,008,344.85	7 " § " " 1873-93	10,499,900.00	
Philadelphia, Reading and Pottsville Tel.	80,790.00	4 " § " " 1878-98	886,600.00	

438

82

East Pennsylvania Railroad Co. stock		[illegible]	
Reading and Columbia Railroad Co. stock		[illegible]	
Allentown Railroad Co. stock		320,582.99	
East Mahanoy Railroad Co. stock		247,295.61	
Mine Hill & Schuyl. Haven Railroad Co. stock		175,297.75	
Phila. and Reading Coal and Iron Co. stock		8,000,000.00	
Phila. and Reading Coal and Iron Co., bond and mortgage, July 1, 1874	29,737,965.53		
Phila. and Reading Coal and Iron Co. bond and mortgage, December 28th, 1876	10,000,000.00		
		39,737,965.53	
Steam-colliers		2,561,245.24	
Susquehanna Canal coal-barges		25,872.80	
Schuylkill Canal coal-barges		437,840.70	
Schuyl. Navigation Co. works and franchises		1,000,000.00	
		101,265,544.16	
Add:			
Schuylkill Canal new barges	22,410.44		
Less:			
Ballance of installments Susquehanna Canal new barges	4,424.35	17,986.09	
			101,283,530.25
ASSETS:			
Cash on hand	228,929.94		
Bills receivable	24,891.09		
Freight and toll bills receivable in December, 1879	778,581.36		
		1,032,402.39	
Stocks and bonds held by the Company		7,083,311.43	
Materials on hand		735,599.99	
Debts due to the Company:			
Sundry branch roads	1,730,298.05		
Philadelphia and Reading Coal and Iron Co	5,177,919.78		
Sundry accounts	1,653,207.19	8,561,425.02	
			17,862,738.83
Funded coupons not yet matured:			
Phila. & Reading Railroad Co. coupons	2,248,889.00		
Schuylkill Navigation Company "	123,000.00		
Susquehanna Canal Company "	230,195.00		
			2,602,084.00
Discount, commission and expenses of general mortgage loan, 1874—1908, issue of $10,000,000 in January, 1876			500,000.00
INCOME ACCOUNTS:			
Loss, per report November 30th, 1878		1,041,440.99	
Add loss year ending November 30th, 1879		1,063,421.73	
			2,104,862.72
			123,853,215.80

6 pr. c. deb. and guaran.	$3,470,[illegible].00			
6 " " " " fret'l	2,948.10			
6 " Gen mtg. gold $ or £	1,733,580.00			
6 " Perk. "guar" "	99,180.00	5,306,738.10		
			17,546,738.10	
Loan of Schuyl. Nav. Co., matu'g 1895		1,200,000.00		
" " " " " 1918		756,650.00		
" " " " " 1915		621,600.00		
		2,578,250.00		
Loan of E. Penna. R. R. Co. mt'g 1888		496,900.00		
			3,074,150.00	
				77,994,761.04
Common stock			32,726,375.28	
Preferred stock			1,551,800.00	
				34,278,175.28
LIABILITIES:				
Floating debt			7,550,079.54	
Debts due by the Company, including rentals, and principally for current business			1,572,665.48	
Wages, materials, drawbacks, and connecting roads for November business			870,911.18	
Coupons and interest on registered loans to December 1st, 1879, inclusive.			805,240.95	
State tax on capital stock and gross receipts			98,165.71	
Sinking fund loan, 1836-82			166,070.45	
Sinking fund Schuylkill Navigation Company improvement bonds			228,000.00	
Credit balance of insurance funds			347,298.65	
Credit balance of renewal fund			11,847.57	
				11,650,279.48
				123,853,215.80

* We have omitted the items which make up this amount, deeming it necessary only to give the aggregate of mortgage indebtedness.

Figure 4–1

A balance sheet of the Philadelphia and Reading Railroad Co., November 30, 1879.

Source: *The Book-Keeper*, 17 August 1880, p. 37.

the relationship between a regulated industries' rate for services and the capital asset rate base caused the issue of fixed asset accounting to be prominent.[5]   A view of the railroad as a quasi-public corporation, and a concern over the result of government influence on rate setting and return on railroad investments, focused attention on the value of capital assets and appropriate methods of accounting for the same. At first, the courts had not recognized the rights of regulated corporations or public service corporations to deduct depreciation in the determination of their rate base. By 1876 the Supreme Court did acknowledge the right of railroads to take depreciation yet it was not perceived to be an expense, in the sense of an expenditure, for railroad accounts were kept primarily on a cash basis. Later courts, in a fashion reflecting the 1898 Supreme Court decision, *Smyth* v. *Ames*, indicated that a "fair return to regulated industry could be based on the 'present value of the property,' " as opposed to historical cost as often used in early uniform systems.[6]

440

Without a depreciation expense concept, companies incurred costs for wear and maintenance and charged the amount to surplus accounts and avoided income statement disclosure. This practice was popular in those years when companies suffered falling profit margins. Moody described the practice as follows:

> In the past, especially, many railroads followed the policy of keeping down their current operating costs including maintenance but at the same time spending the necessary money on their properties and then at the close of the year deducting from the surplus shown above charges the amounts currently spent but not currently charged up. So in the final result they would have no surplus at all, and the item 'surplus above charges' or 'surplus above dividends' would simply be a book-keeping entry (Moody 1916: 170).

Moody goes on to say ". . . it is one of the strong arguments in favor of uniform accounting requirements that railroads coming under the jurisdiction of the interstate commerce commission cannot do this any longer. They are now required to charge to maintenance the items which properly belong there and can only put in improvement or betterment accounts the actual expenditures of such nature."

As early as 1880 business periodicals reviewed the subject of compulsory regulatory accounts. In 1889 an issue of *Office* magazine reported the speech of George Ramsdell, president of the Western Gas Association, regarding the lack of uniformity of gas company accounts and announcing the appointment of an association committee to investigate the lack of systematic accounting. These references suggest an awareness on the part of the practitioners and businessmen for self-regulation of accounting practice.

Concern over the fairness of reporting as indicated by Moody in part explains the justification for the creation of the Interstate Commerce Commission in 1887. In 1894 the commission established a system of accounts entitled, "The Classification of Operating Expenses."[7]

This act evidenced the birth of regulatory agencies, the fourth branch of modern federal government. With this focus on the classification of operating expenses at this point in time, it is evident in the literature of the period that earning capacity was becoming, in the words of John Moody, the factor that should be studied *"in advance of everything else"* (Moody 1916: 18).

How were the accountants to provide leadership in this complex of regulation and legal precedent? Would they be relegated to the status of "busy examiners of detail"? As these early pressures manifested themselves the emerging accounting profession was poorly organized in terms of institutions and literature to cope with public demands for financial reporting. Yet interesting and important precedents were being established. The first consolidated accounts were prepared for the American Cotton Oil Trust in 1886 and Maurice Peloubet suggests that consolidation accounting developed in the United States before it did in Great Britain. In Great Britain the appropriate disclosure for holding companies involved adjusting and amplifying the holding company investment account per se whereas in America there was a growing custom to take a consolidations approach to present a picture of the enterprise as if it were a whole. (Peloubet 1955: 31) This is an example of the ability of American accountants to benefit from the expertise of the British professional and at the same time to innovate, adapt, and progressively determine new and different schemes of disclosure in light of the different environment of the American capital market.

As the trust and holding corporations gained headway (Figure 4-2) popular writers and prominent authorities predicted that such businesses would fail. Their belief was founded upon the view that no one person or board of directors could successfully master such large organizations in a competitive environment. But accounting administrative control systems being developed during this period provided the information and means of direction to place at the disposal of management data factors relevant to operations. Steel companies, rubber companies, munitions works, and transportation, sugar, and refining companies provide examples of the success of such internal

441

management accounting system operations during this period for such large scale enterprises (Wildman 1914). In 1900, Collier surveyed the evolution of the business trust. A summary of his findings suggests the substantial financial structure and the diverse nature of this industrial device:

The Structure of Pre-1900 American Business Trusts

442

Product Process	Number of Trusts	Year(s) Established	Capitalization in Millions		
			Common Stock	Preferred Stock	Bonded Debt
Food	14	1887–1899	252	105	84
Distilling and Brewing	10	1894–1899	123	49	29
Tobacco	5	1890–1899	106	79	4
Paper	6	1898–1899	123	53	26
Textiles	6	1896–1899	160	56	16
Leather and Rubber	5	1892–1899	154	143	10
Wood	3	1892–1896	100	—	1
Glass and Clay	5	1890–1899	84	17	—
Chemicals, Oils and Paints	11	1882–1899	274	96	5
Iron and Steel	18	1887–1899	408	287	55
Machinery and Hardware	8	1893–1899	122	105	—
Electrical Manufacturers	11	1891–1899	140	40	10
Minerals, Metals, and Coal	6	1891–1899	121	47	4
Printing	1	1892	3	3	—
Warehousing	2	1895–1897	20	8	18
Cement, Munitions, and Other	7	1889–1899	119	43	—
			2,309	1,131	352

Source: W. M. Collier, *The Trusts, What Can We Do With Them? What Can They Do For Us?* (New York: Baker and Taylor, 1900), pp. 8–13.

Figure 4–2

Sophisticated techniques such as an estimated bad debts treatment of uncollectible accounts were described as early as 1880 in the periodical literature of accounting. Other examples of internal innovations include the development of loose-leaf and columnar books. These types of records, when compared to bound inflexible style book sets, made it possible to sequence, amend and control information. The voucher system also came into use as a system of controlling cash payments and for determining liability and working capital requirements.

Disclosure

With the settling of the West, the Winchester rifle had become a 443 symbol of the times as a weapon in both hunting and war. The role of accounting information in the mass manufacture of arms at the Winchester Repeating Arms Company is in part portrayed in the rudimentary balance sheets reconstructed by Harold Williamson. The activities sketched by these statements portray some of the important financial events of the company over the period of its early development and growth. The content and structure of the statements suggest the fundamental role of balance sheets in communicating financial information and reveal a step in the evolution of financial reporting and disclosure in America.

As noted in a previous chapter, the writings of Thomas Jones of New York mark the beginnings of the modern period of financial reporting. Jones' instruction emphasized the financial statements as the end result of the system of accounts. In the post–Civil War period the ledger had begun to lose its preeminent position in the system of financial accounting. External capital interests required statements which periodically synthesized the results of changes in the asset position of the firm. This betrayed the increasingly important role played by external capital sources in the financing of large enterprises. As businesses became more widely held and financed, statement extracts of the journals and ledgers were being required in concise, uniform, and understandable form.

Another observation regarding the widespread use and importance of financial information in records of this time can be found in Gressley's *Bankers and Cattlemen*. Gressley points to the fact that his ability to compute the dividends paid by successful land and cattle companies was based on the information on the ledger sheets available from the companies for the periods during the 1870s and

1880s. He determined the average declared dividend as just over 8 percent and thus concluded that few eastern investors found a pot of gold in the West. It is appropriate to observe that since a century later it was possible for Gressley to determine this information it is likely that such information was used immediately for similar evaluations.

Gressley's research additionally reveals that a small percentage of early land and cattle companies did show excellent returns. For example, Marshall Field and Levi Leiter reaped dividends averaging 11 percent on their stock investments over a ten year period in the Pratt-Ferris Cattle Company. Financial records provided a means for the eastern financier to determine the profitability of investment. While more research is needed as to the implications and the significance of such records in these early companies they serve as examples of the likely influence of accounts on investment in non-manufacturing enterprises.

444

Beginning with the post–Civil War period the analytically prudent investor became acquainted with statements of financial information as the object of financial reporting and disclosure systems. Before the turn of the century Peter Earling of Chicago, a pioneer writer in the field of credit analysis, had developed practices useful in bank credit departments and had written a book entitled, *Whom to Trust: A Practical Treatise on Mercantile Credits*. Earling's system was based on the methods and experience of his mercantile credit practice. "Prior to and concurrent with Earling's ideas the amounts of credit to be granted had been estimated from statements submitted by the borrower, but the analysis of the statement appears to have gone no further than a careful reading of the figures and investigation of their accuracy" (Brown 1955: 11). Earling's work illustrated an approach and gave birth to a much more analytical method. He investigated asset valuation and recognized the variation of financial data among industries and also expressed relationships or proportions between assets and liabilities and net worth. This was the dawn of the era of scientific credit granting.

Across a wide spectrum of companies, from arms manufacturers to cattle companies and railroads, examples of increasingly sophisticated accounting disclosures and information are found. Railroad statements provide landmark examples because of the dominant position of railroad securities on trading markets. Railroad reports of this period contain the forerunners of the concept of working capital and funds flow disclosures. Statements based on this type of information can be found beginning as early as the 1870s. Thus by 1893 it is common to find statements entitled, "Statements showing resources and their application during the Year"; the purpose of which was to show changes in the solvency position and the effects of some inter-entity transactions. To the extent that corporations were unresponsive to demands for financial data, regulatory agencies began specifying classifications of accounts relative to legal decisions which affected the basis for the evaluation of assets and the determination of a fair return.

It was not until 1899 that the New York exchange took definite steps to require financial statement reports on a regular basis from listed companies. (Sobel 1965: 177)

Emerging Public Accounting Practice

The accountants of the post–Civil War period were prototypes of the modern professionals. Who were they? What were the elements of their practice? What was the nature of their education? How did they contribute to the overall formation of professional associations and to the legal recognition of accounting? The process of seeking answers to these questions provides the basis for a better understanding of the birth of modern public accounting.

A University of Illinois study on early public accountants published in 1942, conducted by A. C. Littleton, reveals that in 1850, nineteen accountants' names are listed in the city directories of New York, Chicago, and Philadelphia. Considering this low number it would be difficult to support the view that public accounting practice or accounting practice per se was widespread at this time. Consider also that even as late as the 1870s it was common practice for teams of stockholders to make periodic visits to corporate offices as a means of attempting to verify reported information. Stockholder verification of this type was perhaps practical because of the limited size and convenient locale of corporations. As late as 1875 it was still difficult to find a manufacturing company with $10 million in assets whereas over 100 companies had assets exceeding $150 million by the close of the second decade of the twentieth century (Newman 1967: 40). The rapid growth in the size of corporations indicated by these statistics suggests that the demand for public accounting services was only beginning to mount at the start of this era.

Accountants were called on to assist in a wide variety of matters. They became involved in the preparation of disputed cases for arbitration or suit. They were hired to detect improper entries and fraud as well as to discover errors in the books and records of the companies.

Defalcations, breaches of trust, irregularities, and swindling schemes were matters of daily occurrence in this environment. As one practitioner of this era stated:

446

> The professional accountant is an investigator, a looker for leaks, a dissector and a detective in the highest acceptation of the term; he must have a good knowledge of real estate, machinery, buildings and other property. His business is to verify that which is right and to detect and expose that which is wrong; to discover and report facts as they exist, whether they be plainly expressed by clear and distinct records or whether they be concealed by the cunning naive or hidden under plausibly arranged figures or as is frequently the case omitted from the records entirely. He is a reader of hieroglyphics, however written, for every erasure, altercation, (sic) interlining, dot, dash or character may have a meaning. He must interpret, rearrange and produce in simple but distinct from self explanatory and free from mysteries of bookkeeping, the narrative of facts, the relation to each other in results. He is the foe of deceit and the champion of honesty (Keister 1896).

Accounting practice was almost exclusively the province of men. Although records reveal that, after the turn of the century, several women were admitted to practice as certified public accountants, these were exceptions to the rule.[8]

Since expert consulting accountants provided skills and had the experience needed to insure results, the investment community and general public would begin to recognize the need for special talent and training, and the demand for accountants' services would grow. Yet there were too few statutory disclosure laws, professional associations, or publications to assist in the exchange of ideas or development of techniques to meet this new demand.

By 1885 cities and their directories began to reflect an increasing number of persons offering services as expert accountants. The city of Louisville, Kentucky, located at a distance from the financial and commercial centers of the East, listed the services of five practicing accountants. The city directories of New York, Chicago and Philadelphia indicated a rapid growth in the numbers of public accountants, from 81 in 1884, to 322 in 1889. As Ernest Reckitt, an early Chicago practitioner, observed, there was some turnover within these numbers, that is, persons who started and then withdrew from practice. Therefore the total number of individuals who had undertaken to practice publicly would be even greater than indicated. Littleton's study revealed that for the three major cities noted, during the period from 1850 to 1899, some 1,370 different individuals appeared in listings as accountants and 662 of these appeared only once. Despite the high number of nonrepeaters in the listings the number of those that did repeat, in relation to the total population, suggests that this period can be identified as having witnessed the birth of modern public accounting practice. This period also witnessed an unprecedented wave of corporate mergers which peaked in the 1890s. These mergers fueled the demand for accounting services which involved more than the review of clerical accuracy or the detection of fraud. The breadth of accounting services now expanded from the testing of values, financial advising, and various audit services to include report writing, even though statutory disclosure requirements did not exist. In the 1890s the forerunners of at least three of the national public accounting firms were established, and in April 1896, the first state legislation recognizing and establishing the title of certified public accountant was passed in the state of New York.

447

Prior to the merger wave of the 1890s, accountants and auditors, particularly those who had come from Great Britain, benefited from the brewers boom of the 1880s. During this period British capital was attracted to America especially for the purposes of investing in breweries. In such far-flung locations as St. Louis, Chicago, San Francisco, Baltimore, Milwaukee, Denver, Springfield, Indianapolis, and other locations, brewing companies were formed and as a consequence accounting investigations and subsequent audits of considerable length were required.

James T. Anyon, an English bred early CPA leader, suggests that the "back parlor" (moonlighting) nature of many American accounting practices raised doubts among the public about the quality, ability and character of early native accountants. He noted that accountants were viewed as "men of figures"—those who dealt in and loved figures for themselves, who calculated balances in accounts, prepared elaborate statements, and looked for errors. Accountants were viewed as the type of persons who thought figures, sometimes juggled them, and always wrote and talked them.

If this image betrays a lack of popular appeal perhaps it is well to explore the reasons for this perception. During this period accounting work was identified with musty drudgery. The bulky old bound ledgers in which records were kept were complicated affairs. It was quite impossible when starting a new ledger to determine with any accuracy the number of pages that an account might require before another ledger was opened. It was common to forward accounts as they filled up pages such that an account starting on page 10 might be forwarded to page 99, then to page 150, then to page 209, and so on. Unless the account was indexed by page, an outside auditor found it quite difficult to follow. Not until the loose-leaf ledger became practical to employ around the 1880s, was the cumbersome bound ledger replaced. About the same time special journals and voucher journals were achieving wide attention and use. Thus they provided an additional reduction in the repetitive and needless duplication of 448   entry information. Accounting reports rendered during this period were prepared and submitted in longhand, since the popular acceptance of the typewriter did not occur until the mid–1890s. One of the requisite skills of the accountant was to have "an accomplished hand" in penmanship and a modicum of patience. For when multiple copies were required they had to be produced in the same tedious and exacting longhand.

Accountants as might be expected were skeptical as to the advantages of the typewriter when it first appeared. "Why should I pay $125 for a machine when I can buy a pen for two cents?" some asked. Other accountants thought it offensive to be the object of impersonal typewritten correspondence, likening it to receiving a printed public handbill (Reckitt 1953: 9).

Auditing techniques of the period included the following: vouching all cash disbursements, checking all footings and postings, and checking the ledger to the trial balance and the trial balance to the financial statements. As much as three-fourths of the audit time was spent on footings and postings. Experience showed however that about three quarters of the defalcations were hidden by failures to account for income or cash receipts. Frequently books would have been out of balance for months or years and locating errors was a terrible task.

In 1869 *Auditor's Guide*, by H. J. Mettenheim, appeared (Moyer: 1951). Only sixteen pages, it was hardly adequate for the times but it suggested techniques for preventing fraud, including that all entries be clear, full and explicit, that money columns be ruled to prevent slovenly work, and that the cashier be required to use a voucher for every payment. In 1881 Selden R. Hopkins' book, *Manual of Exhibit Bookkeeping*, dealt in part with auditing matters. In 1882 G. P. Greer's *Science of Accounts* contained some significant sections on auditing, including that proof should be sought outside the books in attempting to verify statements of debtors and creditors. Greer went on to specify certain internal control requirements which should be established in corporations, for example, that obligations of the corporation should be authorized by the vote of the directors and that all payments of large amounts should be made by check or draft on a bank of deposit. Greer also noted that when receipts or disbursements passed through the hands of a treasurer, a cashier and a different collecting or disbursing clerk should check and prove each other.

Considering the techniques and the auditing theory of the period, it becomes clear that such early audits were effectively audits of the bookkeepers. The primary targets were error and fraud. Two out of three new audit engagements during the 1890s were likely to reveal defalcations. Such statistics do not come as a surprise in light of the fact that there had been no prior audit, fidelity bonds were not in existence, and few if any internal controls, including the division of duties, existed (Moyer 1951).

449

All of this suggests that the type of services and the qualifications of the individuals practicing public accounting during this period probably varied widely. There was little to prevent someone from advertising as follows in public directories or newspapers:

> Complicated, disputed and confused accounts; also accounts with executors, trustees and estates in assignments investigated and stated. Books opened and closed. Suspected accounts confidentially examined. Partnership settlements made.

Such touting pronouncements were not restricted to public directories and newspapers. Expert account cards were also circulated referring to similar services being offered to include expert work with joint stock companies, banks, and other corporation accounts.

The Institute of Accountants and Bookkeepers formed in New York on July 28, 1882 was the first professional accounting organization in the United States. Its aims during its first decade were almost wholly devoted to education for accounting and providing accounting literature. At institute meetings technical and professional subjects were discussed. Subsequently the institute changed its name to the Institute of Accounts and at the turn of the century published the monthly periodical *Accountics*. The Institute of Accounts required a full test of qualifications before admission. Unfortunately, little is known of the operations of the institute after the turn of the century since its records have not been located and only a few of its examiners are known. Yet for a quarter century, from 1882 until about 1908, the Institute of Accounts provided a professional association which admitted members from public as well as commercial practice. Its membership in 1884 numbered eighty persons, and over the years included such notable members as Charles E. Sprague, Selden Hopkins, Charles Waldo Haskins, Farquhar MacRae, and Henry Harney.

450

Topics of meeting speeches for the period from 1883 to 1887 included the following: "Costs Accounts in Metal Factories," by A. O. Kittredge; "The Unlearned Profession," by Silas S. Packard;" "Documents as Related to Accounts," by Charles E. Sprague; "Account Keeping of Telephone Companies," by Charles Dothan; "Prices and Profits," by Joseph Hardcastle; and "Mechanical Consolidation Items," by Captain Henry Metcalfe. At the meeting of December 15, 1886 Charles Taller, a member of the institute, gave an address entitled "French and American Account Keeping Contrasted". This is the first known professional address on international accounting matters in America. Later during this meeting a catalytic event leading to the formation of an association exclusively serving public accountants occurred. As an interesting sequel to Taller's speech on French and American accounting, Edwin Guthrie, FCA, guest of the evening, gave by request a description of the Institute of Chartered Accountants in England. Guthrie had come to the United States at the invitation of James T. Anyon who had arrived in October of the same year (Webster 1954).

British auditors had begun to reside in America as London firms found it less expensive to provide services on an extended basis by establishing resident offices in major U.S. cities. As business increased, the English firms were slowly Americanized by taking on staff of either British born naturalized Americans or native born Americans. Prior to 1888 such British firms serviced primarily British capital investments in fire insurance, railroad, and mortgage companies via monthly audits. With the subsequent "brewers boom" mentioned above, British firms became involved in the audits of American breweries in several distant points in the United States.

The British contingent served as a nucleus to influence the founding of the American Association of Public Accountants (AAPA). In addition to having known many British practitioners, Anyon had become acquainted with several American accountants of prominent stature, including William Veysey, John Heins, and others. The history of the AAPA, which after several reorganizations and mergers through the twentieth century ultimately became the American

Institute of Certified Public Accountants (AICPA), is well known. The writings of John L. Carey in *The Rise of the Accounting Profession* (vol. I) detail many of the particulars of the early formative matters that were addressed by the AAPA.[9]

At this point only the Institute of Accountants and the American Association of Public Accountants have been cited, but it is also important to note the existence of similar associations across the country during the 1880s. Between November 1874 and January 1886 six bookkeeping and accounting societies were organized in as many cities. Five others were organized in 1887, two in 1888, and three in 1889. These associations were not restricted to public accountants and were located in principal cities, including St. Louis, Chicago, Cleveland, Boston, Dayton, Kansas City, Pittsburgh, Detroit, Chicago, San Francisco, Buffalo and Memphis.

451

Among the most active of these groups was the Bookkeepers Beneficial Association of Philadelphia which was organized in 1874 with thirty-five members and grew to a membership of nearly 300 by 1888. This association celebrated its fiftieth anniversary in 1924 but was dissolved sometime thereafter. It is not clear that this association acted as did the Institute of Accounts to screen membership by a set of rigorous examinations.

Several accounting periodicals serving these organizations also appeared during this period. *The Bookkeeper*, edited and published by Selden R. Hopkins and Charles E. Sprague, appeared in July 1880 and continued until 1883. Other publications included *The American Accounting Room* and *The Treasury*. These were succeeded by *The Office* published by A. O. Kittredge. Each of these reported a circulation of 3,000 or more and extra editions of 10,000 issued as samples were sent out widely to accountants and others.

The certificate of incorporation of the American Association of Public Accountants was filed on September 20, 1887. The first president was James Yalden, an Englishman. The vice-president was John Heins, an American born accountant. The secretary was James T. Anyon and the treasurer was William Veysey. The most formidable obstacle facing public practitioners at this time was a lack of formal legal recognition of their public practice. It is noted by Carey that the existence of the AAPA did little to change things immediately. Both the Institute of Accounts and the AAPA began via separate routes to investigate securing legislation to achieve such legal recognition. Norman Webster and George Wilkinson have provided us with a legacy of details and information regarding the pre–1900 CPA movement. Although some historical essays on the subject of these early years suggest that a noble "onward and upward" spirit existed between British and American accountants, other interpretations do not support this view. The early AAPA was a hybrid of the English Club-Medieval Guild patterned after the Institute of Chartered Accountants. It did not become an "American" organization for several years. Part of the evidence of its lack of acceptance by native Americans before 1900 is found in the fact that it had fewer than 100 members at the turn of the century and these were predominantly English born residents of New York. Accountants from other states were noted in Association records as "non residents." Early professional activities were marked by the existence of these two camps, the British and the American. Although harmony would be forthcoming it is important to note that, in addition to the problem of lack of legal recognition, the professionals themselves had not yet achieved a sense of unity and self-identity. As long as practitioners were thus divided it would be difficult to achieve legal recognition (Wilkinson 1928).

452

A dozen years before the CPA Law of New York was passed, the Institute of Accounts issued certificates to Fellows who had passed the strict practical and technical entrance examinations. The prerequisite of technical competence as a basis of self regulation therefore had been established prior to the existence of a law.

But the professional associations lacked the power and complete authority to control the growing ranks of all practitioners. Therefore in 1895 an initial attempt to obtain CPA legislation was made by both organizations. During the winter of 1894-1895 a rough draft of a bill providing for a professional examination and a distinctive title was prepared by Henry Harney, president of the Institute of Accounts. Many years before Harney had committed to paper some ideas along this line. He appointed Charles E. Sprague to convey the draft to Albany and see what could be done toward having it enacted into legislation. Sprague was a friend of Melville Dewey, secretary of the regents of the University of New York. Dewey advised that the enforcement of the law be put under the jurisdiction of the regents of the University of the State of New York which was the body that had the capability to conduct such examinations. Furthermore, he pointed out that this would give the measure something of an educational character. The legal designation, Certified Public Accountant, was agreed upon at this time.

In the meantime, acting independently in every respect, several members of the AAPA prepared a draft for a bill providing that no person shall practice as a public accountant after the passage of the act unless he be licensed by the regents of the University of the State of New York. No distinctive title was sought under the AAPA bill. This bill was introduced in February 1895, before the senate of the state of New York.

Two weeks later the institute's bill was introduced in the assembly of the state of New York. The institute's bill contained two features which were clearly disadvantageous to the large British born membership of the AAPA. First, it required that CPAs be citizens of the United States and second it provided that only Certified Public Accountants of the state of New York should be appointed or employed to act as examiners of accounts, expert accountants or paid auditors by court administrators, receivers, state, and county or municipal officers.

A meeting was called in March 1895 to attempt to negotiate differences between the two bills and the rival organizations by means 453 of delegating a special committee to resolve the differences between the bills. This "Committee of 14" was to determine the proper action to be taken with regard to the bills before the legislature. Two of the members of the committee representing the AAPA were Anyon and Yalden. Among those representing the institute were Harney and Charles Dutton. There were also nonmember representatives including Silas S. Packard and John E. Hourigan. The committee lost little time in determining that the association's bill proposing a license should be dropped and the institute's bill proposing a title should be pushed. The committee also determined that an attorney should be retained to watch the progress of the bill before the legislature. A subcommittee of the "Committee of 14" retained E. G. Whittaker to represent the committee at the assembly and the subcommittee met with the assembly's committee on general laws to advocate passage of the bill. The subcommittee was unable to influence the legislation. Assemblyman Wylds who had introduced the bill could not be persuaded to report it favorably to the House. Meanwhile, in the senate, the bill which had been substituted for the institute's version failed to receive a majority vote.

The AAPA quickly followed up to reintroduce the provisions of the bill in the following year's meeting of the legislature. Perhaps because the AAPA represented the practicing *public* accountants and not a mixed group of accountants it was deemed most appropriate for them to pursue the passage of the bill in the next session. Frank Broaker became the chairman of the association's subcommittee. He turned the bill over to Senator Albert Ray of Brooklyn, who introduced the bill in the Senate in January 1896. It was referred to the Committee on Judiciary. During the same period a bill under the same title was introduced in the House by Assemblyman Marshall. The bill passed the Assembly on April 3 by almost unanimous vote, passed the Senate on April 7, and was approved by the governor on April 17, 1896.

A significant single amendment to the bill, made as a result of apparent cooperation between the rival professional groups, assured its passage in 1896. The amendment provided that the Certified Public Accounting designation was available to any citizen of the United States or *person who had duly declared his intention to become such a citizen.* The success of the 1896 legislation may have hinged importantly upon that provision which opened the way for many British chartered accountants and other non-Americans who had not as yet secured their papers as U.S. citizens. Without the amendment a split in the support for the bill between American and British professionals might have developed because of the restrictive provisions in the act regarding state directed accounting engagements. When the bill did take effect many British chartered accountants who chose to retain their British citizenship moved to other states to set up their practice.

454

In the years 1896 and 1897, 112 certificates were awarded, 108 under the waiver which had been established by the Board of Regents to grant the CPA certificate to those who could prove they had been in reputable practice as public accountants since January 1, 1890. The waiver certificates were awarded in alphabetical order. Frank Broaker received the first CPA certificate. The first examination under the new law was held in December 1896. Only three of the four who passed this examination are known; they include Edward C. Charles, Joseph Hardcastle, and William H. Jasper (Wilkinson 1903: 9).

The First CPAs	
New York Certificate Number	**Names**
1	Frank Broaker
2	Richard Chapman
3	Leonard Conant
4	William Sanders Davies
5	Rodney S. Dennis
6	Charles Waldo Haskins
7	Brownell McGibbon
8	Frederick Manuel
9	Charles J. Mercer
10	E. W. Sells
11	C. E. Sprague

A typical profile of American born CPA candidates who sat for the exam at the turn of the century would include being thirty years old, attending public schools for grammar education and working as a commercial or government clerk or bookkeeper, before engaging in the public practice of another accountant and/or returning to teaching at a commercial college. Thereafter upon setting up practice in one's own name the CPA exam would be taken and professional activities commenced.

455

Figure 4–3
A lighthearted sketch of Frank Broaker, CPA No. 1.

Source: Souvenir program of the 1906 Annual Meeting of the American Association of Public Accountants, Columbus, Ohio.

State Societies and Legislation

In response to the initial passage of CPA legislation, other states soon followed in obtaining similar legislation. A Pennsylvania CPA law was enacted in 1899. Maryland passed a CPA law in 1900, California in 1901, Washington and Illinois in 1903. Thus by 1921 all states in the Union had CPA legislation. As expected CPAs now began to form separate professional associations. John Hourigan of Albany appears to have been an important catalyst in the formation of the New York State Society of CPAs, whose initial meeting was held at the Hotel Waldorf on March 30, 1897. Earlier Hourigan had solicited via a letter the interest of accountants in the state, to form a society similar to those of physicians, architects and civil engineers. Hourigan served as an incorporator of the New York Society and its first vice-president. (Committee on History 1953a)

456

Although the New Jersey law was not enacted until April 1904, public accountants in the state organized their society in January 1898. This society, through one of its members, Richard Stevenson, a New York CPA practicing in Newark, was instrumental in eventually overcoming the opposition of the New Jersey legislature to achieve passage of the CPA bill.

Leading Figures

The many early CPA movement leaders, including Hopkins, Sprague, Harney, Broaker and MacRae, reflected a diversity of backgrounds. Hopkins for example, had contributed a section to a book entitled, *Dollars and Sense*, written by the famous showman Phineas T. Barnum. Hopkins' section, "Money, Banks and Banking," focused on "where money came from and where it went." In addition, Hopkins was editor of *The Book-Keeper*, a magazine published in the 1880s, and wrote books on the subject of bookkeeping practice. In 1888 he had written a "Horatio Alger" type novel, *A Young Prince of Commerce*.

Charles E. Sprague should be assigned much credit for gaining the instrumental support and advice of Melville Dewey to secure passage of the CPA law. He was a man of many talents. By vocation a banker, he had an interest in foreign languages and also had been involved with Hopkins in the publication of the *Book-Keeper*. Long active in affairs of his alma mater, Union College of Schenectady, he was also the author of the "The Algebra of Accounts," a lengthy series which first appeared in the issues of the *Book-Keeper* in the early

1880s. Sprague achieved fame after the turn of the century as having made a major contribution to the theory of accounts through his algebraic demonstration of the systematic concept of "Assets equal Liabilities plus Proprietorship" (A = L + P) (Sprague 1908: 20). A veteran of the Civil War, he had been wounded at the battle of Gettysburg.

Frank Broaker, the first CPA, was born in Millerstown, Pennsylvania in 1863. He was the son of John Strawbridge but took his stepfather's name. He worked for John Roundy, a Scot accountant, from 1883 to 1887 and then worked in his own name before entering partnership with Richard M. Chapman (the second CPA under the provisions of the 1896 Act). He was active in the American Association of Public Accountants having been vice-president from 1892 to 1896 457 and president and ramrod of the legislative efforts in 1896.

Broaker was involved in a minor scandal relating to the publication of *The American Accountants Manual*, a book which he had prepared in 1897 based on the first CPA examination questions. The manual contained recommended solutions to the examination and sold for three dollars with the proceeds going to his private account. In addition to the matter of revenue, Broaker had been charged with forming a society of accountants with himself as president. It was alleged that he had urged accountants to join the society, and that they were led to expect that if they did so, the regents might be induced to waive the examination as was provided in the law for a person possessing the necessary experience qualifications. In response to complaints about Broaker's actions with regard to the manual, the State Board of Regents effected a reorganization of the State Board of Examiners of Certified Public Accountants by appointing James T. Anyon to replace Broaker and by appointing Charles Waldo Haskins and Charles E. Sprague, who had served on the first board of examiners for the Certified Public Accountant certificate. A published comment in an 1897 issue of *Accountics* notes that the summary dismissal of Broaker for allegedly violating the precedent for treatment of revenues from such a manual was severe and perhaps unwarranted.

Henry Harney, born in Baltimore in 1835, had been the chief accountant of the Bank of Richmond from 1856–1861 and had served in the Civil War on the side of the Confederacy. He became a member of the Institute of Accounts in 1886 and served five successive terms as President. It is interesting and colorful to note that two adversaries in the Civil War, Sprague and Harney, served effectively together to bring the CPA profession into existence.

Farquhar J. MacRae, a native of Brooklyn born in 1862, worked for Selden Hopkins and Henry Harney and was listed as a public accountant in the New York Directory of 1892. MacRae became a member of the Institute of Accounts in 1890, secretary in 1892, and a member of the executive committee in 1897. He served four terms as vice-president. He later became active in the State Society and the Federation of State Societies of Public Accountants after the turn of the century. In 1894 an advertisement by MacRae and Cowan, expert accountants, read as follows:

458

> Forty dollars per week; five years experience; and Members of Institute of Accounts; $20 per week English chartered accountant who has sufficient experience in this country to render them familiar with modern methods of bookkeeping.

As part of his research on the American Association of Public Accountants, Norman Webster lists the backgrounds and important data known about early members of the professional association. One of the most interesting profiles is that of Ferdinand W. Lafrentz. Lafrentz migrated to the United States, living in Chicago, in 1873. Subsequently, he moved West, working in Ogden, Utah, and serving as a member of the Wyoming legislature in 1888. In response to the request of a friend who was traveling to the West Coast, Lafrentz became familiar with the activities of the American Surety Company and was employed as an accountant in 1893. He subsequently became president and chairman of that organization. At the same time he had established a practice in his own name, F. W. Lafrentz and Company. Later Lafrentz's organization was formalized into the American Audit Company with offices located in the Waldorf Astoria. The American Audit Company became F. W. Lafrentz & Company in 1923. Lafrentz continued his service to the American Surety Company past his ninetieth year. He was a poet, having authored a book of poems called *Cowboy Stuff* and a book in German about his boyhood days in Fehmarn, an island in the Baltic Sea just north of the German mainland. Lafrentz received some of his accounting training at a Bryant and Stratton Business College. He was a member of the American Association of Public Accountants and held certificate number 20 in New York State. He also lectured at the New York University School of Commerce, Accounts and Finance.

As the business world moved into the twentieth century, economic theory, the legal system, and society all were shifting their attention toward growth of large enterprises under the system of capitalism. The need for a trained corps of public accountants was becoming recognized and addressed through the passage of CPA legislation and the formation of professional accounting associations. The problems and the challenges were many. For one, the associations of practitioners were not growing as rapidly as key members believed they should. In part this may be attributed to the fact that the rules of admission were rigorous and restrictive. Although some early writers have stated that American public accounting was not in existence before the 1880s, it would be more appropriate to say that public accounting was viable before 1880 but not visible until after 1880. Evidence supplied by Littleton and Webster indicates that accounting activity prior to the 1880s was importantly preparatory for the establishment of a widespread qualified, competent and professional discipline which began to emerge in the 1880s and the 1890s.

459

During these years before the turn of the century the full energies of this small group were devoted to:

1. Organizing at the state, local and national levels.
2. Securing passage of laws and initiating appropriate administration of such laws.
3. Initiating attempts to establish university programs of accounting.

In light of these tasks this young professional group was not sufficiently large to be extensively engaged in matters of developing uniform technical standards, and it would not seem to be a valid criticism of these pioneering CPAs that they did not make headway in the area.

Accounting Education and Textbooks

Business was beginning to require a type of training that existing schools, both high schools and universities, did not supply. In some ways the attitude of businessmen discouraged universities from undertaking business education on a widespread scale. For example, Andrew Carnegie stirred up a controversy which lasted well into the 1890s commenting that "college graduates are not successful businessmen." The old ironmaster thought that young men destined for business ought to be mingling with men who did business.

Prior to 1875 bookkeeping was perhaps the only subject that could be classified as a business topic regularly taught in high schools. Even

after 1875 formal business education was still unknown in universities. In the face of the growing demand for individuals trained in
business procedure to assist large corporations and other developing
business enterprises in the conduct of their affairs, business colleges
sprang up throughout the country during the post–Civil War period
to provide trained personnel. Chain schools such as the Bryant and
Stratton Business Colleges and pioneering business educators including Silas S. Packard, an accountant and later president of the Institute
of Accounts, were among the important names in the business college
movement of the pre-1900 period.

460

Figure 4–4

A classroom scene typical of the post–Civil War era.

Source: *The Countinghouse Arithmetic* (Baltimore, 1889).

In 1883 the first course in accounting to be sustained at the collegiate level was offered at the Wharton School of the University of Pennsylvania, which had started only two years earlier. The contents of the course, which included two terms of instruction, involved several technical requirements, as well as a series of lectures on "The Theory and Practice of Accounting." According to the recollections of one of the first students there were 12 pupils in this first collegiate accounting class. The next offering of the course found two textbooks being used, including Selden Hopkins' *Manual of Exhibit Bookkeeping* and C. C. Marsh's *Theory of Bank Bookkeeping and Joint Stock Accounts*. While the Wharton School initiated sustained university level accounting courses, it should be noted that several other attempts to form schools of commerce had been undertaken at other 461 locations (Lockwood 1938).

Just before the turn of the century the University of Chicago authorized the establishment of a College of Commerce and Politics which was renamed the College of Commerce and Administration. In its initial academic year, 1898–1899, ten students were registered and within three years there were 89 students in total. Henry Rand Hatfield recalled that accounting at the University of Chicago, which he taught, relied upon the early writing of Professor J. F. Schar of Germany, who had written on the matter of single and double entry during the 1890s. The lack of suitable textbooks no doubt hampered the effectiveness of accounting at the university level. The pioneering efforts of the Wharton School, the University of Chicago and, after the turn of the century, the School of Commerce, Accounts and Finance at New York University and the Amos Tuck School at Dartmouth in 1899, provided important first steps in collegiate education in accounting.[10]

Business Colleges

University business programs developed toward the end of the era; the bulk of the training and education of businessmen and accountants *during* the era came by way of the proprietary business colleges. At a banquet for Silas S. Packard, on the occasion of his seventieth birthday in 1896, toasts and testimonials acknowledged his important role in the business college movement. Packard had organized and conducted a general exhibit of the American Commercial and Business Schools at the Chicago World's Fair. For over fifty years Packard had taken upon himself the work of commercial teaching and the promotion of business education. His schools included training the so-called "Packard boys" and young women as well who had an interest in business education. Packard, born in an Ohio log cabin in 1826, was a type of Horatio Alger success story. As one put it, ". . . inspired by poverty in youth he had learned the necessity for labor and for struggle." (Complimentary Banquet: 1896)

Packard wrote texts on accounting and bookkeeping for the chain of business colleges that he established. These books in revised form were still in use through the 1900s. Packard's books are recognized to have had an influence beyond the United States, to include Canada and Japan. Before 1876 William C. Whitney, an American business school proprietor, had journeyed to Japan and established a commercial school at the invitation of the Japanese minister to Washington. Whitney had operated a Bryant and Stratton business college in Newark. He took with him to Japan texts that dealt with the science of accounts. Two such texts which were prominent in the revolution of Japanese accounting during the period include Packard's *Manual of Theoretical Training in the Science of Accounts*, New York 1868, and Folsom's *Logic of Accounts*, New York 1873.

462

Packard had taught at various places before opening his own commercial college as a part of the Bryant and Stratton chain. In 1867 he bought out the interests of his partners, abolished the Bryant and Stratton affiliation, and founded the Packard Business College. This was a step toward terminating chain system influence in business education and laid the foundation for solely owned schools. The chain movement of business schools faltered after the initial success of the Bryant and Stratton system partly because of internal weaknesses involving changes in policies as well as the lack of uniformity with regard to the practices of individual schools under local leadership.

Just as Packard was the patriarch of business education in the East, George Soulé was a patriarch of education for business in the South. New Orleans, which had flourished in the post–Civil War years, also experienced an acute need for persons trained in business subjects. Soulé authored successful and widely used accounting texts as did Packard. Soulé's book was introduced in 1881 with subsequent editions through the early 1900s.

As business colleges began operating on a proprietary and profit basis, they grew rapidly. In 1889 Packard described business colleges as "strong in number and financially prosperous." Response to the success of these colleges included some public school competition to meet the demands heretofore served by the private business colleges. Cities recognized that business college subjects would pay their own way. But the point remains that private business colleges filled the educational void for a significant period.[11]

Textbooks of the Times

An examination of the textbooks that were used to teach account keeping during this period reveals the standardization of the work-sheet step of the accounting cycle. In this step, the pro forma work sheet, based upon the unadjusted trial balance through to adjusted profit and loss and balance sheet columns was used much the same way as we find it in the accounting cycle of today.[12]

A common weakness of the general financial accounting texts of this period seems to have been the lack of technique for dealing with corporation accounts. Even late editions of Soulé's *Science and Practice of Accounts* were oriented to proprietary ownership rather than to capital stock companies. However, some editions did treat opening entries and techniques for capital stock companies.

463

It would seem that the experience of the practicing accountant in the handling of corporate accounts was not yet flowing into the classroom. Practical experience, not academic research, provided the source of technical innovation which was then disseminated through popular textbooks. Most of the native born accountants in the United States who had reached middle life before the turn of the century had graduated from the ranks of the bookkeeper. By the turn of the century the CPA examination emphasizing the theory of accounts, practical accounting, auditing, and commercial law began to assume a leading and conditioning influence as to the educational training pattern suitable for aspiring professionals. High school education followed by "university training in accountancy and its allied branches" was to become the recommended route as early as 1905.

The Birth of Preclassical Theory

The study of theory development during this period leads to the conclusion that several important beginnings in the attempt to conceptualize accounting practice were initiated. Most notable was the appearance of Charles E. Sprague's "Algebra of Accounts" series. This was the forerunner of the theory which was ultimately presented in his important work, *The Philosophy of Accounts*, published shortly after the turn of the century. Sprague's writing in the "Algebra of Accounts" evidences a capability for abstract and axiomatic approaches in accounting thought well before such ideas were popularly recognized. His early works provided a classificatory and deductive framework for notions being widely discussed in the publications of

Carlton & Fowler's Balance Sheet. Set V.

L. Folio	New York, May 31st, 1876.	Ledger Balances Dr.	Cr.	Profit and Loss Losses	Gains	H. L. Carlton Dr.	Cr.	Geo. R. Fowler Dr.	Cr.	State of Affairs Assets	Liabilities
1	H. L. Carlton,	1,164 99	20,100 00				20,100 00	1,164 99			
1	George R. Fowler,										
1	Cash,	2,432 90								2,432 90	
1	Bills Receivable,	1,852 13								1,852 13	
1	Bills Payable,		2,917 50								2,917 50
1	Merchandise,	14,847 01	17,241 88		2,394 87					17,241 88	
2	Interest and Discount,	152 33		152 33							
2	Fixtures and Expenses,	284 50		284 50							
√	Personal Debtors,	2,896 08								2,896 08	
√	Personal Creditors,		612 44						652 68		612 44
		23,629 94	23,629 94	436 83	2,394 87						
				1,305 36			1,305 36	1,164 99	512 31		3,529 94
				652 68					1,164 99		20,893 05
				2,394 87	2,394 87	21,405 36	21,405 36	1,164 99	1,164 99	24,422 99	24,422 99
										24,422 99	

Total Losses and Gains, Firm's Net Gain $1,958 04. { H. L. Carlton's ⅔ gain, Geo. R. Fowler's ⅓ "

Net Capital, $21,405 36

Net Insolvency, 512 31

Firm's Net Capital, { H. L. Carlton's Net Capital, $1,405 36. Geo. R. Fowler's " Insolvency, 512 31.

Total Assets and Liabilities, $1,405 36.

Firm's Net Capital, { H. L. Carlton's Net Capital, $1,405 36. Geo. R. Fowler's " Insolvency, 512 31.

Figure 4-5

Textbook examples of financial reports, 1876.

Source: John Groesbeck. Practical Book-Keeping Single and Double Entry (Philadelphia, 1884).

the time and linked early accounting notions to mathematics and economics.

Sprague began his exposition by noting that accounting "is a history of values." His basic accounting equation, *assets* = *liabilities* + *proprietorship*, appeared in the 1880 series of articles as, "what I have plus what I trust equals what I owe plus what I am worth," which was written symbolically as $H + T = O + X$ (Sprague 1880). Through sets of symbolic equations he provided the reader of accounts a logical and systematic approach to gaining a command over the accounting cycle. Rather than requiring that one memorize an endless series of rules, Sprague emphasized that the keeping of accounts involved certain equations in which addition and cancellation are the central techniques employed. He also noted the importance of uniform value in determining net wealth as follows: 465

> Annals or chronicles merely relate facts which have occurred; but true history groups together facts of the same tendency in order to discover if possible the cause of happiness and misery, prosperity and ruin; so true bookkeeping, being a history, should group together similar values in its equations to discover the causes and effects of Loss and Gain. (Sprague 1880)

He concluded, "In the equation of accounts the answer sought or 'unknown quantity' is what am I worth? This we will represent by the letter X."

Although Sprague's exposition did not go beyond the proprietary model, the forty-two paragraphs of this early treatise included notational operations for balancing and measurement which were suitable for more than proprietary operations.

Sprague's accounting equation ($A = L + P$) was destined to become the starting point of today's approach to accounting education as well as the focal point of subsequent modifications. In this way Sprague axioms have become recognized as the essence of a preclassical school of American accounting theory. His writings were evidence of the unique and essentially complete theory wherefrom modern American accounting developed. It was within this framework that conceptual concerns over issues such as costs and value, income and outlay, inventory and depreciation, would be argued.

As has been noted earlier this is also a crucial time in the debate over the appropriate treatment of what is now recognized as the depreciation of fixed and wasting assets. A comment in the May 1897 issue of *Accountics* betrays the importance and state of the issue at that time. A speech given at a regular meeting of the Institute of

Accounts in New York on Thursday evening January 14, 1897, given by Frederick W. Child, a member of the institute, and attended by a large audience, was the subject of a feature in the magazine. The main point of Child's address was with respect to depreciation of plant, tools, fixtures, and so on, and the plan he recommended for managing the accounts respecting the same. He proposed that such accounts as machinery and tools, buildings and similar items should show the total cost of those items or the amount of the capital invested therein and that the amount written off for wear and tear, depreciation of value, and so forth should be credited to special reserve accounts. "Thus," he noted, "if tools and machinery which cost $27,000 were in the estimation of the managers of the enterprise, depreciated in value by reason of use and other causes to an amount at a certain time equal to 10 percent, then the amount of depreciation ($2700) instead of being credited to tools and machinery account, should be passed to a credit for reserve on tools and machinery." This is one of the earliest publicly discussed examples of reserves for accumulated depreciation in America.

466

Under Child's approach, successive percentages, the results of which were entered during a term of years,would be credited to the reserve account. The allowance for depreciation, he urged, should be regarded as an expense in the factory account and should be spread over the goods produced. He did not believe that satisfactory results from the accounting point of view were ever obtained by carrying the amount of depreciation of machinery and plant into the loss and gain account directly, for he held that depreciation of plant was part of the cost of the product.

The pages of *Accountics* also reveal another discussion in the same year on the subject of goodwill. Although the article focused upon court cases, particularly those in England, it did, after thorough discussion, indicate that the accountants of the period were involved in debating the issue. Other conceptual concerns are also evidenced. Several years earlier at a meeting of the Institute of Accounts in October, 1889, Sprague delivered a lecture on the subject of "income and outlay." He clearly suggests that the appropriate treatment was tied to the principle of *periodicity:*

> The artificiality of profit and loss and its tributaries results partly from their relation to time. The reciprocal action and reaction of outlay and income are continuous, but for convenience we treat them as periodical. We are compelled to cut them into even lengths for purposes of comparison. (Sprague 1889)

In this lecture Sprague distinguished between losses and expenses indicating that if the bookkeeping is that of a business concern then expenditures made under such headings as insurance and so forth are in no sense losses as the title profit and loss suggests. They are, he concluded, business outlays, deliberately made for the purpose of producing income which is hoped will exceed outlay.

As early as 1880, the literature contained subjects of modern interest to include a discussion of a treatment of extraordinary items of expense versus expense items incurred in ordinary operations.

In the writings of Soulé we find descriptions of the use of suspense accounts, in particular a type of allowance for doubtful accounts as a device for treating accounts receivable values. It is also interesting to note that the term "principles" was employed in the description of the methods applicable to accounts as early as 1890.[13]

467

Two notable expositions on the theoretical and valuational aspects of accounting during the post–Civil War period were published before Sprague wrote his important series. The 1868 work of Silas S. Packard entitled, *Manual of Theoretical Training in the Science of Accounts*, and *The Logic of Accounts* written by E. G. Folsom and published in 1873 were forerunners in this preclassical era. Folsom's name is not well known in the history of accounting. What is known about his past begins with his activity as the founder of a business college in Cleveland, Ohio, where he trained two enterprising individuals, Bryant and Stratton, who, as mentioned earlier, later formed their own chain of commercial colleges. In 1875, while proprietor of a different business college in Albany, New York, he published *The Logic Of Accounts*, which had been written in 1873. The book focused on "valuation" problems in accounting. He classified value initially under two headings, commercial value and idea value. As he observed:

> With the view of reducing double entry accounts to an exact science we begin with value as a generic or universal term applicable alike to all things and divided, first into two distinct classes; then each class into species of its own, until ultimate simple values are reached, as shown by the analysis.

It may have become apparent that his notions were not useful or operational in practice, for his message appears to have had no great following. It was not until Sprague's writing that a clear point was made about the value of an asset and that such value could be measured in services given or the cost incurred. Sprague saw both

TOPICAL ANALYSIS OF VALUE.

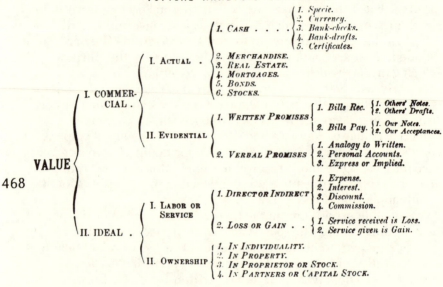

Figure 4–6

Folsom's "value theory chart."

Source: E. G. Folsom, *The Logic of Accounts* (New York, 1873).

the supply and demand aspect of value. Folsom probably saw the distinction between value in use and value in exchange much earlier but only from the supply side. He valiantly tried to incorporate it as the core of his accounting system but, again, his method failed to gain the distinction it merited.

This quarter century of American professional accounting was marked by attempts to establish the role and function of the practicing accountant. Accountants devoted considerable editorial and manuscript attention to what the public accountant *was* and what the public accountant *did*, or to respond to such rhetorical questions as, "What is an accountant, as distinguished from a bookkeeper?" or "What is an auditor?"

The passage of the New York CPA law and the exposition and influence of Sprague's theory of accounts provided the basis upon which to solidify a self view of accounting and its theory.

In this period, in part due to the notions identified with Sprague, it became possible to represent the activities of accounts in a notational and axiomatic fashion which facilitated abstraction and modeling of accounting transactions. Without these achievements it would seem unlikely that the developments of the first thirty years of the next century would have come to pass, particularly in terms of the accounting techniques needed to communicate the financial data and statements that characterized the growth and complexity of the corporation. The influence of Sprague on the writings of later and equally eminent account thinkers may be inferred from the following remarks made by W. A. Paton in referring to Sprague:[14]

> It was these writings that aroused my interest in accounting, and without this spur I am quite certain that I would never have shifted from teaching economic theory to a career primarily in the accounting field. . . .
>
> Above all, he pushed the door ajar to a realization that accounting constitutes the outstanding approach to a pervasive understanding of business enterprises . . . . (Paton 1972: iii, v).

469

Cost and Managerial Accounting

During the 1850s, Paul Garner has noted, industrialism was beginning to have an impact on the character of account keeping. The post–Civil War steel industry boom was a response to the demands of the westward drive of the railroads. For the first time many text writers began to consider accounts related to factory and production costs. John Fleming's *Bookkeeping by Double Entry*, published in Pittsburgh in 1854, included several changes to reflect cost accounting considerations. Fleming changed the name of the merchandise trading account to "factory account" and also attempted to determine the appropriate treatment for factory buildings. Whether these adjustments truly reflected a general need for cost system information because of the many iron and steel mills near Pittsburgh can only be speculated. But at about that time Andrew Carnegie was pioneering the introduction of cost accounting in his mills, and maintaining a considerable staff in his cost department. He was noted to have indicated that his financial success was in part due to his ability to know his costs in the steel industry. (Reckitt 1953: 18)

Up until the 1880s, text writers appeared to neglect industrial accounts at the very time that industry was being revolutionized by the factory system, widespread use of mechanical equipment, and devices for rapid communication and transportation. Perhaps a lack of experience and expertise in this first generation of management accounting explains the lack of writing. One can speculate that prior to 1885 the lack of detailed writings about the methods used by management and factory accountants was assignable to incomplete knowledge or at another extreme, to a desire to retain the advantage of their knowledge by keeping it a secret. Several small societies of accountants and bookkeepers existed even prior to 1880, therefore, there were professional circles through which this information could have circulated. However, there were few professional accounting magazines prior to 1880, and the lack of an effective means of such communication may also have impeded the transfer of knowledge. There is also the possibility that while developments were being achieved in the area of cost controls at this point there was still not a sufficient basis of practice to lend credibility to generalizations about the value of a given approach or system.

470

Recent historical research by H. T. Johnson and W. E. Stone which focuses upon the pre 1880 period and earlier, considers factory records themselves as a device for determining the true state of the management accounting art prior to 1880. Their research indicates that the systems in existence were much more sophisticated than could be determined from the literature and textbooks of the time. Johnson has observed that as the vertical integration of large complex businesses occurred (such that from source supply to consumer, a single organization was involved in transforming the raw material to the final product), it was necessary that an organization structure and an accounting system be developed to integrate the entire effort under a unitary form of managerial accounting that featured independent departments as well as central office communication and control features.

A Bitter View

Not all business writers were content with accounting or the persons who practiced it (Wells 1970). Kirkman, for example, writing in *Railway Expenditures* in 1880, slashed out the following personal attack:

> When I was very young I remember to have been much cast down at the evident want of interest which railway managers manifested in statistical lore. I can recall, now, that my ideal officer was a man of delicate physical structure, of towering intellectual front, with pale, weak eyes and sickly complexion withal, his shoulders bowed with study and the contemplation of the subtle phases of railway polity. My ideal

was, in fact, not a manager at all, but a statistician, a clerk, an accountant. I had not then learned that the class of men I had in mind were never leaders in the affairs of life, but the followers only—the pack-mules, so to speak. The managers of our railways are never of an active statistical turn of mind, and as I said before, it is perhaps fortunate for the owners that this is so (pp. 22–23).

He then notes with alarm

The rapid growth of the railroad interest has developed everywhere embryo accountants in more or less profusion, whose greatest delight seems to have been to introduce in connection with the property with which they were identified all the new and strange forms and obser- 471 vances that occurred to them. In the progress of their work what was before luminous such men make wholly incomprehensible; with them the dawn is ever succeeded by eternal darkness. In this gloom it is their happiness to live; it does not, however, retard their development or decrease their numbers. They multiply indefinitely like bats in a cave. Everywhere they will pursue their theme with industry and enthusiasm, but it will be the enthusiasm of the bigot, born of ignorance and fostered and perpetuated by ignorance.

It is the happy privilege of such a class to believe that they possess the divine power to create. Having no capacity or room for additional knowledge they are consequently insensible to their manifold deficiencies; disregarding that which is, they exercise their circumscribed minds in producing something that does not exist and that ought not to exist. (p. 31).

Kirkman's bitterness toward the inflexible mode of "statistical" accounting which typified railroad financial reports, is an uncharacteristic view, but not unique, particularly among harried railroad managers who found themselves bound by a chain of ledgers and a rote litany of debit and credit passages that seemed to have little to do with the "cash basis success" of the business. Again, quoting Kirkman:

The balance of cash that remains in the treasury after collecting the earnings and paying the operating expenses of a railway company, constitute its net income.

Herein lies the essence of accounting; this is the goal; every thing else is collateral to it. Bookkeeping was an after-thought, a device adopted for the purpose of recording and classifying affairs and preventing roguery. (p. 2)

A Point of Progress

In 1885 there was a turning point in the maturity of American literature in the field of cost accounting. That year Henry Metcalfe, an American army ordinance officer, published a book entitled, *Cost of Manufactures*. Metcalfe's work and his position as an authority were probably recognized in professional circles. For example, during the 1880s he spoke at a meeting of the Institute of Accounts in New York.

In the period 1883–1887 other lecturers at institute meetings often dealt with topics on the subject of management accounting, including accounting for branch stores, account keeping for telephone companies, and cost accounts in metal factories. The institute was not restricted to public practitioners, but included among its members company and managerial accountants.

472

An overview of the practice of cost and managerial accounts as indicated by the records of businesses and by the contents explained in the leading textbooks of the period reveals the following types of cost accounting systems and terminology:

1. *Burden:* The term burden, or overhead, as we know it today, was noted as early as 1862 in the writings of Nassau Senior, an English economist who had developed a theory to distinguish between fixed and variable overhead cost. Overhead was called various names—including "on cost." "On costs" were manufacturing costs which were to be added "on to" the total of labor and material in arriving at total cost.
2. *Depreciation:* Williamson's study of the Winchester Company indicates that its internal accounting practices did not consider depreciation. He also indicates that the first cost controls appear to have been installed in the late 1880's in reaction to competition in the industry so as to determine where costs could be reduced.
3. *Interest:* Certain writers of the period argued for the inclusion of interest on capital employed as a burden cost or cost of manufacturing. Economic theory had not clearly defined whether or not such was appropriately treated as a division of profits or a payment for a factor of production.
4. *Cost Flow:* Studies of the Shelby Iron Works records for the periods from before the Civil War through the 1880s indicate that the management of the firm was able to determine a broad cost of production via aggregative summaries of costs. (The management of Shelby was able to determine cost per ton of pig iron as early as 1847.) There did not appear, however, to be any recognition of cost flow. Their aggregative method of determining cost per ton was essentially an averaging approach and was still used as late as 1887 (Cauley 1949).

By the turn of the century several American writers were contributing to the literature of cost accounting. Even the all-purpose accounting textbooks widely used in business colleges began to refer to cost accounts. This marked the birth of teaching the first specialty subject within the field.

Cost accounting, however, would not begin to mature for several years, subsequent to the wave of corporate mergers and of a unitary form of organization. The typical pre–1900 manufacturing firm was still operating with an accounting system geared to provide information about short run operations. In railroading and textiles it could be observed however that by the 1890s cost systems had become more sophisticated. These industries represented forerunners of the form of future manufacturing and corporate organizations. An 1874 report of the Atchison, Topeka and Santa Fe railroad serves as an example in that it included as an exhibit a table of distribution of

473

WINCHESTER REPEATING ARMS COMPANY*
Estimated Balance Sheet, April 1, 1867

CURRENT ASSETS		
Cash	$ 1,374.65	
Accounts Receivable from New Haven Arms Company	182,234.20	
Inventory	72,447.74	
Chilean-Peruvian Assets	57,000.00	
Stock Subscription Receivable (payable April 1–December 1, 1867)	82,936.99	$395,993.58
LESS: CURRENT LIABILITIES		
Accounts Payable from New Haven Arms Company	188,493.58	
Due Stockholders of New Haven Arms Company	136,500.00	324,993.58
NET WORKING CAPITAL		71,000.00
FIXED ASSETS		
Value of New Haven Arms Company Plant	150,000.00	
Other Assets		
Burnside Rifle Claim[1]	21,000.00	
Mexican Matter[2]	58,000.00	
Patent Rights	150,000.00	379,000.00
NET WORTH (represented by Capital Stock)		$450,000.00

[1] The nature of this claim is not revealed in the Company records.
[2] Amount due from sale of arms and ammunition to Mexico.

Reproduced with permission from Williamson, *Winchester: The Gun That Won the West,* 1952, p. 464, A. S. Barnes.

Figure 4–7

A textbook illustration of a worksheet, 1876.

WINCHESTER REPEATING ARMS COMPANY*
Balance Sheet at December 31, 1889

CURRENT ASSETS		
Cash	$ 575,676.09	
Bills Receivable	83,768.81	
Sundry Receivables	145,706.14	
Inventories	915,963.69	
Investments	630,998.45	$2,352,113.48
LESS: CURRENT LIABILITIES		90,555.48
NET WORKING CAPITAL		2,261,558.07
FIXED ASSETS		
Real Estate, Plant and Machinery, 4/1/67	150,000.00	
Estimated total expenditure from 4/1/67 to		
12/31/89	2,483,444.00	
Patents		
Acquired from O. F. Winchester	150,000.00	
Expenditures from 4/1/67 to 12/31/89	340,176.00	
Investment		
Remington Arms Co.	178,075.00	
TOTAL FIXED CAPITAL		3,301,695.00
ESTIMATED NET WORTH AT DECEMBER 31, 1889		$5,563,255.07

474

(*Note:* As in previous balance sheets the figures above include *total* expenditures on capital assets without allowance for depreciation.)

Reproduced with permission from Williamson, 1952, p. 467, A. S. Barnes.

Figure 4–7–cont.

operating accounts, that is, overhead expense in proportion to revenue from freight service and passenger service.

Still there was a general skepticism about the amount of accuracy that could be obtained from cost accounts. Were they as reliable as commercial accounts? If not, should not integration of cost and financial accounts be avoided? If so, how did one integrate these two systems of accounts? Although instances of integrating commercial and cost records could be found, there was still controversy over whether or not to integrate cost accounts and financial records. In a speech given in 1897, Frank Broaker suggested the use of a double entry technique of integration based on a consumption journal. Such attempts to describe the basis of integration indicate that a generally accepted technique was not yet in existence.

Another important influence on cost accounting during this period was the appearance of "scientific management" techniques. From

1860 to the 1890s factory systems developed increasingly from "systematic" to "scientific" using sophisticated forms of organization for production. In 1890 J. Slatter Lewis's text, *The Commercial Organization of Facilities*, indicated the use of staff-and-line techniques which had become formalized as part of overall management systems. In 1895, Frederick W. Taylor, the father of scientific management, suggested a revolutionary approach to labor costing with the introduction of the piece rate system. This was the start of what was to be scientific labor time and motion efficiency in manufacturing.

    Under this theory of systematic management, the "system" maintained the operation with the aid of the accounting and production records. The logic of processing and supply at each work station   475 therefore dictated the process of the factory's system. Scientific management added the study of efficiency of effort at each station and at each motion of operation, thereby affording the ability to establish standards of performance. The existence of the systematic and scientific management of industrial operations created a need for cost accountants who could develop "price tags" for operations in order to make monetary comparisons within this system of standards.

State and Local Accounting

By the mid 1890s, American cities were growing at a rate about three times as fast as rural areas. By 1920 the census would show that the urban population of America exceeded the rural population. With this unprecedented expansion of cities, the demands for services such as water supply, property protection and public health became apparent. Certificates such as the one shown here for the City of Baltimore, were issued in the larger municipalities. This certificate is evidence of the debt used to fund expansion of a water supply system. Issued in 1874, it was scheduled to mature in 1894.

    In the face of this growth and the need for cities to begin to finance their increasing system of services on a larger and more complex scale, there was a need for uniform accounting and supervised reporting for state and local entities. As early as 1878 and 1879, the states of Minnesota and Massachusetts enacted legislation that affected county administrations, specifying activities that would enhance the efficiency with which county officials fulfilled their duties.

The Minnesota act provided for the appointment of a state examiner to be named by the governor and required that the examiner should be a skilled accountant. The examiner's duties included the inspection of state accounts and the accounts of county officials. He was also charged with enforcing a correct and uniform system of bookkeeping. The Massachusetts act also focused on the financial administration of county officers such that by 1887 the scope of this supervision included the establishment of the Office of Controller of County Accounts (Potts 1976: 50).

476   The influence of these early precedents trickled down to the municipal level and served to define the duties of appropriate officials. Although it was uncommon for cities to issue financial reports prior to the twentieth century, certain examples, notably in the cities of Boston and Milwaukee, do exist for years prior to the turn of the century.

Figure 4–8

City of Baltimore Security, 1894.

Source: *The Countinghouse Arithmetic* (Baltimore, 1889).

Concern over the adequacy of financial disclosure of municipalities served as one cause for the formation of citizen groups that initiated reform movements to change the poor quality of administration in city government. The era of "Boss Tweed" and excessive political patronage that followed the Civil War, impacting most sharply on the large eastern cities, had now reached a point where the public had become restive and was dissatisfied with city administrations. In 1891 James Bryce wrote, "There is no denying that the government of cities is one of the conspicuous failures of the United States." New Yorkers took it upon themselves to slay the Tammany tiger. In 1894 the National Municipal League was formed. The Citizens Union was formed in 1897, representing leading citizens who acted together to bring about better government. By the time of 477 the National Conference on Good City Government in 1896, 245 organizations were functioning. The concern of city dwellers about municipal government served to influence the type of financial and accounting systems that would be forthcoming after the turn of the century. (Dahlberg 1966)

An initial audit of one major city's financial accounts which took place before the turn of the century seems to convey an example of the state of affairs. Ernest Reckitt was invited by R. A. Waller, the controller of the City of Chicago, to make a "spot" audit of the books of the city of Chicago in 1898. For a fee of $2500, an amount not anywhere near sufficient for the size of the operation to be undertaken, Reckitt agreed to start the audit. He immediately employed twelve men for the assignment, which took a period of approximately three months. Among the irregularities Reckitt found was a deficiency of about half a million dollars in the special assessments funds as well as the overall chaotic condition with respect to the payments of city bonds and coupons.

Reckitt recalls that when he requested to examine the actual bonds and interest coupons for one of the periods, he was taken to a vault where all the bonds and coupons paid during a number of years were lying in a disordered array. He observed that it would have been virtually impossible to put the bonds in numerical order so as to commence any audit, and it was therefore impossible to verify the control over the bonded debt and the interest payments of the city.

The reported deficiency in the special assessments funds raised considerable public interest particularly since the investigation had only touched the "high spots" and was specific only with respect to the listing of the balances of all assessments from 1871, the date of the Chicago fire. All prior records had been destroyed in that fire.

As a result of Reckitt's audit the city government commissioned the detailed investigation of all assessment records in both the controller's office and the city clerk's office. The firm of Haskins & Sells was selected, having submitted the lowest bid. Sells later informed Reckitt that the audit had resulted in a considerable financial loss to the firm. However, on an overall basis, in part due to the fact that there was a fee generated from detailed investigations of other city departments, the firm was given an opportunity to recover some of the large loss that it had suffered on the original contract. Such service by public accounting firms within city government resulted in the inauguration of improved systems of accounting so that future audits could be more intelligently and inexpensively con-

478 ducted.

An early American treatise on the subject of governmental accounting, a booklet entitled *Public Accounts*, dealt with the keeping of state and municipal accounts and was written in 1878 by E. S. Mills (Potts 1976: 47). This brief twenty-seven-page work described a double entry system for county treasurers, whom Mills viewed as acting as general business managers for the people. The Mills system was designed to report the following by way of a proposed comprehensive financial system:

1. Cash on hand at the beginning of the period
2. Delinquent taxes due at the beginning of the period
3. Total collections of the past year
4. Receipts from state funds, fines, licenses and other receipts
5. Expenditures for the past year
6. Abated taxes of the last year
7. Delinquent taxes due at the close of the year
8. The cash balance at the end of the period

There is no evidence that Mills' scheme was widely used or regarded. Nevertheless, it presented an early systematic attempt to deal with the perceived problems of municipal accounting. Not until after the turn of the century was a comprehensive municipal accounting system developed, including budgetary accounts. Frederick Cleveland's dual system is recognized as the first of this type.[15]

The Importance of "Gilded Age" Accounting

The year 1877 officially marked the end of the period of reconstruction following the Civil War. It also effectively marked the start of the

era of big cities and big business. It is probably useful to our view of accounting's progress since then to consider that it was only a century ago.

Among the important accomplishments which occurred during the "Gilded Age" was the profession's ability to achieve important gains in public identification and legal recognition. Formal education, standardized textbooks and a system of accounting principles were nascent or nonexistent. Municipal accounting was being shaped by the demands of citizen groups and initial audit engagements in large cities were beginning to provide information which would lead to the passage of legislation to require a more uniform system of accountability.

By the turn of the century the economy was recovering from the severe depression of 1893, and had turned to a policy of "sound money" in the election of 1896. The important role of accounting was being recognized in the financial and business community as corporations began to hire expert auditors to replace the annual audit visit of shareholders. ⁴⁷⁹

The practices of quasi-public enterprises, including transportation and utility companies, were profoundly influenced by the legal arrangements based upon cash receipts less cash disbursements notions of reporting and profit. The precedent of this regulation would serve to underlie the formulation of accounting measurement and policy for years to come. This was true particularly with regard to a view that all accounting information could be rigorously and perfectly prescribed in the form of a cash-like "operating statistic."

Since the early promulgations of the Interstate Commerce Commission (ICC), accountants and businessmen have become increasingly sophisticated as to their notions of value and techniques of measurement in attempting to determine the proper basis for establishing an adequate and fair system of measuring and reporting return on investment. To this day the century old concept of an accounting information system with an objective of providing a "cash statistic" lingers and has led to confusion and contradiction. Is the notion that accounting information should be contained in a cash-like statistic if it is to be useful for measuring return on investment, relevant in light of advances in popular economic knowledge? This cash statistic procedure, a relic of America's early industrial age, does continue to influence our regulatory practice and thinking. Similarly the basic accounting equation developed by Sprague (Assets = Liabilities + Proprietorship) continues to appear in textbooks as a means of explaining the relationship of accounts. Perhaps no two other notions so fully dictate our current practice as the early cash paradigm of regulation and the Sprague equation.

Before long, uniform listing requirements of stock markets would emphasize the need for filing of financial statements by corporations trading their securities. The need to attract capital, along with the increasing attention given by businessmen and legislators to the problem of providing sufficient financial information, would provide dual justification for the unprecedented growth of public accounting practice and periodic financial disclosure.

A popular history of the profession may suggest that 1896, the year in which the first CPA law was passed in New York, represents the birth of the accounting profession in America. Closer examination 480 suggests, however, that the post–Civil War era—the Gilded Age— witnessed the birth of the modern professional societies, all of which have served in part or in whole to establish today's practice.

NOTES

1. By 1880 Standard Oil of Ohio noted that approximately 90% of the oil refining business was under its control.

2. It is important to consider the gilded age as distinct from the years of the Civil War. Too often there is a tendency to equate the origins of the gilded age solely as an aftermath of the Civil War. In fact, the industrial propensity of America was established before the Civil War and even may have been retarded by the Civil War.

3. There is no convincing evidence that the cattle business responded any differently to the peaks and depression of market conditions, investment enthusiasm and overall national economic conditions, than did any other phase of the economy. What has been largely overlooked in economic, business and accounting history is the existence per se of mine, railroad and cattle investment and the part it played in the development of a central capital market.

4. For the last two decades of the nineteenth century the total number of incorporated cattle companies in the west numbered as follows: Montana, 181; Wyoming, 188; Colorado, 324; and New Mexico, 186. The aggregate capitalization for these respective states came to $27 million for Montana, $94 million for Wyoming, $102 million for Colorado and $61 million for New Mexico (Gressley 1971: 105).

5. Several studies by Professor Brief and other sources describe the aspects of the controversy over fixed asset accounting in this period.

6. The prevalent method of rate setting during the 1890s provided for a fixed return for the railroad investment, predominantly in capital assets. It is significant that the increased use of this criterion approximately coincides with the increased use of the retirement method for asset valuation, the demise of the use of appreciation reserves among railroads and a trend toward capitalizing rather than expensing new assets. One concludes therefore, that railroads found it expedient

to use accounting practices for asset valuation which maximized their base for rate setting calculations regardless of the validity of underlying valuation.

Some historians suggest that the Interstate Commerce Commission Act and the potential implications for regulation of the railroads may have been a significant factor in creating financial uncertainties and panics in 1893. Others argue that the classification of operating expenses requirements of the ICC went into effect in 1894, in response to the financial panics of 1893, so as to begin to supply some vestige of uniformity to financial reports of railroads.

7. Deficiencies in railroad reports also pointed to the value basis of assets, as another writer in the *Railroad Gazette* noted: "It's not what a railroad has cost that the stock and bond holders want to know; it is the value in gold, and this will not be given except by legal compulsion." These sentiments were perhaps fanned by the panic of 1893 and may have influenced the Interstate Commerce Commission's first excursion into regulation with its July 1, 1894, implementation of the classification of operating expense format. This action established a precedent for what was to become a system of uniform accounts and standardized reports for railroads under its jurisdiction (Boockholdt 1977).   481

8. One of the difficulties of research about women arises from the fact that names are not always a suitable clue. Florence, for example, though predominantly a feminine name, is occasionally bestowed upon male offspring as well. So when we find Florence Crowley listed as an accountant in the New York Directory in 1797 at 237 Water Street, in 1798 at 59 Cherry Street, and in 1802 at 16 Banker Street, and Florence Crowdy similarly listed in 1801 at 9 Frankford Street, we cannot be sure whether Florence Crowley, or Florence Crowdy, was a man or a woman.

9. Joseph Sterret of Pennsylvania, writing in 1898, is somewhat "cool" about the importance of AAPA: "The association has done some excellent work as a pioneer, but as each state has charge of its own internal affairs (The AAPA was incorporated in New York) it has been found that better results can be accomplished by separate state organizations, and these have been effected in several states."

10. Ohio University established a commercial college coincident with the University of California in 1898.

11. High schools in the post–Civil War period were few in number in relationship to the total population (there were as few as 108 high schools in 1859 and that number had increased to only 536 by 1873, with a total estimated student enrollment of only 40,000). Their curriculum was directed largely at college preparation, not commercial education. The high school had usurped the character of the academies. During the early years of the development of the high school, very little was accomplished toward placing commercial courses in the curriculum. After 1875 however, a gradual increase in commercial course offerings ensued, but these were not deemed sufficiently rigorous, and the training and the status of such a curriculum was deemed inferior by other high school faculty.

12. S. W. Crittenden's 1877 text on bookkeeping and accounting however was not substantially changed from earlier editions which date back to the pre–Civil War period.

13. In 1890 E. D. Moore's *Principles of the Science of Accounts* was published.

14. Paton also considers the works of Hatfield to have been as influential as those of Sprague in determining his career choice.

15. It should be remembered that, prior to the turn of the century, for the most part cash basis public agency systems were in use. There was only a stirring of interest in uniform accounting in the large cities as a form of reaction to public concern over the lack of effective accountability on the part of politicians. Within twenty years of passage of the county administration practices act in Minnesota and Massachusetts, the effects of such legislation were leading to applications of fiscal controls over duties involving public funds at the municipal level. States also began to take an interest in the supervision of municipal accounts in that they were providing examiners with review guidelines.

482

5 THE FORMATION OF AN ACCOUNTING PROFESSION

An excellent monument might be erected to the Unknown Stockholder. It might take the form of a solid stone ark of faith apparently floating in a pool of water. [Felix Riesenberg]

Henry Steel Commager has called the 1890s the watershed of American history. By the turn of the century, the United States had made the change from agrarian simplicity to industrial complexity. The corporate form dominated American industry. Over 70 percent of those working in manufacturing were employed by corporations, and they produced 74 percent of the value added by manufacturing. Technological advances had expanded production possibilities, a nearly complete railroad network permitted mass marketing, and communication improvements facilitated centralization. A large percentage of the country's economic resources were being controlled by a relatively small number of men who managed the industrial trusts. The consolidation of industry led to a reexamination of existing social and economic philosophies and their relevance in a corporate society (Commager, 1950: 406–411).

For many decades Americans had accepted the idea that "commerce had been the world civilizer" and that the interests of both society and the private entrepreneur could be simultaneously promoted by permitting the maximum amount of freedom to the individual.[1] Classical economics provided the English-speaking world with its fundamental economic model. The individual was at center stage. The capitalist, by striving to further his own interests, automatically promoted the public good. In an autonomous competitive market, an automatic mechanism, "the invisible hand", was assumed to result in the most efficient allocation of society's scarce resources. Government's role was passive; competition ensured protection for the public. But, in the 1890's, the effectiveness of competition, given the domination of many industries by a few industrial giants, was open to question.

Social Darwinism exalted individual freedom and was used by some to justify the unequal socio-economic conditions that existed in the United States during the last quarter of the nineteenth century. Industrialist Andrew Carnegie believed that society must accommodate "great inequality in the environment, the concentration of business industrial and commercial enterprises in the hands of a few, and the law of competition between these as being not only beneficial but essential to the future progress of the race." Carnegie modified the harshness of this doctrine by emphasizing the concept of stewardship. "The fundamental idea of the gospel of wealth" he wrote, "is that surplus wealth should be considered a sacred trust to be administered by those into whose hands it falls, during their lives, for the good of the community." But stewardship was purely voluntary, and he did not advocate public accountability.[2]

Similarly, legal theory, prior to the third decade of the twentieth century, reflected concern for individual rights. Agrarian and democratic values combined with a deep respect for the freedom of the individual in the market place to lend credence to the tenets of "individualistic law." Legal theories evolved "to deal with physical harm to ownership or possession of tangible property" but "were totally inadequate to protect the intangible values represented by security interests in the modern corporation" (Green, L., 1937, vol.3: 62ff).

As long as social, economic, and legal theories emphasized the rights of the individual and ignored the community, little demand for the services of independent public accountants was generated. Most businessmen heeded the advice found in [Lowell's] *Bigelow Papers*, which cautioned "no never say nothin' without you're compelled and then don't say nothin' you can be held to" (quoted in Haskins, 1901B). But in the 1890's serious questions were being asked about the validity of the "traditional American creed." It was with the inception of doubt about the ability of such a philosophy to promote the social welfare that public accountants began to have a major role in the United States. An examination of the conditioning environment of this period shows that accountants were in the mainstream of social reform and were given a social obligation necessary for attainment of professional status.

The Rise Of Financial Capitalism

Perhaps the most important development, in retrospect, for the emergence of the public accounting profession, was the rise of financial capitalism. For it became clear that management would become divorced from ownership and that a financier, such as J. P. Morgan, would yield enormous power. Before the panic of 1893, business consolidations were normally effected through vertical integration and internally financed. Among the more important consequences of the panic in that year was the increasing involvement of bankers and outside promoters in the operations of American corporations. Before 1893 it had been rare for a banker or financier to sit on a board of directors. By the eve of World War I, it had become almost common for representatives of investment banking houses or financiers to occupy directors' chairs and sometimes to be in positions of control. By 1913 the "money trust" held 341 directorships in 112 corporations, controlling resources and assets capitalized at around $22 billion (Hacker 1961: 26f).

485

Classical economics emphasized that the amount of capital wealth was fixed and determined the amount of industrial development possible in any given place (Johnson, 1902). This was obviously not the case in the United States where credit markets had evolved which expanded the productivity of industry. The need was apparent for methods to rationally channel capital funds into the nation's credit stream; this need became the genesis for demands that a viable, independent accounting profession be established. Slowly the conviction grew that corporate financial publicity was required to mitigate speculative pressures arising in a situation that encouraged the attitude that finance gimmickry rather than production was the easiest way to make money.

Henry Clews, President of the New York Stock Exchange at the turn of the century, had written that

> The financiers, of course, were still interested in producing goods for sale, but they were likely to be equally if not more interested in profits to be made from issuing securities and powers to be gained in arranging mergers and acquisitions (Clews 1900: 28).

Securities became the vehicles for accumulating wealth. Even those who conceded the need for industrial combinations to extract maximum benefits from economies of scale denounced the "vile demon avarice," which often motivated promoters to realize large profits from nonproductive finance transactions while ignoring manufacturing operations. Contemporary thought became increasingly hostile to those who defended corporate secrecy. Following the failure of one trust after another—tobacco, leather, whiskey, ice, sugar—demands for publicity to enable investors to make informed decisions came from both public and private sources, including progressive leaders within the business community itself. The spectre of "unsocial individualism" mandated regulation of some kind.[3]

Demands for Protection of Investors

486

As early as 1890, Clews had been an avid proponent of publicity of corporate accounts. He believed that this could be accomplished best "by the employment of skilled accountants because the certified results of their examination would be accepted as conclusive." Such examinations would result in verified statements of earnings, profits, expenses, capitalization, indebtedness, dividends, property valuation, liabilities, and assets (Clews 1906). Clews's position that expert accountants in the private sector could provide the requisite services was unique. Most contemporary advocates of reform who did support the publicity of accounts as a viable means of control did not share his confidence in the nascent accounting profession.

Economists, who at that time were the only generally accepted business oriented academicians, also demanded publicity to protect investors' interests. J.B. Clark and Frederick Cleveland declared that publicity provided the best remedy for abuses. The investor was the "most conspicuous of the trusts' victims." Publicity was the "most effective means" of control of the trusts (Cleveland 1905, Clark 1900).

Demands for corporate accountability to stockholders were being echoed in the political sector as progressive reformers advocated and sought public oversight of the activities of coporations. This development worked directly to the benefit of accountants because the vast majority of contemporary reformers did not advocate, and most of them specifically opposed, a direct federal intervention in or regulation of the financial affairs of corporations.[4] The progressive movement was central in identifying a social role and obligation for accountancy.

The Political Climate

Pragmatism has been called the operative philosophy of the progressive impulse. Formulated in a dynamic environment, pragmatism attempted to utilize empirical, investigative techniques of physical science to arrive at philosophical and social "truth." Charles Pierce, William James, and John Dewey defined truth in relation to its practical consequence. Emphasis was on "action rather than logic, immediate practicality rather than theory . . . new solutions rather than holding fast to old standards" (Dewey 1939: 396). Dewey refined earlier pragmatic theories by adding that truth must result in desirable social consequences. Thus truth was relative, but it was not Machiavellian.

Experience and education became key factors in enabling a person to determine truth. Since any data was valid only if it met the needs of practical life, a person must have sufficient experience to be able to recognize those changing conditions which might invalidate what 487 formerly has been considered a normative truth (Dewey 1900: passim). Today pragmatic and expedient are often used interchangeably, but that usage tends to obscure pragmatism's central point: for a theory, conception, policy or idea to meet the test of truth it had to have desirable social consequences. Pragmatism gave philosophic justification to political reformers' demands for government planning within the private sector.

The Progressive Movement

Progressivism is best understood as an eclectic term for an attitude that incorporated such elements as pragmatism, moralism, fundamentalism, socialism, and prohibitionism. Progressive thought embraced "a faith in democracy, a concern for morality and social justice" and expressed an "exuberant belief in progress . . . and the efficacy of education" (Thelan 1969). Fond of speaking in abstractions, the progressives drew support from a broad spectrum of the public including businessmen.[5]

Progressivism, as used here, is not meant to connote "liberalism." The movement did not articulate a single, unified philosophy nor did all progressives embrace a single common cause. There were in fact several progressive movements which are often combined and described as "the quest for social justice." There were few true radicals among the ranks of progressives. Socialism, which gained adherents in Europe, never became a strong political alternative in the United States (McNaught 1966:504).

Progressives and pragmatists both called for government to take an active role in defining social goals in an industrial society. But they never suggested that government assume operational control of business. One of the important themes of progressivism was the "gospel of efficiency." Reformers had a tendency to "turn to the expert as a disinterested person who could divest himself of narrow class or parochial" interests (Grantham 1964). Progressive demands for efficiency in government, regulation of business, and tax reform all had positive effects with respect to the development of the profession of accountancy in the United States. For it was the independent public accountant, the disinterested expert, who could provide the necessary services to implement progressive reforms.

Demands for Government Efficiency

488   Political progressives' conviction that corruption and inefficiency lay at the root of social ills in the United States was reflected in their demands that public officials be held accountable for their actions. Muckrakers like Lincoln Steffens skillfully used popular journalism to stimulate public awareness of the issues. New governmental accounting systems became mandatory under state laws and resulted in significant improvements in the conduct of public business. This kind of activity, which required and obtained the cooperation and participation of accountants, was a major factor in bringing accountancy to public attention.

As early as 1895, when Charles Waldo Haskins and Elijah Watt Sells received Senate commendation for their work on the Dockery Commission, accounting practitioners became a vital force in the reform movement. The National Civic Federation and the National Municipal League received the patronage, interest and participation of accountants. Demands for greater efficiency in federal government brought accountants to national attention. The Keep Commission (1905) had called upon the American Association of Public Accountants for expert advice in plans to reorganize the federal bureaucracy. Official recognition of the association as the national voice of the profession was a milestone in those early days.[6]

The President's Committee on Economy and Efficiency, which Taft proposed in 1911 to facilitate the introduction of business techniques into the federal bureaucracy, immediately called upon leading practitioners to serve on a Board of Consulting Accountants. J.E. Sterret, E.W. Sells, F.F. White, and W.B. Richards were appointed to this board. The President's Secretary, Charles Norton, wrote that "the subject of administration lies largely in your hands," and suggested that accountants allow the commission the "added privilege of submitting written reports for your criticism while we are formulating and starting our constructive program" (U.S., Executive, 1912–1914).

The commission was composed of three political and three expert appointees. Frederick A. Cleveland, the chairman, and Harvey S. Chase, the municipal accounting expert, were primarily responsible for the papers issued on auditing and reporting problems. Conferences were held and opinions submitted on such topics as "constructive recommendations with respect to the principles which should govern expenditure accounting and reporting," issued as Treasury Circular No. 34, 20 May 1911. Many similar questions were discussed and resulted in either Treasury circulars or commission reports (U.S., Congress, 1913, H. Doc. 104).

Chase's work solidified his position as an expert on municipal reform and, like many other early practitioners, he traveled extensively within the United States to act as a consultant to municipalities installing new accounting systems. The American Association of Public Accountants, recognizing the opportunity inherent in administrative reform, established numerous standing committees to provide advice and accounting services for political reform agencies.

The Regulation of Business

Perhaps more important to the development of public accountancy were the political reformers' demands for corporate responsibility. The most universally suggested and accepted remedy for the overt abuses which accompanied the rise of financial capitalism was the publicity of corporate accounts. Both businessmen and government officials preferred that control be left in the private sector. In 1898, with the establishment of the Industrial Commission, it became apparent that accountants had a golden opportunity to join the mainstream of the business reform movement.[7]

The Industrial Commission was established to investigate and to report on questions relating to immigration, labor, agriculture, manufacturing and business. Experts were employed in each field, and it probably was a reflection of the status of accountants in 1898 that none were engaged. But one of the conclusions reached in the commission's preliminary report, which appeared in 1900, was that an independent public accounting profession ought to be established if corporate abuses such as stockwatering and overcapitalization were to be curtailed effectively.

Many of the persons who testified before the Industrial Commission, including most of the businessmen, felt that corporate publicity was the best alternative available for reducing various corporate abuses. Certainly there were a few men who objected vigorously to any form of corporate control and maintained that the doctrine of *caveat emptor* must apply to the investor as well as the consumer. The best known of those who opposed publicity was Henry O. Havemeyer who, however, did little to promote the continuation of government laissez faire.

490 The exchange between Havemeyer and John North, lawyer for the commission, seemed to reinforce rather than mitigate the demand for published financial statements. Havemeyer, president of the American Sugar Refining Company, was asked, "How do you carry on business at a loss and still declare dividends?" Havemeyer responded: "You can carry on business and lose money, you can meet and declare dividends. One is an executive decision and the other is a business matter." Somewhat bewildered, North asked: "Where do you get the money?" "We may borrow it," said Havemeyer. Puzzled, North continued. "How many years can the American Sugar Refining Company keep up the practice?" "That is a problem to everyone," conceded Havemeyer, and explained that "we should either buy or sell (our) stock if we knew that." (U.S. Congress 1900 132f)

Some witnesses had opposed publication of financial reports contending that the information signaled by the payment of dividends was sufficient to permit investors to make informed decisions. Havemeyer's testimony negated that argument and most businessmen conceded that some form of corporate publicity was needed.[8]

Recommendations of the Commission

In its preliminary report, which appeared in 1900, the commission stated that its prime objective would be "to prevent the organizers of corporations or industrial combinations from deceiving investors and the public, either through suppression of material facts or by making misleading statements." The final report, issued in 1902, concluded that:

The larger corporations—the so-called trusts—should be required to publish annually a properly audited report, showing in reasonable detail their assets and liabilities, with profit and loss; such a report and audit under oath to be subject to government regulation (U.S., Congress 1902:650).

A minority report, rejected by the Commission, advocated that a bureau be established in the Treasury Department to register all state corporations engaged in interstate commerce and to secure from each an adequate financial report, to make inspections and examinations of corporate account, and to collate and to publish information regarding such combinations. (U.S. Congress 1902: 649ff)

The only argument presented in opposition to the reporting of financial data, which the commissioners conceded was a convincing one, was that no independent group of technically qualified professionals was available to perform the necessary audits. The lack of an organized accounting profession appeared to preclude reliance on the private sector for adequate, accurate, and reliable information. The conclusions of the Industrial Commission established the need for independent public accountants. After 1902, accountants could also count on the support of businessmen. Although they may have preferred corporate secrecy, the real threat of direct government intervention in corporate affairs rendered the alternative— independent audits by established professional accountants—more attractive.

491

Tax Reform

One of the few permanent progressive reforms was the graduated income tax. For accountants, the 1909 corporate excise tax had become a highly profitable nightmare. The law as passed clearly stated that revenues and expenditures must be calculated on a cash, not an accrual, basis. Accountants objected vigorously and eventually the Treasury issued a regulation that permitted the use of the accrual method of determining net income.

With the ratification of the sixteenth amendment to the constitution, the income tax became a permanent fixture of American life. Accountants, through the American Association, worked closely with the federal government throughout the period to assure no more debacles like the 1909 corporate excise tax.[9] In 1913, Robert H. Montgomery, as president of the association, reminded the Ways and Means Committee of the House of Representatives that "the American Association of Public Accountants . . . shall always be ready and glad to render every assistance in our power to further the preparation of efficient legislation." ("Corporation Tax Returns" *Journal of Accountancy*, Feb. 1913:139).

But the impact of the income tax law on the accounting profession was not as evidently salutary as were calls for reform in the government and corporate sectors. Accountants, who had enhanced their image as being in the mainstream of the social reform movement through municipal and corporate audits, may have lost a little of their perceived independence through the tax reform. There is nevertheless little doubt that tax reform created a very definite need for accounting services and had a dramatic impact on the development of the profession.

The Role of the Accountant in the Reform Movement

492 The progressive movement conferred upon the public accountant a specific social obligation. But this should not be interpreted to mean that all accountants were reformers or progressives. Within accountancy there were divergent opinions as to the value and desirability of progressive reforms. There were few more scathing denunciations of the "money trust" than those found in the editorials of *The Bookkeeper* (May 1899: 11–13). Edward L. Suffern, president of the American Association of Public Accountants, recognized the new "social consciousness" in the nation and advised his colleagues that if accountants were to gain professional status, they must be aware of their social responsibility (Suffern 1912). But although public accountants benefited from the reform movement, the profession remained closely allied to the business community.

Most practitioners readily agreed with the contention that politicians were corruptible and that therefore systems must be installed to insure greater accountability in the public sector; they were less willing to accept any indictment of business morality. They certainly never agreed that government intervention in the private sector was either called for or wise.

This is not surprising since economic theory still did not advocate any form of government planning in the free market. Although the neoclassical economics refined by Alfred Marshall and John Bates Clark added equilibrium analysis, it remained essentially a static theory focusing upon competition to insure the best possible allocation of society's resources. Despite the obvious increase in monopolistic and oligopolistic industries, most economists continued to stress the efficacy of competition. The more radical economic doctrines such as the "economy of abundance" posited by Simon Patten (1907) or institutional theory delineated by Thorstein Veblen and John R. Commons never gained widespread acceptance.[10]

Most accountants empathized with the opinion expressed by the famed jurist Oliver Wendell Holmes, who is purported to have said that the "Sherman Anti-Trust Act is based on pure economic ignorance and the Interstate Commerce Commission isn't fit to have rate making powers" when asked his opinion of government efforts to regulate business (Persons 1958: 273).

Holmes commended Elijah Watt Sells's widely distributed pamphlet, *Corporate Management Compared with Government Control*, which denounced government intervention in the free enterprise system. Sells contended that "it is an unassailable truth that almost anyone of the men who stand at the heart of our great business institutions is far more competent to run the government, and would run it more economically, more wisely, and more honestly than any of those who are in the business of running government"[11] (Sells 1908).

493

Despite the fact that accounting practitioners often expressed a personal belief in the concepts of the "traditional American creed" rather than in the newer social philosophies, they did accept certain assumptions of the reform movement. Three general tenets of progressivism which accountants could accept were (1) a fundamental faith in democracy, a concern for morality and justice and a broad acceptance of the efficacy of education as a major tool in social amelioration; (2) an increased awareness of the social obligation of all segments of society and introduction of the idea of accountability to the public of business and political leaders; and (3) an acceptance of pragmatism as the most relevant operative philosophy of the day (Hofstadter 1944: 318f).

The British Influence

Thus far little has been said about the influence of the English chartered accountants in gaining recognition for accountancy in the United States. Undoubtedly, increased British investments, which required close scrutiny given the wild, free-wheeling business environment in the United States in the 1880s, brought English professional accountants to the United States. But until there was some call for control of business, chartered accountants were not very successful in promoting accounting services. One has only to look at the blatant techniques used by Jay Gould who, when called to account for defrauding English investors of $60,000, simply asked for the return of the stock certificates to verify the amount of investment. When the certificates were returned to him, he promptly shredded them, destroying any evidence against him. There was no strenuous objection voiced in the United States, and it was several years before British investors recovered their losses.

Initial demands for reform did not evolve to protect British investors but rather because social conditions in the United States became intolerable to many. Undoubtedly, the arrival of chartered accountants added to the prestige of the profession, but it seems that the domestic reform movement was more important in gaining recognition for accountancy in the United States. Despite the obvious rhetoric concerning corporate control, no federal corporation law was enacted nor were any statutes similar to the English Companies Acts promulgated.[12]

494   The progressive movement, accompanied by demands for municipal and corporate accountability and the income tax reform all had salutary effects on the development of accountancy. Pragmatism gave philosophic justification to political demands and had a decided impact on the evolution of accounting theory, educational standards, and ethics. Accountants had to provide an institutional framework if the profession was to respond effectively to contemporary demands. Initial efforts here concentrated on securing legislation, which gave statutory recognition to the profession. The first CPA law was passed in New York in 1896 and for the next twenty years efforts to secure similar legislation in the remaining states preoccupied accountants.

The Institutional Framework

In the United States, under our federal system, both professional licensing and education are deemed state prerogatives. Accountants' early organizational efforts, therefore, were oriented to forming viable separate state professional organizations. Thus, after 1896, the American Association of Public Accountants had ceased to be an effective institutional instrument and quickly became moribund even in New York as state societies addressed the major issues confronting the profession. Hostility surfaced between native-born practitioners and the chartered accountants who had gained effective control of the association, and that rift severely hampered its operations. Rivalries developed among different state organizations, and that, too, delayed steps towards professional unity. Three major state societies—New York, Pennsylvania, and Illinois—assumed preeminence in the profession until 1905.

The Emergence of State Societies

There can be little doubt that the existence of these powerful rival societies tended to divisiveness, deterring effective national organization of the profession. A brief examination of the major societies demonstrates that until 1904 (when the International Congress of Accountants convened at St. Louis) efforts at unity were hampered by divergent goals. A pattern did begin to emerge as each state sought, after securing CPA laws, to address the issues of education, university affiliation, and professional publications.

New York State Society of Certified Public Accountants (NYSSCPA)   495

New York's CPA law limited the granting of certificates to "citizens or those who intended to become citizens," which effectively barred many resident British chartered accountants from certification in New York. The waiver privilege was of very short duration and decisions to seek U.S. citizenship had to be made quickly. (See Chapter 4, pp. 100 ff., in this book.)

The NYSSCPA revealed the direction it would take when fifteen men met to incorporate the society in 1897. The American Association (dominated by the British) was virtually unrepresented. Eleven of the fifteen charter members had never joined the association; three of the remaining four who were Association members had joined only for the duration of the effort to secure a CPA law, and all but one were native born. Conspicuous by their absence were men like W. Sanders Davies and Frank Broaker. Davies was a naturalized citizen; Broaker was native born but he studied in Scotland and was closely allied with the British element in the Association (Webster 1954: 336, 343).

New York State practitioners pioneered efforts for cooperation between universities and accountants. Many of the NYSSCPA members had been associated with the abortive New York School of Accounts; most were convinced that a major factor in its failure was its isolation from any established institution.[13] Leaders of the New York state society had approached several universities, often to be met with condescension and ultimately rejection, for accounting was not deemed an appropriate element of a higher education curriculum.

Success, as so often the case during those formative years, was primarily due to the efforts of a single man. In this case, the man was Charles E. Sprague. He rented a faculty house at Washington Square for the summer, near the home of Henry M. McCracken,
a

496

Charles E. Sprague.

president of New York University. Each night, Sprague managed to accompany McCracken on his habitual walk, and never failed to mention the value that a school of commerce would afford citizens of New York (Jones 1933: 357–357). In October 1900, New York University agreed to the proposal advanced by the New York society for a new school of commerce. Accounting practitioners served as guarantors against any and all financial loss and agreed to furnish a large part of the necessary faculty. This pattern was to be emulated by practitioners in other states who held the strong American faith in the efficacy of formal education.

The Pennsylvania Institute of Public Accountants

Pennsylvania practitioners' experiences roughly paralleled those in New York. There, however, the bitterness and hostility toward chartered accountants evident in New York did not arise, for from the beginning the profession in Pennsylvania was in the control of native-born accountants (Ross 1940A: 8–12). The Pennsylvania Institute was incorporated in 1897; a CPA law was enacted in 1898. Inspired by the New York society's example, in 1902 the Pennsylvania institute inaugurated evening courses in accountancy. The institute continued efforts to affiliate with a university, an effort made more imperative when members who taught the courses began to feel the pressures of practicing and teaching, too. Finally, in 1904, the University of Pennsylvania's Wharton School of Finance agreed to take over the institute's program (Bennett 1922: 60–64). 497

Pennsylvania accountants added another dimension to the role of state societies when the institute inaugurated *The Public Accountant.* Although shortlived, the publication was recognition of a real need and foreshadowed early leaders' emphasis on the importance of appropriate professional literature for American practitioners.

The New York and Pennsylvania experiences are somewhat reflective of all early efforts in industrialized states along the east coast, with the exception of Massachusetts. The comparative advantage eastern states enjoyed in securing legal recognition meant that after 1902, practitioners there could focus their energies on a national organization. In other sections of the nation, practitioners' efforts necessarily were concentrated on local issues.[14]

The Illinois Society of Public Accountants

To reply to an obvious question—where did the chartered accountants go after New York State passed its carefully drafted CPA laws?—one has only to look west to Illinois to find a powerful British presence. The Illinois legislature, under strong populist influence, resisted early efforts to enact a CPA law. One state senator, whose notion of equality meant free entry of all into any profession, lack of training or ability notwithstanding, distrusted accountants' motives in seeking a CPA law. The senator was alleged to have announced to George Wilkinson: "I would like to know what youse fellows want; if youse want a lead pipe cinch, I am agin you" (Ross 1940A: 16). Given such attitudes, Illinois practitioners had to demonstrate that they meant to exclude no one. The Illinois state society had earlier opposed incorporated audit companies. In 1903 the society admitted Edward Gore, of the Audit Company of Chicago, and Maurice Kuhns, of the Safeguard Account Company; their influence was needed to lobby for a CPA law. Another result of the political necessity of excluding no one was that chartered accountants, citizens or not, were eligible for membership. In 1903, twenty-one of the society's fifty-three members were from the firm of Price Waterhouse, practitioners who could not be certified in New York State because they were British subjects, but who could be certified in Illinois under broad waiver provisions (Wilkinson 1904). Even after Illinois accountants finally extracted a CPA law from a hostile legislature, practitioners there had to be constantly alert to petitions to undercut certification standards in the interests of persons who complained of discrimination (Reckitt 1953: 73–74).

498

The Illinois society followed the pattern of other states in convincing Northwestern University to inaugurate a school of business and commerce. Practitioners from New York and Pennsylvania joined their Illinois colleagues as guarantors against financial loss to the university. Among the most lasting contribution of the Illinois society was the publication of *The Auditor*, a professional journal later taken over by the American association and renamed *The Journal of Accountancy*.

The Illinois experience reflected the hostility accountants faced in many midwestern and southern states. Efforts in 1902 to bring about a national unity to the profession appeared to have failed largely because regional differences had not been properly appreciated by the national leadership.

The Federation of Societies of Public Accountants in the United States

Practitioners met in 1902 ostensibly to discuss means of forming a national group to promote CPA laws in every state. The fruit of their efforts was the organization of the Federation of Societies of Public Accountants in the United States with the announced intention of promoting uniform CPA laws. But the three major state societies of New York, Pennsylvania, and Illinois were engaged in heated competition. Available evidence suggests that an unnamed objective of the federation had been to mitigate the effects of this legacy of rivalry and bickering which many concerned practitioners feared threatened to undercut professional goals (Suffern 1922). George Wilkinson worked diligently to gain the cooperation of those three powerful states, and is granted the major credit for the federation's organization. The New

York State society, never enthusiastic about the federation and reluctant to surrender any of its prerogatives, made two demands at the organizational meeting which created dissension and almost at once precluded the federation from ever becoming an effective national body. The New York delegates demanded that federation membership be based exclusively upon affiliation with a state society and closed to individuals and also insisted upon an invidious distinction between CPA and non–CPA societies. The first demand was accepted, the second defeated, and it was only after extraordinary efforts by Federation supporters among the New York society members that that state agreed to join the federation (NYSSCPA, *Minutes,* 1902: 17).[15]

The reluctance of the New York state society to participate fully and completely in the federation centered on a fundamental disagreement as to goals. The federation's announced goal was to seek CPA legislation in those states that lacked CPA laws. New York accountants perceived that goal as considerably less important than the development and enforcement of professional standards. In 1904 New York state society members voted 28 to 18 to withdraw from the federation and suggested the unification of existing organizations (NYSSCPA *Minutes,* 1904: 89). This position formed a principal element of the agenda of the 1904 International Congress of Accountants.

499

Meeting in St. Louis

The St. Louis meeting in 1904 was a milestone in the development of accountancy in the United States. It marks the coming of political maturity within the profession's leadership. The most difficult task facing the delegates was to convince practitioners that their professional interests could be best promoted by a national organization. The ability to bring together in a cooperative enterprise men who, by the nature of the profession, were strong-willed and independent, and accustomed to defending personal positions, was critical during those first organizational efforts. Compromise, moderation, discussion, accommodation—perhaps the true politics of any profession— were mandatory. Subsequent to the negotiations at the congress, the federation agreed to merge with the AAPA in 1905. Once again accountants had a single national voice, but fundamental divisions as to goals and priorities remained unresolved.

The American Association of Public Accountants, 1905–1916

Many of those participating in the International Congress viewed the merger of the two national organizations as the first step in obtaining uniform national standards for the accounting profession. But it soon became apparent that the AAPA simply did not have the authority to enforce meaningful standards. The merger had treated but failed to heal bitter regional and ethnic divisions among practitioners.

500

The association's presidential election of 1906 confirmed that chartered accountants were viewed with hostility in most states and would soon be systematically excluded from positions of leadership. The nominees for president that year were Arthur Lowes Dickinson and Elijah Watt Sells. Meeting just before the annual convention of the AAPA, the New York State society threatened to withdraw from the association if Dickinson were elected. A motion was offered stating that the New York society's interests would be best served only if the president of the AAPA was "a distinctly representative American professional accountant . . . familiar with American institutions and customs" (NYSSCPA, *Minutes*, 1906: 160–162). Sells himself was horrified, and moved that the society simply resolve to support whomever was elected. Although Sells's motion was overwhelmingly defeated, he managed to have the original resolution tabled. Webster recalled that this election was especially vitriolic and observed that "those who spoke for or against particular candidates seemed not to have thought of professional ethics" (Webster 1954: 141). One goal of the New Yorkers was achieved in that before 1916 no chartered accountant ever became president of the association. The 1906 election exacerbated anti-British sentiment. It narrowed effective control of the AAPA to a small group of practitioners from New York and Pennsylvania and the national authority the association sought was never realized. Accountants faced severe criticism from outside the profession and the AAPA was powerless to respond adequately and effectively.

Inadequate CPA Legislation

One of the major goals of the association was the standardization of CPA laws. The association had adopted the federation's "model bill for CPA legislation," which John A. Cooper had drafted, and endeavored to use it as a yardstick to determine the effectiveness and acceptability of new state legislation.[16] But the Association could do little to upgrade inadequate legislation or to gain passage of new CPA

501

Lighthearted sketches of Arthur Lowes Dickinson and Elijah Watt Sells.

(Source: program of the 1906 Annual Meeting of the American Association of Public Accountants, Columbus, Ohio.

laws which conformed to Cooper's ideal. The hardworking Committee on State Legislation conducted voluminous correspondence but to no avail. In 1911, Ohio, Georgia and Louisiana enacted CPA laws totally unacceptable to the national leadership. (AAPA, *Yearbook*, 1911: 834) The Association refused to recognize CPA certificates from those states and practitioners in them were not eligible for Association membership. By 1915 the situation had deteriorated to the point that the AAPA would not accept the CPA certificates issued by nine of the forty-two states which had CPA laws.

502
Criticism, especially from federal authorities, that a CPA certificate often was worthless and afforded little protection to the public began to appear in the press. The Association certainly could not argue convincingly that existing legislation could ensure professional competence. The call for more stringent laws became a major factor in reinforcing beliefs that an "eastern establishment" allegedly in control of the association did not care about promoting accountancy nationwide. Southerners and midwesterners argued that, given the strong antipathy among legislators in their states to any CPA law at all, even a bad law was better than none. Insistence upon legislation that conformed to the Cooper model, they argued, meant no CPA law at all.

Disillusioned with the experience of dealing with state legislators, the association attempted to solve the problem by appealing to the federal government. As early as 1889, John A. Cooper had formulated a scheme of federal registration of accountants who met certain qualifications, to be known as Registered Public Accountants.[17] The association's committee on Federal Legislation, under the leadership of Robert Montgomery and Edward L. Suffern, explored that possibility over several years. Practitioners, with few exceptions (among them Cooper), continued to believe that the federal authorities would permit the association to define and control admission standards. Cooper himself had declared it to be an unrealistic assumption and believed that any federal registration plan would probably have to be administered by the Civil Service Commission or a similar body (Cooper 1913). Nothing appeared to move Washington; suddenly, in 1914, Federal Trade Commission Chairman ~~Edwin~~ Hurley announced a plan for the commission to recognize a limited number of accountants as "zone experts." The proposal was a shock, and the association quickly backed off from its earlier enthusiasm for federal recognition (AAPA, *Yearbook*, 1915: 199–200). Hurley's plan for "audits according to rigidly prescribed procedures . . . under a predetermined fee schedule" made accountants wary of the notion that outside authorities could put the profession's house in order without exacting a price.[18]

By 1916 the national organization and its leadership found itself in a critical situation. Legislation proved inadequate in some states; efforts to seek federal recognition almost resulted in government administration of the profession itself. This dilemma alone probably would have been enough to lead to the association's demise. Nevertheless, another issue arose which had serious repercussions throughout the profession: critics outside the profession contended that established practitioners were seeking to secure a monopoly.

Professional Exclusion

503

The charge that in certain states, especially New York and Illinois, established CPAs had restricted entrance into accountancy through unreasonable admission standards, was devastating. When James G. Cannon, president of the Fourth National Bank of New York, publicly charged that CPAs were conspiring to create a monopoly, knowledgeable practitioners were dismayed (AAPA, *Yearbook*, 1908: 120–124). During the 1890s Cannon had been among the first advocates of independent audits for credit purposes, and subsequently had been considered a strong ally of the profession. Many accountants, including most of the officers of the association, were especially sensitive to the allegation that the qualifying examination was a tool for monopoly because they had received their certificates through waiver.

Newspapers in New York and Chicago were especially critical of the profession's alleged policy of deliberate exclusion. The *Chicago Herald* revealed that in Illinois, between 1903 and 1908, 111 persons sat for the CPA examination and only six had passed. Moreover, no less than ninety-eight certificates had been granted by waiver. The situation in New York was, if anything, "worse." The New York State annual failure rate had always been above 90 percent; in 1916, even that record was broken when 3 of 156 candidates were issued CPA certificates. W. Sanders Davies, who rejected the monopoly charge publicly, privately considered the situation intolerable. He contended, ". . . a man in my office . . . doesn't dot his I's or cross his T's just where the examiners require them to be dotted or crossed. This may be alright for schoolboys but not for accountants" (AAPA, *Minutes*, 1916A: 54–55). Had that been Davies's perception alone, reform might not have been necessary. But a New York State examiner corroborated the allegation for picayune grading when he remarked that he allowed "one-fifth for the correctness of an answer and four-fifths for the arrangement" (Suffern 1909).

The American Institute of Accountants

By 1916 a decade of bitter frustration convinced association leaders that the national body must be reorganized to still criticism of the profession. The charges of professional exclusion and meaningless CPA certificates had to be answered if federal intervention was to be averted.

504

A critical element of the reorganization scheme of 1916 was to permit the national organization (hereafter called the institute) to admit new members on an individual basis. Among the requirements for membership was five years of practical experience and passage of the institute's examination. One of the reasons for individual memberships was to give residents of such states as New York and Illinois, notorious for apparently arbitrary CPA examination grading, an opportunity to enter the profession. The same reasoning applied to residents of those states whose CPA qualifying procedures were unacceptable; good men could enter the profession free of the taint of poor standards. A major purpose, overriding others, appeared to be to bring under the control of the institute, all practitioners who for one reason or another had formerly belonged to no professional group at all.[19]

The plan for direct, individual admission to the institute of persons who met its qualifications and passed its examination appeared to many to be an abandonment of nearly a quarter century's effort to gain legislative recognition for the profession.[20] Ironically, the very men who inaugurated the reform of 1916 had also been in the vanguard of the CPA movement in New York, Illinois, and Pennsylvania. They now faced charges of selling out. The 1916 reorganization achieved two major objectives: criticism of a CPA monopoly abated and, for a time, federal intervention was forestalled. But the abandonment of the CPA certificate left the institute open to challenge as the "national" body and a rival organization, the American Society of CPAs, would soon emerge. Therefore, although the reorganization of the national body was politically effective, control over the profession remained illusory. The institute, like the association, had no recognized, legitimate power by which to enforce professional standards.

The Evolution of Professional Standards[21]

"Legislation for a profession only grants opportunity," observed Joseph Sterrett in 1904. He continued, "Education must be underneath and around all our legislation and organization" (Sterrett 1904). His advice reflected native-born practitioners' faith in the efficacy of education, a belief which had a unique influence upon the development of accountancy in the United States.

Early practitioners' view of education's role was influenced by contemporary ideas of the nature of a profession. The most widely accepted definition of a profession at the end of the nineteenth century was " . . . an occupation that involves a liberal education or its equivalent and mental rather than physical labor" (Joplin 1914A). The concept of "liberal education" incorporated the Aristotelean concept of "spiritual condition," and was in its essence ethical. Education imparted not only academic skills but imbued the young person with such values as righteousness, wisdom, and a sense of justice. Experience in the broadest sense completed the educated man. One must keep that background in mind when discussing and evaluating early practitioners' actions and recommendations on education.

505

Accountants at the turn of the century lived during a time of endemic change induced by the economic and social adjustments that rapid industrialization had introduced in the United States. Rapid change can precipitate political and social instability; but it may also promote intellectual flexibility and receptiveness to new ideas. American pragmatism advocated the injection of practical skills into education and provided the necessary philosophical justification for the introduction of accounting into university curricula; the progressive movement advocated the kinds of reforms that created a social need for accountancy.

The major constraint to the fulfillment of practitioners' ideal of placing the profession firmly upon an educational base was the hostility of state legislators. Reluctant even to incorporate rudimentary technical prerequisites in CPA laws they were finally induced to enact, state legislators could not be expected to accept formal educational requirements which lawmakers often interpreted as attempts to restrict free entry into the profession. Before World War I, it was rare for most people to complete high school. In 1900, the median number of school years for the general population was between seven and eight years; the practitioners' ideal of at least a high school diploma for accountants faced insurmountable opposition

American Association of Public Accountants 1910 *Muir Woods*

506

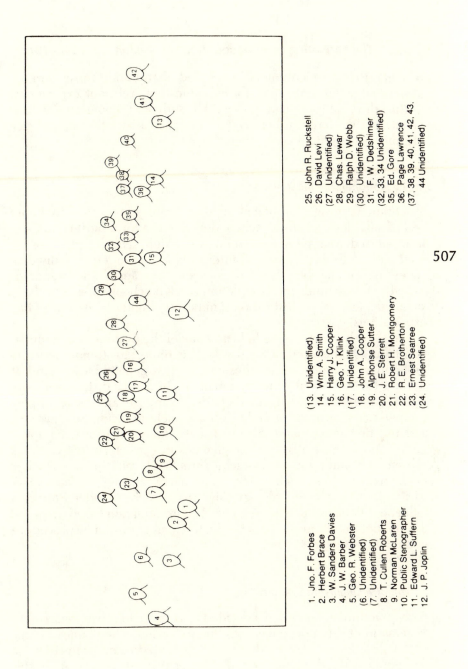

1. Jno. F. Forbes
2. Herbert Brace
3. W. Sanders Davies
4. J. W. Barber
5. Geo. R. Webster
(6. Unidentified)
(7. Unidentified)
8. T. Cullen Roberts
9. Norman McLaren
10. Public Stenographer
11. Edward L. Suffern
12. J. P. Joplin

(13. Unidentified)
14. Wm. A. Smith
15. Harry J. Cooper
16. Geo. T. Klink
(17. Unidentified)
18. John A. Cooper
19. Alphonse Sutter
20. J. E. Sterrett
21. Robert H. Montgomery
22. R. E. Brotherton
23. Ernest Seatree
(24. Unidentified)

25. John R. Ruckstell
26. David Levi
(27. Unidentified)
28. Chas. Lewar
29. Ralph D. Webb
(30. Unidentified)
31. F. W. Dedshimer
(32, 33, 34 Unidentified)
35. Ed. Gore
36. Page Lawrence
(37, 38, 39, 40, 41, 42, 43, 44 Unidentified)

507

(Counts 1922). Practitioners concluded that under those circumstances no single criterion—formal education, relevant experience, passing the CPA examination—could be sufficient. Some combination of criteria therefore was believed necessary to assure the competence of aspiring accountants.

Educational Qualifications

508 Practitioners recognized that at the turn of the century they could not realistically demand a high school diploma; the term most commonly incorporated into CPA legislation was "high school degree or its equivalent." Enforcement and interpretation were left to individual states' examining boards, and consequently applicable standards varied. At that time, the completion of high school appears to have signified a level of sophistication significantly higher than present day expectations.

Most early practitioners held as a model the preliminary examination then administered in Scotland. (It is important to note that the preliminary examination was designed to test general background; it was *not* the CPA qualifying examination). In Scotland, the candidate was required to write from dictation: compose an essay; display competence in arithmetic and algebra to include quadratic equations and the first four books of Euclid; have knowledge of geography, Latin, and English history; and demonstrate mastery in two fields chosen from Latin, Greek, French, German, Italian, Spanism, higher mathematics, physics, chemistry, physiology, zoology, botany, electricity, light and heat, geology, and stenography. Under Sterrett's influence, Pennsylvania implemented an examination based upon the Scot model, but in most states the high school equivalency procedure was a sham (Sterrett 1905).

The CPA Qualifying Examination

Early practitioners revealed a decided reluctance to rely upon a single examination to support entry into the profession. They believed that CPA legislation was justified only if it provided some protection for the public. Standards among the states varied widely, and the comprehensiveness of early examinations often left much to be desired. What concerned practitioners most about the situation was that the public risked relying upon certificates that were meaningless.

Edward Suffern spoke for the most thoughtful practitioners when he wrote that accountants must seek to safeguard "the interests of the public . . . which should not be misled through supposing . . . protection where none exists" (AAPA, *Yearbook*, 1911: 99).

The most common criticism of early CPA examinations was their tendency to be narrowly technical; practitioners were naturally reluctant to place reliance upon such a single prerequisite for entry. John Cooper wrote that

> Not one with any practical knowledge of affairs can argue that a mere passing of an examination is proof of intellectual superiority, and still less that it is a guarantee of judicial temperament, common sense, logical faculty, and professional instincts (Cooper 1970C).

509

To understand this attitude one must recall that these practitioners tended to view the awarding of the CPA certificate as a sign of professional competence. Therefore the candidates' preliminary education and experience became vital elements of the certification process. But the ultimate goal was to combine education and experience, and practitioners looked to universities to provide the requisite educational programs.

University Affiliation

State societies from their inception promoted accounting courses in universities. Practitioners faced the task of convincing university administrators, who shared a common view that only the arts and sciences were proper subjects for higher education, that schools of commerce and business had a legitimate place among more traditional faculties. The business world exhibited a similar skepticism about the value of a college education.[22] Some accountants found it difficult to convince businessmen of the value of education. If anti-intellectualism was not common, there was a definite attitude that long formal educational preparation was neither necessary nor desirable for business careers.

American practitioners had no precedents and no models when it came to outlining the kinds of courses of study the new business schools might offer. As Charles Waldo Haskins pointed out:

> The question could not be answered in Great Britain, because of the absence there of any system of commercial education in which to place it; it could not be answered on the Continent, from which has come the

present wave of activity in economic education, because bureaucratic bookkeeping is still the continental idea of accuracy (Haskins 1901A: 10).

The Role of University Education

The original purpose of the first higher educational programs in accounting was to train practitioners' assistants. After securing acceptance for accounting curricula in universities, accountants began to advocate an expansion of university education to realize the goals of broader, more conceptual programs. Most practitioners considered mastery of the technical procedures of auditing and accounting to be most effectively learned through practical experience; education's role was to develop analytical ability. Accounting, they believed, required a wide range of knowledge and minds trained to think analytically and constructively. They supported a broad program emphasizing theory and philosophy and were disappointed when the evidence accumulated that accounting educators tended to emphasize narrow, technical training.

It was the university accounting educators who moved from the theoretical approach and turned to procedural orientation. As early as 1907 the association's Committee on Education received repeated requests for practitioner-teachers. Practitioners did respond, and most of the faculties in schools of business were composed of practicing CPAs. Academicians supported their requests for practitioner-teachers on the grounds that "professional subjects must be practically applied (and) theoretically oriented professors could not handle accountancy in a satisfactory manner."[23] It is possible, though not certain, that those first academic accountants might have been influenced by contemporary developments in major university law schools. The law schools were restructuring curricula to accommodate the so-called case method of legal instruction, which was designed as a deliberate departure from traditional emphasis on legal theory and philosophy.

After 1910, one specific issue, the ever increasing orientation of academic programs toward the CPA examination, aroused the wrath of most of the national leadership (AAPA, *Yearbook*, 1912: 138f). Some academicians joined with the institute in voicing criticism. Duncan noted that whenever a question on a specific industry—railroads, utilities, breweries—appeared on a CPA examination, accounting departments went searching for an expert to add one more narrowly specialized course to the program (Duncan 1914: 145). In

510

1918 W. Sanders Davies, president of the institute, chided educators for proceeding on the "erroneous assumption (that) preparing men for the CPA examination was what was most needed," and said that as a result academicians "placed too little emphasis on accounting theory" (AIA, *Minutes*, 1917: 46). The debate continued into the 1920s; but the introduction of practice sets and their growing use in accounting courses was clear evidence that Davies's position had lost ground and that accounting curricula had repudiated conceptual approaches in favor of technique and procedure.[24]

Perhaps this change in emphasis in accounting curricula reflected what one might have called a "generation gap." The "first" accountants, who reached maturity and position by 1900, believed in the concept of broad, general and liberal education. The accounting educators of the next generation were influenced by John Dewey and his followers, who stressed practicality and relevance. Unfortunately, "progressive" education became interpreted to mean a kind of vocationalism with little sympathy or use for so-called "classical" subjects. Deeply disappointed with the trends in the university business schools they had done so much to foster, some practitioners advocated yet another reform similar to the present-day movement for professional accounting schools. Interviewed for the *New York Post* in 1921, a disillusioned Joseph Sterrett recommended that "every young man who wishes to take up accounting (ought to) take up, if possible, a full college course in general subjects, followed by post graduate work in accounting" (Watson January 18, 1921).

What may now appear to be the inadequacy of the evolution of accounting curricula notwithstanding, early practitioners made a significant and major contribution to American culture. Accountants, in many states, were responsible for introducing business subjects into universities. They had convinced educators of the legitimacy of business subjects; they had either financed directly or guaranteed against loss of the first university business schools; and they provided faculty. Nevertheless, they did not believe that education alone was sufficient, and retained a deep conviction of the need for practical experience to assure true competence.

The Experience Requirement

A significant development prior to World War I was that, despite the expansion of accounting and applied business courses in institutions of higher education, the recommended practical experience requirement for CPAs was consistently lengthened by both state and national organizations.[25] It is possible that this development was a function of practitioners' efforts to adapt the British apprenticeship system to the American environment.

American practitioners presented what they believed were sound philosophical apologies for the experience requirement. Both the classical tradition of liberal education and the progressive reforms advocated by the Deweyites supported practitioners' advocacy of experience. John Dewey, in "Education and Experience," declared that experience, not formalized education, was the vital factor in developing an educated person. Experience enabled a person to interpret "truth" in different circumstances (Dewey 1939).

512 Among accounting practitioners the principal justification for experience was the need to develop "professional judgment." An actual, functioning accounting practitioner's office was perceived as an ideal environment within which to inculcate in the aspirant a "proper . . . attitude." Also, although no formal programs may have existed, the necessity to sensitize the young accountant to the ethical norms of the profession was another key element in defense of the experience requirement.

Ira Schur remembered his early years with S.D. Leidesdorf, and recalled that developing an appreciation of ethical standards was a fundamental element of a "young man's practical experience." Schur could not explain specifically how it occurred. The attitude "was just there, it was just there." He added that "S.D. told me to watch him closely, if he ever did anything I thought was wrong, to tell him because we all wanted to sleep at night" (Schur 1976).

Practical experience had a second purpose, important to practitioners at a time of varied and uncertain entrance standards, which was to enable established, reputable CPAs to screen aspirants and prevent incompetent or unethical persons from entering the profession. Experience completed the process of professional preparation. (Merino 1977)

Early accountants found no lasting solution to the problem of assuring that all licensed CPAs were competent professionals, but they developed an initial conception of professional "attitude." They accepted the idea that accountants had an obligation to protect the public from unqualified practitioners and concluded that no single instrument could function as a reliable admission standard. They formulated a combination of education, experience, and the CPA qualifying examination as the best of possible compromises. They conceived professional attitude as proceeding from recognition of moral responsibility, which required appreciation of professional ethics.

Ethics

Edward Ross wrote: " . . . the patron of (a) calling which involves the use of highly technical knowledge, since he is not qualified to judge the worth of the services he receives, is in a position of extreme dependence (and requires assurance) of the trustworthiness of the practitioners he engages" (Ross 1918). The stress that practitioners placed upon the need to protect the public's interest was an identifiable theme throughout the progressive era. A clear manifestation of that concern was the reliance early practitioners placed upon ethics to insure acceptable technical standards were maintained. Among the commonest criticism of the profession by outsiders was that accountants considered their discipline to be essentially ethical rather than "scientific" (Smith 1912: 169f).

513

Finding the means to introduce and impress new members with the ethical norms of the profession was not an easy task. There was little agreement over whether it was more effective to rely on informal systems of internalization through monitored experience in a practitioner's office, or to attempt to enforce compliance by adopting a written code of conduct that provided strict sanctions against improper conduct.

Two practitioners, Joseph Sterrett and John Alexander Cooper, became acknowledged spokesmen for the American association on the subject of professional ethics. Although in basic agreement that professional standards must be maintained, they differed in their approach to the problem. Sterrett, in his classic 1907 paper, "Professional Ethics," suggested that a written code of conduct was necessary but expressed some serious reservations.[26] First, he warned his colleagues,

> Let us first divest ourselves of the thought that any system of professional ethics for accountancy . . . can or should supercede or even modify those fundamental principles of right and wrong . . . which from the beginning of time were formulated and given expression in the decalogue (Sterrett 1907).

Secondly, he noted that ethical standards were not absolute, they were evolutionary, and, therefore, rules incorporated into any formal code of ethics must change over time. His position may be called "pragmatic" because he recognized that what was "fair" or "true" or "just" was dependent upon social norms; what one generation considered ethical might not be appropriate for future generations. Sterrett firmly believed that there were absolute fundamental principles that superceded any written rules. At the same time, he maintained that any standards that were set would be viable only so long as they met the social needs of the day, and therefore he supported limited written rules (Sterrett 1907).

The idea that written rules must inevitably be the result of compromise and therefore would only be minimum standards was accepted by many early accountants. John Forbes perhaps expressed the sentiment against written rules best when he said, "I have an abiding impatience with written rules of conduct . . . I have a deep contempt for him whose obedience to a natural principle of right must be regulated by a few poorly constructed lines over the meaning of which he would probably quibble." (AIA Minutes)

514

Cooper, in his 1907 response to Sterrett, insisted that the association should promulgate an ethical code immediately. He felt that every possible rule of conduct that could be codified, should be. Inflexible, sardonic, and totally unwilling to compromise, Cooper often aroused hostility among his colleagues.[27] He continuously introduced rules proscribing contingent fees, advertising, and audit companies which not only were opposed by many accountants but also would have provoked external criticism from those who thought CPAs were trying to create a monopoly by stifling competition.

Historical Foundations

Henry Rand Hatfield perhaps best summed up the prevalent view within the profession when he reviewed Montgomery's *Auditing Theory and Practice* (1912). He mentioned the special section on professional ethics but maintained that the importance placed on professional integrity and personal conduct throughout the book was far more significant (Hatfield 1913). Fundamental and pervasive concepts, such as confidentiality and independence, were not codified. For many believed that to do so meant inevitable dilution of intent. Accountants sought, rather, through the national organization and within the practitioners' offices, to internalize those values so that they were completely accepted and respected by everyone who entered the profession of public accountancy. They believed that independence and confidentiality were absolutes that must apply in all circumstances.[28]

It was assumed that any person permitted into the ranks of accountancy had been conditioned to accept both independence and confidentiality as fundamental norms during his period of practical experience. If that were not the case, then the practitioner-mentor had an ethical and moral responsibility to see that the person who did not measure up was prevented from admission into the profession. Practitioners rejected the idea that by promulgating rules, which by their nature could have dealt only with peripheral matters, either confidentiality or independence could be assured.

To imply that accountants were independent because they observed certain minor prohibitions was considered dangerous. For the public might be misled by assuming that this guaranteed independence, which was not true. The most telling argument appeared to be that if a practitioner was going to be influenced by a relatively minor interest (ownership of stock or a seat on the board of directors of a client company) then he certainly might be equally swayed by the threat of losing the audit fee. (Montgomery 1907)

One could also suggest that since the association had no power to 515 enforce compliance with its rules (its strictest sanction was expulsion of the offending member and to forbid his use of the phrase "member of the American Association of Public Accountants " on business correspondence), any rule was subject to constant violation.[29] In an area such as independence, the benefits of rules that could deal with form only and not substance were considered minimal.

Confidentiality

Confidentiality was the second fundamental concept of the profession. Although there had been at least some discussion of rules to deal with independence, there was no such debate concerning confidentiality. Most practitioners sympathized with this norm and agreed that it was pervasive. Without confidentiality there could be no profession. Practitioners large and small, from all regions, were united in this belief.

In several states, accountants sought statutory recognition of their responsibility to remain silent concerning clients' affairs. Recollections of young men entering the profession are clear on this point. Established practitioners, whether in small or large firms, told their assistants "to keep their mouths shut" about any client's business. There seemed little need for any rule, for any assistant violating a client's confidence faced the prospect of losing his job and thereby expulsion from the profession.

Rules of Conduct

As might be expected, since formal rules of conduct were necessarily the result of compromise, they really did not deal with substantive issues. Only eight written rules were promulgated and they dealt primarily with issues classified today as "other responsibilities and practices." The only agreement which the group was able to reach was that a code of ethics that dealt with overt abuses (which were admittedly not infrequent in this time period) might be beneficial. Minimal standards in some areas were perceived as better than none. But even those rules enacted that dealt with obvious violations of professional conduct were often ignored by state societies.

The most effective means that the national organization had to control practitioners (given its limited power) was not by enforcement of its code of ethics but through a provision incorporated in its bylaws, known as "acts discreditable to the profession," which was a concept broadly interpreted to deter professional misconduct.

516

Acts Discreditable

The observation that early practitioners treated accounting as an "ethical" system and resisted demands for the establishment of uniform technical standards is well founded. In the absence of technical standards, the notion of "acts discreditable" became the primary means of ensuring technical proficiency among practitioners.

The concept of acts discreditable was common to most professions but its application within accounting was unique. The medical and legal professions had specific rules that proscribed any action that threatened to dishonor law or medicine, but these standards referred to the personal conduct of the individual practitioner. Accountants' interpretation of the concept of acts discreditable expanded the idea to cover areas of technical competence. The principal reason for the difference lay in the recognition that accountants were potentially responsible to third parties—investors and creditors—whereas doctors' and lawyers' primary responsibility was to their clients. Accountants noted that the law had not yet evolved to protect the interest of third parties, whereas the client-professional relationship had been clearly delineated by the courts. The lack of a contractual relationship between the accounting practitioner and third parties prohibited the ultimate user from suing for redress in cases of professional incompetence. Despite demands by practitioners as early as 1908 that the situation be remedied by a broader interpretation of accountants' legal liability, the situation was not remedied until the thirties. Accountants, therefore, attempted to develop their own means of policing the profession and protecting third parties from incompetent practice.

When the institute was organized, a general statement was incorporated into its bylaws which permitted the national organization to control the technical quality of accountants' work. The institute "on the written complaint of any person aggrieved, whether a member or not," could expel or suspend a member "guilty of an act discreditable to the profession" (AAPA, *Yearbook*, 1907: 238). This permitted wide latitude in condemning actions which, though not specifically proscribed by the code of ethics, could be construed as harmful to colleagues, clients, or the general public. The council members of the institute took this duty seriously and were not averse to bringing charges against prominent members of the profession. But the lack of power vested in the national body soon became apparent. When James Anyon was suspended, he was furious, and demanded to 517 know what suspension meant. He was told that he could no longer use "member of the A.I.A." on his letterhead. To which he retorted, "I don't use it anyhow," and quit the institute (AIA, *Minutes*, 1918: 25–80; 142–192).

Unfortunately, the only power that the institute might have had—publicity—was closed because of the attitude of some members. There has always been a strong tendency among professionals for "guild selfishness" and "group bias." Within the national organization, a very influential group believed that accountants should not censure their colleagues. A concession made to these opponents of self-policing, which many considered unwise but unfortunately necessary, was that the names of persons or firms found guilty of professional misconduct not be published in the *Journal*. Only the facts of the case and its determination would be reported (AIA, *Minutes*, 1917: 30ff).

The foundation of ethical and educational standards was laid during this trying period, although the issues were not satisfactorily resolved given the institutional framework of the profession. No one body had the power to mandate compliance with professional standards, a problem that was equally perplexing in early efforts to develop accounting theory.

518 **NOTES**

1. See Thomas Cochran, "The History of a Business Society," *The Journal of American History*, June 1967 pp. 5–18, for a discussion of the pervasiveness of business values in the United States.

2. See Andrew Carnegie, *The Gospel of Wealth and Other Timely Essays*, ed. Edward C. Kirkland (Cambridge: Harvard University Press, 1962). Carnegie originally published an essay in two parts in *The North American Review* in 1899 (June, pp. 663–664; December, pp. 682–698). William F. Steed, editor of the *Pall Mall Gazette* supplied the headline "The Gospel of Wealth."

3. Accounting journals were not averse to adding their voices to the growing criticism of the "money trust." One has only to scan the pages of *The Bookkeeper* and *Commerce, Accounts and Finance* to find repeated references to the "evils" being perpetrated by such a concentration of power.

4. See John R. Commons, *Myself* (Madison, Wis: The University of Wisconsin, 1963), p. 56, for discussion for the minority report he wrote for the Industrial Commission recommending governmental audits. Specific rejection of this proposal is found in U.S., Congress, House, *Final Report of the Industrial Commission*. H. Doc. 380, 57th Cong., 1st sess., 1902, pp. 649ff.

5. See Alfred Chandler, "The Origins of Progressive Leadership," in *The Letters of Theodore Roosevelt*, ed. E.E. Morrison (Cambridge: Harvard University Press, 1954), Appendix III. Chandler prepared a profile of progressives and concluded that reformers were primarily middle class, native-born Americans living in urban areas and having a distinct business orientation.

6. For a contemporary discussion of the Keep Commission, see C. H. Forbes Lindsay, "New Business Standards in Washington—Work of the Keep Commission," *The American Review of Reviews* (February 1908), pp. 190–195. For accountants' reaction see AAPA, *Yearbook* (1907), p. 31f. All correspondence referring to the Committee on Economy and Efficiency in this chapter can be found in the National Archives, R.G. 51, Sec. 131, Washington D.C.

7. See U.S., Congress, House, Industrial Commission, *Reports of the Industrial Commission*, 56th and 57th Cong., H. Docs., 19 vols., 1900–1902. The three volumes cited here are *Preliminary Report of the Industrial Commission*, H.

Doc. 476, 56th Cong., 1st sess, 1900; *Report of the Industrial Commission on Transportation*, H. Doc. 178, 57th Cong, 1st sess, 1901; *Final Report of the Industrial Commision*, H. Doc. 380, 57th Cong., 1st sess., 1902.

8. See U.S., Congress, House, *Report of the Industrial Commission on Trusts*, H. Doc. 182, 57th Cong., 1st sess. (Washington, D.C.: Government Printing Office, 1901) for testimony of business leaders. See testimony of A.S. White, president of National Salt Company and Charles Schwab, president of U.S. Steel, who admitted that management could mislead investors by dividend policies. They advocated publication of annual reports and that independent audits or government supervision be employed.

9. See correspondence from accountants to George W. Wickersham and replies from Wickersham, (Deloitte, Haskins & Sells Archival Collection, New York). For the most comprehensive statement of the problems created by this law, see A.M. Sakolski, "The Federal Corporation Tax and Modern Accounting," *The Yale Review* February 1909, pp. 372–389. Treasury Regulations No. 31, December 1910, permitted the use of accrual accounting but the law was not changed.

10. See Simon Patten, *The New Basis for Civilization* (New York: MacMillan Co. 1907; Thorstein Veblen, *The Portable Veblen* (New York: Victory Press, 1950); and John Commons, *Institutional Economics* (Madison, Wis.: The University of Wisconsin Press, 1959) had the most obvious influence upon accounting literature through the work of his student, DR Scott. But Patten published frequently in the *Annals of the American Academy of Social and Political Science* which prior to the turn of the century carried many articles dealing with accounting topics, and, therefore, it must be presumed that some accountants were familiar with his work.

11. See "Scrapbook—Elijah Watt Sells," Haskins & Sells Archival Collection, New York. In a letter dated February 2, 1908, Herbert G. Stockwell criticized Sells's position but most of the voluminous correspondence is laudatory. The scrapbook includes a letter from Oliver Wendell Holmes who commends the author for publication of the pamphlet mentioned above.

12. For interpretation of this absence of federal support, see Michael Chatfield, *A History of Accounting Thought* (Hinsdale, Ill.: The Dryden Press, 1974).

13. A letter from C. W. Haskins to Dr. Henry McCracken of New York University, December 11, 1898, states: "We recall with regret the attempts that have heretofore been made to establish independent schools of accounts. We believe the failure of these attempts has been due to the absence of this very university foundation which we honor to suggest to you." See NYSSCPA, *Ten Year Book* (New York: NYSSCPA, 1907), p. 24.

14. See, for example, L.G. Battelle, *Story of Ohio Accountancy* (Columbus: Ohio Society of CPAs, 1954), for a description of the difficulties faced by most midwestern accountants where populist sentiment was strong.

15. All references to NYSSCPA are to New York State Society of Certified Public Accountants, *Minute Books of Meetings of the Members and of the Board of Directors*—1897-1910, bound handwritten manuscripts; 1911-1920, bound typescripts (New York: NYSSCPA).

16. See AAPA, *Yearbook* (1907): pp. 215–218 for Cooper's "Draft of a Model CPA Law to Regulate the Profession." This is similar to the model law he presented to the Federation (1902) as a guide for uniform CPA legislation.

17. See "Public Accountants in the United States," *The Accountant* (October 17, 1903 pp. 1251–1253), which contains excerpts from Cooper's address, "National Legislation for the Public Accountant," to the Illinois State Society (1899).

18. AIA, *Minutes - 1916*, p. 115ff and AIA, *Minutes - 1917*, p. 30f discuss Hurley's suggestion. Robert Montgomery, who acted as the Devil's advocate, labeled Hurley as an "unknown" quantity in 1916. But by 1917, with federal regulation no longer a serious threat, he lamented the loss of "our boy in Washington" when Hurley resigned. The zone expert scheme can be found in an editorial, *Journal of Accountancy*, August 1915, pp. 129–134.

19. The plan was devised by E. W. Sells and J. E. Sterrett and can be located in the AAPA, *Minutes* (1916), 50ff and in the 1916 *Yearbook of the Institute of Accountants in the United States of America*. Fortunately, the above name was shortened after approximately three months to the American Institute of Accountants (AIA).

20. The AIA modeled its entrance exam on that of New York State. One of its stated objectives was to gain acceptance for a uniform CPA examination in all states. From 1917 to 1919, the institute's examination was comprised of five fields— practice, theory, auditing, business law, and actuarial science. Many states objected to the inclusion of actuarial science and the AIA dropped that section. But, despite this compromise a uniform national exam was not to be realized for more than three decades.

21. This section places heavy reliance on the writings of the presidents of the AAPA and AIA from 1906 to 1918: E.W. Sells, J.E. Sterrett, E.L. Suffern, J.P. Joplin, R.H. Montgomery and W.S. Davies. Establishing professional standards was a responsibility the national organization attempted to assume. Therefore its leadership was extremely influential.

22. See Irvin G. Wyllie, "Social Darwinism and the Businessman," *Proceedings of the American Philosophical Society*, October 1959 p. 633. Wyllie notes that Vanderbilt waited until age 70 to read his first book. Similarly, Daniel Drew wrote that "Book learning is something, but thirteen million dollars is also something, and a mite sight more."

23. See AAPA, "Report of the Committee on Education," *Yearbook* (1912), p. 137ff. The plea was most explicit in this source and the committee had similar requests from 1907 forward.

24. See Robert Montgomery, "An Accountancy Laboratory," *Journal of Accountancy* (June 1914), pp. 405–411 for a discussion of the need for a "practical" orientation in the classroom.

25. For an opposite view which existed as to the merit of such policies, see "Editorial," *Journal of Accountancy*, April 1910, pp. 448–449. The *Journal*, while under the control of Joseph French Johnson, Dean at the School of Commerce and Accounts, New York University, did *not* advocate increasing

experience requirements. The *Journal's* editorials until 1912, when the AAPA took control, often reflected academic opinion that conflicted with practitioners' views.

26. Sterrett's paper, although viewed as a "classic" by John Carey, shows evidence of a decided British influence; see the New Zealand Code of Ethics. E. W. Sells, in his "Inaugural Address," *Journal of Accountancy*, November 1906, pp. 39–41, suggested American auditing and educational standards were far superior to those in Great Britain, but he conceded that the British were far ahead in the field of ethics.

27. Cooper probably lost the 1912 election for President because of his reputation as a scold. AAPA, *Yearbook* (1912), p. 78ff details this election. Cooper was the Association's official nominee (Montgomery seconding his nomination). Arthur Young nominated Alan Smart from Illinois. Montgomery emerged as a compromise candidate and won on the fourth ballot. Since Montgomery suggested in his autobiography that he was the youngest President to that time and this has been widely quoted and his rise sometimes referred to as meteoric in previous histories, it should be mentioned that he was not, in fact, the youngest man to have been elected. Sterrett in 1908 had been younger (38) and Davies in 1887 had been only 35. The age differential is not significant in itself but it is important to note that young men could and did achieve power within the profession quickly at this time.

28. When one reviews only the written rules, conclusions significantly different with respect to both independence and confidentiality are reached. See, for example, Carey 1969, pp. 84–93, and AICPA, Committee on Long Range Objectives, *Profession–1975*, pp. 256–258, 540–549, which suggest little was done during this period with respect to independence or confidentiality.

29. Robert H. Montgomery, "Professional Ethics," *Journal of Accountancy*, December 1907, p. 148. The author suggested that "the only penalty of practical effect is one which would deprive a man from making a living in his profession," a power which the association did not have, only state boards had the authority to revoke a CPA certificate.

521

THE MEANING OF "PUBLIC ACCOUNTANT"

Norman E. Webster

FOR SOME uses a simple and concise dictionary definition of "public accountant" will serve: "An accountant whose services are available to the public." (*Webster's* 1935 edition). For other purposes it may be useful to define public accounting more broadly: "The practice of the art of accounting by men whose services are available to the public for compensation. It may consist in the performance of original work, in the examination and revision of the original work of others (auditing), or in rendering of collateral services for which a knowledge of the art and experience in its practice create a special fitness." (*Accounting Research Bulletin, No 7,* American Institute of Accountants, November, 1940.)

Since some of the work of a public accountant is affected with a public interest, a definition suitable for use in a statute may be needed.

"The public practice of accountancy within the meaning of this article is defined as follows: A person engages in the public practice of accountancy who, holding himself out to the public as an accountant, in consideration of compensation received, or to be received by him, offers to perform or does perform, for other persons services which involve the auditing or verification of financial transactions, books, accounts, or records, or the preparation, verification or certification of financial, accounting and related statements intended for publication or for the purpose of obtaining credit, or who, holding himself out to the public as an accountant, renders professional services or assistance in or about any or all matters of principle or detail relating to accounting procedure or the recording, presentation or certification of financial facts or data." (Sec. 1489, Art. 57, *Education Law of New York,* of April, 1929.)

But the best of definitions necessarily have their limitations. They will indicate the name of a larger group of which the item defined is a part, and they will indicate one or at most a few characteristics which help to differentiate this item from other items in the larger group. No one however, who has special knowledge of the significance of some term, will feel that a definition alone can do the term full justice. The expert will see in his term a much wider connotation than can be brought into a definition. He has an intricate concept in mind; a handful of definitions are not enough to describe it as he knows it. It may be interesting, and possibly useful, therefore, to explore the historical background of the term "public accountant" as reflected in the American literature of accountancy.

Ever since accountants have made their services available to the public, there has been a need for informing that public of the work that a public accountant can do and of the kind of man he is. There are many articles in the early periodical literature that show what the practitioners of these days thought on these subjects. Several extracts are given below about "the scope of the accountant's art," "the functions of the expert accountant," "what an accountant does."

"The full scope of business comprises:
"Designing books of accounts for any special trade, business, or purpose, and opening, balancing and closing the same.
"Auditing the books of accounts of all corporations, . . . and of private individuals and firms.
"Examining into the financial relations existing between all corporations, their branches and agencies.
"Auditing and certifying statements of corporations to stockholders, or for the use of directors, managers and trustees, or as a basis of reports to state officials.
"Auditing and certifying reports made by agents to principals or parent companies in other states or foreign countries.
"Liquidation of the affairs of individuals, private firms and public corporations.
"Investigation and adjustment of disputed accounts and of partnership and joint accounts.
"Examining and reporting upon the statements, facts and financial conditions, upon the strength of which it is proposed to found commercial, manufacturing, mining, financial or other undertakings.
"Examining and reporting on receivers' and trustees' accounts for settlement and acceptance in court.

"Searching books of account by order of court for the purpose of establishing evidence of facts, or for testing probable theories.
"Examining and reporting upon the accounts of insolvents, and upon the value of their assets.
"Estimating and reporting on the value of securities, and comparing them with vouchers and entries upon account-books.
"Supervising and directing inventories of stock and assets, and the proper balancing of sets of books, so as to show the real state of affairs of a business or corporation.
"Examining the affairs of embarrassed but solvent debtors, and of insolvent debtors.
"Preparation of the accounts of executors and administrators, and trustees; ascertaining the respective interests of legatees and other beneficiaries in the estates of deceased persons, both as to principal and income, and their apportionment.
"Overhauling old books of account for stating the interests of minor children, or absent parties and for final settlement.
"Searching for errors, intentional or otherwise, in accounts, and correcting the same." (*The American Counting-Room*, January, 1884, p. 34)

* * * *

"The functions of the expert accountant are, perhaps, less understood by the business community at large than it would be well to have them. They may be summed up under several heads, among which may be mentioned—first, planning and remodeling books so as to adapt them to special requirements; second, auditing books and verifying the balance sheets; third, adjusting and closing books in terms of partnership, dissolution agreements, etc.; and fourth, unravelling books and accounts which are in a tangle. Under the first of these heads the expert occupies a commanding position as compared with the ordinary bookkeeper, from the fact that he has wide and varied experience, and accordingly can do more than even an equally competent man who has been restricted to ordinary lines of practice. Under the second head, the expert's systematic training is a continuous safe-guard against errors and frauds, and a satisfaction as well to those in charge of the cash as to those interested in the profits. Under the third head the expert sees that all questions of depreciations, renewals, drawbacks, doubtful debts and other contingencies are duly considered, while under the fourth head his trained and practiced skill finds clues in a mass of confusion, and soon determines the shortest way out." (*The Office*, September, 1886.)

* * * *

524

"The professional practice of a public accountant embraces within its extensive and varied scope the following, viz.:

"The designing and planning of books and accounts, so as to adapt them to the requirements of any particular business, and thereby show the working of the various departments thereof; also the devising a proper organization to furnish the details necessary to aid the management in obtaining results with the least possible amount of labor, and at the same time insuring correctness in all particulars.

"The critical examination and auditing of the books and accounts of corporations, including railroad companies, banks and insurance companies, municipal corporations, water and gas works, and all other public, mercantile and manufacturing companies, as also those of private individuals and firms; the preparation of balance sheets, trading and profit and loss accounts pertaining thereto for the guidance of stockholders and others interested therein.

"The investigation and adjustment of partnership accounts, for the determination of the respective interests of partners and their representatives.

"Examining and reporting upon statements and conditions upon which it is proposed to found commercial, manufacturing, financial and other undertakings.

"The compilation and examination of receivers' and trustees' accounts for filing in the courts, and also the account of insolvent businesses and the preparation of statements of affairs and deficiency accounts for the purpose of ascertaining the status of the estate, and so guiding creditors in the determination of their interests.

"The settlement of depreciations, renewals, discounts, the provision for doubtful debts and contingencies on the closing of accounts at the termination of the fiscal year, and the incorporating of the same in balance sheets, preparatory to determining the net profits of the year.

"The ascertainment of results in questions of dispute; the elucidation of facts from books and accounts in the adjustment of questions of law where accounts are involved.

"Generally advising and assisting in the organization of offices, in the form of books and other things required for the conduct of business of various descriptions, so that proper safeguards and methods may be adopted to insure correctness with dispatch and the proper classification of details for obtaining results." (Pamphlet by the American Association of Public Accountants, 1888)

* * * *

DUTIES AND RESPONSIBILITIES OF AUDITORS

"Make special or regular audits of books and accounts for principals, treasurers, cashiers, investors, directors, special partners or others.

"Review the balance sheets of firms or corporations, conduct arbitrations, adjust partnership accounts, and make settlements; make partial or thorough investigations and give results in concise and intelligible reports.

"Devise and invent books to meet special requirements; originate printed forms for correspondence and reports; introduce voucher systems and exhibits with plans for saving labor and detecting errors.

"Advise directors of corporations, treasurers, cashiers, trustees, receivers, administrators, auditors or accountants, upon questions arising in the discharge of fiduciary duties; in auditing or examining contested or tangled accounts; opening, closing or keeping the books of firms, corporations, banks, etc.

"Keep the special or private books or ledgers of firms or corporations for partners, principals, officers or directors, making up special or periodical exhibits showing results of operations independent of work of regular bookkeeper.

"Give counsel and assistance in organizing joint-stock companies, attend preliminary meetings, serve temporarily as secretary and assist appointees to official positions in the proper discharge of their trusts.

"Make examinations for clients and report to them on business interests, value of stocks or bonds of incorporated companies, municipal corporations, town, county or other branches of government.

"Prepare and attend to the filing of preliminary reports and final accountings for receivers, assignees, executors, trustees and others filling similar positions." (*Business*, April, 1896, p. 188.)

These statements of what an accountant was prepared to do were made fifty to sixty years ago. When the asserted functions are classified into a few groups it is evident that the practitioners of that time were willing to operate an accounting system (at least to the extent of opening and closing the accounts); design or remodel accounting systems; audit accounts and verify balance sheets (also search out errors, or unravel books in a tangle); give advice and counsel (on fiduciary matters, on organizing joint-stock companies); make investigations and reports. This last service was exceedingly diverse, dealing as it did with: insolvents, receiverships, liquidations, disputed accounts, searching accounts for evidence to be used in court, examining the financial condition of concerns prior to merger or in corporations; reviewing corporation balance sheets; estimating the value of securities.

These descriptions of the services performed tell much more about public accountants than definitions could possibly do. It will help to complete the picture to note also some of the early statements about the personal qualifications of the public accountant.

"According to the best American lexicographers there can be but little difference in the two terms. An accountant is described as a keeper of accounts, while the definition of a book-keeper is a keeper of account-books. We believe it is customary in this country to use the words synonymously. But as to whether our lexicographers have been sufficiently searching in their inquiries, and if possessed of the necessary practical knowledge of the art of keeping and examining accounts to have given a perfectly correct explanation of the two terms, may be a question for discussion. We know that in Great Britain, and, we believe, in British provinces generally, the two words have widely differential meanings—at least they have in their common or practical usages. In England, and also with our cousins just across the northern boundary, the title of accountant is applied to a class of professional persons almost as separate and distinct from the class known as book-keepers as are the judges of courts distinct from the general class of attorneys. A judge must of course be a lawyer, but it is not necessary for that reason that all lawyers must be judges . . . .

"It is expected in the countries referred to, that every accountant must be a book-keeper—so far at least as possessing a knowledge of how books of account should be kept, may extend. And it is expected that he has served a term, and had experience in examining accounts for cases in legal controversy, in liquidations, bankruptcies, etc., which gives him a special qualification." (*The Bookkeeper*, May 23, 1882.)

"Uniformity of reports, however, is but one step in the reform which is necessary. A still more important one is the removal of reports from the possibilities of interested coloring, and this can only be done by the compulsory adoption of the English method of periodical audit by outside professional accountants, duly qualified and sworn. An English corporation elects its auditors, it is true, and to that extent they become officers of the company, but this election is made from the list of Chartered Accountants who have passed examination for capacity, and who are held to a rigid responsibility for the acccuracy of their examinations and reports. They are absolutely independent of the firm or corporations whose accounts they examine and whose balance sheets they prepare for the shareholders. Their reports are looked upon as conclusive, and upon them dividends are declared and public opinion based. We have as yet no Institute of Chartered Accountants, but financial and business men should be roused to an insistence upon some similar organization, and meantime stockholders and bondholders should be assured through independent audit by the best available public accountants, that exact facts are fully disclosed." (*The Office*, January, 1888; part of a letter published by a Wall Street banking house on reform in railway accounts.)

"When the lexicographers gave the definition of accountant as 'one who is skilled in, or keeps accounts,' the compilers of the dictionary covered the ground, but in a partial and general sense. 'Skilled in accounts'—to quote from the definitions—the dangerous latitude of possibility in this gives a significance which is really the key to the mystery of what, to an unthinking person, an accountant really is.

A person to be feared? No; except when, with integrity of purpose, complete knowledge of his duties, adaptability for an emergency which comes from experience and confidence, and a maturity of judgment which weighs cause and effect with justice and discrimination, he seeks for and finds evidence of wrong-doing and fraud which the over-reaching shrewdness of dishonesty has hidden from casual observance.

"A person to be respected? Yes; for the responsibility assumed, the untiring application and industry necessary to fitness for the work undertaken, the constant appreciation of the relations to others against whom he may be searching for damaging evidence, seeking, in many instances, for that which he does not wish to find, and yet with the unerring testimony of the gradually developing facts growing upon the pages before him. Standing as the mentor whose wisdom and impartiality may check the erring or do justice to the wrongfully accused, he is the safeguard to all . . . .

"The accountant has integrity and responsibility as his birthright when he enters the guild, and an independent audit, under similar organization, would disclose the facts, and to a large degree cut short the story of defalcation, irregularity, failure and disaster which is but far too frequently told in America, and which points its own moral—severe and lasting as it is, to those who suffer." (Pamphlet by the American Association of Public Accountants, 1888.)

"The functions of the latter [professional auditors] are analogous to those of a physician to a life office. Before entering upon the risk of insuring a man's life the insuring company requires his condition to be audited by a skilled expert. Such expert—the physician—is enabled by his training to arrive at conclusions generally correct after a short examination of the subject. He knows how to detect by his instruments and soundings the symptoms of the common human diseases, while a similar examination by an unskilled person would lead to no reliable conclusion . . . .

"His duty being, as already indicated, to satisfy himself that the directors place a bona fide statement of the results of their dealings . . . he [the auditor] must be satisfied that the balance sheet is a fair one, properly drawn up; if, however, he be not satisfied he must not alter it except with the consent of the directors. They . . . have the right and the duty to put before the shareholders their view of the results of their management; the auditor's duty, if he does not consider the balance sheet fairly represents those results, and he cannot convert the directors to his view, is to report to the shareholders in what respects he considers it wrong or misleading . . . ."

"From what we have written it will be apparent that auditing, instead of being a matter merely of arithmetic and verification of simple facts, as is generally supposed, requires for its proper performance, trained skill, tact, and judgment of a high order." (*Business*, February, April, May, 1895; reprints from *Bankers Magazine*, London, of a paper by A. H. Gibson, F.C.A.)·

During the meeting in Detroit, on September 17 and 18, 1896, at which there was organized the National Association of Accountants and Bookkeepers, A. J. Horn of Cleveland delivered an address, partly printed in *Business* for October, 1896, page 440, in which he quoted someone whom he identified only as "a prominent manufacturer who knew a good thing when he

saw it." The quotation was the following description of a public accountant.

"A Doctor of Accounts must be a man of good mentality, of keen perception, of sound judgment, and practical business qualifications.

He must be thoroughly posted in all new developments in his profession.

He is accurate in commercial calculations.

He is systematic in the arrangement of accounts, giving the greatest possible information in the most condensed form.

He is a genius in inventing and devising new systems of accounting adaptable to any kind of business.

He examines and probes every matter referred to him.

He is endowed with the faculties of causability and can therefrom locate the causes, ways, wherefores and remedies of adverse business conditions.

He is an excellent counsellor with reference to effecting reform in the administration of affairs.

He is lucid in his reports and expressions.

He has the methodical faculties of a railroad dispatcher in order that the various business operations may not collide in the great road of trade and commerce.

He has the investigating faculties of a detective.

He has the argumentative force of an attorney.

He has the perseverance of an astute politician.

He has more secrets to keep sacred than any other living man.

He is a man of good address, genial temperament, courteous manner, strong character, and honorable motives.

He is a 'hail fellow well met' beloved and respected by the business and civil community."

The extracts given above are all dated prior to the first CPA law. They reflect current opinion of that period regarding the scope of the public accountant's work and his personal qualifications as a professional man. After the New York CPA law became effective (April 17, 1896), there was new reason for defining the term "public accountant." For, so far as has been learned, this was the first statute that included this term. In the first section of the law there were the related expressions, public expert accountant, Certified Public Accountant, and the abbreviation CPA. Section 3 states the following:

"The Regents may in their discretion, waive the examination of any person possessing the qualifications mentioned in Section 1, who shall have been, for more than one year before the passage of this act, practicing in this state on his own account, as a public accountant, and who shall apply in writing for such certificate within one year after the passage of this act."

The administration of this first Certified Public Accountant law was placed with the Regents of the University of the State of New York, which, it may be well to note in passing, is not an educational institution, but a supervisory body for the determination of educational policies, with an administrative organization for making its policies effective.

To make effective the provisions of the new law, the Regents created the Board of Examiners for Certified Public Accountants that was authorized by Section 2 of the Act. Of the first three appointees to the board, two were listed in the 1896 issue of the *New York Business Directory* as public accountants. The minutes of the Board show that it held its first meeting for organization on October 28, 1896.

Two weeks later, on November 12, 1896, the Board adopted rules for its work. Rule 4 provided for the waiver of the required examination upon the "unanimous recommendation of the examiners" if the applicant was "well-known to examiners as meeting professional requirements" and had been in "practice as a public accountant since January 1, 1890." And at its fifth meeting, on December 1, 1896, the Board disapproved application #40 for certification without examination, "he not being in practice as a public accountant upon his own account in this State."

During its first five years to June 30, 1901, the Board rejected 29 such applications, suspended action upon 19 applications for more evidence of practice, and approved 132 applications for waiver of the examination. And, so far as is shown by its minutes, it took such action without

considering it necessary to define the term "public accountant," although on December 22, 1896, it indicated that work similar to that practiced by a public accountant, if performed for a single corporation employer, was not that of a public accountant.

By March 29, 1899, another need for a definition of a public accountant had arisen, for on that date the Pennsylvania CPA Law was approved. Under it there were two reasons for a knowledge of the meaning of the term: first, Section 2 required that three of the board of five examiners "shall be public accountants, who shall have been in practice as such for at least five years"; and second, as in the New York Law, there was a provision for the waiver of the examination in the case of those persons who had been practicing in the state as public accountants for a stated period, which in Pennsylvania was fixed at three years.

Whether or not the Board of Examiners itself formulated a definition of a public accountant, or of the public practice of accountancy, it appears that the earliest organized effort to secure such definition was made in Pennsylvania and only a short time after the organization of the Board of Examiners in that state.

The Public Accountant, publication of the Pennsylvania Institute of Certified Public Accountants in Philadelphia, carried the following editorial in its issue of January 15, 1900, page 43.

"Outside of a limited circle of financial men the utility of the public accountant was little known and appreciated in this country up to a few years ago. But the rapid growth of so-called trusts has helped carry the doctrine all over the United States, and today the public accountant is to be found in practice in all the large cities of the country.

"And yet the question is constantly being asked, 'What is a Public Accountant?' The average financial man in the principal eastern cities knows full well the use of the professional accountant, and knows how important a part he plays in

528

the drama of commercial life, though he is often very reluctant to call in the accountant's services. But the banker, manufacturer and merchant of the middle and western states has until recently had little opportunity of learning the very useful sphere that the public accountant fills, and they have yet to learn that it is far better to call in the public accountant as a physician than as a coroner.

"To elicit an exchange of views as to what a public accountant really is, the editor of this paper has invited several of the leading professional accountants to contribute each a definition. There has been a very generous response to the editor's invitation, and the first six of these definitions are given in this number. The others will follow in detachments of six definitions in each number."

During the months from January to June, 1900, *The Public Accountant* printed answers from 29 accountants in 8 cities. In each issue the answers came from different parts of the country. In this summary the answers from each city are brought together. From Philadelphia seven replies were received.

"A thoroughly capable accountant who is at the service of the public for the solving of any and all bookkeeping problems that arise in mercantile or professional business. His one asset 'ability'; his trade mark 'integrity.'"

William H. Cullen

"A public accountant is one engaged professionally in the practice of accountancy; the term accountancy being understood to cover all forms of investigations of accounts for the determination of financial conditions, detection of frauds or prevention thereof, or for whatever purpose data obtained from the accounts may be required."

William M. Lybrand

"A public accountant is a man fearless and unprejudiced, with the ability to look at both sides of a question; one who will not allow his honest opinions to be changed by client or adverse party; who dictates and is never dictated to; who places his devotion to his profession above the opportunities for gain by questionable means."

Robert H. Montgomery

"One who by reason of intellectual fitness and experience is competent to design and direct systems of accounting; critically examine books of account respecting their accuracy, honesty and

adequacy; prepare therefrom clear and adequate exhibits of financial condition and operations; and, generally to advise in all matters pertaining to accounts."

Adam A. Ross, Jr.

"A public accountant is one who, being skilled in accounts, examines, supervises, adjusts, states and keeps accounts, and designs and inaugurates systems of accounting. His services are not limited to or controlled by one employer, but may be secured by all who require them."

T. Edward Ross.

"A disinterested adviser of the business man. One who can warn him of dangers and protect his interests."

Charles N. Vollum

"A public accountant is one who not only masters the intricacies of the accounts of one business, but who is master of all business and professional accounts, and who is fearless in his knowledge, placing all truths plainly without regard to client or patronage."

Robert B. Vollum

From Pittsburgh there were three answers.

"A person possessing capabilities to successfully ferret out and clearly exhibit the facts involved in some financial tangle; business experience to fit him to advise in, or manage important matters; inventive genius to contrive a neat fitting set of books; detective acumen to scent out unsuspected errors or facts; legal bent to discover and bring out points in a case, and tact to get valuable information without friction and know, from long experience, where to direct his attention."

William W. Edgar

"A public accountant is one who professionally practices the career of an accountant to the general community. He is one who holds himself ready to accept special engagements from the people, in which his advice, discretion, experience, knowledge in the science and skill in the art of accountancy may be deemed desirable and necessary."

"Equity" (described as one of the most prominent accountants of the state)

"One qualified by training and experience in the science and practice of accounting; who originates systems of accounts adapted to special lines of business; who examines, critically, the accounts of corporations and others to verify their correctness, or to detect errors or fraud; and who advises on matters of accountancy."

Francis J. Rebbeck

529

From Chicago there came eleven answers.

"One publicly recognized as having competent knowledge of commercial laws and usages; ability in quickly mastering operating details; ready discernment of improper entries; accurate appreciation of values and mechanical contrivances; reputed integrity toward private confidences. Endowed with a keen sense of equity and unbiased judgment. A thorough student of economics."

H. F. Butler

"Assuming the fundamental tastes and training, he must have a logical, orderly, inquisitive, probing mind; a decisive manner and a resolute will, coupled with a tactful and gracious disposition; a ready approach with discretion and a resourcefulness to meet obstacles; a proper reserve and absolute integrity as to the business intrusted to him. As the eye is the index to the soul, so the public accountants should be the index and guide through the perplexities of commercial life."

John Alexander Cooper

"My understanding of a public accountant is a member of the profession who devotes his entire time to accountancy, who maintains a permanent office in a public place, and whose line of practice is such as to cause him to be recognized as a specialist in all matters pertaining to accounts."

Lawrence A. Jones

"A man's books are the written history of his business. In them are recorded the experience of years. It is important that these records be correct. A public accountant is a specialist in accounts and in the varied and complex interests of our present business life he is a necessity."

Robert Nelson

"A public accountant acknowledges no master but the public, and thus differs from the bookkeeper, whose acts and statements are dictated by his employers. A public accountant's certificate, though addressed to president or directors, is virtually made to the public, who are actually or prospectively stockholders. He should have ability, varied experience and undoubted integrity."

Charles C. Reckitt

"A person whose training enables him to understand and examine into all classes of accounts and books subsidiary thereto, with the object of presenting to his client, without fear or favor, reports and statements accurately setting forth the past workings for a given period, present financial condition, and future prospects."

Ernest Reckitt

"The public accountant should be thoroughly schooled in the practical, as well as the technical application of science of accounts, well read in the laws and ethics of finance and commerce, keen visioned (mentally and physically), capable of hard work, rigidly conscientious, patient, sagacious and be versed in professional etiquette."

George J. Rehm

"One having a natural aptitude for the manifold requirements of the business. Having this, a good education, extensive practical experience, courteous deportment and sterling integrity, he may rightfully claim to be in the full sense of the words, a public accountant."

Allen R. Smart

"A public accountant should be a thorough figure-man and organizer, having an analytical mind, a knowledge of all laws affecting commerce and of the best business methods, able to apply them to any business. In other words should be a thorough business expert, able to practically apply his knowledge."

Walton, Joplin & Co.

"A professional accountant, whose services are available to the public for a fee or per diem remuneration, as may be arranged. To be successful he must be honest, diplomatic, fearless, versatile, indefatigable, experienced, perspicuous and skilled in his craft."

George Wilkinson

"A public accountant is one, who, from a thorough knowledge of the science of accountancy, combined with long experience, is competent to analyze or dissect a set of accounts and verify the correctness or expose the errors or fraud in same. He must, necessarily, be honest, fearless and incorruptible."

H. J. D. Wodrich

From San Francisco two answers came.

"One who is expert in accounts and so entirely familiar with the science of bookkeeping that he can readily apply the principles of that science to the requirements of any business by the most practical and direct methods. One who is fitted by education and experience to examine accounts."

Francis E. Beck

'A public accountant is a person appointed for the purpose of examining into and passing judgment upon books, accounts and general business transactions. This he must do conscientiously and impartially, accompanying his assertions with proper proofs, and gaining by the execution of his duties the respect of friend and foe."

Charles F. Lutgen

From Boston there came one reply.

"An expert specially in matters of account. Keeping an office open at call of public men, being paid for time occupied, not being a salaried book-keeper, having some recognized professional status, in continuous practice for many years on his own account or in the office of another expert."

Wm. Norton Reid

From Newark also one reply came.

"The public accountant is born not made,— should have a natural aptitude for accounts, a fair knowledge of the principles and practice of law, should possess a judicial mind, never swaying from exact truth. His statements should be simple, condensed, and if possible comprehensible to all, perfectly honest."

Richard F. Stevens

From Buffalo again one answer was received.

"A public accountant is a person who renders to others a degree of temporary service so valuable that they could not afford to engage his entire time. His report should be so comprehensive that it will be a retrospective view, a present exposition, and a basis for all future operations."

William G. Mowatt

And from New York City there were three replies.

"A public accountant should be a friend to the erring; a schoolmaster to the ignorant, a spur to the indolent, a warning to the trickster, an eye-opener to the wideawake, a guide to Heaven."

Franklin Allen

"The public accountant is the consulting physician of finance and commerce. He understands the anatomy and physiology of business and the rules of health of corporations, partnerships, and individual enterprises. He diagnoses abnormal conditions, and suggests approved remedies. His study and interest is the soundness of the world of affairs."

Charles W. Haskins

"The ideal public accountant is he who, without trenching on existing authority, systematically examines the accounts and methods of business of the institution in which his patron is interested; renders an intelligible certified report of its financial condition; and, if necessary, suggests a safer or more economical method of accounting."

Elijah W. Sells

Only 7 of these answers mentioned the professional status of the public accountant in that he offers his service to the general public, and only a few particularized as to the nature of the services he offers to render, except that about one-half of the statements say that he is prepared to be an advisor to his clients. But there was a greater unanimity as to what the public accountant should be and how he should act. Generally the replies stressed two things—the qualifications which the public accountant should possess, and the principles which should govern his activities. As to the qualifications, 9 mentioned the desirability that he have educational preparation, 10 that he should be experienced, 13 that he should be thoroughly capable, 7 that he should have tact and courtesy, and 4 that he should possess imagination. And as to governing principles, 10 stressed honesty, 6 that he must be unprejudiced, and 4 that he be fearless.

A similar need for a definition of a public accountant arose from the phrasing of the Illinois CPA law, passed May 15, 1903. Between that date and February, 1905, Dean David Kinley, then chairman of the Committee on Accountancy of the University of Illinois, "sought the opinions of a large number of accountants concerning the proper sphere of the work and duties of the accountant." (*The Auditor*, Chicago, February, 1905, p. 88; also see the *Journal of Accountancy*, July, 1906, p. 87.) This search had a sequel:

In the files of the late George Wilkinson, who in the early years was secretary of the organization that preceded the Illinois Society of Certified Public Accountants, there was found an interesting document which the executor gave to me. It consists of two sheets 14″ × 17″ and is handwritten, apparently by Mr. Wilkinson. It is captioned: "Condensed statement of replies received in answer to query of Dean David Kinley of University of Illinois—What is a public accountant?" The pages are ruled

531

into three columns, which from left to right are headed "Name of Correspondent, Address, Synopsis of Correspondents' Replies." Single alternate lines are used on each sheet, the first sheet containing 21 entries, the second only 7 entries. The names of the correspondents are not arranged alphabetically or grouped by cities. To me it seems that the document includes all the replies that were known to the person who prepared it. Even so, it is of course possible that it is not complete since it lists only 28 replies, whereas Dean Kinley in the *Journal of Accountancy* stated that he received between 30 and 40.

532

It is enlightening to examine forty years later the statements made by practitioners in answer to the question "What is a public accountant?" From Chicago eighteen replies were received.

"A man of wide experience in the science of accounts, one employed by such as require an accountant to open, close or examine books."
Charles W. August

"A competent, skillful, versatile, resourceful, experienced and discreet investigator in the realm of accounts, at the service of the public."
Edwin Rice Baker

"One who by ability, study and experience is enabled to analyze correctly any form of accounts, to determine exact facts, and who has the integrity to report exact conditions. Must have broad knowledge of business conditions."
Robert S. Buchanan

"One who is master of the science of accounts' He must have had practical business training and possess a general perception of business principles."
Gerald L. DeVor

"One who is skilled and learned in creating, devising and recording financial, pecuniary or statistical accounts, not restricting his services to one office or set of accounts."
John Everett

"One who by training and experience has acquired such knowledge of the theory and practical application of theory, of accounts, as to enable him to express a correct opinion on points of accountancy."
Edward E. Gore

"One conversant with the science of accountancy and open to employment by the general public."
A. F. Rattray Greig

"Generally understood to imply expert knowledge by age and experience which a person of 21 years of age cannot possibly have acquired."
Lawrence A. Jones

"He should be a thorough business expert and able to practically apply his knowledge."
J. Porter Joplin

"A professional man whose services are devoted to organizing, examining and reporting upon any and all classes of accounts."
R. O. Macdonald

"Principal function is study of methods of a business and subsequent designing of proper system of accounting."
Henry Millard

"Principal requirements are ability to correct chaotic conditions and present true facts concerning accounts. Experience of business complications a necessity."
Louis G. Peloubet

"An accountant whose services are supposed to be at the command of any person. One versed and skilled in the theory and practice of accounts."
John C. Pirie

"One qualified to act as special commissoner or referee for a court of record, to certify to correctness of accounts required by law. Term is usually applied to professional accountants whose work, however, is virtually the opposite of public —i.e. confidential."
Charles Rudolph

"A person possessing ability to investigate correctness and honest administration of commercial undertakings, of high integrity and wide knowledge of business custom and law."
Philip T. Sandt

"One skilled in accounts, practicing his profession, the word public being used to distinguish him from the accountant employed by a firm or corporation and whose duties are limited to one class of work."
Allen R. Smart

"A scientific, experienced accountant skilled in the work of accountancy and capable of planning and executing any kind of accountancy."
Carrie Snyder

"A person possessed of a thorough knowledge of business principles and methods and the best ways in which to express those principles in the books and other constituent parts of the business to make a harmonious whole."

Seymour Walton

From Springfield, Illinois, the one reply was as follows:

"A person skilled in designing, keeping, adjusting and auditing accounts; versed in commercial law and business in general, who designs, examines and reports on systems of accounts."

Jacob M. Appel

From St. Louis also there was one reply:

"One who by experience has attained a position of authority in the conduct and effect of business transactions. A business counsellor."

John A. Cooper

From Cincinnati two replies were received:

"A person engaged in accountancy as a doctor is in medicine, or a lawyer in law. The prefix public is necessary owing to the fact of bookkeepers calling themselves accountants."

Richard F. Ring

"A public accountant is one holding himself in readiness to serve the public in matters of accountancy. One well versed in matters pertaining to records."

Frank E. Webner

From Philadelphia one reply was received:

"A person skilled in accounts and commercial ways offering his service to the public in auditing, making examinations, designing, installing, and advising concerning accounts."

Joseph E. Sterrett

From New York five answers were as follows:

"One who by training and experience is fitted to perform professional service in devising systems of, installing, auditing, supervising and reporting on accounts.

Frederick A. Cleveland

"A person skilled generally in commercial affairs, and particularly in the accounts relating thereto, who places his service at the disposal of the public."

A. Lowes Dickinson

"One who by study, training and eventual experience has the ability to render professionally services in inaugurating, simplifying, verifying and reporting on accounts."

Frank C. Richardson

"A person skilled in the practice of accountancy whose services are at the disposal of the public."

George Wilkinson

"Degree should be granted only to those having passed CPA examination and having 3 years experience in practicing accountancy in office of expert public accountant.

Henry W. Wilmot

533

Of these 28 definitions only 3 were from accountants who had contributed answers to the *Public Accountant* three or four years earlier. And in the total, which was almost the same as in the earlier list, the answers which mentioned the professional status of the public accountant increased from 7 to 13, whereas fewer particularized as to the nature of the services he rendered. As to qualifications, the answers which called for educational preparation increased from 9 to 13, those which called for experience from 10 to 15, those which stressed ability dropped from 13 to 10, and only 1 mentioned tactfulness instead of 7 as before. And as to governing principles, honesty was mentioned in only 2 answers whereas 10 of the earlier answers called for it, as did 6 that he be unprejudiced and 4 that he be fearless, not mentioned in this list.

This of course was not the end of the attempts at making clear the connotation of the term "public accountant." As shown at the beginning of this article, the problem is still receiving attention. Since the problem remains, it may prove helpful to have a summary such as this to show a cross section of opinion for approximately a decade before and a decade after the date of the first CPA law.

Education and Examination

Early Movements for Accountancy Education

BY NORMAN E. WEBSTER

Much of this article was read at the Fortieth Anniversary Dinner of the School of Commerce, Accounts and Finance of New York University on April 4, 1940. The author has amplified that paper to include all presently known early movements for commercial education of college grade and in particular the circumstances which led to the establishment of the New York School of Accounts, the spiritual ancestor of the present flourishing school.

PRIOR to the early part of the past century, the teaching of bookkeeping was done almost wholly by individual instructors. About the end of the second decade it was more formally organized in business colleges. Some thirty years later, a more fully developed instruction in accounts and related subjects was begun in the chain schools, the first of which was the Bryant and Stratton School, established in 1853.

But a little earlier there had developed a demand for business education of college grade. Schools of law, medicine, and technology had been established in many localities, but pure business had not yet been provided for. In educational policy it seems that there was a relationship between the University of London founded in 1828, the University of the City of New York—now New York University—founded in 1831, and the University of Louisiana——now Tulane—which was founded in 1847. Each sought to offer a preparation for other lines of activity besides the learned professions and statecraft. And between the last two there was this further connection that Dr. Caleb S. Henry, who from 1839 to 1852 served New York University as professor of history and philosophy, was associated in the editorship of the *New York Review* with Francis Lister Hawks, DD, who in 1847 became the first president of the University of Louisiana.

One year earlier, James Dunwoody Brownson DeBow had established in New Orleans a journal popularly known as *Debow's Review*, in which "he addressed himself to promoting the development of the agriculture, industry, and commerce of the South and West through the dissemination of economic, statistical, industrial, commercial, and educational information." It was with this background that President Hawks, in his report for 1848, stated:

"There should be a professorship devoted to *commerce* in all its manifold relations. It presents a vastly extensive field, embracing the general history and statistics of commerce, its relation to the policy of nations, and the consequent happiness of man, its connection with history and influence on civilization, the principles of commercial and maritime law with various other topics that readily suggest themselves. This feature, if adopted, would be peculiar to our University."

With DeBow as professor of political economy, commerce, and statistics, the program was begun in 1851 and with relatively few students was carried on to 1857, when it was abandoned.

During the next decade there were two other movements to provide education for business. In 1866, citizens of Milwaukee tried unsuccessfully to induce the regents of the University of Wisconsin to establish a college of commerce. On January 8, 1869, General Robert E. Lee, President of Washington College at Lexington, Virginia, recommended the addition of a commercial school. He stated, "it is proposed not merely to give instruction in bookkeeping and the forms and details of busi-

535

ness, but to teach the principles of commercial economy, trade and mercantile law." He also submitted a report by a committee of the faculty, one of whom was William Preston Johnston, later president of Louisiana State and Tulane Universities which proposed a curriculum as fellows:

"Course of commerce, consisting of
"1st, Mathematics of accounts, exchange, insurance, annuities, interest, etc.;
"2nd, Geometry and drawing;
"3rd, Bookkeeping and penmanship;
"4th, Commercial correspondence, correct use of the English language;
"5th, Geography applied to production and commerce;
"6th, Commercial technology, or the production of mechanical and chemical manufactures as articles of trade;
"7th, Elements of commercial law, or law of bills, notes, contracts, insurance, corporations, bailments, shipping, etc.;
"8th, Commercial economy, or the administration and financial management of commercial enterprises, banks, insurance and joint stock companies, railroads, canals, ships, steamers, telegraphs, etc.;
"9th, Commercial history and biography;
"10th, Modern languages."

However, because of financial limitations and the death of General Lee in 1870, the proposed school was not established at that time.

Twelve years later, in 1881, the Wharton School of Finance and Economy was established in the University of Pennsylvania. Candidates for admission were required to pass examinations in arithmetic, algebra, geometry, trigonometry, analytical geometry, ancient and modern geography, general history, several branches of English, French, and chemistry. There were also examinations in alternative groups of sub-

jects: either Greek, Latin, and German; or German, French, advanced mathematics, and science. It provided a three-year course and, as stated in its 1881 catalogue, the subjects during each of the years were as follows:

Sub-junior year—English, German, French, Latin, physics, mineralogy, social science, and mercantile practice, the latter including business procedure, management of trusts, and routine of banking.
Junior year—English, German, French, Latin, physics, geology, mental and moral science, and social science, the latter including money, banking, credit system, panics, security markets, taxation, national industry, capital and labor, and related matters.
Senior year—English, mediaeval and modern history, physics, astronomy, law including elementary, mercantile, common carrier, license, land, corporation and constitutional law of the United States and Pennsylvania, and social science including land, labor and monetary questions, socialism and communism with research in the theory and history of such matters.

This curriculum is interesting. It was broad gauge and seems to have warranted the bestowal of the degree of bachelor of science upon those who completed it satisfactorily. Like that of the proposed school at Washington College, it appears to have been designed as a preparation for business. But except for the subjects of mathematics and economics or social science, neither curriculum at first proposed to offer much practical preparation for the professional accountant or anything at all for the auditor.

But very soon thereafter two independent movements were started, both of which looked to the provision of educational facilities in part or in whole for accountants then engaged in public practice or who desired to prepare for such practice.

536

The first was the Institute of Accountants and Bookkeepers of the City of New York, which was incorporated on July 28, 1882, and whose name was shortened to Institute of Accounts on June 23, 1886. Its objects and purposes as stated in its certificate of incorporation were "the elevation of the profession and the intellectual advancement and improvement of its members:

"1st, By the discussion in its councils of technical knowledge and commercial practice;

"2nd, By aiding its members in the performance of their professional and social responsibilities."

Although it was active during twenty-five years or more, very little record of its activities has been found except its charter, its by-laws, a few notices, and some news items in the accounting journals of that period. These show that its membership included a considerable number of accountants in public practice; that for its highest class of membership applicants were required to pass examinations which tradition says were severe; and that it provided technical lectures for its members, often given by experienced accountants from among its own membership. Its aims, at least during the first decade of its life, appear to have been wholly devoted to accountancy education and the provision of accounting literature. Quite naturally, many of the subjects discussed at its meetings were of interest also to accountants in private practice. Some discussions, however, seem to have been wholly for the public practitioner. So far as is known, this was the earliest effort to provide educational opportunities for the profession.

The second movement which looked toward education for the public accountant was the organization of the American Association of Public Accountants, which was incorporated on August 20, 1887. Its certificate of incorporation stated that its object was "to promote the efficiency and usefulness of members of such society, by compelling the observance of strict rules of conduct as a condition of membership, and by establishing a high standard of professional attainments through general education and knowledge and otherwise." For a time its activities as a national association were directed toward securing members throughout the country with a view to the organization of the profession, but by 1891 or 1892 it was moving for the provision of facilities for education for the public practice of accountancy.

On February 10, 1892, when James Yalden was president and Henry R. M. Cook was vice president, a special meeting on charter for an educational institution was held at the office of the president. Upon motion of Louis Yalden, seconded by Frank Broaker, the vice president—who it appears was also chairman of a committee on charter— was authorized to go to Albany "to find out the particulars." No report of his visit has been found, but later records suggest that he conferred with Melvil Dewey, secretary to the Board of Regents, and was advised that the Association should present to the regents a memorial or petition for a charter for the proposed institution, embodying an outline of its form of organization, a statement of the provisions to be made for its financial stability, the curriculum which it would offer to its students, and probably the names of the persons who would constitute its faculty. On February 20, 1892, Harry A. Briggs, Richard F. Stevens, and the committee on charter were constituted a committee on curriculum which, on March 5, 1892, reported that it had agreed upon the course of study. On that date a fund of $5,000 was provided for; on April 6, 1892, John L. N. Hunt was asked to take the chair of commercial law.

No copy of the petition to the regents or of the curriculum has been found.

537

Subsequent records, however, indicate that the petition asked for a charter for a college of accounts, with power to confer degrees, to be located in the City of New York, to have a guaranty of $5,000 against possible deficits, to offer the courses provided for in the curriculum, and to be under the direction and control of the American Association of Public Accountants. Except for provisions which were subsequently deleted or modified, it seems probable that the petition was similar to or perhaps identical with another petition which was presented to the regents about six months later. The petition, together with a list of several hundred banks, bankers, corporations, firms, and individuals of note in this state who had signified in writing their approval of the project, was sent to the regents prior to May 21, 1892, for on that date Vice President Cook informed the trustees that he had been advised that the petition would be acted upon by the regents in Albany on June 8, 1892. The trustees thereupon selected several accountants to address the regents on various subjects as follows:

James Yalden and Henry R. M. Cook on the petition in general
Richard M. Chapman on advantages to the public
George H. Church on judicial accountings
James T. Anyon on mortgage companies
Louis N. Bergtheil on bankruptcy and insolvency
Frank Broaker on equipment and financial ability of the trustees to maintain a college of accounts

On June 8, 1892, these men, excepting Messrs. Church and Anyon, together with Louis Yalden, Mark C. Mirick, William H. Beynroth, W. Sanders Davies, Thomas Bagot, William Trenholm, E. Redgate, and Thomas R. Horley, of New York City, and John Heins of Philadelphia, met at the Kenmore Hotel in Albany and notified Melvil

Dewey, secretary, that they were ready to wait upon the regents. Mr. Dewey informed them that a committee of the regents was in session to receive the petition, but that not all the proposed speakers could be heard. Those who addressed the committee of the regents were James Yalden, Henry R. M. Cook, and Frank Broaker. The regents' minutes show that there was also present at the hearing Charles E. Sprague, a former president of the Institute of Accounts.

The minutes of the regents also show that after the committee reported the results of the hearing in behalf of the charter granted to a delegation of nearly twenty public accountants from New York, it was upon motion of Regent Warren discharged from further consideration of the application. "And after discussion, on motion of Regent Doane, it was voted that the secretary be instructed to inform the petitioners in the matter of the American Association of Public Accountants of New York that the regents are not prepared to endorse the whole proposal in their petition, but are ready to open examinations for such persons as desire to become public accountants."

The reasons for this action by the regents were not set out in their minutes, but Vice President Henry R. M. Cook, in a report to the Association on November 10, 1892, stated at some length four reasons why the regents deferred final action upon the petition. The reasons may be summarized thus:

1. That absences had reduced the meeting of the regents to a bare quorum;

2. That the regents had not had time to construe a recent act of the legislature by which the prior laws defining the powers of the regents had been codified, condensed, and in some instances amended; and
That by law a college of accounts must have an endowment of $500,000;

3. That the proposed constitution of the institution seemed to partake of monopoly; and

4. That the Association did not then have accommodations for the school.

In this report Mr. Cook indicated that he at least was far from being discouraged. He referred to the many years which passed before the English accountants obtained the slightest legislative encouragement, and said, "I think you will all agree with me that this Association is to be congratulated in having obtained actual recognition from the authorities; and in my estimation, judging from the tone of the public prints regarding the matter and the number of letters of inquiry, and written and verbal requests for admission to the proposed school, I think there is no doubt of success."

In the meantime between the meeting with the regents on June 8, 1892, and this report by Vice President Cook on November 10, 1892, it appears that the committee on charter had been giving consideration to changes in the plan. This had progressed so far that on October 6, 1892, four resolutions were adopted upon the motion of Frank Broaker, seconded by Louis N. Bergtheil, as follows:

1. That the following named gentlemen be requested to serve as trustees in the New York School of Accounts, and that the gentlemen whose names are also stated herewith be appointed a committee to confer with them on the subject and report on or before October 15, 1892, to James Yalden and H. R. M. Cook:

Names of Proposed Trustees

John L. N. Hunt, LL.D.
Fred R. Coudert
John A. McCall
John Claflin
Thomas Shearman
Frank B. Thurber
Henry A. Cannon
Horace W. Sibley
C. Christenson

Committee

Henry R. M. Cook
Louis N. Bergtheil
Frank Broaker
James Yalden
George H. Church

2. That the amended petition to the Board of Regents be prepared by Henry R. M. Cook with full power to act, and that the selection of the members of this Association to serve as trustees in the proposed school be left to the discretion of the same gentleman;

3. That the secretary notify the professors of the various departments to prepare a short concise treatise of studies in their respective departments covering instruction of 1,000 hours as stated in petition to the Board of Regents;

4. That Thomas Bagot and Louis Yalden be appointed a committee, with full power to act, to select and hire permanent headquarters for the Association and proposed school of accounts, location to be central, say between 23rd to 48th streets between Lexington and 8th avenues, or at their discretion elsewhere, rental $500 to $1,300 per annum. On October 14, 1892, the committee reported and were instructed to lease two rooms at 122 West 23rd Street and to purchase the necessary furniture and fixtures.

In further preparation for presenting to the regents the revised petition, the trustees of the Association on November 25, 1892, selected six members of the Association to serve as trustees of the New York School of Accounts: James Yalden, Henry R. M. Cook, Louis N. Bergtheil, Richard F. Stevens, Thomas Bagot, and Richard M. Chapman. Apparently all preparations were completed by December 8, 1892, when Mr. Cook submitted:

1. Copy of Certificate of Incorporation of American Association of Public Accountants;
2. Petition of Association for incorporation of New York School of Accounts;

539

445

3. Resolution and guarantee of Association adopted at this meeting;
4. Outline of proposed curriculum of New York School of Accounts; and
5. Guarantee by eleven individuals to make good any monetary deficiency of the school.

On motion of Louis N. Bergtheil, seconded by Frank Broaker, all were approved.

A brief summary of the ten sections of the petition is as follows:

1. It would be to the public interest to establish a professional school for accountants, under the jurisdiction of the regents, the auspices of the Association, and the guidance of members of the profession;
2. Guaranty by the Association against deficits to the extent of $2,500 a year;
3. Nomination as first trustees of the New York School of Accounts of:

Thomas Bagot
Rufus G. Beardslee
Louis N. Bergtheil
Richard M. Chapman
George H. Church
Henry R. M. Cook
John L. N. Hunt
Lucius M. Stanton
Richard F. Stevens
Frank B. Thurber
John B. Woodward
James Yalden

for terms of two years, their succes-

sors to be elected by the Association.
4. Suitable accommodations leased at 122 West 23rd Street, now available;
5. Provision of all necessary furniture, appurtenances, books, and supplies;
6. Full course of instruction to extend over two years, each of forty weeks, 1,000 hours;
7. Provisional charter for two years asked;
8. After two years absolute charter to be asked on endowment of $20,000;
9. School to be self supporting with instruction fee of $100 per annum;
10. Expenses of school estimated at $8,000 or $9,000 per annum, $5,000 subscribed to be used for furnishing the school and establishment of a library, and students estimated at not less than 100, providing an income of $10,000

The outline of the proposed curriculum was too long for incorporation here, but a condensed summary of it, compared with the business courses proposed for the earlier schools twenty and ten years previously, shows that the purpose of the organizers of the New York School of Accounts was to provide a preparation for the public practice of accountancy. The outline included eight sections descriptive of the scope of the course of study and one section showing the time allotted to each during each of the two years.

PROPOSED CURRICULUM

Section 1. Science of double entry: elucidating the principles of original entry and posting and the primary groundwork on which bookkeeping rests.

Section 2. Keeping accounts for sole proprietors, copartnerships, and corporations including the opening, conducting, and closing of books with the preparation of balance-sheets, merchandise, and profit-and-loss accounts and schedules for merchandising, manufacturing, commission and brokerage, construction, and shipping and commission businesses.

Section 3. Corporation accounts, state returns, reorganizations, etc.

Section 4. Judicial accounts (now commonly called fiduciary).

Section 5. Public accounts (now commonly called municipal).

Section 6. Auditing—Examination of accounts for arresting or detecting fraud; reconstruction of systems for insuring greater safety; preparing reports and statements on investigations.

Section 7. Auditing—Analyzing accounts and deducing facts therefrom for making calculations re future course of action; investigation for ascertaining actual earnings of a business; settlement of partnership interests, etc.

Section 8. Law upon mercantile, corporation, banking, judicial accountings, etc., upon matter of accounts as laid down by authorities or N. Y. Statutes.

Section 9. First year: Theory of accounts 5 hours per week for 1st 20 weeks
Profession of pub-
lic accountancy. 5 " per week for last 20 "
Six general classes
of accounts each 2½ " per week for full 40 "
Law............ 2½ " per week for full 40 "
Second year: Substitute auditing and practical reviews for theory and
two general classes of accounts—others as in first year.
Both: Instruction by lectures, dictation, illustration, and texts.

So far this story of the proposed college or school has all been taken from the records of the American Association of Public Accountants, except some details of the hearing on June 8, 1892, found in the minutes of the regents which are also the source of the record of the next action by the regents.

The petition or application with the outline of the proposed curriculum was verified on December 8, 1892, by President James Yalden before George Gordon Battle, notary public, whose certificate was attested by the Clerk of the City and County of New York, William J. McKenna.

The minutes of the regents under date of December 14, 1892, state: "The committee reported that the American Association of Public Accountants had withdrawn the objectionable features in their original proposal and had submitted a petition for a provisional charter for two years for the New York School of Accounts. After discussion it was *voted* that a provisional charter for two years be granted to the New York School of Accounts." The records of the regents also show that the charter was prepared upon an engraved form with three insertions, and when so issued was as follows:

541

"WHEREAS a petition for incorporation as an institution of the university has been duly received, and

"WHEREAS official inspection shows that partial provision has been made for buildings, furniture, equipment and for proper maintenance, and that all other prescribed requirements will be fully met

"THEREFORE, being satisfied that public interests will be promoted by such incorporation, the regents by virtue of the authority conferred on them by law hereby incorporate James Yalden, F. B. Thurber, Thomas Bagot, Rufus G. Beardslee, John L. N. Hunt, Louis M. Bergtheil, Lucius M. Stanton, Richard M. Chapman, Henry R. M. Cook, George H. Church, Richard F. Stevens, John B. Woodward and their successors in office under the corporate name of New York School of Accounts, with all powers, privileges and duties, and subject to all limitations and restrictions prescribed for such corporations by law or by the ordinances of the University of the State of New York. The first trustees of said corporation shall be provisionally the above named twelve original incorporators.

"If all requirements prescribed by law or by the university ordinances be fully met within two years, then this charter shall be made permanent, but otherwise on December 14, 1894, it shall terminate and become void and shall be surrendered to the regents.

"It is also provided that no diplomas, certificate of graduation, or other credentials shall be granted except on such conditions as are from time to time certified under seal of the university as being duly approved by the regents.

"IN WITNESS WHEREOF the regents grant this charter No. 680, under seal of the university at the capitol in Albany, December 14, 1892."

[SEAL]

ANSON JUDD UPSON, *Chancellor*
MELVIL DEWEY, *Secretary*

447

This action of the regents was on December 15, 1892, reported to the trustees of the Association by Henry R. M. Cook, who stated: "I have been in Albany for the past two days, and the Association in the form of a school has now been admitted to the university of this state."

On December 21, 1892, the trustees, acting as a nominating body, recommended to the board of trustees of New York School of Accounts that the undermentioned gentlemen be elected to fill the positions named for the provisional period of two years fixed by the regents of the University of the State of New York in the charter granted to New York School of Accounts:

President, James Yalden	Vice president, Henry R. M. Cook
Secretary, Thomas Bagot	Treasurer, Richard M. Chapman
Dean	John L. N. Hunt
Professor of public accounts	James Yalden
Professor of judicial accounts	Louis N. Bergtheil
Professor of transportation accounts	Richard F. Stevens
Professor of insurance accounts	William M. Brooks
Professor of banking accounts	George H. Church
Professor of mercantile accounts	Frank Broaker
Professor of double-entry accounts	Richard M. Chapman
Professor of double-entry accounts	Louis Yalden
Professor of building-loan accounts	John W. Whitehead

Later records show W. Sanders Davies as another teacher.

Then on January 13, 1893, the president of the Association, Henry R. M. Cook, reported to the trustees that he had received from the regents the provisional charter for two years from December 14, 1892, and had delivered it to James Yalden, president of the New York School of Accounts. The progress that was being made during the next four months was given in the report of James Yalden, president of the School, which was read at the meeting of the Association on May 9, 1893. After noting that the charter was granted "too late to make the necessary arrangements to establish the School during this educational season," President Yalden stated: "The Trustees are now making arrangements to commence in October next. Several consultations relative to the curriculum have been held. A meeting will be called at an early date that the faculty may decide upon the course of study. The dean of the faculty, John L. N. Hunt, thought it advisable to postpone any advertisement of the course until August or September, shortly before the opening of the school. In the meantime we have sent the preliminary prospectus and circulars to all members of the profession, trustees of schools, undergraduates, and other interested parties, to which several replies have been received, and we are in daily correspondence as to our mode of procedure, terms, etc., that will be required of candidates. The trustees are fully alive to the fact that preparations must be made to open the school and they are giving their attention to the requirements."

On October 28, 1893, Louis N. Bergtheil, of the faculty, reported at a meeting of the Association that the New York School of Accounts was opened on October 3, 1893, and that regular sessions had been held since. The minutes of the Association contain no subsequent mention of the school until in June, 1894, but some facts are stated in a recent letter from a member of that faculty.

In this letter he mentioned some of those who taught at the New York School of Accounts and added: "We were all busy men and frequently out of the city, but were definitely charged to find a substitute teacher under such circumstance. The subjects studied were law and business practice, accounting theory and practice. In connection with the latter subject, it was found necessary to sketch the theory of double entry so as to give the students the background necessary for them to prepare trading accounts, profit-and-loss accounts, and balance-sheets. Evening sessions were held each week. I had one evening assigned to me. I do not recall the names of the students except one, a Mr. Wood, who was in the employ of a bank on Long Island. My recollection is that the school lasted only one winter."

At the close of the school year the faculty discussed the question of continuance, and on July 11, 1894, the faculty voted: "That in the opinion of the faculty it is undesirable to continue the School of Accounts, and they recommend that the trustees take such action as they may decide upon, to surrender the charter to the Board of Regents or otherwise."

Then on September 5, 1894, Richard F. Stevens, president of the Association, in an address to the trustees of the New York School of Accounts, said: "A year has passed since the inception of the School of Accounts, and what has been accomplished? A class of seven pupils have gone through the year's course— that is all. Not a business man has come forward to aid us in any way; the whole burden has fallen on the shoulders of a few of our members, now disheartened and disillusioned. The Board of Regents of the University have stood silent and aloof, not a word has been said about commissioning or licensing our members, and communications addressed to them on the subject of legalizing the profession by legislative enactment have remained unanswered. The members, under this state of affairs, naturally have ceased to take interest in the school, the professors have resigned or been slack in their attendance, the scholars supine, and the further con-

tinuance of the school in its present state seems idle." He suggested that, "either of our great universities, Columbia or the College of New York, might receive our little school under its fostering wing." To much the same effect were the comments in the previously noted recent letter from a member of the faculty: "On the whole the school was anything but a success. As a matter of fact, it was a dismal failure." The records in Albany indicate that the temporary charter lapsed automatically at the end of the two years.

That the New York School of Accounts was not a success is as apparent today as it was in the summer and autumn of 1894. And it is not difficult to understand that to its faculty and trustees and to the Association which sponsored it, the outcome then seemed to be a dismal failure. But looking backward over the nearly fifty years which have passed since that time, it appears that while that school may have been a failure, the movement which promoted it was a signal success. Here are the facts.

The first petition which the regents were not prepared to endorse in whole developed the fact that they were "ready to open examinations for such persons as desire to become public accountants." That was on June 8, 1892, and at the first session of the legislature after the temporary charter expired on December 14, 1894, the regents' readiness to open examinations germinated in two bills which though not then enacted blossomed the next year in the C.P.A. act of April 17, 1896.

The C.P.A. act resulted during the next eight months in the issuance of seventy-five certificates in 1896 and was followed by the organization of The New York State Society of Certified Public Accountants, incorporated on January 28, 1897.

Within three years the State Society, on October 9, 1899, began another movement for a school and, acting in accordance with the suggestion of

543

President Stevens in 1894, approached Columbia and New York universities.

The mover of the resolution for this action by the State Society and the chairman of the committee later appointed to carry it forward was Henry R. M. Cook, who eight years earlier was chairman of the charter committee of the American Association which secured the temporary charter for the New York School of Accounts.

Less than ten months later, on July 8, 1900, the School of Commerce, Accounts and Finance of New York University was incorporated and commenced active operation on October 1, 1900.

Whereas in 1892 it was possible to secure for the faculty of the New York School of Accounts only one person outside the ranks of accountants in public practice, namely John L. N. Hunt, who accepted appointment as Dean and Professor of Law and Business Practice, in 1900, nine members of the University Faculty accepted chairs in the School of Commerce, Accounts and Finance and, of the six accountants appointed to the faculty, one was Charles Ezra Sprague who, representing the Institute of Accounts, had attended the first hearing before the regents on June 8, 1892; another was Henry R. M. Cook, who was chairman of the charter committee and vice president of the earlier school and who it appears had refused to lose courage during the intervening years.

While not suggesting that there was any lineal relationship between the two schools it seems clear that the New York School of Accounts was the spiritual ancestor of the School of Commerce, Accounts and Finance.

544

EARLY UNIVERSITY EDUCATION IN ACCOUNTANCY

Jeremiah Lockwood

UNIVERSITY education for business is of recent origin. Forty years ago only one university in this country had a school whose major purpose was to aid in equipping students for careers in the business world. Since then the growth in the number of these schools of university grade has been rapid. Today, thousands of students are attending courses which are classified as business courses in our colleges of commerce, finance and accounts and in our colleges of liberal arts. Accountancy as a business study has moved rapidly toward the front ranks of the business subjects during this period. Only a few years ago, following a survey of courses offered by University Schools of Business, Professor Bossard, of the University of Pennsylvania, said:

Accounting is the most fully developed subject or field of study in our collegiate schools of business. The objectives of accounting departments are usually well defined and clear; the courses in accounting are relatively standardized. Account-

ing is usually the first business subject to be introduced in college curricula. In fact, to many persons accounting stands in a peculiar sense as the Alpha of business education.[1]

These statements concerning accounting were not applicable to the accounting courses during the earlier years of the growth of collegiate schools of business. There were no accounting departments; objectives were not well defined and clear; courses in accounting were not standardized.

The purpose of this paper is to endeavor to shed some light on the contents of accounting courses and on the problems of teaching accounting during the years when the subject was first offered in institutions of higher learning. The period to be covered will be limited to the two decades preceding 1903. This period represents about one-third of the time during

---

[1] *University Education for Business*—J. H. Bossard and F. Dewhurst, p. 390, University of Pennsylvania Press—1931.

which accounting has been taught in these institutions. To shorten the period would result in confining the paper to courses as taught in one or two institutions. During the early years of the new century the courses in accounting were beginning to assume more definite form and content and to increase in number, due partly to the growth of the CPA movement and partly to the growing consciousness of the increasing importance of business education and of accounting in particular. Hence it has not been deemed desirable to lengthen the period beyond the twenty-year span.

The data for this paper secured from college catalogs had to be supplemented by data obtained from other sources. Much interesting material has been obtained by letter and by interview from former teachers and students of accounting. In addition, manuscripts and addresses of some of the earlier teachers of business subjects in universities contained references to difficulties and problems arising in teaching business studies. These sources although valuable have definite limitations. Catalog descriptions, in the main, have been meager, few educators have written on the subject of early accountancy instruction. Many of those who studied or taught the subject years ago have passed on or have had their memories dulled by the passage of time. Fortunately, some of those consulted seemed vividly aware of classroom events of bygone days.

Your president suggested that emphasis be placed on the development of accounting at the Wharton School of Finance and Commerce of the University of Pennsylvania and at the New York University School of Commerce, Accounts and Finance. Before doing this the early development of University Schools of Commerce will be briefly commented upon and some of the factors influencing the development

of University courses in accounting prior to 1900 will be mentioned. The content of early accounting courses offered by some of the other institutions of higher learning will also be noted.

In 1851 a school of commerce was incorporated in the University of Louisiana but was apparently abandoned in 1857.[2] In 1868 the University of Illinois established a school, the name of which became the School of Commerce in 1870, to prepare men for the tasks of business. Bookkeeping was one of the subjects taught. In 1880 the Board of Trustees discontinued the school since "the attempt to construct a University School of Commerce along the lines of a business college have proven unsuccessful. The school had done little more than to prepare clerks and bookkeepers. It had not been realized that the function of a university school of commerce was to prepare for future leadership in economic enterprise, not for clerkships."[3] Twenty-two years later the School of Commerce was reëstablished in this institution.

In 1881 the Wharton School of Finance and Economy was founded through the generosity of Joseph Wharton. Its growth was slow during the early years but its influence was quickly recognized. No other schools of this type were established until 1898 and at the close of 1900 there were but seven such institutions in the country.

The movement in educational circles to establish schools of business encountered much opposition. Many educators sincerely believed that the best training for business consisted of a liberal-arts education to be supplemented by the practical training to be obtained in the business world. This view is held by many even today. In spite of opposition, however, the

---

[2] B. R. Haynes and H. P. Jackson—*History of Business Education in the United States*—Southwestern Publishing Co. 1934, p. 83.
[3] Conference on Commercial Education and Business Progress, University of Illinois, 1913, p. 2.

movement for higher education for business men gained headway due largely to the persistence of Edmund J. James, one time Professor at the Wharton School of Finance and Economy and later President of the University of Illinois. He was a very staunch advocate of university education for business. Speaking before the American Economic Association in 1900 on the subject of the "Relation of our Colleges and Universities to Higher Commercial Education," Dr. James, then professor in the University of Chicago, made the following statement:

> The movement in this country for college and university training for the future business man seems to have entered within the last year or two upon a new era in its history. Twenty years ago, when I first began to insist that our business classes stood in need of higher special or professional education, and that this education should be given in our colleges and universities, my voice was like that of one crying in the wilderness, unheeded either by the business world, on the one hand, or by the college world on the other.[4]

The development of accounting courses was also adversely affected by the attitude of opposition to business courses. It is hardly to be expected that those who did not believe that a break with past educational procedures was desirable should welcome the development of courses in accounting, or, as they were scornfully called, bookkeeping. Professor Henry Rand Hatfield, when Dean of the School of Commerce in the University of Chicago, requested the Mathematics Department of that institution to add a course in bookkeeping thinking that the unquestioned academic standing of the Mathematics Department would remove some of the odium or reproach attached to a course on bookkeeping.[5]

Professor James, in his address before

the American Economic Association, referred to this feeling against accounting when discussing the branches of learning which he would include in the curriculum. He said:

> I should go still further. I should accept any practical subject which can be made a serious intellectual pursuit, if by so doing I could advance practical knowledge and increase intellectual training. Thus, for instance, the whole system of accounting, or as it is sometimes called with a sneering connotation "bookkeeping," I should make an element in all such curricula. The theory of accounting is as strictly a scientific subject as the theory of political economy itself, and steady application to this subject offers a stimulating and valuable mental discipline.[6]

There were a number of other factors hampering the development of accounting courses which should be considered in any discussion of early accounting instruction. Brief mention will be made of some of them.

In the first place there were no accounting textbooks suitable for use in the university classrooms. Although there were many texts on bookkeeping they were usually prepared for use in the business colleges. There were numerous editions of I. I. Hitchcock's *A New Method of Teaching the Art of Bookkeeping* first published in 1823. Many printings of Christopher Columbus Marsh's book, *Science of Double Entry Bookkeeping*, appeared between 1830 and 1886. Fifty editions or printings of Joseph Howard Palmer's *Treatise on Practical Bookkeeping and Business Transactions*, appeared during the period from 1852 to 1884. There were also many printings of books on single- and double-entry by other authors, notably, Peter Duff, Louis L. Williams, Ira Mayhew, John C. Colt and others.[7] However, it is not to be inferred that accounting had

547

---

[4] *Proceedings of the Meeting of the American Economic Association*, at Ann Arbor, Michigan—December 28, 1900. Third Series, Vol. II, No. 1, p. 144.
[5] Letter of Professor Hatfield to the writer—Dated November 27, 1937.

[6] *Proceedings American Economic Association*—1900. *Op. cit.*, p. 158.
[7] H. C. Bentley—*Works on Accounting by American Authors, 1796–1900*, Vol. I.

548

not advanced beyond the bookkeeping stage. A well developed body of accounting knowledge, based on English practices and procedures, was in existence in 1900. American authors had written extensively on the bookkeeping techniques applicable to various types of enterprises and a few books on corporation accounting, cost accounting, auditing, voucher systems and C.P.A. Questions appeared in the two decades between 1880–1900.[7] But these books were unsuited for use in the university courses in accounting. The 1901 catalog of New York University School of Commerce deplored the lack of textbooks on accounting and indicated that the lecture system, pending the preparation of textbooks, would be used in teaching higher accountancy at that institution. An instructor of accounting in the Wharton School prepared his own material for his accounting classes in 1889–1891. Another instructor at the same institution, ten years later, based his accounting course on Woodlock's *Anatomy of a Railroad Report*, which was published in 1895. Dr. Hatfield, of the University of Chicago, reports that he relied upon the earlier writings of Professor J. F. Schär of Germany, who published his book, *Single and Double Entry*, about 1894. The dearth of suitable texts was, no doubt, a hampering influence.

Another factor to be borne in mind in passing judgment upon the early courses in accounting was the difficulty of securing accounting teachers who were familiar with the subject. One of the early teachers of accounting, in discussing the papers which were read before the meeting of the Michigan Political Science Association held in 1903, said:

What is the difference between bookkeeping and higher accounting? It is true that while bookkeeping was formerly held in poor repute, no one was familiar with the subject and it was denied that it had a place in the college curriculum. I

am told that there are college professors not over a thousand miles from here who would not admit bookkeeping into their curriculum unless over their dead bodies.

What is the difference? I do not know. I am teaching "accounting" myself and I can say freely that I don't know what it is and I don't know where to place it.[8]

A very prominent educator, Joseph French Johnson, Dean of the New York University School of Commerce, Accounts and Finance, expressed somewhat similar views at the annual meeting of the American Association of Public Accountants in 1910. During the course of his remarks he gave utterance to the following statements:

Most of you know that many universities in the United States are now teaching or trying to teach accountancy. One of the reasons why I can only say that the Universities are "trying to teach" accountancy is that few men are trained to be teachers . . . and universities have found it an almost impossible task in the past 10 years to find men who can teach accounting. Those who knew it, couldn't teach, and those who could teach didn't know it.[9]

These foregoing remarks are illustrative of many others. They tend to point out some of the handicaps under which the earlier instructors labored. Accountancy as a practical course of instruction was frowned upon. Its growth was exceedingly slow. The instructors of accountancy knew very little about it. Furthermore, the teaching staffs in the newly formed schools of business were small and the burden of teaching the new courses which were being added fell upon the shoulders of a few. Staff members teaching accounting taught other courses such as Economics, Statistics, Modern Industrialism, Transportation, Insurance, Banking, History of Commerce and others. These additional bur-

[8] Dr. H. R. Hatfield, in the *Proceedings of the Michigan Political Science Association*, February 5–7, 1903, Vol. v, p. 183.
[9] *Proceedings of the American Association of Public Accountants*, 1910 Year Book, p. 132.

dens naturally retarded the development of accounting courses. The rapidity with which these courses would have developed if it had not been for the movement toward the legal recognition of accountancy —the C.P.A. movement—and the assistance rendered by practitioners of accountancy, can only be conjectured. There can be no question that the C.P.A. movement revitalized and strengthened materially the educational interest in the field.

With these preliminary thoughts in mind it is fitting that we turn our attention to the courses offered in accounting during its infancy as a course of learning in university schools of business.

EARLY UNIVERSITY INSTRUCTION IN ACCOUNTANCY AT THE UNIVERSITY OF PENNSYLVANIA

The Wharton School of Finance and Commerce of the University of Pennsylvania, originally called the Wharton School of Finance and Economy, was founded in 1881, almost 57 years ago, in order to give a general and professional training to young men who were planning business careers. The reasons motivating Joseph Wharton to found the school and its general organization are too well known to be repeated. In the early years, the courses in business instruction were confined to the junior and senior years of the Arts and Science course but later were extended to four years and the curriculum greatly modified. During 53 of its 57 years accounting has been taught in the school. Since 1887 the subject has been taught continuously.

The first course in accounting taught in the Wharton School was given as a required subject to juniors during the academic year 1883–1884. During the first term the course, which consisted of a series of lectures, was entitled "The Theory and Practice of Accounting." Dur-

ing the second term the work in accounting was devoted to "Expositions of Systems of Bookkeeping in Factories, Banks and Other Corporations and in Municipalities." For the senior year an optional course in Practical Bookkeeping was listed. This course was "taught orally and by requiring the students to keep a set of books according to the most approved forms."[10] Dr. Roland Post Falkner, now Director of the Publication Division of the National Industrial Conference Board, was a student in the first accounting course offered in 1883. During the course of a recent interview, Dr. Falkner stated there were twelve students in that accounting class. The instructor, Chester N. Farr, was a bookkeeper who was very familiar with the principles of debit and credit. Students were required to keep sets of single-entry and double-entry books. The books of original entry were limited to the use of the Day Book, Journal and Sales Book. In this course the principles of debit and credit were applied to the accounts of independent operators and accounts of a partnership, together with an explanation of the methods of allocating partnership profits. During the second term the students were required to keep a set of books for a manufacturer and also operated a theoretical set of blast-furnace books.[11] The next year Seldon R. Hopkins's *Manual of Exhibit Bookkeeping*, published in 1879, and C. C. Marsh's *Theory of Bank Bookkeeping and Joint Stock Accounts* supplemented the material presented in lecture form.[12]

No courses in accounting were given during the academic years 1885–1887. However, the teaching of the subject was renewed in the fall of 1887 and a new in-

549

[10] Catalogue of the University of Pennsylvania, 1883–1884, p. 32.
[11] Interview with Dr. Roland Post Falkner, New York City, November 26, 1937.
[12] Catalogue of the University of Pennsylvania, 1884–1885.

structor, Charles Gilpin, appointed. He taught a course called Methods of Accounting and it is believed he used his own book or pamphlet called The Theory of Double Entry Bookkeeping, which he had published in 1886.

In a report rendered to the Provost of the University of Pennyvania on January 1, 1888, Edmund J. James, Professor of Finance and Administration, reviewed the work of the school during the seven years of its existence and described in detail the nature of the courses which were offered. His statement concerning accounting was as follows:[13]

> A course in the Theory of Accounting, to which are devoted four hours a week throughout the junior year. Practical work is insisted upon only so far as it is necessary to understand the theoretical aspects of the subject and the general principles which underlie all special systems.[13]

The work in accounting during the next few years was under the supervision of Dr. Roland Post Falkner, a graduate of the School, Class of 1885, who had obtained his Ph.D. degree at the University of Halle, Germany, in 1888. At the request of Professor James, Dr. Falkner studied methods of teaching accounting in some of the higher commercial schools in France prior to returning to America. He was appointed Instructor in Bookkeeping on September 4, 1888 and taught the course in Methods of Accounting until he obtained a temporary leave of absence four years later.[14]

Upon taking charge of the accounting work, Dr. Falkner decided that the course should be pitched on a higher plane, if possible, than the courses given by the business colleges. The inquiries made by him concerning methods of teaching accounting in the Superior School of Lyons, France, and his studies of the accounting

books used by this school had a considerable influence on his work as a teacher. American texts on elementary bookkeeping began with day-book entries. The French school's approach to the subject was by means of account analysis. Dr. Falkner believed that the subject could be presented more satisfactorily if he were to begin the subject by analyzing the accounts. This was the method of approach used by him. During the first year of his teaching, Dr. Falkner supplemented his lectures with a textbook. The instruction on journalizing was hampered by the fact that the textbook used listed transactions of a wholesale grocer during a period preceding the Civil War and none of the computations for the transactions were extended. The students were required to make all computations. They also had difficulty in journalizing the many puzzling entries involving bills payable and bills receivable, these entries originating in bills arising through the drawing of drafts or bills by one merchant on another. The unsatisfactory experiences with a text prompted Dr. Falkner to prepare pamphlets giving twelve sets of transactions, all computations being extended. Some of these sets of transactions were prepared to illustrate the operations of individual businesses, partnerships and corporations, all engaged in mercantile operations. The transactions illustrated the use of multiple books of original entry, individual ledgers and the use of a private ledger. The sets also included transactions for a bank, an iron foundry, executors, and for bankruptcy accounting. These bookkeeping sets were not unduly long, only being carried out far enough to illustrate the application of the principles of accounting to various businesses.[15]

In commenting upon Dr. Falkner's course in accounting, the report of the Dean of the College, Dr. Horace Jayne,

---

[13] Annual Report of the Provost of the University of Pennsylvania, including reports of Departments for year ended October 1, 1887.

[14] Roland Post Falkner, *op. cit.*, November 26, 1937.

[15] *Ibid.*

to the Provost of the University, in February 1890, contained the following statement:

The instruction in bookkeeping which was open to criticism in previous years has been put upon a new basis and is now one of the features of the department.[16]

In an address on Schools of Finance and Economy before the Convention of the American Bankers' Association at Saratoga, New York, on September 3, 1890, over 47 years ago, Professor Edmund J. James briefly explained the nature of the business courses taken by the students in the Wharton School. His remarks concerning the accounting course are of interest. Said he—

Finally, parallel with these courses [in history, political science, economics, finance and banking] which are all more or less general in their nature, are the business courses in the narrower sense of the term. . . . They consist of three parts: First, a course in the general theory of accounting; second, in business law; third, in business practice. The first embraces a careful study of the general principles underlying single and double entry, also the study of a dozen or more sets of books carefully selected from leading branches of business and representing the best practice of typical houses. A special point is made of developing the general principles and then illustrating typical variations or applications so that the student can understand with ease any set of books he might have occasion to examine or use. The idea is not so much to make an expert bookkeeper in any one set of books or style of accounting as to train the student so that in a short time he could become expert in any position he might take; and above all so that he can understand with facility and unravel with ease any set of accounts. Another point to which much attention is directed is corporate and public accounting. It is hoped that in course of time a reasonable system of accounting can be introduced into the practice of our cities, counties and state governments.[17]

The course in accounting, to which reference was being made was given four hours a week throughout the year.

[16] Report of the Provost of the University, 1890, p. 73.

[17] Proceedings, addresses, etc.—American Bankers' Association, 1890.

Following Dr. Falkner's temporary absence from the University, this elementary course in accounting was given by others and was not taught by Dr. Falkner until faculty changes made it necessary for him to teach it during the academic year 1899–1900.

On February 7, 1893, Joseph French Johnson, a graduate of Harvard in 1878 and a former newspaper owner, was appointed by the Trustees of the University to be Associate Professor of Business Practice. He was a man of wide experience and, judging from the reports of those associated with him on the faculty, an able teacher who was popular with the students. During his teaching tenure at the Wharton School he taught courses in banking, economic literature, newspaper practice, newspaper law, accounting, business practice and other subjects. His course in accounting and business practice required for one term in the sophomore year dealt with the organization and accounts of corporations, operations of stock exchange brokers, banks and clearing houses.[18]

In 1899 and 1900 the men who had been carrying the burden of teaching accounting resigned from the institution to accept other positions and the Wharton School was forced to build anew its courses in accounting. Courses in Accounting, Advanced Corporation Accounting and in Cost Accounting were established on a firm basis within a few years.

EARLY UNIVERSITY INSTRUCTION IN ACCOUNTANCY AT OTHER UNIVERSITIES

Shortly before the turn of the century other schools of commerce were beginning to appear on the educational horizon. The Wharton School had passed beyond the experimental stage with its courses, in-

[18] Catalogue of the University of Pennsylvania, 1894–1899.

551

cluding accounting, had begun to assume definite form and content. The new institutions establishing their courses in commerce, accounts and finance were ready to begin experimenting on their own behalf. The early courses in accounting offered by them merit attention.

At the University of Chicago, the Department of Political Economy, which was giving some courses in business, offered a course in Railway Accounts, Exchanges, etc., to be given in the autumn quarter of 1898. This course was to be taught by a new instructor, Dr. Henry Rand Hatfield, who had received his Ph.D. degree in 1897. Dr. Hatfield had some experience in the business world, having spent five and one half years in a bank and bond house. During a portion of this time he worked on the books and records, including the general books of the bank. His academic training did not include any courses in bookkeeping or accounting.[19]

The course in Railway Accounts, Exchanges, etc., included a study of the financial methods of leading railroads, training in railroad accounts and auditing, forms of securities, bond tables, and causes regulating the price of bonds and securities. In 1899–1900 its title was changed to Technique of Trade and Commerce, and it was expanded to include discussions on customs regulations, insurance, commercial documents and exchange and arbitrage.[20] The following year saw a very marked change in the work. A course called *Accounting* was offered. In the catalog it was described as follows:

47—Accounting—Winter Quarter. A study of the underlying principles. Some practice work under the guidance of an expert auditor of accounts will be given but only with a view to illustrating the principles discussed in the lectures. Emphasis will be placed on the interpretation of balance sheets and the problems implied therein.[21]

[19] Letter of Dr. H. R. Hatfield, *op. cit.*, November 27, 1937.
[20] Registers of the University of Chicago, 1897–1900.
[21] *Ibid.*, 1900–1901.

The course was given by Dr. Hatfield, assisted by Mr. Trevor Arnett, who was employed in the Comptroller's office of the University. In commenting upon these courses, Dr. Hatfield recently stated—

The beginnings were feeble. I think you can ignore the courses in 1898–1901. I returned to the University in April, 1901 from a six-months' leave, during which I went to Europe to see what the Colleges of Commerce in France and Germany were doing. As a result I offered 47. Accounting on my return and continued to give the course until I left Chicago for California in January, 1904. . . . We used no text book. The class was small. I followed largely the earlier writings of Professor J. F. Schär.[22] [The latter was a German professor who wrote a treatise on single- and double-entry bookkeeping in 1894, which was reprinted in 1901.]

Three years later two accounting courses were offered and were to be preceded by a course in bookkeeping to be given by the Mathematics Department. The courses were becoming very definite and accounting problems were being recognized. In the description of the elementary courses reference is made to reserves, depreciation, valuation questions, capital expenditures and operating expenditures. The advanced course in accounting included discussions of bank accounting, auditing procedure, principal features of railway accounting and discussions of the work of the Public Accountant. This advanced course was to be conducted by experts from Chicago institutions.

In addition to accounting, Dr. Hatfield taught other courses at the University of Chicago. These included courses in Civil Government, Principles of Political Economy, History of Commerce, Processes of American Industries and a course in Banking.

Although the College of Commerce of the University of California was established in 1898, no accounting courses were listed as being taught prior to 1902–1903.

[22] Letter, H. R. Hatfield, *op. cit.*

In this year a course known as Economic 14, called Corporation Finance and Accounting, was offered by Dr. Carl C. Plehn, Associate Professor of Finance and Statistics. This course, given two hours per week for one term, included a study of negotiable securities, examination of bank statements, railroad accounts and available corporation accounts, as well as a study of accounting principles and credit based on methods of large corporations and the government. The course in Corporation Finance and Accounting was one of many courses on Dr. Plehn's roster. He also taught courses in statistics, economics, banking and public finance.[23]

In the following year Henry Rand Hatfield was added to the staff of the University and introduced a course on Principles of Accounting with emphasis on the accounts of the balance sheet and profit-and-loss statement.

Ohio University established its Commercial College about the same time as the University of California. The course was a four-year one, the first two years being preparatory and the last two of collegiate grade. Some work in accounting, typewriting and stenography had been offered in the Commercial Department which preceded the establishment of the Commercial College by four or five years. The course in Theory of Accounts offered in 1896–1897 and continued for a number of years thereafter, was described as follows:

Theory of Accounts—5 hours per week—2 terms. Ample practice is given in the systems of accounts used in various kinds of business from retailing to modern banking. It is the aim of this course to give the student a wide acquaintance with business methods and to secure proficiency in opening and closing books, journalizing, rendering statements, tracing errors, analyzing accounts and drawing business papers.[24]

---

[23] Register of University of California, 1898–1904.
[24] Bulletin—Ohio University, Athens, Ohio, 1896–1897.

A course in Corporation Accounting for one term was added by this institution in 1901–1902. The new course was not limited to accounting but also covered the organization, management and financing of corporations.

The Graduate School of Business Administration, known as the Amos Tuck School of Administration and Finance, was established at Dartmouth through the generosity of Edward Tuck in 1899. Three courses in accounting were listed to be taught in 1900. These courses in accounting were described as follows:

1. PRINCIPLES OF ACCOUNTING.

    A series of lectures on the principles of Railroad and Industrial Accounting as applied to financial and operating administration. Methods of corporation bookkeeping.

2. THEORY AND PRACTICE OF RAILROAD STATISTICS.

    . . . Relation of accounting, auditing and statistics to operation . . . Revenue Accounting, Disbursement Accounting, Store and Car Accounting, General books, side ledgers, . . . organization and methods of accounting office, the division and general office, the shops, storehouse and station agency.

4. ACCOUNTING AND AUDITING.

    Nature of the balance sheet and determination of what constitutes a profit. Accounting methods of corporations. General principles of auditing. Theory of depreciation. Going concerns vs. those that have ceased operations. Economic value of locations.[25]

The next year the Accounting and Auditing courses were reorganized and consisted of—

(1) A series of lectures including a consideration of accounting as a profession.
(2) Theory and Practice of Accounts and Audits. This was a practice course dealing with the general books, opening, conducting and closing accounts of many systems, trial balance, cost, depreciation, auditing

---

[25] Dartmouth College Catalogue, 1900–1901.

and arranging accounts with a view to facilitating audits, etc.

(3) Theory and Practice of Railroad Accounting, which was similar to the course in Theory and Practice of Railroad Statistics offered the preceding year.

These courses stressed the practical side of accounting, under the supervision of professional accountants of Boston and a statistician of the Lehigh Valley Railroad.[26]

The University of Michigan added courses in Commercial Education and Public Administration in 1900, which were open to students in the junior and senior years. Prior to this time, however, courses in Transportation, Finance and Industrial History of the United States had been offered by the Department of Political Economy and Sociology.

A new course, Science of Accounts, to be given two hours per week for one term, was offered during the academic year 1901–1902. The instructor in this course, Durand W. Springer, bore the title Lecturer on Accounts. Mr. Springer, who in later years was Secretary of the American Society of Certified Public Accountants, was a graduate of Albion College, Michigan in 1886. Upon graduation he became a practicing accountant and also taught bookkeeping and accounting at Albion College and at the Ann Arbor High School, joining the teaching staff of the High School in 1893. He was well equipped to teach the subject at the University of Michigan, having a background of fourteen years of practical work and teaching experience. The course in Science of Accounts, which he taught, was limited to theory inasmuch as Dr. Henry Adams, the Chairman of the Economics Department which was giving the course, requested the new instructor to stress theory rather than practice. In the following year, Mr. Springer offered an additional course

in the Science of Accounting for two hours per week during the second term. Mr. Springer's comments on this course follow:

When the additional course was offered, it brought to that course those who had pursued under the writer's direction, the theoretical presentation which had been given the first year. In the group taking accounting for the first time it was found that they had come from families with a variety of business interests. . . . One of the boys came from a family interested in an average country newspaper plant. The father of another one of the boys was interested in a country bank. Still another was interested in a wholesale grocery house. While I do not recall all of the special types of interest I do know that each chap in the class was given the opportunity of making a special study of the accounting involved in the particular business in which he had a special interest. The boys were encouraged to prepare articles with a practical value and at least three that I now recall were awarded prizes in contests that were open to extended competition.[27]

A short course on the Science and Practice of Accounting was given by Mr. Springer to the seniors in the School of Pharmacy. This was a practical course and much stress was placed on record-keeping.

Brief mention will be made of courses in accounting offered by certain other universities from 1900 to 1902. The School of Commerce of the University of Wisconsin offered a one semester course in 1900–1901 in Business Forms and Accounts. This was conducted by the Professor of Theory and Practice of Domestic and Foreign Exchange. In 1901–1902 the title of the course was changed to Accounting and Auditing. Special lecturers assisted the professor in charge of the course. A one-term course in Principles of Accounting was introduced at Harvard University in 1900–1901. This course, under William Morse Cole, consisted of lectures, discussions and reports. It was open only to seniors and graduate students. In 1901 the

---

[26] *Ibid.* 1901–1902.

[27] Letter of Durand W. Springer to the writer, December 13, 1937.

University of Vermont offered a course entitled *Accounting*, which dealt with single and double entry, accounts of an individual, of a partnership, and the, accounting of manufacturers, shippers wholesalers, as well as corporation accounting.

Within the next few years many additional courses were developed by the universities which have been mentioned and by many other institutions. These accounting courses were open to regularly enrolled undergraduates or in a few instances to graduate students. Collegiate instruction in the theory of higher accountancy was not available to non-college men or women. Another institution was to pioneer in this field, to make available to those employed during the day an opportunity to study business subjects at night and to place an additional emphasis on the subject and on the profession of accountancy. That institution was New York University.

EARLY UNIVERSITY INSTRUCTION IN ACCOUNTANCY AT NEW YORK UNIVERSITY

The School of Commerce, Accounts and Finance was approved by the Council of New York University on July 28, 1900 and was opened in the fall of that year. Much of the credit for the founding of the school must go to Charles Waldo Haskins of the accounting firm of Haskins and Sells, and to the New York State Society of Certified Public Accountants.

In 1896 the Legislature of the State of New York passed a bill to recognize, legalize and safeguard a new profession, that of public accountancy. Charles Waldo Haskins was elected president of the first Board of Examiners to pass upon the eligibility of candidates for the degree of Certified Public Accountant. In 1897 the New York State Society of Certified Public Accountants was organized and Mr.

Haskins became its first president. This organization early became interested in educational work and in November 1899 requested President Haskins to approach the Trustees of New York University relative to the organization of classes in accounting, finance and economics. As a result of conferences between the New York Society of Certified Public Accountants and officials of the University, the new School of Commerce, Accounts and Finance was formed. Speaking at the unveiling of a tablet on December 17, 1910, commemorating the services of Charles Waldo Haskins to New York University, Acting-Chancellor John H. MacCracken stated—

555

As I understand it, those who proposed the organization of this School wanted first of all the help of an educational institution in creating and maintaining a new profession—the profession of certified public accountant, and secondly, they wanted instruction which should widen the outlook of young business men, enrich their lives and fit them for the wider opportunities which modern industrial organization affords. I recall that the Chancellor [Henry M. MacCracken] said more than once, that this school differed from all other University Schools of Business in that it had "as its backbone," as he expressed it, the task of preparing men for a definite profession, the profession of the accountant. Mr. Haskins saw ten years ago what the rest of the world has come to see more clearly since—that the intricacies of modern corporate organizations and the multiplying of governmental activities was destined to create a new profession or give a new significance to one already existing in a minor way.[28]

The aim of the new school was two-fold: to raise the standards of business education and to furnish thorough instruction in the more advanced work in professional accountancy. Courses of studies were established in Accounting, Commerce, Finance, Law and Administration. Classes met from 8 P.M. to 10 P.M. Monday to Friday, inclusive, during the academic school year.

[28] Charles Waldo Haskins—*An American Pioneer in Accountancy*, Prentice Hall, 1923, p. 117.

The instruction in accounting during the first year, 1900–1901, included courses in Theory of Accounts, Practice in Accounting and a course in Auditing. The course in theory emphasized the principles of accounting, the purposes of accounting, single and double entry and the different books of account. In the course on Practice the accounts of individuals, partners, and corporations were discussed, as well as municipal accounts, federal accounts, receivership, trusteeship, liquidation and statement of affairs. The course in auditing stressed methods of procedure in examining accounts of individuals, partnerships and corporations, as well as a verification of balance sheets and statements of profit and loss.[29] It should be mentioned in passing that this three fold division of accounting instruction closely paralleled the New York C.P.A. requirements which provided for examinations in Theory of Accounts, Practical Accounting and in Auditing.

The following faculty members were in charge of the work in accounting:

Charles Waldo Haskins, C.P.A.—Dean of the School and Professor of Auditing.
Charles E. Sprague, Ph.D., C.P.A.—Professor of Theory of Accounts.
Ferdinand William Lafrentz, C.P.A.—Professor of Auditing.
Anson O. Kittredge, C.P.A.—Professor of Theory of Accounts.
Henry R. M. Cook, C.P.A.—Professor of Practical Accounting.
Leon Brummer, C.P.A.—Professor of Practical Accounting.

These men were practicing accountants, some of them of many years standing. Dr. Sprague was perhaps the oldest member of the staff teaching accounting, he being about 58 at the time, Professor Kittredge was about 52 and C. W. Haskins, the Dean of the School, was 48. The accounting

courses were conducted on a lecture basis due to the absence of textbooks. In addition to four hours of accounting the work of the first year included four hours of law and two hours of commerce and finance. In courses other than accounting, textbooks were used.

Within two years the curriculum of the School was greatly expanded, the catalog of the University listing eight courses in Accounting, six in Commerce, seven in Business Law and ten in Finance. Additions to the faculty were made—Joseph French Johnson, formerly of the Wharton School, became Professor of Political Economy; Dr. Frederick A. Cleveland and Dr. E. S. Mead, of the Wharton School, were added to the staff as Lecturers in Finance and in Industry, respectively. The expansion in the number of accounting courses and in student enrollment resulted in Messrs. R. M. Chapman, George Young, H. M. C. Vedder and William Dennis being added to the accounting staff, the two latter gentlemen being graduates of the School in 1902.[30] At this time two major courses were offered, one in Accounting and the other in Commerce and Finance. Upon completion of the course the degree of Bachelor of Commercial Science was granted.

Many interesting comments have been gathered concerning the first class which entered the New York University School of Commerce, Accounts and Finance in the fall of 1900. The limitations of this paper will not permit of any extensive comments. Two or three interesting observations will, however, be made. A student in the first class, later a faculty member at the institution, commented as follows:

The first class entered in September, 1900 and was composed of thirty-one men. Twenty-four were graduated in 1902. The average age was around thirty. All were employed during the day

---

[29] *Bi-weekly Bulletin*, New York University, Vol. I, No. 1, February 15, 1901, pp. 295–296.

[30] *Ibid.*, Catalogue of New York University Bulletin of January 15, 1903.

and the school sessions were held in the evening. Five of the class had college degrees. Most of the others had high school training. Two were school teachers, ten bookkeepers, one a social worker. A number were aspiring to the C.P.A. certificate, which seven or eight later received.

All the courses in 1900–1902 . . . were given by lecture and no text books were used that I can remember. The New York C.P.A. questions were not studied, but the professors drew upon their own experiences as practicing accountants. . . . The contact with Professor Sprague and with such men as Haskins, Lafrentz, President of the American Audit Co., Kittredge, President of what was then called the Account Audit Assurance Co., Cook, Auditor of the Board of Education of the City of New York, and Brummer, Secretary of the State Society of C.P.A. and in public practice himself, was a most valuable part of our experience.[31]

Another student, now a Certified Public Accountant and a member of the first graduating class, comments rather interestingly about the accounting work. He says—

Mr. Dennis [later a faculty member] who was himself a student in the first class in the University, organized a class in bookkeeping, the work being done by the students before the regular classes. In common with many of the students I found that the instruction was perhaps a little too far advanced for us. That is, the elements of practical accounting were not stressed enough until Mr. Dennis organized his class. I think that this perhaps was not the fault of the course, but rather that we students had not the proper background at the time and consequently could not entirely grasp the subject matter presented. Some of the students lacked bookkeeping experience entirely, this being particularly true of the two Japanese students who were in the class.[32]

Many interesting recollections were secured from Mr. F. W. Lafrentz who taught in the School. Mr. Lafrentz's background, like that of the other accounting professors, was exceedingly practical. He had taught bookkeeping many years before in one of the Bryant and Stratton Business

Colleges in Chicago, becoming manager of the college in 1881. His public-accounting work began in 1880. He stated that students in his class were quite mature and very earnest in their work. No text was used by him and he drew upon his previous teaching experience and his public-accounting work to illustrate the principles which he developed in his lectures.[33]

Leon Brummer, who was a professor in the New York University School of Commerce, Accounts and Finance during its first year, in the course of an address delivered at New York University on December 17, 1910, made the following remarks regarding the early work in accounting:

I know that, judging from my own class, the accounting knowledge of the students was so ungraded, the knowledge of the teacher and his ability to teach were so uncertain, and the confidence of the scholars, who were continually asking for instruction in higher accountancy, was so wanting that nothing but the persistent efforts and the personal encouragement of Charles Waldo Haskins kept the School from following in the footpaths of those which had gone on before.

As I look upon the scene and upon the inexperience of the early teachers, the absolute absence of guiding precedents, the want of literature, the eagerness of all those students for instruction in accounting, it is not at all surprising that the older and unschooled accountants of today [1910] fear to undertake the duties of a teacher in this school but leave the task mostly for those men who have graduated from the school.[34]

It is to be regretted that time limitations make it impossible to comment further upon the personalities, lectures and development of courses of those entrusted with the early accountancy work at New York University. But to the students of the first two or three classes, Professors Haskins, Sprague, Kittredge, Dennis, Lafrentz, Hardcastle and Deane are more than mere memories. They stand for some-

557

---

[31] Orrin R. Judd, C.P.A. Treasurer of the Kings County Savings Bank—Letter November 30, 1937.
[32] George H. Iffla—Certified Public Accountant, New York—Letter December 6, 1937.

[33] Interview—F. William Lafrentz, Chairman Board of American Surety Co., November 26, 1937.
[34] *Journal of Accountancy*, February 1911, p. 255.

thing significant in the development of accountancy education, an opportunity to acquire from men of wide experience a knowledge of the theory and practice of accountancy at a time when a new profession was beginning to emerge and to secure legal recognition.

In concluding this paper the writer wishes to emphasize again that attitudes toward the introduction of business courses, to accounting in particular, to lack of texts, and to the general unfamiliarity with the subject of accounting were no doubt major factors retarding its development during the early years when taught as a university subject. Those who pioneered in the work were in many cases burdened with other courses and thus prevented from developing accountancy courses more rapidly. Upon the work of these pioneers future teachers and practitioners continued to build, to expand, to define objectives clearly and to develop the accounting departments in our university schools of business. If Accounting is the Alpha of business education much credit for its present position in the curriculum is due to those who strove to teach it in the universities when texts were scarce and when courses in accounting were looked upon with much disfavor.

THE GROWTH OF ACCOUNTING INSTRUCTION SINCE 1900

By C. E. ALLEN, *University of Illinois*

The purpose of this paper is to show the growth of instruction in accounting in American universities and colleges from 1900 to the present. The interest in accounting has also grown rapidly in secondary schools, normal schols, and foreign schools in this same period, but the scope of this study is restricted to American universities and colleges.

The year 1900 was selected as a starting point because instruction in accounting prior to that time was not very important. In fact, even during the first few years following 1900 there was not much development in accounting instruction in our universities; and in such work as was given the art and science of bookkeeping were emphasized rather than the fundamental principles of accounting.

In order to determine the extent of this growth a study was made of the courses in accounting as shown by the catalogues of forty-two of our leading universities and colleges. In this study the catalogues were carefully examined for each year from 1900 to 1926, inclusive. In addition, in order to determine definitely the growth in the number of schools giving courses in accounting, the catalogues of seventy-five additional universities and colleges were studied for the year 1900, 101 for 1910, 303 for 1916, and 575 for 1926. In all about 2,200 catalogues were examined.

The results of this study can be conveniently presented in terms of three periods: first, 1900 to 1910; second, 1910 to 1916; and third, 1916 to 1926.

ACCOUNTING INSTRUCTION FROM 1900 TO 1910

In the year 1900 thirteen universities and colleges* gave courses in accounting for which college credit was given. Six other schools maintained commercial departments on the order of the so-called business college. In the latter institutions the courses in accounting, or, more appropriately, bookkeeping, ranged from five weeks to four years in length, and no credit was given towards a degree.

---

*Dartmouth College, Drake Univ., Harvard Univ., Louisiana State Univ., Univ. of Missouri,, New York Univ., Univ. of Pennsylvania, Temple College, Agricultural College of Utah, Univ. of Utah, Univ. of Vermont, West Virginia Univ., Univ. of Wisconsin.

A certificate was usually granted upon satisfactory completion of the work. The entrance requirements were lax in the case of the latter schools, it being possible for an eighth grade graduate to take the "bookkeeping course."

It is interesting to know that seven of the thirteen schools that had courses in accounting were located in the eastern part of the United States, three in the north central, two in the western, and one in the southern.

These schools gave from one to four courses in accounting. In general these were as follows: Principles of Accounting, Advanced Accounting, Bank Accounting, and Auditing.

560 The elementary course was not called the "Principles of Accounting" in all schools. In fact, the following substitutes were found; "Office Work and Accounting," "Elements of Accounting," "Bookkeeping," "Science of Accounting," "Theory of Accounts," "Principles and Methods of Accounting," "Business Forms and Accounts," and "Business Law and Practice."

As a rule the elementary course covered the principles of debit and credit, the theory and purpose of accounts, use of the journal, daybook and ledger, both single- and double-entry, process of posting, taking a trial balance, making a balance sheet, and closing the ledger. Most of the schools stressed the preparation and use of business forms. The latter included drill in making and using notes, checks, drafts, invoices, bills, receipts, accounts, statements, etc. The schools that maintained so-called commercial departments, the courses of which did not lead towards a degree, laid stress upon penmanship, ruling, spacing, arrangement of work, with special reference to neatness, accuracy and rapidity. A few schools included in the elementary course a careful study of the different books of account. One school took up the study of the principles of railroad and industrial accounting as applied to financial and operating administration. In this case were also covered the methods of corporation bookkeeping, forms of financial organization, and management. The course, however, was only for seniors or graduate students.

Where credit for accounting was given towards a bachelor's degree the elementary course was not offered as a general rule before the sophomore year, and in a few cases it could not be taken before the junior year. Two schools (Harvard and Dartmouth) allowed graduate credit for the completion of the elementary work. Most of the schools required bookkeeping for admission to the elementary course.

The courses were taught largely by the laboratory method supplemented by class discussion. Sets were worked out under the direction of an instructor and ample drills were given in the preparation of forms and the working of exercises. The method of instruction in New York University was an exception to the general rule in that it was "founded upon the use of textbooks and courses of lectures, supplemented by the careful employment of a system of quizzes designed to aid the student's memory."

The course in advanced accounting was offered by five of the thirteen universities. It was described under such titles as "Special   561 Accounting," "Practice in Accounting," "Expert Accounting," and "Advanced Bookkeeping." It covered such phases of accounting as advanced theory, the use of special books of account, controlling accounts, partnership and corporation accounts, and complex financial and partnership adjustments. In some cases it included municipal, federal, receivership, and estate accounting.

It is quite noticeable that the laboratory method of instruction was not used as much in the advanced courses as in the elementary ones. However, there were a few schools that used the laboratory method exclusively in all their accounting courses.

Bank accounting as taught consisted of theoretical work as outlined in a text, and practice as a teller, bookkeeper, etc., in a bank organized in conjunction with the other accounting courses. This subject was not very widely taught and was given primarily by those institutions maintaining so-called commercial or business schools.

The subject of auditing was not offered by many of the schools. Of the thirteen that had courses in accounting, only four (Agri. College of Utah, Dartmouth, New York Univ., and Temple College) gave auditing. It did not always appear under the name "Auditing," however, for some schools combined advanced accounting and auditing and others called it "Expert Accounting and Auditing." The conception of auditing at that time is quite obvious from the following description: "The duties, qualifications and requirements of expert accountants are carefully studied. Books suitable for different kinds of business with the most approved ruling, special columns, etc., are discussed. Much practical work is given in open-

ing and closing sets of books used in various business enterprises."*
One school (Dartmouth) offered auditing under the title "Accounting and Auditing" and from the description of the course it is
evident that most of the time was devoted to the principles of accounting. One institution (John B. Stetson) that did not give
college credit for its accounting courses, had a collection of books
of bankrupt concerns and used them in connection with its course
in auditing.

The description of the course in auditing as given by New York
University conformed quite closely to our present idea of the subject. According to the description the course included a study of
562   methods of procedure in the examination of the accounts of individuals, partnerships, corporations, and municipalities, the verification of balance sheets and profit and loss statements, and the
making of special reports.

In addition to the four courses mentioned in the preceding pages
as being given in 1900, the University of Utah offered a course entitled "School Accounts." It included instruction in double-entry
bookkeeping and the forms of ordinary business paper together
with special instruction in the keeping of district and county school
accounts. It was one semester in length. "Farm Accounting" was
also offered by several schools as a short-term course, continuing
ordinarily from two to four weeks. It was usually given in the
College of Agriculture in connection with the short winter courses
or extension work. The principles of debit and credit were taught
and applied to farm transactions.

It is quite noticeable during the five years following 1900 that
many of our large universities which had not given accounting in
1900 incorporated one or more courses in their curricula. "Corporation Finance and Accounting" was the one new course that
was commonly introduced. It also was found under such titles as
"Corporation Finance, Accounting and Commercial Law," "Corporations," "Corporation Finance and Theory of Accounting," and
Corporation Finance, Securities, and Accounting." In fact this
was the only accounting course offered by many of our large schools.

The content of this course varied with different institutions. In
one school it included a study of the methods of financing employed
in large corporations, with their system of organization and accounting. The accounting phase as a rule was left until the last part

---

*Agricultural College of Utah

of the course and in many cases received little attention. In others it included forms of investment, consolidation, reorganization, nature of balance sheet and profit and loss statement, principles of auditing, theory of depreciation, and accounting systems of special forms of business. The common method of approach to this subject was through the study of reports and financial statements of railway, banking, and industrial corporations. In some schools the course was supplemented by a series of lectures by practical accountants.

In 1902 Professor Sprague of New York University offered a course entitled "Philosophy of Accounts." In this, accountancy was considered from the standpoint of science. Illustrations were freely used but the emphasis was upon the philosophy of the subject as a phase of economic theory. During the course the various arts which depended upon this science were defined and differentiated. The account was defined and analyzed, and accountancy was reviewed. Critical opinions were gathered from different writers as to the purposes of the account, the information furnished, forms of accounts, and the results of accounts. Various theories of debit and credit were studied and used as a basis for argument and explanation.

563

It is interesting to know that as early as 1902 a departure from the regular method of teaching the elementary course was made by a well known teacher of accounting (Professor Hatfield). In this course accounts were studied and interpreted from the point of view of the business man rather than that of the professional bookkeeper. The published statements of railroads and other corporations were used as a means of interpreting the balance sheet and profit and loss statement.

In this same year (1902) "Executor and Trustee Accounting" was given by New York University. The legal rights and duties of trustees, executors, etc., were studied, together with the proper accounting methods. The same school gave a course in "Investment Accounting" in 1903. It included the study of various types of investment institutions, the accounts required by them, and the use of the principles of mathematics as applied to investments. "Special Problems in Accounting" was the title of another course introduced in 1904. It consisted of lectures on such subjects as bank accounting, auditing, appraisal and depreciation, railway accounting, and the public accountant.

In 1904 the subject of cost accounting was introduced in two schools (Univ. of Pennsylvania and New York Univ.) as a separate course. These courses embraced a study of the nature of cost accounts, advantages and methods of cost keeping, the records used for raw materials and perpetual inventories, labor records, distribution of manufacturing expenses, and designing of cost systems.

The greatest progress in accounting instruction as shown by any one school during the period from 1900 to 1905 was by New York University. Beginning in 1900 with three courses in accounting, the number increased to twelve in 1905, and from five semesters' work to fifteen. From 1905 to 1910 the following new courses were given: "Accounting Systems," "Accountant's Reports," "C. P. A. Problems and Questions," and "Railroad Accounting and Auditing."

564

Although the subject of accounting systems was included in many of the advanced courses prior to 1905, no special course having this title was given until 1906 (New York Univ.). This course consisted of a study in detail of various systems of accounting and their construction, and the installation of accounts in cities, theaters, trading companies, commission concerns, etc.

"Accountant's Reports" was the title of a special course given by one institution (New York Univ.) in 1907. It was designed to remedy in part the lack of effectiveness in the presentation of results which often obscures the value of an accountant's work. The lectures dealt with the technique of reports, the proper arrangement of facts and figures, and the means of making clear the treatment of an involved situation and of emphasizing important conclusions. A considerable number of specific cases were taken up for discussion and students were required to write several reports.

The introduction of the study of C. P. A. problems in almost every case closely followed the passage of the state C. P. A. laws. In railroad accounting a study was made of the freight and passenger earnings, operating expenses, fixed charges, and in some cases of the auditing procedure involved.

It is of interest to know in what department or branch of the university the early accounting courses were taught. In the institutions that did not have schools or colleges of commerce, accounting was found listed under "Political Economy," "History and Political Science," "Mathematics," "Economics and Law," "Economics and Social Science," and "History, Geography, and Commerce." In most schools accounting was taught in the department of economics of the college of liberal arts and sciences. There was one school that taught cost accounting in the college of engineering. Farm accounting was usually taught in the department or college of agriculture.

It is quite obvious from the foregoing facts that instruction in accounting was gradually gaining recogniton as an essential subject in our large universities and colleges during this period. No doubt the most important factors causing accounting to take its place beside the old and tried college subjects were: first, the actual need for it because of the industrial and commercial growth of our country; and second, legislative action such as the passage of C. P. A. laws and the establishment of the Interstate Commerce Commission.

ACCOUNTING INSTRUCTION FROM 1910 TO 1916

In 1910 there were fifty-two universities and colleges that gave courses in accounting for which credit was given toward a bachelor's degree. This is an increase of thirty-nine over the number of schools offering accounting in 1900, for which college credit was given. Seventeen institutions granted a bachelor's degree in commerce for which accounting was either required or could be used as an elective. Three schools (Harvard, New York Univ., and Dartmouth) gave a master's degree in commercial science or business administration, and accounting was accepted as fulfilling part of the requirements. Only two institutions (Univ. of Pennsylvania and New York Univ.) permitted accounting to be used as a major toward the bachelor's degree, while only one (New York Univ.) gave a special master's degree in accounting.

Of the fifty-two schools having courses in accounting in 1910, nineteen had only one course, eleven had two courses, five had three and the remaining seventeen had four or more, ranging from eight to nineteen semesters' work. All the fifty-two schools gave at least one course in the elements or principles of accounting, although in three cases these principles were confined to farm transactions, and in two cases—after a short study of the principles—the time was devoted to the study of corporation accounting.

Eight of the schools at this time gave a course in farm accounts. In a few instances, however, it was not listed under that caption, but was a part of the course in farm management. In general it was one semester in length, and consisted primarily of keeping records for the farm, and making farm reports, monthly statements, and annual summaries. The course was designed for the agricultural student to enable him to determine the financial results of his farm operations. One institution went a little further than the above fundamentals by applying cost accounting to farm operations.

Twenty-nine of the fifty-two schools offering accounting in 1910 gave a course in advanced accounting. It was one semester in length as a rule, although a few extended the course throughout the year. In some instances it consisted only of complicated problems, while in others it included such subjects as cost keeping, a study of systems, auditing, partnership and corporation accounting, municipal, public utility, and insurance accounts, and accounting reports. The title of this course was very broad and, as the content showed, might include almost anything in the field of accounting. Eight of the fifty-two schools offered a course in corporation accounting. This consisted of the study of the corporation as to its organization, advantages, and accounts peculiar to it. Special studies were made of corporate records, and of the reports published by telegraph and telephone companies, and by insurance, manufacturing, and transportation corporations. The latter reports were analyzed from the standpoint of accounting and interpretation.

Thirteen of the schools offered a course in auditing, labeled as such. There were five others that included a study of auditing as a part of advanced accounting or corporation accounting. In the latter cases the word "auditing" appeared in the title, "Advanced Accounting and Auditing." In general the course in auditing embraced a study of the duties, qualifications, and responsibilities of the auditor, the various kinds of audits, the procedure involved, and the preparation of the audit report.

Five schools offered "Railroad Accounting." This included the study and use of the forms in this particular field, the audit of passenger and freight receipts, the determination of operating and plant costs and the gathering of various statistical data that could be used by railroad executives. In one institution lectures were given on the reading of railroad reports and statements, and a study was made of the material promulgated by the Interstate Commerce Commission.

Five of the fifty-two schools gave "Cost Accounting." A few

schools, however, included a study of cost accounting in the advanced accounting course. There was not much change in the content since its first introduction in 1904.

A few schools gave such courses as "Trustee and Executor Accounting," "Bank Accounting," "Accounting Systems," "C. P. A. Problems," "Public Accounting," and "Investment Accounting."

Although several schools had a course entitled "Theory of Accounts," a description of the content revealed that more practice than theory was included therein. New York University gave a theory course under the title, "Philosophy of Accounts." The object of the latter was to work out scientifically a consistent theory of accounts "not dependent upon fiction and regardless of tradition." It was shown that each account was in fact an equation, or could be converted into one, and that it was also a portion or sub-equation of a greater equation known as the balance sheet, having for its sphere an entire business universe. In establishing this equation the old rule that assets equal liabilities was disregarded as in most cases fallacious, and the new and accurate one, assets equal liabilities plus proprietorship, was substituted therefor.

567

A course in public accounting was given by two institutions (Dartmouth and Oregon Agri. College) in 1910. It was designed to meet the standard of requirements set by the examining boards of the various states which prescribed certain qualifications for the degree of certified public accountant.

In 1911 such courses as "Cost Accounting for Farmers," "Advanced Railroad Accounting," and "Research in Accounting" came into the curricula of the colleges of commerce. The titles of the courses indicate the content. This is true, as a rule, of the new courses introduced in the succeeding periods, so no description will be given of them except in a few unusual cases.

"Public Service Corporation Accounting" was introduced in 1912 by Northwestern University. Oregon Agricultural College also offered a special course for pharmacy students, in the elements of accounting. In 1913 the special accounting courses introduced for the first time were "Insurance Accounting," "Government Accounting," "Institutional Accounting," "Seminar in Accountancy," and "Municipal Accounting." Although some of these courses had been included to some extent in the earlier ones, still this is the first time they had appeared under these titles. In the seminar course students were required to report on various accounting systems and published reports, and to interpret the accounts of local business establishments. Only one year of accounting was required for admission to the seminar and one year's credit was given for satisfactory completion.

In 1914 accounting courses in "Foreign Exchange, "Auditing Practice," "Analysis of Corporation Reports," "Methods of Teaching Commercial Subjects," and "Cooperative Accounting" were introduced under such titles for the first time. The practical auditing course consisted of practical work for advanced students in auditing the books of charitable institutions. The University of Denver offered a course entitled, "The Accountancy Dispensary." Its purpose was to give the student the experience required by law and at the same time render services to charitable and religious organizations of the City of Denver. Such institutions could obtain the services of student auditors free of charge.

568

Although corporation reports were being analyzed in many accounting courses at this time there was but one school (Univ. of Wisconsin) that gave a specific course in the "Analysis of Corporation Reports." A practical application of accounting and auditing principles to financial reports of railways, public service corporations, and industrial organizations was made. Holding company reports were studied as well as consolidated balance sheets and income statements.

A step towards specialization was made in the introduction of "Cooperative Accounting and Management" (Oregon Agri. College). This course covered the business management of cooperative societies and a study of bookkeeping and cost accounting especially adapted to different types of cooperative associations in the United States such as creamery and cow-testing associations. It was based on the system published by the "Cooperative Union, Limited," of England, adapted to American conditions.

The following new courses came into existence in 1915: "Methods of Teaching Bookkeeping," "Office Practice and Accounting," "Household and Personal Accounts," elements of accounting especially adapted for law and engineering students, "Mine Accounting," and "Advanced Auditing."

Thus we see in this period from 1910 to 1916 the gradual recognition of the importance of accounting as a subject of college grade and in a few cases as a subject that demands the attention of the graduate student. The growth of specialized courses in accounting is also quite noticeable. Likewise the growth in the number of schools teaching accounting indicates without question that the subject has proven its worth in the college curriculum.

Accounting Instruction from 1916 to 1926

The number of colleges and universities giving courses in accounting which were accepted towards a degree increased from fifty-two in 1910 to 116 in 1916. Nearly twenty of these schools allowed accounting to be used as a major towards the bachelor's degree and some four or five accepted it as a major towards the master's degree. These figures are not exact, due to the lack of sufficient information in some college catalogues, but they are sufficiently accurate for the purpose of this study. In addition there were some 569 forty-five or fifty colleges and universities that conducted business departments. A certificate was usually granted for the completion of a course in such a department which required all the way from six weeks to three years to complete. In some cases a bachelor of commercial science degree was granted after the completion of two or three years' work.

Of the 116 schools having courses in accounting in 1916, thirty-three had only one course, twenty-one had two courses, thirteen had three, six had four, and forty-three had five or more. In general these courses were one semester in length. All of the 116 schools gave at least one course in the elements of accounting. In three schools, however, the elementary course was called "Mine Accounting," and in two others "Farm Accounting." In the latter cases the principles of accounting were first studied and then applied to transactions in line with the type of course. About half of the schools continued the elements or principles of accounting throughout the year. The other half studied the elements for only one semester, which was followed in many cases by another semester's work called "Advanced Accounting."

In 1916 forty-eight schools gave a course in accounting problems, in some cases called "C. P. A. Problems." There was a great deal of difference, however, in the content of these courses. Some schools gave "Advanced Accounting Problems" as the second semester of accounting, and, coming at that time, the problems had to be very elementary. Other schools did not give the course until the junior year. The content of the course was naturally much more advanced in these cases, and consisted in the solving of accounting problems that were being used in the state C. P. A. examinations.

Auditing was taught by thirty-six of the 116 schools. The subject was touched upon, however, in fourteen other institutions which combined advanced accounting and auditing. The content of the course had not changed much since 1910. It included a study of the duties of auditors, methods of procedure, the detection of fraud, and the writing of reports. One school (Olivet College) justified its course in auditing by saying,

570

> Accounting, in the narrow sense of the term, is constructive. Auditing is analytical. Students preparing for business life need training in both, even though they do not intend to become auditors. This course aims to give training that will enable the student properly to analyze business operations as shown by the books and statements and to present reports that will clearly and properly visualize the business for the period.

In some schools the practice work in auditing was obtained by searching out and correcting errors made by students in the lower classes, especially where sets had been worked out. Some universities, after the study of the principles of auditing, required their students to make an audit of some local business, arrangement having been made by the institution. Such audits included hotels, clubs, small businesses, churches, hospitals, etc. Other schools made a study of specialized audits after the fundamentals had been covered.

A course in accounting systems was given in fifteen of the 116 schools. It was a one-semester course in nine schools. Leading accounting systems were studied, as building and loan associations, insurance, banking, and trust companies, department stores, municipal and public utilities. One school (Boston Univ.) called the course "System Building." This course provided for training in the designing and installing of modern accounting systems for mercantile and manufacturing businesses.

Cost accounting was offered by thirty-five schools in 1916, five of which extended the course throughout the year. It did not always appear under the title "Cost Acounting," as is noted from the following titles found: "Shop Accounting," "Factory Costs," "Shop Management and Cost Accounting," "Industrial Accounting," and "Commercial Cost Accounting." Many colleges and universities touched upon the study of cost accounting in their advanced accounting courses. Some schools studied only the principles of cost accounting, while others, in addition to the fundamentals, required the student to work out a comprehensive costing problem, and in some cases required him to design his own forms for collecting data.

Six schools offered "Fiduciary Accounting" for one semester. In general the course was open to students who had had one year of accounting. Five colleges and universities gave a course in "Household Accounts," five, in "Municipal Accounting," four, in "Institutional Accounting," four, in "Bank Accounting," ten, in "Theory of Accounts," three, in "Public Utility Accounting," and eighteen, in "Farm Accounting." Of the eighteen schools that offered work in farm accounting, twelve gave the elementary course and six applied cost accounting to farm operations.

Each of the following courses was found in only one or two schools: "Public Accounting," "Forestry Accounts," "Dairy Accounting," "Accounting and Business Policy," "Mine Accounting," "Foreign Exchange Accounting," "Insurance Accounting," "Investment Accounting," "Pharmacy Accounting," "Retail Store Accounting," "Accounting Lectures," "Analysis of Corporation Reports," "Governmental Accounting," "Cooperative Accounting," "Railroad Accounting," "Methods of Teaching Accounting," "History of Accounting," "Research and Seminar in Accounting." 571

In 1917 the following new courses were added: "Advanced Theories of Accounting," "Mathematics of Accounting," "Lumber Accounting," "Retail Accounting," and "Cost Accounting for Printers." "Income Tax Procedure" was introduced by one school (Univ. of Calif.) in 1918 as a one-semester course. One year of accounting was the prerequisite. In 1919 one institution (Univ. of Cincinnati) offered a course entitled "Accounting and Management." It was designed for prospective industrial executives. A study was made of records and their graphical presentation. A detailed analysis was made of the more important industrial questions and their respective accounting records. A similar course entitled "Managerial Accounting" was offered by the University of Chicago in 1920.

Special courses in the interpretation of accounting records and reports were introduced in 1921. Northwestern University had such a course which had as its basis the outlook of the comptroller and public accountant on the construction, control, and interpretation of the accounts of an enterprise. Accounting systems were devised and students who had completed three semesters of accounting were eligible. Another school (Leland Stanford) included in its interpretative course a discussion of the balance sheet and of the income and expense statement from the points of view of the commercial creditor (chiefly the banker) and of the bondholders.

In 1922 the following new courses were given: "Administrative Standards, Reports, and Records," "Organization for Executive Control," "Secretarial Accounting," "Brokerage Accounting," "Auditing Technique," "Advanced Problems in Income Tax," "Syndicate Organization and Accounting," "Accounting Correspondence and Reports," "Overhead Costs," and "Judicial Accounting." As has been previously suggested, the titles of these courses indicate the content. It is interesting to note, however, the description of the course entitled "Accounting Correspondence and Reports." It was intended for students who were specializing in accounting but who intended to remain in the private field. Its purpose was to develop in the student the ability to convey to executives in a clear and convincing manner the ideas that arise in connection with his technical work. It was for seniors only and was listed in the English Department.

From 1923 to 1926 the following new courses were offered: "Public Accountants' Letters and Reports," "Retail Audit and Control," "Wall Street Accounting and Auditing," "Inventories and Capital Assets," "Real Estate Accounts," "Accounting Law," "Elevator Accounting," "Metallurgical and Coal Mine Accounting," "Bank Auditing," "Valuation Accounting," "Consolidated Reports," "Financial and Operating Reports."

Although the content of the above courses is suggested by the titles, it is of interest to note that the same university which introduced a course in 1922 entitled "Accounting Correspondence and Reports," offered in the following year "Public Accountants' Letters and Reports." This was designed for students entering the field of public accounting. Consideration was given to the various types of letters arising in the professional field as well as special atten tion to the use of English in the construction of effective accounting reports. It was also given only to seniors and was offered in the English Department.

There are 335 colleges and universities that are offering courses in accounting this year (1926). Of these 335 institutions at least sixty accept accounting as a major towards the bachelor's degree and thirty allow it as a major for a master's degree. Practically ll of the 335 schools give a course in the principles of accounting.

In some schools it is called "Constructive Accounting," in others, "Accounting and Statistics," and, again, "Accounting Practice." A tendency towards specialization in the elements of accounting is noticeable from such titles as "Accounting for Engineers," "Accounting for Lawyers," etc. About three-fourths of the schools devote one year to the study of the principles of accounting.

Twenty-five institutions offer "Corporation Accounting" as a separate course. In a majority of cases it is only one semester in length. As a rule it is given by those schools offering elementary accounting for only one semester. Many of the latter institutions, however, call the second semester's work "Advanced Accounting;" and this usually consists of a study of corporation accounting. Twenty schools give "Intermediate Accounting," and this in many 573 cases also consists of corporation accounts. Advanced accounting labeled as such is taught in 143 schools. In most cases it extends throughout the year. About seventy of the 335 schools give only two years of áccounting, the second year being called "advanced."

Cost accounting is taught by 147 institutions. It is offered for one semester by ninety-seven schools, and for two semesters by the remaining schools with the exception of one, which offers it for three semesters. In one case it is called "Shop Accounting," in others "industrial" or "factory" accounting. In another school there are two distinct courses in cost accounting, one being titled "Commercial Cost Accounting." It is interesting to note the tendency towards specialization in this field. This is shown by the following: "Printers' Cost Accounting," "Farm Cost Accounting," "Cost Accounting for Engineers," "Problems in Cost Accounting," "Cost Accounting Seminar," and "Petroleum Cost Accounting."

Auditing is now being given by 106 schools and is a one-semester course in eighty-six of them. Several institutions list auditing and advanced accounting problems together. Some combine auditing and public accounting, and others auditing and income tax procedure. The following titles suggest that there is a tendency to specialize in auditing also: "Industrial Auditing," "Retail Auditing," "Bank Auditing," "Wall Street Auditing," and "Income Tax Auditing." A few schools conduct auditing laboratories. One school has an auditing seminar, and another a graduate course in auditing technique.

Income tax accounting is being offered by sixty-six schools. Only ten extend the course throughout the year, the rest offering it for only one semester. A few schools offer advanced work in income tax problems, graduate credit being given for satisfactory completion. A course in accounting problems is given in seventy-three schools. In twenty-two of these the problems are elementary. In the others standard C. P. A. problems are solved. One institution conducts a seminar in accounting problems. Work in accounting systems is offered in forty-one schools, and is a one-semester course in about two-thirds of them.

Twelve colleges and universities have a course in advanced accounting theory, fourteen in "Bank Accounting," eleven, in "Mathematics of Accounting," and fifteen, in "Municipal" or "Government" accounting. An accounting seminar of some sort is conducted in thirty-two schools. Nineteen institutions offer a course in methods of teaching commercial subjects, including accounting, and twelve give a course entitled "Analysis of Financial Statements." A few schools offer "Institutional Accounting," "Investment Accounting," "Managerial Accounting," "Budgetary Control," "Accounting Reports," and "cooperative," "household," "fiduciary," "secretarial," "railway," and "insurance" accounting. Also are found the titles "Accounting Law," "Specialized Accounting," and "Applied Accounting."

574

Each of the following courses is given by only one university or college: "Judicial Accounting," "Real Estate Accounts," "Foreign Exchange Accounting," "Brokerage Accounting," "Elevator Accounting," "Syndicate Organization and Accounting," "Bank Auditing," "Accounting Lectures," "Inventory and Valuation," "Department Store Accounting," "Wall Street Auditing," "Consolidated Reports," and "Petroleum Cost Accounting."

From the foregoing information it is quite evident that the greatest progress in accounting instruction has been made in the period from 1916 to 1926.

SUMMARY

In order to see clearly how rapidly and widely accounting instruction has grown in our American colleges and universities since 1900 it is necessary to summarize the facts previously enumerated.

College credit was given for courses in accounting by thirteen schools in 1900. By 1910 there were fifty-two universities and colleges that accepted accounting towards graduation. In 1916 the number increased to 116, and to 335 in 1926. On a percentage basis the increase from 1900 to 1910 was 300 per cent; from 1910 to 1916 about 125 per cent; and from 1916 to 1926 about 189 per cent.

There were no schools in 1900 that accepted accounting as a major towards a bachelor's or master's degree. In 1910 two allowed it to be used as a major for the bachelor's degree and one for a master's degree. By 1916 about twenty accepted it as a major towards a bachelor's degree and some four or five for a master's degree. At the present time at least sixty institutions allow accounting to be used as a major towards the bachelor's degree and thirty for the master's degree.

Beginning in 1900, five was the highest number of semesters' work offered by any one school. In 1910 the number of semesters' work offered increased to nineteen, in 1916 to thirty, and in 1926 to forty-eight.

Aside from the rapid growth in the number of schools offering elementary and advanced accounting, there is a noticeable increase in the number of schools giving cost accounting and auditing. The former was not given as a separate course in 1900, but five schools offered it in 1910, thirty-five in 1916, and 147 are offering it at the present time. The course in auditing increased from four schools in 1900 to thirteen in 1910, thirty-six in 1916, and 106 in 1926.

Another noticeable increase is found in the course in systems, advanced accounting problems, including C. P. A. problems, theory of accounts, both elementary and advanced, methods of teaching accounting, and income tax procedure. In 1910 three schools gave a course in systems, which increased to fifteen in 1916, and to forty-one in 1926. The increase in the number of schools offering advanced accounting problems was very rapid, beginning in 1910 with two, increasing to twenty in 1916, and to seventy-three in 1926. The course in income tax procedure has been introduced since 1916, there now being sixty-six schools that offer it. Likewise accounting theory is being taught more widely than ever.

Although many schools are now offering specialized courses in accounting it is quite obvious that the fundamental ones have been introduced in our colleges and universities much more rapidly. The specialized courses are given as a rule by our larger schools and in nearly every case by those located in large cities.

575

SOME EARLY ACCOUNTANCY EXAMINERS

NORMAN E. WEBSTER

A s AN indication of time, "early" will not mean the same to all of us. The first Certified Public Accountant examination was given in December, 1896. By the end of 1901 examinations were given in four states. In the next four years 1902–1905, they were given in five more; in the next five years 1906–1910, in thirteen more; and in the next five years 1911–1915, eighteen more; making forty states by the end of 1915. By 1925 these examinations were being given in all the states, territories, and insular possessions.

But these were not the earliest accountancy examinations given in the United States. The Institute of Accounts, organized in 1882, had examiners almost from its beginning. But since its records have been lost and only a very few of its examiners are known, this study has been confined to those who conducted examinations for Certified Public Accountants.

The information available indicates that in the 47 years from 1896 there have been issued in all states about 32,600 certificates, of which about 1,600 were issued upon waiver of examination, perhaps 3,000 upon recognition of certificates issued by other jurisdictions, and 28,000 upon examination, the great majority upon written examination.

In the ten years from 1896 to 1905, seven of the first nine states had issued 644 certificates, largely, of course—and properly, in my opinion—upon waiver of examination. In that period the examiners in those states had decided upon the subjects and scope of their examinations, and in each state they had prepared, given, and rated from one to twenty examinations. Quite likely their bases for ratings differed, but they were in complete agreement upon the scope of the tests. In those first ten years all examinations were in four subjects, Commercial Law, Theory of Accounts, Practical Accounting, and Auditing. Later some states added a few related subjects. In 1907 Pennsylvania combined the last three subjects into one test entitled "General Accounting," and from 1916 to 1942 those states which used the service of the American Institute of Accountants combined the second and third subjects into Accounting Theory and Practice.

It is evident that in the first ten years, 1896 to 1905, the scope at least of the examinations was standardized. This was done by nine states, viz., four Atlantic states: New York, 1896, Pennsylvania, 1899, Maryland, 1900, New Jersey, 1904; two Pacific states: California, 1901, Washington, 1903; two central states: Illinois, 1903, Michigan, 1905; and one Southern state: Florida, 1905. Since the area covered by these states extends from coast to coast and from Canada to the Gulf of Mexico, it seems proper to consider them as representative and to take their examiners in that decade as our subject: Some Early Accountancy Examiners.

The laws of three of these nine states provided that the boards were to be integrated with the state educational systems; in New York and Pennsylvania with the Education Departments and in Illinois with the State University. In the other six states the Boards of Accountancy had other duties and powers. The laws of some states provided that one or two members of their boards should be lawyers or, in a few instances, hold some state office. But this paper is limited to the accountant members of these nine boards.

Although the foregoing facts were easily found in the *Year Books* of the American Association of Public Accountants and in the Accountants' Law Service, the early personnel of the boards was not so readily available. To supplement the information found in old magazines and other publications, the Librarian of the American Institute of Accountants has very kindly carried on a fairly extended correspondence, which in most cases has been successful. In some cases, however, the results would have been funny except that they might be serious. One state reported that it did not have records so far back. Another wrote that its first board was appointed in 1921, whereas the facts are that its first CPA law was enacted in 1907 and the names of its first board were given in the *Journal of Accountancy* in that year. Moreover, two of its present board held certificates issued several years before 1921, the year in which the letter states that its first board was appointed. These instances suggest that the boards of those states, in acting upon current matters, may not be giving consideration to the decisions of their predecessors, or taking them as precedents.

Facts about the individuals were even more difficult to locate. The two editions of the *Accountants' Directory and Who's Who* gave facts about some of the early examiners who were living in 1920 and 1925. Very few biographies or memoirs of accountants have been published. The obituaries which were found were usually highly

578

condensed, and sometimes wholly lauda- tory. What follows is believed to be correct, but almost surely not complete. Perhaps readers will correct its mistakes and supply its deficiencies.

At the present time in 1943, the fifty-two Boards of Examiners are composed of one hundred and ninety-seven members be- sides the nine members of the Board of Examiners of the American Institute of Accountants. In 1905 the nine boards then existing were composed of twenty-nine ac- countant members. And the total of one hundred and thirty member-years repre- sented the services given by forty-six dif- ferent accountants. These are the Early Accountancy Examiners about whom in- formation has been sought as to national- ity, education, training, experience, and terms of service as examiners, with a view to evaluating as far as practicable their qualifications for this service, their points of view, and if possible something of the effects which their service may have had upon accountancy examinations in the first ten years and up to now.

First as to their nationality. Of the forty- six persons, seven were born abroad, two in Germany, Max Teichman of Maryland and Ferdinand W. Lafrentz of New York, and five in England, James T. Anyon of New York, Alfred G. Platt of California, E. G. Shorrock of Washington, Ernest Reckitt of Illinois, and Walter Mucklow of Florida. Apparently the thirty-nine others were native Americans. And since no two of the seven who were born abroad were at one time members of the same board, it seems that the actions of those six boards were not affected greatly, if at all, by the place of birth of the seven members.

Second, as to their educational prepara- tion for the service. Of the seven who were born abroad, Max Teichman, of Maryland, was educated in German institutions ap- parently of college grade, Ernest Reckitt,

of Illinois, at the University of Manchester, England, and Walter Mucklow, of Florida, at Kings College in London. And of the thirty-nine native Americans, the first three examiners in New York were all college men, Charles W. Haskins in the engineering course at Brooklyn Polytech- nic, Charles E. Sprague in the arts course at Union College in Schenectady, and Frank Broaker at City College of New York. Charles N. Vollum of the Pennsyl- vania board was educated at Girard Col- lege in Philadelphia. If the average age of the forty-six accountants was about forty- five when they were named to these early boards, then they were born in the decade from 1850 to 1860, and for seven of the forty-six to have had college training may have been a relatively high proportion in the years 1896 to 1905.

But this does not give the whole picture of their education. Some had been in edu- cational work before their appointment; one of them, John R. Sparrow, of New York, had taught business subjects for fifteen years, and at least seven others were so engaged before or after their service as examiners. And in accountancy literature, Charles E. Sprague and Anson O. Kittredge, both of New York, edited accounting magazines, the latter for twelve years; while Bentley's *Bibliography of Works on Accounting by American Authors* lists four titles by one examiner, two by another, and one each by six others. This record is far ahead of that for the entire profession of accountancy.

Third, as to their training. Of the seven who were born abroad, it seems that five came to this country before or soon after completing their education. But two at least served apprenticeships in England: James T. Anyon, of New York, who be- came an ACA after his service with Thomas, Wade, Guthrie & Company, and E. G. Shorrock, of Washington, who was an FSAA, but concerning whose training we have no information. In the twenty or more years immediately preceding the enactment of the first CPA law, a considerable number of foreign-born public accountants had come here and were in practice. Probably employment by them provided the training obtained by some of the other early examiners. The only one as to whom this is definitely known is Frank Broaker, of New York, who was employed by John Roundy, a public accountant who had come from Scotland. Only a little while after this period there were several such instances, a conspicuous one being that of George Wilkinson, who became a member of the New Jersey Board in 1908. He had received his training first with Veysey & Veysey of New York, beginning in 1887, and some years later with Barrow, Wade, Guthrie & Company, of which firm James T. Anyon was then the senior partner.

Fourth, as to their experience. Old records indicate that a few of the forty-six men who served as examiners in the period 1896 to 1905 gave much or all of their time to activities other than public practice. Some seem to have been in business, one at least was a teacher, and some were city accounting officers. Apparently there were only seven or eight in these latter classes. They will not be named here because the known facts are not sufficient for positive statements about them. And of course all or some of them may have given part of their time to public practice. However, in all states and at all times a majority of the accounting members of the boards were public practitioners. And, so far as has been ascertained, each of them had been in public practice for periods of from eight to twelve years or longer.

Last, as to their terms of service. In those first ten years from 1896 to 1905, twelve examiners served about one year each, ten served two years each, twelve served three years each, four served four

580

years each, four served five years each, two served six years each, and two served seven years each. The forty-six examiners served for a total of one hundred and thirty years, or slightly less than an average of three years each. However, whereas thirty-four served a total of sixty-eight years, or an average of two years each, the other twelve served a total of sixty-two years, or an average of over five years each. Perhaps the influence of the twelve with the longer average service upon the examination work of the boards was greater than that of the thirty-four examiners who averaged only two years in the period studied.

But the twenty-nine examiners who composed the nine boards in 1905 all served one or more years thereafter, some as much as five to ten years. The longest such service among the forty-six early examiners was that of Walter Mucklow of Florida, from 1905 to 1921. Later that record was matched by Charles N. McCulloh of New York, from 1909 to 1925, and was exceeded by Durand W. Springer, from 1913 to 1938. But no other has equalled that of John F. Forbes of California, from 1909 to some year still in the future. These long tenures of position as examiners indicate that their services were satisfactory to the profession and the public, and that, although their work might have been onerous, the examiners found it interesting and inspiring.

Their appointments seem to have been due to various causes. In each of the nine states, one or more of the first examiners had actively promoted the enactment of its CPA law. In some cases nominations were submitted by the State Societies, as has been done in later years. In fewer instances, perhaps, the selections were of persons favorably known to the appointing officer, or upon the recommendation of some one who so advised the appointing officer. Later it was rumored that practical politics occasionally influenced the selection of accountants as examiners, but so far as was learned such was not the case in the naming of the forty-six examiners in the first ten years. Whatever the reason for the early appointments, they seem to have been fortunate selections.

Turning from this survey of the forty-six examiners of the nine boards as a group, to some of the individual examiners, they will be taken up in the reverse of the years in which their boards were created, since of course those who began their service near the end of the first ten years did not have an opportunity to influence the work as did those who began it in 1896.

Florida was the ninth CPA state, its law being approved June 5, 1905. It had three examiners, of whom one was a banker and one an accountant in Tallahassee. But its most outstanding examiner was Walter Mucklow, of Jacksonville. He was born December 9, 1864, in London, England, of Scotch ancestry, and was educated at Kings College, London. In 1866 at the age of twenty-two he located in Jacksonville. In 1909 he was British Vice-Consul and later Consul, and Norway made him a Knight of the Order of St. Olaf. He promoted the Florida CPA law and received Florida certificate No. 1. He was a member of all the accounting societies and an officer in most of them. After serving as president of the State Society from 1905 to 1931 he was made president emeritus. He was chairman of the Florida Board of Examiners from 1905 to 1921, and in 1941 he wrote that "in the report of a survey made in 1915–1916, Florida ranked fourth in the entire country for the originality of its examination questions." The *Accountants' Index* lists three books and twenty-five magazine articles by him. He died June 14, 1941, at Schenectady, New York.

Michigan was the eighth CPA state, its law being approved May 4, 1905. Its first examiners included one lawyer, one ac-

countant in Grand Rapids, and John H. Clegg of Detroit. No record of the latter's birth or education has been found but, as he was a veteran of the Civil War, perhaps he was born about 1840. He was the oldest public practitioner in the state and was active in the organization of the first Michigan association in 1896 and in its re-organizations in 1901 and 1905, having been in 1902 its representative at the meeting in Washington of the Federation of Societies of Public Accountants in the United States. In 1902 and 1903 he had charge of the preparation of a CPA bill for his state. In all these activities from 1901 or earlier he had the active collaboration of Durand W. Springer, of Ann Arbor, whose activities as an accountant, association officer, editor, and member and secretary of the Michigan board from 1913 to 1938 are so well known that it would be superfluous to repeat them in detail. However, it may not be so generally known that he was graduated from Albion College, had taught business subjects, was a member of the National Education Association and of the Commercial Teachers Association, and had been engaged in public practice since 1887. Since he was from thirty-five to forty years of age in the years from 1896 to 1901 it is possible that his educational experience may have had an influence upon John H. Clegg's services as an examiner.

New Jersey was the seventh CPA state, its law being approved April 5, 1904. The three examiners of its first board were accountants, the best known being Frank G. DuBois of Newark. He was born July 27, 1855 in New York; after finishing high school he took the course at Packard's Business College. He received New York CPA certificate No. 177 in 1901. He was the author of the New Jersey law and served as an examiner from 1904 to 1909. When he was president of the board, it adopted a resolution on April 8, 1908, looking to the

581

formation of an Association of CPA Examiners. This object was accomplished at Atlantic City, October 10, 1908: Later in 1916–1917 he was a member of the Board of Examiners of the American Institute of Accountants. He died June 7, 1927.

Illinois was the sixth CPA state, its law being approved May 15, 1903. Its first board included a business man, the manager of an audit company whose directors were bankers, and Ernest Reckitt, of Chicago, who was born on October 8, 1866, in Hull, England, and was graduated with honors at Manchester University. He began public accounting in Chicago in 1891 at the age of twenty-five. He served on the Illinois board from 1903 to 1907 and on the Institute board in 1919–1920. He has contributed many articles on accounting subjects to the magazines. Perhaps his interest in his work as examiner is most clearly evidenced by his close association with Doctor David Kinley, who in 1903 was Dean of the College of Liberal Arts and Science and later President of the University of Illinois, which institution by law had supervision of the Board of Examiners. Illinois was the first state to seek a clear definition of a public accountant, in connection with which endeavor Dean Kinley, presumably with the assistance of Ernest Reckitt, consulted many accountants in Illinois and other states.

Washington was the fifth CPA state, its law being approved March 12, 1903. Its first Board of Examiners numbered five individuals including a corporation treasurer, a banker, a city comptroller, an accountant in Tacoma, and E. G. Shorrock of Seattle, who was born in Blackburn, England. At the age of fifteen he was an office boy with the West Lancashire Railway and in 1899 he moved to Seattle to act for British interests in Alaska. Three years later, in 1902, he began the public practice

of accountancy in Seattle. He had become an FSAA presumably before he left England but details as to his experience are not available. He was an officer of his state society and actively promoted the Washington law. He served as an examiner from 1903 to 1911; and his interest in the literature is evidenced by many magazine articles. He died October 28, 1933.

California was the fourth CPA state, its law being approved March 23, 1901. In the five years from 1901 to 1905 it had eight examiners, of whom one did not become a CPA and two were state or city officials. Norman McLaren served the first year only; A. Wenzelberger and Lester Herrick served two years of the five and also one and three years, respectively, thereafter. But apparently the examiner who exercised the greatest influence during the early years was Alfred G. Platt, of San Francisco, who served from 1901 to 1906. He was born in 1852 in Nottingham, England, and moved to San Francisco in 1872, where he was employed in banking until 1880. In that year, at the age of twenty-eight he began the public practice of accountancy. He actively promoted the California law and his interest in CPA examinations resulted in at least one article on the subject. He died November 10, 1910, at Havre, France.

Maryland was the third CPA state, its law being approved April 10, 1900. There were seven examiners on its board in the six years 1900 to 1905. Of these, two were lawyers, two who received certificates were a banker and an actuary, respectively, and one was a CPA in Baltimore and a member of the American Association of Public Accountants to 1915 but of whom nothing more has been learned. The two others were Max Teichman and Frank Blacklock, both of whom were active in securing the CPA law and were early officers of their state society. No information can be given about Frank Blacklock except that he

582

was born in Baltimore in 1853 and died in 1917, after many years of practice in his city and after having been a frequent contributor to accounting periodicals. Max Teichman was born in Saxony, on June 22, 1860, and was educated in German institutions; after he had moved to the United States in 1883, he was a member of numerous scientific and technological societies besides those of accountants. He was president of the Maryland examiners from 1900 to 1904 and wrote many articles for accounting publications, usually on technical subjects but at least one upon the early history of accounting. He died December 27, 1922.

Pennsylvania was the second CPA state, its law being approved March 29, 1899. In the seven years 1899 to 1905 ten persons, of whom five were lawyers and five were accountants, served on its board of four examiners. These included George R. Heisey, of Lancaster, who served from 1899 to 1903, Frank A. Kimball, of Pittsburg, who served from 1904 to 1905, and Lawrence E. Brown, of Philadelphia, who served from 1904 to 1912. But probably the early activities of the Pennsylvania board were influenced most by John Vaughan of Pittsburgh and Charles N. Vollum of Philadelphia. John Vaughan, after service as a Navy paymaster and several years in business, was on the staff of his brother-in-law, John Heins of Philadelphia, in 1887; he then began his own practice in Pittsburgh. He was an examiner from 1899 to 1903; the state society received his accountancy library upon his death in 1917. Charles N. Vollum was born in Philadelphia, October 4, 1839, and was graduated from Girard College at an early age. Before and after his service in the Civil war he was in business; he began public accounting practice in 1875. He represented the state society in advocating the CPA law. An unknown has told the story thus:

Throughout the session's long and tedious fight
At meld and deal; at shuffle, cut and draw,
Our gallant Vollum strove through half the night,
And thus he got the votes that passed the law.

He served as president of the board from 1899 until his death on October 26, 1911.

New York was the first CPA state, its law being approved April 17, 1896. In the ten years from 1896 to 1905, twelve accountants filled the three places as examiners. James T. Anyon, born in England where he became an ACA, moved here in 1887 and became the head of Barrow, Wade, Guthrie & Co. He was the first secretary of the American Association of Public Accountants in 1887, was an examiner in 1897–1898, published *Recollections of Early Days of American Accountancy* and many magazine articles. He died February 7, 1929. Rodney S. Dennis was a partner in Patterson, Teele & Dennis, was an officer of his state society, served as examiner in 1898–1899 and died March 9, 1904. Anson O. Kittredge was born in Ohio, February 19, 1848, attended Miami Commercial College, was a bookkeeper at the age of eighteen, and became a manufacturer. During his last twenty years he was an editor of accounting and trade journals, and a teacher in New York University. He also was the originator of the course of study of the Institute of Bank Clerks. He was an examiner in 1899–1900 and died March 23, 1903. Henry R. M. Cook and Arthur W. Teele were public practitioners; both served as examiners 1905 to 1907. The former was a member of the New York City Board of Education and was active in promoting the School of Accounts established in New York in 1892, and the School of Commerce, Accounts and Finance of New York University in 1900. He died January 4, 1932. The latter was chairman of the Institute Board of Examiners from 1916 to 1922. John R. Sparrow was born in Brooklyn in 1859, taught accountancy subjects for fifteen years, was accounting adviser to the Comptroller of New York City and was a partner in Sparrow, Harvey & Co. He was an examiner from 1901 to 1905 and died April 9, 1921. John R. Loomis was born in Cambridge, N. Y., January 15, 1846, was in public practice many years, and was an active officer of all societies of accountants. He served as an examiner from 1898 to 1905 and died December 7, 1922. Leonard H. Conant, who was an examiner from 1900 to 1903, and Ferdinand W. Lafrentz who followed him, 1903 to 1907, are both living; these two men, together with Ernest Reckitt of Illinois, are the senior surviving examiners. Mr. Conant was born in Washington, April 25, 1856, and was graduated at Phillips Andover Academy in 1874. After some years in business he began public practice in 1888. Mr. Lafrentz was born in Germany, March 25, 1859, and came here in 1873. In 1879 at the age of twenty he was an instructor in accounting at the Bryant and Stratton School in Chicago. He began public practice in 1899.

The nine New York examiners so far mentioned include all except the first three appointees who made up the first CPA examiners anywhere. Frank Broaker was born in Millerstown, Pa., March 16, 1863, and attended City College, New York. At twenty years of age he was employed by John Roundy of New York, who was a CA of Scotland; upon his employer's death in 1887 he began practice on his own account. He was an early member of the American Association of Public Accountants and participated actively in its efforts to establish the School of Accounts in 1892. Then, in 1895 he and W. Saunders Davies represented all accountants in efforts to secure the New York CPA law. His co-committeeman gave him credit for the successful outcome. Perhaps, though not certainly, he outlined the scope of the examination. This seems probable,

584

because he had worked for a CA and had a complete file of the British magazine, the *Accountant*. He served as an examiner in the year 1896–1897. He died November 11, 1941.

Charles Ezra Sprague was born in New York, October 9, 1842; in 1860 when eighteen he was graduated at Union College with the A.B. degree and a Phi Beta Kappa key; in 1862 he earned the A.M. degree. Union gave him an honorary Ph.D. in 1893, and he became a trustee of the College in 1906. He served in the Union Army from 1862 to 1864 and was discharged as a brevet Colonel. Although his later life was spent as a banker, he was a student of many subjects, including Volapuk—a world language—simplified spelling, and accounting; he was especially interested in accountancy. His acquaintance with the Secretary of the Board of Regents, Melvil Dewey, caused the latter to ask him to be present when the American Association petitioned for a College of Accounts in 1892. His selection as one of the first examiners may have been due to that acquaintance. He was author of *The Philosophy of Accounts*, and *The Accountancy of Investment*. He was a member of the first faculty of the School of Commerce, Accounts and Finance of New York University, but curiously his biography though prepared and published by that institution in 1931 does not mention his service as an examiner in the years 1896 to 1898, though a tablet was erected after he died March 21, 1912.

Charles Waldo Haskins was born in Brooklyn, January 11, 1852, and was graduated as a civil engineer at Brooklyn Polytechnic Institute at the age of fifteen. Thereafter he spent five years as a bookkeeper, two years abroad in the study of art, and about twelve years again as a corporation bookkeeper and internal auditor. He was a member of the Institute of Accounts and started public practice on his own account in 1886. Six years later he and Elijah Watt Sells were engaged by a Congressional Commission to do some special work and out of that association grew a great friendship and professional partnership. From that intimacy Mr. Sells came to know his associate so well that, as is told in the biography, he later urged and had others urge his selection as an examiner, in which capacity he served from 1896 to 1901. In the latter year he resigned to assist in the organization of the School of Commerce, Accounts and Finance, of which he was the first dean. His society offices, his public addresses, and his publications were so many that they cannot be enumerated here. But the minutes of the Board of Examiners show that he was regular in attendance and performed a great quantity of work. With his fellow members, including Sprague, Broaker, Anyon, Loomis, Dennis, Kittredge and Conant, he planned the board's procedure and its rules and practices in connection with waivers of examination, experience requirements for admission, and the issuing of certificates. All this was new. Perhaps however his most important work as an examiner was that of the preparation of the *Certified Public Accountant Syllabus*. This was published in September, 1900, with an attached bibliography that filled forty-seven pages. The *Syllabus* went through two later editions and remained as the standard for the New York CPA examinations until 1935.

Acknowledgments

The editor would like to acknowledge the following for permission to reproduce copyright material in this volume: *University of Illinois Bulletin, The Certified Public Accountant, The Journal of Accountancy, The Accounting Review, The Arthur Young Journal,* the Illinois CPA Society for *Reminiscences of Early Days of the Accounting Profession in Illinois,* Richard D. Irwin, Inc. for excerpts from *Advanced Public Accounting Practice,* © 1966 by Richard D. Irwin, Inc., the AICPA for excerpts from *The Rise of the Accounting Profession,* copyright © 1969 by the American Institute of Certified Public Accountants, and John Wiley & Sons for excerpts from *A History of Accounting in America,* copyright © 1979 by John Wiley & Sons, Inc.

Accounting Books Published by Garland

■■■■■■■■■■■■■■■■■■

NEW BOOKS

■ *Altman, Edward I., *The Prediction of Corporate Bankruptcy: A Discriminant Analysis*.
New York, 1988.

■ Ashton, Robert H., ed. *The Evolution of Accounting Behavior Research: An Overview*.
New York, 1984.

■ Ashton, Robert H., ed. *Some Early Contributions to the Study of Audit Judgement*.
New York, 1984.

■ *Bodenhorn, Diran. *Economic Accounting*.
New York, 1988.

* Included in the Garland series Foundations of Accounting
† Included in the Academy of Accounting Historians, Classics Series, Gary John Previt, ed.

■ *Bougen, Philip D. *Accounting and Industrial Relations: Some Historical Evidence on Their Interaction.*
New York, 1988.

■ Brief, Richard P., ed. *Corporate Financial Reporting and Analysis in the Early 1900s.*
New York, 1986.

■ Brief, Richard P., ed. *Depreciation and Capital Maintenance.*
New York, 1984.

■ Brief, Richard P., ed. *Estimating the Economic Rate of Return from Accounting Data.*
New York, 1986.

■ Brief, Richard P., ed. *Four Classics on the Theory of Double-Entry Bookkeeping.*
New York, 1982.

■ Chambers, R. J., and G. W. Dean, eds. *Chambers on Accounting.*
New York, 1986.
Volume I: Accounting, Management and Finance.
Volume II: Accounting Practice and Education.
Volume III: Accounting Theory and Research.
Volume IV: Price Variation Accounting.
Volume V: Continuously Contemporary
            Accounting.

■ *Clark, John B. (with a new introduction by Donald Dewey). *Capital and Its Earnings.*
New York, 1988.

■ Clarke, F. L. *The Tangled Web of Price Variation Accounting: The Development of Ideas Underlying Professional Prescriptions in Six Countries.*
New York, 1982.

■ Coopers & Lybrand. *The Early History of Coopers & Lybrand.*
New York, 1984.

■ Craswell, Allen. *Audit Qualifications in Australia 1950 to 1979.*
New York, 1986.

■ Dean, G. W., and M. C. Wells, eds. *The Case for Continuously Contemporary Accounting.*
New York, 1984.

■ Dean, G. W. , and M. C. Wells, eds. *Forerunners of Realizable Values Accounting in Financial Reporting.*
New York, 1982.

■ Edey, Harold C. *Accounting Queries.*
New York, 1982.

■ Edwards, J. R., ed. *Legal Regulation of British Company Accounts 1836-1900.*
New York, 1986.

■ Edwards, J. R. ed. *Reporting Fixed Assets in Nineteenth-Century Company Accounts.*
New York, 1986.

■ Edwards, J. R., ed. *Studies of Company Records: 1830-1974.*
New York, 1984.

■ Fabricant, Solomon. *Studies in Social and Private Accounting.*
　　New York, 1982.

■ Gaffikin, Michael, and Michael Aitkin, eds. *The Development of Accounting Theory: Significant Contributors to Accounting Thought in the 20th Century.*
　　New York, 1982.

■ Hawawini, Gabriel A., ed. *Bond Duration and Immunization: Early Developments and Recent Contributions.*
　　New York, 1982.

■ Hawawini, Gabriel A., and Pierre A. Michel, eds. *European Equity Markets: Risk, Return, and Efficiency.*
　　New York, 1984.

■ Hawawini, Gabriel A., and Pierre Michel. *Mandatory Financial Information and Capital Market Equilibrium in Belgium.*
　　New York, 1986.

■ Hawkins, David F. *Corporate Financial Disclosure, 1900-1933: A Study of Management Inertia within a Rapidly Changing Environment.*
　　New York, 1986.

■ *Hopwood, Anthony G. *Accounting from the Outside: The Collected Papers of Anthony G. Hopwood.*
　　New York, 1988.

■ Johnson, H. Thomas. *A New Approach to Management Accounting History.*
　　New York, 1986.

■ Kinney, William R., ed. *Fifty Years of Statistical Auditing.*
New York, 1986.

■ Klemstine, Charles E., and Michael W. Maher. *Management Accounting Research: A Review and Annotated Bibliography.*
New York, 1984.

■ *Langenderfer, Harold Q., and Grover L. Porter, eds. *Rational Accounting Concepts: The Writings of Willard Graham.*
New York, 1988.

■ *Lee, T. A., ed. *The Evolution of Audit Thought and Practice.*
New York, 1988.

■ Lee, T. A., ed. *A Scottish Contribution to Accounting History.*
New York, 1986.

■ Lee, T. A. *Towards a Theory and Practice of Cash Flow Accounting.*
New York, 1986.

■ Lee, T. A., ed. *Transactions of the Chartered Accountants Students' Societies of Edinburgh and Glasgow: A Selection of Writings, 1886-1958.*
New York, 1984.

■ *Loft, Anne. *Understanding Accounting in Its Social and Historical Context: The Case of Cost Accounting in Britain, 1914-1925.*
New York, 1988.

■ McKinnon, Jill L.. *The Historical Development and Operational Form of Corporate Reporting Regulation in Japan.*
New York, 1986.

■ *McMickle, Peter L., and Paul H. Jensen, eds. *The Auditor's Guide of 1869: A Review and Computer Enhancement of Recently Discovered Old Microfilm of America's First Book on Auditing by H. J. Mettenheimer.*
New York, 1988.

■ *McMickle, Peter L., and Paul H. Jensen, eds. *The Birth of American Accountancy: A Bibliographic Analysis of Works on Accounting Published in America through 1820.*
New York, 1988.

■ *Mepham, M.-J. *Accounting in Eighteenth-Century Scotland.*
New York, 1988.

■ *Mills, Patti A., trans. *The Legal Literature of Accounting: On Accounts by Diego del Castillo.*
New York, 1988.

■ *Murphy, George J. *The Evolution of Canadian Corporate Reporting Practices: 1900-1970.*
New York, 1988.

■ *Mumford, Michael J., ed. *Edward Stamp—Later Papers.*
New York, 1988.

■ Nobes, Christopher, ed. *The Development of Double Entry: Selected Essays.*
New York, 1984.

■ Nobes, Christopher. *Issues in International Accounting.*
New York, 1986.

■ Parker, Lee D. *Developing Control Concepts in the 20th Century.*
New York, 1986.

■ *Parker, Lee D., ed. *Financial Reporting to Employees: From Past to Present.*
New York, 1988.

■ *Parker, Lee D., and O. Finley Graves, eds. *Methodology and Method in History: A Bibliography.*
New York, 1988.

■ Parker, R. H. *Papers on Accounting History.*
New York, 1984.

■ Previts, Gary John, and Alfred R. Roberts, eds. *Federal Securities Law and Accounting 1933-1970: Selected Addresses.*
New York, 1986.

■ *Reid, Jean Margo, ed. *Law and Accounting: Nineteenth-Century American Legal Cases.*
New York, 1988.

■ *Sheldahl, Terry K., ed. *Accounting Literature in the United States before Mitchell and Jones (1796): Contributions by Four English Writers, through American Editions, and Two Pioneer Local Authors.*
New York, 1988.

■ Sheldahl, Terry K. *Beta Alpha Psi, from Alpha to Omega: Pursuing a Vision of Professional Education for Accountants, 1919-1945.*
New York, 1982.

■ Sheldahl, Terry K. *Beta Alpha Psi, from Omega to Zeta Omega: The Making of a Comprehensive Accounting Fraternity, 1946-1984.*
New York, 1986.

■ *Sheldahl, Terry K., ed. *Education for the Mercantile Countinghouse: Critical and Constructive Essays by Nine British Writers, 1716-1794.*
New York, 1988.

■ Solomons, David. *Collected Papers on Accounting and Accounting Education (in two volumes).*
New York, 1984.

■ Sprague, Charles F. *The General Principles of the Science of Accounts and the Accountancy of Investment.*
New York, 1984.

■ Stamp, Edward. *Edward Stamp—Later Papers. See* Michael J. Mumford.

■ Stamp, Edward. *Selected Papers on Accounting, Auditing, and Professional Problems.*
New York, 1984.

■ *Staubus, George J. *Activity Costing for Decisions: Cost Accounting in the Decision Usefulness Framework.*
New York, 1988.

■ Storrar, Colin, ed. *The Accountant's Magazine—An Anthology.*
New York, 1986.

■ Tantral, Panadda. *Accounting Literature in Non-Accounting Journals: An Annotated Bibliography.*
New York, 1984.

■ *Vangermeersch, Richard G. *Alexander Hamilton Church: A Man of Ideas for All Seasons.*
New York, 1988.

■ Vangermeersch, Richard, ed. *The Contributions of Alexander Hamilton Church to Accounting and Management.*
New York, 1986.

■ Vangermeersch, Richard, ed. *Financial Accounting Milestones in the Annual Reports of the United States Steel Corporation—The First Seven Decades.*
New York, 1986.

■ *Walker, Stephen P. *The Society of Accountants in Edinburgh, 1854-1914: A Study of Recruitment to a New Profession.*
New York, 1988.

■ Whitmore, John. *Factory Accounts.*
New York, 1984.

■ *Whittred, Greg. *The Evolution of Consolidated Financial Reporting in Australia: An Evaluation of an Alternative Hypothesis.*
New York, 1988.

■ Yamey, Basil S. *Further Essays on the History of Accounting.*
New York, 1982.

■ Zeff, Stephen A., ed. *The Accounting Postulates and Principles Controversy of the 1960s.*
New York, 1982.

■ Zeff, Stephen A., ed. *Accounting Principles Through the Years: The Views of Professional and Academic Leaders 1938-1954.*
New York, 1982.

■ Zeff, Stephen A., and Maurice Moonitz, eds. *Sourcebook on Accounting Principles and Auditing Procedures: 1917-1953 (in two volumes).*
New York, 1984.

■ *Zeff, Stephen a., ed. *The U. S. Accounting Profession in the 1890s and Early 1900s.*
New York, 1988.

REPRINTED TITLES

■ *American Institute of Accountants. *Accountants Index, 1920* (in two volumes).
New York, 1921 (Garland reprint, 1988).

■ American Institute of Accountants. *Fiftieth Anniversary Celebration.*
Chicago, 1937 (Garland reprint, 1982).

■ American Institute of Accountants. *Library Catalogue.*
New York, 1919 (Garland reprint, 1982).

■ Arthur Andersen Company. *The First Fifty Years 1913-1963.*
Chicago, 1963 (Garland reprint, 1984).

■ Bevis, Herman W. *Corporate Financial Reporting in a Competitive Economy.*
New York, 1965 (Garland reprint, 1986).

■ Bonini,. Charles P., Robert K. Jaedicke, and Harvey M. Wagner, eds. *Management Controls: New Directions in Basic Research.*
New York, 1964 (Garland reprint, 1986).

■ *The Book-Keeper and the American Counting Room.*
New York, 1880-1884 (Garland reprint, 1988).

■ Bray, F. Sewell. *Four Essays in Accounting Theory.* London, 1953. *Bound with* Institute of Chartered Accountants in England and Wales and the National Institute of Economic and Social Research. *Some Accounting Terms and Concepts.*
    Cambridge, 1951 (Garland reprint, 1982).

■ Brown, R. Gene, and Kenneth S. Johnston. *Paciolo on Accounting.*
    New York, 1963 (Garland reprint, 1984).

■ Carey, John L., and William O. Doherty, eds. *Ethical Standards of the Accounting Profession.*
    New York, 1966 (Garland reprint, 1986).

■ Chambers, R. J. *Accounting in Disarray.*
    Melbourne, 1973 (Garland reprint, 1982).

■ Cooper, Ernest. *Fifty-seven years in an Accountant's Office. See* Sir Russell Kettle.

■ Couchman, Charles B. *The Balance-Sheet.*
    New York, 1924 (Garland reprint, 1982).

■ Couper, Charles Tennant. *Report of the Trial ... Against the Directors and Manager of the City of Glasgow Bank.*
    Edinburgh, 1879 (Garland reprint, 1984).

■ Cutforth, Arthur E. *Audits.*
    London, 1906 (Garland reprint, 1982).

■ Cutforth, Arthur E. *Methods of Amalgamation.*
    London, 1926 (Garland reprint, 1982).

- Deinzer, Harvey T. *Development of Accounting Thought.*
  New York, 1965 (Garland reprint, 1984).

- De Paula, F.R.M. *The Principles of Auditing.*
  London, 1915 (Garland reprint, 1984).

- Dickerson, R. W. *Accountants and the Law of Negligence.*
  Toronto, 1966 (Garland reprint, 1982).

- Dodson, James. *The Accountant, or, the Method of Bookkeeping Deduced from Clear Principles, and Illustrated by a Variety of Examples.*
  London, 1750 (Garland reprint, 1984).

- Dyer, S. *A Common Sense Method of Double Entry Bookkeeping, on First Principles, as Suggested by De Morgan. Part I, Theoretical.*
  London, 1897 (Garland reprint, 1984).

- *† Edwards, James Don. *History of Public Accounting in the United States.*
  East Lansing, 1960 (Garland reprint, 1988).

- *† Edwards, James Don, and Robert F. Salmonson. *Contributions of Four Accounting Pioneers: Kohler, Littleton, May, Paton.*
  East Lancing, 1961 (Garland reprint, 1988).

- *The Fifth International Congress on Accounting, 1938 [Kongress-Archiv 1938 des V. Internationalen Prüfungs- und Treuhand-Kongresses].*
  Berlin, 1938 (Garland reprint, 1986).

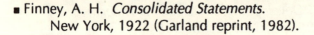

- Finney, A. H. *Consolidated Statements.*
    New York, 1922 (Garland reprint, 1982).

- Fisher, Irving. *The Rate of Interest.*
    New York, 1907 (Garland reprint, 1982).

- Florence, P. Sargant. *Economics of Fatigue and Unrest and the Efficiency of Labour in English and American Industry.*
    London, 1923 (Garland reprint, 1984).

- *Fourth International Congress on Accounting 1933.*
    London, 1933 (Garland reprint, 1982).

- Foye, Arthur B. *Haskins & Sells: Our First Seventy-Five Years.*
    New York, 1970 (Garland reprint, 1984).

- *†* Garner, Paul S. *Evolution of Cost Accounting to 1925.*
    University, Alabama, 1925 (Garland reprint, 1988).

- Garnsey, Sir Gilbert. *Holding Companies and Their Published Accounts.* London, 1923. *Bound with* Sir Gilbert Garnsey. *Limitations of a Balance Sheet.*
    London, 1928 (Garland reprint, 1982).

- Garrett, A. A. *The History of the Society of Incorporated Accountants, 1885-1957.*
    Oxford, 1961 (Garland reprint, 1984).

- Gilman, Stephen. *Accounting Concepts of Profit.*
    New York, 1939 (Garland reprint, 1982).

■ Gordon, William. *The Universal Accountant, and Complete Merchant ...* [Volume II].
> Edinburgh, 1765 (Garland reprint, 1986).

■ Green, Wilmer. *History and Survey of Accountancy.*
> Brooklyn, 1930 (Garland reprint, 1986).

■ Hamilton, Robert. *An Introduction to Merchandise, Parts IV and V (Italian Bookkeeping and Practical Bookkeeping).*
> Edinburgh, 1788 (Garland reprint, 1982).

■ Hatton, Edward. *The Merchant's Magazine; or, Tradesman's Treasury.* London, 1695 (Garland reprint, 1982). Hills, George S. *The Law of Accounting and Financial Statements.*
> Boston, 1957 (Garland reprint, 1982).

■ *A History of Cooper Brothers & Co. 1854 to 1954.*
> London, 1954 (Garland reprint, 1986).

■ Hofstede, Geert. *The Game of Budget Control.*
> Assen, 1967 (Garland reprint, 1984).

■ Howitt, Sir Harold. *The History of the Institute of Chartered Accountants in England and Wales 1880-1965, and of Its Founder Accountancy Bodies 1870-1880.*
> London, 1966 (Garland reprint, 1984).

■ Institute of Chartered Accountants in England and Wales and The National Institute of Social and Economic Research. *Some Accounting Terms and Concepts.* See F. Sewell Bray.

■ Institute of Chartered Accountants of Scotland. *History of the Chartered Accountants of Scotland from the Earliest Times to 1954.*
    Edinburgh, 1954 (Garland reprint, 1984).

■ *International Congress on Accounting 1929.*
    New York, 1930 (Garland reprint, 1982).

■ Jaedicke, Robert K., Yuji Ijiri, and Oswald Nielsen, eds. *Research in Accounting Measurement.*
    American Accounting Association,
    1966 (Garland reprint, 1986).

■ Keats, Charles. *Magnificent Masquerade.*
    New York, 1964 (Garland reprint, 1982).

■ Kettle, Sir Russell. *Deloitte & Co. 1854-1956.* Oxford, 1958. *Bound with* Ernest Cooper. *Fifty-seven Years in an Accountant's Office.*
    London, 1921 (Garland reprint, 1982).

■ Kitchen, J., and R. H. Parker. *Accounting Thought and Education: Six English Pioneers.*
    London, 1980 (Garland reprint, 1984).

■ Lacey, Kenneth. *Profit Measurement and Price Changes.*
    London, 1952 (Garland reprint, 1982).

■ Lee, Chauncey. *The American Accomptant.*
    Lansingburgh, 1797 (Garland reprint, 1982).

■ Lee, T. A., and R. H. Parker. *The Evolution of Corporate Financial Reporting.*
    Middlesex, 1979 (Garland reprint, 1984).

■ *† Littleton, A. C.. *Accounting Evolution to 1900.*
New York, 1933 (Garland reprint, 1988).

■ Malcolm, Alexander. *The Treatise of Book-Keeping, or, Merchants Accounts; In the Italian Method of Debtor and Creditor; Wherein the Fundamental Principles of That Curious and Approved Method Are Clearly and Fully Explained and Demonstrated ... To Which Are Added, Instructions for Gentlemen of Land Estates, and Their Stewards or Factors: With Directions Also for Retailers, and Other More Private Persons.*
London, 1731 (Garland reprint, 1986).

■ Meij, J. L., ed. *Depreciation and Replacement Policy.*
Chicago, 1961 (Garland reprint, 1986).

■ Newlove, George Hills. *Consolidated Balance Sheets.*
New York, 1926 (Garland reprint, 1982).

■ North, Roger. *The Gentleman Accomptant; or, An Essay to Unfold the Mystery of Accompts; By Way of Debtor and Creditor, Commonly Called Merchants Accompts, and Applying the Same to the Concerns of the Nobility and Gentry of England.*
London 1714 (Garland reprint, 1986).

■ *Proceedings of the Seventh International Congress of Accountants.* Amsterdam, 1957 (Garland reprint, 1988).

■ Pryce-Jones, Janet E., and R. H. Parker. *Accounting in Scotland: A Historical Bibliography.*
Edinburgh, 1976 (Garland reprint, 1984).

■ *Reynolds, W. B., and F. W. Thornton. *Duties of a Junior Accountant* [three editions].
New York, 1917, 1933, 1953
(Garland reprint, 1988).

■ Robinson, H. W. *A History of Accountants in Ireland.*
Dublin, 1964 (Garland edition, 1984).

■ Robson, T. B. *Consolidated and Other Group Accounts.*
London, 1950 (Garland reprint, 1982).

■ Rorem, C. Rufus. *Accounting Method.*
Chicago, 1928 (Garland reprint, 1982).

■ Saliers, Earl A., ed. *Accountants' Handbook.*
New York, 1923 (Garland reprint, 1986).

■ Samuel, Horace B. *Shareholder's Money.*
London, 1933 (Garland reprint, 1982).

■ *The Securitites and Exchange Commission in the Matter of McKesson & Robbins, Inc. Report on Investigation.*
Washington, D. C., 1940 (Garland reprint, 1982).

■ *The Securities and Exchange Commission in the Matter of McKesson & Robbins, Inc. Testimony of Expert Witnesses.*
Washington, D. C., 1939 (Garland reprint, 1982).

■ Shaplen, Roger. *Kreuger: Genius and Swindler.*
New York, 1960 (Garland reprint, 1986).

■ Singer, H. W. *Standardized Accountancy in Germany.*
(With a new appendix.)
Cambridge, 1943 (Garland reprint, 1982).

■ *The Sixth International Congress on Accounting.*
London, 1952 (Garland reprint, 1984).

■ Stewart, Jas. C. (with a new introductory note by T. A. Lee). *Pioneers of a Profession: Chartered Accountants to 1879.*
Edinburgh, 1977 (Garland reprint, 1986).

■ Thompson, Wardbaugh. *The Accomptant's Oracle: or, a Key to Science, Being a Compleat Practical System of Book-keeping.*
York, 1777 (Garland reprint, 1984).

■ *Thornton, F. W. *Duties of the Senior Accountant.*
New York, 1932. *Bound with.* John C. Martin. *Duties of Junior and Senior Accountants, Supplement of the CPA Handbook.*
New York, 1953 (Garland reprint, 1988).

■ Vatter, William J. *Managerial Accounting.*
New York, 1950 (Garland reprint, 1986).

■ Woolf, Arthur H. *A Short History of Accountants and Accountancy.*
London, 1912 (Garland reprint, 1986).

■ Yamey, B. S., H. C. Edey, and Hugh W. Thomson. *Accounting in England and Scotland: 1543-1800.*
London, 1963 (Garland reprint, 1982).